Theories of War and Peace

International Security Readers

Strategy and Nuclear Deterrence (1984)

Military Strategy and the Origins of the First World War (1985)

Conventional Forces and American Defense Policy (1986)

The Star Wars Controversy (1986)

Naval Strategy and National Security (1988)

Military Strategy and the Origins of the First World War, revised and expanded edition (1991)

—published by Princeton University Press

Soviet Military Policy (1989)

Conventional Forces and American Defense Policy, revised edition (1989)

Nuclear Diplomacy and Crisis Management (1990)

The Cold War and After: Prospects for Peace (1991)

America's Strategy in a Changing World (1992)

The Cold War and After: Prospects for Peace, expanded edition (1993)

Global Dangers: Changing Dimensions of International Security (1995)

The Perils of Anarchy: Contemporary Realism and International Security (1995)

Debating the Democratic Peace (1996)

East Asian Security (1996)

Nationalism and Ethnic Conflict (1997)

America's Strategic Choices (1997)

Theories of War and Peace (1998)

—published by The MIT Press

Theories of War and Peace

AN *International Security* READER

EDITED BY
Michael E. Brown
Owen R. Coté, Jr.
Sean M. Lynn-Jones
and Steven E. Miller

THE MIT PRESS
CAMBRIDGE, MASSACHUSETTS
LONDON, ENGLAND

Third printing, 2000

The contents of this book were first published in *International Security* (ISSN 0162–2889), a publication of The MIT Press under the sponsorship of The Robert and Renée Belfer Center for Science and International Affairs at Harvard University. Copyright in each of the following articles is owned jointly by the President and Fellows of Harvard College and of the Massachusetts Institute of Technology.

John J. Mearsheimer, "Back to the Future: Instability in Europe After the Cold War," 15:1 (Summer 1990); Stephen Van Evera, "Offense, Defense, and the Causes of War," 22:4 (Spring 1998); Charles L. Glaser, "Realists as Optimists: Cooperation as Self-Help," 19:3 (Winter 1994/95); John M. Owen, "How Liberalism Produces Democratic Peace," 19:2 (Fall 1994); Christopher Layne, "Kant or Cant: The Myth of the Democratic Peace," 19:2 (Fall 1994); Edward D. Mansfield and Jack Snyder, "Democratization and the Danger of War," 20:1 (Summer 1995); Stephen Van Evera, "Hypotheses on Nationalism and War," 18:4 (Spring 1994); David A. Lake and Donald Rothchild, "Containing Fear: The Origins and Management of Ethnic Conflict," 21:2 (Fall 1996); John J. Mearsheimer, "The False Promise of International Institutions," 19:3 (Winter 1994/95); Robert O. Keohane and Lisa Martin, "The Promise of Institutionalist Theory," 20:1 (Summer 1995); Charles A. Kupchan and Clifford A. Kupchan, "The Promise of Collective Security," 20:1 (Summer 1995); John Gerard Ruggie, "The False Premise of Realism," 20:1 (Summer 1995); Alexander Wendt, "Constructing International Politics," 20:1 (Summer 1995); John J. Mearsheimer, "A Realist Reply," 20:1 (Summer 1995); Carl Kaysen, "Is War Obsolete? A Review Essay," 14:4 (Spring 1990); Dale C. Copeland, "Economic Interdependence and War: A Theory of Trade Expectations," 20:4 (Spring 1996); Thomas F. Homer-Dixon, "Environmental Scarcities and Violent Conflict: Evidence from Cases," 19:1 (Summer 1994); John Orme, "The Utility of Force in a World of Scarcity," 22:3 (Winter 1997/98).

Selection and preface, copyright © 1998 by the President and Fellows of Harvard College and of the Massachusetts Institute of Technology.

All rights reserved. No part of this book may be reproduced in any form or by any means, electronic or mechanical, including photocopying, recording, or by any information storage and retrieval system, without permission in writing from The MIT Press. For information, please address The MIT Press Journals Department, Five Cambridge Center, Fourth Floor, Cambridge, Mass. 02142-1493.

Library of Congress Cataloging-in-Publication Data

Theories of war and peace : an international security reader / edited by Michael E. Brown . . . [et al.].
   p. cm. — (International security readers)
  Includes bibliographical references.
  ISBN 0-262-52252-7 (pbk. : alk. paper)
  1. International relations. 2. Security, International. 3. Peace. I. Brown, Michael E. II. Series.
JZ1305.T458 1998
327.1'01—dc21   98-21051
                                                              CIP

Contents

vii
The Contributors

ix
Acknowledgments

xi
Preface   *Sean M. Lynn-Jones*

PART I: REALIST THEORIES OF WAR AND PEACE

3
Back to the Future: Instability in Europe after the   *John J. Mearsheimer*
Cold War

55
Offense, Defense, and the Causes of War   *Stephen Van Evera*

94
Realists as Optimists: Cooperation as Self-Help   *Charles L. Glaser*

PART II: DEMOCRACY AND WAR

137
How Liberalism Produces Democratic Peace   *John M. Owen*

176
Kant or Cant: The Myth of the Democratic Peace   *Christopher Layne*

221
Democratization and the Danger of War   *Edward D. Mansfield
                                                                 and Jack Snyder*

PART III: NATIONALISM, ETHNICITY, AND WAR

257
Hypotheses on Nationalism and War   *Stephen Van Evera*

292
Containing Fear: The Origins and Management of   *David A. Lake and
Ethnic Conflict   Donald Rothchild*

PART IV: INTERNATIONAL INSTITUTIONS, WAR, AND PEACE

329
The False Promise of International Institutions   *John J. Mearsheimer*

384
The Promise of Institutionalist Theory   *Robert O. Keohane and
                                                                 Lisa L. Martin*

397
The Promise of Collective Security   *Charles A. Kupchan and
                                                                Clifford A. Kupchan*

407
The False Premise of Realism   *John Gerard Ruggie*

416
Constructing International Politics   *Alexander Wendt*

427
A Realist Reply   *John J. Mearsheimer*

PART V: WAR AND PEACE IN A CHANGING
INTERNATIONAL SYSTEM

441
Is War Obsolete? A Review Essay   *Carl Kaysen*

464
Economic Interdependence and War: A Theory of   *Dale C. Copeland*
Trade Expectations

501
Environmental Scarcities and Violent Conflict: *Thomas F. Homer-Dixon*
Evidence from Cases

537
The Utility of Force in a World of Scarcity   *John Orme*

The Contributors

MICHAEL E. BROWN teaches in and is Director of Research for the National Security Studies Program, Edmund A. Walsh School of Foreign Service, Georgetown University. From January 1995 until July 1998, he was Associate Director of the International Security Program and Managing Editor of *International Security* at the Belfer Center for Science and International Affairs (BCSIA), Harvard University.

OWEN R. COTÉ, JR. is Co-Editor of *International Security* and Associate Director of the Security Studies Program at the Massachusetts Institute of Technology.

SEAN M. LYNN-JONES is Co-Editor of *International Security* and a Research Associate at BCSIA.

STEVEN E. MILLER is Editor-in-Chief of *International Security* and Director of the International Security Program at BCSIA.

DALE C. COPELAND is Assistant Professor in the Department of Government and Foreign Affairs at the University of Virginia.

CHARLES L. GLASER is Associate Professor at the Harris School of Public Policy Studies at the University of Chicago.

THOMAS F. HOMER-DIXON is Assistant Professor of Political Science at the University of Toronto, where he is Director of the Peace and Conflict Studies Program.

CARL KAYSEN is the David W. Skinner Professor of Political Economy, Emeritus, at the Massachusetts Institute of Technology, where he is a member of the Security Studies Program.

ROBERT O. KEOHANE is James B. Duke Professor of Political Science at Duke University.

CHARLES A. KUPCHAN is Associate Professor of International Relations at Georgetown University and a Senior Fellow at the Council on Foreign Relations.

CLIFFORD A. KUPCHAN is a Professional Staff Member of the Committee on International Relations, U.S. House of Representatives.

DAVID A. LAKE is Professor of Political Science at the University of California at San Diego.

CHRISTOPHER LAYNE is Visiting Associate Professor at the Naval Postgraduate School.

EDWARD D. MANSFIELD is Associate Professor of Political Science at the Ohio State University.

LISA L. MARTIN is Professor of Government at Harvard University.

JOHN J. MEARSHEIMER is R. Wendell Harrison Distinguished Service Professor in the Department of Political Science at the University of Chicago.

JOHN ORME is Professor of Politics at Oglethorpe University in Atlanta, Georgia.

JOHN OWEN is Assistant Professor in the Department of Government and Foreign Affairs at the University of Virginia.

DONALD ROTHCHILD is Professor of Political Science at the University of California at Davis.

JOHN GERARD RUGGIE is Burgess Professor of Political Science at the School of International and Public Affairs at Columbia University.

JACK SNYDER is Professor of Political Science and Chair of the Political Science Department at Columbia University.

STEPHEN VAN EVERA is Associate Professor of Political Science at the Massachusetts Institute of Technology, where he is a member of the Security Studies Program.

ALEXANDER WENDT is Associate Professor of Government at Dartmouth College.

Acknowledgments

The editors gratefully acknowledge the assistance that has made this book possible. A deep debt is owed to all those at the Belfer Center for Science and International Affairs (BCSIA), Harvard University, who have played an editorial role at *International Security*. We are grateful for support from the Carnegie Corporation of New York. Special thanks go to Diane McCree and Meara Keegan Zaheer at BCSIA and International Security Program intern Brett Kitt for their invaluable help in preparing this volume for publication.

Preface | *Sean M. Lynn-Jones*

Why wars occur is one of the oldest and most important issues in the study of international politics. Over the centuries, writers have attempted to find the causes of war in human nature, in the characteristics of particular types of societies and governments, and in the nature of the international system.[1] Different thinkers have proposed numerous theories that explain war and many also have offered prescriptions for peace.[2] It would be difficult or impossible to do justice to every theory of war and peace in a single volume. This volume therefore presents essays on four prominent contemporary approaches to the causes of war. These approaches have generated vigorous debate and discussion in recent years. They have been at the center of much research in political science. The first section of the book offers realist theories. The second presents different perspectives on the connection between democracy and war. The third includes many hypotheses on the causes and prevention of wars of nationalism and ethnicity. The essays in the fourth section debate whether international institutions can promote peace. The final section examines the future of war and how increasing levels of economic interdependence and environmental scarcity will influence the prospects for war and peace.

The first three essays in this volume present realist perspectives on the causes of war and peace. We begin with realist theories because realism has the longest lineage and the greatest prominence among explanations of war.[3] Realist theories tend to regard war as an inevitable feature of international politics. Most realist explanations of war hold that states make decisions for war or peace on the basis of changes in the distribution of capabilities in the international

1. For the classic discussion and analysis of theories in these three categories, see Kenneth N. Waltz, *Man, the State and War: A Theoretical Analysis* (New York: Columbia University Press, 1959).
2. For examples, overviews, and, in some cases, detailed analyses of explanations of war and peace, see Quincy Wright, *A Study of War*, 2nd ed. (Chicago: University of Chicago Press, 1965); Bernard Brodie, *War and Politics* (New York: Macmillan, 1973), chap. 7; Geoffrey Blainey, *The Causes of War*, 3rd ed. (New York: Free Press, 1988); Robert I. Rotberg and Theodore K. Rabb, eds., *The Origin and Prevention of Major Wars* (Cambridge: Cambridge University Press, 1989); Jack S. Levy, "The Causes of War: A Review of Theories and Evidence," in Philip E. Tetlock, Jo L. Husbands, Robert Jervis, Paul C. Stern, and Charles Tilly, eds., *Behavior, Society, and Nuclear War*, Vol. 1 (New York: Oxford University Press, 1989), pp. 209–333; and Stephen Van Evera, *Causes of War, Volume 1: The Structure of Power and the Roots of War* (Ithaca, N.Y.: Cornell University Press, forthcoming 1999).
3. Realist thinkers include Thucydides, Hobbes, and Machiavelli. The most important recent realist theories that bear on the causes of war are presented in Hans J. Morgenthau, *Politics Among Nations: The Struggle for Power and Peace* (New York: Knopf, 1948 and later editions); Kenneth N. Waltz, *Theory of International Politics* (Reading, Mass.: Addison-Wesley, 1979); Waltz, *Man, the State and War;* and Robert G. Gilpin, *War and Change in World Politics* (New York: Cambridge University Press, 1981).

system. Thucydides' claim that the Peloponnesian war became inevitable because of "the growth of Athenian power and the fear which this caused in Sparta" is the classic example of a realist explanation.[4] Contemporary realist theories are not monolithic; realism is a family of theories and it contains different explanations for war.[5] The essays included here exemplify the diversity of realist theories of war and peace.

John Mearsheimer draws upon the structural realism initially advanced by Kenneth Waltz to analyze the implications of the changing international distribution of power in the 1990s. In his well-known article, "Back to the Future: Instability in Europe after the Cold War," he employs neorealist theory to present a pessimistic vision of Europe's future. Mearsheimer contends that Europe has enjoyed peace for the past forty-five years for two key reasons: bipolar systems tend to be peaceful, and the presence of nuclear weapons has induced general caution. If the Soviet Union and the United States withdraw from Europe, he argues, Europe will devolve to multipolarity and a renewed era of wars and major crises may erupt on that continent.[6]

Although Mearsheimer's analysis of the prospects for stability in Europe has, in some ways, been overtaken by events, "Back to the Future" remains an important and useful explication and application of structural realist (or neorealist) perspectives on the causes of war. It also presents a critique of alternative theories of war: economic liberalism, what Mearsheimer calls the theory of "peace-loving democracies," and theories that claim that war is obsolescent.

Mearsheimer argues that war is always possible in the anarchical international system, because no sovereign power exists to prevent states from going

---

4. Thucydides, *History of the Peloponnesian War*, Rex Warner, trans., M.I. Finley, ed. (Harmondsworth, U.K.: Penguin, 1954), p. 49.

5. For a selection of recent examples of and perspectives on realist theory, see Michael E. Brown, Sean M. Lynn-Jones, and Steven E. Miller, eds., *The Perils of Anarchy: Contemporary Realism and International Security* (Cambridge, Mass.: The MIT Press, 1995); and Benjamin Frankel, ed., *Realism: Restatements and Renewal* (London: Frank Cass, 1996).

6. For alternative visions of Europe's future, see Jack Snyder, "Averting Anarchy in the New Europe," *International Security*, Vol. 14, No. 4 (Spring 1990), pp. 5–41; and Stephen Van Evera, "Primed for Peace: Europe After the Cold War," *International Security*, Vol. 15, No. 3 (Winter 1990/91), pp. 7–57. For a more general theoretical rejoinder, see Robert Jervis, "The Future of World Politics: Will it Resemble the Past?" *International Security*, Vol. 16, No. 3 (Winter 1992/92), pp. 39–73. Letters from Stanley Hoffmann, Robert Keohane, Bruce Russett, and Thomas Risse-Kappen replying to Mearsheimer's arguments, as well as Mearsheimer's responses, can be found in "Correspondence: Back to the Future, Part II: International Relations Theory and Post-Cold War Europe," *International Security*, Vol. 15, No. 2 (Fall 1990), pp. 191–199, and "Correspondence: Back to the Future, Part III: Realism and the Realities of European Security," *International Security*, Vol. 15, No. 3 (Winter 1990/91), pp. 216–222.

to war. States start wars when the benefits of going to war are high and the costs and risks of doing so are low. These benefits and costs depend on two factors: the distribution of power among states, and the nature of the military power available to them. The first factor includes the number of great powers in the international system—whether a system is bipolar or multipolar. The second includes whether available weapons are very destructive and whether they tend to favor the offense over the defense. Mearsheimer argues that nuclear weapons give the defense a large advantage, but he believes that for conventional forces offensive and defensive advantages cannot be measured and are irrelevant.

War, according to Mearsheimer, is less likely under bipolarity than under multipolarity. In a bipolar world, where there are only two great powers, the number of potential conflict dyads is lower, because there are only two great powers that could engage in a major war. Under multipolarity, the number of potential conflict dyads is greater. Deterrence of aggression is also easier under bipolarity, because the two great powers do not have to depend on the uncertainties of alliance formation to deter one another. The great powers can balance by internal means and need not worry about unreliable allies, which complicate diplomatic and military calculations under multipolarity. Deterrence is less likely to fail because states will not optimistically go to war in hopes that a coalition will not form to oppose them. Bipolarity also makes it easier to calculate the power of opposing sides in any conflict. Because states do not have to add up the power of several states, they are less likely to make miscalculations of the aggregate power of their adversaries. And because the same two great powers interact repeatedly, they are likely to understand one another's resolve and to accept implicit rules of behavior. All of these peace-promoting factors are absent under multipolarity.

Mearsheimer also argues that nuclear weapons tend to cause peace. Nuclear weapons make conquest extraordinarily difficult. They give defenders a large advantage because states are more likely to risk nuclear war if their survival is at stake. Thus states attempting to defend themselves can credibly threaten to inflict enormous devastation on aggressor states. Nuclear weapons make miscalculation of power capabilities less likely because a numerically smaller nuclear force can still inflict unacceptable destruction.

In a brief review of the history of international politics in Europe before and during the Cold War, Mearsheimer argues that multipolarity and the absence of nuclear weapons contributed to Europe's repeated wars before 1945. States in Europe's multipolar system frequently failed to balance against aggressors and deterrence often failed. The high number of great powers made conflict and miscalculation more likely. During the Cold War, however, the combination of bipolarity and nuclear weapons kept Europe at peace.

Mearsheimer argues that his theory is superior to three alternative theories of war and peace. He first presents a critique of economic liberalism, which argues that "a liberal economic order that allows free economic exchange between states" makes peace more probable.[7] In Mearsheimer's view, economic liberalism rests on the claims that free trade causes prosperity, and prosperous states are more satisfied and more peaceful; that the international regimes or institutions required to maintain free trade foster international peace and co-operation and may even assume more power than states; and that economic interdependence causes peace and cooperation. Mearsheimer faults economic liberalism for assuming that states are motivated mainly by a desire for prosperity. Instead, he argues, the competition for security in an anarchic world drives states into conflict and makes them reluctant to cooperate because they fear that other states will gain relatively more from cooperation. Economic interdependence often causes conflict, not cooperation. Mearsheimer argues that the empirical record shows that economic interdependence has sometimes coincided with war, as it did in 1914. Free trade among the Western powers since 1945 has coincided with peace, but Mearsheimer attributes this outcome to the hegemonic power of the United States and the solidarity produced by the Soviet threat.

Mearsheimer's analysis of a second alternative theory, the "peace-loving democracies theory" (generally known as the democratic peace theory or hypothesis), leads him to conclude that it, too, is inferior to his realist theory. The theory holds that democracies do not go to war with one another because their domestic institutions constrain them from initiating war or because their democratic norms and values rule out war against a fellow democracy.[8] Mearsheimer argues that neither explanation is logically sound. The first would predict that democracies would be more peace-loving in general, but the empirical record suggests that they are just as war-prone as other types of states, even if they do not seem to fight one another. The second explanation is more logically persuasive, but Mearsheimer argues that other factors—such as the need to ally against common threats—account for the absence of war

---

7. For another analysis of economic liberalism, see Dale Copeland's essay in this volume.
8. The democratic peace is discussed in the essays by John Owen, Christopher Layne, and Edward Mansfield and Jack Snyder in this volume.

among democracies. He also notes that democracies have threatened war against other democracies and that the absence of such wars may be due to chance.

Mearsheimer also examines the claim that war has become obsolescent and finds it unpersuasive.[9] He notes that this argument attributes the obsolescence of war to the increased horrors of conventional conflict, not to the destructive effects of nuclear weapons. Mearsheimer points out that the horrors of conventional war are insufficient to render war obsolescent. World War I caused huge casualties, but this did not prevent the outbreak of World War II. Moreover, in conventional war it is still possible to achieve a rapid and decisive victory. The same is not true in nuclear war, because neither side can avoid devastation.

Stephen Van Evera's "Offense, Defense, and the Causes of War" demonstrates that realist theories of war and peace need not focus solely on the distribution of aggregate power among states. Unlike Mearsheimer, Van Evera does not consider the effects of the overall distribution of power or the polarity of the international system. Van Evera examines how the offense-defense balance affects the probability of war. He defines the offense-defense balance as the feasibility of conquest. It is a systemic variable, like those in other realist theories, but it is distinct from measures of aggregate power. The balance is shaped by military factors, geography, domestic social and political factors, and the nature of diplomacy.

Van Evera argues that shifts in the offense-defense balance toward the offense have at least ten effects that make war more likely: (1) empires are easier to conquer; (2) self-defense is more difficult; (3) states become more insecure and thus resist others' expansion more fiercely; (4) first-strike advantages become larger; (5) windows of opportunity and vulnerability open wider; (6) states adopt fait accompli diplomatic tactics; (7) states negotiate less readily and cooperatively; (8) states maintain greater secrecy in foreign and defense policy; (9) arms racing becomes faster and harder; and (10) as conquest grows easier, states adopt policies such as offensive military doctrines, which make conquest even easier, thereby magnifying all the other effects. These effects emerge whether the offensive advantage is real or only perceived. They operate individually or collectively to make war more likely when conquest is easy.

---

9. For other critical analyses of the purported obsolescence of war, see the essays by Carl Kaysen and John Orme in this volume.

What determines the offense-defense balance? Van Evera argues that military factors, such as technology, doctrine, and force posture and deployments have important effects on the balance. For example, the ability to build impregnable fortifications favors the defense. Motorized armor and the doctrine of the blitzkrieg favor the offense. But military factors alone do not determine the offense-defense balance. Geography—especially the presence or absence of defensible borders and natural obstacles to conquest—is also important, as is the domestic political and social order of states. Popular regimes, for example, are better able to organize guerrilla resistance to potential conquest, thereby strengthening the defense. Finally, diplomatic factors influence the offense-defense balance: "collective security systems, defensive alliances, and balancing behavior by neutral states" all "impede conquest by adding allies to the defending side."

Van Evera tests offense-defense theory by looking at three cases: Europe since 1789, ancient China during the Spring and Autumn and Warring States eras, and the United States since 1789. Van Evera deduces three prime predictions from the theory: (1) war will be more common when offense is easy or is perceived to be easy; (2) states that have or think they have offensive opportunities will be more likely to initiate wars than other states; and (3) states will be more likely to initiate wars during periods when they have or believe they have offensive opportunities. The theory also predicts that the ten war-causing effects listed above will be present in eras and states where there is a real or perceived offensive advantage. Although each case can test only some of the theory's predictions, taken together they allow a test of most of the predictions.

The cases offer broad support for offense-defense theory. In Europe since 1789, the amount of war tends to correlate loosely with the offense-defense balance and tightly with perceptions of the balance. States that faced real or perceived offensive opportunities and defensive vulnerabilities were most likely to initiate war. In Ancient China, Van Evera finds that from 722–221 BCE there was a long-term shift in the offense-defense balance that strengthened the offense. As the theory predicts, war became more common as the offense became more powerful. The history of the United States since 1789 also supports the theory. In general, the relative geographical invulnerability of the United States has enabled it to fight only a few great-power wars. Few of the predicted intervening variables—the processes that cause offensive advantages to lead to war—are present in U.S. diplomatic and military history. The United States has fought few preemptive and preventive wars, has been less prone to acquire colonies than other great powers, has not based its diplomacy on fait accompli tactics, has been less secretive than other great powers, and has engaged in arms racing only during the Cold War. The level of U.S. bellicosity also has varied with changes in U.S. perceptions of external threats.

Van Evera concludes that offense-defense theory is a robust theory that can pass some difficult tests. He also contends that it is a useful theory that can be applied to prevent war. Unlike variables such as the polarity of the international system, the state of human nature, or the strength of international institutions, the variables identified by offense-defense theory—especially perceptions of the offense-defense balance—can be manipulated by national policies. Van Evera argues that the theory suggests that war can be limited or prevented if states adopt defensive military doctrines and limit offensive military capabilities through arms control. Defensive alliances, such as U.S. security guarantees in Europe and Asia since 1949, also can make conquest harder and war less likely.

In "Realists as Optimists: Cooperation as Self-Help," Charles Glaser argues that realist theory can explain international peace and cooperation. Realists and their critics have exaggerated the extent to which the nature of the international system makes war likely or inevitable. Both camps have been too pessimistic in their interpretations of realism. In Glaser's view, the logic of realism can lead to predictions of peace and cooperation. Like Van Evera, he argues that these benign outcomes are most likely when the offense-defense balance of military technology favors the defense. This condition creates a mild security dilemma, which enables security-seeking states to pursue security for themselves without undermining it for others. Whether the security dilemma is often mild is an empirical question, not a theoretical one; war is not a necessary consequence of international anarchy and other realist assumptions. Realists who are pessimistic about the prospects for peace and cooperation need to show that the security dilemma is frequently severe. Glaser recognizes that states may not behave peacefully even if international conditions encourage peace, but contends that these outcomes may reflect domestic conditions or state-level pathologies, not the structure of international politics.

The next three essays present different perspectives on the relationship between democracy and war and peace. The apparent absence of wars between democracies—the "democratic peace"—has stimulated considerable research and debate among scholars of war and peace in the 1990s. Many articles and several books have argued over whether the democratic peace is an empirical fact and have attempted to explain it.[10] Some scholars claim that the absence of wars between democracies is close to an "empirical law" of international relations. Others believe that democracies have gone to war and point to examples such as Britain and America in 1812 or Finland and the Western allies in World War II. Even those who agree on the existence of a democratic peace offer contending theories to explain it. Normative explanations attribute the democratic peace to shared liberal and democratic norms that make it impossible for democracies to fight one another. Structural/institutional explanations hold that leaders in democracies are constrained from going to war by the power of legislatures and public opinion.

In "How Liberalism Produces Democratic Peace," John Owen refines and explicates the causal mechanism that generates the democratic peace. He shows how liberal principles and democratic processes work together to make war between democracies virtually impossible.

Owen defines a liberal democracy as a state "where liberalism is the dominant ideology and citizens have leverage over war decisions." Liberalism holds that individuals everywhere should have freedom, and that peace is a necessary condition for freedom. Wars should only be fought in the cause of peace and freedom. Liberals believe that other liberal states act to preserve freedom and thus are pacific and trustworthy. Because liberal states have liberal institutional structures that allow for public control of foreign policy, even illiberal leaders will be unable to lead liberal states into war against other liberal states. Owen also points out that these liberal principles and processes only have a chance to operate when a state actually perceives another state as a liberal democracy. Some alleged wars between liberal democracies (e.g., the War of 1812) took place because at least one state did not see the other as a liberal democracy. He also notes that states may be illiberal democracies—they may

---

10. For a selection of important works on both sides of the issue, see Michael E. Brown, Sean M. Lynn-Jones, and Steven E. Miller, eds., *Debating the Democratic Peace* (Cambridge, Mass.: The MIT Press, 1996). Other important recent works include David L. Rousseau, Christopher Gelpi, Dan Reiter, and Paul K. Huth, "Assessing the Dyadic Nature of the Democratic Peace, 1918–88," *American Political Science Review*, Vol. 90, No. 3 (September 1996), pp. 512–533; Zeev Maoz, "The Controversy over the Democratic Peace: Rearguard Action or Cracks in the Wall?" *International Security*, Vol. 22, No. 1 (Summer 1997), pp. 162–198; Miriam Fendius Elman, ed., *Paths to Peace: Is Democracy the Answer?* (Cambridge, Mass.: The MIT Press, 1997); and Michael W. Doyle, *Ways of War and Peace* (New York: Norton, 1997), pp. 251–311. A helpful review of the literature can be found in Steve Chan, "In Search of Democratic Peace: Problems and Promise," *Mershon International Studies Review: Supplement to the International Studies Quarterly*, Vol. 41, Supplement 1 (May 1997), pp. 59–91.

have representative forms of government without liberal ideologies. Such states will not join the liberal-democratic zone of peace.

Owen deduces several hypotheses from his explanation of how liberalism causes the democratic peace: liberals will trust states they consider liberal and mistrust those they consider illiberal; when liberals observe a foreign state becoming liberal by their own standards, they will expect pacific relations with it; liberals will claim that fellow liberal democracies share their ends, and that illiberal states do not; liberals will not change their assessments of foreign states during crises with those states unless those states change their institutions; liberal elites will agitate for their policies during war-threatening crises; during crises, statesmen will be constrained to follow liberal policy. He then examines four historical cases of troubled relations between liberal states: the Franco-American crisis of 1796–98, and the Anglo-American crises of 1803–12, 1861–65, and 1895–96.[11] The outcomes support Owen's argument. When the U.S. leaders failed to perceive Britain as a democracy in 1812, war broke out. In 1863–65, the British government saw the United States as a liberal democracy and adopted a policy of restraint during the U.S. Civil War. In 1895–96, the United States and Britain saw each other as democracies. They avoided war in the Venezuelan Crisis and laid the foundations for the Anglo-American "special relationship." In each case, the process unfolded in accordance with Owen's hypotheses.

Owen replies to realist critics of the democratic peace. To those who claim that neither the normative or structural/institutional explanation of the democratic peace is adequate, he replies that his integration of the two provides a stronger explanation. He also notes that the existence of threats by one liberal state against another does not invalidate the democratic peace proposition, because such threats are made when liberal states do not recognize each other, or when illiberal leaders are in power. Owen also notes that definitions of democracy are not as malleable in practice as some realists claim. In the crises he examines, American leaders did not suddenly shift their perceptions of other states and redefine them according to exigencies of national interest.

Owen does not dispute that the international distribution of power matters. But he argues that liberalism has an independent effect that sometimes flies in

---

11. For a more detailed discussion of these and other cases, see John M. Owen, IV, *Liberal Peace, Liberal War: American Politics and International Security* (Ithaca, N.Y.: Cornell University Press, 1997).

the face of alleged systemic imperatives. He points out that realist balance-of-threat theory, as proposed by Stephen Walt, is compatible with liberalism.[12]

In "Kant or Cant: The Myth of the Democratic Peace," Christopher Layne argues that the democratic peace proposition does not stand up to empirical scrutiny and is a poor guide for policy. Layne seeks to test the democratic peace by deducing additional, testable hypotheses from its causal logic. He regards the normative variant of the democratic peace proposition as the most promising candidate for further testing. Unlike the structural/institutional explanation, which Layne believes predicts that democracies will be less likely to go to war than other states, the normative explanation only predicts that democracies will not go to war with one another.

To test the normative explanation of the democratic peace, Layne asks which additional predictions can be deduced from its underlying logic. If democratic norms and political culture cause democracies to avoid war with one another, Layne argues, we should expect pairs of democratic states involved in crises with one another to avoid war and resolve these crises peacefully, because these norms constrain their crisis behavior. In other words, Layne tests the democratic peace proposition by asking what it predicts about how democracies will behave in international crises between democracies.[13] He argues that in historical cases of "near misses" of war between democracies the following three factors should be present: pacific public opinion; an absence of military threats and preparations to make such threats; accommodating behavior, including an absence of ultimata, inflexible positions, and coercive diplomacy.

Layne selects four crises in which democracies came close to war: the 1861 "*Trent* Affair" between the United States and Great Britain; the 1895–96 U.S.-British crisis over Venezuela's boundaries; the 1898 Fashoda crisis between France and Great Britain; and the 1923 Ruhr crisis between France and Germany. His review of the historical record concludes that in these cases democracies avoided war, but there is no evidence that they did so because they shared democratic norms. The indicators that should have been present were absent. Instead, the democracies behaved in a manner predicted by realism: they acted on the basis of calculations of national interest; paid attention to

---

12. Stephen M. Walt, *The Origins of Alliances* (Ithaca, N.Y.: Cornell University Press, 1987).
13. In Layne's study, the dependent variable is not whether democracies went to war or not, but how democracies behaved in their diplomatic interactions during crises with one another. These interactions are intervening variables when the democratic peace proposition is used to explain why democracies do not go to war with one another, but they become dependent variables in Layne's study.

strategic concerns, particularly the distribution of military capabilities; and used threats when vital interests were jeopardized.

Layne argues that realism provides a better and more parsimonious explanation of why the democracies involved in the crises did not go to war. He suggests that his findings cast doubt on the democratic peace proposition in general. Although proponents of the proposition claim that they have examined many democratic dyads and found no wars, Layne argues that looking at cases where war was possible is a better way to test the proposition.

Layne also questions whether there have been no wars involving democracies. He classifies the War of 1812 and the U.S. Civil War as wars between democratic states. In addition, he argues that Germany in 1914 was as democratic as France and Britain (at least in the making of foreign policy), and that World War I also should be regarded as a war between democracies.

Layne draws several conclusions for policy from his theoretical and empirical analysis. He cautions against making promoting democracy an aim of U.S. foreign policy. If there is no empirical support for the democratic "zone of peace," it would be a mistake to try to create a democratic world. Attempts to spread democracy to volatile regions would raise risks of war.

In "Democratization and the Danger of War," Edward Mansfield and Jack Snyder present a different type of challenge to the democratic peace proposition. They argue that democratizing states become more likely to go to war. They do not dispute that a democratic peace exists between mature, stable democracies, but they suggest that immature democracies are a force for war, not peace.[14]

Mansfield and Snyder present data indicating that democratizing states are more likely to be involved in war in the years immediately after their democratization begins. This increase becomes greater one, five, and ten years after the start of democratization. When Mansfield and Snyder look at component measures of democratization—competitiveness of participation, executive constraints, and openness of executive recruitment—they find that increases in

---

14. Mansfield and Snyder's argument has stimulated a vigorous debate and further research. See the letters from Reinhard Wolf, Erich Weede, and Andrew Enterline, as well as the reply from Mansfield and Snyder, in *International Security*, Vol. 20, No. 4 (Spring 1996), pp. 176–207; William R. Thompson and Richard M. Tucker, "A Tale of Two Democratic Peace Critiques," *Journal of Conflict Resolution*, Vol. 41, No. 2 (June 1997), pp. 428–451; Edward D. Mansfield and Jack Snyder, "A Reply to Thompson and Tucker," in ibid., pp. 457–461; and Michael D. Ward and Kristian S. Gelditsch, "Democratizing for Peace," *American Political Science Review*, Vol. 92, No. 1 (March 1998), pp. 51–61. Mansfield and Snyder are working on a book (forthcoming from MIT Press) that develops their arguments in more detail and presents additional evidence.

these measures also increase the probability of war. Compared to states that remain or become autocracies, states that make the transition from autocracy to democratization are more than twice as likely to be in a war during the decade after democratization.

Mansfield and Snyder also note that great powers have become more warlike as they have democratized. During the nineteenth century, liberalizing Britain fought the Crimean War and vastly augmented its overseas empire. Napoleon III's France fought a series of wars until it destroyed itself in the Franco-Prussian War. These wars were intended to establish its domestic legitimacy as mass participation grew. In Wilhelmine Germany, domestic political struggles resulting from the political rise of the middle class helped to bring on World War I. Japan's democratization in the 1920s prompted the army to devise and implement a program of imperial expansion to win public support.

According to Mansfield and Snyder, there are four reasons why new democracies get into wars. First, elite groups from the old regime often use appeals to nationalism as they compete for domestic power in the new democratic political arena. Second, new elites find it necessary to resort to similar nationalistic appeals. Third, newly mobilized publics are often hard to control. Fourth, if incipient democracy collapses, the return to autocracy increases the chances of going to war. The basic problem of democratizing states is that they lack the stabilizing institutions of mature democracies. This contributes to a political impasse in new democracies: it becomes hard to form stable coalitions that can stay in power and pursue coherent policies. As a result, elites indulge in short-run thinking and reckless policymaking that can lead to war.

Mansfield and Snyder contend that their findings suggest that promoting democratization may not be the best way to build peace. They present several recommendations for reducing the dangers of democratization. Deposed autocratic leaders of emerging democracies should be exiled and given a "golden parachute" so that they have few incentives to try to regain power by adopting aggressive policies. Former military and economic elites should be given a stake in newly liberalized economies. Guaranteeing a free press and a pluralistic security debate can help to reduce the dangers of nationalist mythmaking. The West should foster an independent and aggressive cadre of journalists in democratizing states.[15]

---

15. For further ideas on how freedom of the press can help to limit the pathologies of democratizing states, see Jack Snyder and Karen Ballentine, "Nationalism and the Marketplace of Ideas," *International Security*, Vol. 21, No. 2 (Fall 1996), pp. 5–40.

The next section of essays examines the connection between nationalism and ethnicity and war. Nationalism and ethnicity appear to be important causes of many internal and international conflicts in the 1990s. After the Cold War ended, nationalist and ethnic strife flared up in the former Yugoslavia, the former republics of the Soviet Union, and Rwanda. Some of these conflicts were new; others had simmered for years in the shadow of the Cold War. As the ideological struggles of the Cold War faded, nationalism and ethnicity took center stage.[16] But the relationship between nationalism, ethnicity, and war remains unclear. There is no single theory of nationalism and war. The essays included here present a wide range of hypotheses.

In "Hypotheses on Nationalism and War," Stephen Van Evera offers a set of hypotheses on the connection between nationalism and war. He addresses the following questions: What types of nationalism cause war? When is it more likely that nationalism will lead to conflict? How can wars of nationalism be prevented? He pays particular attention to the dangers posed by nationalism in post-Cold War Europe.

Van Evera suggests that nationalism poses a greater and more immediate risk of war when some or all of the following factors are present: a high proportion of the state-seeking nationalities are stateless; the nationalities attempt to recover national diasporas through annexationist strategies; the nationalities have hegemonistic goals toward other nationalities and believe that their own national group is racially, culturally, or politically superior; nationalities oppress minorities living in their own states. The more these factors, alone or in combination, are present, the greater the risk that nationalism will provoke war. When nationalist movements have these attributes, the potential for violence is high.

Van Evera identifies many underlying causes that determine whether nationalist movements have these four war-causing attributes. He divides these factors into three categories. The first category, structural factors, is based on the geographic and demographic arrangement of a national group's people. One important factor in this category is whether a national minority has the capability to launch a war for independent statehood and whether the central government can and will resist such an attempt at secession. Other structural factors are whether the populations of national groups are intermingled or not,

---

16. See Michael E. Brown, Owen R. Coté, Jr., Sean M. Lynn-Jones, and Steven E. Miller, eds., *Nationalism and Ethnic Conflict* (Cambridge, Mass.: The MIT Press, 1997); and Michael E. Brown, ed., *The International Dimensions of Internal Conflict* (Cambridge, Mass.: The MIT Press, 1996).

and whether political and communal boundaries can be defended easily. The wars in the former Yugoslavia, for example, started when all three of these factors predicted conflict.

The second category is political-environmental factors—those that arise from how a national group has been treated by its neighbors. When nationalities have committed crimes against one another and these crimes are remembered, war is more likely. Conflict also becomes more probable when states fail to respect minority rights.

Van Evera's third category consists of perceptual factors, especially self-glorifying and chauvinistic myths. When national movements believe in a mythical history that claims that they are superior and uniquely virtuous while others are evil and inferior, they are more likely to oppress or attack other groups. Such beliefs flourished in Germany before the two World Wars, and have been present in contemporary Serbia and Croatia.

Applying his hypotheses, Van Evera forecasts that there is a high risk of continuing nationalist conflict in Eastern Europe. He suggests, however, that these dangers can be controlled. Some of the factors identified by his hypotheses (e.g., intermingling of populations) are hard to change peacefully, but others (e.g., treatment of minorities) can be manipulated by government policies. Van Evera argues that Western democracies should prevent nationalist conflicts in Eastern Europe by making economic relations conditional on acceptance of principles that proscribe war-causing nationalist policies. For example, the West should insist on guarantees of minority rights, the adoption of democratic forms of government and market economies, and renunciation of attempts to change borders by force. Van Evera emphasizes that the West also should insist that Eastern European countries teach history honestly in their schools, so that future generations do not become imbued with war-causing and chauvinistic myths about their nation's past.

The next essay, David Lake and Donald Rothchild's "Containing Fear: The Origins and Management of Ethnic Conflict," attributes ethnic conflict to one important cause: collective fears of the future. When ethnic groups start to fear for their safety, they find themselves in a strategic dilemma. Fears for their own security take hold and are magnified by activists and political entrepreneurs. As ethnic groups attempt to protect themselves, they increase the fears of other groups, producing "a toxic brew of distrust and suspicion that can explode into murderous violence." Lake and Rothchild argue that explanations that attribute ethnic wars to "ancient hatreds" or a sudden release of passions that had been bottled up during the Cold War are incomplete or wrong.

Lake and Rothchild contend that collective fears of the future arise when states cannot arbitrate between ethnic groups or protect minority groups. When this happens, domestic politics starts to resemble the condition of anarchy found in international politics and groups fear for their own survival. Negotiations often fail to resolve political differences between groups because one or more strategic dilemmas prevents an agreement and contributes to violent conflict. According to Lake and Rothchild, the first strategic dilemma is information failure. Ethnic groups often exaggerate their strengths, conceal their weakness, and withhold their plans for victory on the battlefield. Without adequate information, negotiations often collapse and suspicions rise. The second strategic dilemma is the problem of making credible commitments. As the balance of power between ethnic groups shifts, agreements between ethnic groups become harder to enforce. If one group is growing stronger, it has an incentive to abandon an agreement in the future and the other group has an incentive to fight now to preserve the agreement. The third strategic dilemma is the security dilemma, which operates in domestic politics among ethnic groups in a collapsing state, as well as in international politics.[17] Lake and Rothchild define the security dilemma narrowly, suggesting that its core is the idea that incentives to launch preemptive strikes grow when offensive military technologies and strategies have an advantage. In ethnic conflicts, preemptive incentives are particularly likely to emerge when terrain and settlement patterns render groups hard to defend.

According to Lake and Rothchild, all of these strategic dilemmas of interaction between ethnic groups are exacerbated by interactions within groups. As states start to weaken, social polarization often takes place in multi-ethnic societies. Activists and political entrepreneurs within groups exploit political memories, myths, and emotions to gain or maintain political power. By making appeals to ethnic solidarity and portraying other groups as threats, they increase the likelihood of conflict.

Lake and Rothchild prescribe several policies for maintaining ethnic peace. Domestic confidence-building measures can sometimes contain the fears that lead to ethnic conflict. Minority groups must be reassured of their physical and cultural security. Political arrangements such as power-sharing, elections

---

17. See Robert Jervis, "Cooperation Under the Security Dilemma," *World Politics*, Vol. 30, No. 2 (January 1978), pp. 167–213; Barry R. Posen, "The Security Dilemma and Ethnic Conflict," in Michael E. Brown, ed., *Ethnic Conflict and International Security* (Princeton, N.J.: Princeton University Press, 1993), pp. 103–124; and Charles Glaser's essay in this volume.

that reinforce the interdependence of groups, and regional autonomy can achieve this end. Different groups also should offer demonstrations of respect and not show contempt for one another. In the Sudan, for example, the government's decision to impose Islamic law was seen as a sign of disrespect by that country's Christian and animist minority and contributed to the revival of intense ethnic conflict. When domestic policies are insufficient, external intervention may be necessary. Such intervention may be benign and noncoercive. For example, the Western democracies have encouraged Hungary and Romania to mitigate ethnic conflicts by making it clear that oppression of minorities would make it difficult or impossible for Budapest and Bucharest to gain membership in Western international organizations. In other cases, coercive intervention will be necessary to change the balance of power among ethnic groups or to enforce agreements. External actors also can serve as mediators, but civil wars often cannot be ended through negotiations.

Lake and Rothchild conclude by recommending three practical steps to control ethnic conflicts. First, outside states and international organizations should manage the flow of information in countries threatened by ethnic conflict. Radio stations that make inflammatory appeals (as happened in Rwanda before the 1994 genocide) should be jammed. International actors should ensure that objective and unbiased information is freely available. Second, external actors should rescue "failing" states before they collapse. Effective states can often arbitrate between ethnic groups and prevent violence. Once the mechanisms of state power have broken down, ethnic fears intensify and ethnic groups "either turn away from the state or attempt to seize it to further their own quest for security." Third, external actors need to invest more in the implementation of peace agreements between warring groups. Negotiating an agreement often is not enough to maintain ethnic peace. States and international organizations may have to engage in state-building or to at least threaten to intervene to protect ethnic minorities.

For at least two centuries, many proponents of peace have placed their faith in international institutions. In the nineteenth century, the Concert of Europe ameliorated tensions among the great powers. At the turn of the century, treaties of arbitration and the Hague conferences reflected hopes that institutions could prevent war. Woodrow Wilson's ultimately futile effort to create a "league to enforce peace" stands out as perhaps the most ambitious attempt to use international institutions to build peace. The Charter of the United

Nations begins by explicitly proclaiming the goal of freeing the world from the "scourge of war."[18] More recently, theorists of international politics have examined how institutions, including informal regimes and formal organizations, influence international politics and increase the chances of cooperation.[19] The next six essays in this volume debate whether institutions can improve the prospects for peace.

John Mearsheimer's "The False Promise of International Institutions" rebuts arguments that international institutions can reduce the risk of war significantly. Mearsheimer explicates three "anti-realist" arguments for how institutions can promote peace: (1) the liberal-institutionalist claim that international institutions promote cooperation by preventing cheating and providing information; (2) the critical theorists' argument that the adoption of new norms and ideas can eliminate war, even in an anarchic international system; and (3) arguments for collective security, which usually contend that wars would become unlikely if all states pledged to defend any victim of aggression. Mearsheimer does not deny that institutions sometimes matter, but he finds little empirical evidence or logical support for claims that institutions can increase the chances of peace. Instead, he concludes that realist theory correctly suggests that wars will be a recurrent feature of international politics, and that realism more successfully identifies the conditions for peace than any of the contending theories.

The next four essays present vigorous responses to Mearsheimer's arguments and defend the potential of international institutions to bring about peace.

In "The Promise of Institutionalist Theory," Robert Keohane and Lisa Martin begin by pointing to what they believe are flaws in Mearsheimer's version of

---

18. One of the best surveys of the history of international organizations remains Inis L. Claude, Jr., *Swords into Plowshares: The Problems and Progress of International Organization*, 4th ed. (New York: Random House, 1971).

19. See Stephen D. Krasner, ed., *International Regimes* (Ithaca, N.Y.: Cornell University Press, 1983); Robert O. Keohane, *After Hegemony: Cooperation and Discord in the World Political Economy* (Princeton, N.J.: Princeton University Press, 1984); Keohane, *International Institutions and State Power: Essays in International Relations Theory* (Boulder, Colo.: Westview, 1989); Kenneth A. Oye, "Explaining Cooperation under Anarchy: Hypotheses and Strategies" and Robert Axelrod and Robert O. Keohane, "Achieving Cooperation under Anarchy: Strategies and Institutions," both in Oye, ed., *Cooperation Under Anarchy* (Princeton, N.J.: Princeton University Press, 1986); Arthur A. Stein, *Why Nations Cooperate: Circumstance and Choice in International Relations* (Ithaca, N.Y.: Cornell University Press, 1990); Lisa L. Martin, *Coercive Cooperation: Explaining Multilateral Economic Sanctions* (Princeton, N.J.: Princeton University Press, 1992); and John Gerard Ruggie, *Multilateralism Matters: The Theory and Praxis of an Institutional Form* (New York: Columbia University Press, 1993).

realist theory. They note that Mearsheimer's "Back to the Future" (also included in this volume) predicts the demise of NATO and the atrophy of the European Community, now the European Union (EU). Yet these institutions still command large resources from their member states and both are attracting new members. Keohane and Martin point out that Mearsheimer's realism often makes sweeping generalizations that must then be qualified, whereas institutionalism makes more modest, conditional, and accurate claims. According to Keohane and Martin, institutionalist theory does not claim that "institutions can prevent war regardless of the structure in which they operate" and Mearsheimer is mistaken to attack this view.

Keohane and Martin take particular issue with Mearsheimer's argument that institutionalist theory assumes that international politics can be divided into two realms—political economy and security. They argue that institutional theory can be applied to both. They also argue that Mearsheimer greatly overstates the extent to which relative gains impede cooperation. Recognizing that states may worry about relative gains in some circumstances, they argue that those circumstances are limited to cases in which there are only two major actors in international politics or when offense has the advantage over defense. Institutions can alleviate fears of unequal gains and further reduce the importance of relative gains.

Responding to Mearsheimer's argument that empirical research does not support claims for the importance of institutions, Keohane and Martin cite recent studies that show that institutions matter. International treaty rules have reduced the intentional discharge of oil into the oceans. The European Court of Justice has made EU law part of the domestic law of European states. NATO has operated as a security regime in Europe, promoting peace and stable levels of conventional forces. Economic sanctions are easier to apply and enforce when an international organization is involved. Keohane and Martin conclude that "international institutions operating on the basis of reciprocity will be components of any lasting peace."

Charles Kupchan and Clifford Kupchan defend collective security in their "The Promise of Collective Security." They make three replies to Mearsheimer. First, they argue that he defines collective security too narrowly by focusing only on "ideal collective security" in which "states make automatic and legally binding commitments to respond to aggression wherever and whenever it occurs." This definition excludes the type of concert-based collective security system that the Kupchans believe can promote peace by facilitating regulated, institutionalized balancing.[20]

Second, the Kupchans argue that instead of violating the logic of power-balancing, as Mearsheimer claims, collective security is a mechanism for providing more effective balancing than would otherwise occur. The institution of collective security can prevent war because it facilitates the formation of overwhelming coalitions against potential aggressors. By encouraging or requiring states to join coalitions to oppose aggression, collective security systems make it likely that any aggressor will confront a preponderant opposing force. In cases where there is a basic compatibility between the aims of the great powers—as there may be in contemporary Europe—collective security systems also can build trust and deepen international cooperation among their members.

Third, the Kupchans criticize Mearsheimer's realist theory for its failure to take into account domestic politics and ideas. They argue that Mearsheimer incorrectly assumes that all great powers seek power and security in more or less the same way. Instead, domestic politics, norms, and beliefs shape decisions for war and peace. Domestic factors made Germany and Japan aggressor states in the 1930s. Ideology caused Soviet expansionism and the Cold War. When states have compatible domestic political systems and norms, concert-based collective security systems can flourish.

In "The False Premise of Realism" John Gerard Ruggie responds to Mearsheimer by arguing that U.S. policymakers after World War II deliberately created institutions that served peace and U.S. interests. They rejected the kind of anti-institutionalist argument that Mearsheimer makes, and instead accepted that institutions matter. Franklin Roosevelt initially sought to establish a United Nations that would be a hybrid collective security organization with its own military forces. When the Cold War made that impossible, the Eisenhower administration facilitated the creation of UN peacekeeping forces. Eisenhower and later presidents built international regimes to prevent the spread of nuclear weapons. Truman presided over the creation of a NATO that was based on mutual guarantees and an institutionalized integrated command structure. Alternatives such as multiple bilateral alliances between the United States and

---

20. The Kupchans present their complete argument for concert-based collective security in Charles A. Kupchan and Clifford A. Kupchan, "Concerts, Collective Security, and the Future of Europe," *International Security*, Vol. 16, No. 1 (Summer 1991), pp. 114–161.

European states were rejected. Realists like George Kennan argued against many of these institutionalist policies; fortunately for the United States, their advice was not taken.

Ruggie argues that U.S. policymakers emphasized institutional approaches to security problems because they recognized that institutions promised to gradually transform Europe, for example, into a security community that would no longer need U.S. intervention. U.S. leaders understood that it would be difficult for the United States to sustain its overseas involvement when its interests did not seem to be directly affected. By creating institutions, the United States was able to justify its overseas involvement as a means to transform security relations. In the future, the United States should adhere to this vision instead of adopting an anti-institutionalist unilateralism.

Alexander Wendt focuses his reply on Mearsheimer's critique of critical theory. In "Constructing International Politics" he first points out that Mearsheimer has misunderstood critical theory by assuming that it is a single theory. Instead, Wendt explains, there is a family of theories that includes postmodernism, constructivism, neo-Marxism, and feminism. These theories are united by the claims that the fundamental structures of international politics are social, not material, and that these structures shape the identities and interests of actors, not just their behavior. But they differ on many other issues. Wendt identifies himself as a constructivist and does not attempt to speak for other theories.

Wendt does not disagree with Mearsheimer's realist assumptions, but he argues that it is also necessary to look at social relationships as well as the distribution of material capabilities. Social structures depend on shared understandings, expectations, or knowledge. Material capabilities acquire meanings that depend on shared knowledge. For example, the United States is threatened very little by British nuclear weapons but would regard even a handful of North Korean weapons as a major threat. These social structures are not just intellectual; they are embodied in the practice of states. The Cold War was a structure of knowledge that shaped practice for over four decades. Constructivists attempt to explain why social structures exist and how they are related to practice. Mearsheimer is wrong, Wendt claims, to suggest that constructivists are driven solely by a desire to change the world. In addition, Wendt argues that Mearsheimer incorrectly claims that all critical theorists deny that we can have knowledge about the objective world. Postmodernists may hold such views, but constructivists—including Wendt—accept conventional social science.

Wendt argues that constructivist theory does not predict peace, but instead seeks to explain when *realpolitik* practices are used and when they are not. Constructivism emphasizes how agency—what states do—and social structure determine whether international politics will be a state of war or peace. Anarchy alone does not create the insecure, competitive, and war-prone world that Mearsheimer's theory depicts. Social structures and shared knowledge determine whether states are friends or enemies. The fact that social structures are socially constructed does not, however, mean that they can be changed easily.

In "A Realist Reply" John Mearsheimer briefly answers each of the four responses to "The False Promise of International Institutions." He argues that the central issue in the debate is whether institutions can promote peace by encouraging states to abandon balance-of-power logic. Realists say institutions cannot do this; institutionalists say institutions can.

Mearsheimer contends that Ruggie's reply does not address this central issue. Ruggie may be correct in pointing out that some realists gave bad advice on the creation of NATO and other U.S. decisions of the early Cold War, but this does not prove that institutions can foster peace. Mearsheimer agrees that the policies described by Ruggie were wise and successful; they also followed realist logic.

Turning to Keohane and Martin, Mearsheimer suggests that their reply reveals that liberal institutionalist theory is embracing realist ideas. Although liberal institutionalism began as a direct challenge to realist theory, it now seems to be converging with realism. Mearsheimer points out that Keohane and Martin frequently mention that institutions are created in response to state interests and reflect the distribution of capabilities. When institutions settle distributional conflicts and thereby limit the significance of relative gains, they act to make sure that agreements are based on the balance of power. Mearsheimer agrees that "institutions matter" but doubts whether they have a strong independent effect on the probability of war or peace. He points out that few of the examples of institutions cited by Keohane and Martin are relevant to central issues of war and peace.

In response to Charles Kupchan and Clifford Kupchan, Mearsheimer reiterates that collective security systems and concerts are different types of institutions. The Kupchans, Mearsheimer argues, generally accept his critique of the standard logic of collective security. Their attempt to create a form of collective security based on international concerts actually relies on realist principles and logic. It is therefore not a challenge to realism.

Mearsheimer expresses disappointment that Wendt does not answer his criticisms of critical theory but instead describes the theory and explains how it differs from realism. He acknowledges that there are many varieties of critical theory, but points out that they are united by the beliefs that "world politics is socially constructed" and that realist logic need not apply to anarchical international systems. Mearsheimer faults Wendt and critical theory more generally for failing to explain why realist logic has been the dominant discourse in international politics or whether and how it can be replaced by a different, more peaceful and communitarian discourse.

Mearsheimer concludes that it would be folly to base post-Cold War policies on institutional theories. Institutions have failed to stop carnage in Rwanda, Bosnia, and the former Soviet Union. Realist logic offers a better guide to the future, because states that ignore the balance of power do so at their own peril.

The final four essays in this volume address two questions. First, has war become less likely in the international system of the late twentieth century? Second, how do broad contemporary trends, such as increasing international economic interdependence and environmental scarcity, affect the probability of war.

In "Is War Obsolete?" Carl Kaysen argues that war is becoming increasingly unlikely among advanced industrialized countries. His analysis suggests that war is no longer politically or economically profitable for developed countries.

Kaysen begins by reviewing John Mueller's *Retreat from Doomsday*, which argues that war has become "subrationally unthinkable" among modern Western states and this change would have occurred even in the absence of nuclear weapons.[21] Mueller claims that, like duelling and slavery, war is no longer thinkable nor acceptable, at least among advanced industrialized states. The horrors of World War I began this social re-evaluation of war. World War II, which was launched by German and Japanese leaders who still clung to a romantic pre-1914 image of war, reinforced the lessons of World War I. The combined lessons of the two world wars would have been sufficient to render war obsolescent even if nuclear weapons had not been invented.

Although Kaysen agrees with Mueller's conclusion that major wars have become less likely, he is not persuaded by Mueller's claims that war has

---

21. John Mueller, *Retreat from Doomsday: The Obsolescence of Major War* (New York: Basic Books, 1988). See also John Mueller, "The Essential Irrelevance of Nuclear Weapons: Stability in the Postwar World," *International Security*, Vol. 13, No. 2 (Fall 1988), pp. 55–79. Robert Jervis responds to Mueller's argument in "The Political Effects of Nuclear Weapons: A Comment," in ibid., pp. 80–90.

become "subrationally unthinkable." Kaysen criticizes *Retreat from Doomsday* for failing to respond to realist and neorealist arguments that war is an inescapable feature of an anarchic international system. He also faults Mueller for failing to explain how ideas and attitudes about war are influenced by technological, economic, and political changes.

Kaysen's explanation for why war is neither no longer profitable nor likely among the great powers is based on an examination of centuries of social, political, and economic changes. According to Kaysen, war was profitable from the ninth to the fifteenth centuries for traditional European agricultural societies because it was relatively easy to seize and control land without destroying its productive energies. Warrior elites waged wars, which had limited impact on most of the population. This basic pattern remained unchanged through the eighteenth century. Despite the growth of cities and commerce, war still paid, and ruling elites still made the decisions. In the nineteenth century, the industrial revolution ushered in an era of large-scale manufacturing in which capital assumed greater economic importance than land, thereby increasing the scale and cost of war. War entailed larger economic burdens, and the difficulty of organizing a hostile population for continued production in an industrial society reduced the probable economic benefits of war. The gradual spread of democracy changed the basis of political legitimacy. Publics generally sought increased economic welfare, which could not be obtained through war. Attitudes took time to catch up to these changes in society, economy, and polity, but the wars of the twentieth century removed hereditary elites and provided ample evidence that war no longer pays. Far from being irrelevant, the development of nuclear weapons has reinforced these conclusions. Although Kaysen recognizes that internal violence may continue and that wars may rage between nonindustrialized countries, he concludes that there is hope for the emergence of a much more peaceful international system.

Many theorists of war and peace have argued that economic interdependence affects the probability of war. This issue has become prominent again as levels of international trade continue to increase in the 1990s.[22] In "Economic Interdependence and War: A Theory of Trade Expectations," Dale Copeland

---

22. For an important and thoughtful recent statement of this view, see Richard Rosecrance, *The Rise of the Trading State: Commerce and Conquest in the Modern World* (New York: Basic Books, 1986). For a recent reaffirmation and empirical test of the proposition that economic interdependence causes peace, see John R. Oneal and Bruce M. Russett, "The Classical Liberals were Right: Democracy, Interdependence, and Conflict, 1950–1985," *International Studies Quarterly*, Vol. 41, No. 2 (June 1997), pp. 267–293.

reviews the debate between liberals and realists over whether economic inter-dependence leads to war or promotes peace, and presents his own theory on this question. He notes that liberals believe that interdependence makes war less likely because states would rather trade than invade. Realists, on the other hand, argue that economic interdependence may actually increase the risk of war. States' fears for their security are too great to allow economic interdepend-ence to reduce conflict. The mutual dependence and vulnerability inherent in interdependence give states an incentive to initiate wars to maintain access to foreign raw materials and goods. Copeland suggests the timing of the outbreak of the two World Wars shows that neither school is right. The outbreak of World War I coincided with high levels of interdependence and thus casts doubt on the liberal view. But interdependence had been high for thirty years before 1914, calling into question realist claims that interdependence causes war. World War II was initiated by the two major powers (Germany and Japan) that were most dependent on international trade. This fact undermines liberal theories. On the other hand, realist theories that claim interdependence leads to war are unable to explain why these states initiated war in the late 1930s, when their dependence actually was falling.

Copeland's own theory contends that whether interdependence leads to war or to peace depends on what states expect about the future of international trade. He argues that economic interdependence leads to war when states fear that high levels of trade will decline. This condition makes it more likely that highly dependent states will start wars to maintain their access to economic resources and wealth. When economic interdependence is high and states expect that it will remain so, peace is more likely. Copeland suggests that his dynamic theory, which accords central causal significance to changes in expec-tations of future trade, is superior to static theories that focus on the level of economic interdependence at a given time.

Copeland applies his theory to explain Germany's decisions to go to war in 1914 and 1939. He suggests that in the years before World War I Germany greatly feared British, French, Russian, and American efforts to obstruct Ger-man commerce. Individually and collectively, these countries thwarted German expansionist designs in Africa and the Middle East, blocked German invest-ment and trade, and denied Germany the naval supremacy that would have protected German international commerce. Copeland argues that Germany went to war to defeat the powers that denied it greater access to international markets and raw materials. Germany's war aims, as stated in the 1914 "Sep-tember Program" included securing economic dominance in Europe.

In the 1930s, Copeland contends, Germany once again feared its dependence on outsiders for food and raw materials. As protectionism gathered steam in the 1930s, German fears grew. Hitler was obsessed with Germany's need for *lebensraum* ("living space"), because Germany did not have enough land to grow food for its growing population or to provide raw materials to maintain its industrial might. Other Germans shared this basic vision of increasing German economic autarchy to reduce Germany's vulnerability to interruptions of trade. Germany ultimately decided to implement this policy by going to war.

Looking forward, Copeland warns that peace may be imperiled by countries that depend on international trade yet expect trade to decline. China and Japan may fit into this category. The United States and other countries should avoid imposing sanctions on these countries and should attempt to maintain an open international trading system.

In "Environmental Scarcities and Violent Conflict: Evidence from Cases," Thomas Homer-Dixon examines whether scarcities of renewable resources like agricultural land, forests, water, and fisheries will lead to violent internal and international conflicts. He tests three hypotheses. The first suggests that decreasing supplies of resources that can be controlled physically (e.g., clean water or arable land) will provoke international "simple-scarcity" conflicts over these resources. The second hypothesis holds that environmental stresses will cause large population movements, which in turn will lead to "group-identity" conflicts, especially ethnic clashes. Homer-Dixon's third hypothesis suggests that environmental scarcity will increase economic deprivation, thereby causing "deprivation" conflicts such as civil strife and insurgency.[23]

Homer-Dixon tests and refines these hypotheses by examining the impact of six types of environmental change: greenhouse-induced climate change; stratospheric ozone depletion; degradation and loss of good agricultural land; degradation and removal of forests; depletion and pollution of fresh water supplies; and depletion of fisheries. Working with a team of experts, he looked at the connections between environmental scarcity and violent conflict in many countries, including Lesotho, South Africa, Bangladesh, China, Senegal, Mauritania, India, Peru, Haiti, and the Philippines.

Homer-Dixon and his colleagues reach four general conclusions. First, degradation and depletion of agricultural land, forests, water, and fish will cause

---

23. For a more detailed explication of these hypotheses, see Thomas F. Homer-Dixon, "On the Threshold: Environmental Changes as Causes of Acute Conflict," *International Security*, Vol. 16, No. 2 (Fall 1991), pp. 76–116.

more conflict than climate change or ozone depletion. Second, population growth and unequal distribution of resources are often at least as important as environmental change. The three factors together comprise environmental scarcity, and they often interact to cause conflicts. Third, two patterns of interaction among the sources of environmental scarcity are common: "resource capture" and "ecological marginalization." Resource capture occurs when a powerful group in a society uses its influence to control scarce resources and to deny them to weak or minority groups. For example, the Israeli government has restricted the access of Palestinian Arabs to water on the West Bank. Ecological marginalization takes place when unequal access to resources combines with population growth to impel migration to ecologically fragile areas, where further environmental degradation results. Fourth, whether societies can resolve problems of environmental scarcity and avoid conflict depends on their levels of social and technical ingenuity. Unfortunately, developing countries with problems of environmental scarcity lack the social institutions that contribute to social and technical ingenuity: research centers, efficient markets, and capable states.

Homer-Dixon pessimistically concludes that environmental scarcity is likely to increase and will cause more internal and international violence. In combination with population growth and unequal income distribution, environmental scarcities will produce severe internal conflicts. Often these conflicts will cause countries to fragment or to opt for authoritarian rule. Countries that fragment will produce large flows of migrants. Authoritarian regimes may be tempted to initiate international wars to divert attention from their domestic problems.

John Orme's "The Utility of Force in a World of Scarcity" reviews and responds to arguments that war is becoming less likely in the contemporary international system. Orme notes that many observers believe that nuclear weapons have made war unthinkable, that the rise and spread of democracy has forced leaders to abandon dreams of glory through conquest and to focus on satisfying the material needs of their people, and that force cannot be used to achieve prosperity in the current complex global economy. He argues, however, that other trends may return the use of force to a central place in international politics.

Orme suggests three factors will ensure that force continues to play a role in international politics in the early twenty-first century. First, the revolution in military affairs (RMA) will make it easier to use force effectively. The RMA entails increases in the accuracy, range, and lethality of weaponry, improvements in surveillance, reconnaissance, deception, command and control, and enhanced ability to suppress enemy defenses. These advances are due to the application of information technology to modern warfare. Orme suggests that the use of stealth technology and "smart bombs" by the United States in the Gulf War provides a preliminary picture of the scope of the RMA. Further advances will make it even easier to destroy enemy forces effectively without suffering high casualties or inflicting damage on civilian targets. These developments thus will make war a more effective instrument of national policy, at least for states with advanced conventional weapons, and reduce political objections to the use of force. The RMA also appears to shift the offense-defense balance toward the offense.

Second, Orme argues that the projected growth in the world's population—from 5.6 billion in 1998 to as much as 10 billion in 2040—also will increase the likelihood of war. He suggests that societies in which families have many children are more able to accept casualties in war and thus are more likely to go to war. Rapid population growth also creates domestic social and political upheavals that traditionally have been important causes of war. Orme points to the rise in France's population before 1789 and its role in causing the French revolution and subsequent Napoleonic Wars. The current population boom will swell the ranks of the urban poor in developing countries, placing great strains on the political institutions and economies of such countries. Rapid population growth also will strain supplies of global resources, including energy, food, raw materials, and water. Scarcity could produce conflicts over resources and either internal or international conflicts.[24]

Orme identifies a third trend that increases the probability of war: the increasing industrialization of many countries. As more countries industrialize, they will consume more resources, exacerbating scarcities caused by the increase in global population. And industrialization also raises the specter of global warming as more greenhouse emissions are released into the atmosphere.

These three trends lead Orme to conclude that "predictions of the imminent obsolescence of force appear to be premature." In the world Orme envisions, "clubs will be trumps" and prudent leaders will continue to rely on military force to achieve the goals of their states.

The future of international politics will offer plenty of tests of Orme's predictions and those of the other theories presented in this volume. If the past is

---

24. See Thomas Homer-Dixon's essay in this volume for a discussion of how environmental scarcity causes conflict.

any guide, proponents of realism, liberalism, institutionalism, and other approaches will continue to engage in a vigorous theoretical debate over which theory best explains war and peace. Even if international conflicts remain relatively rare, theorists will debate the sources of peace. And it is all too likely that new internal conflicts will emerge and force scholars to reconsider their ideas about wars of nationalism and ethnicity. Policymakers, whether they realize it or not, will find themselves applying insights from the respective theories as they attempt to avoid war and to preserve international and internal stability. We can only hope that their efforts will be successful enough to generate more evidence on the conditions for peace than on the causes of war.

Part I:
Realist Theories of War and Peace

Back to the Future

John J. Mearsheimer

Instability in Europe after the Cold War

The profound changes now underway in Europe have been widely viewed as harbingers of a new age of peace. With the Cold War over, it is said, the threat of war that has hung over Europe for more than four decades is lifting. Swords can now be beaten into ploughshares; harmony can reign among the states and peoples of Europe. Central Europe, which long groaned under the massive forces of the two military blocs, can convert its military bases into industrial parks, playgrounds, and condominiums. Scholars of security affairs can stop their dreary quarrels over military doctrine and balance assessments, and turn their attention to finding ways to prevent global warming and preserve the ozone layer. European leaders can contemplate how to spend peace dividends. So goes the common view.

This article assesses this optimistic view by exploring in detail the consequences for Europe of an end to the Cold War. Specifically, I examine the effects of a scenario under which the Cold War comes to a complete end. The Soviet Union withdraws all of its forces from Eastern Europe, leaving the states in that region fully independent. Voices are thereupon raised in the United States, Britain, and Germany, arguing that American and British military forces in Germany have lost their principal *raison d'être*, and these forces are withdrawn from the Continent. NATO and the Warsaw Pact then dissolve; they may persist on paper, but each ceases to function as an alliance.[1] As a result, the bipolar structure that has characterized Europe since

This article emerged from a paper written for a February 1990 conference at Ditchley Park, England, on the future of Europe, organized by James Callaghan, Gerald Ford, Valéry Giscard d'Estaing, and Helmut Schmidt. An abridged version of this article appears in the *Atlantic*, August 1990. I am grateful to Robert Art, Stacy Bergstrom, Richard Betts, Anne-Marie Burley, Dale Copeland, Michael Desch, Markus Fischer, Henk Goemans, Joseph Grieco, Ted Hopf, Craig Koerner, Andrew Kydd, Alicia Levine, James Nolt, Roger Petersen, Barry Posen, Denny Roy, Jack Snyder, Ashley Tellis, Marc Trachtenberg, Stephen Van Evera, Andrew Wallace, and Stephen Walt for their most helpful comments.

John Mearsheimer is Professor and Chair of the Department of Political Science, University of Chicago.

1. There is considerable support within NATO's higher circles, including the Bush administration, for maintaining NATO beyond the Cold War. NATO leaders have not clearly articulated the concrete goals that NATO would serve in a post–Cold War Europe, but they appear to conceive the future NATO as a means for ensuring German security, thereby removing possible German motives for aggressive policies; and as a means to protect other NATO states against

the end of World War II is replaced by a multipolar structure. In essence, the Cold War we have known for almost half a century is over, and the postwar order in Europe is ended.[2]

How would such a fundamental change affect the prospects for peace in Europe?[3] Would it raise or lower the risk of war?

I argue that the prospects for major crises and war in Europe are likely to increase markedly if the Cold War ends and this scenario unfolds. The next decades in a Europe without the superpowers would probably not be as violent as the first 45 years of this century, but would probably be substantially more prone to violence than the past 45 years.

This pessimistic conclusion rests on the argument that the distribution and character of military power are the root causes of war and peace. Specifically, the absence of war in Europe since 1945 has been a consequence of three factors: the bipolar distribution of military power on the Continent; the rough military equality between the two states comprising the two poles in Europe,

---

German aggression. However, the Germans, who now provide the largest portion of the Alliance's standing forces, are likely to resist such a role for NATO. A security structure of this sort assumes that Germany cannot be trusted and that NATO must be maintained to keep it in line. A united Germany is not likely to accept for very long a structure that rests on this premise. Germans accepted NATO throughout the Cold War because it secured Germany against the Soviet threat that developed in the wake of World War II. Without that specific threat, which now appears to be diminishing rapidly, Germany is likely to reject the continued maintenance of NATO as we know it.

2. I am not arguing that a complete end to the Cold War is inevitable; also quite likely is an intermediate outcome, under which the status quo is substantially modified, but the main outlines of the current order remain in place. Specifically, the Soviet Union may withdraw much of its force from Eastern Europe, but leave significant forces behind. If so, NATO force levels would probably shrink markedly, but NATO may continue to maintain significant forces in Germany. Britain and the United States would withdraw some but not all of their troops from the Continent. If this outcome develops, the basic bipolar military competition that has defined the map of Europe throughout the Cold War will continue. I leave this scenario unexamined, and instead explore what follows from a complete end to the Cold War in Europe because this latter scenario is the less examined of the two, and because the consequences, and therefore the desirability, of completely ending the Cold War would still remain an issue if the intermediate outcome occurred.

3. The impact of such a change on human rights in Eastern Europe will not be considered directly in this article. Eastern Europeans have suffered great hardship as a result of the Soviet occupation. The Soviets have imposed oppressive political regimes on the region, denying Eastern Europeans basic freedoms. Soviet withdrawal from Eastern Europe will probably change that situation for the better, although the change is likely to be more of a mixed blessing than most realize. First, it is not clear that communism will be promptly replaced in all Eastern European countries with political systems that place a high premium on protecting minority rights and civil liberties. Second, the longstanding blood feuds among the nationalities in Eastern Europe are likely to re-emerge in a multipolar Europe, regardless of the existing political order. If wars break out in Eastern Europe, human rights are sure to suffer.

the United States and the Soviet Union; and the fact that each superpower was armed with a large nuclear arsenal.[4] Domestic factors also affect the likelihood of war, and have helped cause the postwar peace. Most importantly, hyper-nationalism helped cause the two world wars, and the decline of nationalism in Europe since 1945 has contributed to the peacefulness of the postwar world. However, factors of military power have been most important in shaping past events, and will remain central in the future.

The departure of the superpowers from Central Europe would transform Europe from a bipolar to a multipolar system.[5] Germany, France, Britain, and perhaps Italy would assume major power status; the Soviet Union would decline from superpower status but would remain a major European power, giving rise to a system of five major powers and a number of lesser powers. The resulting system would suffer the problems common to multipolar systems, and would therefore be more prone to instability.[6] Power inequities could also appear; if so, stability would be undermined further.

The departure of the superpowers would also remove the large nuclear arsenals they now maintain in Central Europe. This would remove the pacifying effect that these weapons have had on European politics. Four principal scenarios are possible. Under the first scenario, Europe would become nuclear-free, thus eliminating a central pillar of order in the Cold War era. Under the second scenario, the European states do not expand their arsenals to compensate for the departure of the superpowers' weapons. In a third scenario, nuclear proliferation takes place, but is mismanaged; no steps are

---

4. It is commonplace to characterize the polarity—bipolar or multipolar—of the international system at large, not a specific region. The focus in this article, however, is not on the global distribution of power, but on the distribution of power in Europe. Polarity arguments can be used to assess the prospects for stability in a particular region, provided the global and regional balances are distinguished from one another and the analysis is focused on the structure of power in the relevant region.
5. To qualify as a pole in a global or regional system, a state must have a reasonable prospect of defending itself against the leading state in the system by its own efforts. The United States and the Soviet Union have enjoyed clear military superiority over other European states, and all non-European states, throughout the Cold War; hence they have formed the two poles of both the global and European systems. What is happening to change this is that both the Soviet Union and the United States are moving forces out of Central Europe, which makes it more difficult for them to project power on the Continent and thus weakens their influence there; and reducing the size of those forces, leaving them less military power to project. Because of its proximity to Europe, the Soviet Union will remain a pole in the European system as long as it retains substantial military forces on its own territory. The United States can remain a pole in Europe only if it retains the capacity to project significant military power into Central Europe.
6. Stability is simply defined as the absence of wars and major crises.

taken to dampen the many dangers inherent in the proliferation process. All three of these scenarios would raise serious risks of war.

In the fourth and least dangerous scenario, nuclear weapons proliferate in Europe, but the process is well-managed by the current nuclear powers. They take steps to deter preventive strikes on emerging nuclear powers, to set boundaries on the proliferation process by extending security umbrellas over the neighbors of emerging nuclear powers, to help emerging nuclear powers build secure deterrent forces, and to discourage them from deploying counterforce systems that threaten their neighbors' deterrents. This outcome probably provides the best hope for maintaining peace in Europe. However, it would still be more dangerous than the world of 1945–90. Moreover, it is not likely that proliferation would be well-managed.

Three counter-arguments might be advanced against this pessimistic set of predictions of Europe's future. The first argument holds that the peace will be preserved by the effects of the liberal international economic order that has evolved since World War II. The second rests on the observation that liberal democracies very seldom fight wars against each other, and holds that the past spread of democracy in Europe has bolstered peace, and that the ongoing democratization of Eastern Europe makes war still less likely. The third argument maintains that Europeans have learned from their disastrous experiences in this century that war, whether conventional or nuclear, is so costly that it is no longer a sensible option for states.

But the theories behind these arguments are flawed, as I explain; hence their prediction of peace in a multipolar Europe is flawed as well.

Three principal policy prescriptions follow from this analysis. First, the United States should encourage a process of limited nuclear proliferation in Europe. Specifically, Europe will be more stable if Germany acquires a secure nuclear deterrent, but proliferation does not go beyond that point. Second, the United States should not withdraw fully from Europe, even if the Soviet Union pulls its forces out of Eastern Europe. Third, the United States should take steps to forestall the re-emergence of hyper-nationalism in Europe.

METHODOLOGY: HOW SHOULD WE THINK ABOUT EUROPE'S FUTURE?
Predictions on the future risk of war and prescriptions about how best to maintain peace should rest on general theories about the causes of war and peace. This point is true for both academics and policymakers. The latter are seldom self-conscious in their uses of theory. Nevertheless, policymakers'

views on the future of Europe are shaped by their implicit preference for one theory of international relations over another. Our task, then, is to decide which theories best explain the past, and will most directly apply to the future; and then to employ these theories to explore the consequences of probable scenarios.

Specifically, we should first survey the inventory of international relations theories that bear on the problem. What theories best explain the period of violence before the Cold War? What theories best explain the peace of the past 45 years? Are there other theories that explain little about pre–Cold War Europe, or Cold War Europe, but are well-suited for explaining what is likely to occur in a Europe without a Soviet and American military presence?

Next, we should ask what these theories predict about the nature of international politics in a post–Cold War multipolar Europe. Will the causes of the postwar peace persist, will the causes of the two world wars return, or will other causes arise?

We can then assess whether we should expect the next decades to be more peaceful, or at least as peaceful, as the past 45 years, or whether the future is more likely to resemble the first 45 years of the century. We can also ask what policy prescriptions these theories suggest.

The study of international relations, like the other social sciences, does not yet resemble the hard sciences. Our stock of theories is spotty and often poorly tested. The conditions required for the operation of established theories are often poorly understood. Moreover, political phenomena are highly complex; hence precise political predictions are impossible without very powerful theoretical tools, superior to those we now possess. As a result, all political forecasting is bound to include some error. Those who venture to predict, as I do here, should therefore proceed with humility, take care not to claim unwarranted confidence, and admit that later hindsight will undoubtedly reveal surprises and mistakes.

Nevertheless, social science *should* offer predictions on the occurrence of momentous and fluid events like those now unfolding in Europe. Predictions can inform policy discourse. They help even those who disagree to frame their ideas, by clarifying points of disagreement. Moreover, predictions of events soon to unfold provide the best tests of social science theories, by making clear what it was that given theories have predicted about those events. In short, the world can be used as a laboratory to decide which theories best explain international politics. In this article I employ the body of theories that I find most persuasive to peer into the future. Time will reveal whether these theories in fact have much power to explain international politics.

The next section offers an explanation for the peacefulness of the post–World War II order. The section that follows argues that the end of the Cold War is likely to lead to a less stable Europe. Next comes an examination of the theories underlying claims that a multipolar Europe is likely to be as peaceful, if not more peaceful, than Cold War Europe. The concluding section suggests policy implications that follow from my analysis.

Explaining the "Long Peace"

The past 45 years represent the longest period of peace in European history.[7] During these years Europe saw no major war, and only two minor conflicts (the 1956 Soviet intervention in Hungary and the 1974 Greco-Turkish war in Cyprus). Neither conflict threatened to widen to other countries. The early years of the Cold War (1945–63) were marked by a handful of major crises, although none brought Europe to the brink of war. Since 1963, however, there have been no East-West crises in Europe. It has been difficult—if not impossible—for the last two decades to find serious national security analysts who have seen a real chance that the Soviet Union would attack Western Europe.

The Cold War peace contrasts sharply with European politics during the first 45 years of this century, which saw two world wars, a handful of minor wars, and a number of crises that almost resulted in war. Some 50 million Europeans were killed in the two world wars; in contrast, probably no more than 15,000 died in the two post-1945 European conflicts.[8] Cold War Europe is far more peaceful than early twentieth-century Europe.

Both Europeans and Americans increasingly assume that peace and calm are the natural order of things in Europe and that the first 45 years of this century, not the most recent, were the aberration. This is understandable,

---

7. The term "long peace" was coined by John Lewis Gaddis, "The Long Peace: Elements of Stability in the Postwar International System," *International Security*, Vol. 10, No. 4 (Spring 1986), pp. 99–142.
8. There were approximately 10,000 battle deaths in the Russo-Hungarian War of October–November 1956, and some 1500–5000 battle deaths in the July–August 1974 war in Cyprus. See Ruth Leger Sivard, *World Military and Social Expenditures 1989* (Washington, D.C.: World Priorities, 1989), p. 22; and Melvin Small and J. David Singer, *Resort to Arms: International and Civil Wars, 1816–1980* (Beverly Hills, Calif.: Sage, 1982), pp. 93–94.

since Europe has been free of war for so long that an ever-growing proportion of the Western public, born after World War II, has no direct experience with great-power war. However, this optimistic view is incorrect.

The European state system has been plagued with war since its inception. During much of the seventeenth and eighteenth centuries war was underway somewhere on the European Continent.[9] The nineteenth century held longer periods of peace, but also several major wars and crises. The first half of that century witnessed the protracted and bloody Napoleonic Wars; later came the Crimean War, and the Italian and German wars of unification.[10] The wars of 1914–45 continued this long historical pattern. They represented a break from the events of previous centuries only in the enormous increase in their scale of destruction.

This era of warfare came to an abrupt end with the conclusion of World War II. A wholly new and remarkably peaceful order then developed on the Continent.

THE CAUSES OF THE LONG PEACE: MILITARY POWER AND STABILITY

What caused the era of violence before 1945? Why has the postwar era been so much more peaceful? The wars before 1945 each had their particular and unique causes, but the distribution of power in Europe—its multipolarity and the imbalances of power that often occurred among the major states in that multipolar system—was the crucial permissive condition that allowed these particular causes to operate. The peacefulness of the postwar era arose for three principal reasons: the bipolarity of the distribution of power on the Continent, the rough equality in military power between those two polar states, and the appearance of nuclear weapons, which vastly expanded the violence of war, making deterrence far more robust.[11]

---

9. For inventories of past wars, see Jack S. Levy, *War In the Modern Great Power System, 1495–1975* (Lexington: University Press of Kentucky, 1983); and Small and Singer, *Resort to Arms.*

10. Europe saw no major war from 1815–1853 and from 1871–1914, two periods almost as long as the 45 years of the Cold War. There is a crucial distinction, however, between the Cold War and these earlier periods. Relations among the great powers deteriorated markedly in the closing years of the two earlier periods, leading in each case to a major war. On the other hand, the Cold War order has become increasingly stable with the passage of time and there is now no serious threat of war between NATO and the Warsaw Pact. Europe would surely remain at peace for the foreseeable future if the Cold War were to continue, a point that highlights the exceptional stability of the present European order.

11. The relative importance of these three factors cannot be stated precisely, but all three had substantial importance.

These factors are aspects of the European state system—of the character of military power and its distribution among states—and not of the states themselves. Thus the keys to war and peace lie more in the structure of the international system than in the nature of the individual states. Domestic factors—most notably hyper-nationalism—also helped cause the wars of the pre-1945 era, and the domestic structures of post-1945 European states have been more conducive to peace, but these domestic factors were less important than the character and distribution of military power between states. Moreover, hyper-nationalism was caused in large part by security competition among the European states, which compelled European elites to mobilize publics to support national defense efforts; hence even this important domestic factor was a more remote consequence of the international system.

Conflict is common among states because the international system creates powerful incentives for aggression.[12] The root cause of the problem is the anarchic nature of the international system. In anarchy there is no higher body or sovereign that protects states from one another. Hence each state living under anarchy faces the ever-present possibility that another state will use force to harm or conquer it. Offensive military action is always a threat to all states in the system.

Anarchy has two principal consequences. First, there is little room for trust among states because a state may be unable to recover if its trust is betrayed. Second, each state must guarantee its own survival since no other actor will provide its security. All other states are potential threats, and no international institution is capable of enforcing order or punishing powerful aggressors.

States seek to survive under anarchy by maximizing their power relative to other states, in order to maintain the means for self-defense. Relative power, not absolute levels of power, matters most to states. Thus, states seek opportunities to weaken potential adversaries and improve their relative power position. They sometimes see aggression as the best way to accumulate more power at the expense of rivals.

This competitive world is peaceful when it is obvious that the costs and risks of going to war are high, and the benefits of going to war are low. Two aspects of military power are at the heart of this incentive structure: the distribution of power between states, and the nature of the military power

---

12. The two classic works on this subject are Hans J. Morgenthau, *Politics Among Nations: The Struggle for Power and Peace*, 5th ed. (New York: Knopf, 1973); and Kenneth N. Waltz, *Theory of International Politics* (Reading, Mass.: Addison-Wesley, 1979).

available to them. The distribution of power between states tells us how well-positioned states are to commit aggression, and whether other states are able to check their aggression. This distribution is a function of the number of poles in the system, and their relative power. The nature of military power directly affects the costs, risks, and benefits of going to war. If the military weaponry available guarantees that warfare will be very destructive, states are more likely to be deterred by the cost of war.[13] If available weaponry favors the defense over the offense, aggressors are more likely to be deterred by the futility of aggression, and all states feel less need to commit aggression, since they enjoy greater security to begin with, and therefore feel less need to enhance their security by expansion.[14] If available weaponry tends to equalize the relative power of states, aggressors are discouraged from going to war. If military weaponry makes it easier to estimate the relative power of states, unwarranted optimism is discouraged and wars of miscalculation are less likely.

One can establish that peace in Europe during the Cold War has resulted from bipolarity, the approximate military balance between the superpowers, and the presence of large numbers of nuclear weapons on both sides in three ways: first, by showing that the general theories on which it rests are valid; second, by demonstrating that these theories can explain the conflicts of the pre-1945 era and the peace of the post-1945 era; and third, by showing that competing theories cannot account for the postwar peace.

THE VIRTUES OF BIPOLARITY OVER MULTIPOLARITY. The two principal arrangements of power possible among states are bipolarity and multipolarity.[15]

---

13. The prospects for deterrence can also be affected by crisis stability calculations. See John J. Mearsheimer, "A Strategic Misstep: The Maritime Strategy and Deterrence in Europe," *International Security*, Vol. 11, No. 2 (Fall 1986), pp. 6–8.

14. See Robert Jervis, "Cooperation Under the Security Dilemma," *World Politics*, Vol. 30, No. 2 (January 1978), pp. 167–214; and Stephen Van Evera, "Causes of War" (unpub. PhD dissertation, University of California at Berkeley, 1984), chap. 3. As noted below, I believe that the distinction between offensive and defensive weapons and, more generally, the concept of an offense-defense balance, is relevant at the nuclear level. However, I do not believe those ideas are relevant at the conventional level. See John J. Mearsheimer, *Conventional Deterrence* (Ithaca: Cornell University Press, 1983), pp. 25–27.

15. Hegemony represents a third possible distribution. Under a hegemony there is only one major power in the system. The rest are minor powers that cannot challenge the major power, but must act in accordance with the dictates of the major power. Every state would like to gain hegemony, because hegemony confers abundant security: no challenger poses a serious threat. Hegemony is rarely achieved, however, because power tends to be somewhat evenly distributed among states, because threatened states have strong incentives to join together to thwart an aspiring hegemon, and because the costs of expansion usually outrun the benefits before domination is achieved, causing extension to become overextension. Hegemony has never

A bipolar system is more peaceful for three main reasons. First, the number of conflict dyads is fewer, leaving fewer possibilities for war. Second, deterrence is easier, because imbalances of power are fewer and more easily averted. Third, the prospects for deterrence are greater because miscalculations of relative power and of opponents' resolve are fewer and less likely.[16]

In a bipolar system two major powers dominate. The minor powers find it difficult to remain unattached to one of the major powers, because the major powers generally demand allegiance from lesser states. (This is especially true in core geographical areas, less so in peripheral areas.) Furthermore, lesser states have little opportunity to play the major powers off against each other, because when great powers are fewer in number, the system is more rigid. As a result, lesser states are hard-pressed to preserve their autonomy.

In a multipolar system, by contrast, three or more major powers dominate. Minor powers in such a system have considerable flexibility regarding alliance partners and can opt to be free floaters. The exact form of a multipolar system can vary markedly, depending on the number of major and minor powers in the system, and their geographical arrangement.

A bipolar system has only one dyad across which war might break out: only two major powers contend with one another, and the minor powers are not likely to be in a position to attack each other. A multipolar system has many potential conflict situations. Major power dyads are more numerous, each posing the potential for conflict. Conflict could also erupt across dyads involving major and minor powers. Dyads between minor powers could also lead to war. Therefore, *ceteris paribus*, war is more likely in a multipolar system than a bipolar one.

Wars in a multipolar world involving just minor powers or only one major power are not likely to be as devastating as a conflict between two major

---

characterized the European state system at any point since it arose in the seventeenth century, and there is no prospect for hegemony in the foreseeable future; hence hegemony is not relevant to assessing the prospects for peace in Europe.

16. The key works on bipolarity and multipolarity include Thomas J. Christensen and Jack Snyder, "Chain Gangs and Passed Bucks: Predicting Alliance Patterns in Multipolarity," *International Organization*, Vol. 44, No. 2 (Spring 1990), pp. 137–168; Karl W. Deutsch and J. David Singer, "Multipolar Power Systems and International Stability," *World Politics*, Vol. 16, No. 3 (April 1964), pp. 390–406; Richard N. Rosecrance, "Bipolarity, Multipolarity, and the Future," *Journal of Conflict Resolution*, Vol. 10, No. 3 (September 1966), pp. 314–327; Kenneth N. Waltz, "The Stability of a Bipolar World," *Daedalus*, Vol. 93, No. 3 (Summer 1964), pp. 881–909; and Waltz, *Theory of International Politics*, chap. 8. My conclusions about bipolarity are similar to Waltz's, although there are important differences in our explanations, as will be seen below.

powers. However, local wars tend to widen and escalate. Hence there is always a chance that a small war will trigger a general conflict.

Deterrence is more difficult in a multipolar world because power imbalances are commonplace, and when power is unbalanced, the strong become hard to deter.[17] Power imbalances can lead to conflict in two ways. First, two states can gang up to attack a third state. Second, a major power might simply bully a weaker power in a one-on-one encounter, using its superior strength to coerce or defeat the minor state.[18]

Balance of power dynamics can counter such power imbalances, but only if they operate efficiently.[19] No state can dominate another, either by ganging up or by bullying, if the others coalesce firmly against it, but problems of geography or coordination often hinder the formation of such coalitions.[20] These hindrances may disappear in wartime, but are prevalent in peacetime, and can cause deterrence failure, even where an efficient coalition will eventually form to defeat the aggressor on the battlefield.

First, geography sometimes prevents balancing states from putting meaningful pressure on a potential aggressor. For example, a major power may not be able to put effective military pressure on a state threatening to cause trouble, because buffer states lie in between.

In addition, balancing in a multipolar world must also surmount difficult coordination problems. Four phenomena make coordination difficult. First, alliances provide collective goods, hence allies face the formidable dilemmas of collective action. Specifically, each state may try to shift alliance burdens onto the shoulders of its putative allies. Such "buck-passing" is a common feature of alliance politics.[21] It is most common when the number of states

17. Although a balance of power is more likely to produce deterrence than an imbalance of power, a balance of power between states does not guarantee that deterrence will obtain. States sometimes find innovative military strategies that allow them to win on the battlefield, even without marked advantage in the balance of raw military capabilities. Furthermore, the broader political forces that move a state towards war sometimes force leaders to pursue very risky military strategies, impelling states to challenge opponents of equal or even superior strength. See Mearsheimer, *Conventional Deterrence*, especially chap. 2.
18. This discussion of polarity assumes that the military strength of the major powers is roughly equal. The consequences of power asymmetries among great powers is discussed below.
19. See Stephen M. Walt, *The Origins of Alliances* (Ithaca: Cornell University Press, 1987); and Waltz, *Theory of International Politics*, pp. 123–128.
20. One exception bears mention: ganging up is still possible under multipolarity in the restricted case where there are only three powers in the system, and thus no allies available for the victim state.
21. See Mancur Olson and Richard Zeckhauser, "An Economic Theory of Alliances," *Review of Economics and Statistics*, Vol. 48, No. 3 (August 1966), pp. 266–279; and Barry R. Posen, *The*

required to form an effective blocking coalition is large. Second, a state faced with two potential adversaries might conclude that a protracted war between those adversaries would weaken both, even if one side triumphed; hence it may stay on the sidelines, hoping thereby to improve its power position relative to each of the combatants. (This strategy can fail, however, if one of the warring states quickly conquers the other and ends up more powerful, not less powerful, than before the war.) Third, some states may opt out of the balancing process because they believe that they will not be targeted by the aggressor, failing to recognize that they face danger until after the aggressor has won some initial victories. Fourth, diplomacy is an uncertain process, and thus it can take time to build a defensive coalition. A potential aggressor may conclude that it can succeed at aggression before the coalition is completed, and further may be prompted to exploit the window of opportunity that this situation presents before it closes.[22]

If these problems of geography and coordination are severe, states can lose faith in the balancing process. If so, they become more likely to bandwagon with the aggressor, since solitary resistance is futile.[23] Thus factors that weaken the balancing process can generate snowball effects that weaken the process still further.

The third major problem with multipolarity lies in its tendency to foster miscalculation of the resolve of opposing individual states, and of the strength of opposing coalitions.

War is more likely when a state underestimates the willingness of an opposing state to stand firm on issues of difference. It then may push the other state too far, expecting the other to concede, when in fact the opponent will choose to fight. Such miscalculation is more likely under multipolarity because the shape of the international order tends to remain fluid, due to the tendency of coalitions to shift. As a result, the international "rules of the road"—norms of state behavior, and agreed divisions of territorial rights and other privileges—tend to change constantly. No sooner are the rules of a given adversarial relationship worked out, than that relationship may become a friendship, a new adversarial relationship may emerge with a previous

---

Sources of Military Doctrine: France, Britain, and Germany between the World Wars (Ithaca: Cornell University Press, 1984).
22. Domestic political considerations can also sometimes impede balancing behavior. For example, Britain and France were reluctant to ally with the Soviet Union in the 1930s because of their deep-seated antipathy to communism.
23. See Walt, *Origins of Alliances*, pp. 28–32, 173–178.

friend or neutral, and new rules must be established. Under these circumstances, one state may unwittingly push another too far, because ambiguities as to national rights and obligations leave a wider range of issues on which a state may miscalculate another's resolve. Norms of state behavior can come to be broadly understood and accepted by all states, even in multipolarity, just as basic norms of diplomatic conduct became generally accepted by the European powers during the eighteenth century. Nevertheless, a well-defined division of rights is generally more difficult when the number of states is large, and relations among them are in flux, as is the case with multipolarity.

War is also more likely when states underestimate the relative power of an opposing coalition, either because they underestimate the number of states who will oppose them, or because they exaggerate the number of allies who will fight on their own side.[24] Such errors are more likely in a system of many states, since states then must accurately predict the behavior of many states, not just one, in order to calculate the balance of power between coalitions.

A bipolar system is superior to a multipolar system on all of these dimensions. Bullying and ganging up are unknown, since only two actors compete. Hence the power asymmetries produced by bullying and ganging up are also unknown. When balancing is required, it is achieved efficiently. States can balance by either internal means—military buildup—or external means—diplomacy and alliances. Under multipolarity states tend to balance by external means; under bipolarity they are compelled to use internal means. Internal means are more fully under state control, hence are more efficient, and are more certain to produce real balance.[25] The problems that attend efforts to balance by diplomatic methods—geographic complications and coordination difficulties—are bypassed. Finally, miscalculation is less likely than in a multipolar world. States are less likely to miscalculate others' resolve, because the rules of the road with the main opponent become settled over time, leading both parties to recognize the limits beyond which they cannot push the other. States also cannot miscalculate the membership of the opposing coalition, since each side faces only one main enemy. Simplicity breeds certainty; certainty bolsters peace.

---

24. This point is the central theme of Waltz, "The Stability of a Bipolar World." Also see Geoffrey Blainey, *The Causes of War* (New York: Free Press, 1973), chap. 3.
25. Noting the greater efficiency of internal over external balancing is Waltz, *Theory of International Politics*, pp. 163, 168.

There are no empirical studies that provide conclusive evidence of the effects of bipolarity and multipolarity on the likelihood of war. This undoubtedly reflects the difficulty of the task: from its beginning until 1945, the European state system was multipolar, leaving this history barren of comparisons that would reveal the differing effects of multipolarity and bipolarity. Earlier history does afford some apparent examples of bipolar systems, including some that were warlike—Athens and Sparta, Rome and Carthage—but this history is inconclusive, because it is sketchy and incomplete and therefore does not offer enough detail to validate the comparisons. Lacking a comprehensive survey of history, we cannot progress beyond offering examples pro and con, without knowing which set of examples best represents the universe of cases. As a result the case made here stops short of empirical demonstration, and rests chiefly on deduction. However, I believe that this deductive case provides a sound basis for accepting the argument that bipolarity is more peaceful than multipolarity; the deductive logic seems compelling, and there is no obvious historical evidence that cuts against it. I show below that the ideas developed here apply to events in twentieth century Europe, both before and after 1945.

THE VIRTUES OF EQUALITY OF POWER OVER INEQUALITY. Power can be more or less equally distributed among the major powers of both bipolar and multipolar systems. Both systems are more peaceful when equality is greatest among the poles. Power inequalities invite war by increasing the potential for successful aggression; hence war is minimized when inequalities are least.[26]

How should the degree of equality in the distribution of power in a system be assessed? Under bipolarity, the overall equality of the system is simply a function of the balance of power between the two poles—an equal balance creates an equal system, a skewed balance produces an unequal system. Under multipolarity the focus is on the power balance between the two leading states in the system, but the power ratios across other potential conflict dyads also matter. The net system equality is an aggregate of the degree of equality among all of the poles. However, most general wars under multipolarity have arisen from wars of hegemony that have pitted the leading state—an aspiring hegemon—against the other major powers in the system. Such wars are most probable when a leading state emerges, and can hope

---

26. This discussion does not encompass the situation where power asymmetries are so great that one state emerges as a hegemon. See note 15.

to defeat each of the others if it can isolate them. This pattern characterized the wars that grew from the attempts at hegemony by Charles V, Philip II, Louis XIV, Revolutionary and Napoleonic France, Wilhelmine Germany, and Nazi Germany.[27] Hence the ratio between the leader and its nearest competitor—in bipolarity or multipolarity—has more effect on the stability of the system than do other ratios, and is therefore the key ratio that describes the equality of the system. Close equality in this ratio lowers the risk of war.

The polarity of an international system and the degree of power equality of the system are related: bipolar systems tend more toward equality, because, as noted above, states are then compelled to balance by internal methods, and internal balancing is more efficient than external balancing. Specifically, the number-two state in a bipolar system can only hope to balance against the leader by mobilizing its own resources to reduce the gap between the two, since it has no potential major alliance partners. On the other hand, the second-strongest state in a multipolar system can seek security through alliances with others, and may be tempted to pass the buck to them, instead of building up its own strength. External balancing of this sort is especially attractive because it is cheap and fast. However, such behavior leaves intact the power gap between the two leading states, and thus leaves in place the dangers that such a power gap creates. Hence another source of stability under bipolarity lies in the greater tendency for its poles to be equal.

THE VIRTUES OF NUCLEAR DETERRENCE. Deterrence is most likely to hold when the costs and risks of going to war are obviously great. The more horrible the prospect of war, the less likely it is to occur. Deterrence is also most robust when conquest is most difficult. Aggressors then are more likely to be deterred by the futility of expansion, and all states feel less compelled to expand to increase their security, making them easier to deter because they are less compelled to commit aggression.

---

27. This point is the central theme of Ludwig Dehio, *The Precarious Balance: Four Centuries of the European Power Struggle,* trans. Charles Fullman (New York: Knopf, 1962). Also see Randolph M. Siverson and Michael R. Tennefoss, "Power, Alliance, and the Escalation of International Conflict, 1815–1965," *American Political Science Review,* Vol. 78, No. 4 (December 1984), pp. 1057–1069. The two lengthy periods of peace in the nineteenth century (see note 10 above) were mainly caused by the equal distribution of power among the major European states. Specifically, there was no aspiring hegemon in Europe for most of these two periods. France, the most powerful state in Europe at the beginning of the nineteenth century, soon declined to a position of rough equality with its chief competitors, while Germany only emerged as a potential hegemon in the early twentieth century.

Nuclear weapons favor peace on both counts. They are weapons of mass destruction, and would produce horrendous devastation if used in any numbers. Moreover, if both sides' nuclear arsenals are secure from attack, creating a mutually assured retaliation capability (mutual assured destruction or MAD), nuclear weapons make conquest more difficult; international conflicts revert from tests of capability and will to purer tests of will, won by the side willing to run greater risks and pay greater costs. This gives defenders the advantage, because defenders usually value their freedom more than aggressors value new conquests. Thus nuclear weapons are a superb deterrent: they guarantee high costs, and are more useful for self-defense than for aggression.[28]

In addition, nuclear weapons affect the degree of equality in the system. Specifically, the situation created by MAD bolsters peace by moving power relations among states toward equality. States that possess nuclear deterrents can stand up to one another, even if their nuclear arsenals vary greatly in size, as long as both sides' nuclear arsenals are secure from attack. This situation of closer equality has the stabilizing effects noted above.

Finally, MAD also bolsters peace by clarifying the relative power of states and coalitions.[29] States can still miscalculate each other's will, but miscalculations of relative capability are less likely, since nuclear capabilities are not elastic to the specific size and characteristics of forces; once an assured destruction capability is achieved, further increments of nuclear power have little strategic importance. Hence errors in assessing these specific characteristics have little effect. Errors in predicting membership in war coalitions also have less effect, since unforeseen additions or subtractions from such coalitions will not influence war outcomes unless they produce a huge change in the nuclear balance—enough to give one side meaningful nuclear superiority.

THE DANGERS OF HYPER-NATIONALISM. Nationalism is best defined as a set of political beliefs which holds that a nation—a body of individuals with characteristics that purportedly distinguish them from other individuals—

---

28. Works developing the argument that nuclear weapons are essentially defensive in nature are Shai Feldman, *Israeli Nuclear Deterrence: A Strategy for the 1980s* (New York: Columbia University Press, 1982), pp. 45–49; Stephen Van Evera, "Why Europe Matters, Why the Third World Doesn't: American Grand Strategy after the Cold War," *Journal of Strategic Studies*, Vol. 13, No. 2 (June 1990, forthcoming); and Van Evera, "Causes of War," chap. 13.

29. See Feldman, *Israeli Nuclear Deterrence*, pp. 50–52; and Van Evera, "Causes of War," pp. 697–699.

should have its own state.[30] Although nationalists often believe that their nation is unique or special, this conclusion does not necessarily mean that they think they are superior to other peoples, merely that they take pride in their own nation.

However, this benevolent nationalism frequently turns into ugly hyper-nationalism—the belief that other nations or nation-states are both inferior and threatening and must therefore be dealt with harshly. In the past, hyper-nationalism among European states has arisen largely because most European states are nation-states—states comprised of one principal nation—and these nation-states exist in an anarchic world, under constant threat from other states. In such a situation people who love their own nation and state can develop an attitude of contempt and loathing toward the nations who inhabit opposing states. The problem is exacerbated by the fact that political elites often feel compelled to portray adversary nations in the most negative way so as to mobilize public support for national security policies.

Malevolent nationalism is most likely to develop under military systems that require reliance on mass armies; the state may exploit nationalist appeals to mobilize its citizenry for the sacrifices required to sustain large standing armies. On the other hand, hyper-nationalism is least likely when states can rely on small professional armies, or on complex high-technology military organizations that do not require vast manpower. For this reason nuclear weapons work to dampen nationalism, since they shift the basis of military power away from pure reliance on mass armies, and toward greater reliance on smaller high-technology organizations.

In sum, hyper-nationalism is the most important domestic cause of war, although it is still a second-order force in world politics. Furthermore, its causes lie largely in the international system.

THE CAUSES OF THE LONG PEACE: EVIDENCE

The historical record shows a perfect correlation between bipolarity, equality of military power, and nuclear weapons, on the one hand, and the long peace, on the other hand. When an equal bipolarity arose and nuclear weapons appeared, peace broke out. This correlation suggests that the bipolarity

---

30. This definition is drawn from Ernest Gellner, *Nations and Nationalism* (Ithaca: Cornell University Press, 1983), which is an excellent study of the origins of nationalism. Nevertheless, Gellner pays little attention to how nationalism turns into a malevolent force that contributes to instability in the international system.

theory, the equality theory, and the nuclear theory of the long peace are all valid. However, correlation alone does not prove causation. Other factors still may account for the long peace. One way to rule out this possibility is to enumerate what the three theories predict about both the pre-war and postwar eras, and then to ask if these predictions came true in detail during those different periods.

BEFORE THE COLD WAR. The dangers of multipolarity are highlighted by events before both world wars. The existence of many dyads of potential conflict provided many possible ways to light the fuse to war in Europe. Diplomacy before World War I involved intense interactions among five major powers (Britain, France, Russia, Austria-Hungary, and Germany), and two minor powers (Serbia, and Belgium). At least six significant adversarial relationships emerged: Germany versus Britain, France, Russia, and Belgium; and Austria-Hungary versus Serbia and Russia. Before World War II five major powers (Britain, France, the Soviet Union, Germany, and Italy) and seven minor powers (Belgium, Poland, Czechoslovakia, Austria, Hungary, Romania, and Finland) interacted. These relations produced some thirteen important conflicts: Germany versus Britain, France, the Soviet Union, Czechoslovakia, Poland, and Austria; Italy versus Britain and France; the Soviet Union versus Finland and Poland; Czechoslovakia versus Poland and Hungary; and Romania versus Hungary. This multiplicity of conflicts made the outbreak of war inherently more likely. Moreover, many of the state interests at issue in each of these conflicts were interconnected, raising the risk that any single conflict that turned violent would trigger a general war, as happened in both 1914 and 1939.

Before World War II Germany was able to gang up with others against some minor states, and to bully others into joining with it. In 1939 Germany bolstered its power by ganging up with Poland and Hungary to partition Czechoslovakia, and then ganged up with the Soviet Union against Poland. In 1938 Germany bullied the Czechs into surrendering the Sudetenland, and also bullied the Austrians into complete surrender.[31] By these successes Germany expanded its power, leaving it far stronger than its immediate neighbors, and thereby making deterrence much harder.

German power could have been countered before both world wars had the other European powers balanced efficiently against Germany. If so, Ger-

---

31. Austria is not a pure case of bullying; there was also considerable pro-German support in Austria during the late 1930s.

many might have been deterred, and war prevented on both occasions. However, the other powers twice failed to do so. Before 1914 the scope of this failure was less pronounced; France and Russia balanced forcefully against Germany, while only Britain failed to commit firmly against Germany before war began.[32]

Before 1939, failure to balance was far more widespread.[33] The Soviet Union failed to aid Czechoslovakia against Germany in 1938, partly for geographic reasons: they shared no common border, leaving the Soviets with no direct access to Czech territory. France failed to give effective aid to the Czechs and Poles, partly because French military doctrine was defensively oriented, but also because France had no direct access to Czech or Polish territory, and therefore could not easily deploy forces to bolster Czech and Polish defenses.

Britain and France each passed the buck by transferring the cost of deterring Germany onto the other, thereby weakening their combined effort. The Soviet Union, with the Molotov-Ribbentrop Pact, sought to turn the German armies westward, hoping that they would become bogged down in a war of attrition similar to World War I on the Western Front. Some of the minor European powers, including Belgium, the Netherlands, Denmark, and the Scandinavian states, passed the buck to the major powers by standing on the sidelines during the crises of 1938 and 1939.

Britain and the United States failed to recognize that they were threatened by Germany until late in the game—1939 for Britain, 1940 for the United States—and they therefore failed to take an early stand. When they finally recognized the danger posed by Germany and resolved to respond, they lacked appropriate military forces. Britain could not pose a significant military threat to Germany until after it built up its own military forces and coordinated its plans and doctrine with its French and Polish allies. In the meantime

---

32. Britain's failure to commit itself explicitly to a Continental war before the July Crisis was probably a mistake of great proportions. There is evidence that the German chancellor, Bethmann-Hollweg, tried to stop the slide towards war once it became apparent that Britain would fight with France and Russia against Germany, turning a Continental war into a world war. See Imanuel Geiss, ed., *July 1914: The Outbreak of the First World War* (New York: Norton, 1967), chap. 7. Had the Germans clearly understood British intentions before the crisis, they might have displayed much greater caution in the early stages of the crisis, when it was still possible to avoid war.

33. See Williamson Murray, *The Change in the European Balance of Power, 1938–1939: The Path to Ruin* (Princeton: Princeton University Press, 1984); Posen, *Sources of Military Doctrine;* and Arnold Wolfers, *Britain and France between Two Wars: Conflicting Strategies of Peace from Versailles to World War II* (New York: Norton, 1968); and Barry R. Posen, "Competing Images of the Soviet Union," *World Politics*, Vol. 39, No. 4 (July 1987), pp. 579–597.

deterrence failed. The United States did not launch a significant military buildup until after the war broke out.

Multipolarity also created conditions that permitted serious miscalculation before both world wars, which encouraged German aggression on both occasions. Before 1914, Germany was not certain of British opposition if it reached for continental hegemony, and Germany completely failed to foresee that the United States would eventually move to contain it. In 1939, Germany hoped that France and Britain would stand aside as it conquered Poland, and again failed to foresee eventual American entry into the war. As a result Germany exaggerated its prospects for success. This undermined deterrence by encouraging German adventurism.

In sum, the events leading up to the world wars amply illustrate the risks that arise in a multipolar world. Deterrence was undermined in both cases by phenomena that are more common under a multipolar rather than a bipolar distribution of power.[34]

Deterrence was also difficult before both wars because power was distributed asymmetrically among the major European powers. Specifically, Germany was markedly stronger than any of its immediate neighbors. In 1914 Germany clearly held military superiority over all of its European rivals; only together were they able to defeat it, and then only with American help. 1939 is a more ambiguous case. The results of the war reveal that the Soviet Union had the capacity to stand up to Germany, but this was not apparent at the beginning of the war. Hitler was confident that Germany would defeat the Soviet Union, and this confidence was key to his decision to attack in 1941.

Finally, the events leading up to both world wars also illustrate the risks that arise in a world of pure conventional deterrence in which weapons of mass destruction are absent. World War I broke out partly because all of the important states believed that the costs of war would be small, and that successful offense was feasible.[35] Before World War II these beliefs were less widespread, but had the same effect.[36] The lesser powers thought war would

---

34. The problems associated with multipolarity were also common in Europe before 1900. Consider, for example, that inefficient balancing resulted in the collapse of the first four coalitions arrayed against Napoleonic France. See Steven T. Ross, *European Diplomatic History, 1789–1815: France Against Europe* (Garden City, N.Y.: Doubleday, 1969).

35. Stephen Van Evera, "The Cult of the Offensive and the Origins of the First World War," *International Security*, Vol. 9, No. 1 (Summer 1984), pp. 58–107. Also see Jack Snyder, *The Ideology of the Offensive: Military Decision-Making and the Disasters of 1914* (Ithaca: Cornell University Press, 1984).

36. Mearsheimer, *Conventional Deterrence*, chaps. 3–4.

be costly and conquest difficult, but the leaders of the strongest state—Germany—saw the prospect of cheap victory, and this belief was enough to destroy deterrence and produce war. Had nuclear weapons existed, these beliefs would have been undercut, removing a key condition that permitted both wars.

What was the role of internal German politics in causing the world wars? So far I have focused on aspects of the international system surrounding Germany. This focus reflects my view that systemic factors were more important. But German domestic political and social developments also played a significant role, contributing to the aggressive character of German foreign policy. Specifically, German society was infected with a virulent nationalism between 1870 and 1945 that laid the basis for expansionist foreign policies.[37]

However, two points should be borne in mind. First, German hyper-nationalism was in part fueled by Germany's pronounced sense of insecurity, which reflected Germany's vulnerable location at the center of Europe, with relatively open borders on both sides. These geographic facts made German security problems especially acute; this situation gave German elites a uniquely strong motive to mobilize their public for war, which they did largely by fanning nationalism. Thus even German hyper-nationalism can be ascribed in part to the nature of the pre-1945 international system.

Second, the horror of Germany's murderous conduct during World War II should be distinguished from the scope of the aggressiveness of German foreign policy.[38] Germany was indeed aggressive, but not unprecedentedly so. Other states have aspired to hegemony in Europe, and sparked wars by their efforts; Germany was merely the latest to attempt to convert dominant into hegemonic power. What was unique about Germany's conduct was its policy of mass murder toward many of the peoples of Europe. The causes of this murderous policy should not be conflated with the causes of the two

---

37. See Ludwig Dehio, *Germany and World Politics in the Twentieth Century*, trans. Dieter Pevsner (New York: Norton, 1967); Fritz Fischer, *War of Illusions: German Policies from 1911 to 1914*, trans. Marian Jackson (New York: Norton, 1975); Paul M. Kennedy, *The Rise of the Anglo-German Antagonism, 1860–1914* (London: Allen and Unwin, 1980), chap. 18; Hans Kohn, *The Mind of Germany: The Education of a Nation* (New York: Harper Torchbook, 1965), chaps. 7–12; and Louis L. Snyder, *German Nationalism: The Tragedy of a People* (Harrisburg, Pa.: Telegraph Press, 1952).
38. There is a voluminous literature on the German killing machine in World War II. Among the best overviews of the subject are Ian Kershaw, *The Nazi Dictatorship: Problems and Perspectives of Interpretation*, 2nd ed. (London: Arnold, 1989), chaps. 5, 8, 9; Henry L. Mason, "Imponderables of the Holocaust," *World Politics*, Vol. 34, No. 1 (October 1981), pp. 90–113; and Mason, "Implementing the Final Solution: The Ordinary Regulating of the Extraordinary," *World Politics*, Vol. 40, No. 4 (July 1988), pp. 542–569.

world wars. The policy of murder arose chiefly from domestic sources; the wars arose mainly from aspects of the distribution and character of power in Europe.

THE COLD WAR RECORD. The European state system abruptly shifted from multipolar to bipolar after 1945. Three factors were responsible: the near-complete destruction of German power, the growth of Soviet power, and the permanent American commitment to the European Continent. The weakening of the German Reich was accomplished by allied occupation and dismemberment. Silesia, Pomerania, East Prussia, and parts of West Prussia and Brandenburg were given to other countries, the Sudetenland was returned to Czechoslovakia, and Austria was restored to independence. The rest of the German Reich was divided into two countries, East and West Germany, which became enemies. This reduction of German power, coupled with the physical presence of American and Soviet military might in the heart of Europe, eliminated the threat of German aggression.[39]

Meanwhile the Soviet Union extended its power westward, becoming the dominant power on the Continent and one of the two strongest powers in the world. There is no reason to think that the Soviets would not have reached for continental hegemony, as the Spanish, French, and Germans did earlier, had they believed they could win a hegemonic war. But the Soviets, unlike their predecessors, made no attempt to gain hegemony by force, leaving Europe in peace.

Bipolarity supplies part of the reason. Bipolarity made Europe a simpler place in which only one point of friction—the East-West conflict—had to be managed to avoid war. The two blocs encompassed most of Europe, leaving few unprotected weak states for the Soviets to conquer. As a result the Soviets have had few targets to bully. They have also been unable to gang up on the few states that are unprotected, because their West-bloc adversary has been their only potential ganging-up partner.

Bipolarity also left less room for miscalculation of both resolve and capability. During the first fifteen years of the Cold War, the rules of the road for the conflict were not yet established, giving rise to several serious crises. However, over time each side gained a clear sense of how far it could push the other, and what the other would not tolerate. A set of rules came to be agreed upon: an understanding on the division of rights in Austria, Berlin,

---

39. See Anton W. DePorte, *Europe between the Superpowers: The Enduring Balance*, 2nd ed. (New Haven: Yale University Press, 1986).

and elsewhere in Europe; a proscription on secret unilateral re-deployment of large nuclear forces to areas contiguous to the opponent; mutual toleration of reconnaissance satellites; agreement on rules of peacetime engagement between naval forces; and so forth. The absence of serious crises during 1963–90 was due in part to the growth of such agreements on the rights of both sides, and the rules of conduct. These could develop in large part because the system was bipolar in character. Bipolarity meant that the same two states remained adversaries for a long period, giving them time to learn how to manage their conflict without war. By contrast, a multipolar world of shifting coalitions would repeatedly have forced adversaries to re-learn how their opponents defined interests, reach new accords on the division of rights, and establish new rules of competitive conduct.

Bipolarity also left less room to miscalculate the relative strength of the opposing coalitions. The composition of possible war coalitions has been clear because only two blocs have existed, each led by an overwhelmingly dominant power that could discipline its members. Either side could have miscalculated its relative military strength, but bipolarity removed ambiguity about relative strength of adversarial coalitions arising from diplomatic uncertainties.

The East-West military balance in Europe has been roughly equal throughout the Cold War, which has further bolstered stability. This approximate parity strengthened deterrence by ensuring that no state was tempted to use force to exploit a power advantage. Parity resulted partly from bipolarity: because the two blocs already encompassed all the states of Europe, both sides have balanced mainly by internal rather than external means. These more efficient means have produced a more nearly equal balance.

Nuclear weapons also played a key role in preventing war in post–World War II Europe.

Western elites on both sides of the Atlantic quickly recognized that nuclear weapons were vastly destructive and that their widespread use in Europe would cause unprecedented devastation. The famous *Carte Blanche* exercises conducted in Germany in 1955 made it manifestly clear that a nuclear war in Europe would involve far greater costs than another World War II.[40] Accordingly, Western policymakers rarely suggested that nuclear war could be "won," and instead emphasized the horrors that would attend nuclear war.

---

40. See Hans Speier, *German Rearmament and Atomic War: The Views of German Military and Political Leaders* (Evanston, Ill.: Row, Peterson, 1957), chap. 10.

Moreover, they have understood that conventional war could well escalate to the nuclear level, and have in fact based NATO strategy on that reality.

Soviet leaders also recognized the horrendous results that a nuclear war would produce.[41] Some Soviet military officers have asserted that victory is possible in nuclear war, but even they have acknowledged that such a victory would be Pyrrhic. Soviet civilians have generally argued that victory is impossible. Furthermore, the Soviets long maintained that it was not possible to fight a purely conventional war in Europe, and that conventional victory would only prompt the loser to engage in nuclear escalation.[42] The Soviets later granted more possibility that a conventional war might be controlled, but still recognized that escalation is likely.[43] Under Gorbachev, Soviet military thinking has placed even greater emphasis on the need to avoid nuclear war and devoted more attention to the dangers of inadvertent nuclear war.[44]

Official rhetoric aside, policymakers on both sides have also behaved very cautiously in the presence of nuclear weapons. There is not a single case of a leader brandishing nuclear weapons during a crisis, or behaving as if nuclear war might be a viable option for solving important political problems. On the contrary, policymakers have never gone beyond nuclear threats of a very subtle sort, and have shown great caution when the possibility of nuclear confrontation has emerged.[45] This cautious conduct has lowered the risk of war.

Nuclear weapons also imposed an equality and clarity on the power relations between the superpowers. This equality and clarity represented a

---

41. See Robert L. Arnett, "Soviet Attitudes Towards Nuclear War: Do They Really Think They Can Win?" *Journal of Strategic Studies*, Vol. 2, No. 2 (September 1979), pp. 172–191; and David Holloway, *The Soviet Union and the Arms Race* (New Haven: Yale University Press, 1983).

42. Thus Nikita Khrushchev explained, "Now that the big countries have thermonuclear weapons at their disposal, they are sure to resort to those weapons if they begin to lose a war fought with conventional means. If it ever comes down to a question of whether or not to face defeat, there is sure to be someone who will be in favor of pushing the button, and the missiles will begin to fly." Nikita Khrushchev, *Khrushchev Remembers: The Last Testament*, trans. and ed. by Strobe Talbott (New York: Bantam, 1976), pp. 603–604.

43. See James M. McConnell, "Shifts in Soviet Views on the Proper Focus of Military Development," *World Politics*, Vol. 37, No. 3 (April 1985), pp. 317–343.

44. See Stephen M. Meyer, "The Sources and Prospects of Gorbachev's New Political Thinking on Security," *International Security*, Vol. 13, No. 2 (Fall 1988), pp. 134–138.

45. See Hannes Adomeit, *Soviet Risk-taking and Crisis Behavior: A Theoretical and Empirical Analysis* (London: Allen and Unwin, 1982); Richard K. Betts, *Nuclear Blackmail and Nuclear Balance* (Washington, D.C.: Brookings, 1987); and McGeorge Bundy, *Danger and Survival: Choices about the Bomb in the First Fifty Years* (New York: Random House, 1988). Also see Joseph S. Nye, Jr., "Nuclear Learning and U.S.-Soviet Security Regimes," *International Organization*, Vol. 41, No. 3 (Summer 1987), pp. 371–402.

marked change from the earlier non-nuclear world, in which sharp power inequalities and miscalculations of relative power were common.[46]

During the Cold War, the United States and the Soviet Union have exhibited markedly less hyper-nationalism than did the European powers before 1945. After World War II, nationalism declined sharply within Europe, partly because the occupation forces took active steps to dampen it,[47] and also because the European states, no longer providing their own security, now lacked the incentive to purvey hyper-nationalism in order to bolster public support for national defense. More importantly, however, the locus of European politics shifted to the United States and the Soviet Union—two states that, each for its own reasons, had not exhibited nationalism of the virulent type found earlier in Europe. Nor has nationalism become virulent in either superpower during the Cold War. In part this reflects the greater stability of the postwar order, arising from bipolarity, military equality, and nuclear weapons; with less expectation of war, neither superpower has faced the need to mobilize its population for war. It also reflects a second effect of nuclear weapons: they have reduced the importance of mass armies for preserving sovereignty, thus diminishing the importance of maintaining a hyper-nationalized pool of manpower.

THE CAUSES OF THE LONG PEACE: COMPETING EXPLANATIONS

The claim that bipolarity, equality, and nuclear weapons have been largely responsible for the stability of the past 45 years is further strengthened by the absence of persuasive competing explanations. Two of the most popular theories of peace—*economic liberalism* and *peace-loving democracies*—are not relevant to the issue at hand.

Economic liberalism, which posits that a liberal economic order bolsters peace (discussed in more detail below), cannot explain the stability of postwar Europe, because there has been little economic exchange between the Soviet Union and the West over the past 45 years. Although economic flows be-

---

46. Some experts acknowledge that nuclear weapons had deterrent value in the early decades of the Cold War, but maintain that they had lost their deterrent value by the mid-1960s when the Soviets finally acquired the capability to retaliate massively against the American homeland. I reject this argument and have outlined my views in John J. Mearsheimer, "Nuclear Weapons and Deterrence in Europe," *International Security*, Vol. 9, No. 3 (Winter 1984/85), pp. 19–46.
47. See Paul M. Kennedy, "The Decline of Nationalistic History in the West, 1900–1970," *Journal of Contemporary History*, Vol. 8, No. 1 (January 1973), pp. 77–100; and E.H. Dance, *History the Betrayer* (London: Hutchinson, 1960).

tween Eastern and Western Europe have been somewhat greater, in no sense has all of Europe been encompassed by a liberal economic order.

The peace-loving democracies theory (also discussed below) holds that democracies do not go to war against other democracies, but concedes that democracies are not especially pacific when facing authoritarian states. This theory cannot account for post–World War II stability because the Soviet Union and its allies in Eastern Europe have not been democratic over the past 45 years.

A third theory of peace, *obsolescence of war*, proposes that modern conventional war had become so deadly by the twentieth century that it was no longer possible to think of war as a sensible means to achieve national goals.[48] It took the two world wars to drive this point home, but by 1945 it was clear that large-scale conventional war had become irrational and morally unacceptable, like institutions such as slavery and dueling. Thus, even without nuclear weapons, statesmen in the Cold War would not seriously have countenanced war, which had become an anachronism. This theory, it should be emphasized, does not ascribe the absence of war to nuclear weapons, but instead points to the horrors of modern conventional war.

This argument probably provides the most persuasive alternative explanation for the stability of the Cold War, but it is not convincing on close inspection. The fact that World War II occurred casts serious doubt on this theory; if any war could have convinced Europeans to forswear conventional war, it should have been World War I, with its vast casualties. There is no doubt that conventional war among modern states could devastate the participants. Nevertheless, this explanation misses one crucial difference between nuclear and conventional war, a difference that explains why war is still a viable option for states. Proponents of this theory assume that all conventional wars are protracted and bloody wars of attrition, like World War I on the Western front. However, it is possible to score a quick and decisive victory in a conventional war and avoid the devastation that usually attends a protracted conventional war.[49] Conventional war can be won; nuclear war cannot be, since neither side can escape devastation by the other, regardless of the outcome on the battlefield. Thus, the incentives to avoid

---

48. This theory is most clearly articulated by John E. Mueller, *Retreat from Doomsday: The Obsolescence of Major War* (New York: Basic Books, 1989). See also Carl Kaysen, "Is War Obsolete? A Review Essay," *International Security*, Vol. 14, No. 4 (Spring 1990), pp. 42–64.

49. See Mearsheimer, *Conventional Deterrence*, chaps. 1–2.

war are far greater in a nuclear than a conventional world, making nuclear deterrence much more robust than conventional deterrence.[50]

Predicting the Future: The Balkanization of Europe?

What new order will emerge in Europe if the Soviets and Americans withdraw to their homelands and the Cold War order dissolves? What characteristics will it have? How dangerous will it be?

It is certain that bipolarity will disappear, and multipolarity will emerge in the new European order. The other two dimensions of the new order—the distribution of power among the major states, and the distribution of nuclear weapons among them—are not pre-determined, and several possible arrangements could develop. The probable stability of these arrangements would vary markedly. This section examines the scope of the dangers that each arrangement would present, and the likelihood that each will emerge.

The distribution and deployment patterns of nuclear weapons in the new Europe is the least certain, and probably the most important, element of the new order. Accordingly, this section proceeds by exploring the character of the four principal nuclear worlds that might develop: a denuclearized Europe, continuation of the current patterns of nuclear ownership, and nuclear proliferation either well- or ill-managed.

The best new order would incorporate the limited, managed proliferation of nuclear weapons. This would be more dangerous than the current order, but considerably safer than 1900–45. The worst order would be a non-nuclear Europe in which power inequities emerge between the principal poles of power. This order would be more dangerous than the current world, perhaps almost as dangerous as the world before 1945. Continuation of the current

---

50. German decision-making in the early years of World War II underscores this point. See Mearsheimer, *Conventional Deterrence*, chap. 4. The Germans were well aware from their experience in World War I that conventional war among major powers could have devastating consequences. Nevertheless, they decided three times to launch major land offensives: Poland (1939); France (1940); and the Soviet Union (1941). In each case, the Germans believed that they could win a quick and decisive victory and avoid a costly protracted war like World War I. Their calculations proved correct against Poland and France. They were wrong about the Soviets, who thwarted their blitzkrieg and eventually played the central role in bringing down the Third Reich. The Germans surely would have been deterred from attacking the Soviet Union if they had foreseen the consequences. However, the key point is that they saw some possibility of winning an easy and relatively cheap victory against the Red Army. That option is not available in a nuclear war.

pattern, or mismanaged proliferation, would be worse than the world of today, but safer than the pre-1945 world.

EUROPE WITHOUT NUCLEAR WEAPONS

Some Europeans and Americans seek to eliminate nuclear weapons from Europe, and would replace the Cold War order with a wholly non-nuclear order. Constructing this nuclear-free Europe would require Britain, France and the Soviet Union to rid themselves of nuclear weapons. Proponents believe that a Europe without nuclear weapons would be the most peaceful possible arrangement; in fact, however, a nuclear-free Europe would be the most dangerous among possible post–Cold War orders. The pacifying effects of nuclear weapons—the security they provide, the caution they generate, the rough equality they impose, and the clarity of relative power they create—would be lost. Peace would then depend on the other dimensions of the new order—the number of poles, and the distribution of power among them. However, the new order will certainly be multipolar, and may be unequal; hence the system may be very prone to violence. The structure of power in Europe would look much like it did between the world wars, and it could well produce similar results.

The two most powerful states in post–Cold War Europe would probably be Germany and the Soviet Union. They would be physically separated by a band of small, independent states in Eastern Europe. Not much would change in Western Europe, although the states in that area would have to be concerned about a possible German threat on their eastern flank.

The potential for conflict in this system would be considerable. There would be many possible dyads across which war might break out. Power imbalances would be commonplace as a result of the opportunities this system would present for bullying and ganging up. There would be considerable opportunity for miscalculation. The problem of containing German power would emerge once again, but the configuration of power in Europe would make it difficult to form an effective counterbalancing coalition, for much the same reason that an effective counterbalancing coalition failed to form in the 1930s. Eventually the problem of containing the Soviet Union could also re-emerge. Finally, conflicts may erupt in Eastern Europe, providing the vortex that could pull others into a wider confrontation.

A reunified Germany would be surrounded by weaker states that would find it difficult to balance against German aggression. Without forces stationed in states adjacent to Germany, neither the Soviets nor the Americans would be in a good position to help them contain German power. Furthermore, those small states lying between Germany and the Soviet Union might fear the Soviets as much as the Germans, and hence may not be disposed to cooperate with the Soviets to deter German aggression. This problem in fact arose in the 1930s, and 45 years of Soviet occupation in the interim have done nothing to ease East European fears of a Soviet military presence. Thus, scenarios in which Germany uses military force against Poland, Czechoslovakia, or even Austria become possible.

The Soviet Union also might eventually threaten the new status quo. Soviet withdrawal from Eastern Europe does not mean that the Soviets will never feel compelled to return to Eastern Europe. The historical record provides abundant instances of Russian or Soviet involvement in Eastern Europe. Indeed, the Russian presence in Eastern Europe has surged and ebbed repeatedly over the past few centuries.[51] Thus, Soviet withdrawal now hardly guarantees a permanent exit.

Conflict between Eastern European states is also likely to produce instability in a multipolar Europe. There has been no war among the states in that region during the Cold War because the Soviets have tightly controlled them. This point is illustrated by the serious tensions that now exist between Hungary and Romania over Romanian treatment of the Hungarian minority in Transylvania, a region that previously belonged to Hungary and still has roughly 2 million Hungarians living within its borders. Were it not for the Soviet presence in Eastern Europe, this conflict could have brought Romania and Hungary to war by now, and it may bring them to war in the future.[52] This will not be the only danger spot within Eastern Europe if the Soviet empire crumbles.[53]

Warfare in Eastern Europe would cause great suffering to Eastern Europeans. It also might widen to include the major powers, because they would

---

51. See, inter alia: Ivo J. Lederer, ed., *Russian Foreign Policy: Essays in Historical Perspective* (New Haven: Yale University Press, 1962); Andrei Lobanov-Rostovsky, *Russia and Europe, 1825–1878* (Ann Arbor, Mich.: George Wahr Publishing, 1954); and Marc Raeff, *Imperial Russia, 1682–1825: The Coming of Age of Modern Russia* (New York: Knopf, 1971), chap. 2.

52. To get a sense of the antipathy between Hungary and Romania over this issue, see *Witnesses to Cultural Genocide: First-Hand Reports on Romania's Minority Policies Today* (New York: American Transylvanian Federation and the Committee for Human Rights in Romania, 1979). The March 1990 clashes between ethnic Hungarians and Romanians in Tîrgu Mures (Romanian Transylvania) indicate the potential for savage violence that is inherent in these ethnic conflicts.

53. See Zbigniew Brzezinski, "Post-Communist Nationalism," *Foreign Affairs*, Vol. 68, No. 5 (Winter 1989/1990), pp. 1–13; and Mark Kramer, "Beyond the Brezhnev Doctrine: A New Era in Soviet-East European Relations?" *International Security*, Vol. 14, No. 3 (Winter 1989/90), pp. 51–54.

be drawn to compete for influence in that region, especially if disorder created fluid politics that offered opportunities for wider influence, or threatened defeat for friendly states. During the Cold War, both superpowers were drawn into Third World conflicts across the globe, often in distant areas of little strategic importance. Eastern Europe is directly adjacent to both the Soviet Union and Germany, and has considerable economic and strategic importance; thus trouble in Eastern Europe could offer even greater temptations to these powers than past conflicts in the Third World offered the superpowers. Furthermore, because the results of local conflicts will be largely determined by the relative success of each party in finding external allies, Eastern European states will have strong incentives to drag the major powers into their local conflicts.[54] Thus both push and pull considerations would operate to enmesh outside powers in local Eastern European wars.

Miscalculation is also likely to be a problem in a multipolar Europe. For example, the new order might well witness shifting patterns of conflict, leaving insufficient time for adversaries to develop agreed divisions of rights and agreed rules of interaction, or constantly forcing them to re-establish new agreements and rules as old antagonisms fade and new ones arise. It is not likely that circumstances would allow the development of a robust set of agreements of the sort that have stabilized the Cold War since 1963. Instead, Europe would resemble the pattern of the early Cold War, in which the absence of rules led to repeated crises. In addition, the multipolar character of the system is likely to give rise to miscalculation regarding the strength of the opposing coalitions.

It is difficult to predict the precise balance of conventional military power that would emerge between the two largest powers in post–Cold War Europe, especially since the future of Soviet power is now hard to forecast. The Soviet Union might recover its strength soon after withdrawing from Central Europe; if so, Soviet power would overmatch German power. Or centrifugal national forces may pull the Soviet Union apart, leaving no remnant state that is the equal of a united Germany.[55] What seems most likely is that

---

54. The new prime minister of Hungary, Jozsef Antall, has already spoken of the need for a "European solution" to the problem of Romania's treatment of Hungarians in Transylvania. Celestine Bohlen, "Victor in Hungary Sees '45 as the Best of Times," *New York Times*, April 10, 1990, p. A8.

55. This article focuses on how changes in the strength of Soviet power and retraction of the Soviet empire would affect the prospects for stability in Europe. However, the dissolution of the Soviet Union, a scenario not explored here in any detail, would raise dangers that would be different from and in addition to those discussed here.

Germany and the Soviet Union might emerge as powers of roughly equal strength. The first two scenarios, with their marked inequality between the two leading powers, would be especially worrisome, although there is cause for concern even if Soviet and German power are balanced.

Resurgent hyper-nationalism will probably pose less danger than the problems described above, but some nationalism is likely to resurface in the absence of the Cold War and may provide additional incentives for war. A non-nuclear Europe is likely to be especially troubled by nationalism, since security in such an order will largely be provided by mass armies, which often cannot be maintained without infusing societies with hyper-nationalism. The problem is likely to be most acute in Eastern Europe, but there is also potential for trouble in Germany. The Germans have generally done an admirable job combatting nationalism over the past 45 years, and in remembering the dark side of their past. Nevertheless, worrisome portents are now visible; of greatest concern, some prominent Germans have lately advised a return to greater nationalism in historical education.[56] Moreover, nationalism will be exacerbated by the unresolved border disputes that will be uncovered by the retreat of American and Soviet power. Especially prominent is that of the border between Germany and Poland, which some Germans would change in Germany's favor.

However, it seems very unlikely that Europe will actually be denuclearized, despite the present strength of anti-nuclear feeling in Europe. For example, it is unlikely that the French, in the absence of America's protective cover and faced with a newly unified Germany, would get rid of their nuclear weapons. Also, the Soviets surely would remain concerned about balancing the American nuclear deterrent, and will therefore retain a deterrent of their own.

THE CURRENT OWNERSHIP PATTERN CONTINUES

A more plausible order for post–Cold War Europe is one in which Britain, France and the Soviet Union keep their nuclear weapons, but no new nuclear powers emerge in Europe. This scenario sees a nuclear-free zone in Central Europe, but leaves nuclear weapons on the European flanks.

---

56. Aspects of this story are recounted in Richard J. Evans, *In Hitler's Shadow: West German Historians and the Attempt to Escape from the Nazi Past* (New York: Pantheon, 1989). A study of past German efforts to mischaracterize history is Holger H. Herwig, "Clio Deceived: Patriotic Self-Censorship in Germany After the Great War," *International Security*, Vol. 12, No. 2 (Fall 1987), pp. 5–44.

This scenario, too, also seems unlikely, since the non-nuclear states will have substantial incentives to acquire their own nuclear weapons. Germany would probably not need nuclear weapons to deter a conventional attack by its neighbors, since neither the French nor any of the Eastern European states would be capable of defeating a reunified Germany in a conventional war. The Soviet Union would be Germany's only legitimate conventional threat, but as long as the states of Eastern Europe remained independent, Soviet ground forces would be blocked from a direct attack. The Germans, however, might not be willing to rely on the Poles or the Czechs to provide a barrier and might instead see nuclear weapons as the best way to deter a Soviet conventional attack into Central Europe. The Germans might choose to go nuclear to protect themselves from blackmail by other nuclear powers. Finally, given that Germany would have greater economic strength than Britain or France, it might therefore seek nuclear weapons to raise its military status to a level commensurate with its economic status.

The minor powers of Eastern Europe would have strong incentives to acquire nuclear weapons. Without nuclear weapons, these Eastern European states would be open to nuclear blackmail from the Soviet Union and, if it acquired nuclear weapons, from Germany. No Eastern European state could match the conventional strength of Germany or the Soviet Union, which gives these minor powers a powerful incentive to acquire a nuclear deterrent, even if the major powers had none. In short, a continuation of the current pattern of ownership without proliferation seems unlikely.

How stable would this order be? The continued presence of nuclear weapons in Europe would have some pacifying effects. Nuclear weapons would induce greater caution in their owners, give the nuclear powers greater security, tend to equalize the relative power of states that possess them, and reduce the risk of miscalculation. However, these benefits would be limited if nuclear weapons did not proliferate beyond their current owners, for four main reasons.

First, the caution and the security that nuclear weapons impose would be missing from the vast center of Europe. The entire region between France and the Soviet Union, extending from the Arctic in the north to the Mediterranean in the south, and comprising some eighteen significant states, would become a large zone thereby made "safe" for conventional war. Second, asymmetrical power relations would be bound to develop, between nuclear and non-nuclear states and among non-nuclear states, raising the dangers that attend such asymmetries. Third, the risk of miscalculation would rise, reflecting the multipolar character of this system and the absence of nuclear weapons from a large portion of it. A durable agreed political order would be hard to build because political coalitions would tend to shift over time, causing miscalculations of resolve between adversaries. The relative strength of potential war coalitions would be hard to calculate because coalition strength would depend heavily on the vagaries of diplomacy. Such uncertainties about relative capabilities would be mitigated in conflicts that arose among nuclear powers: nuclear weapons tend to equalize power even among states or coalitions of widely disparate resources, and thus to diminish the importance of additions or defections from each coalition. However, uncertainty would still be acute among the many states that would remain non-nuclear. Fourth, the conventionally-armed states of Central Europe would depend for their security on mass armies, giving them an incentive to infuse their societies with dangerous nationalism in order to maintain public support for national defense efforts.

NUCLEAR PROLIFERATION, WELL-MANAGED OR OTHERWISE
The most likely scenario in the wake of the Cold War is further nuclear proliferation in Europe. This outcome is laden with dangers, but also might provide the best hope for maintaining stability on the Continent. Its effects depend greatly on how it is managed. Mismanaged proliferation could produce disaster, while well-managed proliferation could produce an order nearly as stable as the current order. Unfortunately, however, any proliferation is likely to be mismanaged.

Four principal dangers could arise if proliferation is not properly managed. First, the proliferation process itself could give the existing nuclear powers strong incentives to use force to prevent their non-nuclear neighbors from gaining nuclear weapons, much as Israel used force to preempt Iraq from acquiring a nuclear capability.

Second, even after proliferation was completed, a stable nuclear competition might not emerge between the new nuclear states. The lesser European powers might lack the resources needed to make their nuclear forces survivable; if the emerging nuclear forces were vulnerable, this could create first-strike incentives and attendant crisis instability. Because their economies are far smaller, they would not be able to develop arsenals as large as those of the major powers; arsenals of small absolute size might thus be vulnerable. Furthermore, their lack of territorial expanse deprives them of possible basing modes, such as mobile missile basing, that would secure their deterrents.

Several are landlocked, so they could not base nuclear weapons at sea, the most secure basing mode used by the superpowers. Moreover, their close proximity to one another deprives them of warning time, and thus of basing schemes that exploit warning to achieve invulnerability, such as by the quick launch of alert bombers. Finally, the emerging nuclear powers might also lack the resources required to develop secure command and control and adequate safety procedures for weapons management, thus raising the risk of accidental launch, or of terrorist seizure and use of nuclear weapons.

Third, the elites and publics of the emerging nuclear European states might not quickly develop doctrines and attitudes that reflect a grasp of the devastating consequences and basic unwinnability of nuclear war. There will probably be voices in post–Cold War Europe arguing that limited nuclear war is feasible, and that nuclear wars can be fought and won. These claims might be taken seriously in states that have not had much direct experience with the nuclear revolution.

Fourth, widespread proliferation would increase the number of fingers on the nuclear trigger, which in turn would increase the likelihood that nuclear weapons could be fired due to accident, unauthorized use, terrorist seizure, or irrational decision-making.

If these problems are not resolved, proliferation would present grave dangers. However, the existing nuclear powers can take steps to reduce these dangers. They can help deter preventive attack on emerging nuclear states by extending security guarantees. They can provide technical assistance to help newly nuclear-armed powers to secure their deterrents. And they can help socialize emerging nuclear societies to understand the nature of the forces they are acquiring. Proliferation managed in this manner can help bolster peace.

How broadly should nuclear weapons be permitted to spread? It would be best if proliferation were extended to Germany but not beyond.[57] Germany has a large economic base, and can therefore sustain a secure nuclear force. Moreover, Germany will feel insecure without nuclear weapons; and Germany's great conventional strength gives it significant capacity to disturb Europe if it feels insecure. Other states—especially in Eastern Europe—may also want nuclear weapons, but it would be best to prevent further proliferation. The reasons are, as noted above, that these states may be unable to

---

57. See David Garnham, "Extending Deterrence with German Nuclear Weapons," *International Security*, Vol. 10, No. 1 (Summer 1985), pp. 96–110.

secure their nuclear deterrents, and the unlimited spread of nuclear weapons raises the risk of terrorist seizure or possession by states led by irrational elites. However, if the broader spread of nuclear weapons proves impossible to prevent without taking extreme steps, the existing nuclear powers should let the process happen, while doing their best to channel it in safe directions.

However, even if proliferation were well-managed, significant dangers would remain. If all the major powers in Europe possessed nuclear weapons, history suggests that they would still compete for influence among the lesser powers and be drawn into lesser-power conflicts. The superpowers, despite the security that their huge nuclear arsenals provide, have competed intensely for influence in remote, strategically unimportant areas such as South Asia, Southeast Asia, and Central America. The European powers are likely to exhibit the same competitive conduct, especially in Eastern Europe, even if they possess secure nuclear deterrents.

The possibility of ganging up would remain: several nuclear states could join against a solitary nuclear state, perhaps aggregating enough strength to overwhelm its deterrent. Nuclear states also might bully their non-nuclear neighbors. This problem is mitigated if unbounded proliferation takes place, leaving few non-nuclear states subject to bullying by the nuclear states, but such widespread proliferation raises risks of its own, as noted above.

Well-managed proliferation would reduce the danger that states might miscalculate the relative strength of coalitions, since nuclear weapons clarify the relative power of all states, and diminish the importance of unforeseen additions and defections from alliances. However, the risk remains that resolve will be miscalculated, because patterns of conflict are likely to be somewhat fluid in a multipolar Europe, thus precluding the establishment of well-defined spheres of rights and rules of conduct.

Unbounded proliferation, even if it is well-managed, will raise the risks that appear when there are many fingers on the nuclear trigger—accident, unauthorized or irrational use, or terrorist seizure.

In any case, it is not likely that proliferation will be well-managed. The nuclear powers cannot easily work to manage proliferation while at the same time resisting it; there is a natural tension between the two goals. But they have several motives to resist. The established nuclear powers will be reluctant to give the new nuclear powers technical help in building secure deterrents, because it runs against the grain of state behavior to transfer military power to others, and because of the fear that sensitive military technology could be turned against the donor state if that technology were further transferred to its adversaries. The nuclear powers will also be reluctant to undermine the legitimacy of the 1968 Nuclear Non-Proliferation Treaty by allowing any signatories to acquire nuclear weapons, since this could open the floodgates to the wider proliferation that they seek to avoid, even if they would otherwise favor very limited proliferation. For these reasons the nuclear powers are more likely to spend their energy trying to thwart the process of proliferation, rather than managing it.

Proliferation can be more easily managed if it occurs during a period of relative international calm. Proliferation that occurred during a time of crisis would be especially dangerous, since states in conflict with the emerging nuclear powers would then have a strong incentive to interrupt the process by force. However, proliferation is likely not to begin until the outbreak of crisis, because there will be significant domestic opposition to proliferation within the potential nuclear powers, as well as significant external resistance from the established nuclear powers. Hence it may require a crisis to motivate the potential nuclear powers to pay the domestic and international costs of moving to build a nuclear force. Thus, proliferation is more likely to happen under disadvantageous international conditions than in a period of calm.

Finally, there are limits to the ability of the established nuclear powers to assist small emerging nuclear powers to build secure deterrents. For example, small landlocked powers cannot be given access to sea-based deterrents or land-mobile missile systems requiring vast expanses of land; these are geographic problems that technology cannot erase. Therefore even if the existing nuclear powers move to manage the proliferation process early and wisely, that process still may raise dangers that they cannot control.

Alternative Theories that Predict Peace

Many students of European politics will reject my pessimistic analysis of post–Cold War Europe and instead argue that a multipolar Europe is likely to be at least as peaceful as the present order. Three specific scenarios for a peaceful future have been advanced. Each rests on a well-known theory of international relations. However, each of these theories is flawed and thus cannot serve as the basis for reliable predictions of a peaceful order in a multipolar Europe; hence the hopeful scenarios they support lack plausibility.

Under the first optimistic scenario, even a non-nuclear Europe would remain peaceful because Europeans recognize that even a conventional war would be horrific. Sobered by history, national leaders will take great care to avoid war. This scenario rests on the "obsolescence of war" theory.

Although modern conventional war can certainly be very costly, there are several flaws in this argument. There is no systematic evidence demonstrating that Europeans believe war is obsolete. However, even if it were widely believed in Europe that war is no longer thinkable, attitudes could change. Public opinion on national security issues is notoriously fickle and responsive to elite manipulation and world events. Moreover, only one country need decide war is thinkable to make war possible again. Finally, it is possible that a conventional war could be fought and won without suffering grave losses, and elites who saw this possibility could believe war is a viable option.

Under the second optimistic scenario, the existing European Community (EC) grows stronger with time, a development heralded by the Single European Act, designed to create a unified Western European market by 1992. A strong EC then ensures that this economic order remains open and prosperous, and the open and prosperous character of the European economy keeps the states of Western Europe cooperating with each other. In this view, the present EC structure grows stronger, but not larger. Therefore, while conflict might emerge in Eastern Europe, the threat of an aggressive Germany would be removed by enmeshing the newly unified German state deeply in the EC. The theory underpinning this scenario is "economic liberalism."

A variant of this second scenario posits that the EC will spread to include Eastern Europe and possibly the Soviet Union, bringing prosperity and peace to these regions as well.[58] Some also maintain that the EC is likely to be so successful in the decade ahead that it will develop into a state apparatus: a unified Western European super-state would emerge and Germany would be subsumed in it. At some future point, the remainder of Europe would be incorporated into that super-state. Either way, suggest the proponents of this second scenario and its variants, peace will be bolstered.

Under the third scenario, war is avoided because many European states have become democratic since the early twentieth century, and liberal democracies simply do not fight against each other. At a minimum, the presence of liberal democracies in Western Europe renders that half of Europe free from armed conflict. At a maximum, as democracy spreads to Eastern Europe and the Soviet Union, it bolsters peace among these states, and between

---

58. Jack Snyder, "Averting Anarchy in the New Europe," *International Security*, Vol. 14, No. 4 (Spring 1990), pp. 5–41.

these states and Western Europe. This scenario is based on the theory that can be called "peace-loving democracies."

ECONOMIC LIBERALISM

THE LOGIC OF THE THEORY. Economic liberalism rejects the notion that the prospects for peace are tightly linked to calculations about military power, and posits instead that stability is mainly a function of international economic considerations. It assumes that modern states are primarily motivated by the desire to achieve prosperity, and that national leaders place the material welfare of their publics above all other considerations, including security. This is especially true of liberal democracies, where policymakers are under special pressure to ensure the economic well-being of their populations.[59] Thus, the key to achieving peace is establishment of an international economic system that fosters prosperity for all states.

The taproot of stability, according to this theory, is the creation and maintenance of a liberal economic order that allows free economic exchange between states. Such an order works to dampen conflict and enhance political cooperation in three ways.[60]

First, it makes states more prosperous; this bolsters peace because prosperous states are more economically satisfied, and satisfied states are more

59. This point about liberal democracies highlights the fact that economic liberalism and the theory of peace-loving democracies are often linked in the writings of international relations scholars. The basis of the linkage is what each theory has to say about peoples' motives. The claim that individuals mainly desire material prosperity, central to economic liberalism, meshes nicely with the belief that the citizenry are a powerful force against war, which, as discussed below, is central to the theory of peace-loving democracies.

60. The three explanations discussed here rest on three of the most prominent theories advanced in the international political economy (IPE) literature. These three are usually treated as distinct theories and are given various labels. However, they share important common elements. Hence, for purposes of parsimony, I treat them as three strands of one general theory: economic liberalism. A caveat is in order. The IPE literature often fails to state its theories in a clear fashion, making them difficult to evaluate. Thus, I have construed these theories from sometimes opaque writings that might be open to contrary interpretations. My description of economic liberalism is drawn from the following works, which are among the best of the IPE genre: Richard N. Cooper, "Economic Interdependence and Foreign Policies in the Seventies," *World Politics*, Vol. 24, No. 2 (January 1972), pp. 158–181; Ernst B. Haas, "Technology, Pluralism, and the New Europe," in Joseph S. Nye, Jr., ed., *International Regionalism* (Boston: Little, Brown, 1968), pp. 149–176; Robert O. Keohane and Joseph S. Nye, Jr., *Power and Interdependence: World Politics in Transition* (Boston: Little, Brown, 1977); Robert O. Keohane, *After Hegemony: Cooperation and Discord in the World Political Economy* (Princeton: Princeton University Press, 1984); David Mitrany, *A Working Peace System* (Chicago: Quadrangle Press, 1966); Edward L. Morse, "The Transformation of Foreign Policies: Modernization, Interdependence, and Externalization," *World Politics*, Vol. 22, No. 3 (April 1970), pp. 371–392; and Richard N. Rosecrance, *The Rise of the Trading State: Commerce and Conquest in the Modern World* (New York: Basic Books, 1986).

peaceful. Many wars are waged to gain or preserve wealth, but states have less motive for such wars if they are already wealthy. Wealthy societies also stand to lose more if their societies are laid waste by war. For both reasons they avoid war.

Moreover, the prosperity spawned by economic liberalism feeds itself, by promoting international institutions that foster greater liberalism, which in turn promotes still greater prosperity. To function smoothly, a liberal economic order requires international regimes or institutions, such as the EC, the General Agreement on Tariffs and Trade (GATT), and the International Monetary Fund (IMF). These institutions perform two limited but important functions. First, they help states to verify that partners keep their cooperative commitments. Second, they provide resources to governments experiencing short-term problems arising from their exposure to international markets, and by doing so they allow states to eschew beggar-thy-neighbor policies that might otherwise undermine the existing economic order. Once in place, these institutions and regimes bolster economic cooperation, hence bolster prosperity. They also bolster themselves: once in existence they cause the expansion of their own size and influence, by proving their worth and selling themselves to states and publics. And as their power grows they become better able to promote cooperation, which promotes greater prosperity, which further bolsters their prestige and influence. In essence, a benevolent spiral-like relationship sets in between cooperation-promoting regimes and prosperity, in which each feeds the other.

Second, a liberal economic order fosters economic interdependence among states. Interdependence is defined as a situation in which two states are mutually vulnerable; each is a hostage of the other in the economic realm.[61] When interdependence is high, this theory holds, there is less temptation to cheat or behave aggressively towards other states because all states could retaliate. Interdependence allows states to compel each other to cooperate on economic matters, much as mutual assured destruction allows nuclear powers to compel each other to respect their security. All states are forced by the others to act as partners in the provision of material comfort for their home publics.

Third, some theorists argue that with ever-increasing political cooperation, international regimes will become so powerful that they will assume an

---

61. See Kenneth N. Waltz, "The Myth of National Interdependence," in Charles P. Kindelberger, ed., *The International Corporation* (Cambridge: MIT Press, 1970), pp. 205–223.

independent life of their own, eventually growing into a super-state. This is a minority view; most economic liberals do not argue that regimes can become so powerful that they can coerce states to act against their own narrow interests. Instead most maintain that regimes essentially reflect the interests of the states that created and maintain them, and remain subordinate to other interests of these states. However, the "growth to super-statehood" view does represent an important strand of thought among economic liberals.

The main flaw in this theory is that the principal assumption underpinning it—that states are primarily motivated by the desire to achieve prosperity— is wrong. States are surely concerned about prosperity, and thus economic calculations are hardly trivial for them. However, states operate in both an international political environment and an international economic environment, and the former dominates the latter in cases where the two systems come into conflict. The reason is straightforward: the international political system is anarchic, which means that each state must always be concerned to ensure its own survival. Since a state can have no higher goal than survival, when push comes to shove, international political considerations will be paramount in the minds of decision-makers.

Proponents of economic liberalism largely ignore the effects of anarchy on state behavior and concentrate instead on economic considerations. When this omission is corrected, however, their arguments collapse, for two reasons.

First, competition for security makes it very difficult for states to cooperate. When security is scarce, states become more concerned about relative gains than absolute gains.[62] They ask of an exchange not, "will both of us gain?" but instead, "who will gain more?"[63] When security is scarce, they reject even cooperation that would yield an absolute economic gain, if the other state would gain more of the yield, from fear that the other might convert its gain to military strength, and then use this strength to win by coercion in later rounds.[64] Cooperation is much easier to achieve if states worry only about absolute gains, as they are more likely to do when security is not so

---

62. See Joseph M. Grieco, "Anarchy and the Limits of Cooperation: A Realist Critique of the Newest Liberal Institutionalism," *International Organization,* Vol. 42, No. 3 (Summer 1988), pp. 485–507; and Grieco, *Cooperation among Nations: Europe, America and Non-Tariff Barriers to Trade* (Ithaca: Cornell University Press, 1990).

63. Waltz, *Theory of International Politics,* p. 105.

64. It is important to emphasize that because military power is in good part a function of economic might, the consequences of economic dealings among states sometimes have important security implications.

scarce. The goal then is simply to insure that the overall economic pie is expanding and each state is getting at least some part of the resulting benefits. However, anarchy guarantees that security will often be scarce; this heightens states' concerns about relative gains, which makes cooperation difficult unless gains can be finely sliced to reflect, and thus not disturb, the current balance of power.

In contrast to this view, economic liberals generally assume that states worry little about relative gains when designing cooperative agreements, but instead are concerned mainly about absolute gains. This assumption underlies their optimism over the prospects for international cooperation. However, it is not well-based: anarchy forces states to reject agreements that result in asymmetrical payoffs that shift the balance of power against them.

Second, interdependence is as likely to lead to conflict as cooperation, because states will struggle to escape the vulnerability that interdependence creates, in order to bolster their national security. States that depend on others for critical economic supplies will fear cutoff or blackmail in time of crisis or war; they may try to extend political control to the source of supply, giving rise to conflict with the source or with its other customers. Interdependence, in other words, might very well lead to greater competition, not to cooperation.[65]

Several other considerations, independent of the consequences of anarchy, also raise doubts about the claims of economic liberals.

First, economic interactions between states often cause serious frictions, even if the overall consequences are positive. There will invariably be winners and losers within each state, and losers rarely accept defeat gracefully. In modern states, where leaders have to pay careful attention to their constit-

---

65. There are numerous examples in the historical record of vulnerable states pursuing aggressive military policies for the purpose of achieving autarky. For example, this pattern of behavior was reflected in both Japan's and Germany's actions during the interwar period. On Japan, see Michael A. Barnhart, *Japan Prepares for Total War: The Search for Economic Security, 1919–1941* (Ithaca: Cornell University Press, 1987); and James B. Crowley, *Japan's Quest for Autonomy* (Princeton: Princeton University Press, 1966). On Germany, see William Carr, *Arms, Autarky and Aggression: A Study in German Foreign Policy, 1933–39* (New York: Norton, 1973). It is also worth noting that during the Arab oil embargo of the early 1970s, when it became apparent that the United States was vulnerable to OPEC pressure, there was much talk in America about using military force to seize Arab oil fields. See, for example, Robert W. Tucker, "Oil: The Issue of American Intervention," *Commentary*, January 1975, pp. 21–31; Miles Ignotus [said to be a pseudonym for Edward Luttwak], "Seizing Arab Oil," *Harpers*, March 1975, pp. 45–62; and U.S. Congress, House Committee on International Relations, *Report on Oil Fields as Military Objectives: A Feasibility Study*, prepared by John M. Collins and Clyde R. Mark, 94th Cong., 1st sess. (Washington, D.C.: U.S. Government Printing Office [U.S. GPO], August 21, 1975).

uents, losers can cause considerable trouble. Even in cases where only winners are involved, there are sometimes squabbles over how the spoils are divided. In a sense, then, expanding the network of contacts among states increases the scope for international disagreements among them. They now have more to squabble about.

Second, there will be opportunities for blackmail and for brinkmanship in a highly dynamic economic system where states are dependent on each other. For example, although mutual vulnerabilities may arise among states, it is likely that the actual levels of dependence will not be equal. The less vulnerable states would probably have greater bargaining power over the more dependent states and might attempt to coerce them into making extravagant concessions. Furthermore, different political systems, not to mention individual leaders, have different capacities for engaging in tough bargaining situations.

THE HISTORICAL RECORD. During two periods in the twentieth century, Europe witnessed a liberal economic order with high levels of interdependence. Stability should have obtained during those periods, according to economic liberalism.

The first case clearly contradicts the theory. The years between 1890 and 1914 were probably the time of greatest economic interdependence in Europe's history. Yet World War I broke out following this period.[66]

The second case covers the Cold War years. During this period there has been much interdependence among the EC states, while relations among these states have been very peaceful. This case, not surprisingly, is the centerpiece of the economic liberals' argument.

The correlation in this second case does not mean, however, that interdependence has *caused* cooperation among the Western democracies. It is more likely that the prime cause was the Cold War, and that this was the main reason that intra-EC relations have flourished.[67] The Cold War caused these results in two different but mutually reinforcing ways.

First, old-fashioned balance of power logic mandated cooperation among the Western democracies. A powerful and potentially dangerous Soviet

66. See Richard N. Rosecrance, et al., "Whither Interdependence?" *International Organization,* Vol. 31, No. 3 (Summer 1977), pp. 432–434.
67. This theme is reflected in Barry Buzan, "Economic Structure and International Security: The Limits of the Liberal Case," *International Organization,* Vol. 38, No. 4 (Autumn 1984), pp. 597–624; Robert Gilpin, *U.S. Power and the Multinational Corporation: The Political Economy of Foreign Direct Investment* (New York: Basic Books, 1975); and Robert A. Pollard, *Economic Security and the Origins of the Cold War, 1945–1950* (New York: Columbia University Press, 1985).

Union forced the Western democracies to band together to meet the common threat. Britain, Germany, and France no longer worried about each other, because all faced a greater menace from the Soviets. This Soviet threat muted concerns about relative gains arising from economic cooperation among the EC states by giving each Western democracy a vested interest in seeing its alliance partners grow powerful, since each additional increment of power helped deter the Soviets. The Soviet threat also muted relative-gains fears among Western European states by giving them all a powerful incentive to avoid conflict with each other while the Soviet Union loomed to the east, ready to harvest the gains of Western quarrels. This gave each Western state greater confidence that its Western partners would not turn their gains against it, as long as these partners behaved rationally.

Second, America's hegemonic position in NATO, the military counterpart to the EC, mitigated the effects of anarchy on the Western democracies and facilitated cooperation among them.[68] As emphasized, states do not trust each other in anarchy and they have incentives to commit aggression against each other. America, however, not only provided protection against the Soviet threat, but also guaranteed that no EC state would aggress against another. For example, France did not have to fear Germany as it rearmed, because the American presence in Germany meant that the Germans were not free to attack anyone. With the United States serving as night watchman, relative-gains concerns among the Western European states were mitigated and, moreover, those states were willing to allow their economies to become tightly interdependent.

In effect, relations among EC states were spared the effects of anarchy—fears about relative gains and an obsession with autonomy—because the United States served as the ultimate arbiter within the Alliance.

If the present Soviet threat to Western Europe is removed, and American forces depart for home, relations among the EC states will be fundamentally altered. Without a common Soviet threat and without the American night watchman, Western European states will begin viewing each other with greater fear and suspicion, as they did for centuries before the onset of the Cold War. Consequently, they will worry about the imbalances in gains as well as the loss of autonomy that results from cooperation.[69] Cooperation in

---

68. See Josef Joffe, "Europe's American Pacifier," *Foreign Policy*, No. 54 (Spring 1984), pp. 64–82.
69. Consider, for example, a situation where the European Community is successfully extended

this new order will be more difficult than it has been in the Cold War. Conflict will be more likely.

In sum, there are good reasons for looking with skepticism upon the claim that peace can be maintained in a multipolar Europe on the basis of a more powerful EC.

PEACE-LOVING DEMOCRACIES

The peace-loving democracies theory holds that domestic political factors, not calculations about military power or the international economic system, are the principal determinant of peace. Specifically, the argument is that the presence of liberal democracies in the international system will help to produce a stable order.[70] The claim is not that democracies go to war less often than authoritarian states. In fact, the historical record shows clearly that such is not the case.[71] Instead, the argument is that democracies do not go to war against other democracies. Thus, democracy must spread to Eastern Europe and the Soviet Union to insure peace in post–Cold War Europe.

It is not certain that democracy will take root among the states of Eastern Europe or in the Soviet Union. They lack a strong tradition of democracy; institutions that can accommodate the growth of democracy will have to be built from scratch. That task will probably prove to be difficult, especially in an unstable Europe. But whether democracy takes root in the East matters

---

to include Eastern Europe and the Soviet Union, and that over time all states achieve greater prosperity. The Germans, however, do significantly better than all other states. Hence their relative power position, which is already quite strong, begins to improve markedly. It is likely that the French and the Soviets, just to name two states, would be deeply concerned by this situation.

70. This theory has been recently articulated by Michael Doyle in three articles: "Liberalism and World Politics," *American Political Science Review*, Vol. 80, No. 4 (December 1986), pp. 1151–1169; "Kant, Liberal Legacies, and Foreign Affairs," *Philosophy and Public Affairs*, Vol. 12, No. 3 (Summer 1983), pp. 205–235; and "Kant, Liberal Legacies, and Foreign Affairs, Part 2," *Philosophy and Public Affairs*, Vol. 12, No. 4 (Fall 1983), pp. 323–353. Doyle draws heavily on Immanuel Kant's classic writings on the subject. This theory also provides the central argument in Francis Fukuyama's widely publicized essay on "The End of History?" in *The National Interest*, No. 16 (Summer 1989), pp. 3–18. For an excellent critique of the theory, see Samuel P. Huntington, "No Exit: The Errors of Endism," *The National Interest*, No. 17 (Fall 1989), pp. 3–11.

71. There is a good empirical literature on the relationship between democracy and war. See, for example, Steve Chan, "Mirror, Mirror on the Wall . . . Are the Freer Countries More Pacific?" *Journal of Conflict Resolution*, Vol. 28, No. 4 (December 1984), pp. 617–648; Erich Weede, "Democracy and War Involvement," in ibid., pp. 649–664; Bruce M. Russett and R. Joseph Monsen, "Bureaucracy and Polyarchy As Predictors of Performance," *Comparative Political Studies*, Vol. 8, No. 1 (April 1975), pp. 5–31; and Melvin Small and J. David Singer, "The War-Proneness of Democratic Regimes, 1816–1965," *The Jerusalem Journal of International Relations*, Vol. 1, No. 4 (Summer 1976), pp. 50–69.

little for stability in Europe, since the theory of peace-loving democracies is unsound.

THE LOGIC OF THE THEORY. Two explanations are offered in support of the claim that democracies do not go to war against one another.

First, some claim that authoritarian leaders are more prone to go to war than leaders of democracies, because authoritarian leaders are not accountable to their publics, which carry the main burdens of war. In a democracy, by contrast, the citizenry that pays the price of war has greater say in the decision-making process. The people, so the argument goes, are more hesitant to start trouble because it is they who pay the blood price; hence the greater their power, the fewer wars.

The second argument rests on the claim that the citizens of liberal democracies respect popular democratic rights—those of their fellow countrymen, and those of individuals in other states. As a result they are reluctant to wage war against other democracies, because they view democratic governments as more legitimate than others, and are loath to impose a foreign regime on a democratic state by force. This would violate their own democratic principles and values. Thus an inhibition on war is introduced when two democracies face each other that is missing in other international relationships.

The first of these arguments is flawed because it is not possible to sustain the claim that the people in a democracy are especially sensitive to the costs of war and therefore less willing than authoritarian leaders to fight wars. In fact, the historical record shows that democracies are every bit as likely to fight wars as are authoritarian states.

Furthermore, mass publics, whether democratic or not, can become deeply imbued with nationalistic or religious fervor, making them prone to support aggression, regardless of costs. The widespread public support in post-revolutionary France for Napoleon's wars of aggression is just one example of this phenomenon. On the other hand, authoritarian leaders are just as likely as democratic publics to fear going to war, because war tends to unleash democratic forces that can undermine the regime.[72] War can impose high costs on authoritarian leaders as well as on their citizenries.

The second argument, which emphasizes the transnational respect for democratic rights among democracies, rests on a weaker factor that is usually

---

72. See, for example, Stanislav Andreski, "On the Peaceful Disposition of Military Dictatorships," *Journal of Strategic Studies*, Vol. 3, No. 3 (December 1980), pp. 3–10.

overridden by other factors such as nationalism and religious fundamental-ism. There is also another problem with the argument. The possibility always exists that a democracy will revert to an authoritarian state. This threat of backsliding means that one democratic state can never be sure that another democratic state will not change its stripes and turn on it sometime in the future. Liberal democracies must therefore worry about relative power among themselves, which is tantamount to saying that each has an incentive to consider aggression against the other to forestall future trouble. Lamentably, it is not possible for even liberal democracies to transcend anarchy.

THE HISTORICAL RECORD. Problems with the deductive logic aside, the his-torical record seems to offer strong support for the theory of peace-loving democracies. There appears to have been no case where liberal democracies fought against each other. Although this evidence looks impressive at first glance, closer examination shows it to be indecisive. In fact, history provides no clear test of the theory. Four evidentiary problems leave the issue in doubt.

First, democracies have been few in number over the past two centuries, and thus there have not been many cases where two democracies were in a position to fight with each other. Only three prominent cases are usually cited: Britain and the United States (1832–present); Britain and France (1832–49, 1871–1940); and the Western democracies since 1945.

Second, there are other persuasive explanations for why war did not occur in those three cases, and these competing explanations must be ruled out before the peace-loving democracies theory can be accepted. While relations between the British and the Americans during the nineteenth century were hardly free of conflict,[73] their relations in the twentieth century were quite harmonious, and thus fit closely with how the theory would expect two democracies to behave towards each other. That harmony, however, can easily be explained by the presence of a common threat that forced Britain and the United States to work closely together.[74] Both faced a serious German threat in the first part of the century, and a Soviet threat later. The same basic argument applies to France and Britain. While Franco-British relations

---

73. For a discussion of the hostile relations that existed between the United States and Britain during the nineteenth century, see H.C. Allen, *Great Britain and the United States: A History of Anglo-American Relations, 1783–1952* (London: Odhams, 1954).
74. For a discussion of this rapprochement, see Stephen R. Rock, *Why Peace Breaks Out: Great Power Rapprochement in Historical Perspective* (Chapel Hill: University of North Carolina Press, 1989), chap. 2.

were not the best throughout most of the nineteenth century,[75] they improved significantly around the turn of the century with the rise of a common threat: Germany.[76] Finally, as noted above, the Soviet threat can explain the absence of war among the Western democracies since 1945.

Third, it bears mention that several democracies have come close to fighting one another, which suggests that the absence of war may be due simply to chance. France and Britain approached war during the Fashoda crisis of 1898. France and Weimar Germany might have come to blows over the Rhineland during the 1920s, had Germany possessed the military strength to challenge France. The United States has clashed with a number of elected governments in the Third World during the Cold War, including the Allende regime in Chile and the Arbenz regime in Guatemala.

Lastly, some would classify Wilhelmine Germany as a democracy, or at least a quasi-democracy; if so, World War I becomes a war among democracies.[77]

Conclusion

This article argues that bipolarity, an equal military balance, and nuclear weapons have fostered peace in Europe over the past 45 years. The Cold War confrontation produced these phenomena; thus the Cold War was principally responsible for transforming a historically violent region into a very peaceful place.

There is no doubt that the costs of the Cold War have been substantial. It inflicted oppressive political regimes on the peoples of Eastern Europe, who were denied basic human rights by their forced membership in the Soviet

---

75. For a good discussion of Franco-British relations during the nineteenth century, see P.J.V. Rolo, *Entente Cordiale: The Origins and Negotiation of the Anglo-French Agreements of 8 April 1904* (New York: St. Martins, 1969), pp. 16–109.

76. Stephen Rock, who has examined the rapprochement between Britain and France, argues that the principal motivating force behind their improved relations derived from geopolitical considerations, not shared political beliefs. See Rock, *Why Peace Breaks Out*, chap. 4.

77. Doyle recognizes this problem and thus has a lengthy footnote that attempts to deal with it. See "Kant, Liberal Legacies, and Foreign Affairs [Part One]," pp. 216–217, n. 8. He argues that "Germany was a liberal state under republican law for domestic issues," but that the "emperor's active role in foreign affairs . . . made imperial Germany a state divorced from the control of its citizenry in foreign affairs." However, an examination of the decision-making process leading to World War I reveals that the emperor (Wilhelm II) was not a prime mover in foreign affairs and that he was no more bellicose than other members of the German elite, including the leading civilian official, Chancellor Bethmann-Hollweg.

empire. It consumed national wealth, by giving rise to large and costly defense establishments in both East and West. It spawned bloody conflicts in the Third World; these produced modest casualties for the superpowers, but large casualties for the Third World nations. Nevertheless, the net human and economic cost of the Cold War order has been far less than the cost of the European order of 1900–45, with its vast violence and suffering.

A Cold War order without confrontation would have been preferable to the order that actually developed; then the peace that the Cold War order produced could have been enjoyed without its attendant costs. However, it was East-West enmity that gave rise to the Cold War order; there would have been no bipolarity, no equality, and no large Soviet and American nuclear forces in Europe without it. The costs of the Cold War arose from the same cause—East-West confrontation—as did its benefits. The good could not be had without the bad.

This article further argues that the demise of the Cold War order is likely to increase the chances that war and major crises will occur in Europe. Many observers now suggest that a new age of peace is dawning; in fact the opposite is true.

The implications of my analysis are straightforward, if paradoxical. The West has an interest in maintaining peace in Europe. It therefore has an interest in maintaining the Cold War order, and hence has an interest in the continuation of the Cold War confrontation; developments that threaten to end it are dangerous. The Cold War antagonism could be continued at lower levels of East-West tension than have prevailed in the past; hence the West is not injured by relaxing East-West tension, but a complete end to the Cold War would create more problems than it would solve.

The fate of the Cold War, however, is mainly in the hands of the Soviet Union. The Soviet Union is the only superpower that can seriously threaten to overrun Europe; it is the Soviet threat that provides the glue that holds NATO together. Take away that offensive threat and the United States is likely to abandon the Continent, whereupon the defensive alliance it has headed for forty years may disintegrate. This would bring to an end the bipolar order that has characterized Europe for the past 45 years.

The foregoing analysis suggests that the West paradoxically has an interest in the continued existence of a powerful Soviet Union with substantial military forces in Eastern Europe. Western interests are wholly reversed from those that Western leaders saw in the late 1940s: instead of seeking the retraction of Soviet power, as the West did then, the West now should hope that the Soviet Union retains at least some military forces in the Eastern European region.

There is little the Americans or the Western Europeans can or are likely to do to perpetuate the Cold War, for three reasons.

First, domestic political considerations preclude such an approach. Western leaders obviously cannot base national security policy on the need to maintain forces in Central Europe for the purpose simply of keeping the Soviets there. The idea of deploying large forces in order to bait the Soviets into an order-keeping competition would be dismissed as bizarre, and contrary to the general belief that ending the Cold War and removing the Soviet yoke from Eastern Europe would make the world safer and better.[78]

Second, the idea of propping up a declining rival runs counter to the basic behavior of states. States are principally concerned about their relative power position in the system; hence, they look for opportunities to take advantage of each other. If anything, they prefer to see adversaries decline, and thus will do whatever they can to speed up the process and maximize the distance of the fall. In other words, states do not ask which distribution of power best facilitates stability and then do everything possible to build or maintain such an order. Instead, they each tend to pursue the more narrow aim of maximizing their power advantage over potential adversaries. The particular international order that results is simply a byproduct of that competition, as illustrated by the origins of the Cold War order in Europe. No state intended to create it. In fact, both the United States and the Soviet Union worked hard in the early years of the Cold War to undermine each other's position in Europe, which would have ended the bipolar order on the Continent. The remarkably stable system that emerged in Europe in the late 1940s was the unintended consequence of an intense competition between the superpowers.

Third, even if the Americans and the Western Europeans wanted to help the Soviets maintain their status as a superpower, it is not apparent that they could do so. The Soviet Union is leaving Eastern Europe and cutting its

---

78. This point is illustrated by the 1976 controversy over the so-called "Sonnenfeldt Doctrine." Helmut Sonnenfeldt, an adviser to Secretary of State Henry Kissinger, was reported to have said in late 1975 that the United States should support Soviet domination of Eastern Europe. It was clear from the ensuing debate that whether or not Sonnenfeldt in fact made such a claim, no administration could publicly adopt that position. See U.S. Congress, House Committee on International Relations, *Hearings on United States National Security Policy Vis-à-Vis Eastern Europe (The "Sonnenfeldt Doctrine")*, 94th Cong., 2nd sess. (Washington, D.C.: U.S. GPO, April 12, 1976).

military forces largely because its economy is foundering. It is not clear that the Soviets themselves know how to fix their economy, and there is little that Western governments can do to help them solve their economic problems. The West can and should avoid doing malicious mischief to the Soviet economy, but at this juncture it is difficult to see how the West can have significant positive influence.[79]

The fact that the West cannot sustain the Cold War does not mean that the United States should abandon all attempts to preserve the current order. The United States should do what it can to direct events toward averting a complete mutual superpower withdrawal from Europe. For instance, the American negotiating position at the conventional arms control talks should aim toward large mutual force reductions, but should not contemplate complete mutual withdrawal. The Soviets may opt to withdraw all their forces unilaterally anyway; there is little the United States could do to prevent this.

POLICY RECOMMENDATIONS

If complete Soviet withdrawal from Eastern Europe proves unavoidable, the West faces the question of how to maintain peace in a multipolar Europe. Three policy prescriptions are in order.

First, the United States should encourage the limited and carefully managed proliferation of nuclear weapons in Europe. The best hope for avoiding war in post–Cold War Europe is nuclear deterrence; hence some nuclear proliferation is necessary to compensate for the withdrawal of the Soviet and American nuclear arsenals from Central Europe. Ideally, as I have argued, nuclear weapons would spread to Germany, but to no other state.

Second, Britain and the United States, as well as the Continental states, will have to balance actively and efficiently against any emerging aggressor to offset the ganging up and bullying problems that are sure to arise in post–Cold War Europe. Balancing in a multipolar system, however, is usually a problem-ridden enterprise, either because of geography or because of significant coordination problems. Nevertheless, two steps can be taken to maximize the prospects of efficient balancing.

The initial measure concerns Britain and the United States, the two prospective balancing states that, physically separated from the Continent, may

---

79. For an optimistic assessment of how the West can enhance Gorbachev's prospects of succeeding, see Jack Snyder, "International Leverage on Soviet Domestic Change," *World Politics*, Vol. 42, No. 1 (October 1989), pp. 1–30.

thus conclude that they have little interest in what happens there. They would then be abandoning their responsibilities and, more importantly, their interests as off-shore balancers. Both states' failure to balance against Germany before the two world wars made war more likely in each case. It is essential for peace in Europe that they not repeat their past mistakes, but instead remain actively involved in maintaining the balance of power in Europe.

Specifically, both states must maintain military forces that can be deployed to the Continent to balance against states that threaten to start a war. To do this they must also socialize their publics to support a policy of continued Continental commitment. Support for such a commitment will be more difficult to mobilize than in the past, because its principal purpose would be to preserve peace, rather than to prevent an imminent hegemony, and the latter is a simpler goal to explain publicly. Moreover, it is the basic nature of states to focus on maximizing relative power, not on bolstering stability, so this prescription asks them to take on an unaccustomed task. Nevertheless, the British and American stake in peace is real, especially since there is a sure risk that a European war might involve large-scale use of nuclear weapons. It should therefore be possible for both countries to lead their publics to recognize this interest and support policies that protect it.[80]

The other measure concerns American attitudes and actions toward the Soviet Union. The Soviets may eventually return to their past expansionism and threaten to upset the status quo. If so, we are back to the Cold War; the West should respond as quickly and efficiently as it did the first time. However, if the Soviets adhere to status quo policies, Soviet power could play a key role in balancing against Germany and in maintaining order in Eastern Europe. It is important that, in those cases where the Soviets are acting in a balancing capacity, the United States recognize this, cooperate with its former adversary, and not let residual distrust from the Cold War interfere with the balancing process.

Third, a concerted effort should be made to keep hyper-nationalism at bay, especially in Eastern Europe. This powerful force has deep roots in Europe and has contributed to the outbreak of past European conflicts. Nationalism has been contained during the Cold War, but it is likely to reemerge once

---

80. Advancing this argument is Van Evera, "Why Europe Matters, Why the Third World Doesn't."

Soviet and American forces leave the heart of Europe.[81] It will be a force for trouble unless it is curbed. The teaching of honest national history is especially important, since the teaching of false chauvinist history is the main vehicle for spreading virulent nationalism. States that teach a dishonestly self-exculpating or self-glorifying history should be publicly criticized and sanctioned.[82]

On this count it is especially important that relations between Germany and its neighbors be handled carefully. Many Germans rightly feel that Germany has behaved very responsibly for 45 years, and has made an honest effort to remember and make amends for an ugly period of its past. Therefore, Germans quickly tire of lectures from foreigners demanding that they apologize once again for crimes committed before most of the current German population was born. On the other hand, peoples who have suffered at the hands of the Germans cannot forget their enormous suffering, and inevitably ask for repeated assurance that the past will not be repeated. This dialogue has the potential to spiral into mutual recriminations that could spark a renewed sense of persecution among Germans, and with it, a rebirth of German-nationalism. It is therefore incumbent on all parties in this discourse to proceed with understanding and respect for one another's feelings and experience. Specifically, others should not ask today's Germans to apologize for crimes they did not commit, but Germans must understand that others' ceaseless demands for reassurance have a legitimate basis in history, and should view these demands with patience and understanding.

None of these tasks will be easy to accomplish. In fact, I expect that the bulk of my prescriptions will not be followed; most run contrary to powerful strains of domestic American and European opinion, and to the basic nature of state behavior. Moreover, even if they are followed, this will not guarantee the peace in Europe. If the Cold War is truly behind us, the stability of the past 45 years is not likely to be seen again in the coming decades.

---

81. On the evolution of nationalistic history-teaching in Europe see Kennedy, "The Decline of Nationalistic History," and Dance, *History the Betrayer.*
82. My thinking on this matter has been influenced by conversations with Stephen Van Evera.

Offense, Defense, and the Causes of War

Stephen Van Evera

2/22

Is war more likely when conquest is easy? Could peace be strengthened by making conquest more difficult? What are the causes of offense dominance?[1] How can these causes be controlled? These are the questions this article addresses.

I argue that war is far more likely when conquest is easy, and that shifts in the offense-defense balance have a large effect on the risk of war. Ten war-causing effects (summarized in Figure 1) arise when the offense dominates. (1) Empires are easier to conquer. This invites opportunistic expansion even by temperate powers (explanation A). (2) Self-defense is more difficult; hence states are less secure. This drives them to pursue defensive expansion (explanation B). (3) Their greater insecurity also drives states to resist others' expansion more fiercely. Power gains by others raise larger threats to national security; hence expansionism prompts a more violent response (explanation C). (4) First-strike advantages are larger, raising dangers of preemptive war (explanation D). (5) Windows of opportunity and vulnerability are larger, raising dangers of preventive war (explanation E). (6) States more often adopt fait accompli diplomatic tactics, and such tactics more often trigger war (explanation F). (7) States negotiate less readily and cooperatively; hence negotiations fail more often, and disputes fester unresolved (explanation G). (8) States enshroud foreign and defense policy in tighter secrecy, raising the risk of

---

Stephen Van Evera teaches international relations in the Political Science Department at the Massachusetts Institute of Technology.

Thanks to Robert Art, Charles Glaser, and an anonymous reviewer for their comments on this article. It is distilled from *Causes of War, Volume 1: The Structure of Power and the Roots of War* (Ithaca, N.Y.: Cornell University Press, forthcoming 1999).

---

1. In this article "offense dominant" means that conquest is fairly easy; "defense dominant" means that conquest is very difficult. It is almost never easier to conquer than to defend, so I use "offense dominant" broadly, to denote that offense is easier than usual, although perhaps not actually easier than defense. I use "offense-defense balance" to denote the relative ease of aggression and defense against aggression. As noted below, this balance is shaped by both military and diplomatic/political factors. Two measures of the overall offense-defense balance work well: (1) the probability that a determined aggressor could conquer and subjugate a target state with comparable resources; or (2) the resource advantage that an aggressor requires to gain a given chance of conquering a target state. I use "offense" to refer to strategic offensive action—the taking and holding of territory—as opposed to tactical offensive action, which involves the attack but not the seizure and holding of territory.

International Security, Vol. 22, No. 4 (Spring 1998), pp. 5–43
© 1998 by the President and Fellows of Harvard College and the Massachusetts Institute of Technology.

miscalculation and diplomatic blunder (explanation H). (9) Arms racing is faster and harder to control, raising the risk of preventive wars and wars of false optimism (explanation I). (10) Offense dominance is self-feeding. As conquest grows easier, states adopt policies (e.g., more offensive military doctrines) that make conquest still easier. This magnifies effects 1–9 (explanation J).

The perception of offense dominance raises these same ten dangers, even without the reality. If states think the offense is strong, they will act as if it were. Thus offense-defense theory has two parallel variants, real and perceptual. These variants are considered together here.

How does this theory perform in tests? Three single case-study tests are performed below. They corroborate offense-defense theory[2] and indicate that it has large theoretical importance: that is, shifts in the offense-defense balance—real or perceived—have a large effect on the risk of war. The actual offense-defense balance has marked effects; the effects of the perceived offense-defense balance are even larger.

What causes offense and defense dominance? Military technology and doctrine, geography, national social structure, and diplomatic arrangements (specifically, defensive alliances and balancing behavior by offshore powers) all matter. The net offense-defense balance is an aggregate of these military, geographic, social, and diplomatic factors.

How can offense dominance be controlled? Defensive military doctrines and defensive alliance-making offer good solutions, although there is some tension between them: offensive forces can be needed to defend allies. Offense dominance is more often imagined than real, however. Thus the more urgent question is: How can illusions of offense dominance be controlled? Answers are elusive because the roots of these illusions are obscure.

On balance, how does offense-defense theory measure up? It has the attributes of good theory. In addition to having theoretical importance, offense-defense theory has wide explanatory range and prescriptive richness. It explains an array of important war causes (opportunistic expansionism, defensive expansionism, fierce resistance to others' expansion, first-strike advantage,

---

2. I use "offense-defense theory" to label the hypothesis that war is more likely when conquest is easy, plus explanatory hypotheses that define how this causation operates. The classic work on the topic is Robert Jervis, "Cooperation under the Security Dilemma," *World Politics*, Vol. 30, No. 2 (January 1978), pp. 167–214 at 169. An overview is Sean M. Lynn-Jones, "Offense-Defense Theory and Its Critics," *Security Studies*, Vol. 4, No. 4 (Summer 1995), pp. 660–691. The theory I frame here subsumes and elaborates on Jervis's theory.

windows of opportunity and vulnerability, faits accompli, negotiation failure, secrecy, arms races, and offense dominance itself) that were once thought to be independent. In so doing, offense-defense theory explains the dangers that these war causes produce and the wars they cause. This simplifies the problem of power and war: a number of disparate dangers are fed by a single taproot. Moreover, both the reality and the perception of easy conquest can be shaped by human action; hence offense-defense theory offers prescriptions for controlling the dangers it frames.

The next section outlines offense-defense theory's ten explanations for war. The following section identifies causes of offense and defense dominance. The fourth section frames predictions that can be inferred from offense-defense theory, and offers three case studies as tests of the theory: Europe since 1789, ancient China during the Spring and Autumn and Warring States periods, and the United States since 1789. The final section assesses the general quality of offense-defense theory.

Hypotheses on the Effects of Offense Dominance

A host of dangers arise when conquest is easy. Some are obvious and some more subtle, some are direct and some indirect. Together they make war very likely when the offense dominates.

A: OPPORTUNISTIC EXPANSIONISM

When conquest is hard, states are dissuaded from aggression by the fear that victory will prove costly or unattainable. When conquest is easy, aggression is more alluring: it costs less to attempt and succeeds more often.[3] Aggressors can also move with less fear of reprisal because they win their wars more decisively, leaving their victims less able to retaliate later. Thus even aggressor states are deterred from attacking if the defense is strong, and even quite benign powers are tempted to attack if the offense is strong.

B AND C: DEFENSIVE EXPANSIONISM AND FIERCE RESISTANCE TO EXPANSION

When conquest is hard, states are blessed with secure borders; hence they are less aggressive and more willing to accept the status quo. They have less need

---

3. Suggesting this hypothesis are Ivan S. Bloch, *The Future of War*, trans. R.C. Long, pref. W.T. Stead (New York: Doubleday and McClure, 1899), pp. xxx–xxxi, lxxix; also George H. Quester, *Offense and Defense in the International System* (New York: John Wiley and Sons, 1977), p. 9. A corroborating test is John J. Mearsheimer, *Conventional Deterrence* (Ithaca, N.Y.: Cornell University Press, 1983).

for wider borders because their current frontiers are already defensible. They have less urge to intervene in other states' internal affairs because hostile governments can do them less harm.

Conversely, when conquest is easy, states are more expansionist because their current borders are less defensible.[4] They covet others' geographic strong points, strategic depth, and sources of critical raw materials. They worry more when hostile regimes arise nearby because such neighbors are harder to defend against. These motives drive states to become aggressors and foreign intervenors.[5] States also resist others' expansion more fiercely when conquest is easy. Adversaries can parlay smaller gains into larger conquests; hence stronger steps to prevent gains by others are more appropriate. This attitude makes disputes more intractable.

The basic problem is that resources are more cumulative when conquest is easy. The ability to conquer others and to defend oneself is more elastic to one's control over strategic areas and resources. As a result, gains are more additive—states can parlay small conquests into larger ones—and losses are less reversible. Hence small losses can spell one's demise, and small gains can open the way to hegemonic dominance. States therefore compete harder to control any assets that confer power, seeking wider spheres for themselves while fiercely resisting others' efforts to expand.

This problem is compounded by its malignant effect on states' expectations about one another's conduct. When conquest is hard, states are blessed with neighbors made benign by their own security and by the high cost of attacking others. Hence states have less reason to expect attack. This leaves states even more secure and better able to pursue pacific policies. Conversely, when the offense dominates, states are cursed with neighbors made aggressive by both temptation and fear. These neighbors see easy gains from aggression and danger in standing pat. Plagued with such aggressive neighbors, all states face

---

4. As Robert Jervis notes, "when the offense has the advantage over the defense, attacking is the best route to protecting what you have...and it will be hard for any state to maintain its size and influence without trying to increase them." Jervis, "Cooperation under the Security Dilemma," p. 211; see also pp. 168–169, 173, 187–199.

5. It also seems possible that states should be more careful to avoid war when conquest is easy, because war then brings greater risk of total defeat. If so, offense dominance should cause more caution than belligerence among states, and should lower the risk of war. Advancing this argument is James Fearon, "The Offense-Defense Balance and War since 1648," paper prepared for the annual meeting of the International Studies Association, Chicago, February 1995, pp. 18–24. Fearon's argument seems deductively sound, but history offers very few examples of policymakers who argued that offense dominance was a reason for caution. This is one of many cases where deduction and the historical record point in opposite directions.

greater risk of attack. This drives them to compete still harder to control resources and create conditions that provide security.

Thus states become aggressors because their neighbors are aggressors. This can proceed reciprocally until no state accepts the status quo.

D: MOVING FIRST IS MORE REWARDING

When conquest is easy, the incentive to strike first is larger because a successful surprise attack provides larger rewards and averts greater dangers. Smaller shifts in ratios of forces between states create greater shifts in their relative capacity to conquer and defend territory. (A reversal in the force ratio between two states from 2 to 1 to 1 to 2 means little if attackers need a 3 to 1 advantage to conquer; it means everything if an attacker needs only a 1.5 to 1 advantage.) Hence a surprise strike that shifts the force ratio in the attacker's favor pays it a greater reward. This expands the danger of preemptive war and makes crises more explosive. States grow more trigger-happy, launching first strikes to exploit the advantage of the initiative, and to deny it to an opponent.[6]

Conversely, if the defense dominates, the first-move dividend is small because little can be done with any material advantage gained by moving first. Most aggressors can be checked even if they gain the initiative, and defenders can succeed even if they lose the initiative. Hence preemptive war has less attraction.

E: WINDOWS ARE LARGER AND MORE DANGEROUS

When conquest is easy, arguments for preventive war carry more weight.[7] Smaller shifts in force ratios have larger effects on relative capacity to conquer or defend territory; hence smaller prospective shifts in force ratios cause greater hope and alarm. Also, stemming decline by using force is more feasible because rising states can be overrun with greater ease. This bolsters arguments for shutting "windows of vulnerability" by war. As a result, all international change is more dangerous. Events that tip the balance of resources in any direction trigger thoughts of war among states that face relative decline.

Conversely, if the defense dominates, arguments for preventive war lose force because declining states can more successfully defend against aggressors even after their decline, making preventive war unnecessary. States are also

---

6. The classic discussion of these dangers is Thomas C. Schelling, *Arms and Influence* (New Haven, Conn.: Yale University Press, 1966), pp. 221–259.
7. For a discussion of the dangers of preventive war, see Jack S. Levy, "Declining Power and the Preventive Motivation for War," *World Politics*, Vol. 40, No. 1 (October 1987), pp. 82–107.

deterred from preventive war by the likelihood that their attack will fail, defeated by their enemy's strong defenses.

F: FAITS ACCOMPLIS ARE MORE COMMON AND MORE DANGEROUS

When conquest is easy, states adopt more dangerous diplomatic tactics—specifically, fait accompli tactics—and these tactics are more likely to cause war.

A fait accompli is a halfway step to war. It promises greater chance of political victory than quiet consultation, but it also raises greater risk of violence.[8] The acting side moves without warning, facing others with an accomplished fact. It cannot retreat without losing face, a dilemma that it exploits to compel the others to concede. But if the others stand firm, a collision is hard to avoid. Faits accomplis also pose a second danger: because they are planned in secret, the planning circle is small, raising the risk that flawed policies will escape scrutiny because critics cannot quarrel with mistaken premises.

Faits accomplis are more common when the offense dominates because the rewards they promise are more valuable. When security is scarce, winning disputes grows more important than avoiding war. Leaders care more how spoils are divided than about avoiding violence, because failure to gain their share can spell their doom. This leads to gain-maximizing, war-risking diplomatic strategies—above all, to fait accompli tactics.

Faits accomplis are more dangerous when the offense dominates because a successful fait accompli has a greater effect on the distribution of international power. A sudden resource gain now gives an opponent more capacity to threaten its neighbors' safety. Hence faits accomplis are more alarming and evoke a stronger response from others. States faced with a fait accompli will shoot more quickly because their interests are more badly damaged by it.

G: STATES NEGOTIATE LESS AND REACH FEWER AGREEMENTS

When conquest is easy, states have less faith in agreements because others break them more often; states bargain harder and concede more grudgingly, causing more deadlocks; compliance with agreements is harder to verify; and

---

8. On fait accompli strategies, see Alexander L. George, "Strategies for Crisis Management," in Alexander L. George, *Avoiding War: Problems of Crisis Management* (Boulder, Colo.: Westview, 1991), pp. 377–394 at 382–383, also pp. 549–550, 553–554. Other discussions of faits accomplis include R.B. Mowat, *Diplomacy and Peace* (London: Williams and Norgate, 1935), chap. 10 (on "sudden diplomacy"); Richard Ned Lebow, *Between Peace and War: The Nature of International Crisis* (Baltimore, Md.: Johns Hopkins University Press, 1981), pp. 57–97 (on "brinkmanship"); and Thomas C. Schelling, *Strategy of Conflict* (New York: Oxford University Press, 1963), pp. 22–28 (on games of "chicken").

states insist on better verification and compliance. As a result, states negotiate less often and settle fewer disputes; hence more issues remain unsettled and misperceptions survive that dialogue might dispel.

States break agreements more quickly when the offense dominates because cheating pays larger rewards. Bad faith and betrayal become the norm. The secure can afford the luxury of dealing in good faith, but the insecure must worry more about short-term survival. This drives them toward back-alley behavior, including deceits and sudden betrayals of all kinds—diplomatic faits accomplis, military surprise attacks, and breaking of other solemn agreements. Hence compliance with agreements is less expected.

When states do negotiate, they bargain harder and concede less when the offense dominates. Agreements must be more finely balanced to gain both sides' agreement, because a relative gain by either side poses greater risks to the other's safety.

Verification of compliance with agreements is both more necessary and more difficult when the offense dominates. States insist on better verification of the other's compliance because smaller violations can have larger security implications; for example, an opponent might convert a small advantage gained by cheating on an arms control agreement into a larger offensive threat. At the same time, verification of compliance is harder because states are more secretive when security is scarce (see explanation G). As a result, the range of issues that can be negotiated is narrowed to the few where near-certain verification is possible despite tight state secrecy.

As a net result, states let more disputes fester when the offense dominates.

H: STATES ARE MORE SECRETIVE

Governments cloak their foreign and defense policies in greater secrecy when conquest is easy. An information advantage confers more rewards, and a disadvantage raises more dangers: lost secrets could risk a state's existence. Thus states compete for information advantage by concealing their foreign policy strategies and military plans and forces.

Secrecy in turn is a hydra-headed cause of war. It can lead opponents to underestimate one another's capabilities and blunder into a war of false optimism.[9] It can ease surprise attack by concealing preparations from the victim. It opens windows of opportunity and vulnerability by delaying states' reac-

---

9. On wars of false optimism, see Geoffrey Blainey, *The Causes of War*, 3d ed. (New York: Free Press, 1988), pp. 35–56.

Figure 1. Offense-Defense Theory
Prime hypothesis: War is more likely when conquest is easy.

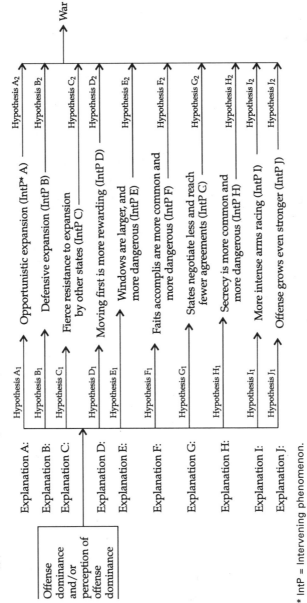

* IntP = Intervening phenomenon.

tions to others' military buildups, raising the risk of preventive war. It fosters policy blunders by narrowing the circle of experts consulted on policy, increasing the risk that flawed policies will survive unexamined. It prevents arms control agreements by making compliance harder to verify.

I: STATES ARMS RACE HARDER AND FASTER

Offense dominance intensifies arms racing, whereas defense dominance slows it down.[10] Arms racing in turn raises other dangers. It opens windows of opportunity and vulnerability as one side or the other races into the lead. It also fosters false optimism by causing rapid military change that confuses policymakers' estimates of relative power. Thus offense dominance is a remote cause of the dangers that arms racing produces.

States have seven incentives to build larger forces when the offense is strong.

- Resources are more cumulative (see explanations B and C). Wartime gains and losses matter more: gains provide a greater increase in security, and losses are less reversible. Therefore the forces that provide these gains and protect against these losses are also worth more.
- Self-defense is more difficult because others' forces have more inherent offensive capability. Hence states require more forces to offset others' deployments.
- States are more expectant of war. Their neighbors are more aggressive (see explanation B), so they must be better prepared for attack or invasion.
- The early phase of war is more decisive. Lacking time to mobilize their economies and societies in the event of war, states maintain larger standing forces.[11] The possibility of quick victory puts a premium on forces-in-being.[12]
- States transfer military resources from defense to offense because offense is more effective (see explanation J). Others then counterbuild because their neighbors' capabilities are more dangerous and so require a larger response. States also infer aggressive intent from their neighbors' offensive buildups, leading them to fear attack and to build up in anticipation.
- States hold military secrets more tightly when the offense dominates (see explanation H). This causes rational overarming, as states gauge their defense efforts to worst-case estimates of enemy strength, on grounds that

---

10. See Jervis, "Cooperation under the Security Dilemma," pp. 172, 188–190.
11. See ibid., pp. 172, 189.
12. General Joseph Joffre argued for a larger French standing force in 1913, because "the affair will already have been settled" by the time reservists were mobilized in three to four weeks. David G. Herrmann, *The Arming of Europe and the Making of the First World War* (Princeton, N.J.: Princeton University Press, 1996), p. 193.

underspending is disastrous whereas overspending is merely wasteful. It also allows national militaries to monopolize defense information more tightly. Given that militaries are prone to inflate threats, states will overspend groundlessly when militaries have an information monopoly that lets them alone assess the threat. Thus "action-reaction" becomes "action-over-reaction-overreaction."

- States reach fewer arms control agreements when the offense dominates, because agreements of all kinds are fewer (see explanation G). Hence states are less able to limit arms competition through agreement.

If the defense dominates, things are reversed. States build smaller offensive forces because offense is less effective, and because other states have less aggressive aims. States are safe without wider empires; hence offensive forces that could provide empires lose utility. The national military therefore grows defense-heavy. This causes other states to feel safer, which in turn makes them less aggressive, further lowering all states' insecurity—hence their need for empire and for offense—up to a point.

States also reduce defensive forces when the defense dominates because defense is easier and attack seems more remote. Moreover, as their neighbors buy less offense, they need even less defense because their defense faces less challenge.

In short, states buy smaller forces in general, and less offense in particular, when the defense dominates. This leads to still smaller forces and still less offense. If information were perfect, arms racing would slow to a crawl if the defense strongly dominated.

J. CONQUEST GROWS STILL EASIER

Offense dominance is self-reinforcing[13] for three main reasons. First, states buy relatively more offensive forces when the offense dominates. They prefer the more successful type of force, so they buy defensive forces when the defense is strong and offensive forces when the offense is strong.[14] This reinforces the initial dominance of the defense or the offense.

---

13. Making this argument is Jervis, "Cooperation under the Security Dilemma," pp. 188, 199, 201.
14. Thus Clausewitz explained: "If attack were the stronger form [of war], there would be no case for using the defensive, since its purpose is only passive. No one would want to do anything but attack. Defense would be pointless." Carl von Clausewitz, *On War*, ed. and trans. Michael Howard and Peter Paret, intro. by Paret, Howard, and Bernard Brodie, commentary by Brodie (Princeton, N.J.: Princeton University Press, 1976), p. 359.

Second, alliances assume a more offensive character[15] when the offense dominates because aggressors can more easily drag their allies into their wars of aggression.[16] Insecure states can less afford to see allies destroyed, so they must support even bellicose allies who bring war on themselves. Knowing this, the allies feel freer to get into wars. As a net result, even de jure defensive alliances operate as defensive-and-offensive alliances. Alliances also assume a more offensive character if the allies adopt purely offensive military doctrines. This hamstrings states that would demand that their allies confine themselves to defensive preparations in a crisis, given that all preparations are offensive.

Third, status quo states are less able to protect their allies from conquest when the offense dominates because attackers can overrun defenders before help can arrive.

Thus offense dominance raises the danger of greater offense dominance. Once entered, an offense-dominant world is hard to escape.

Military offense dominance has one self-limiting effect: it leads status quo powers to cooperate more closely against aggressors.[17] They jump to aid an aggressor's victims because each knows that its neighbor's demise could lead more directly to its own undoing. Conversely, when states think that the defense dominates, they do less to save others from aggression because each expects it can defend itself alone even if others are overrun. As a result, aggressors can more often attack their victims seriatim, which is far easier than defeating a unified coalition. This countervailing effect, however, is more than offset by the several ways that offense dominance feeds itself.

These are the dangers raised by offense dominance. As noted above, these same ten dangers arise when the offense is weak but governments think it dominates. They then act as if it dominates, with comparable effects.

Are offensive capabilities always dangerous? The one-sided possession of offensive capabilities by status quo powers that face aggressors can lower rather than raise the risk of war under some conditions. Most important, status quo powers often need offensive capabilities to defend other states against

---

15. A defensive alliance is conditioned on defensive behavior by the ally; the alliance operates if the ally is attacked but not if it attacks. A defensive-and-offensive alliance operates in the event of war regardless of which side started it. The distinction began with Thucydides, who used "empimachy" to denote defensive alliance, "symmachy" for defensive-and-offensive alliances. G.E.M. de Ste. Croix, *The Origins of the Peloponnesian War* (Ithaca, N.Y.: Cornell University Press, 1972), pp. 60, 72–73, 106–108, 184, 298–302, 328.

16. Developing this point are Thomas J. Christensen and Jack Snyder, "Chain Gangs and Passed Bucks: Predicting Alliance Patterns in Multipolarity," *International Organization*, Vol. 44, No. 2 (Spring 1990), pp. 137–168.

17. Making this argument is ibid.

aggressors (e.g., as France required some offensive capability to defend Czechoslovakia and Poland from Germany in 1938–39). Offensive capabilities in the hands of status quo powers also may provide more deterrence than provocation if the aggressor state knows that it provoked the status quo power's hostility, if the aggressor knows that the status quo power has no bedrock aggressive intentions, and if the aggressor cannot remove the status quo power's offensive threat by force. These conditions are not unknown but they are rare. Hence offensive capabilities usually create more dangers than they dampen.

Causes of Offense and Defense Dominance

The feasibility of conquest is shaped by military factors, geographic factors, domestic social and political factors, and the nature of diplomacy. Discussions of the offense-defense balance often focus on military technology, but technology is only one part of the picture.[18]

MILITARY FACTORS

Military technology, doctrine, and force posture and deployments all affect the military offense-defense balance.[19] Military technology can favor the aggressor or the defender. In past centuries, strong fortification techniques bolstered the defense, and strong methods of siege warfare strengthened the offense. Technologies that favored mass infantry warfare (e.g., cheap iron, allowing mass production of infantry weapons) strengthened the offense because large mass armies could bypass fortifications more easily, and because mass armies fostered more egalitarian polities that could raise loyal popular armies that would not melt away when sent on imperial expeditions. Technologies that favored chariot or cavalry warfare (e.g., the stirrup) strengthened the defense, because cavalry warfare required smaller forces[20] that were more easily stopped by

---

18. For a discussion of the causes of offense and defense dominance, see Jervis, "Cooperation under the Security Dilemma," pp. 176, 194–199.

19. Several measures of the military offense-defense balance could be adopted, such as: (1) the probability that an offensive force can overcome a defensive force of equal cost; (2) the relative cost that attackers and defenders must pay for forces that offset incremental improvements by the other; or (3) the loss ratio when an offensive force attacks a defensive force of equal cost. All three measures (and more are possible) capture the concept of relative military difficulty of conquest and defense. For a list of possible measures, see Charles L. Glaser and Chaim Kaufmann, "What Is Offense-Defense Balance and How Can We Measure It?," *International Security*, Vol. 22, No. 4 (Spring 1998), pp. 44–82.

20. Cavalry warfare was capital intensive; hence it was usually waged by small forces of tax-supported specialists-knights in shining (and expensive) armor on expensive horses. Infantry warfare is more manpower intensive, and is usually waged by larger, less capitalized armies.

fortifications, and fostered hierarchic societies that could not raise armies that would remain loyal if sent on quests for empire.[21] In modern times, technology that gave defenders more lethal firepower (e.g., the machine gun) or greater mobility (e.g., the railroad) strengthened the defense. When these technologies were neutralized by still newer technologies (motorized armor), the offense grew stronger.

Thus when fortresses and cavalry dominated in the late Middle Ages, the defense held the advantage. Cannons then made fortifications vulnerable and restored the strength of the offense. In the seventeenth and eighteenth centuries new fortification techniques strengthened the defense. The mercenary armies of the age also remained tightly tied to logistical tails that kept them close to home: one historian writes that an eighteenth-century army "was like a diver in the sea, its movements strictly limited and tied by the long, slender communicating tube which gave it life."[22] Then revolutionary France's mass armies strengthened the offense because they had greater mobility. Their size let them sweep past border forts without leaving the bulk of their manpower behind for siege duty, and their more loyal troops could be trusted to forage without deserting, so they needed less logistical support. After the conservative restoration in France, Europe abandoned the mass army because it required, and fostered, popular government. This restored the power of the defense, which then waned somewhat as Europe democratized and large mass armies reappeared in the mid-nineteenth century.[23]

The combined effects of lethal small arms (accurate fast-firing rifles and machine guns), barbed wire, entrenchments, and railroads gave the defense an enormous advantage during World War I. The first three—lethal small arms, barbed wire, and trenches—gave defenders a large advantage at any point of attack. The fourth—railroads—let defenders reinforce points of attack faster than invaders could, because invaders could not use the defenders' railroads (given that railroad gauges differed across states, and defenders destroyed rail lines as they retreated) while the defenders had full use of their own lines. During 1919–45 the power of the offense was restored by motorized armor and an offensive doctrine—blitzkrieg—for its employment; this overrode machine

---

21. On the effects of the stirrup on warfare and society in the Middle Ages, see Lynn White, Jr., *Medieval Technology and Social Change* (New York: Oxford University Press, 1964), pp. 1–38. On the general effect of military technology on social stratification, see Stanislav Andreski, *Military Organization and Society* (Berkeley: University of California Press, 1971), pp. 20–74.

22. Harold Temperley, quoted in Blainey, *Causes of War*, p. 188.

23. Large armies aid the offense only up to a point, however. Once armies grow so big that they can cover an entire frontier (as on the western front in World War I), their size aids the defense because offensive outflanking maneuvers against them become impossible.

guns, trenches, and barbed wire. Then after 1945 thermonuclear weapons restored the power of the defense—this time giving it an overwhelming advantage.[24]

Technology and doctrine combined to define these tides of offense and defense. Sometimes technology overrode doctrine, as in 1914–18 and in 1945–91 (when the superpowers' militaries embraced offensive doctrines but could not find offensive counters to the nuclear revolution). Sometimes doctrine shaped technology, as in 1939–45, when blitzkrieg doctrine fashioned armor technology into an offensive instrument.

States shape the military offense-defense balance by their military posture and force deployments. Thus Stalin eased attack for both himself and Hitler during 1939–41 by moving most of the Red Army out of strong defensive positions on the Stalin Line and forward into newly seized territories in Poland, Bessarabia, Finland, and the Baltic states.[25] This left Soviet forces better positioned to attack Germany and far easier for Germany to attack, as the early success of Hitler's 1941 invasion revealed. The U.S. eased offense for both itself and Japan in 1941 when it deployed its fleet forward to Pearl Harbor and bombers forward to the Philippines.[26] Egypt eased Israel's assault by its chaotic forward deployment of troops into poorly prepared Sinai positions in the crisis before the 1967 war.[27]

States also can change the offense-defense balance through their wartime military operations. Aggressive operations can corrode key enemy defenses, and reckless operations can expose one's own defenses. Thus the dangers of offense dominance can be conjured up by unthinking wartime policymakers. For example, General Douglas MacArthur's reckless rush to the Yalu River in 1950 created an offensive threat to China's core territory and, by exposing badly deployed U.S. forces to attack, eased a Chinese offensive.[28]

---

24. Jack Levy provides synoptic history of the military offense-defense balance in "The Offensive/Defensive Balance of Military Technology: A Theoretical and Historical Analysis," *International Studies Quarterly*, Vol. 28, No. 2 (June 1984), pp. 219–238 at 230–234. Other discussions include Quester, *Offense and Defense in the International System*; and Andreski, *Military Organization and Society*, pp. 75–78. A detailed history is needed.

25. Peter Calvocoressi and Guy Wint, *Total War: The Story of World War II* (New York: Pantheon Books, 1972), p. 168.

26. Jonathan G. Utley, *Going to War with Japan, 1937–1941* (Knoxville: University of Tennessee Press, 1985), pp. 84, 163.

27. Donald Neff, *Warriors for Jerusalem: The Six Days That Changed the Middle East* (New York: Simon and Schuster, 1984), pp. 141, 168.

28. Likewise, during the Cold War some worried that NATO might inadvertently threaten the Soviet Union's strategic nuclear deterrent in its effort to defend NATO's Atlantic sea-lanes during

GEOGRAPHY

Conquest is harder when geography insulates states from invasion or strangulation. Hence conquest is hindered when national borders coincide with oceans, lakes, mountains, wide rivers, dense jungles, trackless deserts, or other natural barriers that impede offensive movement or give defenders natural strong points. Human-made obstacles along borders, such as urban sprawl, can also serve as barriers to armored invasion. Conquest is hindered if foes are separated by wide buffer regions (third states or demilitarized zones) that neither side can enter in peacetime. Conquest is hindered when national territories are mountainous or heavily forested, and when populations live mainly in rural settings, easing guerrilla resistance to invaders. Conquest is hindered when states are large and their critical war resources or industries lie far in their interior, where they cannot be quickly overrun. Conquest is hindered when states are invulnerable to economic strangulation. Hence conquest is hindered when states are self-sufficient in supplies of water, energy, food, and critical raw materials, or when their trade routes cannot be severed by land or sea blockade.

The geography of Western Europe, with its mountain ranges and ocean moats, is less favorable to conquest than the exposed plains of Eastern Europe or the open terrain of the Middle East. Israel's geography is especially unfortunate: physically small, its frontiers have few obstacles and much of its industry and population lie on exposed frontiers. Israeli territory is not conducive to guerrilla resistance, and its economy is import dependent. Germany's borders are better but still relatively poor: its eastern frontier is open; its economy is import dependent; and its trade routes are vulnerable. Britain, France, and Italy have formidable frontier barriers that make them relatively defensible. The United States' vast size, ocean-moat frontiers, and independent economy bless it with very defensible geography.

SOCIAL AND POLITICAL ORDER

Popular regimes are generally better at both conquest and self-defense than are unpopular regimes, but these effects do not cancel out. On net, conquest is probably harder among popular than unpopular regimes today, but in past centuries the reverse was likely true.

---

an East-West conventional war. Barry R. Posen, *Inadvertent Escalation: Conventional War and Nuclear Risks* (Ithaca, N.Y.: Cornell University Press, 1991), pp. 129–158. On a related danger, see ibid., pp. 28–67.

Popular governments can better raise larger, more loyal armies that can bypass others' border forts and can operate far from home with less logistical support. This gives popular regimes greater offensive power. Popular regimes can better organize their citizens for guerrilla resistance, making them harder to conquer. Citizen-defense guerrilla strategies are viable for Switzerland or China, but not for Guatemala or ancient Sparta, because these unpopular governments cannot arm their people without risking revolution. The citizens of unpopular oligarchies may actively assist advancing invaders. This gives attackers more penetrating power and makes early losses less reversible. Thus Sparta feared an invading army might grow if it entered Spartan territory, because Spartan slaves and dissident tribes would desert to the enemy.[29]

Unpopular regimes are more vulnerable to subversion or revolution inspired from abroad. Subversion is a form of offense, and it affects international relations in the same way as do offensive military capabilities. Frail regimes are more frightened of unfriendly neighbors, making them more determined to impose congenial regimes on neighboring states. The French revolutionary regime and the oligarchic Austrian regime worried that the other side might subvert them in 1792, causing both sides to become more aggressive.[30] After the Russian Revolution similar fears fueled Soviet-Western conflict, as each side feared subversion by the other.

On balance, is conquest easier in a world of popular or unpopular regimes? Popularity of regimes probably aided offense before roughly 1800 and has aided defense since then. The reversal stems from the appearance of cheap, mass-produced weapons useful for guerrilla war—assault rifles and machine guns, light mortars, and mines. The weapons of early times (sword and shield, pike and harquebus, heavy slow-firing muskets, etc.) were poorly adapted for guerrilla resistance. Guerrilla warfare has burgeoned since 1800 partly because the mass production of cheap small arms has tipped the balance toward guerrillas, allowing the hit-and-run harassment that characterizes guerrilla operations. The defensive power of popular regimes has risen in step with this increase in guerrilla warfare.

---

29. De Ste. Croix, *Origins of the Peloponnesian War*, pp. 89–94. Likewise, Hannibal hoped to defeat Rome by recruiting dissident tribes as he penetrated the Italian peninsula. See R.M. Errington, *Dawn of Empire: Rome's Rise to World Power* (Ithaca, N.Y.: Cornell University Press), pp. 62–64.
30. Stephen M. Walt, *Revolution and War* (Ithaca, N.Y.: Cornell University Press, 1996), pp. 123–124; and T.C.W. Blanning, *The Origins of the French Revolutionary Wars* (London: Longman, 1986), pp. 76, 85–86, 99–101, 111.

DIPLOMATIC FACTORS

Three types of diplomatic arrangements strengthen the defense: collective security systems, defensive alliances, and balancing behavior by neutral states. All three impede conquest by adding allies to the defending side.

States in a collective security system (e.g., the League of Nations) promise mutual aid against aggression by any system member. Such aggressors will face large defending coalitions if the system operates.[31]

States in a defensive alliance promise mutual aid against outside aggressors, leaving such aggressors outnumbered by resisting opponents. Thus during 1879–87 Bismarck wove a network of defensive alliances that discouraged aggression and helped preserve peace throughout central and eastern Europe.

Collective security systems and defensive alliances differ only in the kind of aggressor they target (system members versus outside aggressors). Both kinds of aggressors could be targeted at once, and a hybrid system that did this would offer defenders the most protection.

Neutral states act as balancers when they join the weaker of two competing coalitions to restore balance between them. Aggression is self-limiting when neutrals balance because aggressors generate more opposition as they expand. Britain and the United States traditionally played balancers to Europe, providing a counterweight to potential continental hegemons.

Balancing behavior is more selective than defensive alliance. Balancers balance to avert regional hegemony; hence pure balancers oppose expansion only by potential regional hegemons. Smaller states are left free to aggress. But balancing does contain hegemons and leaves their potential victims more secure. Conversely, if states bandwagon—join the stronger coalition against the weaker one—conquest is easier because aggressors win more allies as they seize more resources.[32]

Diplomatic arrangements have had a large influence on the offense-defense balance in modern Europe, and shifts in diplomatic arrangements have pro-

---

31. An introduction to collective security is Inis L. Claude, Jr., *Swords into Plowshares: The Problems and Progress of International Organizations*, 4th ed. (New York: Random House, 1971), pp. 411–433. A recent advocacy of collective security is Charles A. Kupchan and Clifford A. Kupchan, "Concerts, Collective Security, and the Future of Europe," *International Security*, Vol. 16, No. 1 (Summer 1991), pp. 114–163.

32. On balancing, bandwagoning, and other theories of alliances, see Stephen M. Walt, *The Origins of Alliances* (Ithaca, N.Y.: Cornell University Press, 1987). Historians have often suggested that a "breakdown in the balance of power" caused war. They usually mean (and should recast their claim to say) that states failed to engage in balancing behavior, which made aggression easier, causing war. War occurs not when the balance of power breaks down, but when balancers fail to balance, leaving aggressors unchecked, as in the late 1930s.

duced large shifts in the overall offense-defense balance. Collective security was never effective, but defensive alliances came and went, erecting barriers to conquest when they appeared. Balancing behavior rose and fell as the power and activism of the two traditional offshore balancers, Britain and the United States, waxed and waned. When the United States and/or Britain were strong and willing to intervene against aspiring continental hegemons, conquest on the continent was difficult. To succeed, a hegemon had to defeat both its continental victims and the offshore power. But when Britain and the United States were weak or isolationist, continental powers could expand against less resistance, leaving all states less secure.

Tests of Offense-Defense Theory

What predictions can be inferred from offense-defense theory? How much history does offense-defense theory explain?

PREDICTIONS AND TESTS

Offense-defense theory's predictions can be grouped in two broad types, *prime* predictions and *explanatory* predictions. The theory's prime predictions derive from its prime hypothesis ("War is more likely when conquest is easy"; or, for the theory's perceptual variant, "War is more likely when states think conquest is easy"). Tests of these predictions shed light on whether offense dominance (or perceptions of offense dominance) causes war.

Offense-defense theory's explanatory predictions derive from the hypotheses that comprise its ten explanations. Tests of these predictions shed light on both *whether* and *how* offense dominance (or perceptions of offense dominance) causes war.

PRIME PREDICTIONS. Three prime predictions of offense-defense theory are tested here.

1. War will be more common in periods when conquest is easy or is believed easy, less common when conquest is difficult or is believed difficult.
2. States that have or believe they have large offensive opportunities or defensive vulnerabilities will initiate and fight more wars than other states.
3. A state will initiate and fight more wars in periods when it has, or thinks that it has, larger offensive opportunities and defensive capabilities.

These predictions are tested below in three case studies: Europe since 1789 (treated as a single regional case study), ancient China during the Spring and

Autumn and Warring States eras, and the United States since 1789. I selected these cases because the offense-defense balance (or perceptions of it) varies sharply across time in all three, creating a good setting for "multiple within-case comparisons" tests that contrast different periods in the same case; because the United States is very secure relative to other countries, creating a good setting for a "comparison to typical values" tests that contrasts U.S. conduct with the conduct of average states;[33] and because two of these cases are well recorded (Europe since 1789 and the United States since 1789).

The case of Europe since 1789 allows tests of prime predictions 1 and 2.[34] We can make crude indices of the offense-defense balances (actual and perceived) for Europe over the past two centuries, and match them with the incidence of war (see Table 1). Offense-defense theory predicts more war when conquest is easy or is believed easy. We can also estimate the offensive opportunities and defensive vulnerabilities of individual powers—for example, since 1789 Prussia/Germany has been more vulnerable and has had more offensive opportunity than Spain, Italy, Britain, or the United States—and can match these estimates with states' rates of war involvement and war initiation. Offense-defense theory predicts that states with more defensive vulnerability and offensive opportunity will be more warlike.

The ancient China case allows a test of prime prediction 1. The offense-defense balance shifted markedly toward the offense as China's Spring and Autumn and Warring States periods evolved. Offense-defense theory predicts a parallel rise in the incidence of warfare during these periods.

The U.S. case allows testing of prime predictions 2 and 3. The United States is less vulnerable to foreign military threats than are other states; hence offense-defense theory predicts that it should start fewer wars and be involved in fewer wars than other states. Americans have also felt more vulnerable to foreign military threats in some eras than in others. The U.S. propensity for war involvement and war initiation should co-vary with this sense of vulnerability.

EXPLANATORY PREDICTIONS. Offense-defense theory posits that offense dominance leads to war through the war-causing action of its ten intervening phenomena A–J: opportunistic expansionism, defensive expansionism, fierce

---

33. I say more about the logic of within-case comparisons and comparison to typical values tests in Van Evera, *Guide to Methods for Students of Political Science* (Ithaca, N.Y.: Cornell University Press, 1997), pp. 58–63. On case selection criteria, see pp. 77–88.
34. In principle, prime prediction 3 could also be tested with this case. This, however, would require tracing and describing trends in each state's sense of vulnerability over time—a large task that would fill many pages.

Table 1. The Offense-Defense Balance among Great Powers, 1700s–Present.

Era	Military realities favored	Military realities were thought to favor	Diplomatic realities favored	Diplomatic realities were thought to favor	In aggregate military and diplomatic realities favored	In aggregate military and diplomatic realities were thought to favor	Amount of warfare among great powers
Pre–1792	Defs.	Defs.	Med.	Med.	Med.	Med.	Medium
1792–1815	Aggrs.	Aggrs.	Med.	Aggrs.	Aggrs.	Aggrs.***	High
1816–56	Defs.	Defs.	Defs.	Defs.	Defs.	Defs.	Low
1856–71	Med.	Med.	Aggrs.	Aggrs.	Aggrs.	Aggrs.	Medium
1871–90	Defs.	Med.	Defs.	Defs.	Defs.	Defs.***	Low
1890–1918	Defs.	Aggrs.	Aggrs.	Aggrs.	Aggrs.	Aggrs.	High
1919–45	Aggrs.	Mixed*	Aggrs.	Aggrs.**	Aggrs.	Aggrs.****	High
1945–1990s	Defs.	Med.	Defs.	Defs.	Defs.	Defs.***	Low

Aggrs.: The factor favors aggressors.

Defs.: The factor favors defenders.

Med.: A medium value: things are somewhere in between, cut both ways.

Mixed: Some national elites saw defense dominance, some saw offense dominance.

The perceptions entries are an average of the perceptions of the great power elites. In some cases, the perceptions of these elites varied sharply across states, for example, perceptions of military realities in the 1930s.

* Things varied across states. The German elite recognized the military power of the offensive in the late 1930s; the elites of other great powers thought the defense was dominant.

** Things varied across states. The German elite (above all Hitler) exaggerated the considerable actual diplomatic weakness of the defense; the elites of other great powers recognized this weakness but did not overstate it. These beliefs average to a perception of substantial diplomatic offense dominance.

*** Elites exaggerated the strength of the offense during 1792–1815, 1871–90, and 1945–1990s, but not by enough to give the realities and perceptions of the offense-defense balance different scores.

**** When we aggregate perceptions of the offense-defense balance, the errors of Germany and the other powers cancel each other out. Germany's exaggeration of the diplomatic power of the offense offsets other powers' exaggeration of the military power of the defense, leaving an aggregate perception fairly close to the offense-dominant reality.

resistance to others' expansion, first-strike advantages, windows of opportunity and vulnerability, faits accomplis and belligerent reactions to them, reluctance to solve conflicts through negotiation, policies of secrecy, intense arms racing, and policies that ease conquest, such as offensive force postures and offensive alliances. If offense-defense theory is valid, these intervening phenomena should correlate with the real and perceived offense-defense balance. Two explanatory predictions can be inferred.

1. Phenomena A–J will be more abundant in eras of real or perceived offense dominance: the ten phenomena should increase as offense strengthens and diminish as offense weakens.
2. States that have or believe they have large offensive opportunities or defensive vulnerabilities will more strongly embrace policies that embody phenomena A–J.[35]

Two of the case studies presented here shed light on these explanatory predictions. The case of Europe allows a partial test of both. We can code only two of offense-defense theory's ten intervening phenomena (IntPs A and B, opportunistic and defensive expansionism) for the whole period. We have fragmentary data for values on the other eight intervening variables. Hence the case lets us test explanations A and B fairly completely and offers scattered evidence on explanations C–J. To test explanations A and B, we ask if expansionism correlates over time with periods of real or perceived offense dominance, and if states that were (or believed they were) less secure and more able to aggress were more expansionist.

The case of the United States since 1789 allows a more complete, if rather weak, test of explanatory prediction 2.

TEST 1: EUROPE 1789–1990s

A composite measure of the offense-defense balance in Europe since 1789 can be fashioned by blending the histories of Europe's military and diplomatic

---

35. Explanatory predictions 1 and 2 are inferred from the "left side" of offense-defense theory, that is, from hypotheses A_1–J_1, which frame the claim that offense dominance causes intervening phenomena A–J (see Figure 1). Predictions could also be inferred from hypotheses A_2–J_2, which comprise the "right side" of the theory, and frame the claim that intervening phenomena A–J cause war. For example, we could infer that (6) warfare will be more common in eras and regions where phenomena A–J are more prevalent, and (7) states that embrace policies that embody phenomena A–J will be involved in more wars and will initiate more wars than other states. I leave "right side" hypotheses untested here because the effects of phenomena A–J are less debated than their causes. Most agree that they cause trouble.

offense-defense balances, as outlined above.[36] In sum, the offense-defense balance went through six phases comprising three up-down oscillations after 1789. Conquest was never easy in an absolute sense during these two centuries. Conquest was, however, markedly easier during 1792–1815, 1856–71, and 1930s–1945 than it was during 1815–56, 1871–1920s, and 1945–1990s.

Elite perceptions of the offense-defense balance track these oscillations quite closely, but not exactly. Elites chronically exaggerated the power of the offense, but did so far more in some periods than in others. Most important, they greatly exaggerated the power of the offense during 1890–1918: elites then wrongly thought conquest was very easy when in fact it was very hard. Thus the pattern of reality and perception run roughly parallel, with the major exception of 1890–1918.

Tides of war and peace correlate loosely with the offense-defense balance during this period, and tightly with the perceived offense-defense balance. Expansionism and war were more common when conquest was easy than when it was difficult, and were far more common when conquest was believed easy than when it was believed difficult. Moreover, states that believed they faced large offensive opportunities and defensive vulnerabilities (especially Prussia/Germany) were the largest troublemakers. They were more expansionist, they were involved in more wars, and they started more wars than other states.

1792–1815. During 1792–1815 the offense was fairly strong militarily, as a result of France's adoption of the popular mass army (enabled by the popularity of the French revolutionary government).[37] Moreover, European elites widely exaggerated one another's vulnerability to conquest: at the outset of the War of 1792 all three belligerents (France, Austria, and Prussia) thought their

---

36. My composite index represents my own "author's estimates" based on sources provided throughout this article. I measured the actual and perceived Europe-wide offense-defense balances by asking: (1) Did military technology, force posture, and doctrine favor the offense or the defense? Did elites and publics believe these factors favored the offense or the defense? (2) Did geography and the domestic social and political order of states favor the offense or the defense? Did elites and publics believe they favored the offense or defense? (3) How numerous and powerful were balancer states, and how strongly did they balance? Did elites believe that other states would balance or bandwagon? (4) Did defensive alliances form, and did they operate effectively? Did elites believe that they operated effectively? I gave these factors the same rough relative weight they receive in standard historical accounts.

37. A discussion of the military offense-defense balance in this era is Quester, *Offense and Defense in the International System*, pp. 66–72.

opponents were on the verge of collapse and could be quickly crushed.[38] Defense-enhancing diplomacy was sluggish: Britain, Europe's traditional balancer, stood by indifferently during the crisis that produced the War of 1792, issuing a formal declaration of neutrality.[39] Moreover, French leaders underestimated the power of defense-enhancing diplomacy because they widely believed that other states would bandwagon with threats instead of balancing against them.[40] In short, military factors helped the offense, and this help was further exaggerated; political factors did little to help bolster defenders, and this help was underestimated.

1815–56. After 1815 both arms and diplomacy favored defenders, as outlined above. Mass armies disappeared,[41] British economic power grew, and Britain remained active on the continent as a balancer. Continental powers expected Britain to balance and believed British strength could not be overridden.

This defense-dominant arrangement lasted until midcentury. It began weakening before the Crimean War (1853–56). When war in Crimea broke out, military factors still favored defenders, but elites underestimated the power of the defense: Britain and France launched their 1854 Crimean offensive in false expectation of quick and easy victory.[42] In general, diplomatic factors favored the defense (Britain still balanced actively), but during the prewar crisis in

---

38. Blanning, *Origins of the French Revolutionary Wars*, p. 116. Austrian and Prussian leaders were assured that revolutionary France could be quickly smashed. Ibid., p. 114. One Prussian leader advised his officers: "Do not buy too many horses, the comedy will not last long. The army of lawyers will be annihilated in Belgium and we shall be home by autumn." Ibid., p. 116. Meanwhile, French revolutionaries wrongly expected a pro-French revolutionary uprising of the oppressed peoples of feudal Europe. Ibid., p. 136; R.R. Palmer, *World of the French Revolution* (New York: Harper and Row, 1971), p. 95; and George Rudé, *Revolutionary Europe, 1783–1815* (Glasgow: Fontana/Collins, 1964), p. 209.

39. Blanning, *Origins of the French Revolutionary Wars*, pp. 131–135.

40. As Steven Ross notes, French expansionists thought they could intimidate Europe into coexisting with an expanded French empire in the 1790s: "By inflicting rapid and decisive defeats upon one or more members of the coalition, the [French] directors hoped to rupture allied unity and force individual members to seek a separate peace." Steven T. Ross, *European Diplomatic History, 1789–1815* (Garden City, N.Y.: Anchor Doubleday, 1969), p. 186.

Later Napoleon thought he could compel Britain to make peace by establishing French continental dominion, proclaiming after the Peace of Amiens, "With Europe in its present state, England cannot reasonably make war on us unaided." Geoffrey Bruun, *Europe and the French Imperium, 1799–1814* (New York: Harper and Row, 1938), p. 118. See also Blanning, *Origins of the French Revolutionary Wars*, p. 109.

41. On the post-1815 restoration of pre-Napoleonic warfare, see Quester, *Offense and Defense in the International System*, pp. 73–74; and Michael Howard, *War in European History* (London: Oxford University Press, 1976), pp. 94–95.

42. Richard Smoke, *War: Controlling Escalation* (Cambridge, Mass.: Harvard University Press, 1977), p. 191.

1853, diplomacy favored the offense because Britain and France blundered by giving Turkey unconditional backing that amounted to an offensive alliance. This encouraged the Turkish aggressions that sparked the war.[43]

1856–71. After the Crimean War the offense-defense balance shifted further toward the offense. Changes in the military realm cut both ways. Mass armies were appearing (bolstering the offense), but small arms were growing more lethal and railroads were expanding (bolstering the defense). In the diplomatic realm, however, the power of defenders fell dramatically because defense-enhancing diplomacy largely broke down. Most important, Britain entered an isolationist phase that lasted into the 1870s, and Russia lost interest in maintaining the balance among the western powers.[44] As a result, diplomatic obstacles to continental conquest largely disappeared, giving continental aggressors a fairly open field. This diplomatic change gave France and Sardinia, and then Prussia, a yawning offensive opportunity, which they exploited by launching a series of wars of opportunistic expansion—in 1859, 1864, 1866, and 1870. But defense-enhancing diplomacy had not disappeared completely, and it helped keep these wars short and limited.

In 1859 British and Russian neutrality gave France and Sardinia a free hand, which they used to seize Lombardy from Austria.[45] In 1864 British, Russian, and French neutrality gave Prussia and Austria a free hand, which they used to seize Schleswig-Holstein from Denmark.[46] In 1866 British, French, and Russian neutrality gave Prussia carte blanche against Austria, which Prussia used to smash Austria and consolidate its control of North Germany.[47] Even after war broke out, major fighting proceeded for weeks before any outside

---

43. Ibid., pp. 167, 179–181, 185; Richard Smoke, "The Crimean War," in George, *Avoiding War*, pp. 36–61 at 48–49, 52. The motives of the powers also illustrate offense-defense dynamics. The main belligerents (Britain, France, Russia, and Turkey) were impelled in part by security concerns that would have been allayed had they believed the defense more dominant. Smoke, *War*, pp. 149, 155, 158–159, 162, 190.

44. The harsh Crimean War settlement Britain imposed on Russia turned it into a non–status quo power. Overthrowing that settlement became Russia's chief aim in European diplomacy, superseding its interest in preserving order to the west. M.S. Anderson, *The Eastern Question, 1774–1923* (London: Macmillan, 1966), pp. 144–146.

45. A.J.P. Taylor, *The Struggle for Mastery in Europe 1848–1918* (London: Oxford University Press, 1971), pp. 108, 110.

46. Ibid., pp. 146–154. Britain would have backed Denmark had it found a continental ally but none was available. Ibid., pp. 146–148.

47. Smoke, *War*, pp. 85–92. Britain remained in a semi-isolationist mood in 1866, and Napoleon III thought France would profit from the long, mutually debilitating Austro-Prussian war he expected. Like the Soviets in 1939, Napoleon underestimated the danger of a quick, lopsided victory by either side. Ibid., pp. 87–90.

state even threatened intervention.[48] As A.J.P. Taylor notes, Bismarck's 1866 diplomatic opportunity—a wide-open field for unopposed expansion—was "unique in recent history."[49]

In 1870 Bismarck ensured the neutrality of the other European powers by shifting responsibility for the war to France and convincing Europe that the war stemmed from French expansionism.[50] As a result, Prussia again had a free hand to pursue its expansionist aims. It used this to smash France, seize Alsace-Lorraine, and consolidate control over South Germany.[51]

1871–90. For some twenty years after the Franco-Prussian War, the defense dominated because of Bismarck's new diplomacy and Britain's renewed activism. In the military area the cult of the offensive had not yet taken hold. In diplomacy Bismarck wove a web of defensive alliances that deterred aggressors and calmed status quo powers after 1879.[52] British power waned slightly, but this was offset by the recovery of Britain's will to play the balancer. The "war-in-sight" crisis of 1875 illustrates the change: Britain and Russia together deterred a renewed German attack on France by warning that they would not allow a repeat of 1870–71.[53]

1890–1919. After 1890 military realities increasingly favored the defense, but elites mistakenly believed the opposite. Diplomatic realities swung toward the offense, and elites believed they favored the offense even more than they did.

---

48. Ibid., p. 86.
49. Taylor, *Struggle for Mastery*, p. 156. Moreover, Bismarck stopped the 1866 war partly because he feared French or Russian intervention if Prussia fought on too long or conquered too much. Smoke, *War*, pp. 101–102. Thus lack of defense-enhancing diplomacy helped cause the war while Prussian fear of such diplomacy shortened and limited the war.
50. William Carr, *The Origins of the Wars of German Unification* (London: Longman, 1991), p. 202; and Michael Howard, *The Franco-Prussian War: The German Invasion of France, 1870–1871* (New York: Granada, 1961), p. 57. Austria also stayed neutral because Hungarian Magyar influence was growing inside the Dual Monarchy, and the Magyars felt that the more Austria was pushed out of Germany, the stronger the position of the Magyars within it would be. R.R. Palmer and Joel Colton, *A History of the Modern World*, 4th ed. (New York: Alfred A. Knopf, 1971), p. 574.
51. On Prussia's free hand, see Smoke, *War*, pp. 133–136; Norman Rich, *The Age of Nationalism and Reform, 1850–1890*, 2d ed. (New York: W.W. Norton, 1977), p. 140; and W.E. Mosse, *European Powers and the German Question* (New York: Octagon, 1969), pp. 291, 295.
52. Bismarck formed defensive alliances with Austria, Italy, and Romania, and a more limited defensive accord with Russia—specifically, a reciprocal agreement not to join a war against the other unless the other attacked France (in the German case) or Austria (in the Russian case). Synopses include Paul M. Kennedy, *The Rise and Fall of the Great Powers: Economic Change and Military Conflict from 1500 to 2000* (New York: Random House, 1987), pp. 249–250; and Robert E. Osgood and Robert W. Tucker, *Force, Order, and Justice* (Baltimore, Md.: Johns Hopkins University Press, 1967), pp. 80–81. For a longer account, see Taylor, *Struggle for Mastery*, pp. 258–280, 316–319.
53. Imanuel Geiss, *German Foreign Policy, 1871–1914* (Boston: Routledge and Kegan Paul, 1976), p. 28.

European militaries were seized by a "cult of the offensive." All the European powers adopted offensive military doctrines, culminating with France's adoption of the highly offensive Plan XVII in 1913 and with Russia's adoption of the highly offensive Plan 20 in 1914. More important, militaries persuaded civilian leaders and publics that the offense dominated and conquest was easy. As a result, elites and publics widely believed the next war would be quickly won by a decisive offensive.

Bismarck's defensive alliances withered or evolved into defensive-and-offensive alliances after he left office in 1890, largely because the cult of the offensive made defensive alliances hard to maintain. Pacts conditioned on defensive conduct became hard to frame because states defended by attacking, and status quo powers shrank from enforcing defensive conduct on allies they felt less able to lose. For example, Britain and France felt unable to enforce defensive conduct on a Russian ally that defended by attacking and that they could not afford to see defeated. Elites also thought that aggressors could overrun their victims before allies could intervene to save them, making defensive alliances less effective. Thus Britain seemed less able to save France before Germany overran it, leading Germany to discount British power. Lastly, German leaders subscribed to a bandwagon theory of diplomacy, which led them to underestimate others' resistance to German expansion. Overall, the years before 1914 were the all-time high point of perceived offense dominance.

Nine of the ten intervening phenomena predicted by offense-defense theory (all except phenomenon G, nonnegotiation) flourished in this world of assumed offense dominance. Opportunistic and defensive expansionist ideas multiplied and spread, especially in Germany. Russia and France mobilized their armies preemptively in the 1914 July crisis. That crisis arose from a fait accompli that Germany and Austria instigated in part to shut a looming window of vulnerability. This window in turn had emerged from a land arms race that erupted during 1912–14. The powers enshrouded their military and political plans in secrecy—a secrecy that fostered crisis-management blunders during July 1914. These blunders in turn evoked rapid, violent reactions that helped drive the crisis out of control. Belief in the offense fueled offensive military doctrines throughout the continent and impeded efforts to restrain allies. Together these dangers formed a prime cause of the war: they bore the 1914 July crisis and helped make it uncontrollable.

1919–45. The interwar years were a mixed bag, but overall the offense gained the upper hand by 1939, and the German elite believed the offense even stronger than in fact it was.

Military doctrine and technology gave the defense the advantage until the late 1930s, when German blitzkrieg doctrine combined armor and infantry in an effective offensive combination. This offensive innovation was unrecognized outside Germany and doubted by many in Germany, but the man who counted most, Adolf Hitler, firmly believed in it. This reflected his faith in the offense as a general principle, imbibed from international social Darwinist propaganda in his youth.[54]

More important, the workings of interwar diplomacy opened a yawning political opportunity for Nazi expansion. Britain fell into a deep isolationism that left it less willing to commit this declining power to curb continental aggressors.[55] The United States also withdrew into isolation, removing the counterweight that checked Germany in 1918.[56] The breakup of Austria-Hungary in that year created a new diplomatic constellation that further eased German expansion. Austria-Hungary would have balanced against German

---

54. Hitler often echoed international social Darwinist slogans on the short, precarious lives of states, for example, "Politics is in truth the execution of a nation's struggle for existence," and "Germany will either be a world power or there will be no Germany." Quoted in P.M.H. Bell, *The Origins of the Second World War in Europe* (London: Longman, 1986), p. 81; and in Anthony P. Adamthwaite, *The Making of the Second World War* (London: George Allen and Unwin, 1977), p. 119.

Hitler's faith in the offense differed from that of the pre-1914 cultists of the offensive in three ways. First, he saw offensive capabilities arising from a long search for offensive methods, not from permanent properties of war. In his mind offense could be created, but also had to be; Germany would discover offensive answers only after a long effort. In contrast, the pre-1914 cultists thought offense inherently easier than defense; deep thought need not be given to how to make it superior, because it already was. Second, Hitler's offensive optimism was based on racism and social prejudice, as well as on assessment of military factors. Specifically, his contempt for Slavs and Jews led him to expect that the Soviets would quickly collapse under German attack. Third, Hitler's concerns for German security focused on fear of conquest by economic strangulation, not conquest by French or Soviet blitzkrieg. He thought German security was precarious, but for reasons rooted more in the political economy of war than in the nature of doctrine or weaponry. These differences aside, the logical implications of Hitler's offensive cult were the same as those of the pre-1914 cult. He exaggerated both German insecurity and the feasibility of imperial solutions to redress it.

55. Prime Minister Neville Chamberlain of Great Britain said in 1937 that he "did not believe we could, or ought . . . to enter a Continental war with the intention of fighting on the same lines as in the last," meaning that Britain would deploy no large ground force on the continent. Bell, *Origins of the Second World War in Europe*, p. 177. Britain had only two divisions available to send to the continent during the 1938 Munich crisis, and the four-division force it actually sent in 1939 was smaller and less well trained than its small expeditionary force of 1914. These four divisions were a drop in the bucket relative to the 84 French and 103 German divisions then deployed. Ibid., p. 175.

56. The United States also proclaimed this isolationism in four neutrality laws passed during 1935–39, giving Hitler a clear if misleading signal of American indifference to his aggression. On these laws a synopsis is Thomas A. Bailey, *A Diplomatic History of the American People*, 9th ed. (Englewood Cliffs, N.J.: Prentice-Hall, 1974), pp. 701–702, 715.

expansion, but its smaller successor states tended to bandwagon.[57] This let Hitler extend German influence into southeast Europe by intimidation and subversion.

The Soviet Union and the Western powers failed to cooperate against Hitler.[58] Ideological hostility divided them. Britain also feared that a defensive alliance against Hitler would arouse German fears of allied encirclement, spurring German aggressiveness. This chilled British enthusiasm for an Anglo-French-Soviet alliance.[59]

Hitler exaggerated the already-large advantage that diplomacy gave the offense because he thought bandwagoning prevailed over balancing in international affairs. This false faith colored all his political forecasts and led him to vastly underestimate others states' resistance to his aggressions. Before the war he failed to foresee that Britain and France would balance German power by coming to Poland's rescue.[60] Once the war began he believed Germany could intimidate Britain into seeking alliance with Germany after Germany crushed France—or, he later held, after Germany smashed the Soviet Union.[61] He thought the United States could be cowed into staying neutral by the 1940 German-Japanese alliance (the alliance had the opposite effect, spurring U.S. intervention).[62] In short, Hitler's false theories of diplomacy made three of his most dangerous opponents shrink to insignificance in his mind.

These realities and beliefs left Hitler to face temptations like those facing Bismarck in 1866 and 1870. Hitler thought he could conquer his victims seriatim. He also thought his conquests would arouse little countervailing opposition from distant neutral powers.[63] As a result, he believed he faced a yawning opportunity for aggression.

---

57. Explaining why weaker states are more prone to bandwagon than are stronger states is Walt, *Origins of Alliances*, pp. 29–30.

58. Bell, *Origins of the Second World War in Europe*, pp. 172, 224, 260; and Adamthwaite, *Making of the Second World War*, pp. 60, 69. This failure greatly eased Hitler's aggressions, because geography made Britain's 1939 guarantees to Poland and Romania unenforceable without a Soviet alliance. Ibid., pp. 86, 91.

59. Raymond J. Sontag, *A Broken World, 1919–1939* (New York: Harper and Row, 1971), p. 361.

60. On August 22, 1939, Hitler assured his generals that "the West will not intervene" to defend Poland. Jeremy Noakes and Geoffrey Pridham, eds., *Nazism, 1919–1945: A History in Documents and Eyewitness Accounts*, 2 vols. (New York: Schocken Books, 1988), vol. 2, p. 741.

61. See Jack Snyder, *Myths of Empire: Domestic Politics and International Ambition* (Ithaca, N.Y.: Cornell University Press, 1991), p. 94.

62. Noakes and Pridham, *Nazism*, vol. 2, p. 797. Some German leaders also hoped that Germany could win decisively in Europe before the United States could bring its power to bear. Thus in September 1940 Hitler's naval commander in chief voiced the hope that Britain could be beaten "before the United States is able to intervene effectively." Ibid., p. 794.

63. The fine-grained pattern of events during 1938–40—who attacked whom and when—also fits the predictions of offense-defense theory (specifically, prime prediction 3). The Western allies stood

Unlike 1914, the late 1930s were not a pure case of perceived offense domi-nance. Instead, the 1930s saw status quo powers' perceptions of defense domi-nance create real offensive opportunities for an aggressor state. Hitler thought the offense strong and even exaggerated its strength, but other powers (the Soviet Union, Britain, and France) underestimated its strength. Their percep-tions of defense dominance relaxed their urge to jump the gun at early signs of threat (as Russia did in 1914); this made things safer. But this perception also relaxed their will to balance Germany, because they found German expan-sion less frightening. This weakened the coalition against Hitler, leaving him wider running room.[64]

1945–1990s. After 1945 two changes swung the offense-defense balance back toward the defense. First, the end of American isolationism transformed Euro-pean political affairs. The United States replaced Britain as continental bal-ancer, bringing far more power to bear in Europe than Britain ever had. As a result, Europe in the years after 1945 was unusually defense dominant from a diplomatic standpoint.

Second, the nuclear revolution gave defenders a large military advantage—so large that conquest among great powers became virtually impossible. Con-quest now required a nuclear first-strike capability (the capacity to launch a nuclear strike that leaves the defender unable to inflict unacceptable damage in retaliation). Defenders could secure themselves merely by maintaining a second-strike capability (the capacity to inflict unacceptable damage on the attacker's society after absorbing an all-out strike). The characteristics of nu-clear weapons—their vast power, small size, light weight, and low cost—ensured that a first-strike capability would be very hard to attain, while a second-strike capability could be sustained at little cost. As a result, the great powers became essentially unconquerable, and even lesser powers could now stand against far stronger enemies. Overall, the nuclear revolution gave de-fenders an even more lopsided advantage than the machine gun–barbed wire–entrenchments–railroad complex that emerged before 1914.

---

without attacking Germany in 1938 and again in 1939–40 because they doubted they could win a decisive victory. Germany stood without attacking westward in the fall of 1939 for the same reason, and finally attacked in May 1940 after German military leaders developed a plausible plan for decisive attack. Mearsheimer, *Conventional Deterrence*, pp. 67–133.

64. Would the risk of war have fallen had all powers believed the offense was dominant in the late 1930s? This seems unlikely. The status quo powers would have balanced harder against Hitler, offering him more discouragement, but they also would have been jumpier, making early crises more dangerous. One of these crises—Hitler's remilitarization of the Rhineland, the Spanish civil war, or the German seizure of Austria or Czechoslovakia—probably would have served as the "Sarajevo" for World War II, with the Allies moving first as Russia did in 1914.

American and Soviet policymakers grasped this cosmic military revolution only slowly, however. At first many feared nuclear weapons would be a boon to aggressors. When this fear proved false, the vast advantage they gave defenders was only dimly recognized, partly because scholars strangely failed to explain it. Thus the nuclear revolution changed realities far more than they did perceptions. As a result, state behavior changed only slowly, and both superpowers competed far harder—in both Central Europe and the third world—than objective conditions warranted. The Cold War was far more peaceful than the preceding forty years, but could have been still more peaceful had Soviet and U.S. elites understood that their security problems had vastly diminished and were now quite small.

In sum, the events of 1789–1990s clearly corroborate offense-defense theory predictions—specifically, prime predictions 1 and 2, as well as both explanatory predictions. These conclusions rest on rather sketchy data—especially regarding the explanatory predictions—but that data confirm offense-defense theory so clearly that other data would have to be very different to reverse the result.

- The incidence of war correlates loosely with the offense-defense balance and very tightly with perceptions of the offense-defense balance (for a summary see Table 1).
- Europe's less-secure and more offensively capable continental powers were perennial troublemakers, while more secure and less offensively capable offshore powers were perennial defenders of the status quo. Prussia/Germany was cursed with the least defensible borders and faced the most offensive temptations. It started the largest number of major wars (1864, 1866, 1914, 1939, and shared responsibility for 1870 with France). France and Russia, with more defensible borders and fewer temptations, started fewer major wars.[65] Britain and the United States, blessed with even more insulating borders, joined a number of European wars but started none.[66] Spain, Sweden, and Switzerland, also insulated from other powers by mountains or oceans, fought very little.

Thus the timing of war and the identities of the belligerents tightly fit prime predictions 1 and 2.

---

65. France can be assigned prime responsibility for 1792 and 1859, and shared responsibility for Crimea and 1870. Russia deserves prime responsibility for the Cold War and shared responsibility for Crimea and the 1904–05 Russo-Japanese War.
66. Britain does share responsibility for the Crimean War with Russia, France, and Turkey.

- Sketchy evidence suggests that opportunistic and defensive expansionism were more prominent during the periods of perceived offense dominance (1792–1815, 1859–71, 1890–1914, 1930s–1945) than at other times. The years 1792–1815 saw a strong surge of French expansionism, nearly matched at the outset by parallel Prussian expansionism.[67] The mid-nineteenth century saw large opportunistic expansionism in Prussia and some French expansionism. The years 1890–1914 saw vast expansionist ambitions develop in Wilhelmine Germany,[68] matched by fierce resistance to this German expansionism in Russia and France, and by lesser French and Russian expansionism. Large German expansionism then reappeared under the Nazis in the 1930s. During other periods European expansionism was more muted: European powers had smaller ambitions and acted on them less often. This supports explanatory prediction 1.
- Opportunistic and defensive expansionism were prominent among those states that saw the clearest defensive vulnerability and offensive opportunity (especially Prussia/Germany, also revolutionary France), while being more muted among states with more secure borders and fewer offensive opportunities (Britain, the United States, the Scandinavian states, and Spain). This corroborates explanatory prediction 2.

How strong is this test? The strength of a passed test depends on the uniqueness of the predictions tested. Do other theories predict the outcome observed, or is the prediction unique to the tested theory? The predictions tested here seem quite unique. There is no obvious competing explanation for the periodic upsurges and downsurges in European expansionism and warfare outlined above. Offense-defense theory has the field to itself. Particular domestic explanations have been offered to explain the aggressiveness of specific states—for example, some argue that Wilhelmine Germany was aggressive because it was a late industrializer, that revolutionary France was aggressive because its regime came to power through mass revolution, and so forth[69]—but no competing theory claims to explain the general cross-time and cross-state pattern of war involvement that we observe. Hence this test seems strong.

What importance does this evidence assign to offense-defense theory? That is, how potent is offense dominance as a cause of war? In Europe since 1789, the nature of international relations has gyrated sharply with shifts in the

---

67. On Prussia's expansionism, see Blanning, *Origins of the French Revolutionary Wars*, pp. 72–82; on French expansionism, see ibid., passim.
68. A summary of Wilhelmine German aims and policies is Geiss, *German Foreign Policy*.
69. On Germany as late industrializer, see Snyder, *Myths of Empire*, pp. 66–111; and on France as a revolutionary state, see Walt, *Revolution and War*, pp. 46–128.

perceived offense-defense balance. War is far more common when elites believe that the offense dominates, and states are far more belligerent when they perceive large defensive vulnerabilities and offensive opportunities for themselves. This indicates that perceptions of the offense-defense balance have a large impact on international relations. Offense-defense theory is important as well as valid.

How much history does this evidence suggest that offense-defense theory can explain? Explanatory power is partly a function of the prevalence of the theory's cause: abundant causes explain more history than scarce causes. In Europe since 1789 the offense has seldom been really strong, but it was believed strong quite often—often enough to cause considerable trouble.

TEST 2: ANCIENT CHINA
The ancient Chinese multistate system witnessed a long-term shift from defense dominance to offense dominance across the years 722–221 BCE.[70] Offense-defense theory predicts that warfare should have increased as this transformation unfolded (see prime prediction 1). This prediction is fulfilled: diplomacy grew markedly more savage and international relations grew markedly more violent as the power of the offense increased.

Before roughly 550 BCE the defense held the upper hand among China's many feudal states. Four related changes then strengthened the offense: feudalism declined,[71] mass infantry replaced chariots as the critical military force, conscription was introduced, and armies grew tremendously in size.[72] The two largest Chinese states deployed enormous armies of more than a million men, and some smaller states had armies numbering in the hundreds of thousands.[73] As armies grew, border forts had less stopping power against infantry because invaders could sweep past, leaving a smaller portion of their force behind to besiege the forts. Forts also lost stopping power as improved siege-engines appeared—battering rams, catapults, and rolling towers—that further eased the conquest of fortified positions.[74] The decline of feudalism eased offensive operations by reducing social stratification, which increased troop loyalty to

70. Concurring is Andreski, *Military Organization and Society*, p. 76.
71. Noting the decline of feudalism are Samuel B. Griffiths, "Introduction," in Sun Tzu, *The Art of War* (London: Oxford University Press, 1971), p. 33; and Dun J. Li, *The Ageless Chinese: A History*, 3d ed. (New York: Charles Scribner's Sons, 1978), p. 64.
72. On the growth of armies, the introduction of conscription, and the rise of infantry, see Li, *Ageless Chinese*, p. 56; Griffiths, "Introduction," pp. 28, 33; and Wolfram Eberhard, *A History of China* (Berkeley: University of California Press, 1977), p. 49.
73. Li, *Ageless Chinese*, p. 56.
74. Andreski, *Military Organization and Society*, p. 76.

regimes; this meant troops could be trusted to conduct long-distance offensive operations without deserting.

The outcomes of battles and wars reveal the shift toward the offense that these technical and social changes produced. The number of independent Chinese states declined from two hundred in the eighth century BCE to seven in the late fifth century, to one in the late third century—a clear measure of the growing power of the offense.[75] Before 550 BCE defenders were often victorious. Thus the states of Tsin and Ch'i fought three great battles, in 632, 598, and 567 BCE, each won by the defender. Dun J. Li concludes, "If the three battles indicate anything, they meant that neither side was able to challenge successfully the other's leadership in its own sphere of influence."[76] In contrast, the state of Ch'in conquered all of China in a rapid campaign lasting only nine years at the end of the Warring States period (230–221 BCE).[77]

This increase in the power of the offense coincides with a stark deterioration in international relations. During the Spring and Autumn period (722–453 BCE) interstate relations were fairly peaceful, and wars were limited by a code of conduct. The code confined warfare to certain seasons of the year and forbade killing enemy wounded. It was considered wrong to stoop to deceit, to take unfair advantage of adversaries, to "ambush armies," or to "massacre cities."[78] The subsequent Warring States period (453–221 BCE) was perhaps the bloodiest era in Chinese history. Warfare raged almost constantly,[79] becoming a "fundamental occupation" of states.[80] Restraints on warfare were abandoned. Casualties ran into hundreds of thousands, and prisoners of war were massacred en masse.[81] Diplomatic conduct deteriorated; one historian writes that "diplomacy was based on bribery, fraud, and deceit."[82]

In short, the shift toward offense dominance in China during 722–221 BCE correlates tightly with a dramatic breakdown of China's international order.

TEST 3: UNITED STATES 1789–1990S

Since 1815 the United States has been by far the most secure of the world's great powers, blessed with two vast ocean moats, no nearby great powers, and

---

75. Li, *Ageless Chinese*, pp. 50, 59.
76. Ibid., p. 52.
77. Ibid., p. 59.
78. Griffiths, "Introduction," p. 30.
79. Ibid., p. 21.
80. Ibid., p. 24, quoting Shang Yang, Prime Minister of Ch'in, who conceived war and agriculture to be the two fundamental occupations.
81. Li, *Ageless Chinese*, pp. 56, 58–59.
82. Griffiths, "Introduction," p. 24.

(after 1890) the world's largest economy. In the nineteenth century the United States also had substantial offensive opportunities, embodied in chances for continental and then Pacific expansion against weak defenders. However, America's security endowments were quite extraordinary, while its offensive opportunities were more ordinary. Offense-defense theory predicts that such a state will exhibit perhaps average offensive opportunism but markedly less defensive belligerence than other states. Hence, on net, it will start fewer wars and be involved in fewer wars than others (see prime prediction 2).

This forecast is confirmed, although not dramatically, by the pattern of past U.S. foreign policy. The United States has fought other great powers only three times in its two hundred–year history—in 1812, 1917, and 1941—a low count for a great power.[83] The 1812 war stemmed mainly from U.S. belligerence, but the wars of 1917 and 1941 resulted mainly from others' belligerence. The United States did start some of its lesser wars (1846 and 1898), but it joined other wars more reactively (Korea and Vietnam).

Offense-defense theory also predicts that while the United States will pursue some opportunistic expansionism (intervening phenomenon A), it will embrace few policies that embody offense-defense theory's other intervening phenomena (B–J) (explanatory prediction 2). Where the record allows judgments, this forecast is borne out. Regarding expansionism, the United States has confined itself largely to opportunistic imperialism against frail opponents. Defensive expansionism has been muted, and overall, expansionist ideas have held less sway in the United States than in other powers. This is reflected in the relatively small size of the U.S. empire. The modern American empire has been limited to a few formal colonies seized from Spain in the 1890s and an informal empire in the Caribbean/Central American area, with only intermittent control exerted more widely—a zone far smaller than the vast empires of the European powers.

The U.S. impulse to engage in preemptive and preventive war has been small. In sharp contrast to Germany and Japan, the United States has launched a stealthy first strike on another major power just once (in 1812) and has jumped through only one window of opportunity (in 1812). Surprise first strikes and window-jumping were considered on other occasions (e.g., preventive war was discussed during 1949–54, and surprise attack on Cuba was considered during the Cuban missile crisis), but seldom seriously.

---

83. Britain, France, Russia, and Prussia/Germany fought other great powers an average of five times over the same two hundred years, by my count. None fought as few as three times.

American diplomacy has been strikingly free of fait accompli tactics. American foreign and security policy has generally been less secretive than those of the European continental powers, especially during the late Cold War, when the United States published military data that most powers would highly classify as state secrets. The U.S. arms raced with the Soviet Union energetically during the Cold War, but earlier maintained very small standing military forces—far smaller than those of other great powers. Overall, intervening phenomena B–J of offense-defense theory are strikingly absent in the U.S. case.

In sum, the United States has not been a shrinking violet, but it has been less bellicose than the average great power. Compare, for example, U.S. conduct with the far greater imperial aggressions of Athens, Rome, Carthage, Spain, Prussia/Germany, Japan, Russia, and France.

Offense-defense theory further predicts that levels of American bellicosity should vary inversely with shifts over time in America's sense of security and directly with the scope of perceived external threats (see prime prediction 3)—as in fact they have.

During 1789–1815 the United States saw large foreign threats on its borders and large opportunities to dispel them with force. It responded with a bellicose foreign policy that produced the 1812 war with Britain.

During 1815–1914 the United States was protected from the threat of a Eurasian continental hegemon by Britain's active continental balancing, and protected from extracontinental European expansion into the Western hemisphere by the British fleet, which was the de facto enforcer of the Monroe Doctrine. The United States responded by withdrawing from European affairs and maintaining very small standing military forces, although it did pursue continental expansion before 1898 and limited overseas imperial expansion after 1898.

During 1914–91 Britain could no longer maintain the European balance. This deprived the United States of its shield against continental European aggressors. Then followed the great era of American activism—fitful at first (1917–47), then steady and persistent (1947–91). This era ended when the Soviet threat suddenly vanished during 1989–91. After 1991 the United States maintained its security alliances, but reduced its troops stationed overseas and sharply reduced its defense effort.

WHAT THESE TESTS INDICATE
Offense-defense theory passed the tests these three cases pose. Are these tests positive proof for the theory or mere straws in the wind?

We learn more from strong tests than from weak ones. The strength of a passed test is a function of the uniqueness of the predictions that the test corroborated. The more numerous and plausible are contending explanations for the patterns that the test theory predicted and the test revealed, the weaker the test.

The three case study tests reported here range from fairly weak to quite strong. They each lack Herculean power but in combination they pose a strong test. The test posed by the ancient China case is weak because our knowledge of ancient Chinese society and politics is fairly thin. This leaves us unable to rule out competing explanations for the rise of warfare in the Warring States period that point to causes other than the rise of offense. The test posed by the U.S. case is a little stronger but still rather weak overall. Alternative explanations for the rise and fall of American global activism are hard to come up with, leaving the offense-defense theory's explanation without strong competitors, so this element of the test posed by the U.S. case is fairly strong. Plausible contending explanations for other aspects of the U.S. case can be found, however. For example, some would argue that America's more pacific conduct is better explained by its democratic domestic structure than by its surfeit of security. Others would contend that the United States has fewer-than-average conflicts of interest with other powers because it shares no borders with them, and it fights fewer wars for this reason. Hence this element of the test posed by the U.S. case is weak: U.S. lower-than-average bellicosity is only a straw in the wind.

As noted above, the case of Europe since 1789 offers a fairly strong test. Some competing explanations for Germany's greater bellicosity are offered—as noted above, the lateness of German industrialization is sometimes suggested as an alternative cause, as is German culture. However, there is no obvious plausible competing explanation for the main pattern we observe in the case—the rise of warfare during 1792–1815, 1856–71, and 1914–45, and the greater periods of peace in between. The fit of this pattern with prime prediction 1 of offense-defense theory lends it strong corroboration.

WHAT PRESCRIPTIONS FOLLOW?
If offense dominance is dangerous, policies that control it should be pursued. Governments should adopt defensive military force postures and seek arms control agreements to limit offensive forces. Governments should also maintain defensive alliances. American security guarantees in Europe and Asia have made conquest much harder since 1949 and have played a major role in

preserving peace. A U.S. withdrawal from either region would raise the risk of conflict.

Conclusion: Offense-Defense Theory in Perspective

Offense-defense theory has the attributes of a good theory. First, it has three elements that give a theory claim to large explanatory power. (1) Large importance, that is, its posited cause has large effects. Variance in the perceived offense-defense balance causes large variance in the incidence of warfare. Variance in the actual offense-defense balance has less impact because policymakers often misperceive it, but it has a potent effect when policymakers perceive it accurately. (2) Wide explanatory range. The theory explains results across many domains of behavior—in military policy, foreign policy, and crisis diplomacy.[84] It governs many intervening phenomena (e.g., expansionism, first-move advantage, windows, secrecy, negotiation failures, crisis management blunders, arms races, tight alliances) that have been seen as important war causes in their own right. Thus offense-defense theory achieves simplicity, binding a number of war causes under a single rubric. Many causes are reduced to one cause with many effects. (3) Wide real-world applicability. Real offense dominance is rare in modern times, but the perception of offense dominance is fairly widespread. Therefore, if perceived offense dominance causes war it causes lots of war, and offense-defense theory explains much of international history.

Second, offense-defense theory has large prescriptive utility, because the offense-defense balance is affected by national foreign and military policy; hence it is subject to political will. Perceptions of the offense-defense balance are even more malleable, being subject to correction through argument. Both are far more manipulable than the polarity of the international system, the strength of international institutions, the state of human nature, or other war causes that have drawn close attention.

Third, offense-defense theory is quite satisfying, although it leaves important questions unanswered. In uncovering the roots of its ten intervening phenom-

---

84. Moreover, offense-defense theory might be usefully adapted for application beyond the domain of war, for example, to explain international economic competition (or cooperation), or even intra-academic competition. Suggesting its application to economics is Jitsuo Tsuchiyama, who writes of the "prosperity dilemma"—a cousin of the security dilemma in which measures taken by one state to increase its economic well-being decrease another's economic well-being. See Jitsuo Tsuchiyama, "The U.S.-Japan Alliance after the Cold War: End of the Alliance?" unpublished manuscript, Olin Institute, Harvard University, 1994, p. 27.

ena, offense-defense theory offers a more satisfying (and simpler) explanation than do interpretations pointing directly to these phenomena. However, it also raises another mystery: Why is the strength of the offense so often exaggerated?

History suggests that offense dominance is at the same time dangerous, quite rare, and widely overstated. It further suggests that this exaggeration of insecurity, and the bellicose conduct it fosters, are prime causes of national insecurity and war. States are seldom as insecure as they think they are. Moreover, if they are insecure, this insecurity often grows from their own efforts to escape imagined insecurity.

The rarity of real insecurity is suggested by the low death rate of modern great powers. In ancient times great powers often disappeared, but in modern times (since 1789) no great powers have permanently lost sovereignty, and only twice (France in 1870–71 and in 1940) has any been even temporarily overrun by an unprovoked aggressor.[85] Both times France soon regained its sovereignty through the intervention of outside powers—illustrating the powerful defensive influence of great-power balancing behavior.

The prevalence of exaggerations of insecurity is revealed by the great wartime endurance of many states that enter wars for security reasons, and by the aftermath of the world's great security wars, which often reveal that the belligerents' security fears were illusory. Athens fought Sparta largely for security reasons, but held out for a full nine years (413–404 BCE) after suffering the crushing loss of its Sicilian expedition—an achievement that shows the falsehood of its original fears. Austria-Hungary held out for a full four years under allied battering during 1914–18, a display of toughness at odds with its own prewar self-image of imminent collapse. With twenty-twenty hindsight we can now see that modern Germany would have been secure had it only behaved itself. Wilhelmine Germany was Europe's dominant state, with Europe's largest and fastest-growing economy. It faced no plausible threats to its sovereignty except those it created by its own belligerence. Later, interwar Germany and Japan could have secured themselves simply by moderating their conduct. This would have assured them of allies, hence of the raw materials supplies they sought to seize by force. America's aggressive and often costly Cold War interventions in the third world now seem hypervigilant in light of the defensive benefits of the nuclear revolution, America's geographic

---

85. France helped trigger the 1870 war; hence one could argue for removing France in 1870 from the list of unprovoking victims of conquest, leaving only France in 1940.

invulnerability, and the strength of third world nationalism, which precluded the Soviet third world imperialism that U.S. interventions sought to prevent.

Paradoxically, a chief source of insecurity in Europe since medieval times has been this false belief that security was scarce. This belief was a self-fulfilling prophecy, fostering bellicose policies that left all states less secure. Modern great powers have been overrun by unprovoked aggressors only twice, but they have been overrun by provoked aggressors six times—usually by aggressors provoked by the victim's fantasy-driven defensive bellicosity. Wilhelmine and Nazi Germany, Imperial Japan, Napoleonic France, and Austria-Hungary were all destroyed by dangers that they created by their efforts to escape from exaggerated or imaginary threats to their safety.[86]

If so, the prime threat to the security of modern great powers is . . . themselves. Their greatest menace lies in their own tendency to exaggerate the dangers they face, and to respond with counterproductive belligerence. The causes of this syndrome pose a large question for students of international relations.

---

86. Mussolini also provoked his own destruction, but his belligerence was not security driven.

Realists as Optimists | *Charles L. Glaser*

Cooperation as Self-Help

Structural realists are pessimistic about the prospects for international cooperation; they believe that competition between the major powers in the international system is the normal state of affairs. The structural-realist argument is driven by the implications of international anarchy, that is, the lack of an international authority capable of enforcing agreements. Responding to the pressures of anarchy, during peacetime countries will be inclined to deal with adversaries by arms racing and gaining allies, rather than by cooperating via arms control or other approaches for realizing common interests. Anarchy discourages cooperation because it requires states to worry about the relative gains of cooperation and the possibility that adversaries will cheat on agreements. In short, the standard structural-realist argument predicts that cooperation between adversaries, while not impossible, will be difficult to achieve and, as a result, will be rare and contribute relatively little to states' well-being.[1]

This characterization of structural realism is offered by both its proponents and its detractors. Kenneth Waltz argues that self-help systems "make the cooperation of parties difficult. . . . Rules, institutions, and patterns of cooperation . . . are all limited in extent and modified from what they might otherwise be." Summarizing the views of realists, Joseph Grieco says, "realism presents a fundamentally pessimistic analysis of the prospects for international coop-

Charles L. Glaser is Associate Professor and Acting Dean of the Irving B. Harris Graduate School of Public Policy Studies at the University of Chicago.

For helpful comments on earlier drafts, I would like to thank Matt Evangelista, Jim Fearon, Lloyd Gruber, Ted Hopf, Chaim Kaufmann, Barbara Koremenos, Andy Kydd, John Mearsheimer, Jonathan Mercer, Robert Powell, Duncan Snidal, Ivan Toft, Brad Thayer, Steve Walt, and Ken Yao, and participants in seminars at the University of Chicago's Program on International Politics, Economics and Security and at Stanford's Center for International Security and Arms Control.

1. Structural realists are sometimes referred to as neorealists. Kenneth N. Waltz, *Theory of International Politics* (New York: Random House, 1979) remains the most important statement of these arguments. Some authors want to reserve "neorealism" to refer to the theory as articulated by Waltz, while using structural realism to refer to a broader family of systemic theories; see Barry Buzan, Charles Jones and Richard Little, *The Logic of Anarchy: Neorealism to Structural Realism* (New York: Columbia University Press, 1993). In this essay, I use "structural realist" as an ideal type—an analyst who believes that only international or systemic-level factors influence international politics. I recognize, however, that virtually all structural realists actually believe that other levels of analysis have some influence.

International Security, Winter 1994/95 (Vol. 19, No. 3), pp. 50–90
© 1995 by the President and Fellows of Harvard College and the Massachusetts Institute of Technology.

eration." Critics essentially agree. Robert Keohane concludes that, "realism sometimes seems to imply, pessimistically, that order can be created *only* by hegemony. If the latter conclusion were correct . . . at some time in the foreseeable future, global nuclear war would ensue. . . . No serious thinker could, therefore, be satisfied with Realism." Steve Weber declares that structural realism claims that any cooperation that emerges under anarchy will "be tenuous, unstable, and limited to issues of peripheral importance."[2]

I argue that this pessimism is unwarranted. Contrary to the conventional wisdom, the strong general propensity for adversaries to compete is not an inevitable logical consequence of structural realism's basic assumptions. Structural realism properly understood predicts that, under a wide range of conditions, adversaries can best achieve their security goals through cooperative policies, not competitive ones, and should, therefore, choose cooperation when these conditions prevail.

This article focuses on states' military-policy options during peacetime. In this context, "cooperation" refers to coordinated policies designed to avoid arms races,[3] while competition refers to unilateral military buildups, which are likely to generate arms races, and to alliance formation.[4]

The implications of my reevaluation are not limited to peacetime policies, however. Adversaries find peacetime cooperation desirable because it enables

---

2. Kenneth N. Waltz, "Reflections on *Theory of International Politics:* A Response to My Critics," in Robert O. Keohane, ed., *Neorealism and Its Critics* (New York: Columbia University Press, 1986), p. 336; Joseph M. Grieco, *Cooperation Among Nations: Europe, America and Non-tariff Barriers to Trade* (Ithaca, N.Y.: Cornell University Press, 1990), p. 27; Robert O. Keohane, "Theory of World Politics: Structural Realism and Beyond," in Ada W. Finiter, ed., *Political Science: The State of the Discipline* (Washington, D.C.: American Political Science Association, 1983), p. 532, reprinted in Keohane, *Neorealism and its Critics;* and Steve Weber, "Realism, Detente, and Nuclear Weapons," *International Organization,* Vol. 44, No. 1 (Winter 1990), pp. 58–59. Weber claims further that realism "cannot comfortably encompass the more constraining provisions of SALT," the Strategic Arms Limitation Treaty.

3. In other contexts, cooperation can refer to decisions to make concessions during a crisis and to decisions to forgo launching a war. Cooperation—including both formal and informal reciprocated restraint—is not the only alternative to competitive policies. Uncoordinated but unthreatening, and therefore uncompetitive, policies can sometimes be a second key alternative. For example, if defensive forces have an advantage over offensive forces, then countries could choose defense, independent of others' choices.

4. I consider alliance formation to be a type of competition because, although the allies are cooperating with each other, they are competing with a common adversary. Since balancing in the form of alliance formation is probably the most prominent and widely accepted prediction of structural realism, the standard pessimism about cooperation presumably does not count alliances as cooperation. The key questions about cooperation therefore focus on cooperation between adversaries. However, because today's ally could be an adversary in the future, the line between allies and adversaries is not always sharp, and under certain conditions concern about relative gains could inhibit cooperation between allies.

them to moderate causes of war that already exist or to avoid competition that would intensify causes of war. Consequently, beyond being more optimistic about the prospects for peacetime cooperation, my alternative structural-realist analysis, which I label *contingent realism*, is also more optimistic about the likelihood of avoiding war than is the standard structural-realist analysis.

My argument draws on various strands of international relations theory, including arguments about the security dilemma, costly signaling, relative-gains constraints, arms control, and cooperation under anarchy. I develop a number of specific arguments that are required to apply these strands of theory to the security realm and to integrate them fully into a structural-realist argument. However, the overall argument is bigger than the sum of the individual strands: it offers a direct and thorough challenge to the standard structural-realist explanation of the prevalence of international competition.

Recent critics of structural realism have come to be viewed as advancing a competing theory, instead of correcting flaws within structural realism.[5] In part, this is because the critics have emphasized factors such as institutions and regimes that structural realists believe have little explanatory power, and have underplayed factors that structural realists believe are critical, such as the relative gains of cooperation. This article focuses more closely on the elements that structural realists identify as most important. Therefore, my argument should be understood as identifying basic corrections that follow deductively from structural realism's core assumptions, not as another theory being counterposed against structural realism.

Contingent realism challenges neo-institutionalists, who see institutions as the key to cooperation, by explaining international cooperation without focusing on institutions. Moreover, to the extent that institutions facilitate cooperation, contingent realism explains why they are necessary and how they help.

The first section of this article summarizes the "standard" structural realist explanation for competition. The next section presents the three arguments that together constitute contingent realism. The first argument shows that the stan-

---

5. One challenge comes from cooperation theory, which employs game theory to study the implications of potential cheating. Robert Axelrod, *The Evolution of Cooperation* (New York: Basic Books, 1984), provides the foundation for much of this work. Key works include Robert O. Keohane, *After Hegemony: Cooperation and Discord in the World Political Economy* (Princeton, N.J.: Princeton University Press, 1984); and Kenneth A. Oye, ed., *Cooperation Under Anarchy* (Princeton, N.J.: Princeton University Press, 1986). Cooperation theory has been criticized for overlooking constraints imposed by concern over relative gains; see Grieco, *Cooperation Among Nations*. David A. Baldwin, ed., *Neorealism and Neoliberalism: The Contemporary Debate* (New York: Columbia University Press, 1993), includes many of the key articles in this debate. Robert Powell, "Anarchy in International Relations Theory: The Neorealist-Neoliberal Debate," *International Organization*, Vol. 48, No. 2 (Spring 1994), pp. 313–44, explores many of the key issues.

dard explanation is biased, because it emphasizes the benefits of competition while overlooking its risks, and it implies that "self-help" necessitates competition; in fact, cooperative policies are an important type of self-help. The second corrects problems with how the standard formulation deals with states' military capabilities, specifically their ability to perform military missions. In assessing their security, states should focus on their ability to perform military missions. However, the standard structural-realist argument is cast in terms of power.[6] Power influences mission capability, but is only the beginning of the story. Contingent realism corrects this mis-specification by integrating offense-defense variables into structural-realist theory. This integration shows that, as the security-dilemma literature argues, cooperation can be a country's best option, and identifies the conditions under which states should prefer arms control or unilateral defensive policies to arms racing.

The third argument shows that basic structural-realist assumptions leave open the possibility that a country can use its military policy to communicate information that should lead its adversaries to reassess its motives and intentions. Thus, contrary to the standard argument, countries should not focus solely on capabilities, but also on motives. Consequently, countries should sometimes exercise self-restraint and pursue cooperative military policies, because these policies can convince a rational opponent to revise favorably its view of the country's motives. I explore the conditions under which these considerations favor cooperation.

The third section of this article addresses the three major arguments that structural realists use to support their standard prediction of competition, and that could be used to counter the conclusions that flow from my reformulation. These potential counter-arguments are: 1) states try to maximize relative power, which creates a zero-sum situation that usually precludes cooperation; 2) states' concerns over relative gains make security cooperation especially difficult; and 3) states adopt competitive policies because the possibility of cheating makes cooperation too risky. I explain how each of these arguments is seriously flawed, holding only under certain conditions, and not under others.

---

6. To avoid confusion, it is important to distinguish the role that power plays in two major strands of realism. Classical realists hold that power is an end in itself; in contrast, structural realists hold that security is an end, and according to the standard argument, states measure their ability to achieve this end in terms of power. My discussion accepts the structural-realist assumption that security is the end, and explores problems that arise from focusing on power as the means to this end. Hans J. Morgenthau is often credited with presenting the fullest statement of classical realism; see his *Politics Among Nations*, 5th ed. (New York: Knopf, 1973). Robert O. Keohane, "Realism, Neorealism and the Study of World Politics," pp. 7–16, in Keohane, ed., *Neorealism and Its Critics*, compares classical and structural realism.

The final section briefly considers implications for theoretical and policy debates. Contingent realism emphasizes that offense-defense variables and the security dilemma are central to the logic of structural realism, not a separate body of theory. Integrating these variables yields a set of conditional structural-realist predictions about when states should compete and when they should cooperate. Because structural realism is a parsimonious theory of rational behavior, these predictions establish an important baseline against which to compare theories that are less parsimonious or that deal with sub-optimal behavior. The thrust of my argument is not that contingent realism necessarily explains states' behavior correctly, but rather that such a baseline is essential for assessing the explanatory power of structural realism relative to theories built on other assumptions and at other levels of analysis.

Contingent realism makes clear that the standard structural-realist claim about the strong tendency for states to pursue competitive military policies is at best incomplete. Because contingent realism makes conditional predictions about cooperation and competition, a structural-realist case against cooperation must demonstrate that the conditions necessary for cooperation have not occurred; structural-realists have not provided this type of evidence. Furthermore, contingent realism contradicts the conventional wisdom that while structural realism does a good job of explaining the Cold War, it is severely challenged by the end of the Cold War, which runs counter to the theory's supposed predictions of competitiveness. Contingent realism suggests that structural realism, correctly understood, can explain the end of the Cold War relatively easily, but has greater difficulty explaining the latter half of the Cold War. The need for additional theories is clearest when trying to explain this competitive period. In terms of the future, contingent realism provides more optimistic predictions than those now often associated with structural realism.

Review of the "Standard" Structural-realist Argument

Structural realism is built on a small number of basic assumptions: that states can be viewed as essentially rational unitary actors; that states give priority to insuring their security; and that states confront an international environment that is characterized most importantly by anarchy.[7] Structural realism is a

---

7. This formulation is consistent with Waltz, *Theory of International Politics.* For Waltz's view on rationality, see "Reflections on *Theory of International Politics*," pp. 330–331. Waltz does make other assumptions and basic arguments that significantly influence his conclusions, including claims that power is fungible. For discussion and criticism of his formulation see Buzan, Jones, and Little, *The Logic of Anarchy.* For useful discussions of the assumptions of realism, see Keohane, "Theory of

third-image theory: the constraints and opportunities created by the international system are used to explain states' behavior; and states view each other as "black boxes"—they focus on other states' observable behavior, not their type of government, the quality of their decision-making, or particular features of their leaders.[8]

Structural realism does not preclude the possibility that states have important motives in addition to security. States must worry that others have non-security ("greedy") motives that call for expansionist policies,[9] but structural realism does not assume the presence of greedy states in the system.[10] Central to the structural realist argument is the conclusion that security competition and war are possible even when there are no greedy states in the system, since states might seek to increase their security through expansion.

THE STANDARD ARGUMENT

Working from these basic assumptions,[11] structural realists argue that states live in a "self-help" world that results from international anarchy: without an

---

World Politics," pp. 163–169, and Robert G. Gilpin, "The Richness of the Tradition of Political Realism," pp. 304–305, both in Keohane, *Neorealism and Its Critics.* Another common assumption is that states are the major actors in the international system. I do not include this as an assumption, preferring to leave open to analysis the question of whether states would create or allow other actors that would replace them as the major actors.

8. On the third image, see Kenneth N. Waltz, *Man, the State and War* (New York: Columbia University Press, 1959), esp. chaps. 6 and 7. Other useful discussions of levels of analysis include J. David Singer, "The Level-of-Analysis Problem in International Relations," in James N. Rosenau, ed., *International Politics and Foreign Policy* (New York: The Free Press, 1969), pp. 20–29; and Robert Jervis, *Perception and Misperception in International Politics* (Princeton, N.J.: Princeton University Press, 1976), chap. 1.

9. Because expansion can be motivated by greed as well as insecurity, I do not use the terms "expansionist" and "aggressive" to define types of states. For similar reasons, I do not use the term "status quo" to define states that are motived only by insecurity; pure security seekers may be unwilling to accept the status quo. For more on these points, see Charles L. Glaser, "Political Consequences of Military Strategy: Expanding and Refining the Spiral and Deterrence Models," *World Politics,* Vol. 44, No. 4 (July 1992), pp. 497–538.

10. Although the standard structural-realist explanation says little about the probability and severity of greedy states in the system, these variables and states' beliefs about them would influence their choices between cooperation and competition; see Glaser, "Political Consequences of Military Strategy," and the discussion below. Therefore, a more complete theory would incorporate variations in greed and generate a family of predictions, while holding other variables constant. In this spirit, see Randall L. Schweller, "Bandwagoning for Profit: Bringing the Revisionist State Back In," *International Security,* Vol. 19, No. 1 (Summer 1994), pp. 72–107.

11. The following description of the standard argument does not include some important nuances and it blurs some differences between authors that I have lumped together as contributors to the standard structural-realist analysis. Nevertheless, I believe that it captures the basic thrust of the standard argument. For a good summary of the realist literature, see Arthur A. Stein, *Why Nations Cooperate: Circumstances and Choice in International Relations* (Ithaca, N.Y.: Cornell University Press, 1990), pp. 4–13.

international authority capable of protecting them, major powers must look out for themselves.[12] The standard interpretation equates self-help with states' pursuit of unilateral, competitive policies.[13] This inclination toward competition is reinforced by doubts about the adversary's motives and intentions. Intentions are unknowable, and even if known, could be different tomorrow. This uncertainty works against cooperation.[14] States must not overlook the possibility that potential adversaries will use their full capabilities against them, and they therefore must focus on adversaries' capabilities instead of their intentions. Thus, at a minimum, cooperation is difficult because states are sensitive to how it affects their current and future relative capabilities;[15] moreover, cooperation is often impossible because states find military advantages to be especially valuable and thus compete to acquire them.[16] Making matters still worse, falling behind in this competition can carry extremely high costs: it invites war and, in the worst case, a major power can lose its sovereignty.[17] Consequently, competition tends to be intense and cooperation is rare because the risks of being cheated are large.

In short, according to the standard structural-realist explanation, states prefer competitive policies for multiple, reinforcing reasons. Arms races occur because

12. On the nature and implications of self-help, see Waltz, *Theory of International Politics*, pp. 105–107, 111–112. The necessity of self-help also depends on the assumption that states do not believe that other states are highly altruistic—specifically, that they would be willing to risk their own security to guarantee others' security. If they were, then even under anarchy, states would not have to rely entirely on self-help; instead, they could count on others coming to their aid, even when the other states' security was not in jeopardy. However, altruism is not the key issue for structural realists; under anarchy, the more immediate concern is the extent of opposing states' current and future malign intentions; states cannot count on others being benign, let alone altruistic.
13. For example, Christopher Layne, "The Unipolar Illusion: Why New Great Powers Will Rise," *International Security*, Vol. 17, No. 4 (Spring 1993), p. 11, argues: "Because it is anarchic, the international political system is a self-help system in which states' foremost concern must be with survival. In an anarchic system, states must provide for their own security and they face many real or apparent threats. International politics is thus a competitive realm." In his critique of structural realism, Alexander Wendt, "Anarchy is What States Make of It: The Social Construction of Power Politics," *International Organization*, Vol. 46, No. 2 (Spring 1992), p. 392, argues: "The self-help corollary to anarchy does enormous work in neorealism, generating the inherently competitive dynamics of the security dilemma and collective action problem." See also ibid, p. 396. Waltz appears to agree that self-help leads to competition: "In self-help systems, the pressures of competition weigh more heavily than ideological preferences or internal political pressures." Waltz, "Reflections on *Theory of International Politics*," p. 329; see also the quotation previously cited in fn. 2.
14. Waltz, *Theory of International Politics*, p. 105.
15. Waltz, *Theory of International Politics*, p. 105; Grieco, *Cooperation Among Nations*, p. 45.
16. John J. Mearsheimer, "Back to the Future: Instability in Europe After the Cold War," *International Security*, Vol. 15, No. 1 (Summer 1990), p. 12.
17. For example, Mearsheimer, "Back to the Future," p. 12, argues "there is little room for trust among states because a state may be unable to recover if its trust is betrayed."

states must rely on their own means; because states must avoid reductions in their capabilities and often desire military advantages; and because, even if interested in avoiding a race, states must insure against falling behind if the adversary cheats on agreements. In its most succinct version, the standard argument sees the search for security that flows from anarchy as sufficient to explain competition: "realists argue that states are preoccupied with their security and power; *by consequence*, states are predisposed toward conflict and competition."[18] Cooperation between adversaries, although not impossible, will be rare and limited to areas of at best secondary importance.

This conclusion is implicit in Waltz's focus on arms competition and alliance formation. In broad terms, states can choose from three approaches for acquiring and maintaining the military capabilities required to meet their security needs: building arms, gaining allies, and reaching arms control agreements.[19] In principle, the approaches could be equally important. Waltz acknowledges that some cooperation (i.e., arms control) is possible,[20] but he then excludes cooperation with adversaries from the basic alternatives available to states in a self-help system:

States, or those who act for them, try in more or less sensible ways to use the means available in order to achieve the ends in view. Those means fall into two categories: internal efforts (moves to increase economic capability, to increase military strength, to develop clever strategies) and external efforts (moves to strengthen and enlarge one's own alliance or to weaken and shrink an opposing one).[21]

Contingent Realism

Although widely accepted as an accurate statement of structural realism, the standard structural-realist argument is deeply flawed. A more complete and

---

18. Grieco, *Cooperation Among Nations*, p. 4 (emphasis added).
19. "Arms control" is used here to refer to the full range of reciprocated restraint in the deployment, operation, and monitoring of forces; it is not restricted to formal agreements. On this broader definition see Thomas C. Schelling and Morton H. Halperin, *Strategy and Arms Control* (New York: Twentieth Century Fund, 1961), pp. 2–5; on the relative strengths of formal agreements and tacit bargaining, see George W. Downs, David M. Rocke, and Randolph M. Siverson, "Arms Control and Cooperation," in Oye, ed., *Cooperation Under Anarchy*.
20. Waltz, *Theory of International Politics*, pp. 115–116; also, Waltz, "A Response to My Critics," p. 336.
21. Waltz, *Theory of International Politics*, p. 118; see also Waltz, "The Origins of War in Neorealist Theory," in Robert I. Rotberg and Theodore K. Rabb, eds., *The Origin and Prevention of Major Wars* (Cambridge: Cambridge University Press, 1989), p. 43: "Their individual intentions aside, collectively their actions yield arms races and alliances."

balanced assessment, while starting from the same structural-realist assumptions, leads to quite different conclusions. Under a wide range of conditions, cooperation should be a country's preferred option; significantly, two or more countries could simultaneously reach this conclusion, thereby making security cooperation feasible. The following discussion also demonstrates that under other conditions structural realism does not identify a clear preference for competition versus cooperation.

My contingent-realist analysis develops three lines of argument. First, it eliminates the unwarranted bias toward competition that exists in the standard argument. Second, to capture more faithfully the logic that flows from structural realism's basic assumptions, contingent realism focuses on military capabilities—the ability to perform military missions—instead of on power.[22] This is accomplished by more fully integrating the security dilemma into structural realism. Third, contingent realism recognizes that the rational-actor assumptions that form the foundation of structural realism allow states to use military policy to communicate information about their motives. As a result, states seeking security should see benefits in cooperative policies that can communicate benign motives.

ELIMINATING THE "COMPETITION" BIAS

The standard argument focuses on the risks of cooperation; by underplaying and overlooking the risks of competition, it contains an unwarranted bias toward competition. The bias is the result of several mistakes. First, although the standard argument equates self-help with pursuit of competitive policies, in fact cooperative policies are an important type of self-help. For example, an adversary will engage in reciprocal restraint only if arms control promises to provide it with greater security than the competitive alternatives; this is possible only if the adversary believes that an arms race would be risky. Consequently, a country gets an adversary to cooperate by relying on its own resources—through self-help—since the country's ability to engage in an

---

22. To avoid confusion, I stress that the term "military capabilities" refers to the capability to perform military missions. Some authors use "military capabilities" to refer to military forces, that is, as a measure of the forces a country has deployed, not as a measure of the ability of forces to perform missions against an adversary's forces. As an example of the former use, Waltz explains that "capabilities are attributes of units [states]" and he includes "military strength" among the components of overall capability; Waltz, *Theory of International Politics*, pp. 98, 131. The distinction is very important because a state's ability to perform military missions is not determined by the size, type, and quality of its own military forces or resources, but by how these resources compare with and would fight against the adversary's forces.

arms race is a central condition for its adversary's belief that arms racing is risky, and thus for its willingness to cooperate. Thus, by itself, self-help tells us essentially nothing about whether states should prefer cooperation or competition.

Second, although the standard argument is correct in maintaining that the desire to avoid losses of capability and to gain military advantages can force states to compete, it is also true that this desire can lead states to cooperate. If military advantages are extremely valuable, then military disadvantages can be extremely dangerous. Therefore, when uncertain about the outcome of an arms race, which it would like to win, a risk-averse state could prefer an arms control agreement that accepted the current military status quo to gambling on prevailing in the arms race.[23] In addition, countries can prefer cooperation even when they are sure that they would not lose the arms race. For example, a country concerned about maintaining its military capabilities could prefer arms control when an arms race would result in advances in weapons technology that, when deployed by both countries, would have the unfortunate effect of leaving both countries more vulnerable to attack. And a country could prefer arms control when equal increases in the size of forces might decrease, not increase, its ability to defend itself.[24] The central message of modern arms control theory is that under certain conditions *both* countries could prefer these kinds of cooperation.[25]

Third, although it is correct in stating that uncertainty about the adversary's motives creates reasons for a state to compete, the standard argument fails to recognize that uncertainty about motives also creates powerful reasons for states to cooperate. Each faces uncertainty about the other's motives; such

---

23. Doubts about the outcome of the race could reflect uncertainties about which country is wealthier, better able to extract resources for military purposes, or better able to develop and exploit military technologies.

24. Moreover, the choice of arms racing over cooperation must compare arms racing not only to the military status quo but also to the possibility that reductions from the status quo might improve capabilities. Of course, the choice between arms racing, arms control and allies will also be influenced by domestic factors. For example, a country might prefer to avoid an arms race, which would not reduce its security, simply to avoid the economic costs of further arming. On domestic factors in the choice between arming and allies, see James D. Morrow, "Arms Versus Allies: Tradeoffs in the Search For Security," *International Organization*, Vol. 47, No. 2 (Spring 1993), pp. 207–233.

25. See Schelling and Halperin, *Strategy and Arms Control;* and Donald G. Brennan, ed., *Arms Control, Disarmament and National Security* (New York: George Braziller, 1961). Thomas C. Schelling, "A Framework for the Evaluation of Arms-Control Proposals," *Daedalus*, Vol. 104, No. 3 (Summer 1975), pp. 187–200, explores the implications of a country's preferences for an arms race, an unmatched unilateral buildup, or the military status quo.

uncertainty is dangerous because it can fuel insecurity, which structural realism identifies as the key source of international conflict. This generates two reasons for a state to cooperate. Even if cooperation leaves the adversary's uncertainty about a state's motives unchanged, cooperation is valuable if it reduces the adversary's insecurity by reducing the military threat it faces. Moreover, cooperation is valuable if it can reduce the adversary's uncertainty, convincing it that the first state is motivated more by insecurity than by greed; this would further reduce the probability of conflict caused by an opponent's insecurity. The benefits of competition, specifically gaining military advantages, must be weighed against these benefits of cooperation. This tradeoff lies at the core of the security dilemma, is a central component of structural realism, and cannot be generally resolved in favor of competition.

In sum, eliminating the bias in the standard structural-realist argument shows that states face a variety of countervailing pressures for cooperation as well as competition. Nothing in the basic structural-realist argument resolves these tradeoffs in general in favor of competition. The standard argument stresses only the risks of cooperation, but both cooperation and competition can be risky. Launching an arms buildup can make the adversary more insecure and, therefore, harder to deter. Pursuing military advantages forgos the possibility of avoiding an arms race in which the state could fall temporarily or permanently behind. When the risks of competition exceed the risks of cooperation, states should direct their self-help efforts toward achieving cooperation. Thus, contingent realism makes it clear that we need to replace essentially unconditional predictions of competition with conditional predictions of when states should cooperate and when they should compete.

SHIFTING THE FOCUS FROM POWER TO MILITARY CAPABILITIES: BRINGING IN CONSIDERATIONS OF OFFENSE AND DEFENSE

A security-seeking state that is comparing competition and cooperation must confront two fundamental questions. First, which will contribute more to its military capabilities for deterring attack, and for defending if deterrence fails? Second, appreciating the pressures created by anarchy and insecurity, the state should ask which approach is best for avoiding capabilities that threaten others' abilities to defend and deter, while not undermining its military capabilities? The tension that can exist between these two objectives lies at the core of the security dilemma.

WHY REFORMULATION IS NECESSARY. According to the standard structural-realist argument, states evaluate their ability to achieve security in terms of power.[26] Great powers are defined in terms of aggregate resources, including size of population, economic and industrial assets, and military assets. Power is defined in terms of the distribution of these resources among the states in the system. States seeking security endeavor to maintain their position in the system, and therefore they seek to maintain their relative resource rankings.[27]

This formulation is problematic because, as noted above, security-seeking states should assess their military requirements in terms of their ability to perform necessary military missions and to forgo the ability to perform certain other missions. Considerations of power do influence the answers to these questions, but they only begin to tell the story. For example, under certain conditions, two equally powerful states might have good prospects for defending against each other, while under other conditions their prospects for defending successfully could be relatively poor.

To shift from a structural theory based on power to one based on military capabilities and strategy, we need to include the dimensions of the security dilemma—the offense-defense balance and offense-defense distinguishability—as key variables. The offense-defense balance determines how much military-mission capability a country can get from its power; more specifically, for a country with a given amount of power, including the offense-defense balance in our analysis improves our ability to evaluate the country's prospects for defending itself. The offense-defense balance can be defined in terms of the investment in forces that support offensive missions that an opponent must make to offset a defender's investment in forces that support defensive missions. Defense enjoys a larger advantage when the required investment in offense is larger. The offense-defense balance is the ratio of the cost of the offensive forces to the cost of the defensive forces.[28]

---

26. We need to be clear on whether power is a "relational concept" defined in terms of the ability to influence another's actions, or a "property concept," something that can be defined and measured without reference to other countries. See David A. Baldwin, *Economic Statecraft* (Princeton, N.J.: Princeton University Press, 1985), esp. pp. 18–24. I am using "power" as a relational concept, which is consistent with Waltz, who defines power in terms of the *distribution* of capabilities (by which he means resources) in *Theory of International Politics*, pp. 98, 192. However, "power" is often used to refer to a state's resources, in which case assessments of influence need to be cast in terms of relative power.

27. Waltz, *Theory of International Politics*, pp. 131, 98, 192, and 126; Grieco, *Cooperation Among Nations*, pp. 10, 39–40. What I am referring to as resources, Waltz refers to as capabilities; see note 22 for why I avoid using "capabilities."

28. Robert Jervis, "Cooperation Under the Security Dilemma," *World Politics*, Vol. 30, No. 2 (January 1978), p. 188; on the variety of definitions of the offense-defense balance and potential problems that this creates see Jack S. Levy, "The Offense/Defense Balance of Military Technology: A Theoretical and Historical Analysis," *International Studies Quarterly*, Vol. 28, No. 2 (Spring 1990), pp. 222–230.

Therefore, the defender's power (which is a function of the ratio of its aggregate resources to the adversary's aggregate resources) multiplied by the offense-defense balance tells us much more about the defender's prospects for maintaining effective defensive capabilities than does considering power alone. Put slightly differently, the offense-defense balance provides information about the ratio of resources required by a country to maintain the military capabilities that are necessary for deterrence and defense. As the advantage of defense grows, the ratio of resources required by the defender decreases.

Including offense-defense distinguishability in our analysis enables us to consider whether states can choose to convert their power into different types of military capability, specifically, offensive or defensive-mission capability. When offense and defense are completely distinguishable, the forces that support offensive missions do not support defensive missions, and vice versa; when offense and defense are not at all distinguishable, the forces that support offensive missions can be used as effectively in defensive missions. Therefore, the extent to which military power can be disaggregated, making offense and defense distinguishable, is important for answering a key question—whether defenders can avoid having offensive-mission capabilities while maintaining defensive ones.

These offense-defense variables depend on a variety of factors, significantly including the nature of military technology and geography.[29] Integrating them into a structural-realist analysis enables us to shift from a *balance-of-power* theory to a *military-capabilities* theory, specifically a theory cast in terms of countries' abilities to perform military missions.[30] This transformation constitutes an important advance because security is much more closely correlated with mission capabilities than with power.

Some implications of variation in these two key dimensions of the security dilemma have been explored previously.[31] Moreover, some analysts have sug-

---

29. Other factors that may influence the overall offense-defense balance include the cumulativity of resources and strategic beliefs, in particular, states' beliefs about others' propensity to balance versus bandwagon. See, for example, Ted Hopf, "Polarity, the Offense-Defense Balance and War," *American Political Science Review*, Vol. 85, No. 2 (June 1991), pp. 475–494; and Jack Snyder, *Myths of Empire: Domestic Politics and International Ambition* (Ithaca, N.Y.: Cornell University Press, 1991).

30. I say "capabilities" here instead of "balance of capabilities" because states should care most about their capabilities for performing necessary missions, not about relative capabilities or a balance in capabilities. For example, a state that has high confidence in its ability to defend may not care about whether its potential adversary has even greater confidence in its ability to defend; security does not depend on a balance of capabilities. The key qualification arises when an "imbalance" in capabilities would leave one state more vulnerable to an arms race.

31. See John H. Herz, "Idealist Internationalism and the Security Dilemma," *World Politics*, Vol. 2, No. 2 (January 1950), pp. 157–180; George Quester, *Offense and Defense in the International System* (New York: John Wiley & Sons, 1977); Jervis, "Cooperation Under the Security Dilemma," pp. 167–

gested the need to combine security-dilemma considerations with overall power to generate predictions about state behavior. They have not, however, explored all of the implications for the predictions of structural realism, especially regarding security cooperation between adversaries.[32] Two basic points should be emphasized.

First, the basic argument of structural realism is not altered by using the dimensions of the security dilemma to shift from a focus on power to a focus on military capabilities. Indeed, to capture the central logic of the structural-realist argument requires that we assess how much and what types of military capability a state can produce with its power, since security-seekers should evaluate the international environment and their policy options in terms of military capabilities. Bringing in offense-defense variables is not optional, but necessary. Specifying the theory primarily in terms of power has distorted the insights that should flow deductively from structural realism's assumptions. Contingent realism eliminates this distortion.

Second, explicitly including the dimensions of the security dilemma as variables increases the ability of a structural theory to explain variations in states' choices between competitive and cooperative options for acquiring necessary military capabilities.[33] In contrast, Waltz's formulation focuses on a single variable—the degree of polarity—and explores its implications for the probability of war.[34] However, the preceding arguments suggest that states' choices

---

214; Stephen W. Van Evera, "Causes of War" (Ph.D. dissertation, University of California, Berkeley, 1984), esp. chap. 3; and Glaser, "Political Consequences of Military Strategy." Important criticisms of offense-defense arguments include Levy, "The Offense/Defense Balance of Military Technology: A Theoretical and Historical Analysis," pp. 137–168; and Jonathan Shimshoni, "Technology, Military Advantage and World War I," *International Security*, Vol. 15, No. 3 (Winter 1990/91), pp. 187–215.

32. However, Snyder makes an argument similar to the one I am presenting here in *Myths of Empire*, pp. 11–12 and 21–26, although he focuses on the question of expansion and suggests that defense usually has the overall advantage, largely because of states' propensity to balance. See also Sean Lynn-Jones, "The Implications of Security Dilemma Theory as a Theory of International Politics" (unpublished memo, September 1993). Others who have combined offense-defense considerations with structural-realist logic include Barry R. Posen, *The Sources of Military Doctrine* (Ithaca, N.Y.: Cornell University Press, 1984); Thomas J. Christensen and Jack Snyder, "Chain Gangs and Passed Bucks: Predicting Alliance Patterns in Multipolarity," *International Organization*, Vol. 44, No. 1 (Spring 1990), pp. 137–168; and Stephen M. Walt, *The Origins of Alliances* (Ithaca, N.Y.: Cornell University Press, 1987).

33. Other variables also matter in assessing capabilities: for example, the level of uncertainty about key variables, including the forces the adversary has deployed and the rate at which it could build additional forces, and the offense-defense balance. In addition, if states suffer evaluative biases, then this type of theory will still be inadequate for explaining behavior. Thus, for example, Christensen and Snyder, "Chain Gangs and Passed Bucks," include the quality of states' perceptions as an additional variable.

34. Waltz, *Theory of International Politics*, esp. chaps. 5 and 8:

between arms racing and arms control could vary substantially even when the degree of polarity does not vary, for example, within a bipolar system.

To appreciate the central role of variations in the severity of the security dilemma in structural-realist theory, consider the implications of anarchy if there were no security dilemma. States that were seeking only security could deploy adequate military capabilities without threatening other states. Moreover, uncertainty about motives would be reduced, if not eliminated, since security-seekers would not need offensive capabilities. Insecurity could be virtually eliminated.[35] Competition would arise only if one or more major powers were motivated by greed, rather than security.

IMPLICATIONS OF VARIATION IN THE DIMENSIONS OF THE SECURITY DILEMMA. Under what conditions should security-seeking states find cooperative policies to be desirable and feasible?[36] The types of policies that states can choose from depend on whether the forces required to support offensive strategies are distinguishable from those required to support defensive strategies. If they are distinguishable, then states can choose to build offense, defense, or both; they can also engage in arms control to limit offensive forces, defensive forces, or both. Given these choices, three approaches for gaining security are especially interesting: cooperation via arms control; unilateral defense, that is, deploying

---

35. Jervis makes this point in "Cooperation Under the Security Dilemma," p. 187, and provides qualifications. Waltz notes that, as a result of their situation, states face a security dilemma; he thereby gives it standing as part of a systemic explanation. See, for example, Waltz, *Theory of International Politics*, pp. 186–187; and Waltz, "The Origins of War in Neorealist Theory," pp. 41–42. However, he says little about the implications of variations in its severity. Waltz also argues that changes in military technology, including nuclear weapons, are a unit-level change. Waltz, "Reflections on *Theory of International Politics*," in Keohane, *Neorealism and Its Critics*, p. 327; and Waltz, "The Origins of War in Neorealist Theory," pp. 50–51. This seems problematic, however, since these changes influence the security dilemma, which is a systemic variable. This problem is noted by Joseph S. Nye, Jr., "Neorealism and Neoliberalism," *World Politics*, Vol. 40, No. 2 (January 1988), p. 243; and Daniel Deudney, "Dividing Realism: Structural Realism versus Security Materialism on Nuclear Security and Proliferation," *Security Studies*, Vol. 2, No. 3/4 (Spring/Summer 1993), pp. 13–14.

36. The following discussion assumes that states motivated primarily by security would prefer situations in which all countries lack effective offensive capabilities to situations in which all countries have effective offensive capabilities. However, pure security seekers might see some benefits in offensive capabilities under a variety of circumstances. For example, offense might contribute to deterrence by providing the capability to credibly threaten a punishing counteroffensive, might enhance the country's ability to defend its territory by providing the capability to regain lost territory, and might enable a declining state to insure its security by launching a preventive war. These benefits would have to be weighed against the dangers of increasing the adversary's insecurity. In addition, given the choice of both states having or both lacking offense, each state needs to consider the dangers posed by an increase in the adversary's offensive capability. On factors that influence this choice see Stephen Van Evera, "Offense, Defense, and Strategy"; Posen, *The Sources of Military Doctrine*, pp. 67–71; and Glaser, "Political Consequences of Military Strategy."

defensive forces independent of the strategy one's adversary chooses; and arms racing.[37] On the other hand, if offense and defense are indistinguishable, the basic choice facing states is whether to build larger forces, and risk generating an arms race, or to pursue arms control that reduces or caps the size of their forces.[38]

Arms control can be especially useful when the forces that support offensive missions can be distinguished from forces that support defensive missions.[39] If they can be distinguished, then agreements can restrict offensive capabilities by limiting specific types of forces; both countries will have better defensive capabilities and appear less threatening than if they had both deployed offensive forces.

Whether arms control is the preferred policy will vary with the offense-defense balance. When defense has a large advantage, arms control will be largely unnecessary. Countries can instead pursue unilateral defense, choosing to deploy defensive forces independent of whether their adversaries do. Even if one country decides to pursue offense, the competition should be mild due to the advantage of the defense. Two countries motivated primarily by security are both likely to choose unilateral defense, resulting in even less intense military competition.

In contrast, if offense has an advantage over defense, arms control has far more to contribute. Limiting offensive weapons while allowing defensive ones would establish a military status quo in which both countries are better able to defend themselves and in which first-strike incentives are smaller than if the countries invested primarily in offensive forces.[40] Arms control would likely be necessary to avoid this emphasis on offensive forces and on the arms race that could ensue, since both countries would find it difficult, technically or economically, to counter the adversary's offense with defense. Beyond improving the military status quo, arms control could help avoid some of the

---

37. Unilateral defense has much in common with cooperative policies in that it does not threaten the adversary's security, and usually will not generate threatening reactions from an adversary motivated primarily by security. However, pursuit of unilateral defense is not cooperation because the defender can productively pursue unilateral defense without coordinating with the adversary. Unilateral defensive policies therefore reflect a situation of harmony, not cooperation; see Keohane, *After Hegemony*, pp. 51–55.
38. To simplify the discussion, I do not address qualitative arms control that limits technological innovation.
39. Robert Jervis, "Security Regimes," *International Organization*, Vol. 36, No. 2 (Spring 1982), p. 362, comments on some of the following points.
40. On the dangers of offense see Stephen Van Evera, "The Cult of the Offensive and the Origins of the First World War," *International Security*, Vol. 9, No. 1 (Summer 1984), pp. 58–107.

"dynamic" risks that an arms race itself could generate. When defense does not have the advantage, falling temporarily behind in a race, which creates a "window" of disadvantage, becomes more dangerous.[41]

This case for arms control is not entirely clear-cut, however, because countries face an increasingly severe tradeoff as the advantage of offense increases. This is because cheating poses a greater danger: as the advantage of offense grows, a given amount of cheating would provide a larger advantage and, therefore, allowing the adversary to gain a headstart in a renewed arms race is more dangerous. This makes it more difficult to monitor an agreement satisfactorily, which makes it harder for arms control to increase the states' security.

Therefore, in addition to the clear benefits that arms control could provide with regard to the military status quo, states must compare the dynamic risks of arms control and arms racing. When offense and defense are distinguishable, countries can reduce the dangers of cheating, and therefore the requirements for monitoring, by allowing large defensive forces while banning offensive ones, creating a defensive barrier to cheating. However, there is no general resolution of the tradeoff between these dynamic considerations; it will depend on the specifics of monitoring capabilities and the rates at which countries can break out of agreements, as well as the effectiveness of a defensive barrier.[42] Nevertheless, because arms control can definitely improve the military status quo, states should be inclined to prefer arms control.

When the forces required for offensive and defensive missions are not distinguishable, arms control is less clearly useful. Agreements that limit the size of forces may leave offensive and defensive capabilities essentially unchanged, in which case they would have little effect on a country's ability to deter.[43] In contrast to the case in which offense and defense are distinguishable, arms control cannot promise to improve the military status quo. However, this observation applies equally to arms racing: competition that increases the size of the countries' forces may not increase their deterrent capabilities. Thus, when

---

41. On windows see Van Evera, "Causes of War," esp. chap. 2; and Charles L. Glaser, *Analyzing Strategic Nuclear Policy* (Princeton, N.J.: Princeton University Press, 1990), pp. 150–155.
42. A defensive barrier increases the time required to gain an offensive advantage, but does not necessarily reduce the benefits of cheating. However, if there are uncertainties about relative rearmament rates, then defensive barriers would increase uncertainty about whether breaking out of an agreement will provide military advantages, which could contribute to deterrence. See Thomas C. Schelling, *Arms and Influence* (New Haven, Conn.: Yale University Press, 1966), pp. 248–259; and Glaser, *Analyzing Strategic Nuclear Policy*, pp. 178–179.
43. This depends on whether the the offense-defense balance varies with the size of deployed forces. To see that it can, consider the deterrence requirements of nuclear forces, or force-to-space requirements of conventional forces designed to defeat breakthrough battles.

offense and defense are indistinguishable, there is no general conclusion about whether states should prefer arms control or arms racing. To analyze specific cases, states would have to perform net assessments of the variation in mission capability as a function of force size.[44]

Here again, the offense-defense balance matters. When defense has a large advantage, countries will find that arms control is largely unnecessary for avoiding competition. Because large unmatched increases in forces are required to gain significant military advantages, military competition should be mild and countries should enjoy high levels of security.[45] When offense has the advantage, arms control will be necessary for avoiding arms races, but will be harder to achieve and riskier than in the case in which offense and defense are distinguishable. Reaching agreement on the forces that will be permitted will be harder because, as noted above, limits are less likely to improve military capabilities and small differences in force size may be more important. Agreements will be riskier than in the case in which offense and defense are distinguishable because large defensive forces cannot be deployed as a hedge against cheating.

In sum, adding offense-defense variables does not shift the basic emphasis of structural theories, but instead eliminates distortions that result when the theory is cast primarily in terms of power. Considering not just power, but also how much and what types of military capability a state can produce with its power, is essential for understanding the pressures and opportunities that countries face when seeking security in an anarchic system. Given this formulation, a country's concern about its military capabilities should lead it to reject competitive policies under a range of conditions. In fact, contrary to the standard structural-realist analysis, arms racing is only clearly preferred to less competitive policies under rather narrow conditions: when offense has the advantage and is indistinguishable from defense, and when the risks of being cheated exceed the risks of arms racing.

INCORPORATING MOTIVES AND INTENTIONS: MILITARY POLICY AND SIGNALING

A state seeking security should be concerned about whether its adversary understands that its motivations are benign. Uncertainty about the state's motives, or even worse, the incorrect belief that the state is motivated by greed

---

44. However, even when larger forces are desirable, it is unclear that states should prefer truly competitive policies. One alternative is simply to coordinate increases in force size up to but not above a level at which both countries believe their deterrent capabilities would be enhanced.
45. See Malcolm W. Hoag, "On Stability in Deterrent Races," *World Politics*, Vol. 13, No. 4 (July 1961), pp. 505–527.

rather than security concerns, will increase the adversary's insecurity, which in turn will reduce the state's own security. Thus, structural realism suggests that states should be very interested in demonstrating that their motives are benign. The problem, according to the standard formulation, is that states acting within the constraints imposed by the international structure cannot communicate information about motives;[46] this type of information is seen as available only at the unit level.

Here again, however, the conventional wisdom is flawed. The rational actors posited by structural realism can under certain conditions communicate information about their motives by manipulating their military policies.[47]

Because greedy states have an incentive to misrepresent their motives, a pure security seeker can communicate information about its motives only by adopting a policy that is less costly for it than it would be for a greedy state.[48] A greedy state would like to mislead its adversaries into believing that it is interested only in security, since its adversaries would then be more likely to pursue policies that leave them vulnerable, enabling the greedy state to meet its expansionist objectives. However, when the policies that indicate that a state is not greedy are more costly for greedy states than for pure security seekers, greedy states are less likely to adopt them. Consequently, by adopting such a policy a state can communicate information about which type of state it is, that is, about its motives.

States can try to communicate their benign intentions via three types of military policies: arms control, unilateral defense, and unilateral restraint.[49] Agreeing to limit offensive capabilities, when offense has the advantage, can shift the adversary's assessment of the state's motives. Although a greedy state might accept this arms control agreement, because limits on its adversary's offense would increase its security, the agreement is costly for a greedy state because it reduces its prospects for expansion. Thus, although both states that are pure security-seekers and states that are motived by greed as well as

46. This view plays a central role in Wendt, "Anarchy is What States Make of It," pp. 391 and 392.
47. For formal treatments that focus on this possibility see George W. Downs and David M. Rocke, *Tacit Bargaining, Arms Races, and Arms Control* (Ann Arbor: University of Michigan Press, 1990), chap. 4; and Andrew Kydd, "The Security Dilemma, Game Theory, and WWI," paper presented at the 1993 annual meeting of the American Political Science Association. See also Robert Jervis, *The Logic of Images in International Relations* (Princeton, N.J.: Princeton University Press, 1970); and Jervis, "Cooperation Under the Security Dilemma."
48. On "costly signals," see James Dana Fearon, "Threats to Use Force: Costly Signals and Bargaining in International Crises" (Ph.D. dissertation, University of California, Berkeley, 1992).
49. See also Glaser, "Political Consequences of Military Strategy."

security might accept such an agreement, the costs of agreement are higher for the greedy state; moreover, the greedier the state was, the less likely it would be to accept the agreement. Consequently, although accepting the arms agreement should not entirely convince the adversary that it does not face a greedy state, it does nevertheless provide valuable information. By comparison, agreeing to limit offense when defense has the advantage provides less information, since an arms race is less likely to make expansion possible. Consequently, a greedy state would find such an agreement less costly, narrowing the cost-differential between greedy and non-greedy states, and thus limiting the information conveyed by such a policy.

Agreeing to limit the size of forces when offense and defense are indistinguishable can also communicate information about motives. Assuming that both countries have some chance of gaining an offensive military advantage in the race, the costs of accepting limits on force size will be greater for greedier states. The clearest signal will come from a state that has good prospects for winning the race, but nevertheless agrees to some form of parity.

Under certain conditions, a country may be able to communicate more effectively with unilateral defensive policies than with arms control. When offense has the advantage, a country that decides to meet its military requirements with defensive means will have to make larger investments in military forces than if it had chosen the offensive route. Compared to the arms control approach, this state will have indicated not only its willingness to forgo offensive capabilities, but also a willingness to invest greater resources to send this message.[50]

Finally, a country can try to communicate benign motives by employing unilateral restraint—that is, by reducing its military capability below the level it believes would otherwise be necessary for deterrence and defense.[51] This should send a clear message for two reasons: the state has reduced its offensive capability, which a greedy state would be less likely to do; and the state has incurred some risk, due to the shortfall in military capabilities, which the adversary could interpret as a further indication of the value the state places on improving relations. Of course, this security risk will make states reluctant to adopt an ambitious policy of unilateral restraint. Consequently, states are

---

50. Of course, if its adversary also shifts to a defensive policy, the cost of sustaining the defensive policy will be similar to the costs under an arms control agreement.

51. The uses of unilateral restraint are emphasized by Charles E. Osgood, *An Alternative to War or Surrender* (Urbana: University of Illinois, 1962). In *Tacit Bargaining, Arms Races and Arms Control*, pp. 41–51, Downs and Rocke assess Osgood's arguments.

likely to turn to unilateral restraint only when other options are precluded, e.g., when unilateral defense is impossible because offense and defense are indistinguishable, or when it is unaffordable, because offense has a large advantage over defense, or when they conclude that an especially dramatic gesture is necessary.

In short, the essentially rational actors posited by structural realism will under certain conditions be able to use cooperative or other unthreatening military policies to improve understanding of their motives. For states motivated primarily by security, such opportunities will be especially attractive when cooperative policies can also enhance their military capabilities. By comparison, when communication of benign motives requires a state to reduce necessary military capabilities, states face a much more difficult choice, especially since they must worry not only about deterring, but also about defending if deterrence fails.

The standard structural-realist argument overlooks the possibility of clarifying motives. Although uncertainty about the adversary's motives can sometimes call for competitive policies, the adversary's uncertainty about the state's motives can call for the opposite. A balanced assessment of alternative approaches must weigh these potentially countervailing pressures, as well as the possibility of acquiring improved military mission capabilities via cooperative means.

Flaws in the Standard Structural-realist Counter-arguments

Three major arguments are commonly used in support of the standard structural-realist argument, and could be used to counter the overall thrust of contingent realism. However, each argument suffers serious flaws or limitations; none weakens contingent realism.

"STATES TRY TO MAXIMIZE RELATIVE POWER, WHICH CREATES A ZERO-SUM SITUATION THAT MAKES COOPERATION DIFFICULT"

Although the claim that states try to maximize relative power has been rejected by some prominent structural realists, most notably Waltz,[52] it has been presented forcefully by others. For example, John Mearsheimer argues that "states seek to survive under anarchy by maximizing their power relative to other

---

52. Waltz, "Theory of International Politics," p. 118, 126, and 127; and Waltz, "Reflections on *Theory of International Politics*," in Keohane, *Neorealism and its Critics*, p. 334. See also Robert Gilpin, *War and Change in International Politics* (Cambridge: Cambridge University Press, 1981), esp. pp. 86–88.

states, in order to maintain the means for self-defense."[53] If states try to maximize relative power, international relations will be highly competitive, since states will then "seek opportunities to weaken potential adversaries and improve their relative position."[54] Adversaries attempting to maximize their relative power face a zero-sum situation—increases in one state's relative power necessarily result in decreases in the other's relative power. Cooperative policies will be rare because they preempt the possibility of achieving advantages in relative power.

The key to assessing this claim is to recognize that, for structural realists, conclusions about maximizing power are conclusions about means, not ends. Structural realism assumes that, in an anarchic system, security is the end to which states will give priority. States may pursue other goals, but structural realism does not assume that they do. Consequently, showing that structural realism predicts that states try to maximize relative power requires demonstrating that doing so is the best way for states to gain security.

Three arguments suggest that pursuing increases in relative power is not always the best way to increase security. First, the claim in favor of maximizing relative power overlooks the security dilemma: a state that increased its relative power might nevertheless decrease its security because its increased relative power could make its adversary less secure, which could in turn increase the value its adversary places on expansion. War could become more likely, since any deterrent value of increased relative power might be outweighed by the increased benefits that a security-seeking adversary would see in expansion. Consequently, a country could reasonably conclude that accepting rough parity in military capabilities would provide greater security than maximizing its relative power. Notwithstanding the claim that states try to maximize power, structural realism leaves this question wide open.[55]

---

53. Mearsheimer, "Back to the Future," p. 12. See also Fareed Zakaria, "Realism and Domestic Politics: A Review Essay," *International Security*, Vol. 17, No. 1 (Summer 1992), pp. 193–194. In this argument, "power" is being used as a property concept, not a relational concept; see footnote 26. Although I prefer the relational use, in this section I use relative power to maintain consistency with the quotations.
54. Mearsheimer, "Back to the Future," p. 12.
55. Factors important in resolving this tradeoff include: 1) the extent of increases in relative power: military advantages that are so overwhelming that they clearly deny the adversary any chance of victory probably reduce the probability of war, whereas smaller military advantages that leave some doubt about the adversary's prospects for victory might increase the probability of war; 2) the offense-defense balance, as discussed above; 3) the adversary's motives: military advantages will be less valuable against states motivated primarily by insecurity and more valuable against states motivated primarily by greed; and 4) the quality of the adversary's evaluative capabilities, which influences the extent of insecurity that launching an arms buildup or arms race would generate.

Second, trying to maximize power could increase the probability of losing an arms race. Even a country that would prefer to win an arms race—that is, that would prefer superiority to parity—might choose cooperation over arms racing to avoid the risk of losing the race.

Third, by failing to distinguish between offensive and defensive potential, the claim that states try to maximize relative power disregards the fact that maximizing relative power may not maximize the military capabilities that a country needs for defense and deterrence. Consider the case in which, to maximize its power, a country must compete in the deployment of offensive capabilities, and its alternative is to accept parity in defensive capabilities. The offensive race could decrease the winner's security by reducing its ability to defend against attack and by increasing crisis instability. Thus, even setting aside dangers that could result from decreasing the adversary's security and losing a race, maximizing power could decrease one's own security.

In short, states motivated primarily by security should not as a general rule try to maximize their relative power. Proponents of the relative-power–maximization argument sometimes try to defend their claim by adding the qualification that states maximize relative power when they can. This qualification is actually quite significant, suggesting that the claim is about what states want, not about how they behave. If so, their claim is potentially quite misleading, since constraints on state behavior can create a large gap between what a state would like to achieve and what it actually tries to achieve. Moreover, the qualification is inadequate because it does not deal with the first and third arguments presented in this section. Therefore, analyses that start from the claim that states try to maximize relative power exaggerate the extent to which structural realism predicts that international politics will be highly competitive.

"STATES' CONCERN OVER RELATIVE GAINS MAKES SECURITY COOPERATION ESPECIALLY DIFFICULT"

Structural realists believe that states must be concerned not only about whether cooperation will provide them with gains, but also with how these gains will be distributed.[56] If cooperation enables a state's adversary to gain more, the adversary may be able to convert this advantage into a capability for effectively coercing the state or, in extreme cases, defeating it in war. As a result, states

---

56. Waltz, *Theory of International Politics,* pp. 105, 175; Grieco, *Cooperation Among Nations;* Grieco, "Anarchy and the Limits of Cooperation: A Realist Critique of the Newest Liberal Institutionalism," *International Organization,* Vol. 42, No. 3 (Summer 1988), pp. 485–507.

must be concerned about relative gains, that is, about which state gains more from cooperation. States may conclude that the danger of relative losses exceeds the benefit of absolute gains, making cooperation undesirable. Relative-gains problems are generally believed to be more severe in the security realm than in the economic realm, thereby making security cooperation especially difficult.[57]

The following arguments, however, show that under a wide range of conditions, states interested in security cooperation should not be constrained by a relative-gains problem.[58]

THE RELATIVE-GAINS PROBLEM IS NOT ABOUT RELATIVE MILITARY ASSETS. The key to understanding relative gains in the security realm is to frame the issue correctly. We first must distinguish the instruments of policy from the ends of policy, that is, the value the policy produces. In the security realm, military assets are instruments of policy, while security is the end. In the economic realm, tariffs and other barriers to trade are instruments of policy, while wealth is the end.[59] A policy provides a state with "gains" when it increases what the state values, not when it increases the instruments the state has available or employs.

Consider the tradeoff posed by the relative-gains problem. In describing states' concern for relative gains, Waltz argues that states "are compelled to ask not 'Will both of us gain?' but 'Who will gain more?'"[60] The first question focuses on absolute gains, the second on relative gains. The implication is that if only absolute gains mattered, then states would need to answer only the first question to determine whether cooperation was desirable. Desirability would

---

57. For example, Grieco, *Cooperation Among Nations*, p. 46, argues that, "a state's sensitivity to gaps in gains is also likely to be greater if a cooperative venture involves security matters than economic well-being"; see also ibid, p. 14. This view of the conventional wisdom is also described by Robert Powell, "Absolute and Relative Gains in International Relations Theory," *American Political Science Review*, Vol. 85, No. 4 (December 1991), p. 1303.

58. Moreover, they also suggest that concern about relative gains will be less constraining in security cooperation, specifically in arms control, than in economic cooperation.

59. For the sake of contrast, I am using "security realm" to refer to policies that influence the size and type of forces, and "economic realm" to refer to policies that influence the type and severity of trade barriers. I do not mean to imply that policies in the economic realm lack security implications and vice versa. Thus, these statements include important simplifications: they exaggerate the extent to which manipulation of instruments in one realm produces only one type of value. For example, policies in the economic realm can generate changes in relative wealth, which can in turn have security implications; moreover, cooperation in the security realm can have implications for future relative wealth. I address the implications below.

60. Waltz, p. 105. A state really only needs to ask "will I gain?" to determine whether cooperation is desirable; however, it may need to ask "will both of us gain?" to assess whether cooperation is feasible.

be determined by "gains," which must therefore refer to the value produced by cooperation.[61]

This formulation helps us correct a common mistake: analysts argue that states care a great deal about relative changes in military assets, and then conclude that countries are highly sensitive to relative gains.[62] However, although states do care about relative changes in military assets, this concern is not due to a relative-gains problem. A state evaluating the impact of cooperation on relative force size is comparing changes in instruments, not changes in the achievement of ends. This does not reflect a relative-gains problem, since states are concerned with relative gains when they compare relative changes in their achievement of things they value, not when they compare the instruments employed. The analogous but perhaps more obvious mistake in the economic realm would be to evaluate relative gains by comparing the extent to which trade barriers were loosened instead of comparing the economic benefits that this loosening would generate. This error is rarely made in economic analysis.

Consequently, although I agree with proponents of the flawed formulation that states care about relative military assets, I explain this concern in a different, more straightforward way. Correctly formulated, in the security realm the "absolute gains" from cooperation refer to an increase in security.[63] When cooperation would result in a relative loss in military assets, and when this loss reduces mission capability and security, the state will refuse to cooperate.[64]

---

61. We can reach the same conclusion by considering the evolution of the debate over absolute and relative gains. Grieco, "Anarchy and the Limits of Cooperation" argued that neoliberals focused on absolute gains in the repeated prisoner's dilemmas, while overlooking relative gains in establishing the preference orderings in their two-by-two games. Because preferences in these games are defined across outcomes produced by cooperation and defection, "absolute gains" must refer to the value produced by policies, not to increases in the means employed.

62. This formulation also helps to clarify a closely related point of confusion: the first two arguments of this section—(1) that states maximize relative power and (2) that states are constrained by concern about relative gains—are sometimes thought to be the same argument. However, the first argument focuses on states' choices regarding policies that manipulate means— the instruments that can produce security—whereas the second argument focuses on states' concern about relative achievement of value.

63. Absolute gain could also refer to economic savings, if the arms control agreement enables the country to reduce investment in military forces. However, although saving money is one of the three classic objectives of arms control, security is usually the priority goal of cooperation. On the classic objectives see Schelling and Halperin, *Strategy and Arms Control*, p. 2. For a dissenting view on the role of saving money see Bernard Brodie, "On the Objectives of Arms Control," *International Security*, Vol. 1, No. 1 (Summer 1976), pp. 17–36.

64. Three points are worth noting briefly: (1) as discussed below, losses in relative military assets might not reduce the state's security if they increase the adversary's security; (2) a state's sensitivity to relative losses in military assets will depend on the offense-defense balance; (3) a state's military capability could increase, even if it suffers a relative loss in military assets, if the offense-defense balance varies with force size.

However, this refusal would reflect the failure of cooperation to increase security, that is, to provide absolute gains, not the state's concern over relative gains.[65]

In short, although the relative-gains problem is often apparently viewed in terms of concern over relative gains in military assets, this is the wrong way to formulate the issue. If there is a relative-gains problem in the security realm, it must lie elsewhere. The two possibilities, discussed below, are relative gains in security and relative gains in wealth resulting from security cooperation. However, exploration of these areas casts serious doubt on whether relative-gains concerns are severe in the security realm and suggests further that states will usually not be constrained by them.

RELATIVE SECURITY GAINS AND COMPARISONS OF SECURITY. Since the goal of cooperation is to increase security, relative-gains logic suggests that we explore whether concern over the distribution of security gains should inhibit cooperation. A country is concerned about relative gains in security if cooperation would increase its adversary's security more than its own, and if this relative loss in security would in turn reduce its own security. If we narrowly equate security with military capability, then this situation could arise if an arms control agreement increased both countries' denial capabilities, but not equally.

However, following security-dilemma logic, all else being equal, increases in the adversary's security often increase one's own security because a more secure adversary has smaller incentives for pursuing an expansionist foreign policy, and therefore will pose a smaller threat. This argument does not depend on whether the increase in the adversary's security exceeds or trails the increase in the defender's security, because the change in the adversary's motives reflects its absolute security, not a relative measure of its security compared to the defender's.

Objections and qualifications to this argument focus on two types of cases. First, when facing an adversary that is motivated by greed, as well as security, increasing the adversary's security could increase its willingness to pursue its expansionist objectives. This danger could result from cooperation that attempted to increase both countries' security by reducing both countries' offensive capabilities. The defender's denial capability would be enhanced, but its ability to deter via punishment would likely be reduced, since mutual reduc-

---

65. One possible counter to this argument is that mission capability, and therefore, security are themselves relative, not absolute measures. This is incorrect. Although a country's ability to perform military missions depends on how its forces compare to the adversary's, we measure mission capability in absolute terms. For example, an estimate of the probability that a country can defeat an invasion is an absolute measure.

tions in offense would reduce the defender's counteroffensive capability. An adversary that was especially impressed by the risks posed by punishment capabilities might conclude that the deterrent value of the defender's military capabilities had been reduced.[66]

Although important, the issue raised by this case is not about relative gains, but rather about whether cooperation that reduces both countries' offensive capabilities would provide the defender with absolute gains in security. If this cooperation reduces the defender's ability to deter, then the defender would not achieve an absolute gain in security, thus making cooperation undesirable. The problem is not that the adversary gains more security, but rather that the defender does not gain.

The second type of case comes closer to presenting the defender with a relative-gains problem. In these cases, the countries have conflicts of interest that lie beyond their primary security interests, that is, beyond their concern for protecting their homelands and possibly their major allies. Relative gains in security could influence countries' abilities to prevail in these secondary conflicts, if the advantaged country is willing to risk major war to prevail. A country's credibility in this competition in risk-taking will depend on the costs of major war. Therefore, cooperation that provides a country with relative gains in security by reducing the costs of major war could advantage that country in these secondary disputes. Nevertheless, the country that suffers a relative loss in security could still favor cooperation, since its primary security interests would be better protected.

In short, contrary to the problem identified by the logic of the relative-gains problem, if cooperation increases a country's security, then increases in the adversary's security are usually desirable, whether or not they exceed increases in the defender's security. In the security realm, instead of a relative-gains problem, we often have a mutual-gains benefit.

RELATIVE ECONOMIC SAVINGS AND ECONOMIC GROWTH. The second line of argument shifts the focus of the relative-gains argument from comparisons of security gains to comparisons of economic growth that are made possible by

---

66. On the value of counteroffensive capabilities for deterrence, see Samuel P. Huntington, "Conventional Deterrence and Conventional Retaliation in Europe," *International Security*, Vol. 8, No. 3 (Winter 1983/84), pp. 32–56; and Barry R. Posen, "Crisis Stability and Conventional Arms Control," *Daedalus*, Vol. 120, No. 1 (Winter 1991), pp. 217–232. The overall effect on the defender's prospects for deterrence would then depend on weighing countervailing factors: even a greedy adversary would be easier to deter, because increasing its security would reduce its interest in expansion; the defender, however, would be left with a less effective mix of deterrent capabilities.

security cooperation. This argument traces the danger in security cooperation through relative increases in the adversary's wealth, which the adversary can eventually convert into superior military forces. More specifically, when security cooperation saves the adversary greater resources than it saves the defender, the adversary will be able to redirect greater resources into future security competition, which will enable it eventually to pose a greater security threat than if cooperation had never occurred.

Although this argument appears to hinge on differences in savings, in fact it hinges on the relationship between reduced defense spending and economic growth. Assume that both countries reserve their savings for a future arms race. If the agreement breaks down, the country that saved more cannot compete more effectively than if an agreement had never been reached, since it has only the resources it would have invested earlier. The agreement defers the arms race, but does not advantage the country that saves more. Consequently, savings can have security implications only if they generate economic growth. In this case, the country that saves more can achieve relative gains in GNP. If the agreement then breaks down, the countries' abilities to engage in an arms race would have changed.

The problem with this line of argument is that studies have not established a strong relationship between defense spending and economic growth.[67] The basic concern is that defense spending crowds out private investment, which would otherwise contribute more to economic growth. However, there is no agreement on whether even U.S. defense spending during the Cold War slowed the growth of the American economy.[68] Moreover, if the country that would save less from an arms agreement were nevertheless worried about the long-term growth implications, it could adopt a variety of economic policies that would reduce the risks.[69]

---

67. Aaron L. Friedberg, "The Political Economy of American Strategy," *World Politics*, Vol. 41, No. 3 (April 1989), pp. 395–405; Charles A. Kupchan, "Empire, Military Power, and Economic Decline," *International Security*, Vol. 13, No. 4 (Summer 1989), pp. 40–47; and Steve Chan, "The Impact of Defense Spending on Economic Performance: A Survey of Evidence and Problems," *Orbis*, Vol. 29, No. 2 (Summer 1985), pp. 403–434.

68. For opposing views see Kenneth A. Oye, "Beyond Postwar Order and New World Order," in Kenneth A. Oye, Robert J. Lieber, and Donald Rothchild, *Eagle in a New World* (New York: HarperCollins, 1992), pp. 7–11; David Gold, *The Impact of Defense Spending on Investment, Productivity and Economic Growth* (Washington, D.C.: Defense Budget Project, 1990) and Friedberg, "The Political Economy of American Strategy," pp. 398–405.

69. These could include policies that would encourage savings and investment. See, for example, Friedberg, "The Political Economy of American Strategy," p. 400.

The feasibility of such policies depends on the size of the differential in saved defense spending: the smaller the relative loss in savings, the easier it is to compensate by revising domestic economic policy. Consequently, it is significant that an arms agreement can rarely promise to save a significant percentage of GNP. An agreement that saved the United States one percent of GNP per year would have to be quite dramatic.[70] An agreement that resulted in a difference in savings of this magnitude would have to be at least as dramatic and highly asymmetric in its effect on savings, which is unlikely.

In sum, although it is analytically sound to focus on the possibility that security cooperation could generate relative gains in economic growth, it appears that the dangers posed by this possibility should rarely, if ever, be a major barrier to security cooperation. This should be especially true for states that give priority to security, since they should be more willing to adjust domestic economic policies if necessary to gain the immediate security benefits of cooperation.

FACTORS THAT WOULD INFLUENCE THE SECURITY IMPLICATIONS OF RELATIVE ECONOMIC GAINS. In cases in which security cooperation would generate differential economic growth, three additional considerations influence whether the risks would outweigh the defender's direct gains in security, thereby making security cooperation undesirable. The first consideration applies only to security cooperation, while the latter two apply to economic cooperation as well. First, the beneficial effects of the adversary's increased security make its increased relative economic strength less threatening, since it would be less inclined to use this economic potential for security-driven expansion. Thus, the defender should find relative economic losses produced by security cooperation somewhat less threatening than comparable relative losses produced by economic cooperation.

Second, the magnitude of relative gains influences the potential security threat. Small relative gains, compared to GNP, would rarely pose a major threat. If cooperation breaks down, the disadvantaged country would be able to offset any increased military threat made possible by growth in the adversary's GNP by increasing the percentage of GNP that it spends on defense. Thus, when the adversary's relative economic gains are small, the defender risks a loss of prosperity, but not of security. If the agreement (while it holds) provides large security gains, risking this loss would usually be warranted.

---

70. For example, during much of the Cold War the United States spent approximately one percent of its GNP on nuclear forces; an agreement to ban nuclear weapons might therefore have saved approximately this much per year.

Third, the offense-defense balance influences the security implications of relative economic gains.[71] Relative economic gains matter less as the advantage of defense grows, because acquiring effective offensive capabilities requires the adversary to make increasingly disproportionate investments in military forces. Thus, when defense has a large advantage over offense, the possibility of relative gains should do little to inhibit economic or security cooperation.[72] Consequently, countries that possess large nuclear arsenals and that rely heavily on nuclear deterrence for their security should not be inhibited from security or economic cooperation by security-related relative-gains constraints, since nuclear weapons create a very large advantage for the defense.[73]

These arguments suggest that under most conditions countries should focus on the absolute security gains offered by security cooperation, since these gains would rarely be jeopardized by relative economic gains. Exceptions are most likely when gains in relative economic growth would be significant in terms of overall national wealth and when the offense-defense balance favors offense.

"STATES ARE COMPETITIVE BECAUSE THE POSSIBILITY OF CHEATING MAKES
COOPERATION TOO RISKY; INSTITUTIONS CANNOT SOLVE THE PROBLEM"
The third broad argument, that states will not engage in extensive security cooperation focuses on the danger posed by the adversary's ability to cheat on arms control agreements (whether formal or tacit). The possibility of cheating is important only for cases in which cooperation, assuming it holds, would increase the country's security, and therefore is desirable. Thus, the implications of cheating matter only after the preceding standard structural-realist arguments have been rejected.

The standard structural-realist argument notes that since under anarchy there is no authority that can enforce agreements, states will cheat when doing so serves their interests. The possibility of cheating means that a country's true choice may not be between successful arms control and arms racing, but

---

71. A second structural factor that can influence the implications of relative gains is the number of major states in the system. See Duncan Snidal, "Relative Gains and the Pattern of International Cooperation," *American Political Science Review*, Vol. 85, No. 3 (September 1991), pp. 701–726.
72. Powell, "Absolute and Relative Gains in International Relations Theory," pp. 1303–1320, reaches a similar conclusion, but has cast it in terms of the cost of fighting, not the offense-defense balance. See also Helen Milner, "International Theories of Cooperation Among Nations: Strengths and Weaknesses," *World Politics*, Vol. 44, No. 3 (April 1992), pp. 483–484. Waltz, *Theory of International Politics*, p. 195, suggests this logic but does not spell it out.
73. For similar points, see Kenneth N. Waltz, "The Emerging Structure of International Politics," *International Security*, Vol. 18, No. 2 (Fall 1993), p. 74. Layne, "The Unipolar Illusion," pp. 44–45, appears to disagree.

instead between risking being left behind when the adversary cheats and racing from the start to insure that the adversary fails to gain a lead. The standard structural-realist argument emphasizes the dangers of being cheated and suggests that this will usually prevent significant cooperation, especially security cooperation, since states are especially reluctant to risk shortfalls in military capability.[74]

We have already seen that contingent realism rejects cheating as a dominating influence. Correcting the bias in the standard argument requires, among other things, emphasizing the risks of arms racing, as well as the risks of arms control, and specifically of cheating; this correction creates a balance that is missing in the standard argument. In addition, exploring the implications of incorporating the security dilemma into structural realism showed that the risks of cheating, and therefore its implications for cooperation, vary with offense-defense considerations. Thus, contingent realism recognizes that the possibility of cheating matters, but proceeds to focus on the conditions under which major powers are likely to find that, when all factors are considered, cooperation remains desirable. The following subsection draws on two bodies of literature that help to elaborate the overall thrust of this analysis.

ARMS CONTROL THEORY.   The literature on modern arms control theory recognizes the danger posed by the adversary's cheating.[75] But, as Schelling and Halperin argue, the risks of cheating must be weighed against the benefits the agreement would provide, assuming it holds. They argue that the danger of cheating depends on: the probability of detecting violations of a given size; the strategic implications of a given degree of cheating, which depends upon the level and type of forces allowed by the agreement; and the ability to respond to violations by joining the renewed arms race.[76]

To reduce the risks of cooperation, a formal arms control agreement could include provisions for monitoring that insure the ability to react before the advantage of cheating becomes too large, that is, to ensure that the benefits of

---

74. This view of the role of cheating in making security cooperation more difficult than economic cooperation is supported by important articles in cooperation theory; for example, Robert Jervis, "Security Regimes," in Stephen Krasner, ed., *International Regimes* (Ithaca, N.Y.: Cornell University Press, 1983); and Charles Lipson, "International Cooperation in Economic and Security Affairs," *World Politics*, Vol. 37, No. 1 (October 1984), pp. 1–23, esp. 12–18. Both articles do, however, point to conditions that increase the probability of security cooperation.

75. See Schelling and Halperin, *Strategy and Arms Control*, esp. 67–74, 91–106; see also Abram Chayes, "An Inquiry Into the Working of Arms Control Agreements," *Harvard Law Review*, Vol. 85, No. 5 (March 1972), pp. 905–969, esp. 945–961; and James A. Schear, "Verification, Compliance, and Arms Control: The Dynamics of the Domestic Debate," in Lynn Eden and Steven E. Miller, eds., *Nuclear Arguments* (Ithaca, N.Y.: Cornell University Press, 1989).

76. Schelling and Halperin, *Strategy and Arms Control*, pp. 67–74.

taking the first step in the arms race are not too large. If, however, the countries' independent national monitoring capabilities already provide information that makes the benefits of cheating small, deals to accept the military status quo may not require formal agreement, but can instead be accomplished by uni-lateral statements that a state plans to build only if the adversary builds. Schelling and Halperin conclude that "it cannot be assumed that an agreement that leaves some possibility of cheating is necessarily unacceptable or that cheating would necessarily result in strategically important gains."[77]

Although this line of argument was well established by the early 1960s, the standard structural-realist argument neither incorporates it nor seriously dis-putes it. The burden to confront these conclusions lies with the structural-real-ists, since none of the essential elements of arms control theory run counter to structural realism's basic assumptions. Some critics will fall back on self-help as an argument, but, as we have seen, cooperation is an important type of self-help, and this includes cooperation in monitoring agreements. Moreover, as argued below, the types of institutions that might be required to make arms control desirable are not precluded by structural realism.

COOPERATION THEORY. Support for contingent realism also comes from the literature that uses game theory to explore cooperation under anarchy.[78] Coop-eration theory provides insights that parallel those offered by arms control and offense-defense theories, and emphasizes the importance of each countries' beliefs about its adversary's preferences. A simple model of the choice between an arms control agreement and an arms race assumes that if an agreement is reached and cheating is then detected, the arms race begins and is not halted again by another agreement.[79] Given this assumption, the country comparing the value of the arms agreement and the risks of being cheated faces four possible outcomes: the agreement prevails (CC); the adversary cheats, leaving the country one step behind in the ensuing arms race (CD); an equal arms race (DD); or, the country cheats, gaining a one step lead in the arms race (DC).[80]

---

77. Schelling and Halperin, *Strategy and Arms Control*, p. 69.
78. See citations in fn. 5; also Schelling, "A Framework for the Evaluation of Arms-Control Proposals."
79. More complex assumptions would allow for reestablishing an agreement at any point during the ensuing race. Although renegotiation would be possible, the simplified assumption seems to do an adequate job of capturing the options that states would consider in joining and breaking out of a major arms control agreement. Relaxing this simplifying assumption opens up the possibility in iterated-game models of tit-for-tat type strategies, which play a central role in the literature on cooperation under anarchy, but not in this discussion.
80. "C" stands for cooperation, which in this example means abiding by the agreement; "D" stands for defection, which in this example means cheating on the agreement. CC refers to the outcome in which both countries cooperate; DD refers to the outcome in which both countries defect; and DC and CD refer to outcomes in which one country cooperates and the other defects.

A country is concerned with the implications of cheating only if it prefers the arms agreement to the equal arms race, CC > DD.[81] If in addition, the country prefers the arms agreement to an arms race in which it gets a one-step lead (CC > DC), and if its adversary has the same preference ordering, then the countries face a "stag hunt."[82]

Unlike the prisoner's dilemma, in a stag hunt it can be individually rational for two countries to cooperate.[83] However, cooperation is not assured if the countries are unsure of each other's preference orderings. For example, a country with stag-hunt preferences believing that it faces a country with prisoner's-dilemma preferences should defect. A country that is unsure about its adversary's preferences, and therefore unsure about whether the adversary will abide by the arms agreement, should consider the magnitude of the differences between its payoffs.[84] This is when the magnitude of the danger posed by cheating comes into play.

To determine when the risks of cooperation are "too large," the defender compares an arms race in which it starts one step behind (CD) to both an arms race started on equal footing (DD) and to the arms agreement (CC). The country's willingness to risk cooperation grows as: (1) the difference between falling behind by a step and running an equal arms race (CD-DD) decreases; and (2) the difference between the arms control agreement and the equal arms race (CC-DD) increases. As discussed in the arms control and security dilemma literatures, the difference between CD and DD depends on the forces allowed by the agreement, the offense-defense balance, and the quality of monitoring and reaction capabilities. For example, improving the country's ability to monitor an agreement reduces the difference between the adversary getting a lead and starting the race on equal footing, that is, it reduces CD-DD, thereby making cooperation more desirable.

To translate this argument into the kind of model that is commonly used in cooperation theory, we can envision the arms control–arms race choice as a

---

81. Standard structural-realist arguments argue that this condition is not fulfilled. For example, the argument that cooperation theory is flawed because it fails to take into account countries' concerns about relative gains amounts to saying that for one country DD > CC.

82. This also includes the reasonable assumption that DC > DD > CD. For a discussion of how a stag hunt compares to other games where cooperation is necessary for states to achieve mutual gains, see Kenneth A. Oye, "Explaining Cooperation Under Anarchy: Hypotheses and Strategies," in Oye, *Cooperation Under Anarchy*, pp. 6–9.

83. For a discussion of when competition will nevertheless occur in a stag hunt, see Downs, Rocke, and Siverson, "Arms Races and Arms Control," pp. 133–137.

84. The country must also worry about whether its adversary correctly understands its own preferences, since misunderstanding could lead a country that would otherwise cooperate to defect.

series of decisions made over time; each decision constitutes a single play of a game, which is then repeated.[85] The simplifying assumption used above—that once cheating is detected the arms race begins and is not halted again by another agreement—translates into a model in which each country's strategy is to always defect after its adversary's first defection. The prospects for cooperation depend on the countries' preferences in the game. Cooperation should occur if the countries believe they are playing stag hunt. However, cooperation can also be possible if the countries believe they are playing prisoner's dilemma, since, given their strategy for dealing with defection, the overall game that results with iteration can be a stag hunt.[86] Thus, a way to get the stag hunt discussed in the previous paragraphs is from an iterated prisoner's dilemma played under certain conditions.

In sum, the arguments presented in the arms control literature and later in the cooperation theory literature make it clear that whether the dangers of cheating more than offset the potential benefits of arms control depends on a variety of specific factors, including the terms of the agreement and the countries' abilities to monitor it and to respond to breakout. Thus, according to contingent realism, although the possibility of cheating could make cooperation undesirable under certain conditions, under other conditions arms control would remain preferable to arms racing.

INSTITUTIONS. Contingent realism does not establish an important role for institutions. This clarification is necessary because influential cooperation theorists have emphasized the importance of institutions and regimes in making

---

85. However, the assumption of this type of model, that the payoffs do not change over time, can be problematic for certain arms agreements and races. For example, in an agreement that establishes low levels of forces, a given amount of cheating in the first play of the game could have dramatically different implications than cheating of the same magnitude once the renewed arms race has continued through many plays. In addition, because a war could stop the repetition of the game, a model that includes the possibility of war after each play of the game might capture more of what we care about. The probability of war after each move would depend on the countries' military capabilities at that stage of the race, thereby reflecting the cumulative nature of the arms race. Powell, "Absolute and Relative Gains in International Relations Theory" develops this type of model for cooperation on trade issues. This type of model would be unnecessary, however, if states' preferences for each outcome incorporate their assessment of the probability of war as an element of their security.

86. On this possibility and complications see David M. Kreps, *A Course in Microeconomic Theory* (Princeton, N.J.: Princeton University Press, 1990), pp. 503–515. Whether it is a stag hunt or a prisoners' dilemma depends on the cost of being cheated in a single play and on the country's discount rate. The intuition is as follows: assuming a prisoner's dilemma for each iteration of the game, although a country can do better than mutual cooperation by cheating on the first move, it does less well than mutual cooperation on each following move. If the first move is not valued much more than future moves (that is, if the discount rate is sufficiently low), then eventually the costs suffered in all following moves will outweigh the gains of taking advantage in the first move. In effect, the prospect of restarting and prosecuting the race is sufficient to deter initial cheating.

cooperation feasible.[87] In contrast, contingent realism leaves open the question of whether institutions will play a role in making cooperation possible.[88] Although the prospects for cooperation vary with the quality of information about cheating, whether states need to cooperate to make this information available varies greatly with the specific case. For example, the invention of satellites made available information that was critical for strategic arms agreements, but required little cooperation. Moreover, even when cooperation is required, *ad hoc* agreements, which would not by themselves count as institutions,[89] could provide the necessary information.

Further, the type of institutions in question—those that provide information and reduce transaction costs—do not pose a problem for structural realism. Nothing about the roles performed by this type of institution conflicts with structural realism's basic assumptions. States remain the key actors, and anarchy remains unchanged; from this perspective the role played by these institutions is modest. If institutions of this type would make cooperation desirable, then structural realism predicts that states would create them for essentially the same reason that under certain conditions they should pursue advances in technology or increases in force size: these policies would enhance their military capabilities. The more ambitious purposes of institutions—for example, changing states' motives from self-interest to altruism, instilling confidence in benign shifts in motives, or eliminating anarchy by granting tremendous control to an international authority—appear to violate structural realism's core assumptions or its basic insights. But the debate between neorealists and neoinstitutionalists is not primarily over these more ambitious institutions. Therefore, if there is really anything to disagree over, this debate needs to be refocused.

---

87. Key works include Keohane, *After Hegemony;* Robert Axelrod and Robert O. Keohane, "Achieving Cooperation under Anarchy: Strategies and Institutions," in Oye, *Cooperation Under Anarchy;* and Krasner, ed., *International Regimes.* The relationship between the literatures on regimes and institutions and that on structural realism is complex, because although their assumptions are not logically inconsistent, their connotations are different. See Stephen D. Krasner, "Global Communications and National Power: Life on the Pareto Frontier," *World Politics,* Vol. 43, No. 3 (April 1991), pp. 360–362, who explains that, "the connotation of a research program suggests which questions are most important, what kind of evidence should be gathered, and, often tacitly, which issues should be ignored."

88. Keohane seems to waver on this issue, sometimes arguing only that institutions help make cooperation possible, while elsewhere suggesting the much stronger position that cooperation is possible only when institutions are present. For example, *After Hegemony,* p. 245: "Institutions are necessary, even on these restrictive premises, in order to achieve *state* purposes"; see also pp. 13, 78, and 245–247.

89. On the distinction between *ad hoc* agreements and institutions see Keohane, *After Hegemony,* pp. 51–54.

Contingent realism helps us to understand the confusion. The standard structural-realist argument predicted less cooperation than structural realism should have, leaving a gap that was filled by institutionalist arguments, which purported to diverge from structural realism.[90] In effect, contingent realism reclaims much of the territory that the standard argument gave to neoinstitutionalists.

However, more is at issue than deciding which arguments belong to which theories, because contingent realism identifies the possibility of extensive cooperation without focusing on institutions. This is not because structural realism finds that institutions do not matter. Rather, contingent realism sees institutions as the product of the same factors—states' interests and the constraints imposed by the system—that influence whether states should cooperate. Consequently, it sees institutions not as having much explanatory power of their own, but instead as part of what is being explained. Structural realism can, therefore, provide a partial foundation for a theory of international institutions.

Implications for Structural-realist Arguments

Contingent realism has a number of implications for the study and application of structural theories. First, because contingent realism predicts cooperation under certain conditions and competition under others, a structural-realist case against cooperation must demonstrate that the conditions necessary for cooperation have not occurred or will not occur in the future. This empirical assessment should be a key component of the argument explaining the prevalence of international competition. However, the standard structural-realist case about the competitive nature of international politics has not been built on this type of evidence.[91] These arguments are therefore incomplete; whether their conclusions are nevertheless correct remains an open question.

---

90. For example, Robert Keohane, "Institutionalist Theory and the Realist Challenge After the Cold War," in Baldwin, *Neorealism and Neoinstitutionalism*, p. 277, states that "institutionalism accepts the assumptions of realism about state motivation and lack of common enforcement power in world politics, but argues that *where common interests exist,* realism is too pessimistic about the prospects for cooperation and the role of institutions."

91. Nevertheless, the debate over the competitive policies that preceded World War I can be read from this perspective with Scott D. Sagan, "1914 Revisited: Allies, Offense, and Instability," *International Security,* Vol. 11, No. 2 (Fall 1986), pp. 151–176, arguing the greater explanatory power of structural explanations, and Van Evera, "The Cult of the Offensive and the Origins of the First World War," and Jack Snyder, *The Ideology of the Offensive: Military Decision Making and the Disasters of 1914* (Ithaca, N.Y.: Cornell University Press, 1984), emphasizing the shortcomings.

Second, development of an improved structural-realist baseline improves our ability to explore the value of alternative explanations for competitive and cooperative policies.[92] For example, since contingent realism predicts cooperation in certain cases, alternative and complementary explanations for cooperation—for example, institutions and regimes—could become less compelling. On the other hand, in cases where contingent realism predicts extensive cooperation but little occurs, other theories that explain competition become more important. A variety of important possibilities have received extensive attention—for example, that greedy motives, in addition to insecurity, make cooperation less likely if not impossible, and that a variety of individual and state-level misperceptions could lead countries to pursue undesirable competition.[93] Our ability to compare the explanatory strength of these theories depends on having established a structural-realist baseline that explains cooperation, as well as competition, and the conditions under which each is predicted.

Third, because contingent realism identifies countervailing pressures, it will, at least sometimes, not clearly prescribe either competitive or cooperative policies. In these cases, other levels of analysis will necessarily play a more important role in explaining state behavior. Structural pressures will bound the possibilities, while leaving states with substantial choice between more cooperative and more competitive approaches. Although the levels-of-analysis debate is often viewed as a competition between different levels of explanation, this argument suggests that they are often necessarily complementary. A related point focuses on implications for policy analysis: when structural arguments do not provide clear guidance, the choice between cooperative and competitive policies could hinge on the anticipated effects of various policy options on the opponent's domestic politics.[94]

Fourth, contrary to what appears to be the conventional wisdom, structural realism, properly understood, has more trouble explaining the competitive military policies the superpowers pursued during the latter half of the Cold War than it does explaining the less competitive policies that have followed it.

---

92. Noting the importance of a "rationalist baseline," although focusing on different issues, is Fearon, "Threats to Use Force," chap. 2.

93. On individual misperceptions see Jervis, *Perception and Misperception in International Politics;* on national-level explanations see Snyder, *Myths of Empire,* and Van Evera, "Causes of War."

94. On the interaction between international policy and domestic politics see Peter Gourevitch, "The Second Image Reversed: The International Sources of Domestic Politics," *International Organization,* Vol. 32, No. 4 (Autumn 1978); Jack Snyder, "International Leverage on Soviet Domestic Change," *World Politics,* Vol. 42, No. 1 (October 1989), pp. 1–30; and Glaser, "Political Consequences of Military Strategy," pp. 519–525.

Because structural realism is commonly understood to predict highly competitive international relations, the end of the Cold War was interpreted as a severe defeat for structural-realist theories and as a boost for unit-level, country-specific theories. For the same reason, some analysts argued that even the limited cooperation that did occur during the Cold War could not easily be explained by structural realism.[95] Others argued that the limited contribution of arms control to slowing the superpowers' military buildups and reducing the probability of war provides support for the standard structural-realist claim that cooperation can play only a marginal role in major powers' security policies.[96]

However, contingent realism suggests that it is the competition that occurred during the latter half of the Cold War that poses the more serious challenge to structural realism properly understood. The security dilemma facing the United States and Soviet Union was greatly reduced, if not entirely eliminated, by the superpowers' acquisition of assured destruction capabilities, which appeared virtually certain to occur by the mid-1960s at the latest: the superpowers' deployment of large survivable nuclear arsenals established clear defense-dominance, and the technology of nuclear weapon delivery systems and various types of offensive counterforce provided the opportunity to distinguish offense and defense.[97] At the same time, bipolarity reduced the complexity of the arms control agreements that were required to slow competition. Under these conditions, instead of a marginal role, contingent realism predicts a major role for arms control or other non-competitive policies. The nuclear arms race should have ground to a halt and the full spectrum of the most threatening nuclear forces should have been limited either by arms control agreements or unilaterally. Thus, rather than providing support, the continuing military competition cuts against structural realism and must be explained by other theories.

In addition, the U.S. need to protect Western Europe should have been seriously questioned, if not terminated, since the United States would have been able to protect its homeland against a conventional attack by a European

---

95. For example, Weber, "Realism, Detente and Nuclear Weapons."

96. See, for example, John J. Mearsheimer, "Correspondence: Back to the Future, Part II: International Relations Theory and Post–Cold War Europe" *International Security*, Vol. 15, No. 2 (Fall 1990), p. 197, footnote 6; in disagreeing with Mearsheimer on this point I do not intend to endorse the position he is arguing against—that institutions necessarily play a major role in security cooperation.

97. This conclusion depends on judgments about U.S. requirements for counterforce to extend deterrence and on implications for the security dilemma facing the United States. See Glaser, *Analyzing Strategic Nuclear Policy*, pp. 94–99, 207–256.

hegemon.[98] Likewise, the Soviet need to control Eastern Europe should have been greatly reduced or eliminated, since the Soviet Union would have been able to deter a Western invasion without using Eastern Europe as a security buffer. Thus, it is the ending of the Cold War rather than the latter half of the Cold War that is in many ways easier for structural realism to explain.[99]

A fifth implication of contingent realism is that, contrary to the standard interpretation, structural-realist analysis offers generally optimistic predictions about the future of conflict between Europe's major powers. For example, because states pursue security, not advantages in relative power, structural realism does not predict that the West will try to take advantage of current Russian weakness. This is fortunate because military competition and a lack of economic cooperation would risk an increase in future threats to Western security: Russia already has large nuclear forces and is likely eventually to regain economic strength and with it the wherewithal to maintain large modern conventional forces. Competitive Western policies designed to keep Russia down are likely to be counterproductive, leaving Russia with enormous military capability, while signaling that the West is a threat to Russian economic and political well-being. By contrast, the cooperative policies the West is now pursuing—providing economic support, continuing with arms control instead of launching an arms race, and coordinating on foreign policy—hold better prospects for advancing its long-term security interests.

In addition, contingent realism finds that security-driven concern over relative economic gains should not damage trading relations among Western Europe's major powers, and between the United States and these countries, and therefore should not be a source of political tension. The large defensive advantages provided by nuclear weapons should dwarf any security risk that might otherwise result from advantages in relative economic growth. This is especially true since Germany is the focus of fears about disproportionate economic growth, but the other major Western powers have nuclear weapons.

Furthermore, this analysis suggests that the dangers of a shift to multipolarity in Europe have been exaggerated because offense-defense considerations have not been adequately integrated with polarity arguments. Many of the dangers that can be generated by multipolarity do not arise when defense has

---

98. Robert J. Art, "A Defensible Defense: America's Grand Strategy After the Cold War," *International Security*, Vol. 15, No. 4 (Spring 1991), pp. 11–23; Charles L. Glaser and George W. Downs, "Defense Policy: U.S. Role in Europe and Nuclear Strategy," in Oye, Lieber, and Rothchild, *Eagle in a New World*, pp. 72–78.
99. For elements of such an argument, see Daniel Deudney and G. John Ikenberry, "The International Sources of Soviet Change," *International Security*, Vol. 16, No. 3 (Winter 1991/92), pp. 74–118.

a large advantage:[100] uncertainties about whether allies will meet their commitments matter less because countries can maintain adequate deterrent capabilities on their own; increases in the miscalculation of capabilities will be smaller because capabilities are less sensitive to differences in the size and quality of forces; and the ability of major powers to gain military superiority by ganging up against other major powers is greatly reduced if not eliminated.[101] Because nuclear weapons provide very large advantages for the defense, a multipolar Europe can largely avoid these problems.

Finally, this analysis also indicates a likely source of tension. Current nuclear powers will face conflicting pressures if other major or intermediate powers—most obviously, Germany and Ukraine—decide they need nuclear weapons. On the one hand, structural arguments hold that the nuclear powers should welcome the security that nuclear weapons can provide to other major powers. On the other hand, the acquisition of nuclear capabilities will reduce the ability of current nuclear powers to deter conventional attacks, or at least their confidence in their abilities,[102] and might increase the damage they would suffer if war occurs. At least initially, therefore, proliferation is likely to be an unwelcome change and to strain relations in Europe. Fortunately, there is a readily available solution for avoiding these strains in the case of Germany. Preserving NATO, and thereby U.S. security guarantees to Germany, should essentially eliminate Germany's need for nuclear weapons.[103] Unfortunately, there is no comparable solution for Ukraine's security requirements.[104]

In closing, contingent realism paints a picture that diverges dramatically from that offered by the standard structural-realist argument. Instead of a strong propensity toward security competition, we find that states' choices

---

100. Even without including the offense-defense balance, the overall deductive case against multipolarity is mixed; see Stephen Van Evera, "Primed for Peace: Europe After the Cold War," *International Security*, Vol. 15, No. 3 (Winter 1990/91), pp. 33–40. For a different challenge to the explanatory value of polarity arguments see Hopf, "Polarity, the Offense-Defense Balance and War."

101. Mearsheimer, "Back to the Future," notes these points but does not fully integrate them into his predictions about the shift to multipolarity; Waltz, "The Emerging Structure of International Politics," p. 74, agrees that nuclear weapons transform the implications of multipolarity.

102. The argument here follows the logic of the stability-instability paradox. There is, however, a sound argument that nuclear powers should not be very worried about their ability to deter; see Robert Jervis, *The Meaning of the Nuclear Revolution* (Ithaca, N.Y.: Cornell University Press, 1989), pp. 19–22.

103. I present the case for NATO in Glaser, "Why NATO is Still Best: Future Security Arrangements for Europe," *International Security*, Vol. 18, No. 1 (Summer 1993), pp. 5–50.

104. For competing views on Ukrainian proliferation see John J. Mearsheimer, "The Case for a Ukrainian Nuclear Deterrent," and Steven E. Miller, "The Case Against a Ukrainian Nuclear Deterrent," both in *Foreign Affairs*, Vol. 72, No. 3 (Summer 1993), pp. 50–66 and 67–80.

between cooperation and competition are highly conditional, with no general preference for competition. This conclusion flows from the same assumptions that are employed in the standard structural-realist analysis. However, by eliminating the bias in that analysis, integrating offense-defense considerations to determine how much and what types of military capability countries can generate from their power, and explaining how military policies can signal valuable information about motives, contingent realism corrects a variety of shortcomings. It provides a set of conditional structural-realist predictions that improve our ability to explore past cooperation and competition, are necessary for assessing competing explanations, and provide better guidance for designing future policies.

Part II:
Democracy and War

How Liberalism Produces Democratic Peace

John M. Owen

The proposition that democracies seldom if ever go to war against one another has nearly become a truism. The "democratic peace" has attracted attention for a number of reasons. It is "the closest thing we have to an empirical law in the study of international relations," reports one scholar.[1] It poses an apparent anomaly to realism, the dominant school of security studies. And it has become an axiom of U.S. foreign policy. "Democracies don't attack each other," President Clinton declared in his 1994 State of the Union address, meaning that "ultimately the best strategy to insure our security and to build a durable peace is to support the advance of democracy elsewhere." Clinton has called democratization the "third pillar" of his foreign policy.[2]

The democratic peace proposition is vulnerable in at least three ways, however. First, it contains two inherent ambiguities: How does one define democracy? What counts as a war? The slipperiness of these terms provides a temptation to tautology: to define them so as to safeguard the proposition. Indeed, some challengers to the proposition claim that democracies have been at war with each other several times.[3] A second challenge is that the

John M. Owen is a fellow at the Center for International Security and Arms Control at Stanford University.

This article was written under the auspices of the Center for International Affairs at Harvard University. The author wishes to thank the Olin Institute for Strategic Studies for its generous support. He also wishes to thank Robert Art, Michael Desch, Gil Merom, Daniel Philpott, Randall Schweller, and David Spiro for comments on a previous draft.

1. Jack S. Levy, "Domestic Politics and War," in Robert I. Rotberg and Theodore K. Rabb, *The Origin and Prevention of Major Wars* (New York: Cambridge University Press, 1989), p. 88. See also Bruce Russett, *Grasping the Democratic Peace: Principles for a Post–Cold War World* (Princeton: Princeton University Press, 1993), pp. 3–23; and James Lee Ray, "Wars between Democracies: Rare or Nonexistent?" *International Interactions*, Vol. 18, No. 3 (Spring 1988), pp. 251–276.
2. "Excerpts from President Clinton's State of the Union Message," *New York Times*, January 26, 1994, p. A17; "The Clinton Administration Begins," *Foreign Policy Bulletin*, Vol. 3, No. 4/5 (January–April 1993), p. 5.
3. See for example Christopher Layne, "Kant or Cant: The Myth of the Democratic Peace," *International Security*, Vol. 19, No. 2 (Fall 1994), pp. 5–49; Kenneth N. Waltz, "The Emerging Structure of International Politics," *International Security*, Vol. 18, No. 2 (Fall 1993), p. 78; Jack Vincent, "Freedom and International Conflict: Another Look," *International Studies Quarterly*, Vol. 31, No. 1 (March 1987), pp. 102–112; and Henry S. Farber and Joanne Gowa, "Polities and Peace," unpublished manuscript, Princeton University, January 11, 1994. Claiming that democracies have never fought one another is Ray, "Wars between Democracies."

International Security, Vol. 19, No. 2 (Fall 1994), pp. 87–125
© 1994 by the President and Fellows of Harvard College and the Massachusetts Institute of Technology.

lack of wars among democracies, even if true, is not surprising. Wars are so rare that random chance could account for the democratic peace, much as it could account for an absence of war among, say, states whose names begin with the letter K.[4] A third critique points out that the democratic peace lacks a convincing theoretical foundation. No one is sure why democracies do not fight one another and yet do fight non-democracies.[5] That we do not really know the causal mechanism behind the democratic peace means we cannot be certain the peace is genuine. It may be an epiphenomenon, a by-product of other causal variables such as those suggested by realist theories of international politics.[6]

In this article I defend the democratic peace proposition by attempting to remedy the last problem. I do not rebut the argument that the proposition is tautological, although it is worth noting that most democratic peace theorists are meticulous in their definitions, and that their critics are also susceptible to the tautological temptation. I also leave aside the "random chance" argument, except to point out with its proponents that democracies also appear more likely to align with one another. Rather, I argue that liberal ideas cause liberal democracies to tend away from war with one another, and that the same ideas prod these states into war with illiberal states. I derived the argument by testing propositions from existing democratic peace theories[7] on historical cases, then using the results to formulate a new theory.

---

4. David Spiro, "The Insignificance of the Liberal Peace," *International Security*, Vol. 19, No. 2 (Fall 1994), pp. 50–86; John J. Mearsheimer, "Back to the Future: Instability in Europe after the Cold War," *International Security*, Vol. 15, No. 1 (Summer 1990), p. 50. Spiro does not believe random chance accounts for war; he also argues that liberal states do tend to align with one another.

5. Melvin Small and J. David Singer, "The War-proneness of Democratic Regimes," *Jerusalem Journal of International Relations*, Vol. 1, No. 4 (Summer 1976), pp. 50–69. R.J. Rummel maintains that democracies are *generally* less prone to war. Rummel, "Libertarianism and International Violence," *Journal of Conflict Resolution*, Vol. 27, No. 1 (March 1983), pp. 27–71.

6. Mearsheimer, "Back to the Future," pp. 48–51; Farber and Gowa, "Polities and Peace," pp. 3–8. See also Michael Desch, "War and State Formation, Peace and State Deformation?" unpublished manuscript, Olin Institute for Strategic Studies, Harvard University, November 1993.

7. See Immanuel Kant, "Perpetual Peace, a Philosophical Sketch," in *Perpetual Peace and Other Essays*, trans. Ted Humphrey (Indianapolis: Hackett Publishing Company, 1983), pp. 107–143; Michael Doyle, "Kant, Liberal Legacies, and Foreign Affairs, Part I," *Philosophy and Public Affairs*, Vol. 12, No. 3 (Summer 1983), pp. 205–235; Doyle, "Liberalism and World Politics," *American Political Science Review*, Vol. 80, No. 4 (December 1986), pp. 1151–1169; Russett, *Grasping the Democratic Peace*; Bruce Bueno de Mesquita and David Lalman, *War and Reason: Domestic and International Imperatives* (New Haven: Yale University Press, 1992), chap. 5; David A. Lake, "Powerful Pacifists: Democratic States and War," *American Political Science Review*, Vol. 86, No. 1 (March 1992), pp. 24–37; Randall L. Schweller, "Domestic Structure and Preventive War: Are

The cases are war-threatening crises involving the United States from the 1790s through World War I.[8]

I define a liberal democracy as a state that instantiates liberal ideas, one where liberalism is the dominant ideology and citizens have leverage over war decisions. That is, liberal democracies are those states with a visible liberal presence, and that feature free speech and regular competitive elections of the officials empowered to declare war. I argue that liberal ideology and institutions work in tandem to bring about democratic peace. Liberals believe that individuals everywhere are fundamentally the same, and are best off pursuing self-preservation and material well-being. Freedom is required for these pursuits, and peace is required for freedom; coercion and violence are counter-productive. Thus all individuals share an interest in peace, and should want war only as an instrument to bring about peace. Liberals believe that democracies seek their citizens' true interests and that thus by definition they are pacific and trustworthy. Non-democracies may be dangerous because they seek other ends, such as conquest or plunder. Liberals thus hold that the national interest calls for accommodation of fellow democracies, but sometimes calls for war with non-democracies.

When liberals run the government, relations with fellow democracies are harmonious. When illiberals govern, relations may be rockier. Even then, if war is threatened with a state that the liberal opposition considers a fellow democracy, liberals agitate to prevent hostilities using the free speech allowed them by law. Illiberal leaders are unable to rally the public to fight, and fear that an unpopular war would lead to their ouster at the next election. On the other hand, if the crisis is with a state believed to be a non-democracy, the leaders may be pushed toward war.

This argument improves on previous accounts of the democratic peace in several ways. First, it grounds liberal ideology in an Enlightenment concept of self-interest. Second, it opens the "black box" of the state to show how democratic structures translate liberal preferences into policy even when

Democracies More Pacific?" *World Politics*, Vol. 44, No. 2 (January 1992), pp. 235–269; T. Clifton Morgan and Sally Howard Campbell, "Domestic Structure, Decisional Constraints, and War: So Why Kant Democracies Fight?" *Journal of Conflict Resolution*, Vol. 35, No. 2 (June 1991), pp. 187–211; R.J. Rummel, *Understanding Conflict and War*, Vol. 4 (Beverly Hills: SAGE Publications, 1974).
8. The crises on which I tested the explanations were: U.S.-Britain 1794–96, U.S.-France 1796–98, U.S.-Britain 1803–12, U.S.-Britain 1845–46, U.S.-Mexico 1845–46, U.S.-Britain 1861–63, U.S.-Spain 1873, U.S.-Chile 1891–92, U.S.-Britain 1895–96, U.S.-Spain 1898, U.S.-Mexico 1914–16, and U.S.-Germany 1916–17. See John M. Owen, "Testing the Democratic Peace: American Diplomatic Crises, 1794–1917," Ph.D. dissertation, Harvard University, 1993.

statesmen are themselves illiberal. Third, it takes into account the importance of perceptions. For my argument to hold, liberals must consider the other state democratic. My argument also answers several criticisms of the democratic peace thesis. It shows that the inadequacy of either democratic structures or norms alone to explain democratic peace does not prove that the democratic peace is spurious. It shows how illiberal leaders of democracies can make threats against one another and yet still be domestically constrained from attacking one another. It explains several supposed exceptions to the democratic peace by taking account of actors' perceptions; for example, the War of 1812 was fought at a time when almost no Americans considered England a democracy.

I begin by briefly reviewing previous theories of democratic peace and attempts to test them. I then summarize the foundations of liberalism and the foreign policy ideology it produces. In so doing, I explore the perceptual aspect of the causal mechanism. Next I describe how democratic institutions make it likely that liberal ideology will influence policy during a war-threatening crisis. I then illustrate the argument in four historical cases: the Franco-American crisis of 1796–98, and the Anglo-American crises of 1803–12, 1861–63, and 1895–96. I answer realist critics of the democratic peace proposition, and suggest possible ways to synthesize realism and liberalism. I conclude by cautioning that although democratic peace is real, threats to liberalism itself mean that it is not a certain precursor to perpetual peace.

Previous Attempts to Explain Democratic Peace

Typically, theories of the democratic peace are divided into *structural* and *normative* theories. Structural accounts attribute the democratic peace to the institutional constraints within democracies. Chief executives in democracies must gain approval for war from cabinet members or legislatures, and ultimately from the electorate. Normative theory locates the cause of the democratic peace in the ideas or norms held by democracies. Democracies believe it would be unjust or imprudent to fight one another. They practice the norm of compromise with each other that works so well within their own borders.[9]

---

9. Some explanations, including those of Kant, Doyle, and Rummel (fn. 7), contain both structural and normative elements. However, these writers disagree as to what constitutes a democracy and why they forgo wars against one another; they do not take perceptions into account; and they underspecify how democratic structures work.

On balance, statistical tests of these two theories have yielded no clear winner.[10] Moreover, although quantitative studies provide a necessary part of our evaluation of these theories by identifying correlations, by their nature they cannot tell us the full story. First, they often must use crude proxy variables that are several steps removed from the phenomena being measured.[11] Second, they infer processes from statistical relationships between these variables, but do not examine those processes directly. Overcoming these limitations requires looking at the actual processes in historical cases, or "process tracing."[12] Joseph Nye writes that democratic peace "need[s] exploration via detailed case studies to look at what actually happened in particular instances."[13] One way to carry out such tests is to ask: If the theory is true, then what else should we expect to observe happening?[14]

In carrying out such process-tracing on a dozen cases, I uncovered problems in both structural and normative accounts. I found that democratic structures were nearly as likely to drive states to war as to restrain them from it. Cabinets, legislatures, and publics were often more belligerent than the government heads they were supposed to constrain. I found that the normative theory neglected to take perceptions into account. Often states which today's researchers consider democratic did not consider each other democratic. Thus the anticipated normative check on war was frequently absent.[15]

---

10. Studies favoring some form of structural theory include Bueno de Mesquita and Lalman, *War and Reason;* and Morgan and Campbell, "So Why Kant Democracies Fight?" Favoring normative theory are Zeev Maoz and Bruce Russett, "Normative and Structural Causes of Democratic Peace, 1946–1986" *American Political Science Review,* Vol. 87, No. 3 (September 1993), pp. 624–638; and William J. Dixon, "Democracy and the Peaceful Settlement of Conflict," *American Political Science Review,* Vol. 88, No. 1 (March 1994), pp. 14–32.

11. For example, Maoz and Russett infer democratic norms from regime stability and from levels of internal social and political violence. Maoz and Russett, "Normative and Structural Causes," p. 630.

12. Alexander George and Timothy J. McKeown, "Case Studies and Theories of Organizational Decision Making," in *Advances in Information Processing in Organizations,* Vol. 2 (Greenwich, Conn.: JAI Press, 1985); see also David Dessler, "Beyond Correlations: Toward a Causal Theory of War," *International Studies Quarterly,* Vol. 35, No. 3 (September 1991), pp. 337–345; James Lee Ray, *Democracy and International Conflict: An Evaluation of the Democratic Peace Proposition* (Columbia: University of South Carolina Press, 1995), chapter 4.

13. Joseph S. Nye, Jr., *Understanding International Conflicts* (New York: HarperCollins, 1993), p. 40.

14. See Gary King, Robert O. Keohane, and Sidney Verba, *Designing Social Inquiry: Scientific Inference in Qualitative Research* (Princeton: Princeton University Press, 1994).

15. See Owen, "Testing the Democratic Peace." For a summary of the findings, see Owen, "Is the Democratic Peace a Matter of Luck?" paper presented at the annual meeting of the American Political Science Association, Washington, D.C., September 1993.

These findings do not kill the democratic peace thesis. Logically, that neither structures nor norms by themselves explain the democratic peace does not imply that the two in tandem cannot do so. The structure/norms typology used by the literature is used merely for analytic convenience. If in trying to determine whether an automobile will run I separate its gasoline from its engine, then find that neither component by itself suffices to run the automobile, I cannot then conclude that the car will not run. It could still be that liberal ideology motivates some citizens against war with a fellow democracy, and democratic institutions allow this ideology to affect foreign policy.

Some of the cases suggest such a synergy, I found, but only when the actors' perceptions are taken into account. For example, most Americans in the nineteenth century thought in terms of *republics* and *monarchies* rather than *democracies* and *non-democracies*. When in 1873 the United States nearly went to war with Spain during the *Virginius* affair, many Americans, including the secretary of state, explicitly argued for peace precisely because Spain was at the time a republic.[16] Again in 1892, when President Benjamin Harrison asked Congress to declare war on Chile after the *Baltimore* affair, many Americans expressed opposition based on the fact that Chile was a republic.[17]

These considerations combine with quantitative evidence to suggest that democratic peace is a genuine phenomenon that simply needs a better explanation. Multivariate analysis indicates that it is not the product of some omitted variable. In separate studies, Bremer and Maoz and Russett found that democracy as an independent variable still had explanatory power after controlling for an impressive array of competitors. Variables suggested by realism such as relative power, alliance status, and the presence of a hegemon did not erase the effects of democracy.[18]

---

16. See especially the attitude of Hamilton Fish, the U.S. secretary of state, in Allan Nevins, *Hamilton Fish: The Inner History of the Grant Administration* (New York: Dodd, Mead, 1936), pp. 668–674. The fullest treatment of the crisis is in Richard H. Bradford, *The "Virginius" Affair* (Boulder: Colorado Associated University Press, 1980).

17. E.g., in opposing Harrison, Representative William Breckinridge of Kentucky told Congress: "War . . . is only the last resort, especially so when the war must be with a republic like our own, anxious for liberty, desiring to maintain constitutional freedom, seeking progress by means of that freedom." 52d Congress, 1st sess., *Congressional Record*, Vol. 23 (January 26, 1892), p. 550. See also Joyce S. Goldberg, *The "Baltimore" Affair* (Lincoln: University of Nebraska Press, 1986).

18. Stuart Bremer, "Democracy and Militarized Interstate Conflict, 1816–1965," *International Interactions*, Vol. 18, No. 3 (Spring 1993), pp. 231–249; Zeev Maoz and Bruce Russett, "Alliances, Contiguity, Wealth, and Political Stability: Is the Lack of Conflict between Democracies a Statistical Artifact?" *International Interactions*, Vol. 17, No. 3 (Spring 1992), pp. 245–267.

As explained at the end of this article, however, I do not argue that power politics has no force in determining the foreign policies of liberal democracies. Rather, I describe a second force—liberalism—which prods democracies toward peace with each other, and toward war with non-democracies. In looking within the state, I suggest domestic foundations for those studies that have explored the international systemic aspects of the democratic peace.[19]

Liberalism as the Cause of Democratic Peace

Liberal ideas are the source—the independent variable—behind the distinctive foreign policies of liberal democracies. These ideas give rise to two intervening variables, liberal ideology and domestic democratic institutions, which shape foreign policy. Liberal ideology prohibits war against liberal democracies, but sometimes calls for war against illiberal states. Democratic institutions allow these drives to affect foreign policy and international relations.[20]

LIBERAL IDEAS

Liberalism is universalistic and tolerant. Liberal political theory, such as that of Hobbes, Locke, Rousseau, and Kant, typically begins with abstract man in a state of nature in which he is equal to all other men. Although beliefs and cultures may differ, liberalism says, all persons share a fundamental

---

19. On the level of the international system, this model is compatible with others which essentially present democracies as constrained (for various reasons) to prevent disputes among themselves from turning into wars. For Bruce Bueno de Mesquita and David Lalman, for example, democracies know each other to be prevented by domestic checks and balances from initiating war. This knowledge makes cooperation the rational choice in the "international interactions game." At the same time, democracies know that non-democracies, which are unconstrained, have the same knowledge and are prone to exploit them for that reason. Democracies thus may find it rational pre-emptively to attack non-democracies for fear of being taken advantage of. See Bueno de Mesquita and Lalman, *War and Reason*, chap. 5; see also William J. Dixon, "Democracy and the Peaceful Settlement"; and D. Marc Kilgour, "Domestic Political Structure and War Behavior: A Game-Theoretic Approach," *Journal of Conflict Resolution*, Vol. 35, No. 2 (June 1991), pp. 266–284.

20. See Judith Goldstein and Robert O. Keohane, *Ideas and Foreign Policy: Beliefs, Institutions, and Political Change* (Ithaca: Cornell University Press, 1993), pp. 13–17. See also Spiro, "Insignificance," for the importance of liberal conceptions of national interest.

interest in self-preservation and material well-being.[21] There is thus a harmony of interests among all individuals. To realize this harmony, each individual must be allowed to follow his or her own preferences as long as they do not detract from another's freedom. People thus need to cooperate by tolerating one another and forgoing coercion and violence.[22] Since true interests harmonize, the more people are free, the better off all are. Liberalism is cosmopolitan, positing that all persons, not just certain subjects of one's own state, should be free. The spread of liberalism need not be motivated by altruism. It is entirely in the individual's self-interest to cooperate.[23] In sum, liberalism's ends are life and property, and its means are liberty and toleration.

Liberals believe that not all persons or nations are free, however. Two things are needed for freedom. First, persons or nations must be themselves enlightened, aware of their interests and how they should be secured.[24] Second, people must live under enlightened political institutions which allow their true interests to shape politics.[25] Liberals disagree over which political institutions are enlightened. Kant stressed a strict separation of the executive from the legislative power.[26] For most Americans in the nineteenth century,

---

21. John Locke, for example, writes: "The great and *chief end* therefore, of Mens uniting into Commonwealths, and putting themselves under Government, *is the Preservation of their Property.*" Locke, *Second Treatise of Government*, chap. 9, para. 124. Locke says "property" includes one's "Life, Liberty, and Estate"; ibid., chap. 7, para. 87. In Locke, *Two Treatises of Government*, ed. Peter Laslett (New York: Cambridge University Press, 1988), pp. 350–351, 323.

22. Immanuel Kant, who deduced a zone of peace among republics in the 1790s, argues that over time, the devastation of conflict teaches them that it is best to cooperate with others so as to realize their full capacities. See for example Kant, "Idea for a Universal History with a Cosmopolitan Intent," in *Perpetual Peace*, pp. 31–34. See also Locke, *Second Treatise*, chap. 2, para. 5, p. 270. By "harmony," I do not imply that uncoordinated selfish action by each automatically results in all being better off (a "natural" harmony). All individuals are interested in peace, but enlightenment, the right institutions, and cooperation are necessary to bring peace about. On the distinction between uncoordinated harmony and cooperation, see Robert O. Keohane, *After Hegemony: Cooperation and Discord in the World Political Economy* (Princeton: Princeton University Press, 1984), pp. 49–64.

23. Kant says a republic is possible "even for a people comprised of devils (if only they possess understanding)." Kant, *Perpetual Peace*, p. 124. See also Alexis de Tocqueville, "How the Americans Combat Individualism by the Doctrine of Self-interest Properly Understood," *Democracy in America*, ed. J.P. Mayer, trans. George Lawrence (New York: Harper and Row, 1988), part 2, chap. 8, pp. 525–528.

24. See Kant, "An Answer to the Question: What Is Enlightenment?" in Kant, *Perpetual Peace*, pp. 41–48.

25. For a brief history of the view that selfish rulers rather than ordinary people are responsible for war, see Michael Howard, *War and the Liberal Conscience* (New Brunswick, N.J.: Rutgers University Press, 1978), pp. 14–18.

26. Kant, "Perpetual Peace," pp. 112–115. Kant calls such states "republics," but by his definition monarchies may be republics.

only republics (non-monarchies) were "democracies" or "free countries."[27] Today, Westerners tend to trust states that allow meaningful political competition. Central to all these criteria is the requirement that the people have some leverage over their rulers. That is, nineteenth-century republics and today's liberal democracies share the essential liberal goal of preventing tyranny over individual freedom.

LIBERAL FOREIGN POLICY IDEOLOGY

Liberalism gives rise to an ideology that distinguishes states primarily according to regime type: in assessing a state, liberalism first asks whether it is a liberal democracy or not.[28] This is in contrast to neorealism, which distinguishes states according to capabilities. Liberalism, in looking to characteristics other than power, is similar to most other systems of international thought, including communism, fascism, and monarchism.[29]

Liberalism is, however, more tolerant of its own kind than these other systems. Once liberals accept a foreign state as a liberal democracy, they adamantly oppose war against that state. The rationale follows from liberal premises. *Ceteris paribus*, people are better off without war, because it is costly and dangerous. War is called for only when it would serve liberal ends—i.e., when it would most likely enhance self-preservation and well-being. This can only be the case when the adversary is not a liberal democracy. Liberal democracies are believed reasonable, predictable, and trustworthy, because they are governed by their citizens' true interests, which harmonize with all individuals' true interests around the world. Liberals believe that they understand the intentions of foreign liberal democracies, and that those intentions are always pacific toward fellow liberal democracies.

---

27. See for example David M. Fitzsimons, "Tom Paine's New World Order: Idealistic Internationalism in the Ideology of Early American Foreign Relations," unpublished manuscript, University of Michigan, 1994.

28. I have benefited from conversations with Sean Lynn-Jones on many of these points. For an attempt to reformulate liberal international relations theory based on distinctions among domestic political orders, see Andrew Moravcsik, "Liberalism and International Relations Theory," Working Paper, Center for International Affairs, Harvard University, 1992.

29. Traditional realists such as E.H. Carr and Hans Morgenthau, ancient Greeks, medieval Muslims, and communists all see state-level distinctions as important. Carr, *The Twenty Years' Crisis* (London: Macmillan, 1946), p. 236; Morgenthau, *Politics among Nations*, 3d ed. (New York: Alfred A. Knopf, 1965), p. 131; Sohail Hashmi, "The Sixth Pillar: Jihad and the Ethics of War and Peace in Islam," Ph.D. dissertation, Harvard University, 1994; Robert Jervis, "Hypotheses on Misperception," *World Politics*, Vol. 20, No. 3 (April 1968), p. 467.

Again, it is not necessary that liberals be motivated by justice, only by self-interest.[30]

Illiberal states, on the other hand, are viewed *prima facie* as unreasonable, unpredictable, and potentially dangerous. These are states either ruled by despots, or with unenlightened citizenries. Illiberal states may seek illiberal ends such as conquest, intolerance, or impoverishment of others. Liberal democracies do not automatically fight all illiberal states in an endless crusade to spread freedom, however. Usually, they estimate that the costs of liberalizing another state are too high, often because the illiberal state is too powerful.[31] Liberal democracies do not fully escape the imperatives of power politics.

THE IMPORTANCE OF PERCEPTIONS. That a state has enlightened citizens and liberal-democratic institutions, however, is not sufficient for it to belong to the democratic peace: if its peer states do not believe it is a liberal democracy, they will not treat it as one. History shows many cases where perceptions tripped up democratic peace. For example, as Christopher Layne demonstrates, the French after World War I did not consider Germany a fellow liberal democracy, even though Germans were governed under the liberal Weimar constitution. The salient fact about Germany, in the French view of 1923, was not that it had a liberal constitution, but that it was peopled by Germans, who had recently proven themselves most unenlightened and were now reneging on reparations agreements.[32]

Thus, for the liberal mechanism to prevent a liberal democracy from going to war against a foreign state, liberals must consider the foreign state a liberal democracy. Most explanations of democratic peace posit that democracies recognize one another and refuse to fight on that basis; but the researchers never test this assumption.[33] In fact, often it does not hold. The refusal to

---

30. Here my argument differs from that of Michael Doyle, who writes that "domestically just republics, which rest on consent, presume foreign republics to be also consensual, just, and therefore deserving of accommodation." Doyle, "Kant, Part I," p. 230.
31. Compare this with the Union's attitude toward Britain in the Civil War, described below. For explanations that see democratic prudence as more central to the democratic peace, see Schweller, "Democracy and Preventive War"; and Lake, "Powerful Pacifists."
32. See Layne, "The Myth of the Democratic Peace." More research needs to be done on the question of how a state with democratic institutions comes to be regarded by its peers as liberal.
33. For example, Bueno de Mesquita and Lalman assert: "The presence of the constraint is not alone sufficient to ensure cooperation or harmony. However, it is common knowledge whether a given state is a liberal democracy." In *War and Reason*, p. 156. The same assumption is used (less explicitly) by Doyle, "Liberalism and World Politics"; Russett, *Grasping the Democratic Peace;* Ray, "Wars between Democracies"; Lake, "Powerful Pacifists"; Schweller, "Domestic Structure and Preventive War"; and Rummel, "Libertarianism and International Violence."

take this into account keeps the democratic peace literature from understanding apparent exceptions to democratic peace, such as the War of 1812, the American Civil War, and the Spanish-American War.[34] My argument explains these apparent exceptions. As shown below, most Americans did not consider England democratic in 1812 because England was a monarchy. In 1861, Southern slavery prevented liberals in the Union from considering the Confederacy a liberal democracy.[35] Almost no Americans considered Spain a democracy in 1898. To determine which states belong to the pacific union, we must do more than simply examine their constitutions. We must examine how the liberals themselves define democracy.

Skeptics would immediately counter that the subjectivity inherent in terms such as "democracy" and "despotism" means that these concepts have no independent causal force. When leaders want war, they simply define the rival state as despotic; when they want peace, they define the friend as democratic. Thus Joseph Stalin became "Uncle Joe" when Americans needed to justify fighting alongside the Soviet Union against Germany in World War II.

In fact, however, democracy and despotism are not wholly subjective. Liberals have relatively stable conceptions of what a democracy looks like. In the nineteenth century, most Americans applauded when other states became republican, and anticipated friendly relations with those states. More recently, the attitude of the Western democracies toward Russia shows the independent power that liberalization has on expectations of hostility. The failed August 1991 coup and subsequent breakup of the Soviet Union did not cause the vast Soviet nuclear arsenal to disappear. Yet James Baker, then U.S. secretary of state, announced on February 5, 1992:

The Cold War has ended, and we now have a chance to forge a democratic peace, an enduring peace built on shared values—democracy and political and economic freedom. The strength of these values in Russia and the other

---

34. Kenneth Waltz asserts that the War of 1812 and the Civil War were fought between democracies; Waltz, "Emerging Structure," p. 78. David Lake, who argues for the democratic peace proposition, calls the Spanish-American War a war between democracies. Lake, "Powerful Pacifists," p. 33.

35. As the nineteenth century reached its midpoint, slavery came to be seen by such Southern figures as John C. Calhoun as "the most safe and stable basis for free institutions in the world." It mattered a great deal to Northerners that the South was illiberal. Thus the *New York Tribune* in 1855 could write: "We are not one people. We are two peoples. We are a people for Freedom and a people for Slavery. Between the two, conflict is inevitable." See Eric Foner, *Politics and Ideology in the Age of the Civil War* (New York: Oxford University Press, 1980), pp. 40–41, 52–53.

new independent states will be the surest foundation for peace—and the strongest guarantee of our national security—for decades to come.[36]

ILLIBERAL DEMOCRACIES. The importance of liberal ideology is evident from other supposed exceptions to democratic peace. It has been considered a puzzle, for example, that ancient Greek democracies waged war against one another.[37] But Thucydides reveals that the ancient Athenians were not liberal. They valued heroism and conquest over self-preservation and well-being. The Corinthians tell the oligarchical Spartans that they are more sluggish than the Athenians, who "are adventurous beyond their power, and daring beyond their judgment, and in danger they are sanguine. . . . Their bodies they spend ungrudgingly in their country's cause . . . and to them laborious occupation is less of a misfortune than the peace of a quiet life."[38] The Athenian good life consisted in what Charles Taylor calls the warrior ethic.[39] In this world view, all persons are not fundamentally the same, and there is no harmony of interests among them.[40] Ancient democracy as a result is a restive, adventurous, conquering regime, to be trusted by no one.

A similar illiberalism is evident in many "democracies" today. Balkan peoples live in popularly-governed polities; yet they define themselves primarily not as abstract individuals, but according to religious categories: Serbs are Orthodox Christian, Croats are Roman Catholic, and Bosnians are Muslim. The lack of commonality means no democratic peace among these peoples. Iranians live in a state with universal adult suffrage and vigorous parliamentary debate, yet they do not view the world through a liberal lens, where all

---

36. On April 21, 1992, Baker declared, "Real democracies do not go to war with each other." Quoted in Russett, *Grasping the Democratic Peace*, pp. 128–129.
37. See Bruce Russett and William Antholis, "The Imperfect Democratic Peace of Ancient Athens," in Russett, *Grasping the Democratic Peace*, pp. 43–71.
38. Thucydides, *The Peloponnesian War* I, 70, ed. T.E. Wick, trans. Richard Crawley (New York: Random House, 1982), p. 40.
39. "There is . . . a warrior (and later warrior-citizen) morality, where what is valued is strength, courage, and the ability to conceive and execute great deeds, and where life is aimed at fame and glory, and the immortality one enjoys when one's name lives for ever on men's lips." This ethic, dominant in the era of Homer, was still very much alive at the time of Pericles, as evidenced by Plato's arguments against it. Charles Taylor, *Sources of the Self: The Making of the Modern Identity* (Cambridge: Harvard University Press, 1987), pp. 115–118.
40. As Russett and Antholis write, "the citizens of most democratic cities probably did not think of democracy as a trans-Hellenic project, at least at the outset of the Peloponnesian War. The individual liberties central to liberal democracy were not so universalized in the ancient world." Russett, *Grasping the Democratic Peace*, p. 45. See Aristotle, *The Politics*, trans. Carnes Lord (Chicago: University of Chicago Press, 1984), Book I, chaps. 4–6, pp. 39–43 on how certain persons are slaves by nature.

individuals are best off cooperating to pursue self-preservation and well-being. Other new democracies, such as those arising from the ruins of the Soviet Union, may be illiberal as well. If so, democratic peace will not emerge in that area of the world.

DEMOCRATIC INSTITUTIONS

The domestic structures that translate liberal preferences into foreign policy are likewise a product of liberal ideas. Liberalism seeks to actualize the harmony of interests among individuals by insuring that the freedom of each is compatible with the freedom of all. It thus calls for structures that protect the right of each citizen to self-government. Most important for our purposes are those giving citizens leverage over governmental decision makers. Freedom of speech is necessary because it allows citizens to evaluate alternative foreign policies. Regular, competitive elections are necessary because they provide citizens with the possibility of punishing officials who violate their rights. Liberalism says that the people who fight and fund war have the right to be consulted, through representatives they elect, before entering it.[41]

DEMOCRATIC INSTITUTIONS. When those who govern hold the liberal ideology prohibiting war against fellow liberal democracies, then the role of democratic institutions is limited simply to putting these liberals in office. Liberal American presidents have included Thomas Jefferson and Woodrow Wilson. These men sought to implement liberal foreign policies, including harmonious relations with those states they considered liberal and confrontation with those they considered illiberal.

Not everyone in every liberal democracy, however, necessarily holds the liberal ideology. Some may instead be political realists, who view power as more important than freedom. Some others may simply want good relations with economic partners, regardless of regime type.[42] When such illiberals govern liberal democracies, they may lead the nation into disputes with fellow liberal democracies. They can do so because the general public pays little attention to everyday foreign policy.

---

41. "If . . . the consent of the citizenry is required in order to determine whether or not there will be war, it is natural that they consider all its calamities before committing themselves to so risky a game." Kant, "Perpetual Peace," p. 113.

42. An explanation of why not everyone in a regime necessarily holds the dominant ideology is beyond the scope of this article. Here I simply take it as empirically obvious that not all citizens of liberal democracies are liberal, just as not all citizens of communist states are communist.

ELITES AND EVERYDAY FOREIGN POLICY. Day-to-day foreign policy is mostly the province of elites. Ordinary citizens have good reason for ignoring relations with other nations. Since relations with most nations have little perceptible impact on the individual citizen, the expected payoff to each is not worth the time investment.[43] This collective-action problem means that normal foreign policy is delegated to representatives.

In making everyday foreign policy, the main domestic influences on these representatives are elites. Together, representatives and elites form what James Rosenau calls *opinion leaders:* people "who occupy positions which enable them regularly to transmit, either locally or nationally, opinions about any issue to unknown persons outside of their occupational field or about more than one class of issues to unknown professional colleagues." They include "government officials, prominent businessmen, civil servants, journalists, scholars, heads of professional associations, and interest groups."[44] In liberal democracies, these include staunch liberals who always desire to see good relations with fellow liberal democracies, and often desire confrontation with those states they consider illiberal. Without the leverage provided by public attention, the liberal elite has no special advantage over other elites, such as special interests.[45] The state may thereby fall into a crisis with a fellow liberal democracy.

WHEN WAR IS THREATENED: LIBERAL ELITES AND THE PUBLIC. At the point where war is threatened, however, it becomes in the interest of each citizen to pay attention. War costs blood and treasure, and these high costs are felt throughout society. It also requires public mobilization. Those statesmen and elites who want war must persuade public opinion that war is necessary. In democracies, this persuasion typically includes arguments that the adversary state is not democratic. When the prior liberal consensus is that the adversary *is* a liberal democracy, however, these illiberal statesmen find that they cannot mobilize the public.

This is in part because they face strong opposition from liberal opinion leaders. Using the tools allowed them by domestic institutions—the media,

43. This reasoning follows that of Anthony Downs, *An Economic Theory of Democracy* (New York: Harper and Row, 1957), pp. 207–276.
44. James Rosenau, *Public Opinion and Foreign Policy: An Operational Formulation* (New York: Random House, 1961), pp. 35–39; Michael Leigh, *Mobilizing Consent: Public Opinion and American Foreign Policy, 1937–1947* (Westport, Conn.: Greenwood Press, 1976), pp. 4–5.
45. For a theory of how special interests can "hijack" foreign policy, see Jack Snyder, *Myths of Empire: Domestic Politics and International Ambition* (Ithaca: Cornell University Press, 1991), pp. 31–55.

public speeches, rallies, and so on—liberal elites agitate against war with fellow liberal democracies. They prevent illiberal elites from persuading the public that war is necessary.[46] Illiberal statesmen find that war with a liberal democracy would be extremely unpopular. Moreover, they begin to fear electoral ouster if they go to war against a fellow liberal democracy. Even illiberal statesmen are then compelled to act as liberals and resolve the crisis peacefully.[47]

Alternatively, there may be times when liberals desire war with an illiberal state, yet illiberal statesmen oppose such a war. Using the same institutions of free discussion and the threat of electoral punishment, liberals may force their leaders into war. Such was the case in the Spanish-American War.[48]

This part of my argument conforms to recent research on public opinion and foreign policy, which indicates a dialectic among elites, the general public, and policy makers. A number of studies indicate that opinion changes precede policy changes, suggesting that the former cause the latter rather than vice versa.[49] Moreover, a recent work finds that in the 1970s and 1980s the greatest influences on aggregate shifts in U.S. public opinion were television news commentators and experts. For example, television commentators' statements on crises in Vietnam in 1969 and the Middle East in 1974–75 and 1977–78 evidently swayed public opinion. Often these media commentators opposed official governmental policy.[50] Together, these findings suggest that, at least in the United States, an opinion elite at times shapes public positions on issues, thus constraining foreign policy.

Figure 1 illustrates the argument. Liberal ideas form the independent variable. These ideas produce the ideology which prohibits war with fellow liberal democracies and sometimes calls for war with illiberal states. The ideas also give rise to democratic institutions. Working in tandem, the ideology and institutions push liberal democracies toward democratic peace.

---

46. On the importance of free speech to democratic peace, see Stephen Van Evera, "Primed for Peace: Europe After the Cold War," *International Security*, Vol. 15, No. 3 (Winter 1990/91), p. 27.
47. Works that have used the assumption that elected officials value re-election above all else include Downs, *Economic Theory*; and David R. Mayhew, *Congress: The Electoral Connection* (New Haven: Yale University Press, 1974).
48. See John L. Offner, *An Unwanted War: The Diplomacy of the United States and Spain over Cuba, 1895–1898* (Chapel Hill: University of North Carolina Press, 1992).
49. For a summary, see Lawrence R. Jacobs and Robert Y. Shapiro, "Studying Substantive Democracy," *PS*, Vol. 27, No. 1 (March 1994), pp. 9–10.
50. Popular presidents had strong effects, while unpopular ones had little effect. Interestingly, special interest groups usually caused public opinion to move in a *contrary* direction. Benjamin I. Page, Robert Y. Shapiro, and Glenn R. Dempsey, "What Moves Public Opinion," *American Political Science Review*, Vol. 81, No. 1 (March 1987), pp. 23–43.

Figure 1. Causal Pathways of Liberal Democratic Peace.

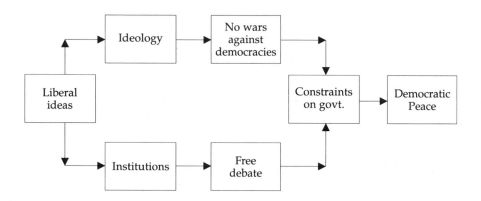

Hypotheses on Democratic Peace

To reiterate, I define liberal democracies as those states that are dominated by liberal ideology, and that feature, in both law and practice, free discussion and regular competitive elections. Signs that a state is dominated by liberalism may be institutional, such as equality of all citizens before the law. Or they may be informal, such as the predominance of appeals to personal freedom, self-preservation, and prosperity in debates about public life. Some states with liberal elements may be undemocratic, such as Great Britain before the 1832 Great Reform Act. Some democratic states may be illiberal, such as the Confederate States of America during the Civil War. Not all liberal democracies will forgo war with one another. A liberal democracy will only avoid war with a state that *it believes to be liberal*.

A causal mechanism such as I describe may be logically coherent yet empirically false. I now turn to the search for clues that this liberal mechanism really exists and works. As I did with previous theories of democratic peace, I ask: If this argument were valid, what would we expect to observe in the foreign policy processes in liberal democracies? I check these expectations or hypotheses against real historical cases. If the hypotheses are falsified—if history does not bear out my expectations—then my argument is like its predecessors inadequate.[51] The hypotheses are:

Liberals will trust states they consider liberal and mistrust those they consider illiberal. I argue that liberal ideology divides the world's states into liberal democracies and illiberal states. Because they share the enlightened ends of self-preservation, material well-being, and liberty, liberal democracies are seen as trustworthy and pacific. States ruled by despots and those populated by unenlightened citizens seek illiberal ends, and are believed potentially dangerous.

When liberals observe a foreign state becoming liberal by their own standards, they will expect pacific relations with it. Although definitions of democracy vary across time and space, these definitions are relatively stable rather than arbitrary. If a state once thought despotic adopts the right institutions, or comes to be dominated by liberals, liberals in other states will begin to trust it more.

Liberals will claim that fellow liberal democracies share their ends, and that illiberal states do not. Specifically, liberals will say that liberal democratic states seek the preservation and well-being of their citizens, that they love peace and freedom, and that they are cooperative. They will say of illiberal states that they seek conquest to the detriment of their citizens' true interests, disdain peace, and are treacherous.

Liberals will not change their assessments of foreign states during crises with those states unless those states change their institutions. When a liberal democracy is embroiled in a dispute with a state it considers a fellow liberal democracy, its liberals will not switch to viewing the state as illiberal. Similarly, when a liberal democracy is in a dispute with a state it considers illiberal, its liberals will not suddenly decide that the state is liberal after all, unless its domestic institutions change. (If this hypothesis is not borne out, the democratic peace is illusory, because power politics or some other force would actually be determining what label liberals attached to foreign states.)

Liberal elites will agitate for their policies during war-threatening crises. In a crisis with a fellow liberal democracy, liberals will use the news media and other fora to persuade leaders and the public to resolve the crisis peacefully. In a crisis with an illiberal state, liberals may agitate in favor of war if they believe it would serve liberal ends.

---

51. See King, Keohane, and Verba, *Designing Social Inquiry*.

During crises, statesmen will be constrained to follow liberal policy. When officials are themselves liberal, they will simply find a way to defuse crises with liberal democracies, or they may escalate them if the other state is illiberal. When officials are not liberal, they will still be pressured by public opinion, which has been aroused by a liberal elite, to forgo war with a liberal democracy; or, if the foreign state is illiberal, they may be spurred into war.

Four Cases

Four historical cases illustrate the argument: Franco-American relations in 1796–98, and Anglo-American relations during 1803–12, 1861–63, and 1895–96. These are four of the twelve cases from which I derived the argument.[52] I chose the twelve original cases because, first, they hold the identity of one state, the United States, constant. The United States has throughout its history been dominated by liberalism and featured free elections. Second, the cases allow the perceptions and governmental systems of the other state in each crisis to vary. In some crises, liberal Americans had previously considered the foreign state liberal; in others, they had not; in still others, opinion was divided. Moreover, in some of the cases the other state was dominated by liberalism and had free elections, and in others it did not. Third, choosing cases from before 1945 allows me to rule out the effects of bipolarity and nuclear weapons, two powerful confounding factors.

I chose these four cases because they have been written about extensively, and my claims are easily tested. The causal factors in my argument also vary across the four. I do not consider France in 1796–98 or Britain in 1803–12 liberal-democratic; but I do consider Britain in 1861–63 and 1895–96 to be so. These cases also point up the importance of perceptions to democratic peace. Most Americans did not consider Britain liberal-democratic in either 1803–12 or 1861–63; and most British did not consider the Union liberal in 1861, but they changed their minds in the fall of 1862. In addition, the three Anglo-American cases have all been cited as evidence *against* democratic peace.[53]

Strictly speaking, one cannot test an argument on the very cases from which it was derived. Such a "test" would be biased in favor of the argument.

---

52. The cases are listed in fn. 8.
53. On the War of 1812, see Waltz, "Emerging Structure"; on 1861 and 1895–96, see Layne, "Kant or Cant."

A true test involves fresh cases. Thus I use the following four cases to illustrate the argument rather than provide a crucial trial of its validity.

FRANCO-AMERICAN RELATIONS, 1796–98

In 1798 the United States initiated what became known as the Quasi-War with France, in which the two nations fought a series of naval battles in the Caribbean Sea. The American action was in response to French seizures of U.S. merchant vessels on the high seas, and to the "XYZ Affair" in which the French government attempted to extort thousands of dollars from three U.S. envoys in Paris. The French, then at war with England, had taken these actions in retaliation for the Jay Treaty, in which the Americans promised the British not to trade with France.[54] Here I argue that liberal ideology in the form of republican solidarity prevented France and the United States from engaging in full-scale war.

The United States in the late 1790s qualifies as a liberal democracy. Although suffrage in most states was limited to white males who owned property, regular elections were mandated by law, and Republican opposition to the Federalist government was lively. Republicans held to liberal tenets. They considered only republics—non-monarchies—to be liberal states, and they viewed France as a sister republic.[55]

They did so even though France does not qualify by my definition as a liberal democracy. The Constitution of the Year III (1795) mandated regular elections, and the French press was free, but the Executive in effect destroyed any institutional claim France had to democracy. In September 1797 and again in March 1798, radicals in the Directory ordered *coups d'état* expelling members of the executive and legislature who opposed them.[56] French foreign policy making is therefore not of direct interest here. Instead, I only

---

54. Accounts of the origins of the conflict may be found in Alexander DeConde, *The Quasi-War: The Politics and Diplomacy of the Undeclared War with France 1797–1801* (New York: Charles Scribner's Sons, 1966); Albert Hall Bowman, *The Struggle for Neutrality: Franco-American Diplomacy during the Federalist Era* (Knoxville: University of Tennessee Press, 1974); William C. Stinchcombe, *The XYZ Affair* (Westport, Conn.: Greenwood Press, 1980); E. Wilson Lyon, "The Directory and the United States," *American Historical Review,* Vol. 43, No. 3 (April 1938), pp. 514–532; and James A. James, "French Opinion as a Factor in Preventing War between France and the United States, 1795–1800," *American Historical Review,* Vol. 30, No. 1 (October 1924), pp. 44–55.
55. See for example Bowman, *Struggle for Neutrality,* pp. 25–30.
56. Georges Lefebvre, *The Thermidoreans and the Directory,* trans. Robert Baldick (New York: Random House, 1964), pp. 176–179; R.R. Palmer, *The Age of the Democratic Revolution* (Princeton: Princeton University Press, 1964), pp. 214–217, 255–259.

show that processes in the United States conform to the hypotheses derived from my argument.

U.S. REPUBLICANS TRUSTED FRANCE AND MISTRUSTED GREAT BRITAIN. Even after the French maritime depredations and the XYZ Affair, the Republicans forgave the French even as they excoriated the British. Their rationale was that France remained a sister republic, and England remained a monarchy. One Republican newspaper averred: "There is at present as much danger of an invasion from the French, as from the inhabitants of Saturn."[57] Thomas Jefferson, vice president and leader of the Republicans, applauded rumors of a pending French invasion of Britain, because it would "republicanize that country" so that "all will be safe with us."[58]

REPUBLICANS HAD CHEERED THE FRENCH REVOLUTION AND EXPECTED PACIFIC RELATIONS WITH THEIR SISTER REPUBLIC. In 1789, American support for the French Revolution had been nearly unanimous. With the execution of Louis XVI and establishment of the First Republic in 1793, Federalists turned against the French, but most Republicans remained staunch supporters. One historian writes:

Democratic papers commenced a calculated program of justifying those in power in Paris. This practice was consciously pursued throughout the remainder of the decade and must be acknowledged in order to assess the part of foreign relations in the political propaganda of the period. A defense was found for every French action, from Robespierre's Feast of the Supreme Being to the seizures of American ships.[59]

Republicans did not simply decide in 1798 to oppose war with France and invent an ideological justification for that position; they had been well disposed toward France since 1789.

REPUBLICANS CLAIMED THAT THE FRENCH SHARED THEIR ENDS, AND THAT THE BRITISH DID NOT. The Republicans saw the Anglo-French struggle as one between the principles of monarchy and republicanism more than between two European powers, and thus as part and parcel of the same struggle they had themselves fought only a decade before.[60] During the debate over the

---

57. *Independent Chronicle* (Boston), March 4, 1798, quoted in Donald H. Stewart, *The Opposition Press of the Federalist Period* (Albany: State University of New York Press, 1969), pp. 442–443.
58. Stinchcombe, *XYZ Affair*, p. 118.
59. Stewart, *Opposition Press*, p. 120.
60. See Jerald Combs, *The Jay Treaty* (Berkeley: University of California Press, 1970), pp. 110–111; Samuel Flagg Bemis, *Jay's Treaty: A Study in Commerce and Diplomacy* (New York: Macmillan, 1923; repr. ed., Westport, Conn.: Greenwood Press, 1975), pp. 95–96.

Jay Treaty in 1796, one Virginian told his fellow Congressmen: "As it has not been in the power of the United States to assist their Republican allies, *when fighting in fact their battles*, the least they can do . . . must be, that they will not put the enemies [the British] of those allies into a better condition than they were."[61]

REPUBLICANS DID NOT CHANGE THEIR FAVORABLE ASSESSMENT OF FRANCE DURING THE CRISIS, DESPITE FEDERALIST EFFORTS. Much American public opinion of France had soured after the XYZ Affair, but Republican elites stood by France against England. One newspaper declared that "'our Pharaohs' still wishfully looked for the downfall of the Republic and were ready to 'lend a hand to effect it'." Another said of the Federalists: "The tory faction will endeavour to torture fact, in order to excite our feelings against the cause of liberty and the revolution. . . . Let us be calm."[62]

REPUBLICANS AGITATED AGAINST WAR WITH FRANCE. In Congress, the party of Jefferson used all its energy to stave off a war declaration. Accusing President Adams of trying to declare war by himself, they introduced resolutions stating that "it is not expedient for the United States to resort to war against the French Republic."[63] The Republican press shrieked in protest against the possibility of a Franco-American war.[64]

THE PRESIDENT AND THE CONGRESSIONAL FEDERALISTS WERE CONSTRAINED BY THE REPUBLICANS FROM DECLARING WAR ON FRANCE. In the spring of 1798, Adams wanted war with France. In March he drafted a war message to Congress saying, "All men will think it more honorable and glorious to the national character when its existence as an independent nation is at stake that hostilities should be avowed in a formal Declaration of War."[65] Yet the president never presented the message to Congress. He could not do so, because he knew he did not have the votes to obtain a war declaration. Not everyone in Congress opposed Adams: the "high Federalists" had wanted war long before he had. It was the Republicans and the moderate Federalists who would not vote for war.

The Republican motivation is already clear. The moderate Federalists opposed war in part because the nation was so divided—i.e., because Republican opposition was so adamant. Believing only a united effort would enable

---

61. 4th Cong., 1st sess., *Annals of Congress* (April 20, 1796), Vol. 5, p. 1099. Emphasis added.
62. Stewart, *Opposition Press*, p. 286.
63. 5th Cong., 2d sess., *Annals of Congress* (March 27, 1798), Vol. 2, p. 1329.
64. Stewart, *Opposition Press*, pp. 289–290.
65. DeConde, *Quasi-War*, pp. 66–68.

the nation to fight France effectively, the moderates were in effect constrained by a liberal ideology they did not even hold. As one moderate put it after the defeat of a test vote in the House of Representatives in July 1798, "we should have war; but he did not wish to go on faster to this state of things than the people of this country, and the opinion of the world would justify."[66]

ANGLO-AMERICAN RELATIONS, 1803–12

Another Anglo-French war, begun in 1803, likewise entangled the U.S. merchant marine. Both the British and French were again humiliating the United States by seizing U.S. cargoes, and the British were impressing American sailors into service as well. Ultimately, under the presidency of James Madison, the United States went to war.[67] The War of 1812 is often cited by critics of the democratic peace proposition as an example of two democracies at war.[68] By my definition, however, Britain cannot be considered a liberal democracy.[69] Moreover, even a cursory examination of the events leading up to the war shows that very few Americans, and virtually no British, considered Great Britain a democracy at the time. Here again, Republicans in the United States act as my argument would predict.

REPUBLICANS MISTRUSTED ENGLAND, AND SOME STILL TRUSTED NAPOLEONIC FRANCE. Thomas Jefferson, president from 1801 to 1809, wrote privately to a friend in 1810 that the nature of the British government rendered England unfit "for the observation of moral duties," and that it would betray any agreement with the United States. Napoleon, on the other hand, was safe: "A *republican* Emperor, from his affection to republics, independent of motives of expediency, must grant to ours the Cyclops' boon of being the last devoured."[70]

---

66. Ibid., p. 106.
67. See Reginald Horsman, *The Causes of the War of 1812* (Philadelphia: University of Pennsylvania Press, 1962); Roger H. Brown, *The Republic in Peril: 1812* (New York: Norton, 1971); Bradford Perkins, *Prologue to War* (Berkeley: University of California Press, 1961).
68. See for example Waltz, "Emerging Structure," p. 78.
69. Elections in pre-reform Britain were uncompetitive. Many seats in the House of Commons represented tiny boroughs where one patron determined who was elected; other towns were entirely disenfranchised. Votes in the Commons were effectively bought and sold in an open market. The House of Lords, an unelected body, could veto legislation. Moreover, the cabinet, which possessed war powers, was responsible to the king rather than to parliament. See E.L. Woodward, *The Age of Reform 1815–1870* (Oxford: Clarendon Press, 1938), pp. 18–28.
70. Robert W. Tucker and David C. Hendrickson, *Empire of Liberty: The Statecraft of Thomas Jefferson* (New York: Oxford University Press, 1990), pp. 329–330.

REPUBLICANS CLAIMED THAT ENGLAND DID NOT SHARE THEIR ENDS. With few exceptions, Republicans blasted England for opposing the cause of liberty.[71] One Congressman exclaimed that "the standard of freedom had never been raised in any country without [England's] attempting to pull it down."[72] Republicans believed England was trying to wipe republicanism from the face of the earth. One newspaper asserted:

Not only the rights of the nation, but the character of the government, are involved in the issue. . . . The deliberations of Congress "at this momentous era," will perhaps, do more to stamp the character of genuine republican governments, than has been effected in this respect since the creation of the world.

Republicans feared that continued foreign humiliation would lead to a Federalist government which would align the United States with England and set up a monarchy.[73]

REPUBLICANS DEFINED ENGLAND AS NON-DEMOCRATIC BEFORE AND DURING THE CRISIS. Far from changing their views of the British to suit the moment, Jeffersonians had consistently hated the mother country since before the American Revolution. In 1806 one Congressman rhetorically asked if his colleagues could tolerate "that same monarch [George III] . . . who, instead of diminishing, has added to the long and black catalogue of crimes set forth in our Declaration of Independence."[74]

REPUBLICANS AGITATED FOR WAR. Both Jefferson and James Madison, Republican president from 1809 to 1817, preferred economic sanctions to war. But the 1811 War Hawk Congress decided with Madison that force had to be used to punish the British. Henry Clay, John C. Calhoun, and other young Republican Congressmen demanded war, as did the Republican press.[75]

STATESMEN FOLLOWED REPUBLICAN IDEOLOGY. Since Republicans controlled the executive and Congress, they did not need to be forced by democratic institutions to initiate war. Public support for war was certainly not unanimous; New England in particular was vehemently opposed. But Madison and the War Hawks declared war anyway. One biographer writes of Madison:

---

71. One prominent exception was John Randolph, the eccentric Virginian, who agreed with Federalists that England rather than France was fighting for the liberties of the world. See Brown, *Republic in Peril,* pp. 151–155.
72. 12th Cong., 1st sess., *Annals of Congress,* Vol. 23 (January 6, 1812), p. 688.
73. Brown, *Republic in Peril,* pp. 74–84.
74. 9th Cong., 1st sess., *Annals of Congress,* Vol. 15 (March 7, 1806), pp. 609–610.
75. Horsman, *Causes of the War of 1812,* chapter 13.

To have submitted to [Britain's] unilateral decrees, her discriminatory trade regulations, or her naval outrages would have . . . ratified unjust principles in international law and emboldened antirepublican forces in Britain and the United States, thus threatening, in Madison's opinion, the survival of free government anywhere in the world.[76]

Realists at the time opposed the War of 1812, and in fact realists ever since have had difficulty accounting for it. Morgenthau calls it "the sole exception" to the rule that the United States has followed realist tenets in dealing with Europe.[77] In their 1990 book, Robert Tucker and David Hendrickson chide Jefferson for throwing America's lot in with France rather than Britain during the Napoleonic Wars. The United States would have avoided trouble, had it

publicly recognized that England was in truth engaged in a contest for public liberty and international order, and that by virtue of its own stance against Napoleon Britain protected the United States from the peculiar menace that Bonaparte embodied. . . . Jefferson would not say this because he did not believe it.[78]

That is, the Republican conception of the national interest ultimately required war because Britain was a monarchy.

ANGLO-AMERICAN RELATIONS, 1861–63

Fifty years later, Americans still mainly saw the world's nations as republics and monarchies.[79] Britain remained a monarchy and therefore a despotism. At several points during the American Civil War, Britain and the Union teetered on the brink of war. In none of these crises did liberal affinity for England play much of a role in keeping the Union from attacking Britain. And in the first, the *Trent* affair,[80] British liberal affinity for the Union was

---

76. Ralph Ketcham, *James Madison* (New York: Macmillan, 1971), p. 530.
77. Hans J. Morgenthau, *In Defense of the National Interest* (New York: Knopf, 1951), p. 5.
78. Tucker and Hendrickson, *Empire of Liberty*, pp. 226–227.
79. Sources on this case include Ephraim Douglass Adams, *Great Britain and the American Civil War*, 2 vols. (New York: Longmans, Green and Co., 1925); Brian Jenkins, *Britain and the War for the Union*, 2 vols. (Montreal: McGill-Queen's University Press, 1974 and 1980); Howard Jones, *Union in Peril: The Crisis over British Intervention in the American Civil War* (Chapel Hill: University of North Carolina Press, 1992); Norman B. Ferris, *The "Trent" Affair: A Diplomatic Crisis* (Knoxville: University of Tennessee Press, 1977); Martin P. Claussen, "Peace Factors in Anglo-American Relations, 1861–1865," *Mississippi Valley Historical Review*, Vol. 26 (March 1940), pp. 511–522.
80. The crisis occurred when a Union ship seized the British mail packet *Trent* as it carried two Southern emissaries to London to try to negotiate formal recognition of the Confederacy. The British were almost unanimously outraged, and clearly would have declared war had Lincoln not apologized and returned the emissaries. See Ferris, *Trent*.

rather weak as well, which in turn fed Union hostility toward England. The resolution of the *Trent* crisis can be explained without reference to democratic peace theory: the administration of Abraham Lincoln backed down to a British ultimatum because it could not afford war with such a powerful foe over such an issue.[81] With the Union fighting for its life against the Confederacy, Lincoln and his cabinet prudently decided that no liberal purpose would be served by an Anglo-American war.

By my definition, Britain in the 1860s was a liberal democracy. The 1832 Reform Act had made elections fairer, and had made the cabinet responsible to parliament rather than to the Crown. This meant the executive was ultimately responsible to the electors, giving the public leverage over war decisions.[82]

British liberal sympathy for the Union was weak during *Trent* because most British took Lincoln at his word that the Civil War was about restoring the Union—a cause uninspiring to the British—rather than abolition.[83] British of all classes had supported the abolition of slavery since the 1830s. Then in September 1862, Lincoln issued the preliminary Emancipation Proclamation, declaring that as of January 1, 1863, all slaves in the rebellious states would be free. Although it was condemned by pro-Confederates as likely to provoke a slave insurrection, the Proclamation cause British opinion to shift to the Union side. This shift helped prevent Britain from intervening in the Civil War. Christopher Layne's account of Anglo-American relations in this time misses this because he only looks at the *Trent* affair.

BRITISH LIBERALS TRUSTED THE UNION. Even before the Emancipation Proclamation, the Union had its staunch supporters among the Philosophical Radicals, notably John Bright and Richard Cobden. Bright told Parliament in early 1862, "there probably never has been a great nation in which what is familiarly termed mob law is less known or has had less influence. . . . Understand, I confine my observations always to the free States of the

---

81. See Layne, "The Myth of the Democratic Peace," Again, I do not argue that liberals will continually seek war against states they consider illiberal. Liberalism determines the ends, but power politics may circumscribe the means.
82. The shift in cabinet responsibility was *de facto* rather than *de jure*; since 1832, no monarch has ever dismissed a ministry. See Robert Livingston Schuyler and Corinne Comstock Weston, *British Constitutional History since 1832* (Princeton: D. Van Nostrand, 1957), pp. 26–44.
83. In his first inaugural address, Lincoln said: "I have no purpose, directly or indirectly to interfere with the institution of slavery in the States where it exists. I believe I have no lawful right to do so, and I have no inclination to do so." Quoted in Adams, *Great Britain and the Civil War*, Vol. 1, p. 50.

North."[84] Bright's view gained wide acceptance after the Proclamation, because abolitionists viewed slaveholding states as aggressive by nature.[85]

AFTER THE EMANCIPATION PROCLAMATION, LIBERALS WANTED BETTER RELATIONS WITH THE UNION, AND BELIEVED THE UNION SHARED LIBERAL ENDS. Britain's *Morning Star* newspaper summarized the change in October: "The inevitable has come at last. Negro emancipation is formally and definitively adopted as the policy in war and peace of the United States."[86] The *Daily News* predicted that now "the most audacious Secessionists" in England would shy away from proposing recognition of the "confederated Slave States." All through the war the Union had blockaded the Confederacy, preventing cotton from reaching England and causing extreme distress in the Lancashire textile region. Yet after the Proclamation, England's working class newspapers shifted over to the Union's side, proclaiming that the Union's cause, liberation of the masses, was their cause. One paper said the most dangerous problem facing Britain was now "the recognition of the slaveholding Confederate States, and, as an almost necessary consequence, an alliance with them against the Federal States of America."[87]

LIBERALS AGITATED AGAINST INTERVENTION AFTER THE PROCLAMATION. As the Proclamation energized evangelical Christian and other emancipation groups in Britain, Bright stated that the "anti-slavery sentiment" of his country was finally being "called forth."[88] One historian writes that "there took place meeting after meeting at which strong resolutions were passed enthusiastically endorsing the issue of the emancipation proclamation and pledging sympathy to the cause of the North."[89] In Manchester, a rally at the end of 1862 approved a missive to Lincoln congratulating him for the "humane and righteous course" he had taken in furthering America's founding concept that "all men are created equal." In London during the spring of 1863, a rally of 2,500 or more workers pledged themselves "to use their 'utmost efforts' to prevent the recognition of any government 'founded on human slavery'."[90]

THE BRITISH CABINET WAS CONSTRAINED BY LIBERALISM FROM INTERVENING IN THE CIVIL WAR. Shortly after the Proclamation, the cabinet was considering

---

84. *Hansard's Parliamentary Debates* (Commons), 3d Ser., Vol. 165 (February 17, 1862), col. 382.
85. See, e.g., the remarks of Goldwin Smith in the Venezuelan crisis, below.
86. Jenkins, *Britain and the War*, Vol. 2, p. 152.
87. Ibid., p. 216; Philip Foner, *British Labor and the American Civil War* (New York: Holmes and Meier, 1981), p. 69.
88. Jenkins, *Britain and the War*, Vol. 2, pp. 209–211.
89. Adams, *Great Britain and the Civil War*, Vol. 2, p. 107.
90. Foner, *British Labor*, pp. 41, 61.

a French proposal to offer joint mediation to end the Civil War. All knew that the Union would almost certainly refuse, and armed intervention would have to follow to enforce mediation. Advocates of intervention, including Lord John Russell and William Gladstone, wanted to end the Union blockade of the South. They were also sickened at the brutality of the war, and supported the Southerners' right to self-determination.[91] Other advocates also argued that a permanently divided and weakened America was in long-term British interests.[92] Viscount Palmerston, the prime minister, had at times supported intervention as well.[93] But in late October, he soured on the prospect.

Palmerston gave many reasons, but significantly, his main obstacle seems to have been the shift in public opinion caused by the Emancipation Proclamation. In October, Palmerston wrote privately to Russell that slavery was now England's "great difficulty" in trying to put together peace terms. Could the cabinet, he asked, "without offence to many People here recommend to the North to sanction Slavery and to undertake to give back Runaways, and yet would not the South insist upon some such Conditions after Lincoln's Emancipation Decree"? The French were readier to intervene, he wrote, because they were freer from the "Shackles of Principle and of Right & Wrong on these Matters, as on all others than we are."[94]

To be sure, Palmerston heard other arguments against intervention. His secretary for war, George Cornewall Lewis, was primarily concerned that British recognition of the Confederacy would set a bad international legal precedent. Lewis also argued that the European powers would have difficulty forcing the Union to accept terms. Also on Palmerston's mind was the progress of the war itself, which had recently not gone well for the South.[95] But as Palmerston had said to the Russian ambassador to London in 1861, there were "two Powers in this Country, the government & public opinion, and that both must concur for any great important steps."[96]

---

91. Jones, *Union in Peril*, pp. 178–179, 184–185, 203; Adams, *Great Britain and the Civil War*, Vol. 1, pp. 212–215; Jenkins, *Britain and the War*, Vol. 2, pp. 168–169.
92. For example, William Lindsay, a member of Parliament, said he desired intervention because he "desired the disruption of the American Union, as every honest Englishman did, because it was too great a Power and England sh'd not let such a power exist on the American continent." Jones, *Union in Peril*, p. 134.
93. Ibid., pp. 150–151.
94. Ibid., pp. 191, 206.
95. Ibid., pp. 210–217.
96. Ferris, *Trent*, p. 158.

After the autumn of 1862, public opinion rendered British intervention impossible. Russell himself stopped Britain from selling ironclad warships to the Confederacy in the spring of 1863, writing privately to a colleague: "If we have taken part in interventions, it has been in behalf of the independence, freedom and welfare of a great portion of mankind. I should be sorry, indeed, if there should be any intervention on the part of this country which could bear another character."[97] Even Gladstone argued against intervention during the summer: "A war with the United States . . . ought to be unpopular on far higher grounds, because it would be a war with our own kinsmen for slavery."[98]

ANGLO-AMERICAN RELATIONS, 1895-96

Just over thirty years later, Britain and the United States were again close to war.[99] President Grover Cleveland and Richard Olney, his secretary of state, saw a boundary dispute between British Guiana and Venezuela as an opportunity to assert U.S. power in the New World. Cleveland and Olney demanded U.S. arbitration in the dispute, arguing that England was violating the Monroe Doctrine by trying to expand its territory in the New World. After Lord Salisbury, British prime minister and foreign minister, told Cleveland that it was no affair of the United States', Congress voted unanimously in December 1895 to fund an American commission to decide the boundary, with its recommendations to be enforced by whatever means necessary. War fever was loose for a few days in America. But the crisis was resolved peacefully over the next few months, and never again would these two nations seriously consider war with each other.

Because both states were liberal democracies, and sizable populations in each state considered the other liberal, I consider the foreign policy processes in both.

AMERICANS HAD OBSERVED BRITAIN DEMOCRATIZING IN THE 1880S AND HAD BEGUN TO EXPECT BETTER RELATIONS. Many Americans in the 1890s still

---

97. Jenkins, *Britain and the War*, Vol. 2, p. 241.
98. *Hansard's Parliamentary Debates* (Commons), 3d ser., Vol. 171 (June 30, 1863), cols. 1805–1806.
99. Accounts of this crisis are found in Ernest R. May, *Imperial Democracy: The Emergence of America as a Great Power* (Chicago: Imprint Publications, 1991); Allen, *Great Britain and the United States;* Dexter Perkins, *The Monroe Doctrine 1867–1907* (Baltimore: Johns Hopkins University Press, 1937); A.E. Campbell, *Great Britain and the United States 1895–1903* (Westport, Conn.: Greenwood Press, 1960); and Marshall Bertram, *The Birth of Anglo-American Friendship: The Prime Facet of the Venezuelan Boundary Dispute* (Lanham, Md.: University Press of America, 1992).

viewed Britain mainly as a monarchy and thus not democratic. But others had begun to challenge this old view after the Third Reform Act in 1884 enormously expanded the franchise in Britain. Andrew Carnegie then proclaimed, "Henceforth England is democratic," and predicted that "British democracy is to be pacific, and that the American doctrine of non-intervention will commend itself to it."[100] On the eve of the Venezuelan crisis, Joseph Pulitzer, publisher of the *New York World*, decried a senator's proposal that the United States align with Russia and wage war against England:

Russia represents the worst despotism that civilization has permitted to survive, except possibly that of Turkey. England represents Anglo-Saxon liberty and progress only in less degree than does our own government. We have much in common with the English. We have nothing whatever in common with Russia.[101]

A liberal elite desired good relations with England precisely because the nation had democratized.

MOST BRITONS NOW SAW THE UNITED STATES AS TRUSTWORTHY. One reason was the end of slavery. The scholar Goldwin Smith wrote during the crisis, "I am firmly convinced that since the abolition of slavery there prevails among them no desire for territorial aggrandizement."[102] Another was democratization in Britain itself. A historian writes, "Anti-Americanism, traditionally associated with a disappearing social order, had long been on the wane . . . Thus in all the tensions of the period, and particularly in the Venezuela dispute, the most important influence for amity and peace was the new English democracy." Fear of Russia and Germany influenced this desire for American friendship, but the point is that the new Britain was more inclined than the old to choose America as friend.[103] William Vernon Harcourt, Liberal leader in the House of Commons, often referred to "we semi-Americans" when writing to his friend Joseph Chamberlain, the Liberal colonial secretary.[104] On both sides of the Atlantic, Anglo-Saxon chauvinism played a strong role in this affinity.[105]

---

100. Andrew Carnegie, "Democracy in England," *North American Review*, Vol. 142, No. 1 (January 1886), p. 74.
101. *Public Opinion*, November 21, 1895, p. 21. One publicist called England "the Crowned Republic." Moncure D. Conway, "The Queen of England," *North American Review*, Vol. 145, No. 2 (August 1887), p. 121.
102. *New-York Times*, December 25, 1895, p. 3.
103. Allen, *Great Britain and the United States*, p. 525.
104. A.G. Gardiner, *The Life of Sir William Vernon Harcourt* (London: Constable and Co., 1923), Vol. 2, pp. 396–397.
105. Campbell, *Great Britain and the United States*, pp. 9–10.

AMERICAN LIBERALS CONTINUED TO SEE ENGLAND AS LIBERAL DURING THE CRISIS. Neither Cleveland nor Olney was part of the liberal pro-British elite in the United States, and much of the American public wanted war at the beginning of the crisis. But the U.S. ambassador to London, Thomas F. Bayard, was a pro-British liberal who viewed the United States and Great Britain as the "two guardians of civilization." During the crisis, Bayard stressed his well-known views that England was to be trusted because, unlike Venezuela, it was governed by law.[106] In Congress, Senator Edward O. Wolcott of Colorado declared Venezuela one of South America's "so-called republics" in which the "rulers are despots and suffrage a farce." He hoped the Venezuelan mines would be governed by "English common law" with its "certainty of enforcement."[107]

Most pro-British liberals were found outside government, however. Prominent among these was Pulitzer, whose *New York World* said on December 21:

There is not a hothead among the jingoes who does not know that England is more likely to become a republic than the United States are to revert to monarchism. The entire trend of government for the past fifty years has been toward democracy. . . . Observe the working of the leaven of democracy in England.[108]

"In a word," commented the *Nation*, "the American Secretary of State's references to Venezuelan republicanism and friendship and English monarchy and hostility have no more to do with the facts than with the planet Jupiter."[109]

BRITISH LIBERALS CONTINUED TO SEE THE UNITED STATES AS LIBERAL THROUGH THE CRISIS. The British press expressed general revulsion at the prospect of war with the United States. The *Standard* gave a typical opinion:

We feel confident that a vast majority of the Americans will soon be profoundly sorry for what Mr. Cleveland has done. He has travestied and damaged a principle that they hold dear, and has made the Republic which we have all honored on account of its supposed attachment to peace and

---

106. Charles Callan Tansill, *The Foreign Policy of Thomas F. Bayard* (New York: Fordham University Press, 1940), p. 716.
107. 54th Cong., 1st sess., *Congressional Record* (December 20, 1895), Vol. 28, Pt. 1, pp. 859–860.
108. John L. Heaton, *The Story of a Page* (New York: Harper and Bros., 1913), p. 114.
109. *The Nation*, January 2, 1896, p. 5.

non-intervention, figure in the eyes of Europe as a gratuitously aggressive and reckless champion of war.[110]

The *Daily Telegraph* calmly stated, "We are perfectly satisfied to rely upon the straightforward, high-bred simplicity of Lord Salisbury's diplomacy and the good sense, widespread honesty, intelligence, and kindliness of the American people."[111]

AMERICAN LIBERALS AGITATED FOR PEACE. Pulitzer led the peace movement, sending cablegrams to influential British asking their opinions on the crisis. On Christmas Day the *World*'s front page featured a selection of responses under the headline "PEACE AND GOOD WILL," expressing horror at the thought of an Anglo-American war.[112] There was, moreover, an interactive effect as Americans observed this British good will. In January 1896 the *Philadelphia Press* asserted, "Nothing in the succession for a month past of discussion, declaration and feeling, personal and public, private and National, has so moved the American Nation as a whole as the sudden revelation which has been made of English horror of war with this country."[113]

BRITISH LIBERALS AGITATED FOR PEACE. Not only the British press, but also Joseph Chamberlain, the colonial secretary who had originally agreed with Salisbury to rebuff Cleveland and Olney, "determined to move heaven and earth to avert conflict between the two English-speaking peoples," one biographer writes.[114] In a speech in Birmingham, Chamberlain proclaimed:

War between the two nations would be an absurdity as well as a crime. . . . The two nations are allied more closely in sentiment and in interest than any

---

110. Quoted in the *New York Times*, December 21, 1895, p. 6. It is also interesting to note that the London *Review of Reviews* took great pains to counter those Americans who claimed England was not democratic. "The superstition that the United States is in a peculiar sense Republican, whereas we are Monarchical, is being utilized for all it is worth in order to bolster up the case for intervention in Venezuela. If British subjects in Guiana would but repudiate their allegiance to the British Empire, and set up in business as a British republic, no American citizen would object to them eating their way into the heart of Venezuela. All the difficulty arises from the prejudice against the monarchy—a prejudice that is as old as George III., and ought to have been buried with him." *Review of Reviews* (London), December 14, 1895, pp. 484–485.
111. *New-York Times*, December 19, 1895, p. 3.
112. Heaton, *The Story of a Page*, p. 114; W.A. Swanberg, *Pulitzer* (New York: Charles Scribner's Sons, 1967), p. 199. This is in stark contrast to Pulitzer's behavior two years later in the crisis with Spain, a country few if any Americans considered democratic. In agitating for war, the *World* declared, "War waged on behalf of freedom, of self-government, of law and order, of humanity, to end oppression, misrule, plunder and savagery, is a holy war in itself." Heaton, *Story of a Page*, p. 162.
113. *Public Opinion*, Vol. 20 (January 23, 1896), p. 107.
114. J.L. Garvin, *The Life of Joseph Chamberlain*, Vol. 3 (London: Macmillan, 1934), p. 67.

other nations on the face of the earth. . . . I should look forward with pleasure to the possibility of the Stars and Stripes and the Union Jack floating together in defence of a common cause sanctioned by humanity and justice.[115]

His friend Harcourt made it clear that he would make the crisis a major issue in the upcoming session of Parliament. He urged Chamberlain to grant the Americans all they wanted.[116]

RESOLUTION OF THE CRISIS. Especially in the United States, liberals had a difficult task. Not only were Cleveland and Olney unimpressed by British democratization, but much of the American public, especially Irish-Americans, roared its approval at this "tweaking of the lion's tail." One cannot prove what drove officials on either side of the Atlantic defuse the crisis. What can be said is that on January 2, 1896, Cleveland appointed a distinguished commission to adjudicate the Venezuelan-British Guianan border, with only one member who could be construed as anglophobic. Since the president could have appointed a much more inflammatory commission, this must be seen as a conciliatory step.

The British cabinet voted on January 11, over the objections of Salisbury, to accept the U.S. commission's jurisdiction. It was the liberals on the cabinet, led by the pro-American Chamberlain, who favored the settlement. Salisbury, a realist with no affinity for American democracy, would have accepted war, and he nearly resigned in protest when the cabinet outvoted him.

The resolution of the Venezuelan border crisis was the beginning of the apparently permanent Anglo-American friendship. Today, realists argue that Britain appeased the Americans here and elsewhere because it could no longer sustain its "splendid isolation" in the face of rising threats from Germany and Russia.[117] That argument begs the question of why the British aligned with the United States rather than with Germany. Germany threatened British interests in Africa, but the United States threatened British interests in the New World. Liberalism offers an answer: British liberals trusted the democratic United States more than imperial Germany. During the Venezuelan crisis, the German emperor sent the infamous Krüger telegram congratulating the Boers in southern Africa for repelling the British Jameson raid. In a striking contrast to its calm reaction to Cleveland and

---

115. May, *Imperial Democracy*, pp. 44–45, 53–54.
116. Ibid., p. 49; Gardiner, *Life of Harcourt*, pp. 396–397; Garvin, *Chamberlain*, p. 161; Bertram, *Anglo-American Friendship*, p. 83. Harcourt had always admired the United States, and argued vigorously against British intervention in the U.S. Civil War.
117. Layne, "The Myth of the Democratic Peace."

Olney's provocations, the British public was outraged. One historian writes, "when 'Yankee Doodle' was cheered and 'Die Wacht am Rhein' hissed in London, it demonstrated clearly how utterly different was popular feeling towards the two countries."[118]

Appeasement of the United States was no arbitrary choice. Now that Britain was more democratic than ever, its government and people trusted democratic America more than ever.[119]

Democratic Peace and the Realist Challenge: The Liberal Response

Many realists have declared democratic peace a fantasy. Permanent peace between mutually recognized liberal democracies, they argue, is not possible. Liberal states, like all others, must base foreign policy on the imperatives of power politics. Some realists argue that there is no theoretically compelling causal mechanism that could explain democratic peace. Others claim that even if there were, the foreign policy processes of democracies show that such a "mechanism" is empirically impotent.[120] Realist skeptics make a number of claims:

First, they claim that if neither democratic structures nor norms alone can explain the democratic peace, then there is no democratic peace.[121] I have already pointed out the logical fallacy behind this claim. The structural/ normative distinction is epistemological, not ontological. I argue that structure and norms work in tandem: liberal ideas proscribe wars among democracies, and democratic institutions ensure that this proscription is followed.

Realists claim that if there were a democratic peace, then liberal democracies would never make threats against one another.[122] The claim is that the logic of the democratic peace proposition implies that liberal democracies will never try to coerce one another. But of course, there is no inherent

---

118. Allen, *Great Britain and the United States*, p. 354.
119. Stephen Rock writes: "Englishmen, who could agree on practically nothing else, were in fact almost unanimous in their distaste for the German political system, its ideology, and its methods. . . . Both [Germany and the United States] were rising imperial powers with growing navies. . . . Yet Britons, while they detested and feared Germany, almost universally admired the United States and felt minimal apprehension at her ambitions." Rock, *Why Peace Breaks Out: Great Power Rapprochement in Historical Perspective* (Chapel Hill: University of North Carolina Press, 1989), pp. 86–87.
120. See Mearsheimer, "Back to the Future"; Waltz, "Emerging Structure"; Layne, "The Myth of the Democratic Peace"; Farber and Gowa, "Polities and Peace."]
121. Layne, "Kant or Cant."
122. Ibid.

"logic" of democratic peace independent of an explicit argument about how it works. My argument answers realism in two ways. First, liberal democracies do not always consider each other liberal. What a scholar in 1994 considers democratic is not always what a statesman in 1894 considered democratic. Second, liberal democracies are sometimes governed by illiberal leaders who are somewhat autonomous in implementing foreign policy. Such leaders may make threats; they are simply unable to mobilize the nation for war, due to the constraints of democratic institutions.

Realists claim that if there were democratic peace, then public opinion in liberal democracies would never want war with a fellow liberal democracy.[123] Like the previous claim, this one makes two assumptions: that all citizens of liberal democracies are liberal, and that they agree on which foreign states are also liberal. Neither assumption is true, and neither is necessary for democratic peace to occur. All that is necessary for statesmen to be constrained is that they believe war would be too unpopular. For this, a nation's population need not all be liberal.

Realists claim that when power politics requires war with a democracy, liberals will redefine that state as a despotism; when power politics requires peace with a non-democracy, they will redefine that state as a democracy.[124] That is, ideological labels are sugar-coating to make otherwise bitter policies easier to swallow. Statesmen's public rationales for foreign policy are solely rhetorical; one must look at their confidential statements to understand their true motives. In this article, however, I have shown that in crises liberals hang fast to the ideological labels they previously gave foreign states. Republicans stood by France after the XYZ Affair. They mistrusted England from the time of the American Revolution up to the end of the War of 1812 (and beyond). Many Americans began to see England as democratic in the 1880s, and continued to do so during the Venezuelan crisis. Britons began admiring the United States well before the rise of Germany "forced" them to make friends in the late 1890s. The one case where liberals changed their opinion of a foreign state during a crisis was in the Civil War. There, British opinion shifted to the Union side after the Emancipation Proclamation. The cause of this shift was not power politics, but the Emancipation Proclamation,

---

123. Ibid.
124. This is implied in Hans Morgenthau's argument that Woodrow Wilson led the United States into World War I "not to make the world safe for democracy," but because "Germany threatened the balance of power. . . . Wilson pursued the right policy, but he pursued it for the wrong reason." Morgenthau, *National Interest,* pp. 25–26.

which signified that the Union was fighting for abolition, a liberal cause the British had long supported.

Realists claim that "strategic concerns and the relative distribution of military capabilities . . . should crucially—perhaps decisively" affect the outcomes of crises between liberal democracies, and moreover that "broader geopolitical considerations pertaining to a state's position in international politics should, if implicated, account significantly for the crisis's outcome."[125] I do not contest the relevance of power politics to the foreign policies of liberal democracies. These realist hypotheses, however, imply that during a crisis, statesmen will be able either to ignore liberals or to persuade them to change their minds. But liberal ideology and institutions clearly had independent power in 1798, when John Adams could not ask Congress for war against France due to staunch Republican opposition. In 1862, Palmerston privately admitted to being constrained by pro-Union opinion from intervening in the Civil War. Realism would and did counsel the British to work to keep the United States divided and weak, but they passed up the opportunity. In 1895–96, war would clearly have been highly unpopular, especially in England, and Salisbury was thwarted by Liberals in his own cabinet from confronting the United States.

Realists claim that states that view each other as liberal-democratic will still balance against each other.[126] Realists who posit that states balance solely against capabilities must explain why Britain conciliated the United States rather than Germany. As explained below, a more nuanced realism, such as balance-of-threat theory, could account for this outcome. In assessing whether a foreign states is a threat, liberals such as Chamberlain look at, among other things, the state's regime type.

Realists claim that Wilhelmine Germany was a democracy, and therefore democracies fought one another in World War I.[127] There is not the space to address this claim fully, but two things may briefly be said. First, even before the war, most British and Americans saw Germany as undemocratic. The British abhorred German ideology, and although many Americans admired Germany's progressive social policies, most viewed the country as politically backward. "Germany is mediæval," said one magazine in 1912. "'Divine

---

125. Layne, "Kant or Cant."
126. Waltz, "Emerging Structure," pp. 66–67, predicts that Japan and Germany will acquire nuclear capabilities to balance against the United States.
127. Layne, "The Myth of the Democratic Peace."

Rights' is written on the brow of the Kaiser. . . . This is the trinity that rules Germany: a mediæval king, a feudal aristocracy, and the pushing parvenus of coal dust and iron filings."[128] Second, the chancellor was responsible to the Emperor William rather than the legislature. The electorate had little leverage over war decisions. The press was not wholly free, as illustrated when William suppressed an antiwar book in 1913. The emperor also controlled the upper chamber of the legislature, the Bundesrat, which had veto power over the legislation of the lower house.[129] Thus, by neither the standards of its time nor those of this study can Germany be called a liberal democracy in 1914.

IS A REALIST-LIBERAL SYNTHESIS POSSIBLE?
Both realists and liberals who have written about democratic peace have been loath to cede any ground to the opposing side. Yet my argument and evidence suggest that both camps are describing real forces in international politics, namely, power politics and liberal ideas. It is conceivable that these two forces sometimes push in different directions in a particular case, yielding a weak effect in favor of one or the other. Jon Elster discusses such dynamics in a very different context: suppose a weak aggregate tendency was discovered for people to donate more to charity when others do so. The weak tendency may well be due to the existence of two different types of people with opposite tendencies: one, slightly dominant, that gives much more when observing others give (following a norm of reciprocity), and one that gives less (following a utilitarian norm). The combined effect conceals two strong mechanisms working at cross purposes.[130] Similarly, it could be that *Realpolitik* pushes policy into one direction and liberalism in another, and that the combined effect weakly favors one or the other. Consistent with this, my cases indicate that some actors are realist, some liberal.

A key to synthesizing the two theories would seem to be that liberals define national interest in such a way that cooperation with fellow liberal

128. *World's Work*, June 1912, p. 146.
129. John L. Snell, *The Democratic Movement in Germany, 1789–1914* (Chapel Hill: University of North Carolina Press, 1976), pp. 165, 212–219, 237–238, 343, 366; *Literary Digest*, June 14, 1913, pp. 1332–1333. For an argument that the German political system contributed to the coming of war, see Paul Kennedy, "The Kaiser and German *Weltpolitik*," in J. Rohl and N. Sombert, eds., *Kaiser Wilhelm II: New Interpretations* (Cambridge: Cambridge University Press, 1982), pp. 143–168.
130. Jon Elster, *Political Psychology* (Cambridge: Cambridge University Press, 1993), pp. 2–7. I thank David Dessler for bringing this source to my attention.

democracies is required. Given this premise, two synthetic approaches seem promising. First, the balance-of-threat theory of Stephen Walt could incorporate states' estimates of regime type. Walt writes that a state's alliance decisions are based not only on the aggregate and offensive power and geographic proximity of foreign states, but also on how aggressive their intentions are. He cites the Eyre Crowe memorandum of 1907, which stated that the British welcomed the growth of German power *per se*, but were concerned about German intentions.[131] My argument holds that liberals judge foreign states' intentions in part based on whether those states are liberal democracies. Had Eyre Crowe considered Germany liberal, he would not have been so worried.

A second approach would use the ideational framework of Alexander Wendt, David Lumsdaine, and others. Essentially, this approach postulates that international anarchy does not necessarily lead to self-help and power politics. Rather, these features are derivative of states' practices, particularly the ways they define themselves and their interests. That is, even absent a world sovereign, states must hold certain beliefs about each other before they fear each other.[132] Neorealism posits that these beliefs are always a product of power factors and thus not an independent variable. But the evidence that there is democratic peace and that it is a product of liberal ideas suggests neorealism is wrong. Power would not drop out of a framework that claims ideational sources of national interest. It would simply be one of several forces, filtered through an ideational lens.

Conclusion

That no one has directly observed a causal mechanism preventing democracies from going to war against one another has damaged the democratic peace thesis. In this article, I have argued that there is indeed such a mechanism. Fundamentally it is the liberal ideas undergirding liberal democracies. Liberalism says that all persons are best off pursuing self-preservation and material well-being, and that freedom and toleration are the best means to

---

131. Stephen M. Walt, *The Origins of Alliances* (Ithaca: Cornell University Press, 1987), pp. 21–25.
132. See Alexander Wendt, "Anarchy Is What States Make of It: The Social Construction of Power Politics," *International Organization*, Vol. 46, No. 2 (Spring 1992), pp. 391–425; and David Halloran Lumsdaine, *Moral Vision in International Politics: The Foreign Aid Regime, 1949–1989* (Princeton: Princeton University Press, 1993), pp. 3–29.

these ends. The liberal commitment to individual freedom gives rise to foreign policy ideology and governmental institutions that work together to produce democratic peace.

Ideologically, liberals trust those states they consider fellow liberal democracies and see no reason to fight them. They view those states they consider illiberal with suspicion, and sometimes believe that the national interest requires war with them. In different countries at different times, liberals have differed on the form of a liberal democracy, but the essential ideology is the same. Institutionally, liberalism brings about democratic structures that give citizens leverage over governmental decisions. Sometimes liberals run the government and simply implement their view of the national interest. Even when they do not, the institutions of free speech and regular, competitive elections allow liberal elites to force even illiberal leaders of democracies to follow liberal ideology. When a liberal democracy is in a war-threatening crisis with a state it considers liberal-democratic, its liberal elites agitate against war. Illiberal leaders find they cannot persuade the public to go to war, and moreover fear they will lose the next election if they do go to war. By the same process, they may be goaded into war with states that liberals believe to be illiberal.

This model was illustrated in four war-threatening crises involving the United States. In three of these, liberalism helped to prevent war. In one (Anglo-American relations from 1803–12), liberalism helped bring on war. Among other things, these cases illustrate the importance of perceptions.

Although I argue that realists are wrong in denying the existence of the democratic peace, I do not argue that power politics has no role in liberal-democratic foreign policy. The balance of power matters to liberals as well as to realists, but liberals view it as part of a larger picture of international politics. It appears that a synthesis of realism and liberalism is possible, as least concerning democratic peace.

The democratic peace provides strong evidence that ideas matter in international relations, both as shapers of national interest and as builders of democratic institutions. Thomas Paine claimed that the American Revolutionaries "have it in our power to begin the world all over again."[133] He may have been overreaching: the hostile relations between France and the United States in the 1790s, sister republics of the first democratic peace, show how

---

133. In "Common Sense," January 1776, quoted in Michael H. Hunt, *Ideology and U.S. Foreign Policy* (New Haven: Yale University Press, 1987), p. 19.

the world of power politics can stymie the harmonious plans of liberals. Yet it looks as though a force does rise up within liberal democracies capable of steering conflict off of its usual trajectory.

Still, this study does not show that the democratic peace necessarily leads to perpetual peace. Threats to liberalism itself should engender caution. Historically, one threat has come from liberalism's inability to fulfill the material expectations it raises. When peace does not bring prosperity, as in Weimar Germany, war begins to look more attractive and liberalism may collapse. A second threat may lie in liberalism's tendency to destroy traditional ways of life and sources of meaning. Islamic fundamentalists, for example, simply reject the individualism that undergirds the democratic peace, and there are signs that many within the West itself reject it also.[134] Despite its stunning recent successes,[135] and arguments that it has triumphed over its philosophical competitors,[136] it is not at all clear that liberalism has brought an end to History.

---

134. For a synopsis of threats to liberalism and thus to democratic peace, see Samuel P. Huntington, "No Exit: The Errors of Endism," *The National Interest*, No. 17 (Fall 1989), pp. 3–11.
135. For a theoretical treatment of the spread of democracy, see Samuel P. Huntington, *The Third Wave: Democratization in the Late Twentieth Century* (Norman: University of Oklahoma Press, 1991).
136. See Francis Fukuyama, *The End of History and the Last Man* (New York: The Free Press, 1992).

Kant or Cant | *Christopher Layne*
The Myth of the Democratic Peace

$\mathbf{T}$ne theory of the "Democratic Peace" raises important theoretical issues:[1] the contention that democratic states behave differertly toward each other than toward non-democracies cuts to the heart of the international relations theory debate about the relative salience of second-image (domestic politics) and of third-image (systemic structure) explanations of international political outcomes. Democratic peace theory has also come to have a real-world importance as well: Policymakers who have embraced democratic peace theory see a crucial link between America's security and the spread of democracy, which is viewed as the antidote that will prevent future wars. Indeed some democratic peace theorists, notably Bruce Russett, believe that in an international system comprising a critical mass of democratic states, "It may be possible in part to supersede the 'realist' principles (anarchy, the security dilemma of states) that have dominated practice to the exclusion of 'liberal' or 'idealist' ones since at least the seventeenth century."[2] Because of its theoretical claims and

Christopher Layne of Los Angeles is an unaffiliated scholar. He is presently a consultant to the government contracts practice group of the law firm of Hill, Wynne, Troop and Meisinger, which represents major firms in the defense industry.

I am extremely grateful to the following colleagues who reviewed various drafts of this paper and offered helpful criticisms: John Arquilla, Ted Galen Carpenter, Kerry Andrew Chase, Jeffry Frieden, John Mearsheimer, Benjamin C. Schwarz, Jack Snyder, Stephen Walt, and Kenneth Waltz. I also thank Stephen Van Evera and David Spiro for providing me copies of, and permission to quote from, their unpublished works.

1. I use the term "democratic peace theory" because it is a convenient shorthand term. However, strictly speaking, the claim that democracies do not fight democracies is a proposition, or hypothesis, rather than a theory. Democratic peace "theory" proposes a causal relationship between an independent variable (democratic political structures at the unit level) and the dependent variable (the asserted absence of war between democratic states). However, it is not a true theory because the causal relationship between the independent and dependent variables is neither proven nor, as I demonstrate in this article, adequately explained. See Stephen Van Evera, "Hypotheses, Laws and Theories: A User's Guide," unpub. memo, Department of Political Science, MIT.
2. Bruce Russett, *Grasping the Democratic Peace: Principles for a Post–Cold War World* (Princeton: Princeton University Press, 1993), chap. 7; and Russett, "Can A Democratic Peace Be Built?" *International Interactions*, Vol. 18, No. 3 (Spring 1993), pp. 277–282.

International Security, Vol. 19, No. 2 (Fall 1994), pp. 5–49
© 1994 by the President and Fellows of Harvard College and the Massachusetts Institute of Technology.

policy implications, the democratic peace theory merits careful examination.[3] In this article, I focus primarily on a critique of the persuasiveness of democratic peace theory's causal logic and ask whether democratic peace theory or realism is a better predictor of international outcomes. I then briefly assess the robustness of democratic peace theory's empirical evidence in light of my conclusions about the strength of its explanatory power.

I begin by reviewing the explanations of the Democratic Peace advanced by democratic peace theorists. There are two strands to the theory's causal logic. One attributes the absence of war between democracies to institutional constraints: the restraining effects of public opinion, or of the checks and balances embedded in a democratic state's domestic political structure. The other posits that it is democratic norms and culture—a shared commitment to the peaceful adjudication of political disputes—that accounts for the absence of war between democratic states. As I demonstrate, the institutional-constraints argument fails to provide a compelling explanation for the absence of war between democracies. Thus, democratic peace theory's explanatory power rests on the persuasiveness of the contention that democratic norms and culture explain why, although democratic states fight with non-democracies, they do not go to war with each other.

This article's centerpiece is a test of the competing explanations of international outcomes offered by democratic peace theory and by realism. This test is based on case studies of four "near misses"—crises where two democratic states almost went to war with each other. These four cases are well-documented instances of democratic great powers going to the brink of war without going over it. As such, they present an opportunity to determine which of the competing hypotheses advanced respectively by democratic peace theory and realism best account for international political outcomes.[4]

---

3. In this article, I build upon and expand the criticisms of democratic peace theory found in John J. Mearsheimer, "Back to the Future: Instability in Europe After the Cold War," *International Security*, Vol. 15, No. 1 (Summer 1990), pp. 5–56; and Kenneth N. Waltz, "America as Model for the World? A Foreign Policy Perspective," *PS* (December 1991), pp. 667–670.

4. Other cases of crises between democratic great powers that might be studied include Anglo-French relations during the Liberal *entente cordiale* of 1832–48, Franco-Italian relations during the late 1880s and early 1890s and, if Wilhelmine Germany is classified as a democracy, the Moroccan crises of 1905–06 and 1911 and the Samoan crises of 1889 and 1899. These cases would support my conclusions. For example, from 1832 to 1848, the Foxite legacy disposed England's Whigs to feel a strong commitment to France based on a shared liberal ideology. Yet Anglo-French relations during this period were marked by intense geopolitical rivalry over Belgium, Spain, and the Near East, and the threat of war was always a factor in the calculations of policymakers in both London and Paris. Foreign Minister Lord Palmerston profoundly distrusted French ambitions and constantly urged that England maintain sufficient naval power to defend its

Moreover, they present an easy case for democratic peace theory and a hard case for realism. The selected cases favor democratic peace theory because, in each, the pacifying effect of democratic norms and culture was bolstered by complementary factors (e.g., economic interdependence, or special ties linking the disputants). I deduce, from both the democratic norms and culture argument and from realism, sets of indicators—testable propositions— that should be present if a crisis's outcome is explained by either of the two theories. Using a process-tracing approach, I examine each crisis in detail.

I conclude that realism is superior to democratic peace theory as a predictor of international outcomes. Indeed, democratic peace theory appears to have extremely little explanatory power in the cases studied. Doubts about the validity of its causal logic suggest that the empirical evidence purporting to support democratic peace theory should also be revisited. Democratic peace theorists contend that the theory is validated by a large number of cases. However, a powerful argument can be made that the universe of cases from which it can be tested is actually quite small. This is a crucial issue, because if the theory's empirical support is based on a small-N universe, this magnifies the importance of possible exceptions to the rule that democracies do not fight each other (for example, World War I, the War between the States, the War of 1812). I conclude by discussing democratic peace theory's troublesome implications for post–Cold War American foreign policy.

The Case for a Democratic Peace: Its Claims and its Logic

Democratic peace theory does not contend that democratic states are less war-prone than non-democracies; they are not. The theory does, however, make two important claims, first, that democracies never (or rarely; there is

interests against a French challenge. See Kenneth Bourne, *Palmerston: The Early Years, 1784–1841* (New York: Macmillan, 1982), p. 613. Also see Roger Bullen, *Palmerston, Guizot and the Collapse of the Entente Cordiale* (London: Athlone Press, 1974); and Sir Charles Webster, *The Foreign Policy of Palmerston*, Vol. I: *1830–1841, Britain, The Liberal Movement and The Eastern Question* (London: G. Bell & Sons, 1951). Italy challenged France for Mediterranean ascendancy although the two nations were bound by liberalism, democracy, and a common culture. The two states engaged in a trade war and came close to a real war. France apparently was dissuaded from attacking Italy in 1888 when the British Channel Fleet was sent to the Italian naval base of La Spezia. Italy was prevented from attacking France by its military and economic weakness. See C.J. Lowe and F. Marzari, *Italian Foreign Policy, 1870–1940* (London: Routledge & Kegan Paul, 1975, chap. 4; C.J. Lowe, *The Reluctant Imperialists: British Foreign Policy 1879–1902* (London: Routledge & Kegan Paul, 1974), Vol. I, pp. 147–150; John A.C. Conybeare, *Trade Wars: The Theory and Practice of International Commercial Rivalry* (New York: Columbia University Press, 1987), pp. 183–188.

a good deal of variation about this) go to war with other democracies.[5] As Jack S. Levy observes, the "absence of war between democracies comes as close as anything we have to an empirical law in international relations."[6] Second, when democracies come into conflict with one another, they only rarely threaten to use force, because it is "illegitimate" to do so.[7] Democratic peace theory explicitly holds that it is the very nature of democratic political systems that accounts for the fact that democracies do not fight or threaten other democracies.

THE CAUSAL LOGIC

Democratic peace theory must explain an anomaly: democracies are no less war-prone than non-democratic states. Yet, while they will readily threaten and fight non-democracies, they do not threaten or fight other democracies. The key challenge for the theory, then, is to identify the special characteristics of democratic states that restrain them from using coercive threats against, or actually going to war with, other democracies. The theory advances two alternative explanations: (1) institutional constraints; and (2) democratic norms and cultures.[8]

There are two major variants of the institutional constraints argument. Michael Doyle, building on Immanuel Kant, explains that democratic governments are reluctant to go to war because they must answer to their

---

5. Melvin Small and J. David Singer first observed the pattern of democracies not fighting democracies in a 1976 article: Small and Singer, "The War-proneness of Democratic Regimes, 1816–1865," *Jerusalem Journal of International Relations*, Vol. 1, No. 4 (Summer 1976), pp. 50–69. Their finding has been the subject of extensive further empirical testing which has produced a consensus around the propositions stated in the text. See Stuart A. Bremer, "Dangerous Dyads: Conditions Affecting the Likelihood of Interstate War, 1816–1865," *Journal of Conflict Resolution*, Vol. 36, No. 2 (June 1992), pp. 309–341; Steve Chan, "Mirror, Mirror on the Wall . . . Are the Freer Countries More Pacific?" *Journal of Conflict Resolution*, Vol. 28, No. 4 (December 1984), pp. 617–648; Zeev Maoz and Nasrin Abdolali, "Regime Type and International Conflict," *Journal of Conflict Resolution*, Vol. 33, No. 1 (March 1989), pp. 3–35; R.J. Rummel, "Libertarianism and International Violence," *Journal of Conflict Resolution*, Vol. 27, No. 1 (March 1983), pp. 27–71; Erich Weede, "Democracy and War Involvement," *Journal of Conflict Resolution*, Vol. 28, No. 4 (December 1984), pp. 649–664.
6. Jack S. Levy, "Domestic Politics and War," in Robert I. Rotberg and Theodore K. Rabb, eds., *The Origin and Prevention of Major Wars* (Cambridge: Cambridge University Press, 1989), p. 88.
7. Russett, *Grasping the Democratic Peace*, p. 33; Michael W. Doyle, "Kant, Liberal Legacies and Foreign Affairs," Part I, *Philosophy and Public Affairs*, Vol. 12, No. 3 (Summer 1983), p. 213.
8. This is the terminology employed by Russett, *Grasping the Democratic Peace*; also see Bruce Russett and Zeev Maoz, "Normative and Structural Causes of Democratic Peace," *American Political Science Review*, Vol. 87, No. 3 (September 1993), pp. 624–638. Russett points out (pp. 40–42) that, although analytically distinct, these two explanations are intertwined.

citizens.[9] Citizens pay the price for war in blood and treasure; if the price of conflict is high, democratic governments may fall victim to electoral retribution. Moreover, in democratic states, foreign policy decisions carrying the risk of war are debated openly and not made behind closed doors, which means that both the public and policymakers are sensitized to costs of fighting. A second version of the institutional constraints argument focuses on "checks and balances"; it looks at three specific features of a state's domestic political structure: executive selection, political competition, and the pluralism of the foreign policy decisionmaking process.[10] States with executives answerable to a selection body, with institutionalized political competition, and with decisionmaking responsibility spread among multiple institutions or individuals, should be more highly constrained and hence less likely to go to war.

The democratic norms explanation holds that "the *culture, perceptions, and practices* that permit compromise and the peaceful resolution of conflicts without the threat of violence *within countries* come to apply across national boundaries toward other democratic countries."[11] Democratic states assume both that other democracies also subscribe to pacific methods of regulating political competition and resolving disputes, and that others will apply these norms in their external relations with fellow democracies. In other words, democratic states develop positive perceptions of other democracies. Consequently, Doyle says, democracies, "which rest on consent, presume foreign republics to be also consensual, just and therefore deserving of accommodation."[12] Relations between democratic states are based on mutual respect

---

9. Doyle, "Kant, Liberal Legacies, and Foreign Affairs," pp. 205–235. See also Doyle, "Liberalism and World Politics," *American Political Science Review*, Vol. 80, No. 4 (December 1986), pp. 1151–1169; Russett, *Grasping the Democratic Peace*, pp. 38–40.
10. T. Clifton Morgan and Sally H. Campbell, "Domestic Structure, Decisional Constraints and War: So Why Kant Democracies Fight?" *Journal of Conflict Resolution*, Vol. 35, No. 2 (June 1991), pp. 187–211; and T. Clifton Morgan and Valerie L. Schwebach, "Take Two Democracies and Call Me in the Morning: A Prescription for Peace?" *International Interactions*, Vol. 17, No. 4 (Summer 1992), pp. 305–420.
11. Russett, *Grasping the Democratic Peace*, p. 31 (second emphasis added).
12. Doyle, "Kant, Liberal Legacies, and Foreign Affairs," p. 230. It is also argued that the predisposition of democratic states to regard other democracies favorably is reinforced by the fact that liberal democratic states are linked by mutually beneficial ties of economic interdependence. Democracies thus have strong incentives to act towards each other in a manner that enhances cooperation and to refrain from acting in a manner that threatens their stake in mutually beneficial cooperation. Ibid., pp. 230–232; Rummel, "Libertarianism and International Violence," pp. 27–28. For the "interdependence promotes peace" argument see Richard Rosecrance, *The Rise of the Trading State* (New York: Basic Books, 1986). In fact, however, for great powers economic interdependence, rather than promoting peace, creates seemingly important

rooted in the fact that democracies perceive each other as dovish (that is, negotiation or the status quo are the only possible outcomes in a dispute). This perception, it is argued, is based on a form of learning. Democratic states benefit from cooperative relations with one another and they want to expand their positive interactions. In turn, this desire predisposes them to be responsive to the needs of other democratic states, and ultimately leads to creation of a community of interests. As democracies move towards community, they renounce the option to use (or even to threaten to use) force in their mutual interactions.[13]

The democratic ethos—based on "peaceful competition, persuasion and compromise"—explains the absence of war and war-like threats in relations between democratic states.[14] Conversely, the absence of these norms in relations between democracies and non-democracies, it is said, explains the paradox that democracies do not fight each other even though in general they are as war-prone as non-democracies: "When a democracy comes into conflict with a nondemocracy, it will not expect the nondemocratic state to be restrained by those norms [of mutual respect based on democratic culture]. It may feel obliged to adapt to the harsher norms of international conduct of the latter, lest it be exploited or eliminated by the nondemocratic state that takes advantage of the inherent moderation of democracies."[15] Thus it is a fundamental postulate of democratic peace theory that democracies behave in a qualitatively different manner in their relations with each other than they do in their relations with non-democracies.

The Realist Case: The Same Things Over and Over Again

If history is "just one damn thing after another," then for realists international politics is the same damn things over and over again: war, great power security and economic competitions, the rise and fall of great powers, and the formation and dissolution of alliances. International political behavior is characterized by continuity, regularity, and repetition because states are con-

---

interests that must be defended by overseas military commitments (commitments that carry with them the risk of war). See Christopher Layne and Benjamin C. Schwarz, "American Hegemony—Without an Enemy," *Foreign Policy*, No. 92 (Fall 1993), pp. 5–23.
13. Doyle, "Kant, Liberal Legacies, and Foreign Affairs"; and Harvey Starr, "Democracy and War: Choice, Learning and Security Communities," *Journal of Peace Research*, Vol. 29, No. 2 (1992), pp. 207–213.
14. Maoz and Russett, "A Statistical Artifact?" p. 246.
15. Russett, *Grasping the Democratic Peace*, p. 33.

strained by the international system's unchanging (and probably unchangeable) structure.

The realist paradigm explains why this is so.[16] International politics is an anarchic, self-help realm. "Anarchy," rather than denoting chaos or rampant disorder, refers in international politics to the fact that there is no central authority capable of making and enforcing rules of behavior on the international system's units (states). The absence of a rule-making and enforcing authority means that each unit in the system is responsible for ensuring its own survival and also that each is free to define its own interests and to employ means of its own choice in pursuing them. In this sense, international politics is fundamentally competitive. And it is competitive in a manner that differs crucially from domestic politics in liberal societies, where the losers can accept an adverse outcome because they live to fight another day and can, therefore, ultimately hope to prevail. In international politics, states that come out on the short end of political competition face potentially more extreme outcomes, ranging from constraints on autonomy to occupation to extinction.

It is anarchy that gives international politics its distinctive flavor. In an anarchic system, a state's first goal is to survive. To attain security, states engage in both internal and external balancing for the purpose of deterring aggressors, and of defeating them should deterrence fail. In a realist world, cooperation is possible but is hard to sustain in the face of the competitive pressures that are built into the international political system's structure. The imperative of survival in a threatening environment forces states to focus on strategies that maximize their power relative to their rivals. States have powerful incentives both to seek the upper hand over their rivals militarily and to use their edge not only for self-defense but also to take advantage of others. Because military power is inherently offensive rather than defensive in nature, states cannot escape the security dilemma: measures taken by a state as self-defense may have the unintended consequence of threatening others. This is because a state can never be certain that others' intentions are benign; consequently its policies must be shaped in response to others' capabilities. In the international system, fear and distrust of other states is the normal state of affairs.

---

16. Classic explications of realism are Kenneth N. Waltz, *Theory of International Politics* (Reading, Mass.: Addison-Wesley, 1979) and Hans J. Morgenthau, rev. by Kenneth W. Thompson, *Politics Among Nations: The Struggle for Power and Peace,* 6th ed. (New York: Knopf, 1985).

Here democratic peace and realism part company on a crucial point. The former holds that changes within states can transform the nature of international politics. Realism takes the view that even if states change internally, the structure of the international political system remains the same. As systemic structure is the primary determinant of international political outcomes, structural constraints mean that similarly placed states will act similarly, regardless of their domestic political systems. As Kenneth Waltz says: "In self-help systems, the pressures of competition weigh more heavily than ideological preferences or internal political pressures."[17] Changes at the unit level do not change the constraints and incentives imbedded at the systemic level. States respond to the logic of the situation in which they find themselves even though this may result in undesirable outcomes, from the breakdown of cooperation to outright war. States that ignore the imperatives of a realist world run the risk of perishing. In a realist world, survival and security are always at risk, and democratic states will respond no differently to democratic rivals than to non-democratic ones.

Testing Democratic Peace Theory

Institutional constraints do not explain the democratic peace. If democratic public opinion really had the effect ascribed to it, democracies would be peaceful in their relations with all states, whether democratic or not. If citizens and policymakers of a democracy were especially sensitive to the human and material costs of war, that sensitivity should be evident whenever their state is on the verge of war, regardless of whether the adversary is democratic: the lives lost and money spent will be the same. Nor is democratic public opinion, *per se*, an inhibitor of war. For example, in 1898 it was public opinion that impelled the reluctant McKinley administration into war with Spain; in 1914 war was enthusiastically embraced by public opinion in Britain and France. Domestic political structure—"checks and balances"—does not explain the democratic peace either. "This argument," as Morgan and Schwebach state, "does not say anything directly about the war-proneness of democracies," because it focuses on an independent variable—decisional constraints embedded in a state's domestic political structure—that is associated with, but not exclusive to, democracies.

---

17. Kenneth N. Waltz, "A Reply to My Critics," in Robert O. Keohane, ed., *Neorealism and Its Critics* (New York: Columbia University Press, 1986), p. 329.

Because these explanations fall short, the democratic norms and culture explanation must bear the weight of the democratic peace theory's causal logic. It is there we must look to find that "something in the internal makeup of democratic states" that explains the democratic peace.[18]

Democratic peace theory not only predicts a specific outcome—no war between democracies—but also purports to explain why that outcome will occur. It is thus suited to being tested by the case study method, a detailed look at a small number of examples to determine if events unfold and actors act as the theory predicts. The case study method also affords the opportunity to test the competing explanations of international political outcomes offered by democratic peace theory and by realism. To test the robustness of democratic peace theory's causal logic, the focus here is on "near misses," specific cases in which democratic states had both opportunity and reason to fight each other, but did not.

The case studies in this article use the process-tracing method (opening up the "black box") to identify the factors to which decisionmakers respond, how those factors influence decisions, the actual course of events, and the possible effect of other variables on the outcome.[19] As Stephen Van Evera says, if a theory has strong explanatory power, process-tracing case studies provide a robust test because decisionmakers "should speak, write, and otherwise behave in a manner consistent with the theory's predictions."[20]

Democratic peace theory, if valid, should account powerfully for the fact that serious crises between democratic states ended in near misses rather than in war. If democratic norms and culture explain the democratic peace, in a near-war crisis, certain indicators of the democratic peace theory should be in evidence: First, public opinion should be strongly pacific. Public opinion is important not because it is an institutional constraint, but because it is an indirect measure of the mutual respect that democracies are said to have for each other. Second, policymaking elites should refrain from making military threats against other democracies and should refrain from making preparations to carry out threats. Democratic peace theorists waffle on this point by

18. Maoz and Russett, "Normative and Structural Causes," p. 624.
19. Alexander L. George and Timothy J. McKeown, "Case Studies and Theories of Organizational Decision Making," in Robert F. Coulam and Richard A. Smith, eds., *Advances in Information Processing in Organizations*, Vol. 2 (Greenwich, Conn.: JAI Press, 1985), p. 35.
20. Stephen Van Evera, "What Are Case Studies? How Should They Be Performed?" unpub. memo, September 1993, Department of Political Science, MIT, p. 2.

suggesting that the absence of war between democracies is more important than the absence of threats. But this sets the threshold of proof too low. Because the crux of the theory is that democracies externalize their internal norms of peaceful dispute resolution, then especially in a crisis, one should not see democracies threatening other democracies. And if threats are made, they should be a last-resort option rather than an early one. Third, democracies should bend over backwards to accommodate each other in a crisis. Ultimata, unbending hard lines, and big-stick diplomacy are the stuff of *Realpolitik*, not the democratic peace.

A realist explanation of near misses would look at a very different set of indicators. First, realism postulates a ratio of national interest to democratic respect: in a crisis, the more important the interests a democracy perceives to be at stake, the more likely that its policy will be shaped by realist imperatives rather than by democratic norms and culture. When vital interests are on the line, democracies should not be inhibited from using threats, ultimata, and big-stick diplomacy against another democracy. Second, even in a crisis involving democracies, states should be very attentive to strategic concerns, and the relative distribution of military capabilities between them should crucially—perhaps decisively—affect their diplomacy. Third, broader geopolitical considerations pertaining to a state's position in international politics should, if implicated, account significantly for the crisis's outcome. Key here is what Geoffrey Blainey calls the "fighting waterbirds' dilemma," involving concerns that others watching from the sidelines will take advantage of a state's involvement in war; that war will leave a state weakened and in an inferior relative power position *vis-à-vis* possible future rivals; and that failure to propitiate the opposing state in a crisis will cause it to ally with one's other adversaries or rivals.[21]

I have chosen to study four modern historical instances in which democratic great powers almost came to blows: (1) the United States and Great Britain in 1861 ("the *Trent* affair"); (2) the United States and Great Britain in 1895–96 (the Venezuela crisis); France and Great Britain in 1898 (the Fashoda crisis); and France and Germany in 1923 (the Ruhr crisis).[22] I focus on great

---

21. Geoffrey Blainey, *The Causes of War*, 3rd ed. (South Melbourne: Macmillan Co. of Australia, 1988), pp. 57–67. As the parable goes, while the waterbirds fight over the catch, the fisherman spreads his net.
22. My classification of the United States in 1861 and 1895 and of Germany in 1923 as great powers might be challenged. By the mid-nineteenth century British policymakers viewed the United States, because of its size, population, wealth, and growing industrial strength (and

powers for several reasons. First, international relations theory is defined by great powers: they are the principal components of the international system, and their actions—especially their wars—have a greater impact on the international system than do those of small powers.[23] Moreover, while democratic peace theory should apply to both great and small powers, realist predictions about great power behavior are not always applicable to small powers, because the range of options available to the latter is more constrained.[24] Crises between democratic great powers are a good head-to-head test because democratic peace theory and realism should both be applicable.[25]

The cases selected should favor democratic peace theory for more than the obvious reason that none of them led to war. In each crisis, background factors were present that should have reinforced democratic peace theory's predictions. In the two Anglo-American crises, a common history, culture and language, and economic interdependence were important considerations.[26] In the Fashoda crisis, the factors that led to the 1904 Anglo-French entente were already present and both countries benefited significantly from their economic relations.[27] The Franco-German Ruhr crisis tested both the Wilsonian prescription for achieving security in post–World War I Europe and the belief (increasingly widespread among French and German business elites, and to a lesser extent the political elites) that the prosperity of both states hinged on their economic collaboration.

---

latent military power), as "a great world power," notwithstanding the fact that it was not an active participant in the European state system. Ephraim Douglass Adams, *Great Britain and the American Civil War* (New York: Russell and Russell, 1924), Vol. I, p. 10. In 1895 the perception of American power had heightened in Britain and in other leading European powers. In 1923, Germany, although substantially disarmed pursuant to Versailles, remained Europe's most economically powerful state. As most statesmen realized, it was, because of its population and industry, a latent continental hegemon. Democratic peace theorists have classified all eight states as having been democracies at the time of their involvement in the crises under discussion. See Doyle, "Kant, Liberal Legacies, and Foreign Affairs," part I, pp. 214–215. Russett, *Grasping the Democratic Peace*, pp. 5–9, briefly discusses the Venezuela and Fashoda crises, but his bibliography has few historical references to these two crises (and related issues), and omits most standard sources.
23. Waltz, *Theory of International Politics*, pp. 72–73.
24. See Robert L. Rothstein, *Alliances and Small Powers* (New York: Columbia University Press, 1968), especially chap. 1.
25. As noted above, other such crises also support my argument.
26. For a brief discussion of the cultural, social, and economic bonds between Britain and the United States during the mid-nineteenth century, see Martin Crawford, *The Anglo-American Crisis of the Mid-Nineteenth Century: The Times and America, 1850–1862* (Athens: University of Georgia Press, 1987), pp. 39–55.
27. Stephen R. Rock, *Why Peace Breaks Out: Great Power Rapprochement in Historical Perspective* (Chapel Hill: University of North Carolina Press, 1989), pp. 91–119.

ANGLO-AMERICAN CRISIS I: THE *TRENT* AFFAIR, 1861

In 1861, tensions arising from the War Between the States brought the Union and Britain to the brink of war. The most important causes of Anglo-American friction stemmed from the Northern blockade of Confederate ports and the consequent loss to Britain of the cotton upon which its textile industry depended. The immediate precipitating cause of the Anglo-American crisis, however, was action of the *USS San Jacinto* which, acting without express orders from Washington, intercepted the British mail ship *Trent* on November 8, 1861. The *Trent* was transporting James M. Mason and John Slidell, the Confederacy's commissioners-designate to Great Britain and France; they had boarded the *Trent*, a neutral vessel, in Havana, Cuba, a neutral port. A boarding party from the *San Jacinto*, after searching the *Trent*, placed Mason and Slidell under arrest. The *Trent* was allowed to complete its voyage while the *San Jacinto* transported Mason and Slidell to Fort Warren in Boston harbor, where they were incarcerated.

When word was received in Britain, the public was overcome with war fever. "The first explosion of the Press, on receipt of the news of the *Trent*, had been a terrific one."[28] An American citizen residing in England reported to Secretary of State William H. Seward, "The people are frantic with rage, and were the country polled I fear 999 men out of 1000 would declare for war."[29] From Edinburgh, another American wrote, "I have never seen so intense a feeling of indignation in my life."[30]

The British government was hardly less bellicose than the public and the press. Fortified by legal opinions holding that Mason and Slidell had been removed from the *Trent* in contravention of international law, the Cabinet adopted a hard-line policy that mirrored the public mood. Prime Minister Lord Palmerston's first reaction to the news of the *Trent* incident was to write to the Secretary of State for War that, because of Britain's "precarious" relations with the United States, the government reconsider cuts in military expenditures planned to take effect in 1862.[31] At the November 29 Cabinet meeting, Palmerston reportedly began by flinging his hat on the table and

---

28. Adams, *Britain and the Civil War,* Vol. I, p. 216.
29. Quoted in Gordon H. Warren, *Fountain of Discontent: The Trent Affair and Freedom of the Seas* (Boston: Northeastern University Press, 1981), p. 105.
30. Quoted in Adams, *Britain and the Civil War,* Vol. I, p. 217.
31. Quoted in Norman B. Ferris, *The Trent Affair: A Diplomatic Crisis* (Knoxville: University of Tennessee Press, 1977), p. 44.

declaring to his colleagues, "I don't know whether you are going to stand this, but I'll be damned if I do!"[32]

The Cabinet adopted a dual-track approach towards Washington: London used military threats to coerce the United States into surrendering diplomatically, while on the diplomatic side, Foreign Secretary Lord John Russell drafted a note to the Union government in which, while holding firm to the demand that Mason and Slidell be released, he offered Washington an avenue of graceful retreat by indicating that London would accept, as tantamount to an apology, a declaration that the *San Jacinto* had acted without official sanction. Nevertheless, the note that was actually transmitted to Washington was an ultimatum. Although the British minister in Washington, Lord Lyons, was instructed to present the communication in a fashion calculated to maximize the chances of American compliance, his charge was clear: unless within seven days of receipt the Union government unconditionally accepted Britain's demands, Lyons was to ask for his passports and depart the United States. As Russell wrote to Lyons: "What we want is a plain Yes or a plain No to our very simple demands, and we want that plain Yes or No within seven days of the communication of the despatch."[33]

Although some, notably including Russell, hoped that the crisis could be resolved peacefully, the entire Cabinet recognized that its decision to present an ultimatum to Washington could lead to war. The British believed that there was one hope for peace: that Washington, overawed by Britain's military power and its readiness to go to war, would bow to London's demands rather than resisting them.[34] As the Undersecretary of State for Foreign Affairs stated, "Our only chance of peace is to be found in working on the fears of the Government and people of the United States."[35]

Driven by the belief that Washington would give in only to the threat of force, London's diplomacy was backed up by ostentatious military and naval preparations. Anticipating a possible conflict, the Cabinet embargoed the export to the United States of saltpeter (November 30) and of arms and ammunition (December 4). Underscoring the gravity of the crisis, for only

---

32. Ibid., p. 109; Howard Jones, *Union in Peril: The Crisis Over British Intervention in the Civil War* (Chapel Hill: University of North Carolina Press, 1992), pp. 84–85.
33. Quoted in Jones, *Union in Peril*, p. 85.
34. Jenkins, *War for the Union*, p. 214.
35. Quoted in Kenneth Bourne, *Britain and the Balance of Power in North America, 1815–1908* (Berkeley: University of California Press, 1967), p. 219.

the fourth time in history the Cabinet created a special war committee to oversee strategic planning and war preparations. Urgent steps were taken to reinforce Britain's naval and military contingents in North America. Beginning in mid-December, a hastily organized sealift increased the number of regular British army troops in Canada from 5,000 to 17,658, and Royal Navy forces in North American waters swelled from 25 to forty warships, with 1,273 guns (compared to just 500 before the crisis).[36] These measures served two purposes: they bolstered London's diplomacy and, in the event diplomacy failed, they positioned Britain to prevail in a conflict.

London employed big-stick diplomacy because it believed that a too-conciliatory policy would simply embolden the Americans to mount increasingly serious challenges to British interests.[37] Moreover, British policymakers believed that England's resolve, credibility, and reputation were at stake internationally, not just in its relations with the United States. The comments of once and future Foreign Secretary Lord Clarendon were typical: "What a figure . . . we shall cut in the eyes of the world, if we lamely submit to this outrage when all mankind will know that we should unhesitatingly have poured our indignation and our broadsides into any weak nation . . . and what an additional proof it will be of the universal . . . belief that we have two sets of weights and measures to be used according to the power or weakness of our adversary."[38] Thus "the British were prepared to accept the cost of an Anglo-American war . . . rather than sacrifice their prestige as a great power by headlong diplomatic defeat."[39]

London's hard-line policy was fortified by its "general optimism about the ultimate outcome" of an Anglo-American war.[40] Queen Victoria said a war would result in "utter destruction to the North Americans" and Secretary of

---

36. The figures are from Warren, *Fountain of Discontent*, pp. 130, 136. For an overview of British military and naval activities during the Trent crisis see Kenneth Bourne, "British Preparations for War with the North, 1861–1862," *English Historical Review*, Vol. 76, No. 301 (October 1961), pp. 600–632.

37. Ferris, *Trent Affair*, p. 56; Wilbur Devereux Jones, *The American Problem in British Diplomacy, 1841–1861* (London: Macmillan, 1974), p. 203. In international relations theory terms, London's view of Anglo-American relations was based on a deterrence model rather than a spiral model. See Robert Jervis, *Perception and Misperception in International Politics* (Princeton: Princeton University Press, 1976), pp. 58–111. Coexisting uneasily with the positive view of an Anglo-American community was the British image of the United States as a vulgar "mobocracy" that, unless firmly resisted, would pursue a rapacious and bullying foreign policy. Warren, *Fountain of Discontent*, pp. 47–51.

38. Quoted in Bourne, *Balance of Power*, p. 247.

39. Bourne, "British Preparations," p. 631.

40. Bourne, *Balance of Power*, p. 247.

State for War George Cornewall Lewis said "we shall soon *iron the smile* out of their face."[41] Palmerston was therefore untroubled by the discomfiture imposed on the Union by London's uncompromising policy. In his view, regardless of whether the crisis was resolved peacefully or resulted in war, Britain's interests would be upheld. He wrote to Queen Victoria:

If the Federal Government comply with the demands it will be honorable to England and humiliating to the United States. If the Federal Government refuse compliance, Great Britain is in a better state than at any former time to inflict a severe blow upon, and to read a lesson to the United States which will not soon be forgotten.[42]

In late 1861, the war against the Confederacy was not going well for Washington and the one major engagement, the first Battle of Manassas, had resulted in a humiliating setback for the Union army. Whipped up by Secretary of State Seward, who was a master at "twisting the lion's tail" for maximum domestic political effect, Northern opinion was hostile in London and resented especially Queen Victoria's May 1861 neutrality proclamation, which Northerners interpreted as *de facto* British recognition of Southern independence. News of the seizure of Mason and Slidell had a double effect on Northern public opinion. First, it was a tonic for sagging Northern morale. Second, it was seen as a warning to Britain to refrain from interfering with the Union's prosecution of the war against the Confederacy. Thus, although some papers (notably the *New York Times* and the *New York Daily Tribune*) urged that Washington should placate the British, public opinion strongly favored a policy of standing up to London and refusing to release Mason and Slidell.[43] In response to Britain's hard line, "a raging war cry reverberated across the Northern states in America."[44] Charles Francis Adams, Jr., whose father was U.S. minister in London at the time, wrote later of the affair: "I do not remember in the whole course of the half-century's retrospect . . . any occurrence in which the American people were so completely swept off their feet, for the moment losing possession of their senses, as during the weeks which immediately followed the seizure of Mason and Slidell."[45]

---

41. Quoted in ibid., pp. 245–246, emphasis in original.
42. Quoted in Jenkins, *War for the Union*, p. 216.
43. Ferris, *Trent Affair*, pp. 111–113.
44. Norman B. Ferris, *Desperate Diplomacy: William H. Seward's Foreign Policy, 1861* (Knoxville: University of Tennessee, 1976), p. 194.
45. Quoted in Adams, *Britain and the Civil War*, Vol. I, p. 218.

The Lincoln administration was aware of the strength of anti-British sentiment among the public and in Congress (indeed, in early December, Congress passed a resolution commending the *San Jacinto's* captain for his action). There is some evidence that in order to placate public opinion, President Lincoln was inclined toward holding on to Mason and Slidell, notwithstanding the obvious risks of doing so.[46] Nevertheless, after first toying with the idea of offering London arbitration in an attempt to avoid the extremes of war or a humiliating climb-down, the United States elected to submit to Britain's demands. Given that Washington "could not back down easily," it is important to understand why it chose to do so.

The United States bowed to London because, already fully occupied militarily trying to subdue the Confederacy, the North could not also afford a simultaneous war with England, which effectively would have brought Britain into the War Between the States on the South's side.[47] This was clearly recognized by the Lincoln administration when the cabinet met for two days at Christmas to decide on the American response to the British note. The cabinet had before it two critical pieces of information. First, Washington had just been informed that France supported London's demands (ending American hopes that Britain would be restrained by its own "waterbird" worries that France would take advantage of an Anglo-American war).[48] Second, Washington had abundant information about the depth of the pro-war sentiment of the British public. The American minister in London, Charles Francis Adams, wrote that the English "were now all lashed up into hostility" and that: "The leading newspapers roll out as much fiery lava as Vesuvius is doing, daily. The Clubs and the army and the navy and the people in the streets generally are raving for war."[49] Senator Charles Sumner passed on to the Lincoln administration letters from the noted Radical members of parliament, Richard Cobden and John Bright. While deploring their government's policy and the tenor of British public opinion, both Cobden and Bright

---

46. Warren, *Fountain of Discontent*, pp. 184–185; Adams, *Britain and the Civil War*, p. 231. Howard Jones, however, suggests that Lincoln probably intended to give up Mason and Slidell and that he may have been posturing in order to shift to other members of his cabinet the onus of advancing the argument for surrendering them. Jones, *Union in Peril*, pp. 91–92.
47. Ferris, *Trent Affair*, pp. 177–182; Jenkins, *War for the Union*, pp. 223–226; Warren, *Fountain of Discontent*, pp. 181–182.
48. See Jenkins, *War for the Union*, pp. 225–226.
49. Quoted in Ferris, *Trent Affair*, pp. 154, 147 and see also pp. 66–67, 139–141; Jones, *Union in Peril*, p. 89.

stressed that war would result unless the United States gave in to London. Cobden observed:

Formerly England feared a war with the United States as much from the dependence on your cotton as from a dread of your power. *Now* the popular opinion (however erroneous) is that a war would give us cotton. And we, of course, consider your power weakened by your Civil War.[50]

Facing the choice of defying London or surrendering to its demands, Washington was compelled to recognize both that Britain was serious about going to war and that such a war almost certainly would result in the Union's permanent dissolution. During the cabinet discussions, Attorney General Edward Bates suggested that Britain was seeking a war with the United States in order to break the Northern blockade of Southern cotton ports and he worried that London would recognize the Confederacy. The United States, he said, "cannot afford such a war." He went on to observe, "In such a crisis, with such a civil war upon our hands, we cannot hope for success in a . . . war with England, backed by the assent and countenance of France. We must evade it—with as little damage to our own honor and pride as possible."[51] Secretary of State Seward concurred, stating that it was "no time to be diverted from the cares of the Union into controversies with other powers, even if just causes for them could be found."[52] When the United States realized that Britain's threat to go to war was not a bluff, strategic and national interest considerations—the "waterbird dilemma"—dictated that Washington yield to Britain.

The *Trent* affair's outcome is explained by realism, not democratic peace theory. Contrary to democratic peace theory's expectations, the mutual respect between democracies rooted in democratic norms and culture had no influence on British policy. Believing that vital reputational interests affecting its global strategic posture were at stake, London played diplomatic hardball, employed military threats, and was prepared to go to war if necessary. Both the public and the elites in Britain preferred war to conciliation. Across the Atlantic, public and governmental opinion in the North was equally bellicose. An Anglo-American conflict was avoided only because the Lincoln admin-

---

50. Quoted in ibid., p. 172 (emphasis in original). Bright's letter warned: "If you are resolved to succeed against the South, *have no war with England.*" Quoted in Adams, *Britain and the Civil War,* p. 232 (emphasis in original).
51. Quoted in ibid., p. 182.
52. Quoted in Jenkins, *War for the Union,* p. 224.

istration came to understand that diplomatic humiliation was preferable to a war that would have arrayed Britain with the Confederacy and thus probably have secured the South's independence.

ANGLO-AMERICAN CRISIS II: VENEZUELA, 1895–96

In 1895–96, the United States and Great Britain found themselves embroiled in a serious diplomatic confrontation arising out of an obscure long-standing dispute between London and Caracas over the Venezuela–British Guiana boundary. By 1895, Caracas was desperately beseeching Washington to pressure London to agree to arbitrate the dispute. The Cleveland administration decided to inject the United States diplomatically into the Anglo-Venezuelan disagreement, but not out of American solicitude for Venezuela's interests or concern for the issue's merits.[53] For the United States, the Anglo-Venezuelan affair was part of a larger picture. By 1895, American policymakers, conscious of the United States's status as an emerging great power, were increasingly concerned about European political and commercial intrusion into the Western Hemisphere.[54] For Washington, the controversy between London and Caracas was a welcome pretext for asserting America's claim to geopolitical primacy in the Western hemisphere. It was for this reason that the United States provoked a showdown on the Anglo-Venezuelan border dispute.[55]

The American position was set forth in Secretary of State Richard Olney's July 20, 1895, note to the British government.[56] The United States stated that its "honor and its interests" were involved in the Anglo-Venezuelan dispute, "the continuance of which it cannot regard with indifference." Washington demanded that London submit the dispute to arbitration. In grandiloquent terms, Olney asserted that the Monroe Doctrine not only gave the United

53. Walter LaFeber demonstrates that the United States injected itself into the crisis to protect its own interests, not Venezuela's. LaFeber, *The New Empire: An Interpretation of American Expansion, 1860–1898* (Ithaca: Cornell University Press, 1963), chap. 6.
54. The relationship between security concerns and American foreign and strategic policy is discussed in Richard D. Challener, *Admirals, General and Foreign Policy, 1898–1914* (Princeton: Princeton University Press, 1973) and J.A.S. Grenville and George B. Young, *Politics, Strategy, and American Diplomacy: Studies in American Foreign Policy, 1873–1917* (New Haven: Yale University Press, 1966).
55. Walter LaFeber, "The Background of Cleveland's Venezuelan Policy: A Reinterpretation," *American Historical Review*, Vol. 66 No. 4 (July 1961), p. 947; Ernest R. May, *Imperial Democracy: The Emergence of America as a Great Power* (New York: Harcourt, Brace and World, 1961), p. 34.
56. The full text of the note can be found in *Foreign Relations of the United States, 1895* (Washington, D.C.: U.S. Government Printing Office), Vol. I, pp. 542–576.

States the right to intervene in the Venezuela affair but also a more general right to superintend the affairs of the Western hemisphere.

In challenging Britain, President Grover Cleveland and his secretary of state realized they were taking a serious step. Although they almost certainly hoped to score a peaceful diplomatic victory, their strategy was one that could have led instead to an armed confrontation. Olney's July 20 note (praised by Cleveland as "the best thing of the kind I have ever read") was deliberately brusque and, as Henry James pointed out, under prevailing diplomatic custom, London could justifiably have regarded it as an ultimatum.[57] Moreover, Washington intended Olney's note for publication. Olney and Cleveland believed that their strong language would get London's attention and that, by using the Monroe Doctrine as a lever, the United States could ram a diplomatic settlement down Britain's throat.[58] Cleveland and Olney expected London to back down and agree to arbitration and they hoped that Britain's positive response could be announced when Congress reconvened in December.

To the administration's consternation, however, London refused to give in to Washington's demands. British Prime Minister and Foreign Secretary Salisbury's unyielding reply prompted Cleveland's December 17, 1895, message to Congress. While acknowledging that the prospect of an Anglo-American war was an unhappy one to contemplate, the president declared there was "no calamity which a great nation can invite which equals that which follows a supine submission to wrong and injustice and the consequent loss of national self-respect and honor beneath which are shielded and defended a people's safety and greatness." Cleveland strongly defended the validity of the Monroe Doctrine, which he described as vital to America's national security and to the integrity of its domestic political institutions. He asserted that London's exercise of jurisdiction over any territory that the United States determined to belong properly to Venezuela was "willful aggression upon [America's] rights and interests."

In taking this position, Cleveland declared that he was "fully alive to the responsibility incurred and keenly realize[d] all the consequences that may follow." Notwithstanding his strong rhetoric, however, Cleveland did leave

---

57. Henry James, *Richard Olney and His Public Service* (New York: DaCapo Press, 1971, reprint ed.), p. 109. President Cleveland quoted in May, *Imperial Democracy*, p. 40.
58. Gerald C. Eggert, *Richard Olney: Education of a Statesman* (University Park: Pennsylvania State University Press, 1974), pp. 202, 212–213.

the British with some maneuvering room. Before acting against Britain, he said, the United States would set up a commission to investigate the Anglo-Venezuelan dispute and Washington would take no steps until the commission's report was made and accepted. Nevertheless, the import of Cleveland's message was clear: the United States was willing to fight Britain if necessary in order to establish America's primacy in the Western hemisphere.[59]

As Kenneth Bourne points out, during the Venezuela crisis the risk of war was quite real.[60] Salisbury flatly rejected the terms for resolving the crisis set out in Olney's July 20 note. J.A.S. Grenville wrote: "nothing could be plainer than Salisbury's rejoinder to Olney: the United States had no business interfering in the dispute, the Monroe Doctrine had no standing as an international treaty and did not in any case apply to the controversy; the British government would accordingly continue to refuse arbitration of the Venezuelan claims as a whole."[61] Salisbury understood the risk that Washington would maintain its stance and that the crisis would escalate. But as Grenville points out, he was willing to run this risk because "he did not believe the danger to Britain would be serious. The country and empire would have united in defence of British possessions, and in the face of their determination he believed the United States would give way."[62] Either Washington would understand the significance of the disparity between its military power and Britain's, or the United States would be defeated.

In late 1895 Britain and the United States clearly were on a collision course, and conflict almost certainly would have occurred had Britain held fast to the policy line adopted by Salisbury in November 1895. London did not do so, however, and by late January 1896 London and Washington had embarked upon a diplomatic process that culminated in November 1896 in an amicable settlement of Anglo-American differences. The crucial question is, why did Britain suddenly reverse course at the beginning of 1896?

---

59. Both Walter LaFeber and Ernest May come to this conclusion. See LaFeber, *The New Empire,* p. 268 and May, *Imperial Democracy,* p. 42.
60. Kenneth Bourne, *Balance of Power,* p. 319. It should be noted that not all historians agree with Bourne. For example, J.A.S. Grenville has argued that the Venezuelan crisis was synthetic and that there was no real risk of war during the crisis; Grenville, *Lord Salisbury and Foreign Policy at the Close of the Nineteenth Century* (London: Athlone Press, 1964), p. 55. However, in later work, Grenville wrote: "Given the mood of the British Cabinet . . . a serious Anglo-American conflict seemed inevitable." Grenville and Young, *Politics, Strategy and American Diplomacy,* p. 169.
61. Grenville, *Lord Salisbury,* p. 63.
62. Ibid., p. 65.

Although there is no "smoking gun," compelling circumstantial evidence supports the historians' consensus opinion that Britain was constrained from going to war in 1896 by an unfavorable distribution of military capabilities *vis-à-vis* the United States and by a deteriorating international situation. London, Lord Salisbury excepted, had become concerned about the outcome of an Anglo-American war because of Britain's inability, due to threats elsewhere, to spare warships to reinforce its naval presence in North American waters; fears that Canada would be conquered by the United States; and fears that in a prolonged war, the United States would be able to force a stalemate and possibly even prevail because of its enormous economic strength.[63] Moreover, between November 1895 and mid-January 1896, Britain's international position took a sharp turn for the worse: "England stood completely isolated at the beginning of 1896. Her position was scarcely endurable."[64] Anglo-German relations had been plunged into crisis by the Krueger telegram that Kaiser Wilhelm II had dispatched in the wake of the Jameson raid on the Transvaal. Elsewhere, the threats from Britain's main rivals, Russia and France, seemed only slightly less menacing.

Britain concluded that it must settle with Washington because it could not afford yet another enemy. At the critical January 11, 1896, Cabinet meeting, Salisbury remained steadfastly committed to his November "no negotiations" policy, but his colleagues decided to resolve the crisis with Washington peacefully. As Grenville and Young point out: "In November they believed that Britain held all the trump cards [but] the mood was no longer confident. The Cabinet was now inclined to cut Britain's losses in a world which appeared to have become suddenly hostile."[65] Overruled by the Cabinet, Salisbury—who believed that eventual war with the United States was "some-

---

63. See Bourne, *The Balance of Power in North America*, p. 340–341; A.E. Campbell, *Britain and the United States*, pp. 29–40; Eggert, *Richard Olney*, pp. 232–233; Paul Kennedy, *The Realities Behind Diplomacy: Background Influences on British External Policy, 1865–1980* (London: George Allen & Unwin, 1981), pp. 107–109; Arthur J. Marder, *The Anatomy of British Sea Power: A History of British Naval Policy in the Pre-Dreadnought Era, 1880–1905* (New York: Knopf, 1940), pp. 254–257. In an early January 1896 letter to Theodore Roosevelt, Lord Bryce said that nothing could be farther from his countrymen's minds than interfering with America's rights or the hemispheric balance of power because: "Our hands are more than sufficiently full elsewhere." Quoted in A.E. Campbell, *Britain and the United States*, pp. 59–60.
64. Marder, *Anatomy of British Sea Power*, p. 257.
65. Grenville and Young, *Politics, Strategy and American Diplomacy*, p. 170; Grenville, *Lord Salisbury*, pp. 67–69.

thing more than a possibility"—apparently considered resigning the premiership.[66]

There is virtually no evidence that supports a democratic peace theory explanation of the Venezuela crisis's outcome. Although the crisis ended before either London or Washington could make war-like threats, both the United States and Britain began planning militarily for a possible conflict.[67] This suggests that both British and American policymakers considered that war, or at least the preparation for it, was a legitimate component of their diplomatic strategies.

It does not appear, either, that public opinion affected policy on either side of the Atlantic. In Britain, the Cleveland administration's demands initially were greeted with hostility. Nevertheless, even before January 1896, British public opinion overwhelmingly favored a peaceful settlement of the Anglo-American crisis. There is, however, no evidence in the historical record that public opinion had any effect on the Cabinet's January 11 decision to resolve the crisis peacefully. Indeed, during the Venezuela crisis, Britain's policy-making elite had a different view of Anglo-American relations than did the British public. At the time of the Venezuela crisis there was still "an enormous gulf" between the advocates of an Anglo-American rapprochement based on racial kinship "and the hard-headed realism of the school of professional politicians and strategists headed by Salisbury."[68]

On the American side of the Atlantic, Cleveland's bellicose December 17 message elicited widespread public support. As Walter LaFeber notes, "Expansionist-minded Americans heartily endorsed the President's message, though most of them also fully shared his hopes that no war would result."[69] However the public's enthusiasm rather quickly subsided, and important groups, especially the churches and some elements of the financial and manufacturing sectors, recoiled at the prospect of an Anglo-American war. Nevertheless, if war had occurred, the public would probably have united behind the Cleveland administration. American public opinion viewed the prospect of war with England "not with enthusiasm but as, though regret-

---

66. See J.L. Garvin, *Life of Joseph Chamberlain* (London: Macmillan, 1934), Vol. III, p. 161; Salisbury quoted in Bourne, *The Balance of Power in North America*, p. 339.
67. Both London and Washington planned for a North American war during early 1896. American planning focused on invading Canada, Britain's on defending it. See Bourne, *The Balance of Power in North America*, pp. 319–331.
68. Bourne, *Balance of Power*, p. 340. Marder, *Anatomy of British Sea Power*, pp. 254–255, shows that Britain's national security elites took a very hard-line stance during the Venezuela crisis.
69. LaFeber, *New Empire*, p. 270.

table, necessary if there were no other way of establishing the paramount position of the United States in the western hemisphere."[70]

Recent generations have come to regard the Anglo-American "special relationship" as an immutable fact of international life. Indeed, in some ways it is considered an archetype of relations between democratic states. The "great rapprochement" upon which the special relationship was built was the epilogue to the Venezuelan crisis. But whatever Anglo-American relations arguably have become, the impetus for the rapprochement between London and Washington (like the impetus for the settlement of the Venezuelan crisis itself) was, as C.S. Campbell points out, rooted in geostrategic concerns and not in the considerations that underlie democratic peace theory.[71]

By 1898, the effects of Britain's by then not-so-splendid isolation were being painfully felt, and London's overtures to Washington must be viewed as part of the dramatic "end of isolation" process of strategic and diplomatic readjustment that London undertook after the Boer War.[72] The British did not welcome the rapid expansion of American power; rather they reconciled themselves to something they could not prevent and which, unlike the German, Russian and French challenges, did not seem immediately threatening to vital British interests. The Anglo-American rapprochement was possible because on every issue in dispute between them, London yielded to Washington's demands. As Bourne dryly observes, "All this was not simply or even perhaps at all significant of any special goodwill towards the United States."[73] Britain could not afford to make any more enemies, and least of all could London afford to incur the enmity of the United States, with which the British knew they could no longer compete geopolitically. For London, the "special relationship" was a myth devised "to enable Britain

---

70. A.E. Campbell, *Britain and the United States*, p. 41.
71. Charles S. Campbell, *Anglo-American Understanding, 1898–1903* (Baltimore: Johns Hopkins University Press, 1957), pp. 8–24. Kenneth Bourne and Paul Kennedy both point out that many of the same non-strategic factors underlying the Anglo-American rapprochement ("Anglo-Saxonism," economic interdependence) had been strongly present since at least 1850. They did not, however, noticeably mitigate Anglo-American hostility. These factors only came into play *after* the changing international situation forced London to reassess its grand strategy. Bourne, *Balance of Power*, p. 343; Kennedy, *Realities Behind Diplomacy*, p. 118.
72. There is strong consensus on this point among diplomatic historians. Bourne, *Balance of Power*, pp. 409–410; A.E. Campbell, *Britain and the United States*, p. 208; C.S. Campbell, *Anglo-American Understanding*, p. 346, 184–185; Bradford Perkins, *The Great Rapprochement: England and the United States, 1895–1914* (New York: Atheneum, 1968) pp. 156–157; Kennedy, *Realities Behind Diplomacy*, pp. 118–119.
73. Bourne, *Balance of Power*, p. 343.

to withdraw gracefully" from those areas where British interests clashed with Washington's, and its function was to make the "pill" of appeasing the United States "more palatable to swallow."[74]

The outcome of the Venezuelan crisis is better explained by realism than by democratic peace theory. Consistent with realist expectations, both Britain and the United States began planning for war. Although, as democratic peace theory would predict, there was no war fever in either Britain or the United States, there is no evidence that public opinion played any role in London's decision-making process. It was London's decision to reverse its initially uncompromising stance and instead seek an amicable diplomatic solution with Washington that allowed Britain and the United States to avoid war. All available evidence supports the realist explanation that London made this decision solely for strategic reasons.

THE ANGLO-FRENCH STRUGGLE FOR CONTROL OF THE NILE: FASHODA, 1898

The Fashoda crisis marked the culmination of the Anglo-French struggle for supremacy over Egypt and the headwaters of the Nile.[75] Until 1882 Egypt, although nominally part of the Ottoman Empire, had been administered by an Anglo-French condominium. In 1882, Britain intervened unilaterally to suppress a nationalist revolt. Because the Suez canal was the vital artery linking Britain with India and its other far eastern imperial interests, strategic considerations overrode London's initial inclination to withdraw quickly from Egypt after the 1882 intervention. By the early 1890s, Lord Salisbury and other British policymakers had determined that in order to safeguard Egypt, Britain had to exert control over the Nile's source and its entire valley.

For France, Britain's post-1882 Egyptian primacy was an affront and, spurred by France's colonial party, Paris periodically looked for ways in which it could compel London to honor its pledge to withdraw from Egypt.

---

74. Ronald Hyam, *Britain's Imperial Century, 1815–1914: A Study of Empire and Expansion* (London: B.T. Batsford, 1976), pp. 202, 205; C.J. Lowe and M.L. Dockrill, *The Mirage of Power: British Foreign Policy, 1902–1914*, Vol. I (London: Routledge and Kegan Paul, 1972), p. 99.

75. For accounts of the Fashoda crisis and its background, the following are excellent sources: William L. Langer, *The Diplomacy of Imperialism, 1890–1902*, 2d ed. (New York: Knopf, 1965), pp. 101–144, 259–302; Ronald Robinson and John Gallagher with Alice Denny, *Africa and the Victorians: The Official Mind of Imperialism* (London: Macmillan, 1981, rev. ed.), pp. 76–159, 290–306; G.N. Sanderson, *England, Europe, and the Upper Nile, 1882–1899* (Edinburgh: Edinburgh University Press, 1965), chaps. 12–15; and Sanderson, "The Origins and Significance of the Anglo-French Confrontation at Fashoda," in Prosser Gifford and William Roger Louis, eds., *France and Britain in Africa: Imperial Rivalry and Colonial Rule* (New Haven: Yale University Press, 1971), pp. 285–332.

The immediate impetus for the French expedition to Fashoda appears to have come from a January 1893 talk given by the hydraulic engineer Victor Prompt at the Egyptian Institute in Paris, which suggested that the flow of water to Egypt could be restricted by damming the Upper Nile. After reviewing Prompt's speech, President of the French Republic Sadi Carnot exclaimed, "we must occupy Fashoda!"[76]

The plan to advance on Fashoda was eagerly embraced by Theophile Delcassé during his 1893–95 tenure first as undersecretary and then as minister for colonies. As a journalist and as a politician, he had been obsessed by the Egyptian question. For Delcassé and other French colonialists, France's prestige and its Mediterranean interests required an end to Britain's occupation of Egypt.[77] In 1896, a plan by marine captain Jean-Baptiste Marchand for an overland expedition to establish French control at Fashoda was approved by Foreign Minister Gabriel Hanotaux and Colonial Minister Emile Chautemps. They did not seek to precipitate an armed confrontation with Britain; they favored an eventual Anglo-French rapprochement and entente. However, they were convinced that French opinion would not accept an entente unless the two powers could reach settlement on the points of dispute between them, including Egypt. Thus, for Hanotaux and Delcassé, the Fashoda expedition was conceived as a lever to force the British to negotiate the Egyptian question and thus to increase France's great-power prestige.

In September 1898, Delcassé was foreign minister. As the conflict loomed, he hoped that it might be averted by Marchand's failure to reach his objective or, if the French expedition did run into British forces, by an agreement that the crisis would be settled diplomatically by London and Paris, not militarily by the opposing forces at Fashoda. Apparently relying on Salisbury's reputation for making "graceful concessions," Delcassé hoped to defuse the crisis by exchanging Marchand's withdrawal for Britain's agreement to reopen the Egyptian question and to discuss giving France an outlet on the Nile.[78] The British, however, had no intention of negotiating. London's position was simple: "Marchand should go, without quibbles or face saving."[79]

---

76. Quoted in A.J.P. Taylor, "Prelude to Fashoda: The Question of the Upper Nile, 1894–5," *English Historical Review*, Vol. 65, No. 254 (January 1950), p. 54.
77. Christopher Andrew, *Theophile Delcassé and the Making of the Entente Cordiale: A Reappraisal of French Foreign Policy, 1898–1905* (New York: Macmillan, 1968), pp. 21–25.
78. Ibid., p. 100; Roger Glenn Brown, *Fashoda Reconsidered: The Impact of Domestic Politics on French Policy in Africa* (Baltimore: Johns Hopkins University Press, 1970), pp. 92–93.
79. Robinson and Gallagher, *Africa and the Victorians*, p. 371.

French policymakers "deluded themselves" into thinking that by taking Fashoda they could force London to negotiate the Egyptian issue.[80] As early as March 1895, when London had its first intimations about French designs on the upper Nile, Sir Edward Grey, then parliamentary undersecretary for foreign affairs, had stated bluntly that such a move "would be an unfriendly act and would be so viewed in England."[81] In spring 1898, responding to reports that France was driving on the upper Nile, London decided on an all-out reconquest of Sudan.

After victory at Khartoum, Field Marshal Lord Kitchener was ordered to advance to Fashoda and instructed, in the event he encountered French forces, to do nothing that "would in any way imply a recognition on behalf of Her Majesty's Government of a title on behalf of France . . . to any portion of the Nile Valley."[82] On September 19, 1898, Kitchener's forces reached Fashoda, where they were greeted by Marchand's band. Although the opposing forces treated each other with elaborate military courtesy, their meeting plunged London and Paris into a deep diplomatic crisis. The Anglo-French "quarrel was not about Fashoda, or about the fate of the Sudan, or even about the security of the Nile waters and of Egypt; it was about the relative status of France and Britain as Powers."[83]

Once the crisis began, Delcassé quickly recognized that France was in an untenable position. The British ambassador in Paris reported that Delcassé was "prepared to retreat . . . if we can build him a golden bridge."[84] Delcassé believed his maneuvering room was seriously circumscribed by the potentially volatile domestic political situation in France stemming from the Dreyfus affair. To accept a humiliating diplomatic defeat would probably mean the Brisson cabinet's fall and, it was widely feared, even a military coup.[85] Delcassé reportedly begged London, "Do not drive me into a corner."[86] On October 11, he told the British ambassador that if London made it easy for

---

80. Langer, *Diplomacy of Imperialism,* pp. 550–551.

81. Quoted in James Goode, *The Fashoda Crisis: A Survey of Anglo-French Imperial Policy on the Upper Nile Question, 1882–1899* (Ph.D. diss., North Texas State University, 1971), p. 150; and Darrell Bates, *The Fashoda Incident of 1898: Encounter on the Nile* (New York: Oxford University Press, 1984), p. 24.

82. Lord Salisbury's instructions quoted in Robinson and Gallagher, *Africa and the Victorians,* p. 368.

83. Sanderson, "Origins and Significance of Fashoda," p. 289.

84. Quoted in Sanderson, *The Upper Nile,* p. 346.

85. Brown, *Fashoda Reconsidered,* pp. 99–100, 127.

86. Quoted in T.W. Riker, "A Survey of British Policy in the Fashoda Crisis," *Political Science Quarterly,* Vol. 44, No. 1 (March 1929), p. 63.

him "in form he would be conciliatory in substance."[87] On October 27 the French ambassador to London, telling Salisbury that Marchand would soon leave Fashoda, pleaded for Britain to make some concession in return.[88]

Meanwhile, notwithstanding both the pleading tone of French diplomacy and the possible repercussions of Britain's stance on French internal politics, London adamantly refused to give Paris an alternative to the bleak choice of ordering Marchand's humiliating withdrawal or going to war. On September 18, the British ambassador in Paris told Delcassé "categorically" that London would not consent to any compromise of the Fashoda dispute.[89] On September 30, responding to Delcassé's statement that France would fight rather than submit to a British ultimatum, the British ambassador reiterated that there could be no discussions until Marchand withdrew from Fashoda. Salisbury was determined "to compel, rather than persuade, the French to withdraw."[90]

London's hard-line diplomacy was overwhelmingly supported by bellicose public opinion. Even before Fashoda, because of the tensions engendered by the Anglo-French colonial rivalry, "war with France was not exactly desired in England, but it would be accepted without hesitation if the occasion arose."[91] Once the crisis began, the press overwhelmingly supported the government's decision to refuse negotiations with France, and during the crisis "the British popular press indulged in an orgy of scurrility."[92] "There was plenty of warlike spirit in the country," and British public opinion was "aggressively jingoistic" over Fashoda.[93] "The unequivocal expression of British opinion" was solidly behind the Cabinet's hard-line policy.[94] This no doubt was true because the British public believed England's prestige was at stake and consequently was "in a mood to respond vigorously" to the French challenge.[95]

The public mood was matched by that of Britain's political elite. As Chancellor of the Exchequer Michael Hicks Beach said on October 19, "The country

---

87. Quoted in Keith Eubank, "The Fashoda Crisis Re-examined," *The Historian*, Vol. 22, No. 2 (February 1960), p. 152.
88. Quoted in ibid., p. 154.
89. Quoted in Robinson and Gallagher, *Africa and the Victorians*, p. 370.
90. Sanderson, *The Upper Nile*, p. 334.
91. Ibid., p. 372.
92. Ibid.; Riker, "British Policy in the Fashoda Crisis," pp. 65–67; Sanderson, *The Upper Nile*, p. 348.
93. Robinson and Gallagher, *Africa and the Victorians*, p. 376; Sanderson, *The Upper Nile*, p. 354.
94. Riker, "British Policy in the Fashoda Crisis," pp. 66–67.
95. Sanderson, "Origins and Significance of Fashoda," pp. 295, 300.

has put its foot down."[96] The government's uncompromising stance was supported strongly by the opposition Liberal Imperialists, notably Lord Rosebery, H.H. Asquith, and Sir Edward Grey.[97] Rosebery, a former prime minister and foreign secretary, recalled that his Cabinet had warned the French away from the Upper Nile in 1895 and declared that any Cabinet that showed signs of conciliating Paris over Fashoda would be replaced within a week. Indeed when, in the crucial October 27 Cabinet meeting, Salisbury left the impression in some minds that he was leaning towards compromise with Paris, the majority of ministers quickly poured cold water on that idea and the Admiralty was ordered to put the navy on a war footing.

The British knew that if Paris did not capitulate, armed conflict would ensue. London regarded that prospect with equanimity and, indeed, confidence. Because they believed both Britain's credibility and its reputation as a great power to be at stake, the British felt they had no alternative to forcing a showdown with the French: "Had Britain followed a less intransigent policy in the circumstances of October 1898, there would certainly have been a temptation, not only in Paris but also in St. Petersburg and Berlin, to write her off as a Power who would never risk a war, however great the provocation."[98]

In October 1898 the British navy enjoyed a decisive superiority over the French fleet in both numbers and quality, and the outcome of an Anglo-French war was a foregone conclusion.[99] London manifested no reluctance in pressing its strategic advantage. During October, the Royal Navy made preparations for a war with France.[100] On October 15, the Channel fleet was assembled. By October 26, the Royal Navy had drawn up detailed war plans. On October 28 the reserve squadron was activated and concentrated at Portland; soon the Channel fleet was deployed to Gibraltar and the Mediterranean fleet was moved to Malta. As these measures became known in Paris from intelligence reports and stories in the British press, they made a strong impression on French policymakers.

There is no question that France was finally compelled to accept a crushing diplomatic defeat because of its military inferiority *vis-à-vis* Britain. The Royal

---

96. Quoted in Langer, *Diplomacy of Imperialism,* p. 553.
97. Langer, *Diplomacy of Imperialism,* pp. 552–553; Robinson and Gallagher, *Africa and the Victorians,* pp. 376–378; Riker, "British Policy in the Fashoda Crisis," p. 67; Sanderson, *The Upper Nile,* p. 347.
98. Sanderson, "Origin and Significance of Fashoda," pp. 301–302.
99. On the Royal Navy's advantages and London's confidence in British sea power, see Marder, *Anatomy of British Sea Power,* pp. 320–331; Langer, *Diplomacy of Imperialism,* pp. 559–560.
100. Marder, *Anatomy of British Sea Power,* pp. 321–328.

Navy's power contrasted sharply with the numerical and qualitative deficiencies, and unpreparedness, of the French fleet. When Paris calculated the prevailing Anglo-French military balance, an embarrassing diplomatic climbdown emerged as a more attractive alternative than decisive defeat in a war.[101] As Delcassé admitted, he and President of the Republic Fauré were compelled to order Marchand's withdrawal by "the necessity of avoiding a naval war which we are absolutely incapable of carrying on, even with Russian help."[102] In the end, "Delcassé had no real alternative but to yield; except as an irrational gesture of defiance, war with England was not a possible choice."[103] The Fashoda crisis's outcome was, as Grenville says, "a demonstration of British power and French weakness."[104]

The outcome of the Fashoda crisis is explained by realism, not by democratic peace theory. Believing that vital strategic and reputational interests were at stake, the British ruled out diplomatic accommodation with Paris notwithstanding Delcassé's pleas to be given a face-saving way to extricate France from the crisis. Britain's intransigence runs directly counter to democratic peace theory's expectation that relations between democratic states are governed by mutual respect based on democratic norms and culture. Backed strongly by public and elite opinion, London adopted a policy that left Paris with two stark choices: diplomatic humiliation or military defeat in a war. Counter to democratic peace theory's expectations, but consistent with those of realism, Britain made, and was prepared to carry out, military threats against France. Paris caved in to British demands rather than fight a war it could not win.

FRANCO-GERMAN CRISIS: THE RUHR, 1923

The Ruhr occupation, culmination of the post-1918 cold peace, "practically amounted to the renewal of war."[105] The occupation arose from the collision

---

101. Two other factors weighed heavily in Britain's favor: First, Kitchener had an enormous local superiority over Marchand on the ground at Fashoda. Second, France's Russian ally made it clear that it would not support Paris and, in any event, even if St. Petersburg had wanted to intervene there was little the Russian navy could do to offset Britain's maritime superiority. See Langer, *Diplomacy of Imperialism*, pp. 559–563; Marder, *Anatomy of British Sea Power*, pp. 323, 328–329. As Paul Kennedy observes, "all the best cards were in Britain's hands." Kennedy, *Realities Behind Diplomacy*, pp. 112–113.
102. Quoted in Andrew, *Theophile Delcassé*, pp. 102–103. Fauré's reaction to Britain's naval preparations is described in Brown, *Fashoda Reconsidered*, pp. 115–116.
103. Sanderson, *The Upper Nile*, p. 362.
104. Grenville, *Lord Salisbury*, p. 218.
105. Royal J. Schmidt, *Versailles and the Ruhr: Seedbed of World War II* (The Hague: Martinus Nijhoff, 1968), p. 17; Marshall M. Lee and Wolfgang Michalka, *German Foreign Policy, 1917–1933:*

of France's policy of security and Germany's policy of seeking revision of the Versailles Treaty system. The reparations issue was the immediate cause of the Ruhr occupation, but although it had economic significance in itself, its true importance was that Paris and Berlin regarded it as symbolic of the geopolitical competition between them.[106]

For Paris, compelling Germany to adhere strictly to its reparations obligations was seen as crucial to maintaining the Versailles system. Moreover reparations were, as the Ruhr occupation demonstrated, a lever for France to revise Versailles in its favor by imposing political and territorial sanctions on Germany when Berlin defaulted on its payments. For Germany, obtaining modification of reparations was a wedge to open the issue of revising the entire Versailles framework. The "fulfillment" policies adopted by Berlin were designed to force revision by demonstrating that strict compliance with reparations obligations was beyond Germany's capacity and would lead inevitably to Germany's financial and economic collapse.[107]

Although Germany had been defeated and its short-term power constrained by the Versailles settlement, the underlying sources of its geopolitical strength—its industrial base and population—remained intact. French policymakers were obsessed about the resurgence of a German security threat and determined to prevent it by imposing military, territorial and economic restrictions on Germany.

France's postwar German policy was rooted in the aims that Paris had pursued during the war. As early as 1915, Foreign Minister Delcassé had envisioned breaking up the German Reich into a number of small states, coupled with annexation by France, Holland, and Belgium of the Rhine's left bank.[108] By late 1917, Paris had decided to leave a truncated Reich intact while annexing Alsace-Lorraine and the Saar, and creating an independent

Continuity or Break? (Leamington Spa, U.K.: Berg, 1987), p. 47; Detlev J.K. Peukert, *The Weimar Republic: The Crisis of Classical Modernity*, trans. Richard Deveson (New York: Hill and Wang, 1992), p. 61; Hermann J. Rupieper, *The Cuno Government and Reparations, 1922–1923: Politics and Economics* (The Hague: Martinus Nijhoff, 1979) p. 96.

106. Peukert, *Weimar Republic*, p. 55; Marc Trachtenberg, *Reparation in World Politics: France and European Economic Diplomacy, 1916–1923* (New York: Columbia University Press, 1980), p. 122; Stephen A. Schuker, *The End of French Predominance in Europe: The Financial Crisis of 1924 and the Adoption of the Dawes Plan* (Chapel Hill: University of North Carolina Press, 1976), p. 6.

107. On Berlin's strategy of seeking revision through fulfillment, see David Felix, *Walther Rathenau and the Weimar Republic: The Politics of Reparations* (Baltimore: Johns Hopkins University Press); and Rupieper, *The Cuno Government*.

108. D. Stevenson, *French War Aims Against Germany, 1914–1919* (Oxford: Clarendon Press, 1982), pp. 26–27.

French satellite state in the Rhineland.[109] France's military and economic security would be enhanced by imposing reparations on Germany and by giving France control of the iron and coal that were crucial to West European industrial supremacy.

After the war, France's objectives did not change. Paris sought military security, reparations, and the establishment of France as Europe's leading steel producer. At Versailles, to avoid alienating Britain and the United States, France abandoned its annexationist aspirations in the Rhineland; however, throughout the period from the Armistice to the Ruhr occupation, Paris covertly supported Rhenish separatism while continuing to harbor hopes of controlling the left bank.[110] Even while appearing to abandon France's territorial claims in the Rhineland, French Premier Clemenceau had achieved much of their essence by coupling the reparations and security issues: under the Versailles Treaty's provisions, as long as Germany remained in default on reparations, French troops could remain in the Rhineland.

The government's German policy was strongly supported by the French public. French public opinion had demanded a peace settlement that would "impose the greatest possible restrictions on Germany's influence and power," and the French public's Germanophobia carried over into the postwar period.[111] Public and policymakers alike believed that Germany should be forced to pay all of the costs France had sustained in connection with the war (including reconstruction of German-occupied French territory), and official and public opinion were mutually reinforcing. Indeed, French public opinion, which French Prime Minister Poincaré had done much to shape, was so anti-German in late 1922 that it is doubtful that he would have survived politically had he not moved to occupy the Ruhr.[112]

The French military invasion of the Ruhr was prompted by Paris's mounting frustration with Germany's campaign to obtain a significant reduction of its reparations obligations. Although there is some disagreement as to the exact nature of Poincaré's objectives in occupying the Ruhr, the balance of

---

109. On French war aims see Walter A. McDougall, *France's Rhineland Diplomacy, 1914–1924: The Last Bid for a Balance of Power in Europe* (Princeton: Princeton University Press, 1978), p. 25; Schmidt, *Versailles to the Ruhr*, pp. 22–23; Stevenson, *French War Aims*, pp. 38–39.

110. Stevenson, *French War Aims*, pp. 195–196. The definitive account of France's Rhenish policy is McDougall, *Rhineland Diplomacy.*

111. Stevenson, *French War Aims*, pp. 135–136. Leaders such as Poincaré actively promoted anti-German attitudes, not a particularly difficult task. See Schmidt, *From Versailles to the Ruhr*, p. 231.

112. Rupieper, *The Cuno Government*, pp. 88, 96; Schmidt, *From Versailles to the Ruhr*, p. 52.

opinion is that the Ruhr occupation was undertaken in an attempt to advance France's goals of revising the Versailles system in its favor. The Ruhr occupation clearly was intended to bolster French security by crippling Germany's economy while simultaneously enabling Paris to realize its ambition of establishing France as Europe's leading economic power. At a minimum, Paris hoped that the Ruhr occupation would inflame Rhenish separatism and lead the Rhineland to break away from the Reich; there is some evidence that the Ruhr occupation was undertaken specifically to advance the French aims of annexing the Rhineland and dissolving the Reich.[113] Once the Ruhr crisis commenced, France actively abetted the Rhenish separatists.

In the Ruhr crisis, France did not hesitate to use military force against democratic Weimar Germany in pursuit of French security interests. Indeed, what leaps out from histories of the period between 1915 (when French policymakers began to think seriously about their war aims) and 1923 is the repeated French rejection of "second image" arguments that France's postwar security position would be enhanced if Germany were transformed into a democracy. Unlike the British, who soon after the war came to believe a democratic Germany was the key to maintaining the peace in Europe, France preferred to put German democracy at risk rather than abandon its strategy of protecting its security with tangible guarantees. As Walter McDougall observes:

The Quai d'Orsay perceived little connection between forms of government and foreign policies. The Wilsonian idea that democracies choose peaceful foreign policies, while authoritarian regimes are aggressive, found few disciples in the French government and military . . . . A strong united Germany, whether monarchist or republican, would pose a threat to France and surely come to dominate the economies of the Danubian and Balkan regions.[114]

The French military occupation of the Ruhr provoked a major crisis—if not a Franco-German war, at least a quasi-war. A real war was avoided only because Germany lacked the capabilities to wage it. Still the Germans resisted the occupation fiercely. If anything united the fractious Germans of the

---

113. McDougall argues that Rhenish separation from the Reich was Poincaré's hope but not his specific goal in the Ruhr operation. McDougall, *Rhineland Diplomacy*, pp. 247–249. Schmidt argues that Poincaré undertook the Ruhr occupation for the specific purpose of gaining permanent territorial control of the Ruhr and Rhineland and promoting the Reich's disintegration. Schmidt, *From Versailles to the Ruhr*, pp. 232–233.

114. McDougall, *Rhineland Diplomacy*, p. 114.

Weimar Republic, it was hatred for the Versailles system and a determination to overturn it. The Germans believed that the French move was designed to bring about the dissolution of the Reich. Because of Germany's military weakness, the Reichswehr ruled out a policy of active resistance to the French occupation; however, steps were taken to facilitate military resistance in the event the French attempted to advance beyond the Ruhr.[115] Although unable to oppose France militarily, the Berlin government did adopt a policy of resistance to the French occupation, based on the noncooperation of German workers, civil servants, and railway personnel with French occupation authorities. The resistance was not entirely passive; the Reichswehr coordinated an active campaign of sabotage against the French occupation forces.[116] To sustain the resistance, the Berlin government provided the Ruhr population with food and unemployment subsidies. Passive resistance was financed by printing money, a practice that triggered Germany's financial collapse (due to hyperinflation and the concomitant collapse of the mark); this ultimately compelled Berlin to abandon its resistance to the Ruhr occupation. Over the long term, the Ruhr occupation had even more important effects on German domestic politics and public opinion: France's hard line policies strengthened the position of the right-wing nationalist parties in Germany and served to discredit the Weimar democracy.

The Ruhr crisis strongly disconfirms democratic peace theory. In World War I's aftermath, both the public and the elites in France perceived Germany as a dangerous threat to France's security and its great power status, even though Weimar Germany was a democracy. What mattered to the French was Germany's latent power, not its domestic political structure. Contrary to democratic peace theory's predictions, French policy toward democratic Germany reflected none of the mutual respect based on democratic norms and culture that democracies are supposed to display in their relations with each other. On the contrary, driven by strategic concerns, the French used military power coercively to defend the Versailles system upon which they believed their safety depended, rather than entrust their national security to

---

115. See F.L. Carsten, *The Reichswehr and Politics, 1918 to 1933* (Oxford: Clarendon Press, 1966) pp. 154–155. German preparations included mobilization of reserve units (whose existence was illegal under the terms of Versailles), the purchase of fighter aircraft from Holland and seaplanes from Sweden, and the training of secret units to conduct guerrilla operations behind the lines of any French advance beyond the Ruhr.
116. Ibid., pp. 154–155.

the hope that Germany's postwar democratic institutions would mitigate the geopolitical consequences flowing from the underlying disparity between German and French power.

Theoretical Conclusions

Proponents have made sweeping theoretical claims for, and have drawn important policy conclusions from, democratic peace theory. These claims rest on a shaky foundation, however. The case studies presented above subject both democratic peace theory and realism to a robust test. It is striking that in each of these four cases realism, not democratic peace theory, provides the more compelling explanation of why war was avoided. Indeed, the democratic peace theory indicators appear not to have played *any* discernible role in the outcome of these crises.

In each of these crises, at least one of the democratic states involved was prepared to go to war (or, in the case of France in 1923, to use military force coercively) because it believed it had vital strategic or reputational interests at stake. In each of these crises, war was avoided only because one side elected to pull back from the brink. In each of the four crises, war was avoided not because of the "live and let live" spirit of peaceful dispute resolution at democratic peace theory's core, but because of realist factors. Adverse distributions of military capabilities explain why France did not fight over Fashoda, and why Germany resisted the French occupation of the Ruhr passively rather than forcibly. Concerns that others would take advantage of the fight (the "waterbirds dilemma") explain why Britain backed down in the Venezuela crisis, and the Union submitted to Britain's ultimatum in the *Trent* affair. When one actually looks beyond the *result* of these four crises ("democracies do not fight democracies") and attempts to understand *why* these crises turned out as they did, it becomes clear that democratic peace theory's causal logic has only minimal explanatory power.

Although democratic peace theory identifies a correlation between domestic structure and the absence of war between democracies, it fails to establish a causal link. Because democratic peace theory's deductive logic lacks explanatory power, a second look at the theory's empirical support is warranted to see if the evidence is as strong as is commonly believed. The statistical evidence that democracies do not fight each other seems impressive but in fact, it is inconclusive, because the universe of cases providing empirical support for democratic peace theory is small, and because several important cases of wars between democratic states are not counted for reasons that are not persuasive.

QUANTITATIVE SUPPORT FOR THE THEORY: HOW BIG AN N?

Democratic peace theory purports to be validated by a large number ("N") of cases. A large N is achieved by aggregating the number of possible democratic dyads. Thus Switzerland and Sweden, or Austria and Israel, count as democratic dyads validating democratic peace theory. The result is the appearance of a large number of interactions with little or no conflict between democracies. Notwithstanding the theory's claim, however, the universe of supporting cases is small. There are three reasons why this is so. First, between 1815 and 1945 there were very few democracies (and the N would shrink further if only dyads involving democratic great powers are considered). Second, the possibility of *any* dyad (whether democratic, mixed, or non-democratic) becoming involved in a war is small, because wars are a relatively rare occurrence. States, even great powers, do not spend most of their time at war.[117] As David Spiro points out, if all nations are unlikely to fight wars, the claim that democracies do not fight each other loses much of its power. He states that if nations are rarely at war, and liberal dyads are a small proportion of all possible pairings of nation-states, then perhaps we should be surprised if democracies ever do go to war, but not at the absence of wars among democracies.[118]

Third, not all dyads are created equal. For the purposes of testing democratic peace theory, a dyad is significant only if it represents a case where there is a real possibility of two states going to war. To fight, states need both the *opportunity* (that is, the ability to actually project their power to reach an opponent) and a *reason* to do so. Only dyads meeting these preconditions are part of the appropriate universe of cases from which democratic peace theory can be tested.

---

117. On the striking decline in the frequency of great power war during the past two centuries see Jack S. Levy, *War and the Modern Great Power System, 1495–1975* (Lexington: University Press of Kentucky, 1983), chap. 6.

118. David E. Spiro, "The Insignificance of the Liberal Peace," *International Security*, Vol. 19, No. 2 (Fall 1994), pp. 50–86. Spiro concludes that the statistical evidence for the liberal peace is weak: either the data are ambiguous, or random chance would predict the absence of wars between democracies. Spiro is sympathetic to the democratic peace theory. He suggests that the tendency of liberal states to ally with, instead of opposing, each other is important and probably is rooted in liberal norms.

WARS BETWEEN DEMOCRACIES: BIG EXCEPTIONS IN A SMALL-N WORLD. The size of the N is an important question. If the effective universe of cases from which democratic peace theory can be tested is a small N, the importance of exceptions to the rule that democracies do not fight each other is heightened. Here, by their own admissions, democratic peace theorists are on thin ice. For example, referring specifically to the classification of the War of 1812 as one not involving two democracies, Bruce Russett acknowledges that this decision "may seem like a cheap and arbitrary escape" but asserts it is not.[119] It is only intellectual suppleness—the continual tinkering with definitions and categories—that allows democratic peace theorists to deny that democratic states have fought each other.[120]

An important example of this is the War Between the States, which the democratic peace theorists generally rule out on the grounds that it was an internal conflict within a state rather an international conflict between sovereign states.[121] Yet the events of 1861–65 seem especially relevant because the theory is based explicitly on the premise that the norms and culture that operate within democracies are externalized by them in their relations with other democratic states.[122] Democratic peace theory itself makes relevant the

---

119. Russett, *Grasping the Democratic Peace*, p. 16. However, sometimes things *are* exactly as they seem. Russett excludes the War of 1812 on the grounds that, prior to the Reform Bill of 1832, Britain was not a democracy. Yet, until the "revolution" that followed Andrew Jackson's 1828 election to the presidency, the United States was not appreciably more democratic than Britain. *The Federalist* and the Constitution itself, in its provision for an Electoral College and indirect election of senators, reflect the desire of the framers to circumscribe egalitarian democratic impulses. In early nineteenth-century America, suffrage was significantly restricted by property and other qualifications imposed at the state level. See Clinton Williamson, *American Suffrage: From Property to Democracy, 1750 to 1860* (Princeton: Princeton University Press, 1960); Paul Kleppner, et al., *The Evolution of American Electoral Systems* (Westport, Conn.: Greenwood Press, 1981).
120. A good example is James L. Ray, "Wars Between Democracies: Rare, or Nonexistent?" *International Interactions*, Vol. 18, No. 3 (1993), pp. 251–276. After readjusting the definition of democracy, Ray takes a brief look at five of the nineteen alleged exceptions to the rule that democratic states do not fight each other and concludes that over the last 200 to 250 years there are no exceptions to the rule.
121. Russett's comments (*Grasping the Democratic Peace*, p. 17) notwithstanding, after secession the War Between the States did take on the cast of an international conflict between two sovereign democratic entities. It certainly was so regarded by contemporaneous observers (and had the Confederacy prevailed, it certainly would be so regarded today). For example, no less a figure than Prime Minister William Gladstone, the arch-apostle of British Liberalism, observed that: "Jefferson Davis and other leaders of the South have made an army; they are making, it appears, a navy; and they have made what is more than either: they have made a nation." Quoted in James M. McPherson, *Battle Cry of Freedom: The Civil War Era* (New York: Oxford University Press, 1988), p. 552.
122. Democratic peace theory "*extends to the international arena* the cultural norms of live-and-let-

issue of whether democratic norms and culture do, in fact, result in the peaceful resolution of disputes within democracies. The War Between the States cuts to the heart of the democratic peace theory's causal logic: if democratic norms and culture fail to prevent the outbreak of civil war within democracies, what reason is there to believe that they will prevent the outbreak of interstate wars between democracies?

In the case of the Union and the Confederacy, the characteristics at the heart of democratic peace theory—the democratic ethos of respect for other democracies, a political culture that emphasizes the non-violent dispute resolution, the shared benefits of cooperation, the restraining effect of open debate and public opinion—failed conspicuously to assure a peaceful result. Indeed, if a democracy as tightly knit—politically, economically, culturally—as the United States was in 1861 could split into two warring successor states, we should have little confidence that democracy will prevent great power conflicts in an anarchic, competitive, self-help realm like international politics.

An even more important example is the issue of whether Wilhelmine Germany was a democracy. Even if World War I were the only example of democracies fighting each other, it would be so glaring an exception to democratic peace theory as to render it invalid. As even Michael Doyle concedes, the question of whether Wilhelmine Germany was a democracy presents a "difficult case."[123] Indeed, it is such a difficult case that, in a footnote, Doyle creates a new category in which to classify Wilhelmine Germany—that of a bifurcated democracy: pre-1914 Germany was, he says, democratic with respect to domestic politics but not in the realm of foreign policy.[124] Doyle does not consider Imperial Germany to have been a democracy for foreign policy purposes because the executive was not responsible to the Reichstag and, consequently, the foreign policy making process remained, he argues, autocratic.

---

live and peaceful conflict resolution that operate *within* democracies." Ibid., p. 19 (emphasis added).
123. Doyle, "Kant, Liberal Legacies and Foreign Affairs," part I, p. 216, fn 8.
124. Ibid. I do not address the issue of whether any state can in fact have such a tightly compartmentalized political system that it can be democratic in domestic politics but not in foreign policy. I know of no other example of a bifurcated democracy. If this concept of bifurcated democracy were accepted, proponents of democratic peace theory could defend their argument by asserting that, while democratic in the realm of domestic policy, in 1914 Britain and France, like Wilhelmine Germany, also were non-democratic in terms of foreign policy.

In fact, however, with respect to foreign policy, Wilhelmine Germany was as democratic as France and Britain. In all three countries, aristocratic or upper-middle-class birth and independent wealth were prerequisites for service in the diplomatic corps and the key political staffs of the foreign office.[125] In all three countries, foreign policy was insulated from parliamentary control and criticism because of the prevailing view that external affairs were above politics.

In democratic France, the Foreign Minister enjoyed virtual autonomy from the legislature, and even from other members of the cabinet.[126] As Christopher Andrew notes, "On the rare occasions when a minister sought to raise a question of foreign policy during a cabinet meeting, he was accustomed to the remark: 'Don't let us concern ourselves with that, gentlemen, it is the business of the foreign minister and the President of the Republic.'"[127] Treaties and similar arrangements were ratified by the president of the Republic (that is, by the cabinet) and the legislature played no role in the treaty making process (although the Senate did have the right to ask to be informed of treaty terms insofar as national security permitted).[128] Notwithstanding the formal principle of ministerial responsibility, the French legislature possessed no mechanisms for effectively supervising or reviewing the government's conduct of foreign policy.[129] Even in democratic France, the executive enjoyed unfettered power in the realm of foreign policy. This concentration of foreign policy-making power in the executive had a profound effect on the chain of events leading to World War I. The terms of the Franco-Russian alliance and military convention—the "fateful alliance" that ensured that an Austro-Russian war in the Balkans could not remain localized—were kept secret from the French legislature, public, and press.[130]

In democratic Britain, too, as in France and Germany, crucial foreign policy decisions were taken without consulting Parliament. Notwithstanding the

---

125. See Lamar Cecil, *The German Diplomatic Service, 1871–1914* (Princeton: Princeton University Press, 1976); Paul Gordon Lauren, *Diplomats and Bureaucrats: The First Institutional Responses to Twentieth Century Diplomacy in France and Germany* (Stanford: Hoover Institution Press, 1976), pp. 27–29; Frederick L. Schuman, *War and Diplomacy in the French Republic: An Inquiry into Political Motivations and the Control of Foreign Policy* (New York: Whittlesy House, 1931); Zara S. Steiner, *The Foreign Office and Foreign Policy, 1898–1914* (Cambridge: Cambridge University Press, 1969); and Steiner, "The Foreign Office under Sir Edward Grey," in F.H. Hinsley, ed., *British Foreign Policy Under Sir Edward Grey* (Cambridge: Cambridge University Press, 1977), pp. 22–69.
126. Schuman, *War and Diplomacy*, pp. 21, 28–32.
127. Andrew, *Theophile Delcassé*, p. 64.
128. Ibid., p. 22; Lauren, *Diplomats and Bureaucrats*, p. 29.
129. Lauren, *Diplomats and Bureaucrats*, p. 29.
130. Schuman, *War and Diplomacy*, p. 143.

profound implications of the Anglo-French staff talks, which began in January 1906, Foreign Secretary Sir Edward Grey and Prime Minister H.H. Asquith did not inform the Cabinet of their existence.[131] Grey and Asquith feared (and rightly so) that a Cabinet majority would oppose the staff talks and indeed the very idea of more intimate Anglo-French strategic relations. When questioned in Parliament in 1910, 1911, and 1913 about the Anglo-French military discussions, Grey and Asquith consistently gave false or evasive answers that kept hidden both the nature and the implications of the strategic agreements between London and Paris.[132] Even when Grey and Asquith had to account to the Cabinet, after it learned in November 1911 of the existence of staff talks, they left their colleagues with the incorrect impression that London had undertaken no binding obligations to France.[133] Notwithstanding Grey's and Asquith's constant reiteration (to the French, to Cabinet, and to Parliament) that London retained unimpaired freedom of maneuver, they had, in fact, undertaken a portentous commitment through a constitutionally doubtful process. In the Cabinet's debates about whether Britain should go to war in August 1914, Grey's argument that the Entente, and the concomitant military and naval agreements, had morally obligated Britain to support France proved decisive.[134]

It is apparent that before World War I, the most important and consequential grand strategic decisions made by both Paris (on the Russian alliance) and London (on the entente and military arrangements with France) were made without any legislative control or oversight, notwithstanding both countries' democratic credentials. Form should not be confused with substance. In the realm of foreign policy, France and Britain were no more and no less democratic than the Second Reich.[135]

---

131. See Samuel R. Williamson, *The Politics of Grand Strategy: Britain and France Prepare for War, 1904–1914* (Cambridge: Harvard University Press, 1969).
132. Ibid., pp. 134, 137–138, pp. 202–204, 330–331.
133. Ibid., pp. 198–200.
134. Grey threatened to resign from the Cabinet unless it agreed to take Britain into the war on France's side. Grey's resignation threat was determinative because the non-interventionist Cabinet Radicals realized that their refusal to declare war would lead to the Cabinet's replacement either by a Conservative-Unionist government or by a coalition between the Conservatives and the Liberal Imperialists. See K.M. Wilson, "The British Cabinet's Decision for War, 2 August 1914," *British Journal of International Studies*, Vol. 1, No. 2 (July 1975), pp. 148–159.
135. The classification of Wilhelmine Germany as a democracy is also supported by an analysis of the foreign policy making process of its successor, the Weimar Republic. Although the Weimar Republic invariably is classified as a democracy, in crucial respects, it closely resembled the Second Reich. During the Weimar Republic, the Foreign Office and the Army collaborated to ensure that the processes of formulating foreign policy and grand strategy were insulated from

The case of Wilhelmine Germany suggests that democratic great powers indeed have gone to war against one another (and could do so again in the future). Yet the prevailing view that the Second Reich was not a democracy has powerfully influenced the international relations–theory debate both on the broad question of how domestic political structure affects international outcomes and the specific issue of whether there is a "democratic peace." However, the received wisdom about pre–World War I Germany has been badly distorted by a combination of factors: the liberal bias of most Anglo-American accounts of German history between 1860–1914; the ideologically tinged nature of post-1960 German studies of the Wilhelmine era; and the residual effects of Allied propaganda in World War I, which demonized Germany.[136] The question of whether Wilhelmine Germany should be classified as a democracy is an important one and it deserves to be studied afresh.

AN ALTERNATIVE HYPOTHESIS: THE SECOND IMAGE REVERSED

From a realist perspective, democratic peace theory has mistakenly reversed the linkage between international systemic constraints and domestic political institutions. Otto Hintze made the realist argument that a state's internal political structure is highly influenced by external factors.[137] This creates a selection process that explains why some states become democracies while others do not. States that enjoy a high degree of security, like Britain and the United States at the beginning of the twentieth century, can afford the more minimalist state political structures of classical Anglo-American liber-

the Reichstag's oversight and control. The leading study is Gaines Post, Jr., *The Civil-Military Fabric of Weimar Foreign Policy* (Princeton: Princeton University Press, 1973). Post observes (p. 358) that the Weimar Republic stands as a "model for the virtual exclusion of the parliamentary or legislative level from politico-military activity in a representative system of government." If Weimar Germany is considered to be a democracy, then how can Wilhelmine Germany be classified as a non-democracy?

136. For a discussion of the leftist ideological biases that color the writings of Fritz Fischer's disciples and a critique of Fischer, Berghahn, Kehr, and Wehler, see Wolfgang J. Mommsen, "Domestic Factors in German Foreign Policy before 1914," *Central European History*, Vol. 6, No. 1 (March 1973), pp. 4–18. An insightful critique of the "failure of liberalism" school is Klaus P. Fischer, "The Liberal Image of German History," *Modern Age*, Vol. 22, No. 4 (Fall 1978), pp. 371–383.

137. This thesis is developed in Otto Hintze, "The Formation of States and Constitutional Development: A Study in History and Politics"; Hintze, "Military Organization and the Organization of the State"; and Hintze, "The Origins of the Modern Ministerial System: A Comparative Study," in Felix Gilbert, ed., *The Historical Essays of Otto Hintze* (New York: Oxford University Press, 1975).

alism, because there is no imminent external threat that necessitates a powerful governmental apparatus to mobilize resources for national security purposes. States that live in a highly threatening external environment are more likely to choose either more statist forms of democracy or even authoritarian structures, precisely because national security concerns require that the state have available to it the instruments for mobilizing national power resources.[138] The greater the external threat a state faces (or believes it does), the more "autocratic" its foreign policymaking process will be, and the more centralized its political structures will be.

If this hypothesis is true, it suggests that democratic peace theory is looking through the wrong end of the telescope. States that are, or that believe they are, in high-threat environments are less likely to be democracies because such states are more likely to be involved in wars, and states that are likely to be involved in wars tend to adopt autocratic governmental structures that enhance their strategic posture.[139] Thus, as realist theory would predict, international systemic structure is not only the primary determinant of a state's external behavior but may also be a crucial element in shaping its domestic political system. This hypothesis may provide a more useful approach than democratic peace theory to investigating the links between domestic structure and foreign policy.

Policy Conclusions: Why It Matters

The validity of democratic peace theory is not a mere academic concern. Democratic peace theory has been widely embraced by policymakers and foreign policy analysts alike and it has become a lodestar that guides Amer-

---

138. This argument is developed in Brian M. Downing, *The Military Revolution and Political Change: Origins of Democracy and Political Change* (Princeton: Princeton University Press, 1992).

139. There is another way of visualizing this phenomenon. The more threatened a state is (or believes it is) the more it will move toward more centralized domestic structures. A state may move so far that it ceases to be democratic and becomes autocratic. This hypothesis conforms with the experience of liberal democratic great powers in this century. In both World Wars, the exigencies of conflict resulted in such a concentration of state power in both the United States and Britain that, for a time, arguably, both became autocratic. The Cold War, similarly, impelled the United States to become a "national security state," still a democracy but one where the power of the state was vastly enhanced and the executive's predominance over the legislature in the sphere of foreign policy was decisively established. Quincy Wright came to a similar conclusion about the effect of external environment on domestic political structure and observed that "autocracy, at least in the handling of foreign affairs, has been the prevailing constitutional form." Wright, *A Study of War* (Chicago: University of Chicago Press, 1964, abridged ed.), p. 158.

ica's post–Cold War foreign policy. Michael Doyle's 1983 conception of a democratic "zone of peace" is now routinely used in both official and unofficial U.S. foreign policy pronouncements. Following the Cold War, a host of commentators have suggested that the export or promotion of democracy abroad should become the central focus of American's post–Cold War foreign policy.[140] From Haiti to Russia, America's interests and its security have been identified with democracy's success or failure. National Security Adviser Anthony Lake said that America's post–Cold War goal must be to expand the zone of democratic peace and prosperity because, "to the extent democracy and market economics hold sway in other nations, our own nation will be more secure, prosperous and influential."[141]

Those who want to base American foreign policy on the extension of democracy abroad invariably disclaim any intention to embark on a "crusade," and profess to recognize the dangers of allowing policy to be based on excessive ideological zeal.[142] These reassurances are the foreign-policy version of "trust me." Because it links American security to the nature of other states' internal political systems, democratic peace theory's logic inevitably pushes the United States to adopt an interventionist strategic posture. If democracies are peaceful but non-democratic states are "troublemakers" the conclusion is inescapable: the former will be truly secure only when the latter have been transformed into democracies, too.

Indeed, American statesmen have frequently expressed this view. During World War I, Elihu Root said that, "To be safe democracy must kill its enemy when it can and where it can. The world cannot be half democratic and half autocratic."[143] During the Vietnam War, Secretary of State Dean Rusk claimed that the "United States cannot be secure until the total international environment is ideologically safe." These are not isolated comments; these views reflect the historic American propensity to seek absolute security and to

---

140. See for example Joshua Muravchik, *Exporting Democracy: Fulfilling America's Destiny* (Washington, D.C.: AEI Press, 1991); and Larry Diamond, "Promoting Democracy," *Foreign Policy*, No. 87 (Summer 1992), pp. 25–46.

141. "Remarks of Anthony Lake," Johns Hopkins School of Advanced International Studies, Washington, D.C., September 21, 1993 (Washington, D.C.: National Security Council Press Office).

142. Lake stated that the Clinton administration does not propose to embark on a "democratic crusade." Both Doyle and Russett acknowledge that democratic peace theory could encourage democratic states to pursue aggressive policies toward non-democracies, and both express worry at this. Doyle, "Kant, Liberal Legacies, and Foreign Affairs," part II; Russett, *Grasping the Democratic Peace*, p. 136.

143. Quoted in Russett, *Grasping the Democratic Peace*, p. 33.

define security primarily in ideological (and economic) terms. The political culture of American foreign policy has long regarded the United States, because of its domestic political system, as a singular nation. As a consequence, American policymakers have been affected by a "deep sense of being alone" and they have regarded the United States as "perpetually beleaguered."[144] Consequently, America's foreign and defense policies have been shaped by the belief that the United States must create a favorable ideological climate abroad if its domestic institutions are to survive and flourish.[145]

Democratic peace theory panders to impulses which, however noble in the abstract, have led to disastrous military interventions abroad, strategic overextension, and the relative decline of American power. The latest example of the dangers of Wilsonianism is the Clinton administration's Partnership for Peace. Under this plan, the asserted American interest in projecting democracy into East Central Europe is advanced in support of NATO security guarantees and eventual membership for Poland, Hungary, and the Czech Republic (and some form of U.S. security guarantee for Ukraine). The underlying argument is simple: democratic governments in these countries will guarantee regional peace in the post–Cold War era, but democracy cannot take root unless these countries are provided with the "reassurance" of U.S. or NATO security guarantees.

In fact, however, East Central Europe is bound to be a highly volatile region regardless of whether NATO "moves east." The extension of NATO guarantees eastward carries with it the obvious risk that the United States will become embroiled in a future regional conflict, which could involve major powers such as Germany, Ukraine, or Russia. There is little wisdom in assuming such potentially risky undertakings on the basis of dubious assumptions about the pacifying effects of democracy.[146]

---

144. William Appleman Williams, *Empire As A Way of Life: An Essay on the Causes and Character of America's Present Predicament Along With a Few Thoughts About An Alternative* (New York: Oxford University Press, 1980), p. 53.

145. Lloyd C. Gardner, *A Covenant With Power: America and World Order from Wilson to Reagan* (New York: Oxford University Press, 1984), p. 27. For an excellent critique of the notion that America's domestic ideology must be validated by its foreign policy, see Michael H. Hunt, *Ideology and U.S. Foreign Policy* (New Haven: Yale University Press, 1987).

146. It could be argued that if Hintze's argument is correct (that secure states are more likely to become, or remain, democratic), then extending security guarantees to states like Ukraine, or preserving extant alliances with states like Germany, Japan, and South Korea, is precisely what the United States should do. Indeed, the Bush and Clinton administrations have both subscribed to a worldview that holds that the United States, as the sole remaining superpower, must take responsibility for maintaining regional power balances in Europe and East Asia. By

Democratic peace theory is dangerous in another respect, as well: it is an integral component of a new (or more correctly, recycled) outlook on international politics. It is now widely believed that the spread of democracy and economic interdependence have effected a "qualitative change" in international politics, and that war and serious security competitions between or among democratic great powers are now impossible.[147] There is therefore, it is said, no need to worry about future great power challenges from states like Japan and Germany, or to worry about the relative distribution of power between the United States and those states, unless Japan or Germany were to slide back into authoritarianism.[148] The reason the United States need not be concerned with the great-power emergence of Japan and Germany is said to be simple: they are democracies and democracies do not fight democracies.

Modern-day proponents of a liberal theory of international politics have constructed an appealing vision of perpetual peace within a zone of democracy and prosperity. But this "zone of peace" is a peace of illusions. There is no evidence that democracy at the unit level negates the structural effects of anarchy at the level of the international political system. Similarly, there is no evidence that supports the sister theory: that economic interdependence leads to peace. Both ideas have been around for a long time. The fact that they are so widely accepted as a basis for international relations theory shows that for some scholars, "theories" are confirmed by the number of real-world tests that they fail. Proponents of liberal international relations theory may contend, as Russett does, that liberal approaches to international politics have not failed, but rather that they have not been tried.[149] But this is what disappointed adherents of ideological worldviews always say when belief is overcome by reality.

---

preventing the "renationalization" of other states' security policies and by foreclosing the possibility of regional power vacuums, the United States, it is argued, can preserve the kind of international environment that is conducive to the spread of democracy and economic interdependence. For critiques of this policy see Christopher Layne, "The Unipolar Illusion: Why New Great Powers Will Rise," *International Security*, Vol. 17, No. 4 (Spring 1993), pp. 5–51; Layne, "American Grand Strategy After the Cold War: Primacy or Blue Water?" in Charles F. Hermann, ed., *American Defense Annual* (New York: Lexington Books, 1994); and Layne and Schwarz, "American Hegemony."

147. Robert Jervis, "The Future of World Politics: Will It Resemble the Past?" *International Security*, Vol. 16, No. 3 (Winter 1991/92), pp. 39–73.

148. For an example of this argument see James M. Goldgeier and Michael McFaul, "A Tale of Two Worlds: Core and Periphery in the Post–Cold War Era," *International Organization*, Vol. 46, No. 3 (Spring 1992), pp. 467–491.

149. Russett, *Grasping the Democratic Peace*, p. 9, says that Kantian and Wilsonian principles have not been given a real chance to operate in international politics.

If American policymakers allow themselves to be mesmerized by democratic peace theory's seductive—but false—vision of the future, the United States will be ill prepared to formulate a grand strategy that will advance its interests in the emerging world of multipolar great power competition. Indeed, as long as the Wilsonian worldview underpins American foreign policy, policymakers will be blind to the need to have such a grand strategy, because the liberal theory of international politics defines out of existence (except with respect to non-democracies) the very phenomena that are at the core of strategy: war, the formation of power balances, and concerns about the relative distribution of power among the great powers. But in the end, as its most articulate proponents admit, liberal international relations theory is based on hope, not on fact.[150] In the final analysis, the world remains what it always has been: international politics continues to occur in an anarchic, competitive, self-help realm. This reality must be confronted, because it cannot be transcended. Given the stakes, the United States in coming years cannot afford to have either its foreign policy, or the intellectual discourse that underpins that policy, shaped by theoretical approaches that are based on wishful thinking.

---

150. Russett, *Grasping the Democratic Peace*, p. 136, argues that, "understanding the sources of democratic peace can have the effect of a self-fulfilling prophecy. Social scientists sometimes create reality as well as analyze it. Insofar as norms do guide behavior, repeating those norms helps to make them effective. *Repeating the norms as descriptive principles can help to make them true.*" (Emphasis added.)

Democratization and the Danger of War

Edward D. Mansfield and Jack Snyder

One of the best-known findings of contemporary social science is that no democracies have ever fought a war against each other, given reasonably restrictive definitions of democracy and of war.[1] This insight is now part of everyday public discourse and serves as a basis for American foreign policymaking. President Bill Clinton's 1994 State of the Union address invoked the absence of war between democracies as a justification for promoting democratization around the globe. In the week following the U.S. military landing in Haiti, National Security Adviser Anthony Lake reiterated that "spreading democracy . . . serves our interests" because democracies "tend not to abuse their citizens' rights or wage war on one another."[2]

It is probably true that a world where more countries were mature, stable democracies would be safer and preferable for the United States. However, countries do not become mature democracies overnight. More typically, they go through a rocky transitional period, where democratic control over foreign policy is partial, where mass politics mixes in a volatile way with authoritarian elite politics, and where democratization suffers reversals. In this transitional phase of democratization, countries become more aggressive and war-prone, not less, and they do fight wars with democratic states.

Edward D. Mansfield is Associate Professor of Political Science at Columbia University and author of Power, Trade, and War *(Princeton University Press, 1994). Jack Snyder is Professor of Political Science and Director of the Institute of War and Peace Studies at Columbia University. His most recent book is* Myths of Empire: Domestic Politics and International Ambition *(Cornell University Press, 1991).*

The authors thank Sergei Tikhonov for assistance with computer programming; Liv Mansfield for preparing the figures; Richard Betts, Miriam Fendius Elman, David Lake, Bruce Russett, Randall Schweller, David Spiro, Randall Stone, Celeste Wallander, and participants at seminars at Harvard and Columbia for helpful comments; and the Pew Charitable Trusts for financial support.

---

1. Michael Doyle, "Liberalism and World Politics," *American Political Science Review,* Vol. 80, No. 4 (December 1986), pp. 1151–1169; Bruce Russett, *Grasping the Democratic Peace* (Princeton: Princeton University Press, 1993). For skeptical views, see David E. Spiro, "The Insignificance of the Liberal Peace," *International Security,* Vol. 19, No. 2 (Fall 1994), pp. 50–86; and Christopher Layne, "Kant or Cant: The Myth of the Democratic Peace," *International Security,* Vol. 19, No. 2 (Fall 1994), pp. 5–49. They are rebutted by Bruce Russett, "The Democratic Peace: 'And Yet It Moves'," *International Security,* Vol. 19, No. 4 (Spring 1995), pp. 164–175.
2. "Transcript of Clinton's Address," *New York Times,* January 26, 1994, p. A17; Anthony Lake, "The Reach of Democracy: Tying Power to Diplomacy," *New York Times,* September 23, 1994, p. A35.

International Security, Vol. 20, No. 1 (Summer 1995), pp. 5–38
© 1995 by the President and Fellows of Harvard College and the Massachusetts Institute of Technology.

The contemporary era shows that incipient or partial democratization can be an occasion for the rise of belligerent nationalism and war.[3] Two pairs of states—Serbia and Croatia, and Armenia and Azerbaijan—have found themselves at war while experimenting with varying degrees of partial electoral democracy. Russia's poorly institutionalized, partial democracy has tense relationships with many of its neighbors and has used military force brutally to reassert control in Chechnya; its electorate cast nearly a quarter of its votes for the party of radical nationalist Vladimir Zhirinovsky.

This contemporary connection between democratization and conflict is no coincidence. Using the same databases that are typically used to study the democratic peace, we find considerable statistical evidence that democratizing states are more likely to fight wars than are mature democracies or stable autocracies. States like contemporary Russia that make the biggest leap in democratization—from total autocracy to extensive mass democracy—are about twice as likely to fight wars in the decade after democratization as are states that remain autocracies. However, reversing the process of democratization, once it has begun, will not reduce this risk. Regimes that are changing toward autocracy, including states that revert to autocracy after failed experiments with democracy, are also more likely to fight wars than are states whose regime is unchanging.

Moreover, virtually every great power has gone on the warpath during the initial phase of its entry into the era of mass politics. Mid-Victorian Britain, poised between the partial democracy of the First Reform Bill of 1832 and the full-fledged democracy of the later Gladstone era, was carried into the Crimean War by a groundswell of belligerent public opinion. Napoleon III's France, drifting from plebiscitary toward parliamentary rule, fought a series of wars designed to establish its credentials as a liberal, popular, nationalist type of empire. The ruling elite of Wilhelmine Germany, facing universal suffrage but limited governmental accountability, was pushed toward World War I by its escalating competition with middle-class mass groups for the mantle of German nationalism. Japan's "Taisho democracy" of the 1920s brought an era of mass politics that led the Japanese army to devise and sell an imperial ideology

---

3. Zeev Maoz and Bruce Russett, "Normative and Structural Causes of the Democratic Peace, 1956–1986," *American Political Science Review*, Vol. 87, No. 3 (September 1993), pp. 630, 636; they note that newly created democracies, such as those in Eastern Europe today, may experience conflicts, insofar as their democratic rules and norms are not adequately established. See also Russett, *Grasping the Democratic Peace*, p. 134, on post-Soviet Georgia.

with broad-based appeal.[4] In each case, the combination of incipient democratization and the material resources of a great power produced nationalism, truculence abroad, and major war.

Why should democratizing states be so belligerent? The pattern of the democratizing great powers suggests that the problem lies in the nature of domestic political competition after the breakup of the autocratic regime. Elite groups left over from the ruling circles of the old regime, many of whom have a particular interest in war and empire, vie for power and survival with each other and with new elites representing rising democratic forces. Both old and new elites use all the resources they can muster to mobilize mass allies, often through nationalist appeals, to defend their threatened positions and to stake out new ones. However, like the sorcerer's apprentice, these elites typically find that their mass allies, once mobilized, are difficult to control. When this happens, war can result from nationalist prestige strategies that hard-pressed leaders use to stay astride their unmanageable political coalitions.[5]

The problem is not that mass public opinion in democratizing states demonstrates an unvarnished, persistent preference for military adventure. On the contrary, public opinion often starts off highly averse to war. Rather, elites exploit their power in the imperfect institutions of partial democracies to create *faits accomplis*, control political agendas, and shape the content of information media in ways that promote belligerent pressure-group lobbies or upwellings of militancy in the populace as a whole.

Once this ideological connection between militant elites and their mass constituents is forged, the state may jettison electoral democracy while retaining nationalistic, populist rhetoric. As in the failure of Weimar and Taisho democracy, the adverse effects of democratization on war-proneness may even heighten after democracy collapses. Thus, the aftershock of failed democratization is at least one of the factors explaining the link between autocratization and war.

---

4. Asa Briggs, *Victorian People*, rev. ed. (Chicago: University of Chicago, 1970), chaps. 2–3; Geoff Eley, *Reshaping the German Right* (New Haven: Yale University Press, 1980); Alain Plessis, *De la fête impériale au mur des fédérés, 1852–1871* (Paris: Editions du seuil, 1973), translated as *The Rise and Fall of the Second Empire, 1852–1871* (Cambridge: Cambridge University Press, 1985); Jack Snyder, *Myths of Empire: Domestic Politics and International Ambition* (Ithaca: Cornell University Press, 1991), chaps. 3–5.
5. Hans Ulrich Wehler, *The German Empire, 1871–1918* (Dover, N.H.: Berg, 1985); Jack S. Levy, "The Diversionary Theory of War: A Critique," in Manus Midlarsky, ed., *Handbook of War Studies* (Boston: Unwin Hyman, 1989), pp. 259–288.

In developing these arguments, we first present our statistical findings showing that democratizing states have been disproportionately likely to fight wars. We then explain why democratizing states are so war-prone, drawing illustrations from the history of the great powers. Finally, we offer suggestions for reducing the risks of transitions to democracy.

Quantitative Analysis: Definitions, Measures, and Techniques

Much of the research on the democratic peace has relied on statistical tests, which indicate that democracies become involved in wars about as frequently as other states, but that by reasonably restrictive definitions, they have never fought each other. Using similar methods and the same databases (covering the period from 1811 to 1980), we find that *democratizing* states—those that have recently undergone regime change in a democratic direction—are much more war-prone than states that have undergone no regime change, and are somewhat more war-prone than those that have undergone a change in an autocratic direction. In this section, we distinguish between *democratic* and *democratizing* regimes and explain how we set up our statistical tests. We then report our statistical findings.

Definitional issues have been central to the debate on the democratic peace. Even fairly minimal definitions of democracy require periodic elections between candidates who compete fairly for the votes of a substantial portion of the adult population, and whose outcome determines who makes state policy, including foreign and military policy.[6] Thus, the War of 1812 does not count as a war between democracies because Britain's suffrage was too narrow. Conversely, although the German Reichstag of 1914 was elected by universal suffrage with voter turnout over 90 percent, the war between France and Germany is excluded because German cabinet officials were chosen by the Kaiser. Nonetheless, in light of the current enthusiasm about the prospects for promoting peace by encouraging democratization, it is important not simply to discard cases that are not yet mature democracies, but to analyze democratization as a significant category in its own right.

Ted Robert Gurr's Polity II database on regime characteristics is commonly used to study the democratic peace, and is especially well-suited to measuring

---

6. Joseph Schumpeter, *Capitalism, Socialism, and Democracy*, 2d ed. (New York: Harper, 1947); Samuel P. Huntington, *The Third Wave: Democratization in the Late Twentieth Century* (Norman: University of Oklahoma Press, 1991), pp. 5–13, esp. p. 6; see also Russett, *Grasping the Democratic Peace*, pp. 16–18, and Michael Doyle, "Liberalism and World Politics," esp. p. 1164.

gradations of regime change toward or away from democracy.[7] Gurr created measures of democracy and autocracy (with values from 0 to 10) based on the competitiveness of political participation, the strength of the rules regulating participation in politics, the competitiveness of the process for selecting the chief executive, the openness of executive recruitment, and the strength of the constraints on the chief executive's power. Bruce Russett has combined these measures to develop a composite index of a state's regime type.[8] Based on this index and following Gurr, Russett distinguishes among democracies, autocracies, and "anocracies," political systems in which democratic and autocratic features are mixed, or in which very little power is concentrated in the hands of public authorities.[9] Some of the anocracies discussed by Russett include Iran under Mossadegh, Indonesia after Sukarno's first election, Goulart's Brazil, and Allende's Chile.[10] Victorian Britain is coded as close to fully democratic on some dimensions, but anocratic on others.[11]

We consider states to be *democratizing* if, during a given period of time, they change from autocracy to either anocracy or democracy, or if they change from anocracy to democracy. Conversely, states are *autocratizing* if they change from democracy to autocracy or anocracy, or from anocracy to autocracy.

We conduct separate analyses based on the composite index of regime change and on three of its components, because we are interested in both their combined and their separate effects on war. The first of these components is the openness of executive recruitment. In Gurr's definition, "recruitment of the chief executive is 'open' to the extent that all the *politically active* population has an opportunity, in principle, to attain the position through a regularized process."[12] The second component, executive constraints, measures "the insti-

---

7. Ted Robert Gurr, *Polity II: Political Structures and Regime Change, 1800–1986,* Inter-University Consortium for Political and Social Research No. 9263 (1990).

8. Russett, *Grasping the Democratic Peace,* p. 77; see also Maoz and Russett, "Normative and Structural Causes of the Democratic Peace, 1956–1986." This index is: PCON(DEM − AUT), where DEM is a state's score on the summary measure of democracy, AUT is a state's score on the summary measure of autocracy, and PCON is a measure of the extent to which power in a regime is monopolized by state authorities, which takes on values ranging from 0 to 10. This index therefore takes on values ranging from 100 (maximal democracy) to −100 (maximal autocracy).

9. More specifically, Russett classifies as democracies those states with values of the index of regime type described in footnote 8 ranging from 30 to 100, those with scores ranging from −25 to −100 as autocracies, and those with scores ranging from −24 to 29 as anocracies. See Russett, *Grasping the Democratic Peace,* p. 77; and Ted Robert Gurr, "Persistence and Change in Political Systems," *American Political Science Review,* Vol. 68, No. 4 (December 1974), pp. 1482–1504.

10. Russett, *Grasping the Democratic Peace,* pp. 121–122.

11. Gurr, *Polity II,* p. 11.

12. Gurr, *Polity II,* p. 11; emphasis in original. This variable is coded, based on a four-point scale ranging from closed to open. Closed regimes and regimes in which the recruitment of executives

tutionalized constraints that exist on the decision-making powers of chief executives, whether individuals or collectivities."[13] The greater these constraints, the more democratic is the polity.[14] The third component, the competitiveness of political participation, "refers to the extent to which alternative preferences for policy and leadership can be pursued in the political arena."[15] The greater the competitiveness, the more democratic is the polity.[16]

Although Gurr's selection of indicators and his classification of cases are not beyond dispute, they are generally considered to be better documented and more discriminating than other compilations.[17] Moreover, by using Gurr's data, we insure that none of the cases included in our analysis were coded with an eye toward confirming the hypothesis that democratization promotes war.

Like most research on the democratic peace, we rely on the Correlates of War (COW) Project data on war.[18] Most of these studies have focused on wars

---

is unregulated were coded autocratic; regimes characterized by hereditary succession and an executive chief minister chosen by either "executive or court selection" or "electoral selection" were coded anocratic; and open regimes were coded democratic. This sometimes leads to counterintuitive coding of cases. Partly for this reason, Britain's composite score remains anocratic until 1922. However, recoding cases piecemeal would be fraught with dangers. Rather than dealing with possible validity problems through recoding, we checked for the impact of any particular coding quirks by running separate tests for the various component indices and for different time periods. The fact that we obtained roughly parallel results from these various tests suggests that possible biases in the coding of specific regimes or the measurement of specific indicators were not decisively influencing our findings.

13. Gurr, *Polity II,* p. 15.

14. Regimes are coded using a seven-point scale. Polities in which executives are vested with unlimited authority and those classified as falling between these regimes and those in which limited constraints exist on the executive are coded autocratic. Polities in which "accountability groups have effective authority equal to or greater than the executive in most areas of activity" (Gurr, *Polity II,* p. 16), and those classified as falling between these regimes and those in which substantial constraints exist on executive authority, are coded democratic. All polities falling between these extremes are coded anocratic.

15. Gurr, *Polity II,* p. 18.

16. The competitiveness of political participation is coded on a five-point scale ranging from "suppressed competition" to "competitive competition." We code the former polities as autocratic, the latter polities as democratic, and all polities in between these extremes as anocratic.

17. We are unaware of any data set that is better suited to our purposes. For example, Michael Doyle's data on democracies emphasize normative features of a polity rather than the institutional features on which we focus. Further, since these data do not distinguish among the regime types of non-democracies, it is not possible to identify countries that underwent periods of democratization but failed to become mature democracies. Arthur Banks's data do not tap the institutional factors emphasized in our analysis as well as the Polity II data developed by Gurr. And, as Russett points out, although measures of regime type based on Gurr's and Banks's data are moderately related to one another, Banks's "simpler categorization, compiled earlier than that of Gurr et al. and less fully documented, is probably less discriminating." See Russett, *Grasping the Democratic Peace,* p. 78; Doyle, "Liberalism and World Politics"; and Banks, *Cross-Polity Time-Series Data* (Binghamton: State University of New York, Center for Comparative Political Research, 1986).

18. See Melvin Small and J. David Singer, *Resort to Arms: International and Civil Wars, 1816–1980* (Beverly Hills, Calif.: Sage Publications, 1982).

between states. However, we also assessed whether democratizating states fight non-state actors, as in a colonial war.[19] Consistent with the COW definition, we consider as a war any military conflict that led to at least 1,000 battle fatalities.[20]

Because we view democratization as a gradual process, rather than a sudden change, we analyze whether democratization during periods of one, five, and ten years is associated with involvement in war over subsequent periods of one, five, and ten years, respectively. Insofar as the effects of democratization on domestic coalitions, interest groups, and ideologies might unfold gradually after the initial political opening, the likelihood of war might increase gradually over the following decade. We compare the first and last year of each time period to identify cases of democratization, autocratization, and no regime change. We then examine whether a war involving that state began in the subsequent period. We carry out this analysis for each measure of democratization discussed above, and for both interstate wars and all wars, during the period from 1811 to 1980, the only era common to Gurr's Polity II data and the COW data.[21]

---

19. Since the correlation between the COW data sets of interstate wars and all wars is quite modest, the relationship between democratization and all wars need not be similar to that between democratization and interstate wars. See Edward D. Mansfield, *Power, Trade, and War* (Princeton: Princeton University Press, 1994), chap. 2. Most of the literature on the democratic peace, especially that which focuses on the role of norms, is cast at the dyadic level of analysis and therefore analyzes wars between pairs of states. Thus, it necessarily ignores wars between states and non-state actors. Our tests, however, are not dyadic, but rather address the characteristics of individual states. We will analyze dyadic relationships of democratizing states in a subsequent study.

20. To be counted as a participant, each state involved in an interstate war must have suffered at least 100 fatalities or sent at least 1,000 troops into active combat. States involved in wars against non-state actors must have sustained (in combination with any allies) at least 1,000 deaths in battle during each year of the conflict. On these coding procedures, see Small and Singer, *Resort to Arms*, pp. 55–57.

21. The COW data on war cover the period from 1816 to 1980, whereas Gurr's data cover the period from 1800 to 1986. As a result, our analysis based on one-year periods begins in 1815, and our analyses based on five-year and ten-year periods begin in 1811. In the case of five-year periods, the first observation measures democratization between 1811 and 1815 and war between 1816 and 1820. In the case of ten-year periods, the first observation measures democratization from 1811 to 1820 and war from 1821 to 1830. In order to observe the need for statistical independence among the observations, non-overlapping periods are used in each set of analyses. Certain countries were formed during this period (e.g., Italy, Germany, the Soviet Union), whereas others dissolved (e.g., Austria-Hungary, the Ottoman Empire, Serbia, Germany). Small and Singer agree with Gurr that some countries should be treated separately (Austria-Hungary and Austria; Russia and the Soviet Union; Germany, West Germany, and East Germany; the United Arab Republic and Egypt; Cambodia and Kampuchea; and Tanganyika and Tanzania). We therefore follow this procedure in our analyses. In other cases, however, Small and Singer disagree with Gurr. We analyzed these countries in two ways. First, the Ottoman Empire and Turkey, Sardinia and Italy, Prussia and Germany, and Serbia and Yugoslavia were considered a single country during the period from 1811 to 1980. Second, we treated each country in every pair separately. Since there was little

To assess the strength of the relationship between regime change and war, we construct contingency tables to determine whether democratization and autocratization are each statistically independent of a state's subsequent involvement in war. The null hypothesis is that the probabilities are identical that a democratizing state, an autocratizing state, and a regime with no change will become involved in a war. To test this hypothesis, we calculate the expected frequency of each outcome (democratization and war, democratization and no war, autocratization and war, autocratization and no war, no regime change and war, no regime change and no war) assuming that the probability of war is the same, whether the regime changes or not. We then compare these expected frequencies to the corresponding observed frequencies. A Pearson chi-square statistic (χ^2) is calculated, the value of which indicates the extent of the difference between these frequencies.[22] The greater the value of this statistic, the lower is the probability that regime change and war are statistically independent.[23]

DEMOCRATIZATION AND WAR: STATISTICAL FINDINGS

We found that democratizing states were more likely to fight wars than were states that had undergone no regime change. As shown in Figures 1 and 2, the probability of war for democratizing states always exceeds that for states undergoing no regime change. On average, democratizing states were about two-thirds more likely to go to war than were states that did not experience a regime change. For example, during any given ten-year period, a state that had not experienced a regime change during the previous decade had about one chance in six of fighting a war; in the decade following democratization, a state's chance of fighting a war was about one in four. The relationship between

---

difference in the results based on these two sets of tests, we report the results based on the latter procedure, which is consistent with that of Gurr.

22. More formally, $\chi^2 = \Sigma[(f - e)^2 / e]$, where f is the observed frequency for each outcome, e is the expected frequency for each outcome, and sigma (Σ) refers to the summation of this value for all outcomes.

23. The null hypothesis of statistical independence is rejected if $\Sigma[(f - e)^2 / e] > \chi^2_{.05}$, if we rely on the .05 level of statistical significance. This statistic has degrees of freedom equal to $(r - 1)(c - 1)$, where r refers to the number of rows and c refers to the number of columns in the contingency table. The use of this statistic is appropriate only if the expected frequency for each outcome exceeds one, a condition which is met in all of the following tests. Indeed, the expected frequency of war usually exceeds five when five-year and ten-year periods are analyzed. On this issue, see Stephen E. Fienberg, *The Analysis of Cross-Classified Categorical Data* (Cambridge, Mass.: The MIT Press, 1980), p. 170.

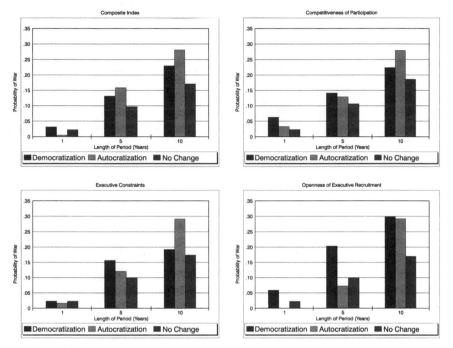

Figure 1. **Effect of Regime Change (or No Change) on the Probability of All Wars.**

democratization and war was strongest for ten-year periods and weakest for one-year periods.

These findings are not very sensitive to our decision to distinguish autocratizing regimes from those experiencing no change. When we compared the probability of war for democratizing states with that of all countries that were not democratizing (i.e., autocratizing countries and those experiencing no change), democratization gave rise to a higher probability of war than the absence of democratization in every instance. Democratizing states were, on average, about 60 percent more likely to go to war than states that were not democratizing.

Although our results provide strong support for the hypothesis that democratization promotes war, the strength of this relationship differs depending on the measure of democratization used and the length of time that is analyzed.

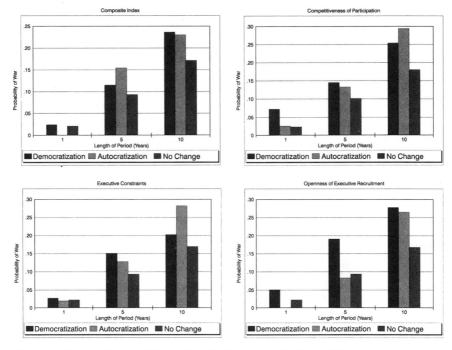

Figure 2. Effect of Regime Change (or No Change) on the Probability of Interstate Wars.

Based on the composite index, states undergoing democratization were, on average, about one-third more likely to go to war than states experiencing no regime change, regardless of whether all wars or interstate wars are considered. The effects of democratization were somewhat stronger when the three components of regime change (discussed earlier) are analyzed separately. Based on the openness of executive recruitment, the probability of both interstate wars and all wars was, on average, about twice as large for states in the process of democratization as for states undergoing no regime change. Based on the competitiveness of political participation, the probability that democratizing states would fight any type of war was, on average, about 75 percent greater than for states undergoing no regime change. The probability of interstate wars for countries in the process of democratization was, on average, about twice as large as for countries experiencing no regime change. Based on the constraints placed on a chief executive, states undergoing democratization were, on average, about 35 percent more likely to become engaged in both interstate wars and all wars than states experiencing no regime change.

The strength of the relationship between democratization and war also varies depending on the length of time that is analyzed. Our results were statistically significant in three out of eight tests based on one-year periods; in four out of eight tests based on five-year periods; and in six out of eight tests based on ten-year periods.[24] (The latter results are presented in Table 1.) Further, based on the composite index, the percentage change in the probability of war associated with democratization and that associated with the absence of regime change increases as the period of time analyzed becomes longer: it is greatest based on ten-year periods and lowest based on one-year periods.

These results are quite robust. Our findings about democratization and war did not change significantly when we excluded changes from autocracy to anocracy from the category of democratization; when we excluded changes from democracy to anocracy from the category of autocratization; when we excluded states that underwent transitions in both directions, toward democracy and autocracy, in a given five-year or ten-year period; when we analyzed the periods before and after World War I separately; nor when we analyzed great powers and other states separately.[25]

---

24. Only our results based on the competitiveness of participation fail to conform to this tendency for the strength of the relationship between regime change and war to increase as the period of time we analyzed becomes longer. In this case, however, our results are statistically significant only when one-year periods are considered (for all wars, $\chi^2 = 5.44$ ($p < .10$); for interstate wars, $\chi^2 = 7.54$ ($p < .05$)) and, for interstate wars, when ten-year periods are analyzed (see Table 1).

25. For a description of the criteria used to code states as great powers and a list of these states, see Small and Singer, *Resort to Arms*, pp. 44–45. One reason that we conducted separate tests based on pre–World War I cases is that a few of the cases of democratizing states that went to war in the period after World War I seemed on the surface to be causally questionable. For example, after World War II, Greece became democratic and subsequently became involved in the Korean War. Though events in Greece and Korea were connected through the larger contest between democratic and communist states, it hardly seems correct to say that Greek democratization caused the Korean War. Rather than throwing out such cases in *ad hoc* manner, we checked to see whether these cases were substantially influencing our overall findings by examining the seemingly less problematic pre-1914 cases separately. In addition, we checked whether states initially autocratized and subsequently, during the following five or ten years, democratized to a sufficient extent that the state was coded as democratizing. Under these circumstances, we would not be able to determine whether to attribute a war to the initial autocratization or the subsequent democratization. Fortunately, there were few cases in which multiple fluctuations occurred within a given period, and they did not noticeably influence our results. To analyze their influence, we first omitted these periods, and then coded them on the basis of the last fluctuation that occurred in each period. The only marked changes in our results due to multiple fluctuations occurred when the composite index and ten-year periods were analyzed. In these cases, the results became substantially stronger (for all wars, $\chi^2 = 11.54$ ($p < .01$); for interstate wars, $\chi^2 = 7.75$ ($p < .05$)).

Table 1. Contingency Tables of the Relationships Between Regime Change and War, Based on Ten-Year Periods, 1811–1980.

Regime Change	War	No War	Total
A. All Wars			
Composite Index ($\chi^2 = 7.99**$)			
Democratization	22 (17.8)	62 (66.2)	84
Autocratization	25 (16.6)	53 (61.4)	78
No Change	142 (154.6)	586 (573.4)	728
Total	189	701	890
Openness of Executive Recruitment ($\chi^2 = 9.10**$)			
Democratization	17 (10.4)	33 (39.6)	50
Autocratization	10 (6.2)	20 (23.8)	30
No Change	140 (150.4)	584 (573.6)	724
Total	167	637	804
Competitiveness of Participation ($\chi^2 = 3.09$)			
Democratization	14 (12.2)	41 (42.8)	55
Autocratization	14 (9.7)	30 (34.3)	44
No Change	137 (143.1)	510 (503.9)	647
Total	165	581	746
Executive Constraints ($\chi^2 = 6.17**$)			
Democratization	14 (13.4)	50 (50.6)	64
Autocratization	20 (12.6)	40 (47.4)	60
No Change	135 (143.0)	548 (540.0)	683
Total	169	638	807
B. Interstate Wars			
Composite Index ($\chi^2 = 3.51$)			
Democratization	20 (15.4)	64 (68.6)	84
Autocratization	18 (14.3)	60 (63.7)	78
No Change	125 (133.3)	603 (594.7)	728
Total	163	727	890
Openness of Executive Recruitment ($\chi^2 = 5.58*$)			
Democratization	14 (9.0)	36 (41.0)	50
Autocratization	8 (5.4)	22 (24.6)	30
No Change	122 (129.7)	602 (594.3)	724
Total	144	660	804
Competitiveness of Participation ($\chi^2 = 4.92*$)			
Democratization	14 (10.6)	41 (44.4)	55
Autocratization	13 (8.5)	31 (35.5)	44
No Change	117 (124.9)	530 (522.1)	647
Total	144	602	746
Executive Constraints ($\chi^2 = 5.03*$)			
Democratization	13 (11.6)	51 (52.4)	64
Autocratization	17 (10.9)	43 (49.1)	60
No Change	116 (123.6)	567 (559.4)	683
Total	146	661	807

NOTE: Cell entries are observed frequencies of war and no war with expected frequencies in parentheses. χ^2 is the Pearson chi-square statistic for tests of statistical independence. In all cases, there are two degrees of freedom. The total number of observations differs among the tables due to variations across states in the availability of data on the features of regime change analyzed here.

* Significant at the .10 level.
** Significant at the .05 level.

We also analyzed whether the relationship between democratization and war depends on either a state's regime type prior to this transition or the magnitude of the regime change. To do this, we computed the probability of war separately for each of the three types of regime change in a democratic direction: that is, from anocracy to democracy, autocracy to democracy, and autocracy to anocracy. Likewise, we computed separately the probability of war for states that, during a given period of time, remained autocracies, anocracies, and democracies. Consistent with our other findings, democratization increased the probability of both interstate wars and all wars, especially based on five-year and ten-year periods. Consistent with the findings of other scholars,[26] stable democracies were, on average, no more and no less likely to go to war than other states. In addition, the probability of war for regimes that remained autocracies, anocracies, or democracies during a given period of time was roughly similar.

Our findings based on ten-year periods are presented in Table 2. Depending on which index is used to measure democratization, a change from anocracy to democracy increased the probability of any type of war by roughly 15 to 100 percent, and of interstate war by roughly 35 to 115 percent, compared to a state that remained anocratic. A change from autocracy to democracy increased the probability of any type of war by approximately 30 to 105 percent, and of interstate war by approximately 50 to 135 percent, compared to a state that remained autocratic. A change from autocracy to anocracy increased the probability of war by about 70 percent compared to states that remained autocratic, based on the openness of executive recruitment, whereas it slightly decreased the likelihood of war based on the other three indices. Moreover, on average, the percentage increase in the probability of war was smallest for countries making transitions from autocracy to anocracy and greatest for countries making the dramatic leap from autocracy to democracy. More dramatic transitions toward democracy therefore seem more likely to promote wars than do less profound changes of this sort.

---

26. See, for example, Bruce Bueno de Mesquita and David Lalman, *War and Reason: Domestic and International Imperatives* (New Haven: Yale University Press, 1992); Steven Chan, "Mirror, Mirror on the Wall . . . Are the Freer Countries More Pacific?" *Journal of Conflict Resolution*, Vol. 28, No. 4 (December 1984), pp. 617–648; Jack S. Levy, "Domestic Politics and War," in Robert I. Rotberg and Theodore K. Rabb, eds., *The Origin and Prevention of Major Wars* (New York: Cambridge University Press, 1989), pp. 83–88; Zeev Maoz and Nasrin Abdolali, "Regime Types and International Conflict, 1816–1976," *Journal of Conflict Resolution*, Vol. 33, No. 1 (March 1989), pp. 3–35; and Melvin Small and J. David Singer, "The War-Proneness of Democratic Regimes," *Jerusalem Journal of International Relations*, Vol. 1, No. 1 (Summer 1976), pp. 50–69.

Table 2. Probability of War for Autocracies, Anocracies, Democracies, States Undergoing Democratization, and States Undergoing Autocratization, Based on Ten-Year Periods, 1811–1980.

	Composite Index	Openness of Executive Recruitment	Competitiveness of Participation	Executive Constraints
A. All Wars				
No Change in Regime Type				
Autocracy	.24	.22	.27	.21
Anocracy	.16	.31	.20	.16
Democracy	.19	.16	.20	.23
Democratization				
Autocracy to Anocracy	.22	.38	.21	.20
Anocracy to Democracy	.33	.39	.27	.18
Autocracy to Democracy	.33	.29	.50	.43
Autocratization				
Democracy to Anocracy	.25	.25	.13	.20
Anocracy to Autocracy	.32	.50	.35	.37
Democracy to Autocracy	.67	.28	.50	.33
B. Interstate Wars				
No Change in Regime Type				
Autocracy	.21	.19	.23	.18
Anocracy	.14	.23	.16	.14
Democracy	.19	.15	.20	.19
Democratization				
Autocracy to Anocracy	.20	.25	.21	.17
Anocracy to Democracy	.30	.31	.27	.18
Autocracy to Democracy	.33	.29	.50	.43
Autocratization				
Democracy to Anocracy	.17	.25	.13	.20
Anocracy to Autocracy	.24	.50	.35	.34
Democracy to Autocracy	.33	.17	0	.11

AUTOCRATIZATION AND WAR: STATISTICAL FINDINGS

Although democratization increases the probability of war, autocratization is also dangerous. Autocratizing states were more likely to go to war than countries experiencing no regime change, based on the results of 16 out of 24 tests, which are presented in Figures 1 and 2. However, autocratization tends to be a somewhat less combustible process than democratization. States in the process of democratization are more likely to go to war than those in the process of autocratization, based on the results of 17 out of 24 tests that we conducted.

Like the effects of democratization on war, the effects of autocratization vary across the different indices and periods of time that we analyzed. For example, on average, autocratization yields about a 35 percent greater likelihood of war than does the absence of regime change, when we focus on a state's competitiveness of participation, and about a 25 percent increase in the probability of war, when we focus on a polity's constraints on its executive. In contrast, autocratization decreases the likelihood of war in many cases compared to a country that experienced no regime change, based on the composite index and on the openness of executive recruitment.

Our findings also indicate that autocratization is less likely to lead to war over the short run than in the long run. Regardless of whether all wars or interstate wars are analyzed, autocratization occurring over a one-year period substantially decreases the probability of war compared to states experiencing no regime change, based on every measure except the competitiveness of participation. In contrast, as the results in Table 1 show, autocratization over a ten-year period yields a marked percentage increase in the probability of war in every instance.

The results in Table 2 likewise show that autocratization over a ten-year period is associated with an increased probability of war. States making the large change from democracy to autocracy were especially likely to fight in all wars, compared to countries that remained democratic. States changing from anocracy to autocracy were especially likely to fight interstate wars. However, states changing from democracy to anocracy were not especially war-prone at all. In combination with our earlier results, these findings suggest that the biggest leaps in democratization disproportionately increase the likelihood that a country will engage in an *interstate* war, whereas the most dramatic types of autocratization disproportionately increase the likelihood that a state will fight *non-state opponents.*

In short, although democratizing states are, on average, somewhat more likely to engage in war than their autocratizing counterparts, states experiencing either type of change run a greater risk of war than those experiencing no change.

How Democratization Causes War

Why are democratization and autocratization associated with an increased chance of war? What causal mechanism is at work? Based on case studies of four great powers during their initial phases of democratization, we argue that threatened elites from the collapsing autocratic regime, many of whom have parochial interests in war and empire, use nationalist appeals to compete for mass allies with each other and with new elites. In these circumstances, the likelihood of war increases due to the interests of some of the elite groups, the effectiveness of their propaganda, and the incentive for weak leaders to resort to prestige strategies in foreign affairs in an attempt to enhance their authority over diverse constituencies. Further, we speculate that transitional regimes, including both democratizing and autocratizing states, share some common institutional weaknesses that make war more likely. At least in some cases, the link between autocratization and war reflects the success of a ruling elite in using nationalist formulas developed during the period of democratization to cloak itself in populist legitimacy, while dismantling the substance of democracy. In explaining the logic behind these arguments, we draw on some standard theories about the consequences of different institutional arrangements for political outcomes.

We illustrate these arguments with some contemporary examples and with cases drawn from four great powers at early stages in the expansion of mass political participation: mid-Victorian Britain, the France of Napoleon III, Bismarckian and Wilhelmine Germany, and Taisho Japan. In each of these cases, elections were being held and political leaders were paying close attention to public opinion in the making of foreign policy, yet some key aspects of democratic control over policy were absent or distorted. We do not claim that these four cases constitute a systematic test of our hypotheses. Our definition of democratization is a broad one, and these are not the only instances of democratization among the great powers. France has been "democratizing" in fits and starts between 1789 and the Fifth Republic, sometimes fighting wars linked to surges of democratization and sometimes not. Moreover, there are cases where great powers democratized peacefully when circumstances were propitious: for example, West Germany and Japan after 1945. Though the qualitative part of our study does show that democratization and war have often been linked in the history of the great powers, its main task is less to test the strength of this relationship than to trace how democratization and war were linked in several important cases.

Nor do we claim that these great powers are necessarily representative of all democratizing states. However, as mentioned earlier, in order to assess the robustness of our statistical results, we analyzed separately the relationship between democratization (and autocratization) and war for great powers, and for other states. We found few significant differences between the results based on great powers and those based on other states. Further, it is especially important to have a theory about democratizing great powers, because they have such a huge impact on world politics, and because Russia—and perhaps soon China—is in a democratizing phase.

The features of democratization captured in Gurr's data are echoed in the arguments we derive from the case studies, but they do not correspond in every respect. In discussing the case studies, we used concepts that seemed most useful in illuminating the patterns we found, rather than strictly applying Gurr's categories. Sometimes the fit between Gurr's concepts and our own is quite close. For example, Gurr's category of "factional competition," which is the mid-point on his scale of the competitiveness of a country's political participation, is similar to our concept of interest-group jockeying and logrolling in a democratizing setting. In contrast, however, elements such as ideology play a large role in our argument, but are ignored in Gurr's data.

In the following sections, we first explain why the institutional structures of democratizing states produce a different pattern of policy outcomes than in fully democratic states. We then show how this affects the strategies of domestic interest groups, patterns of coalition politics, and foreign policy outcomes in the context of the collapse of an autocratic state.

Democratic versus Democratizing Institutions

Well-institutionalized democracies that reliably place ultimate authority in the hands of the average voter virtually never fight wars against each other. Moreover, although mature democracies do fight wars about as frequently as other types of states, they seem to be more prudent: they usually win their wars; they are quicker to abandon strategic overcommitments; and they do not fight gratuitous "preventive" wars.[27] Explanations for these tendencies focus variously on the self-interest of the average voter who bears the costs of war, the norms of bargaining and conflict resolution inherent in democracy, the moderating impact of constitutional checks and balances, and the free marketplace of ideas.[28]

---

27. David Lake, "Powerful Pacifists," *American Political Science Review,* Vol. 86, No. 1 (March 1992), pp. 24–37; Snyder, *Myths of Empire,* pp. 49–52; Randall Schweller, "Domestic Structure and Preventive War: Are Democracies More Pacific?" *World Politics,* Vol. 44, No. 2 (January 1992), pp. 235–269.
28. Russett, *Grasping the Democratic Peace;* Miles Kahler, "Introduction," in Miles Kahler, ed., *Liberalization and Foreign Policy* (forthcoming); Jack Snyder, "Democratization, War, and Nationalism in the Post-Communist States," in Celeste Wallander, ed., *The Sources of Russian Conduct after the Cold War* (Boulder: Westview, forthcoming).

However, these happy solutions typically emerge only in the very long run. In the initial stages of expanding political participation, strong barriers prevent the emergence of full-fledged democratic processes and the foreign policy outcomes associated with them. The two main barriers are the weakness of democratic institutions and the resistance of social groups who would be the losers in a process of full-fledged democratization.

Popular inputs into the policymaking process can have wildly different effects, depending on the way that political institutions structure and aggregate those inputs.[29] It is a staple of political science that different institutional rules —for example, proportional representation versus single-member districts, or congressional versus executive authority over tariffs—can produce different political outcomes, even holding constant the preferences of individual voters. In newly democratizing states, the institutions that structure political outcomes may allow for popular participation in the policy process, but the way they channel that input is often a parody of full-fledged democracy. As Samuel Huntington has put it, the typical problem of political development is the gap between high levels of political participation and weak integrative institutions to reconcile the multiplicity of contending claims.[30] In newly democratizing states without strong parties, independent courts, a free press, and untainted electoral procedures, there is no reason to expect that mass politics will produce the same impact on foreign policy as it does in mature democracies.

In all of the democratizing great powers, public inputs were shaped and aggregated in ways that differed from those of mature democracies. In mid-Victorian Britain, rural areas had greater representation than urban areas, the ballot was not secret, and only propertied classes could vote.[31] In rural France under Napoleon III, the local prefect, appointed in Paris, stood at the ballot box and exercised control over voters' choices.[32] In Wilhelmine Germany, the parties that won the elections could not name governmental ministers; rather, they had to use their limited powers over the budget to bargain over policy with ministers named by the kaiser.[33] In Taisho Japan, the electoral franchise

29. Kenneth Shepsle, "Studying Institutions: Some Lessons from the Rational Choice Approach," *Journal of Theoretical Politics,* Vol. 1, No. 2 (April 1989), pp. 131–147.
30. Samuel Huntington, *Political Order in Changing Societies* (New Haven: Yale University Press, 1968).
31. D.C. Moore, "The Other Face of Reform," *Victorian Studies,* Vol. 5, No. 1 (September 1961), pp. 7–34.
32. Theodore Zeldin, *The Political System of Napoleon III* (New York: Norton, 1958), pp. 84–85, 91–94, 135.
33. Wehler, *German Empire.*

was widened, but the choice of who would govern was left to the oligarchs who had founded the Meiji state.[34] And in Russia today almost none of the major institutions of representative government work in a reliable way: constitutional rules change to fit the needs of the moment; constitutional courts take sides on transparently political grounds; elections are postponed or announced on short notice; and political parties are transitory elite cliques, not stable organizations for mobilizing a mass coalition. Moreover, in all of these cases, the political press was to some degree bribed or censored by the government or had not yet institutionalized the objectivity, knowledge, and professionalism needed to create a full and fair public debate.[35]

As a result of these institutional deformations, ruling circles in these democratizing great powers were only haphazardly accountable to the electorate. Typically, elite groups reached out intermittently and selectively for mass support but were able to buffer themselves from systematic accountability through the ballot box. In Britain both the Whig and Tory parties were still dominated by landed oligarchs, who refused to entertain the notion of anything more than issue-specific alignments with the parliamentary representatives of middle-class radical opinion. Similarly, in Wilhelmine Germany the ruling elite bargained with mass groups like the Catholic Center Party over specific horse-trades, for example, exchanging support on the naval budget for concessions on Catholic rights. The Center Party was not, however, offered ministerial portfolios.

As a consequence, public groups in all of these polities tended to organize as narrow pressure groups or single-issue lobbies, such as the Anti-Corn Law League in Britain in the 1840s, or the Navy and Agrarian Leagues in pre-1914 Germany. These groups often worked outside the electoral system, making direct demands on public authorities, since the democratic path to power was rigged against them. This tendency toward direct action in the streets or in smoke-filled back rooms rather than through the ballot box is typical of what Huntington calls the "praetorian society," where pressures for participation are strong but institutions for effective participation are weak.[36]

---

34. Peter Duus, *Party Rivalry and Political Change in Taisho Japan* (Cambridge, Mass.: Harvard University Press, 1968).

35. Lynn M. Case, *French Opinion on War and Diplomacy during the Second Empire* (Philadelphia: University of Pennsylvania Press, 1954), pp. 2–6; Stephen Koss, *The Rise of the Political Press in England* (London: Hamish Hamilton, 1981), pp. 72–80.

36. Patricia Hollis, ed., *Pressure from Without in Early Victorian England* (London: Edward Arnold, 1974); Huntington, *Political Order in Changing Societies*, pp. 78–92.

To some extent this weakness of democratic institutions simply reflects the difficulty of building effective structures from scratch. Well-developed organizations, skilled cadres to staff them, and habits of democratic action are not acquired overnight by journalists, parliamentarians, judicial officials, and party politicians. Nor is trust in the efficacy and objectivity of such institutions easily acquired. As rational-choice analysts of the creation of institutional structures have convincingly and repeatedly shown, "transaction costs" and dilemmas of collective action hinder the emergence of institutions to facilitate bargaining that would make everyone better off.[37]

Of course, the development of efficient democratic institutions is hindered further by the fact that everyone is *not* made better off by effective democratic reforms. Many social groups, including many powerful ones, are likely to be losers from the strengthening of democratic institutions.[38] These include the autocratic rulers themselves, state bureaucrats of the old regime who might fear that their function would lose its importance in a transformed polity, social and economic elites whose privileges might diminish in a more open system, or even mass special interest groups who would lose from reforms that the average voter might find attractive. In the nineteenth and early twentieth centuries, constituencies having an interest in holding back full democratization typically included kings, nobles, landowners, owners of industrial capital, militaries that were closely tied to old elites or the old regime, and artisans and other middle-class groups that benefited from the guild-type economic restrictions backed by the old regime.[39] In contemporary post-communist states, the analogous cast of characters has, in one place or another, included national and local former Communist party officials, the military, ministries or firms controlling obsolete industrial capital, workers in such sectors, and people living and working in the regions where such sectors predominate.

The strength of these groups' incentives to hold back democratic change depends in large part on the mobility of their assets and skills. British landowners were comparatively relaxed about the expansion of democratic rights: the relative mobility of their substantial commercial investments allowed many

---

37. Todd Sandler, *Collective Action* (Ann Arbor: University of Michigan, 1992); Robert Keohane, *After Hegemony: Cooperation and Discord in the World Political Economy* (Princeton: Princeton University Press, 1984).
38. For a rational choice perspective emphasizing distributional issues, see Jack Knight, *Institutions and Social Conflict* (Cambridge: Cambridge University Press, 1992).
39. The classic study is Barrington Moore, Jr., *Social Origins of Dictatorship and Democracy* (Boston: Beacon, 1966).

of them to accept the end of agricultural protection and to profit from a liberalizing, free-trading political alliance with the commercial middle classes. In contrast, Germany's Junker landowning elite, who largely staffed the Prussian state, had very few attractive economic prospects outside of their relatively inefficient agricultural holdings, and thus had a larger stake in using state-backed protectionism and political repression to maintain their social position.[40] In Russia today, some former Communist elites have shown agility in adapting to a privatized economy, where they have devised ways to maintain control over or profit from the disposal of many of the elite's economic assets. However, the military has suffered greatly in status and organizational cohesion from the opening of the political system. And even the elites who *are* doing well in the transition have a stake in making the transition a controlled, partial one, where profiteering is not too fettered by democratic scrutiny or rule of law.

Both in the nineteenth century cases and in the contemporary post-communist ones, it is striking that many of the groups with an interest in retarding democratization are also those with a parochial interest in war, military preparation, empire, and protectionism. This is not accidental. Most of the benefits of war, military preparations, imperial conquest, and protectionism—e.g., in career advancement or in protection from foreign economic competition—are disproportionately concentrated in specific groups.[41] Any special interest group, including the military, that derives parochial benefits from a public policy has to feel wary about opening up its affairs to the scrutiny and veto of the average voter, who pays for subsidies to special interests. Whenever the costs of a program are distributed widely, but the benefits are concentrated in a few hands, democratization may put the program at risk.

When autocratic states start to democratize, many of the interests threatened by democratization are military in nature. As Charles Tilly says, "war made the state and the state made war."[42] In early modern Europe, military organizations occupied a privileged position in the state, which was built to serve their needs. Moreover, ruling aristocracies were intertwined with military in-

---

40. In addition to Moore, *Social Origins*, see David Spring, ed., *European Landed Elites in the Nineteenth Century* (Baltimore: Johns Hopkins University Press, 1977); and Robert Moeller, ed., *Peasants and Lords in Modern Germany* (Boston: Allen & Unwin, 1986).
41. Snyder, *Myths of Empire*, pp. 32–35, 49–52; Lance Davis and Robert Huttenback, *Mammon and the Pursuit of Empire: The Political Economy of British Imperialism, 1860–1912* (Cambridge: Cambridge University Press, 1986).
42. Charles Tilly, "Reflections on the History of European State-Making," in Charles Tilly, ed., *The Formation of National States in Europe* (Princeton: Princeton University Press, 1975), p. 42.

stitutions, so democratization inherently challenged the vested social, economic, and bureaucratic interests of an old elite that was at its core a military elite. Joseph Schumpeter constructed a whole theory of imperialism on the atavistic interests of the military-feudal aristocracy.[43] It is true that middle-class reformers sometimes wanted to build up the state's military power: this was a rallying cry of English radicals in the Crimean War, and of German middle-class officers before 1914. However, they wanted to replace aristocratic deadwood with middle-class rationalizers. Democratization led by proponents of military power was thus nearly as much of a threat to the old army as democratization led by pacifists like Richard Cobden.[44]

THE POLITICAL IMPASSE OF DEMOCRATIZATION

This situation of social change, institutional weakness, and threatened interests tends to produce a political impasse along the route toward democracy: it becomes difficult to form stable political coalitions with coherent policy platforms and sufficient support to stay in power. This impasse, which breeds the kind of short-run thinking and reckless policymaking that lead to war, occurs for four reasons.

WIDENING THE POLITICAL SPECTRUM. First, the social changes impelling democratization create a wider spectrum of politically significant groups with diverse, incompatible interests. Kings, aristocrats, peasants, and artisans may share the historical stage with industrialists, an urban working class, and a middle-class intelligentsia. Or in the contemporary post-communist cases, former party apparatchiks, atavistic heavy industrialists, and downwardly mobile military officers may share the stage with populist demagogues, free-market entrepreneurs, disgruntled workers, and newly mobilized ethnic groups. In principle, a fully institutionalized democracy can integrate even the widest spectrum of interests through party competition for the favors of the median voter. But where democracy is only incipient and partial, the wide spread of politically mobilized social interests characteristic of a transition to democracy may make the formation of stable coalitions extremely difficult.

For example, in Britain during the period leading up to the Crimean War, neither Whigs nor Tories could form a governing coalition that was more than temporary, because so many groups refused to enter into stable political alli-

---

43. Joseph Schumpeter, *Imperialism and Social Classes* (New York: Kelly, 1950; orig. ed. 1919).
44. Olive Anderson, *A Liberal State at War: English Politics and Economics during the Crimean War* (New York: St. Martin's, 1967).

ances with each other. None of the old elites would coalesce with the parliamentary bloc of radicals elected by British urban middle-class and Irish voters. Moreover, protectionist Tories would not unite with free-trading Tories or Whigs. Thus, the social and political mid-Victorian "equipoise" between traditional and modern Britain created a temporary political stalemate, as groups found it impossible to compromise vital interests in the construction of a ruling coalition.[45]

An even more serious example is the stalemate in Wilhelmine-era electoral politics. In principle, coalitions of the left and the right might have formed to vie for the median voter, thus driving policy in a moderating direction. In fact, both the left and the right were too divided internally to mount effective coalitions with internally consistent policies. Progressives dreamed of a bloc extending "from Bassermann to Bebel," from the liberal-democratic middle classes through the Marxist working classes, but the differences between labor and capital chronically barred this development. Conservatives had more success in forging a "marriage of iron and rye," but fundamental differences between military-feudal Junkers and Ruhr industrialists, ranging from the distribution of tax burdens to military strategy, made their policies incoherent. Germany wound up with plans for a big army, a costly navy, and nobody willing to pay for it.[46]

In more recent times, incipient democratization has caused political impasse by widening the political spectrum to include too many irreconcilable political forces. In the final days of Yugoslavia, efforts by moderates like Ante Markovic to promote compromise on a federalist, democratic, economic reformist platform were hindered not only by ethnic divisions but also by the cleavage between market-oriented business interests, on the one hand, and party bosses and military officers, on the other.[47]

INFLEXIBLE INTERESTS AND SHORT TIME HORIZONS. Groups threatened by social change and democratization, including still-powerful elites, are often compelled to take a very inflexible view of their own interests, especially when their assets cannot be readily adapted to changing political and economic

---

45. W.L. Burn, *The Age of Equipoise* (London: George Allen & Unwin, 1964).

46. Eckart Kehr, *Economic Interest, Militarism, and Foreign Policy* (Berkeley: University of California Press, 1977); David D'Lugo and Ronald Rogowski, "The Anglo-German Naval Race and Comparative Constitutional 'Fitness'," in Richard Rosecrance and Arthur Stein, eds., *The Domestic Bases of Grand Strategy* (Ithaca: Cornell University Press, 1993), pp. 65–95, esp. 81–83.

47. V.P. Gagnon, Jr., "Ethnic Nationalism and International Conflict: The Case of Serbia," *International Security,* Vol. 19, No. 3 (Winter 1994/95), pp. 130–166; Branka Magas, *The Destruction of Yugoslavia: Tracking the Break-Up, 1980–1992* (London: Verso, 1993).

conditions. In extreme cases, there may be only one solution that will maintain the social position of the group. For the Prussian landowners, it was agricultural protection in a non-democratic state; for the Japanese military, organizational autonomy in an autarkic empire; for the Serbian military and party elites, a Serbian nationalist state. Compromises that may lead down the slippery slope toward social extinction or irrelevance have no appeal, despite the danger that taking an intransigent stance might provoke a hostile encirclement by great-power opponents. This adds to the difficulty of finding an exit from the political impasse.

COMPETITIVE MASS MOBILIZATION. In a period of democratization, threatened elite groups have an overwhelming incentive to mobilize allies among the mass of people, but only on their own terms, using whatever special resources they still retain. These have included monopolies of information (e.g., the German Navy's unique "expertise" in making strategic assessments); propaganda assets (the Japanese Army's public relations blitz justifying the invasion of Manchuria); patronage (British Foreign Secretary Palmerston's gifts of foreign service postings to the sons of cooperative journalists); wealth (Krupp steel's bankrolling of mass nationalist and militarist leagues); organizational skills and networks (the Japanese army's exploitation of rural reservist organizations to build a social base); and the ability to use the control of traditional political institutions to shape the political agenda and structure the terms of political bargains (the Wilhelmine ruling elite's deal with the Center Party, eliminating anti-Catholic legislation in exchange for support in the Reichstag on the naval budget).[48]

This elite mobilization of mass groups takes place in a highly competitive setting. Elite groups mobilize mass support to neutralize mass threats (e.g., patriotic leagues to counter workers' movements) and to counter other elite groups' successful efforts at mass mobilization (e.g., the German Navy League, as a political counterweight to the Junker-backed Agrarian League). Thus, the elites' resources allow them to influence the direction of mass political participation, but the imperative to compete for mass favor makes it difficult for a single elite group to control the outcome of this process. For example, mass groups that gain access to politics through elite-supported nationalist organizations often try to outbid their erstwhile elite sponsors. By 1911, German popular nationalist lobbies were in a position to claim that if Germany's foreign

48. Snyder, *Myths of Empire*, pp. 103, 140–141, 205; Louise Young, "Mobilizing for Empire: Japan and Manchukuo, 1931–1945," Ph.D. dissertation, Columbia University, 1992.

foes were really as threatening as the ruling elites had portrayed them, then the government had sold out German interests in reaching a compromise settlement of the Moroccan dispute with France.[49] In this way, the process of elite mobilization of the masses adds to the ungovernability and political impasse of democratizing states.

Ideology takes on particular significance in the competition for mass support. New participants in the political process may be uncertain of where their political interests lie, because they lack established habits and good information, and are thus fertile ground for ideological appeals. Ideology can yield particularly big payoffs, moreover, when there is no efficient free marketplace of ideas to counter false claims with reliable facts. Elites try out all sorts of ideological appeals, depending on the social position that they need to defend, the nature of the mass group that they want to recruit, and the type of appeals that seem plausible in the given political setting. A nearly universal element in these ideological appeals is nationalism, which has the advantage of positing a community of interest that unites elites and masses, thus distracting attention from class cleavages.

Nationalist appeals have often succeeded even though the average voter was not consistently pro-war or pro-empire. For example, the French public was not keen to enter the Crimean War when it began in January 1854, and after sustaining 100,000 war-related deaths by 1855, the public's war-weariness led Napoleon to make concessions to Russia at the bargaining table. Likewise, the French public was initially opposed to participation in the Italian and Austro-Prussian Wars, fearing a disruption of the economy.[50] Mass opinion was similarly pacifist and anti-imperial in Britain during the high tide of Richard Cobden's Anti-Corn Law League, which succeeded in linking foreign military intervention and military budgets to the popular issues of free trade and democracy.[51] In Japan, too, the Naval Arms Limitation Treaty of 1930 was initially popular with the public.[52] And even in Germany, where public opinion was more consistently bellicose, the two largest mass parties, the Social Democrats and the Catholic Center Party, had no interest in imperialism. Though the

---

49. Eley, *Reshaping the German Right*, chap. 10.

50. William E. Echard, *Napoleon II and the Concert of Europe* (Baton Rouge: Louisiana State University Press, 1983), pp. 31, 37, 49; Case, *French Opinion*, pp. 54–56, 64–65, 71, 273.

51. Peter Cain, "Capitalism, War and Internationalism in the Thought of Richard Cobden," *British Journal of International Studies*, Vol. 5 (October 1979), pp. 229–247.

52. Tatsuji Takeuchi, *War and Diplomacy in the Japanese Empire* (Garden City, N.Y.: Doubleday, 1935), pp. 303–304.

German leaders' strategy is often called "social" imperialism, its appeal was almost entirely to the middle classes, not the workers. And Catholics backed the fleet not out of conviction, but to get side-payments on domestic issues.[53]

Since mass opinion was typically mobilized into politics by elite interest groups rather than by broad-based parties competing for the median voter, mass voices tended to reinforce the pattern of elite interests, rather than to check them: in Germany, the Agrarian League clamored for grain tariffs, the Navy League for a fleet, the imperial groups for settler colonies abroad, and the Pan-German League for a bigger army. In cases where mass opinion has been articulated through different channels, such as the institutionalized two-party competition in twentieth century Britain and the United States, its impact on foreign policy has been very different.

THE WEAKENING OF CENTRAL AUTHORITY. The political impasse and reckless-ness of democratizing states is exacerbated further by the weakening of the state's authority. Autocratic power is in decline *vis-à-vis* both the elite interest groups and mass groups, but democratic institutions lack the strength to integrate these contending interests and views. Parties are weak and lack mass loyalty. Elections are rigged or intermittent. Institutions of public political participation are distrusted, because they are subject to manipulation by elites and to arbitrary constraints imposed by the state, which fears the outcome of unfettered competition.

In each of the historical great-power cases, the problem was not excessive authoritarian power at the center, but the opposite. The Aberdeen coalition that brought Britain into the Crimean War was a makeshift cabinet headed by a weak leader with no substantial constituency. Likewise, on the eve of the Franco-Prussian War, Napoleon III's regime was in the process of caving in to its liberal opponents, who dominated the parliament elected in 1869. As Europe's armies prepared to hurtle from their starting gates in late July 1914, Austrian leaders, perplexed by the contradictions between the German Chan-cellor's policy and that of the German military, asked "Who rules in Berlin?" The 1931 Manchurian Incident was a *fait accompli* by the local Japanese military; Tokyo was not even informed.[54] Today, the return to imperial thinking in

---

53. Jonathan Steinberg, *Yesterday's Deterrent* (London: Macdonald, 1965), pp. 190–191; David Black-bourn, *Populists and Patricians* (London: Allen & Unwin, 1987), pp. 161–162, 190, 211.
54. J.B. Conacher, *The Aberdeen Coalition, 1852–1855* (London: Cambridge University Press, 1968); Zeldin, *The Political System of Napoleon III*, pp. 3, 135; Gerhard Ritter, *The Sword and the Sceptre: The Problem of Militarism in Germany*, Vol. 2 (Coral Gables: University of Miami Press, 1969), pp. 257–263; Sadako Ogata, *Defiance in Manchuria* (Berkeley: University of California Press, 1964).

Moscow is the result of Yeltsin's weakness, not his strength. As Sergei Karaganov has recently argued, the breakdown of the Leninist state "has created an environment where elite interests influence [foreign] policy directly."[55] In each of these cases, the weak central political leadership resorts to the same strategies as do the more parochial elite interests, using nationalist ideological appeals and special-interest payoffs to maintain their short-run viability, despite the potential long-run risks associated with these strategies.

IMPLICATIONS FOR WAR-PRONENESS

Political leaders in the great powers resorted to a typical syndrome of expedients in their attempts to deal with the political impasse of democratization. These tactics—logrolling, squaring the circle, and prestige strategies—tended to breed recklessness in foreign relations and the resort to war.

LOGROLLING. In these democratizing states, the power of elite groups was strengthened relative to the weakened autocratic center, yet the power of mass groups was not yet institutionalized as in a mature democracy. This created the incentive to make policy by logrolling among elite interest groups. Elite logrolling often yielded policies of war, military preparation, and imperial expansion, in part because many of the interest groups created in the process of weakening and breaking up the autocratic state were its military-feudal detritus: the army, the navy, and the aristocratic elites that staffed them. Similar military interest groups also figure in some of the post-communist cases, especially Yugoslavia and Russia. Militaries do not necessarily favor war, especially when they feel unprepared to win quickly and decisively. However, because of militaries' typically zero-sum view of security, they often recommend offensive military strategies that inadvertently lead the state down the path toward war.[56]

Moreover, logrolling works by giving each group what it wants most, so that even if only some of the groups in the coalition favored policies leading to war

---

55. Sergei A. Karaganov, "Russia's Elites," in Robert Blackwill and Sergei A. Karaganov, eds., *Damage Limitation or Crisis? Russia and the Outside World* (Washington, D.C.: Brassey's, 1994), p. 42; see also Robert Legvold, "The Russian Question," in Vladimir Baranovsky, ed., *Russia and Europe: Emerging Security Agenda* (N.Y.: Oxford University Press, forthcoming in 1995).

56. Stephen Van Evera, "Causes of War," Ph.D. dissertation, University of California at Berkeley, 1984. This does not seem to apply in cases of military dictatorship. Rather, it is when the military acts as a cartel in political logrolling or as an actor in the politics of the democratization process that the military's political role makes war more likely. See Stanislav Andreski, "On the Peaceful Disposition of Military Dictatorships," *Journal of Strategic Studies*, Vol. 3, No. 3 (December 1980), pp. 3–10.

and expansion, that would be enough to make their adoption likely. The classic example is the Wilhelmine iron-and-rye logroll, where the navy and heavy industry insisted on a fleet that alienated Britain, the Junkers got grain tariffs that sowed discord with Russia, and the army got the offensive Schlieffen Plan, which threatened all of Germany's neighbors. Another instance is the logroll between the Japanese imperial army and navy, which overtaxed the economy and embroiled Japan with enemies on all azimuths.[57]

SQUARING THE CIRCLE, OR INTEGRATING OPPOSITES. Since democratizing states typically comprise such a broad spectrum of social interests, would-be ruling coalitions must often be cobbled together from diverse or even contradictory bases of support. For this reason, one of the characteristic problems of the leadership of transitional, democratizing states is explaining away the self-contradictory aspects of a coalition or policy that must integrate antithetical elements. In foreign affairs, this often means sweeping tough trade-offs under the rug, pretending that contradictory policies actually make sense or cannot be avoided. As a consequence, the foreign policies of democratizing states are often overcommitted, provoking too many enemies at the same time, while claiming that the resulting conflicts are due to the others' inherent hostility. For example, Wilhelmine iron-and-rye policies leading to a hostile encirclement of Germany were explained away in two ways: first, that the hostility was inherent in the nature of Germany's opponents, and that German policy had done nothing to provoke it; and second, that the way to break apart the hostile coalition was to issue threats, rather than to make concessions that would have jeopardized the policies of the iron-and-rye coalition.[58]

Palmerston and Louis Napoleon faced a somewhat different problem of integrating opposites. Their strategies required winning over substantial middle-class backers to a strategy of social conservatism to safeguard the interests of old elites in an era of mass politics. In part, the rise of the working-class threat made this alliance possible. But in order to win converts from middle-class radicalism, Palmerston and Napoleon both had to show that their conservative policies were somehow actually liberal. The simplest way to do this was to back liberal goals abroad, such as national self-determination and the expansion of commercial opportunities, while fighting a rear-guard action against them at home. This was convenient because liberal goals abroad could easily

57. Michael Barnhart, *Japan Prepares for Total War: The Search for Economic Security, 1919–1941* (Ithaca: Cornell University Press, 1987).
58. Snyder, *Myths of Empire*, pp. 85–89.

be made to dovetail with geopolitical goals that Palmerston and Napoleon wanted to pursue anyway.[59] However, liberals were not completely passive dupes of this strategy. In Britain, for example, they used the Crimean War to force an opening of the administration of the war office to middle-class rationalizers, a move that Palmerston could hardly prevent in light of the way he had justified his foreign policy.[60]

In Russia today, foreign policy is likewise providing glue for an emerging "red-brown" coalition of nationalists and neo-communists. The Soviet system created organized vested interests in a particular pattern of industrial investment, a large military establishment, a working class protected from market forces, a local elite that served as a substitute for the market in administering the economy, and a division of labor on an imperial scale. The collapse of the Marxist-Leninist state took away the ideological underpinnings of this collection of interests, but many of these interests remain in place. The doctrines of nationalism and of the distinctiveness of Russia from the liberal West provide natural ideological justification for reasserting imperial control and retaining at least some of the strong-state, limited-market tendencies from Russia's past. It may also help to justify a truncated approach to democratization, which would help secure these traditional elite interests.

PRESTIGE STRATEGIES. One of the simplest but most risky strategies for a hard-pressed regime in a democratizing country is to shore up its prestige at home by seeking victories abroad. Johannes Miquel, who revitalized the iron-rye coalition at the turn of the century, argued that "successes in foreign policy would make a good impression in the Reichstag debates, and political divisions would thus be moderated."[61] The domestic targets of such strategies often share this view. Cobden, for example, argued that military victories abroad would confer enough prestige on the military-feudal landed elite to allow them to raise food tariffs and snuff out democracy: "Let John Bull have a great military triumph, and we shall have to take off our hats as we pass the Horse Guards for the rest of our lives."[62]

Prestige strategies make the country hypersensitive to slights to its reputation. As the kaiser found out in the First and Second Moroccan Crises, stiff foreign resistance can produce not cheap victories but embarrassing defeats,

---

59. Plessis, *De la fête*, p. 189; Snyder, *Myths of Empire*, pp. 180–183.
60. Anderson, *A Liberal State at War.*
61. J.C.G. Rohl, *Germany without Bismarck* (Berkeley: University of California, 1967), p. 250.
62. Letter to John Bright, October 1, 1854, quoted in John Morley, *The Life of Richard Cobden*, abridged ed. (London, n.d.), pp. 311–312.

which further complicate domestic governance. In another instance, Napoleon III was easily goaded into a fateful declaration of war in 1870 by Bismarck's insulting editorial work on a leaked telegram from the kaiser.[63]

If the public itself is wary of war, the prestige-enhancing venture may have to be mounted in the face of initial domestic opposition. Nonetheless, the gamble may be worth it. The Crimean victory created the conditions for what is acknowledged to be the high point of Napoleon III's rule, despite the popular reluctance and war-weariness that accompanied it.[64] Napoleon learned this lesson well, and tried to recapitulate his success when he saw his popularity waning in January 1859. On the eve of French military intervention in the Italian struggle with Austria, Napoleon told his cabinet, "On the domestic front, the war will at first awaken great fears; traders and speculators of every stripe will shriek, but national sentiment will [banish] this domestic fright; the nation will be put to the test once more in a struggle that will stir many a heart, recall the memory of heroic times and bring together under the mantle of glory the parties that are steadily drifting away from one another day after day."[65] Napoleon was trying to lead public opinion to become bellicose, not just to follow opinion, but in order to stir a national feeling that would enhance the state's ability to govern a split and stalemated political arena.

Autocratization and Great Power War

Though democratization has been a cause of great power war, reversing that process is not an effective antidote. At least four times, great powers have undergone sharp reversals of incipient democratization: France under Napoleons I and III, Nazi Germany, and Japan in the 1930s. Each then embarked on an aggressive foreign adventure. It is true that the reassertion of traditional autocracy under the Concert of Europe after 1815 produced a period of comparative peace. However, this merely postponed domestic and international conflicts, which returned with the democratizing trend after the revolutionary uprisings of 1848.[66]

---

63. Case, *French Opinion*, p. 267.
64. Thompson, *Louis Napoleon*, pp. 144–145.
65. Alain Plessis, *The Rise and Fall of the Second Empire, 1852–1871* (Cambridge: Cambridge University Press, 1985), pp. 146–147.
66. Charles A. Kupchan and Clifford A. Kupchan, "Concerts, Collective Security, and the Future of Europe," *International Security*, Vol. 16, No. 1 (Summer 1991), pp. 114–161.

How should the link between autocratization and war be interpreted? It is possible that any regime change increases the likelihood of war, whether it is on the dimension of democratization and autocratization, or on any other dimension. Regime change more generally may lead to some of the same war-causing pathologies that are present in democratizing states, including policy stalemates, threatened elites, and other social groups with shortened time horizons. Since political scientists have barely begun to address this question, this interpretation cannot be ruled out.[67]

However, at least some wars of autocratization can be best understood as wars of failed or perverted democratization. In each of these great power cases, the autocratizing ruler's foreign policy was either a tool that helped him to overcome the political impasse of the democratizing regime, or else it grew out of ideas that had arisen in the political context of the preceding period of democratization. For example, explanations of Nazi foreign policy can be grouped into two general categories: "structuralist" ones that see Nazi policies as functional responses to the political impasse of Weimar society, and "intentionalist" ones that see such policies as the implementation of racist, nationalist ideas spawned in the coffeehouses of the late Wilhelmine and Weimar periods.[68] In either case, the warlike character of the new autocracy grew out of a flaw in the democratizing society that preceded it.

These new autocrats, unlike traditional monarchs, all claimed to rule in the name of people, while shutting down democratic institutions. Napoleon I exploited the popular nationalism of the French Revolution, promising to spread its ideals throughout Europe even as he extinguished them in France. The Japanese army invented a populist ideology, rooted in the nation's imperial myths, designed to solidify the army's links to a rural mass constituency and to denigrate the commercially-oriented Taisho democrats. Thus, the foreign policy of these autocratizing states was at least partially shaped by the character of the democratic political system that they were escaping. In some cases, it was a means for accomplishing that escape. In this sense, the wars of re-autocratization can be seen as part of the larger phenomenon of wars of democratization.

---

67. Addressing one aspect of this question is Zeev Maoz, "Joining the Club of Nations: Political Development and International Conflict, 1816–1976," *International Studies Quarterly*, Vol. 33, No. 2 (June 1989), pp. 199–231.
68. John Hiden and John Farquharson, *Explaining Hitler's Germany: Historians and the Third Reich* (Totowa, N.J.: Barnes and Noble, 1983).

Implications for Policy

In light of these findings, it would be hard to maintain a naive enthusiasm for spreading peace by promoting democratization. Pushing nuclear-armed great powers like Russia or China toward democratization is like spinning a roulette wheel, where many of the potential outcomes are likely to be undesirable. However, in most cases the initial steps on the road to democratization will not be produced by the conscious policy of the United States, no matter what that policy may be. The roulette wheel is already spinning for Russia, and perhaps China, regardless of what the West does. Moreover, reversals of democratization are nearly as risky as democratization itself. Consequently, the international community needs a strategy not so much for promoting or reversing democratization as for managing the process in ways that minimize its risks and facilitate smooth transitions.

What might be some of these mitigating conditions, and how might they be promoted? The association of democratization with war is probabilistic. Democratization can lead either to war or to peace, depending on a variety of factors, such as the incentives facing the old elites during the transition process, the structure of the marketplace of foreign policy ideas, the speed and thoroughness of the democratic transition, and the character of the international environment in which democratization occurs. Some of these features may be subject to manipulation by astute democratic reformers and their allies in the international community.

One of the major findings of scholarship on democratization in Latin America is that the process goes most smoothly when elites that are threatened by the transition, especially the military, are given a "golden parachute."[69] Above all, they need a guarantee that if they relinquish power they will not wind up in jail. The history of the democratizing great powers broadens this insight. Democratization was least likely to lead to imprudent aggression in cases where the old elites saw a reasonably bright future for themselves in the new social order. British aristocrats, for example, had more of their wealth invested in commerce and industry than they did in agriculture, so they had many interests in common with the rising middle classes. They could face democratization with relative equanimity. In contrast, Prussia's capital-starved, small-

---

69. On the importance of bargaining with and co-opting old elites (giving them incentives, a "golden parachute," to depart from power), see the literature summarized in Doh Chull Shin, "On the Third Wave of Democratization: A Synthesis and Evaluation of Recent Theory and Research," *World Politics*, Vol. 47, No. 1 (October 1994), pp. 135–170, esp. 161–163.

scale Junker landholders had no choice but to rely on agricultural protection and military careers.

In today's context, finding benign, productive employment for the erstwhile Communist *nomenklatura*, military officer corps, nuclear scientists, and smoke-stack industrialists ought to rank high on the list of priorities. Policies aimed at giving them a stake in the privatization process and subsidizing the conversion of their skills to new, peaceful tasks in a market economy seem like a step in the right direction. According to some interpretations, Russian Defense Minister Pavel Grachev was eager to use force to solve the Chechen confrontation in order to show that Russian military power was still useful and that increased investment in the Russian army would pay big dividends. Instead of pursuing this reckless path, the Russian military elite needs to be convinced that its prestige, housing, pensions, and technical competence will rise if and only if it transforms itself into a western-style military, subordinate to civilian authority and resorting to force only in accordance with prevailing international norms. Moreover, though old elites need to be kept happy, they also need to be kept weak. Pacts should not prop up the remnants of the authoritarian system, but rather create a niche for them in the new system.

A top priority must also be placed on creating a free, competitive, yet responsible marketplace of ideas in the newly democratizing states. Most of the war-prone democratizing great powers had pluralistic public debates, but the terms of these debates were skewed to favor groups with money, privileged access to the media of communication, and proprietary control over information, ranging from historical archives to intelligence about the military balance. Pluralism is not enough. Without an even playing field, pluralism simply creates the incentive and opportunity for privileged groups to propound self-serving myths, which historically have often taken a nationalist turn. One of the rays of hope in the Chechen affair was the alacrity with which Russian journalists exposed the true costs of the fighting and the lies of the government and the military about it. Though elites should get a golden parachute in terms of their pecuniary interests, they should be given no quarter on the battlefield of ideas. Mythmaking should be held up to the utmost scrutiny by aggressive journalists who maintain their credibility by scrupulously distinguishing fact from opinion and tirelessly verifying their sources. Promoting this kind of journalistic infrastructure is probably the most highly leveraged investment that the West can make in a peaceful democratic transition.

Our research offers inconclusive results about the wisdom of speed and thoroughness in transitions to democracy. On the one hand, we found that states making the big jump from autocracy to democracy were much more war-prone than those moving from autocracy to anocracy. This would seem to favor a strategy of limited goals. On the other hand, the experience of the former Communist states suggests that those that have gone farthest and fastest toward full democracy are less nationalistic and less involved in militarized quarrels. This is a question that needs more research.

Finally, what kind of ruling coalition emerges in the course of democratization depends a great deal on the incentives that are created by the international environment. Both Germany and Japan started on the path toward liberal, stable democratization in the mid-1920s, encouraged in part by abundant opportunities for trade and investment from the advanced democracies and by credible security treaties that defused nationalist scare-mongering in domestic politics. But when the international supports for free trade and democracy were yanked out in the late 1920s, their liberal coalitions collapsed. Especially for the case of contemporary China, whose democratization may occur in the context of sharply expanding economic ties to the West, the steadiness of the Western commercial partnership and security presence is likely to play a major role in shaping the incentives of proto-democratic coalition politics.

In the long run, the enlargement of the zone of stable democracy will probably enhance the prospects for peace. But in the short run, there is a lot of work to be done to minimize the dangers of the turbulent transition.

Hypotheses on Nationalism and War

Stephen Van Evera

Scholars have written
widely on the causes of nationalism[1] but said little about its effects, especially
its effects on international politics. Most strikingly, the impact of nationalism
on the risk of war has barely been explored. Most authors take the war-
causing character of nationalism for granted, assuming it without proof or
explanation.[2] Factors that govern the size of the dangers posed by nationalism
are neglected. What types of nationalism are most likely to cause war? What
background conditions catalyze or dampen this causal process? These ques-

Stephen Van Evera teaches in the political science department at the Massachusetts Institute of Technology.

Thanks to Robert Art, Don Blackmer, David Laitin, John Mearsheimer, Barry Posen, Jack Snyder, and Stephen Walt for sharing their thoughts on nationalism and their comments on this paper. A version of this article will appear in 1994 in a Council on Foreign Relations volume edited by Charles Kupchan.

1. A survey is Anthony D. Smith, _Theories of Nationalism,_ 2nd ed. (New York: Harper & Row, 1983). Prominent recent works include: Ernest Gellner, _Nations and Nationalism_ (Ithaca: Cornell University Press, 1983); Anthony D. Smith, _The Ethnic Origins of Nations_ (Oxford: Basil Blackwell, 1986); E.J. Hobsbawm, _Nations and Nationalism Since 1780_ (New York: Cambridge University Press, 1990); Benedict Anderson, _Imagined Communities: Reflections on the Origin and Spread of Nationalism,_ rev. ed. (London: Verso, 1991); Liah Greenfeld, _Nationalism: Five Roads to Modernity_ (Cambridge: Harvard University Press, 1992); and Barry R. Posen, "Nationalism, the Mass Army, and Military Power," _International Security,_ Vol. 18, No. 2 (Fall 1993), pp. 80–124. However, the nationalism literature leaves ample room for more work on nationalism's causes: much of it fails to frame hypotheses clearly and much does not systematically test hypotheses against empirical evidence; hence the literature leaves many questions unresolved.
2. Thus Anthony Smith notes that "the prevailing image of nationalism in the West today is mainly negative," and Boyd Shafer states his "belief that nationalism, especially when carried to extremes, leads to war and destruction." Smith, _Theories of Nationalism,_ p. 8; Boyd C. Shafer, _Faces of Nationalism_ (New York: Harcourt Brace Jovanovich, 1972), p. xiii. Yet the entry under "Nationalism and War" in Louis Snyder's 435-page _Encyclopedia of Nationalism_ fills only two pages, and its bibliography lists no works focused on the topic. Louis L. Snyder, _Encyclopedia of Nationalism_ (New York: Paragon, 1990), pp. 248–250. Exceptions exist: a few scholars have held a less purely critical view of nationalism, arguing that it has the potential for both good and evil. See, for example, Carlton J.H. Hayes, _Essays on Nationalism_ (New York: Macmillan, 1926), pp. 245–275; Hayes's views are summarized in Snyder, _Encyclopedia of Nationalism,_ pp. 132–133. And the impact of nationalism on the risk of war is now receiving more attention: see especially Jack Snyder, "Nationalism and the Crisis of the Post-Soviet State," _Survival,_ Vol. 35, No. 1 (Spring 1993), pp. 5–26; and Barry R. Posen, "The Security Dilemma and Ethnic Conflict," _Survival,_ Vol. 35, No. 1 (Spring 1993), pp. 27–47. The Snyder and Posen pieces are also published in Michael E. Brown, ed., _Ethnic Conflict and International Security_ (Princeton: Princeton University Press, 1993).

International Security, Vol. 18, No. 4 (Spring 1994), pp. 5–39
© 1994 by the President and Fellows of Harvard College and the Massachusetts Institute of Technology.

tions are largely undiscussed, hence the causal nexus between nationalism and war presents an important unsolved riddle.

This article explores that nexus. I define nationalism as a political movement having two characteristics: (1) individual members give their primary loyalty to their own ethnic or national community;[3] this loyalty supersedes their loyalty to other groups, e.g., those based on common kinship or political ideology; and (2) these ethnic or national communities desire their own independent state.[4] I leave the origins of nationalism unexplored, instead focusing on its effects on the risk of war. Seven questions are addressed: Does nationalism cause war? If so, what types of nationalism are most likely to cause war? How and why do they cause war? What causes these war-causing nationalisms? Under what conditions are they most dangerous? How, if at all, can the war-causing attributes of nationalism be suppressed

---

3. My usage of "ethnic community" follows Anthony Smith, who suggests that an ethnic community has six characteristics: a common name, a myth of common ancestry, shared memories, a common culture, a link with a historic territory or homeland (which it may or may not currently occupy), and a measure of common solidarity. See Smith, *Ethnic Origins of Nations*, pp. 22–30. Summarizing Smith nicely is Michael E. Brown, "Causes and Implications of Ethnic Conflict," in Brown, ed., *Ethnic Conflict and International Security*, pp. 3–26 at 4–5.

Smith's second criteria (myth of common ancestry) would exclude immigrant societies of diverse origin that have developed the other five characteristics of ethnic community, such as the immigrant peoples of the United States, Cuba, Argentina, Chile, and Brazil. However, the common usage of "nation" and "nationalism" includes these groups as nations that can have a nationalism, e.g., "American nationalism," "Argentine nationalism," "Chilean nationalism." I define nationalism as a movement of a "national community" as well as an "ethnic community" in order to include these nationalisms. My usage of "national" follows the *Dictionary of the Social Sciences*, which defines "nation" as "the largest society of people united by a common culture and consciousness," and which "occupies a common territory." Julius Gould and William L. Kolb, eds., *A Dictionary of the Social Sciences* (New York: Free Press of Glencoe, 1964), p. 451.

4. The academic literature defines nationalism in an annoyingly wide range of ways. My definition follows no other exactly, but it amalgamates the more prominent definitions: each of these include at least one element of my definition, that prime loyalty is owed to one's ethnic/ culture group, and/or that the group to which prime loyalty is given should have its own state. My usage most closely follows Rupert Emerson and Richard Cottam, who define nationalism (in Cottam's words) as "a belief on the part of a large group of people that they comprise a community, a nation, that is entitled to independent statehood, and a willingness of this group to grant their community a primary and terminal loyalty"; quoted in Shafer, *Faces of Nationalism*, p. 4. Similar is Hans Kohn, whose nationalists give "supreme loyalty" to their own nationality, and who see "the nation-state as the ideal form of political organization." Ibid. Also similar are E.J. Hobsbawm and Ernest Gellner, who define nationalism as "primarily a principle which holds that the political and national unit should be congruent." Hobsbawm, *Nations and Nationalism since 1780*, p. 9, quoting and adopting Gellner's definition. However, their definition, by describing nationalism as an idea holding that states and nationalities should be coterminous, omits the many nationalisms that would claim their own state while also denying the statehood aspirations of other nationalities, and also omits more modest nationalisms that are content to allow a diaspora beyond their state borders.

or neutralized? How large are the risks to peace posed by nationalism in today's Europe, and how can these risks be minimized? In answer I offer unproven hypotheses that I leave untested for now. Our stock of hypotheses on the consequences of nationalism is meager, hence our first order of business should be to expand it. This can set the stage for empirical inquiry by others.[5]

Causes of war or peace can be classified as proximate (causes that directly affect the odds of war) or remote (causes of these proximate causes, or background conditions required for their activation.) I explore proximate causes first, then turn to remote causes. Specifically, the next section of this article identifies varieties of nationalism that are most likely to cause war (including both civil and inter-state war). The section that follows it identifies the causes of these dangerous varieties of nationalism and the conditions that govern the size of the dangers they produce. Twenty-one hypotheses are proposed in all—nine main hypotheses and twelve sub-hypotheses. Some focus on the impact of the environment that surrounds nationalist movements; this environment can incline the movement toward peaceful or toward warlike behavior. Others focus on the impact of the movement's internal character, especially its ideology and vision of history; this, too, can incline the movement toward peace or war. These hypotheses are highlighted because they are deductively sound, survive plausibility probes, and in some cases generate policy prescriptions. They are summarized in Table 1.[6] Viewed together, they suggest that the effects of nationalism are highly varied: some types of nationalism are far more dangerous than other types, all types of nationalism are more dangerous under some conditions than under others, and nationalism can even dampen the risk of war under some conditions.

If accepted, these hypotheses provide a checklist for assessing the dangers posed by a given nationalist movement or by the spread of nationalism in a given region. To illustrate, I use them in the concluding section to assess the risks that nationalism now poses in Europe, because Europe is a region in flux whose future is much debated. This exercise suggests that nationalism

---

5. A similar exercise whose example influenced my design is Robert Jervis, "Hypotheses on Misperception," *World Politics,* Vol. 20, No. 3 (April 1968), pp. 454–479; reprinted in Robert J. Art and Robert Jervis, ed., *International Politics: Anarchy, Force, Political Economy, and Decision Making,* 2nd ed. (Glenview, Ill.: Scott, Foresman, 1985), pp. 510–526.
6. The text of this article identifies factors that govern the size of the risk posed by nationalism, and explains the proposed causal relationship. Table 1 restates these factors and explanations as hypotheses.

Table 1. Hypotheses on Nationalism and War: Summary.

I. IMMEDIATE CAUSES

1. The greater the proportion of state-seeking nationalities that are stateless, the greater the risk of war.
2. The more that nationalities pursue the recovery of national diasporas, and the more they pursue annexationist strategies of recovery, the greater the risk of war.
3. The more hegemonistic the goals that nationalities pursue toward one another, the greater the risk of war.
4. The more severely nationalities oppress minorities living in their states, the greater the risk of war.

II. CAUSES OF THE IMMEDIATE CAUSES AND CONDITIONS REQUIRED FOR THEIR OPERATION

Structural Factors:

1. Stateless nationalisms pose a greater risk of war if they have the strength to plausibly reach for freedom, and the central state has the will to resist their attempt.
2. The more densely nationalities are intermingled, the greater the risk of war.
   a. The risks posed by intermingling are larger the more local (house-by-house) rather than regional (province-by-province) the pattern of intermingling.
   b. The risks posed by intermingling are larger if the rescue of diasporas by homelands is difficult but possible; smaller if rescue is either impossible or easy.
3. The greater the defensibility and legitimacy of borders, and the greater the correspondence between these political borders and communal boundaries, the smaller the risk of war.
   a. The less secure and defensible the borders of emerging nation-states, the greater the risk of war.
   b. The greater the international legitimacy of the borders of emerging nation-states, the smaller the risk of war.
   c. The more closely the boundaries of emerging nation-states follow ethnic boundaries, the smaller the risk of war.

---

poses very little danger of war in Western Europe, but poses large dangers in the East, especially in the former Soviet Union. Current Western European nationalisms are benign, and the conditions required for a return to the malignant nationalisms of 1870–1945 are almost wholly absent. In contrast, many Eastern nationalisms have many (though not all) of the attributes that

---

Table 1, cont.

Political/Environmental Factors:

4. The greater the past crimes committed by nationalities toward one another, the greater the risk of war.
   a. The better these crimes are remembered by the victims, the greater the risk of war.
   b. The more that responsibility for past crimes can be attached to groups still on the scene, the greater the risk of war.
   c. The less contrition and repentance shown by the guilty groups, the greater the risk of war.
   d. The greater the coincidence of power and victimhood, the greater the risk of war.
5. The more severely nationalities oppress minorities now living in their states, the greater the risk of war. (This restates Hypothesis No. I.4; I list it twice because it operates as both a direct and a remote cause of war.)

Perceptual Factors:

6. The more divergent are the beliefs of nationalities about their mutual history and their current conduct and character, the greater the risk of war.
   a. The less legitimate the governments or leaders of nationalist movements, the greater their propensity to purvey mythical nationalist beliefs, hence the greater the risk of war.
   b. The more the state must demand of its citizens, the greater its propensity to purvey mythical nationalist beliefs, hence the greater the risk of war.
   c. If economic conditions deteriorate, publics become more receptive to scapegoat myths, hence such myths are more widely believed, hence war is more likely.
   d. If independent evaluative institutions are weak or incompetent, myths will more often prevail, hence war is more likely.

I argue make nationalism dangerous; hence the risk of large-scale violence stemming from the now-rising tide of Eastern nationalism is substantial.

What prescriptions follow? The character and consequences of nationalism are not written in stone. The Western powers have some capacity to influence the character and consequences of Eastern nationalist movements, and should try to channel it in benign directions. Most importantly, the Western powers should promote full respect for minority rights, democracy, and official respect for historical truth; if Eastern nationalisms adopt these programs, the risks they pose will sharply diminish.

Varieties of Nationalism: Which Cause War?

Four primary attributes of a nationalist movement determine whether it has a large or small potential to produce violence. These are: (1) The movement's political status: is statehood attained or unattained? (2) The movement's stance toward its national diaspora (if it has one): if the movement has a national state, but some members of the nation are dispersed or entrapped beyond the state's borders, does the nation accept continued separation from this diaspora, or does it seek to incorporate the diaspora in the national state? And if it seeks the diaspora's incorporation, will it accomplish this by immigration or by territorial expansion? (3) The movement's stance toward other nations: does it respect or deny other nationalities' right to national independence? (4) The movement's treatment of its own minorities: are these minorities respected or abused?

IS NATIONAL STATEHOOD ATTAINED OR UNATTAINED?
Nationalist movements without states raise greater risks of war because their accommodation requires greater and more disruptive change. Their struggle for national freedom can produce wars of secession, which in turn can widen to become international wars. Their freedom struggle can also injure the interests of other groups, displacing populations whose new grievances sow the seeds of future conflict, as Zionism's displacement of the Palestinian Arabs in 1948 sowed the seeds of later Arab-Israeli wars. Finally, the appearance of new states creates a new, less mature regional international system that lacks "rules of the game" defining the rights and obligations of its members toward one another, and norms of international conduct; these rights, obligations, and norms can take years to define, raising the risk of crises and collisions in the meantime.

The international system tolerates change poorly, but the accommodation of new nationalist movements requires it.[7] Thus the first measure of the risks

---

7. The dichotomy between stateless and state-possessing nationalist movements is analogous to the dichotomy in international relations between "satisfied" and "dissatisfied" powers; the latter disturb the peace in their effort to gain satisfaction, while the former cause less trouble.

to the peace of a region posed by nationalism is found in the proportion of its nationalist movements that remain unfulfilled in statehood, a factor expressed in the nation-to-state ratio. Are the supply of and demand for states in equilibrium or disequilibrium? Peace in a region is more likely the more closely a supply/demand equilibrium is approached.[8] Modern nationalism disrupted peace over the past two centuries partly because so many of the world's current nationalist movements were stateless at the outset, requiring vast change to accommodate their emergence. Nationalism still threatens peace because its full accommodation would require vast additional change: the number of states in the world has more than tripled since World War II (up from the 50 signers of the UN Charter in 1945, to 180-odd states today), but many nationalities remain stateless; the world has some 6000 language groups,[9] many of which have dormant or manifest aspirations for statehood.

In Western Europe the transition of nations to statehood is largely behind us: that region's remaining stateless nationalities are relatively few and weak. In Eastern Europe and the former Soviet Union, the problem is more serious because the transition to statehood, while largely fulfilled, is still incomplete. The bulk of these stateless nationalities are found in the former Soviet Union; 15 of the 104 nationalities in the former USSR have attained states, but the other 89 have not; these stateless nationalities total 25.6 million people, comprising 10 percent of the former USSR's total population.[10] Most of these nationalities are not potential candidates for statehood (e.g., the Jews) but

---

8. Wars can result from having too many states, as well as too few. If states are too many, wars of national unification will result, as they did in Germany and Italy in the nineteenth century, and as they might someday in the Arab world. In Europe, however, the problem everywhere is an excess of demand for states over the supply.

9. Alan Thein Durning, *Guardians of the Land: Indigenous Peoples and the Health of the Earth*, Worldwatch Paper No. 112 (Washington, D.C.: Worldwatch Institute, December 1992), p. 9. Durning reports that measured by spoken languages the world has 6000 cultures. Of these some 4000–5000 are indigenous, and comprise some 10 percent of the world's population. See also Michael Krauss, "The Language Extinction Catastrophe Just Ahead: Should Linguists Care?" paper presented at the 15th International Congress of Linguists, Quebec City, Quebec, Canada, August 10, 1992. For another estimate see Gunnar P. Nielsson, "States and 'Nation-Groups': A Global Taxonomy," in Edward A. Tiryakian and Ronald Rogowski, eds., *New Nationalisms of the Developed West* (Boston: Allen and Unwin, 1985), pp. 27–56. He identifies a global total of 589 ethnic groups, most of which are stateless (p. 33). He also found that only 41 of 161 states surveyed were ethnically homogeneous (in which one ethnic group comprises over 95 percent of the state's population); see ibid., Table 2.1, pp. 30–31.

10. These figures are for 1979, and are calculated from John L. Scherer, ed., *USSR Facts and Figures Annual*, Vol. 5 (Gulf Breeze, Fla.: Academic International Press, 1981), pp. 51–52. Of these stateless groups the ten largest are the Tatar (6.3 million), German (1.9 million), Jewish (1.8 million), Chuvash (1.8 million), Dagestan (1.7 million), Bashkir (1.4 million), Mordvin (1.2 million), Polish (1.2 million), Chechen (.8 million), and Udmurt (.7 million).

some might be (e.g., the Tatars, Chechen, Ingush, and Ossetians), and their reach for statehood could sow future friction.

ATTITUDE TOWARD THE NATIONAL DIASPORA: IS PARTIAL OR TOTAL NATIONAL UNITY PURSUED? ARE IMMIGRATIONIST OR EXPANSIONIST TACTICS USED?
Does the nationalist ideology posit that all or only a part of the national ethnic community must be incorporated in the national state? And if the whole nationality must be incorporated, will this be accomplished by immigration (bringing the diaspora to the state) or by territorial expansion (bringing the state to the diaspora)?

These questions suggest a distinction among three types of nationalism: "diaspora-accepting," "immigrationist," and "diaspora-annexing." Some nationalisms (the diaspora-accepting variety) are content with partial union (e.g., Chinese nationalism);[11] such nationalisms are less troublesome because they make fewer territorial demands on their neighbors. Some nationalisms (the immigrationist type) seek to incorporate their diasporas in the national state, but are content to pursue union by seeking immigration of the diaspora (current German nationalism and Zionist Jewish nationalism.) Such immigrationist nationalisms are also easy to accommodate. Finally, some nationalisms seek to incorporate their diasporas by means of territorial expansion (pre-1914 Pan-Germanism and current Pan-Serbianism are examples.) Such diaspora-annexing nationalisms are the most dangerous of the three, since their goals and tactics produce the greatest territorial conflict with others. Thus one scenario for war in the former Soviet Union lies in the possible appearance of a Pan-Russian nationalism that would seek to reincorporate by force the vast Russian diaspora now living in the non-Russian republics. This diaspora includes some 24 million Russians, or 17 percent of all Russians.[12] The future hinges heavily on whether Russian nationalism accepts separation from this diaspora (or seeks to ingather it by immigration), or instead forcibly seeks to annex it.[13]

---

11. The Chinese state has historically left the overseas Chinese to their own political devices. John E. Wills, "Maritime Asia, 1500–1800: The Interactive Emergence of European Domination," *American Historical Review*, Vol. 98, No. 1 (February 1993), pp. 83–105, at p. 87.
12. Calculated from Scherer, *USSR Facts and Figures Annual*, pp. 49–51.
13. Russia's extensive military meddling in the affairs of the other former Soviet republics during 1992–94 and the political rise of Vladimir Zhirinovsky in 1993 warns that a new Russian expansionism is already emerging. On this military meddling see Thomas Goltz, "Letter From Eurasia: The Hidden Russian Hand," *Foreign Policy*, No. 92 (Fall 1993), pp. 92–116.

ATTITUDE TOWARD OTHER INDEPENDENT NATIONALITIES:
TOLERANT OR HEGEMONISTIC?

Does the ideology of the nationalism incorporate respect for the freedom of other nationalities, or does it assume a right or duty to rule them? In other words, is the national ideology symmetrical (all nationalities deserve states) or asymmetrical (only our nationality deserves statehood; others should be denied it)?

Hegemonistic, or asymmetrical, nationalism is both the rarest and the most dangerous variety of nationalism. Interwar Nazi nationalism in Germany, fascist nationalism in Mussolini's Italy, and militarist nationalism in imperial Japan illustrate such hegemonistic nationalism; the wars they caused illustrate its results.[14] No European nationalism today displays such hegemonism, but the vast trouble that it caused in the past advises alertness to its possible reappearance in Europe or elsewhere.

THE DEGREE OF NATIONAL RESPECT FOR MINORITY RIGHTS: HIGH OR LOW?

Is the nationalism minority-respecting, or minority-oppressing? A minority-respecting nationalism grants equal rights to other nationalities lying within the boundaries of its claimed state; it may even grant their right to secede and establish their own state. A minority-oppressing nationalism denies such rights to these other nationalities, subjugating them instead. Many of the nationalisms of immigrant nations (American, Anglo-Canadian) have been relatively minority-respecting (in the Canadian case this includes a tacit right to secession, which the Quebecois may soon exercise.) Non-immigrant nationalisms often display far less tolerance for their minorities: prominent current examples include Iraq's and Turkey's oppression of their Kurdish minorities, Bulgaria's oppression of its Turks, China's cruelties in Tibet, Croatia's intolerance toward its Serb minority, and Serbian oppression of its

---

14. On twentieth-century German nationalism, see Louis L. Snyder, *German Nationalism: The Tragedy of a People*, 2nd ed. (Port Washington, New York: Kennikat Press, 1969); Louis L. Snyder, *From Bismarck to Hitler: The Background of Modern German Nationalism* (Williamsport: Bayard Press, 1935); and Hans Kohn, *The Mind of Germany: The Education of a Nation* (New York: Harper and Row, 1960). On official ideas and perceptions in fascist Italy see Denis Mack Smith, *Mussolini's Roman Empire* (Harmondsworth, U.K.: Penguin, 1977). On domestic currents in imperial Japan see Saburo Ienaga, *The Pacific War, 1931–1945* (New York: Pantheon, 1978); and Ienaga, "The Glorification of War in Japanese Education," *International Security*, Vol. 18, No. 3 (Winter 1993/94), pp. 113–133. Nationalism is not, of course, the only possible source of claims against neighbors. These can also arise from non-nationalist expansionist political ideologies (communism), from hegemonistic religious ideas (the crusading Christianity of the middle ages), from safety concerns arising from the security dilemma, from economic greed, and so forth.

Slavic Moslem and Albanian minorities. Nazi German nationalism was an extreme case of a minority-oppressing nationalism.

The first three attributes—is statehood attained? attitude toward diaspora? attitude toward other independent nationalities?—define the scope of a nationalist movement's claims against others; conversely, the fourth attribute—policy toward minorities?—helps determine the scope of others' claims against the movement. The larger these others' goals become, the more they will collide with the movement's goals, raising the risk of war. Minority-oppressing nationalism can cause war in two ways: (1) by provoking violent secessions by its captive nations; or (2) by spurring the homelands of these captive nations to move forcefully to free their oppressed co-nationals[15] (as Croatian threats against the Serb minority in Croatia helped spawn the Serb attack on Croatia in 1991).[16] Minority-oppressing nationalism is most dangerous if the oppressed minorities have nearby friends who have the capacity to protect the oppressed nation by force. (The Serbo-Croat war exploded partly because Croatia's Serbs had such a friend in Serbia). The attitude of many nationalisms in Eastern Europe and the former Soviet Union toward their minorities remains undefined, and the future hinges on whether they evolve toward minority respect or oppression.

These four attributes can be used to create a nationalism "danger-scale," expressing the level of danger posed by a given nationalism, or by the spread of nationalism in a given region. If all four attributes are benign, the nationalism poses little danger of war, and may even bolster peace. Specifically, a nationalism is benign if it has achieved statehood; has limited unity goals (i.e., accepts the existence of any unincorporated diaspora) or adopts an immigrationist strategy for ingathering its diaspora; posits no claim to rule other nationalities living beyond its national territory; and respects the rights of minorities found in this territory. Multiplied, such nationalisms may even dampen the risk of war, by making conquest more difficult: where these nationalisms are prevalent, conquest is harder because nation-states are

---

15. Thus the second and fourth attributes are related: if some states oppress their minorities (the fourth attribute) this affects other states' propensity to pursue diaspora recovery (the second attribute).

16. On the war's origins, including the important role of Croatia's pre-war threats against its Serb minority, see Misha Glenny, "The Massacre of Yugoslavia," *New York Review of Books*, January 30, 1992, pp. 30–35, at 30–31; and Misha Glenny, *The Fall of Yugoslavia: The Third Balkan War* (London: Penguin, 1992), pp. 12–14, 123. An account stressing international aspects of the war's origins is Morton H. Halperin and David J. Scheffer with Patricia L. Small, *Self-Determination in the New World Order* (Washington, D.C.: Carnegie Endowment, 1992), pp. 32–38.

among the most difficult type of state to conquer (since nationalism provides an inspirational liberation doctrine that can be used to mobilize strong popular resistance to conquest).[17] As a result strong states will be deterred from reaching for regional or global hegemony, and will also be less fearful that others might achieve it; hence all states will compete less fiercely with one another.[18] In contrast, a nationalism is bound to collide with others if all four attributes are malign: If the nationalism has no state, the risk of civil war arising from its struggle for national independence is increased; this also raises the risk of inter-state war, since civil war can widen to engulf nearby states. If, after achieving statehood, the nationalism seeks to incorporate a diaspora by force, oppresses minorities found in its claimed national territory, and seeks hegemony over nationalities lying beyond that territory, violence between the nationalism and its neighbors is inevitable.

Causes and Conditions for War-Causing Nationalism

What factors determine whether these four variables will have benign or malignant values? What conditions are required for malignant values to have malignant effects? The deciding factors and conditions are grouped below into three broad families: structural (those arising from the geographic and demographic arrangement of a nation's people); political-environmental (those arising from the past or present conduct of a people's neighbors); and perceptual (those arising from the nationalist movement's self-image and its

---

17. On the greater peacefulness of a defense-dominant world, see Robert Jervis, "Cooperation Under the Security Dilemma," *World Politics*, Vol. 30, No. 2 (January 1978), pp. 167–214.

18. Thus the evident power of nationalism helped dampen Soviet-American competition during the Cold War, by persuading some in the West that nationalism imposed a natural limit on Soviet expansion. These observers argued that the Western powers need not actively check Soviet expansionism at every point because local nationalism could defeat it alone, nor move actively to roll back Soviet gains, because these gains would eventually be rolled back by indigenous nationalism, and in the meantime nationalist resistance would bleed Soviet power. For example, George Kennan took a calm approach to containment partly because he believed that resistant local nationalism would check Soviet expansion in the short run, and would rend the Soviet empire in the long run. See John Lewis Gaddis, *Strategies of Containment: A Critical Appraisal of Postwar American National Security Policy* (New York: Oxford University Press, 1982), pp. 42–48. Other arguments for Cold War restraint that rested in part on the power of nationalism included Arthur M. Schlesinger, *The Bitter Heritage: Vietnam and American Democracy 1941–1968*, rev. ed. (Greenwich: Fawcett, 1968), pp. 78–80; Jerome Slater, "Dominos in Central America: Will They Fall? Does It Matter?" *International Security*, Vol. 12, No. 2 (Fall 1987), pp. 105–134, at 113; and Stephen M. Walt, "The Case for Finite Containment," *International Security*, Vol. 14, No. 1 (Summer 1989), pp. 3–49, at 26–27. Had nationalism been weaker, these arguments would have lost force, leaving a stronger case for more aggressive American policies.

images of others, including its images of both sides' past and present conduct and character).

STRUCTURAL FACTORS: THE GEOGRAPHIC, DEMOGRAPHIC, AND MILITARY SETTING

The size of the risks posed by nationalism is influenced by the balance of power and of will between stateless nationalisms and the central states that hold them captive; by the degree and pattern of regional ethnic intermingling; by the defensibility and legitimacy of the borders of new national states; and by the correspondence of these borders with ethnic boundaries.

THE DOMESTIC BALANCE OF POWER AND OF WILL. Unattained nationalisms are more troublesome under two conditions: (1) the movement has the strength to reach plausibly for statehood; and (2) the central state has the will to resist this attempt.

Stateless nationalisms whose statehood is unattainable will lie dormant, their emergence deterred by the power of the central state.[19] Nationalism becomes manifest and can produce war when the power-balance between the central state and the captive nationalism shifts to allow the possibility of successful secession. Thus two safe conditions exist: where national statehood is already attained; and where it is not attained, but clearly cannot be. The danger zone lies between, in cases where statehood has not been attained yet is attainable or appears to be.[20] In this zone we find wars of nationalist secession.[21] Such conflicts can, in turn, grow into international wars: examples include the 1912–14 Balkan secessionist struggles that triggered World War I, and the 1991–92 Serbo-Croatian conflict.

---

19. If nationalism is unattainable it may not even appear: the captive nation will submerge the nationalist thought. This is similar to the realist argument that imperialism is a function of capability: states imperialize simply when and where they can. Likewise, and conversely, nationalism is in part simply a function of capability: it emerges where it can.

20. We can scale up this logic from single states to regions by asking: do nations have states in proportion to their power? That is, does the state-to-nation ratio correspond with the state-to-nation power ratio? Or do nations have fewer states than their power justifies? If the former is the case, peace is more likely. But if nations have fewer states than their power would allow, trouble results in the form of wars of secession.

21. Overall, then, three variables matter: (1) the supply of states; (2) the demand for states; (3) the capacity of submerged nations to acquire states. Peace is stronger if supply and demand are in equilibrium; or if supply and capacity are in equilibrium. In one case, nationalism is satisfied; in the other, it is dissatisfied but impotent. Dangers arise if both supply and demand, and supply and capacity, are not in equilibrium. We then have submerged nationalisms that both desire and can assert the demand for statehood.

The Third World nationalisms of the twentieth century erupted partly because the spread of small arms and literacy shifted the balance of power in favor of these nationalisms, and against their imperial captors. Nationalism emerged because it could. Likewise, nationalism exploded in the former Soviet Union in the late 1980s partly because Soviet central power had waned.

War is inevitable if central states have the will to resist emerging nationalist/ secessionist movements, but these movements can win freedom without violence if that will is missing. Many sub-Saharan African states gained freedom in the 1960s without violence because the European colonial powers lost their imperial will. Likewise, the emergence of non-Russian nationalisms in the former Soviet Union was accompanied by (and encouraged by) the loss of imperial will in Moscow; this loss of will at the center allowed the non-Russians to escape the Soviet empire without waging wars of secession. French decolonization was far more violent, spawning large wars in Vietnam and Algeria, because the French metropole retained its will even after nationalism gained momentum in the French empire.

The will of the central state is largely governed by its domestic politics, but is also determined partly by demographic facts. Specifically, central governments can allow secession more easily if secession would leave a homogeneous rump central state, since permitting secession then sets a less damaging precedent. Thus the Czechs could accept Slovak independence without fear of setting a precedent that would trigger another secession, since there is no potential secessionist group in the rump Czech Republic. Likewise, the United States could grant independence to the Philippines fairly easily in 1946 because the United States had few other colonies, and none of these were large or valuable, hence Philippine independence set no dangerous precedents. Conversely, the Austro-Hungarian empire strongly resisted secessions before 1914 because the empire contained many potential secessionists who might be encouraged if any secession were allowed.

THE DEMOGRAPHIC ARRANGEMENT OF NATIONAL POPULATIONS: ARE THEY INTERMINGLED OR HOMOGENEOUS? Are nationality populations densely intermingled? If they are, does this create large or small national diasporas? Intermingling raises the risk of communal conflict during the struggle for national freedom, as groups that would be trapped as minorities in a new national state oppose its reach for freedom. Dispersion and intermingling will also trap some co-ethnics outside the boundaries of their nation-states; this raises the danger that new nation-states will pursue diaspora-recovering expansionism after they gain statehood, and the possibility that their abuse of minorities will trigger attack from outside.[22]

These dangers are reduced if national populations are compact and homogenous—diasporas and minorities then occur only if political boundaries fail to follow ethnic boundaries. They are intensified if the nationality is dispersed abroad, and intermingled with others at home. The Czechs, for example, can pursue nationalism with little risk to the peace of their neighborhood, because they have no diaspora abroad, and few minorities at home. They need not limit their goals or learn to accommodate minorities. The 1947 partition of India was a far bloodier process than the 1992 Czech-Slovak divorce partly because Hindus and Moslems were far more intermingled than Czechs and Slovaks. The partition of Yugoslavia has been especially violent partly because nationalities in former Yugoslavia are more densely intermingled than any others in Eastern or Western Europe outside the former Soviet Union.[23]

Overall, nationalism poses greater dangers in Eastern than Western Europe because the peoples of Eastern Europe are more densely intermingled. A survey of Eastern Europe reveals roughly a dozen minority group pockets that may seek independence or be claimed by other countries.[24] The ethno-

---

22. The scope and structure of intermingling governs the acuteness of what might be called the "inter-ethnic security dilemma": this dilemma is posed where one group cannot achieve physical security without diminishing the physical security of other groups. It is analogous to the inter-state security dilemma of international relations, except that the clashing units are ethnic or culture groups, not states.

23. Moreover, Yugoslavia's one easy secession—that of Slovenia—was easy because the Slovene population was not intermingled with others. An excellent ethnographic map of the former Yugoslavia that details its intermingling is Central Intelligence Agency, "Peoples of Yugoslavia: Distribution by Opstina, 1981 Census," Map No. 505956 9-83 (543994). A useful though less detailed ethnographic map covering all of Eastern Europe including former Yugoslavia is Central Intelligence Agency, "Ethnic Majorities and Minorities," in Central Intelligence Agency, *Atlas of Eastern Europe* (Washington, D.C.: U.S. Government Printing Office [U.S. GPO], August 1990), p. 6. A good ethnographic map of the former USSR is National Geographic Society, "Peoples of the Soviet Union," supplement to *National Geographic*, Vol. 149, No. 2 (February 1976), p. 144A; back issues of *National Geographic* containing this map are available from the National Geographic Society, Washington, D.C.

24. These include Hungarians in Romania, Slovakia, and Serbia; Poles in Lithuania, Belarus, Ukraine, and the Czech Republic; Germans in Poland and the Czech Republic; Turks in Bulgaria; Greeks in Albania; Albanians in Serbia and Macedonia; Croats in Bosnia-Herzegovina; and Serbs in Croatia and Bosnia-Herzegovina. Summaries include F. Stephen Larrabee, "Long Memories and Short Fuses: Change and Instability in the Balkans," *International Security*, Vol. 15, No. 3 (Winter 1990/91), pp. 58–91; Istvan Deak, "Uncovering Eastern Europe's Dark History," *Orbis*, Vol. 34, No. 1 (Winter 1989), pp. 51–65; Barry James, "Central Europe Tinderboxes: Old Border Disputes," *International Herald Tribune*, January 1, 1990, p. 5; and the CIA map cited above, "Ethnic Majorities and Minorities, 1990."

graphic structure of the former Soviet Union is even more ominous; an ethnographic map of the former USSR reveals massively intermingled nationalities, scattered in scores of isolated pockets, a mosaic far more tangled and complex than any found elsewhere in Europe except the former Yugoslavia.[25]

Two aspects of intermingling determine the size of the dangers it poses: the scope of intermingling, and the pattern of intermingling. All intermingling causes trouble, but some patterns of intermingling cause more trouble than others.

Groups can be intermingled on a regional scale (regions are heterogeneous, small communities are homogeneous) or local scale (even small communities are heterogeneous, as in Sarajevo.) Regional intermingling is more easily managed, because inter-group relations can be negotiated by elites. In contrast, elites can lose control of events when intermingling extends to the local level: conflict can flare against the wishes of elites when unofficial killers seize the agenda by sparking a spiral of private violence. Local intermingling can also produce conflict-dampening personal friendships and inter-ethnic marriages, but the Bosnian conflict shows the limits of this tempering effect. Overall, local intermingling is more dangerous.

The most dangerous pattern of regional intermingling is one that leaves elements of one or both groups insecurely at the mercy of the other, but also allows for the possibility of forcible rescue—either by self-rescue (secession) or external rescue (intervention by an already-free homeland).

If rescue is impossible, then the goal of secession or reunion with a homeland will be abandoned. Israel cannot rescue Soviet Jewry, except by immigration, and Ukraine cannot rescue the Ukrainian diaspora in Russia; hence neither considers forceful rescue. This lowers the risk of war.

If rescue is easy, it may not be attempted, since the threat of rescue is enough to deter abuse of the diaspora. Russia could fairly easily rescue the Russian minority in the Baltics and perhaps elsewhere on the Russian periphery, because much of the Russian diaspora lies clustered near the Russian

---

25. See the maps cited in note 23 above. Overall, 16 percent of the titular peoples of the 15 successor states of the former Soviet Union, totalling 39 million people, live outside their home states ("titular peoples": the peoples after whom republics are named, e.g., Armenians, Kazakhs, Russians, etc.). Calculated from Scherer, *USSR Facts and Figures Annual*, pp. 49–51. And, as noted above, another 10 percent of the former Soviet population (26 million people) are members of the 89 smaller nationalities without titular home republics ("titular home republic": a republic named after the nationality).

border, and Russia holds military superiority over its neighbors. These power realities may deter Russia's neighbors from abusing their Russian minorities, leaving Russia more room to take a relaxed attitude.[26]

It is in-between situations—those where rescue is possible, but only under optimal conditions—that are most dangerous. This situation will tempt potential rescuers to jump through any windows of opportunity that arise. Forceful rescue is then driven by both fear and opportunity—fear that later the abuse of diasporas cannot be deterred by threatening to rescue them (since the difficulty of rescue will rob that threat of credibility), and by the opportunity to rescue the diaspora now by force.[27] Thus Serbia would have probably been unable to rescue the Serb diaspora in normal times: Serbia is too weak, and the Serbian diasporas in Croatia and Bosnia are too distant from Serbia. But rescue was feasible if Serbia made the attempt at a moment of peak Serbian military advantage. Such a moment emerged in 1990, after Serbia consolidated the weaponry of the Yugoslav army under its control, but before the Croatian and Bosnian states could organize strong militaries.[28] In contrast, such a moment may never emerge for Russia, because it can always rescue large parts of its diaspora should the need ever arise, leaving less need to seize an early opportunity.

These in-between situations are most troublesome when the diaspora is separated from the homeland by lands inhabited by others: wars of rescue then cause larger injury. In such cases rescue requires cutting a secure corridor through these lands; this, in turn, requires the forcible expulsion of the resident population, with its attendant horrors and cruelties. In 1991 the Serbian diaspora in Croatia and Bosnia was cut off from the Serb homeland by walls of Moslem-inhabited territory,[29] and the vast Serbian cruelties against the Bosnian Moslems during 1992–93 grew mainly from Serbia's effort to punch corridors through these walls in order to attach these diasporas to Serbia proper. In contrast, more of Russia's diaspora is contiguous to Russia, hence a Russian war of rescue would do relatively less harm to others innocently in the way (though it would still do plenty of harm).

---

26. Making this argument is Posen, "The Security Dilemma and Ethnic Conflict," pp. 32–35.
27. See Posen, "The Security Dilemma and Ethnic Conflict," pp. 32–38.
28. The intensification of fighting between Armenia and Azerbaijan in 1991–92 had similar origins: Armenia moved to free Nagorno-Karabakh at a moment that Armenia's power relative to Azerbaijan's was at its peak.
29. See Central Intelligence Agency, "Peoples of Yugoslavia."

BORDERS: DEFENSIBILITY, LEGITIMACY, AND BORDER/ETHNIC CORRESPON-
DENCE. The risks to peace posed by a nationalism's emergence are governed
partly by the defensibility and international legitimacy of the nation's borders, and by the degree of correspondence between these political borders
and ethnic boundaries.

The satisfaction of national demands for statehood extends international
anarchy by creating more states: hence nationalism's effects are governed
partly by the character of the extended anarchy that it creates. Some anarchies
are relatively peaceful, others more violent. The acuteness of the security
dilemma is a key factor governing the answer. Anarchy is a precondition for
international war, hence extending anarchy may expand the risk of war, but
this is not always the case: the fragmentation of states can deepen peace if
it leaves the world with states that are more difficult to conquer, hence are
more secure, than the older states from which they were carved. The character of boundaries helps decide the issue: if the new borders are indefen-
sible, the net impact of the creation of new national states will be warlike; if
borders are highly defensible, the net impact may be peaceful.[30]

Defensible boundaries reduce the risk of war because they leave new states
less anxious to expand for security reasons, while also deterring others from
attacking them. The nations of Western Europe can be more peaceful than
those of the East because they are endowed with more defensible borders:
the French, Spanish, British, Italian, and Scandinavian nations have natural
defenses formed by the Alps and the Pyrenees, and by the waters of the
English Channel, the Baltic, and the North Sea. Icelandic nationalism is
especially unproblematic because geography makes Iceland unusually secure,
and almost incapable of attack. In contrast, the nationalities living on the
exposed plains of Eastern Europe and western Asia contend with a harsher
geography: with few natural barriers to invasion, they are more vulnerable
to attack, hence are more tempted to attack others in preemptive defense.[31]
They are therefore more likely to disturb the status quo, or to be victims of
other disturbers.

The international legitimacy of a new nation's borders helps determine the
level of danger raised when it gains independence: if borders lack interna-

---

30. The new states may also be more defensible than their parent states because they can call
upon nationalism as a mobilizing defensive force, as their multi-ethnic parent states could not.
31. Likewise, Germany has produced the most troublesome Western nationalism partly because
German borders are relatively exposed.

tional legitimacy or are unsettled altogether, demands for border changes will arise, providing new occasions for conflict. The successor states of the former Soviet Union find themselves with borders drawn by Stalin or other Bolshevik rulers; these have correspondingly small legitimacy. Israel's post-1948 boundaries at first lacked international legitimacy because they had no historical basis, having arisen simply from truce lines expressing the military outcome of the 1948 war. In contrast, the borders of the recently-freed states of Eastern Europe have greater legitimacy because they have firmer grounding in history, and some were the product of earlier international negotiation and agreement.

Borders may bisect nationalities, or may follow national demographic divides. Nation-bisecting borders are more troublesome, because they have the same effect as demographic intermingling: they entrap parts of nationalities within the boundaries of states dominated by other ethnic groups, giving rise to expansionism by the truncated nation. Thus Hungary's borders bisect (and truncate) the Hungarian nation, giving rise to a (now dormant but still surviving) Hungarian revanchism against Slovakia, Serbia, and Rumania.[32] The Russian/Ukrainian border bisects both nationalities, creating the potential for movements to adjust borders in both countries.

The borders of new states can arise in two main ways: from violent military struggle (e.g., Israel) or as a result of cession of sovereignty to existing administrative units whose boundaries were previously defined by the parent multiethnic state (e.g., former Soviet Union). War-born borders often have the advantage of following ethnic lines, because the cruelties of war often cause ethnic cleansing, and offensives lose strength at ethnic boundaries; inherited administrative borders (e.g., the boundaries of Azerbaijan, which entrap the Armenians of Nagorno-Karabakh) more often plant the charge of future conflict by dividing nations and creating diasporas. The peaceful dissolution of the former Soviet Union was thus a mixed blessing: its successor states emerged without violence, but with borders that captured unhappy diasporas behind them.

---

32. On latent Hungarian revanchism see, for example, Judith Ingram, "Boys Impatient for 'Great Hungary' to Take Wing," *New York Times*, January 15, 1993, p. A4. On its official manifestations see Stephen Engelberg with Judith Ingram, "Now Hungary Adds Its Voice to the Ethnic Tumult," *New York Times*, January 25, 1993, p. A3.

POLITICAL/ENVIRONMENTAL FACTORS: HOW HAVE NEIGHBORS BEHAVED?
HOW DO THEY NOW BEHAVE?

The conduct of nationalities and nation-states mirrors their neighbors' past and present conduct.

PAST CONDUCT: WERE GREAT CRIMES COMMITTED? The degree of harmony or conflict between intermingled nationalities depends partly on the size of the crimes committed by each against the other in the past; the greater these past crimes, the greater the current conflict. Memories of its neighbors' cruelties will magnify an emerging nation's impulse to ingather its diaspora, converting the nation from a diaspora-accepting to a diaspora-annexing attitude. Thus the vast Croatian mass-murders of Serbs during the 1940s were the taproot that fed violent pan-Serbianism after 1990: Serbs vowed "never again," and argued that they must incorporate the Serbian diaspora in Croatia to save it from new pogroms.[33] Past suffering can also spur nations to oppress old tormentors who now live among them as minorities, sparking conflict with these minorities' home countries. Thus the past horrors inflicted on the Baltic peoples by Stalinism fuels their discrimination against their Russian minorities today;[34] this discrimination, in turn, feeds anti-Baltic feeling in Russia. In contrast, non-victim nations are less aggressive toward both neighbors and minorities. Czech nationalism is benign partly because the Czechs have escaped real victimhood; Quebec nationalism is mild for the same reason.

Mass murder, land theft, and population expulsions are the crimes that matter most. Past exterminations foster diaspora-recovering ideologies that are justified by self-protection logic. Past land theft fosters territorial definitions of nationhood (e.g., the Israeli Likud's concept of "the Land of Israel," a place including once-Jewish lands that Likud argues were wrongfully taken by others) and claims to land that excludes the rights of peoples now on that land (the Likud rejects equal rights for the Palestinian inhabitants of these

---

33. See Bette Denich, "Unbury the Victims: Nationalist Revivals of Genocide in Yugoslavia," Paper presented at the American Anthropological Association Annual Meeting, Chicago, Illinois, November 1991.
34. On the Baltic states' policies see Steven Erlanger, "Baltic Identity: Russians Wonder If They Belong: New Citizenship Rules May in Effect Expel the Ex-'Occupiers'," *New York Times*, November 22, 1992, p. 1. This Baltic anti-Russian discrimination reflects the great cruelties inflicted on the Baltic peoples by Stalin's government: during the years 1940–49 some 36 percent of the indigenous population of Latvia, 33 percent of the indigenous population of Estonia, and 32 percent of the indigenous population of Lithuania were killed, deported, or driven into exile. Dag Sebastian Ahlander, "Help Baltics Deal with Russian Minority," *New York Times* (letter to the editor), December 6, 1992, p. E18.

once-Jewish lands; Serbs likewise reject equal rights for Albanian Kosovars who Serbs claim wrongfully took Serb land). Past expulsions and dispersions feed diaspora-intolerance: if others created the diaspora, it is argued, then others should pay the price for restoring the diaspora to the nation by making territorial concessions.

The scope of the dangers posed by past crimes is a function, in part, of whether these crimes are remembered, and whether victims can attach responsibility for crimes to groups that are still present. Crimes that have faded in the victims' memories have a less corrosive effect on intergroup relations; thus mayhem that occurred before written records poses fewer problems than more recent crimes that are better-recorded.[35]

Crimes committed by groups still on the scene pose more problems than crimes committed by vanished groups. This, in turn, is a matter of interpretation: who committed the crime in question? Can inherited blame be attached to any present group? Thus the Ukrainians can assess responsibility for Stalin's vast murders of Ukrainians in several ways.[36] Were they committed by a crazed Georgian? This interpretation is benign: it points the finger at a single man who is long gone from the scene. Were they committed by that now-vanished tribe, the Bolsheviks? This interpretation is also benign: those responsible have miraculously disappeared, leaving no target for violence. Or, more ominously, were these the crimes of the Russian empire and the Russian people? This interpretation would guarantee bitter Russian-Ukrainian conflict, because the crimes in question were so enormous, and many of the "criminals" live in Ukraine,[37] making ready targets for hatred, and setting the stage for a Russian-Ukrainian conflict-spiral. Such a spiral is more likely because Russians would not accept the blame assigned them: they count themselves among the victims, not the perpetrators, of Bolshe-

---

35. For example, native Americans can coexist, albeit uneasily, with European immigrants partly because the enormous horrors that the Europeans inflicted on the natives have faded into the mists of history. On these horrors see David E. Stannard, *American Holocaust: Columbus and the Conquest of the New World* (New York: Oxford University Press, 1992). Stannard estimates that the native population of the Americas fell by roughly 95 percent—in absolute numbers by about 71–95 million people—after the European arrival in 1492 (p. 268). If so, this was the greatest human-caused human death in world history.
36. On these murders see Robert Conquest, *The Harvest of Sorrow: Soviet Collectivization and the Terror-Famine* (New York: Oxford University Press, 1986). Stalin's other crimes are covered in Robert Conquest, *The Great Terror: A Reassessment* (New York: Oxford University Press, 1990).
37. Ukraine contains 10.5 million Russians, 21 percent of its total population. Calculated from Scherer, *USSR Facts and Figures Annual*, p. 49.

vism's crimes, and they would view others' demands that they accept blame as a malicious outrage.

The danger posed by past crimes also depends on the criminal group's later behavior: has it apologized or otherwise shown contrition? Or has it shown contempt for its victims' suffering? Nazi Germany's crimes were among the greatest in human history, but Germany has re-established civil relations with its former victims by acknowledging its crimes and showing contrition, e.g., by postwar German leaders' public apologies and symbolic acts of repentance. Conversely, Turkey has denied the great crimes it committed against the Armenian people during World War I;[38] this display of contempt has sustained an Armenian hatred that is still expressed in occasional acts of violent anti-Turkish retribution.

A final significant factor lies in the degree of coincidence of power and victimhood. Are the groups with the greatest historic grievances also the groups with the greatest power today? Or is past victimhood confined to today's weaker groups? Things are more dangerous when power and aggrievement coincide, since this combination brings together both the motive and the capacity to make trouble; when power and aggrievement are separated, grievances have less effects. On this count the past crimes of the Russian and Bolshevik states leave a less dangerous legacy than the crimes committed in the former Yugoslavia during World War II, because the strongest group in the former Soviet Union (the Russians) is the least aggrieved; in contrast, in former Yugoslavia the strongest group (the Serbs) is the most aggrieved.

CURRENT CONDUCT: ARE MINORITY RIGHTS RESPECTED? As noted earlier, nations are less diaspora-accepting if others abuse the rights of that diaspora; such abuse magnifies the impulse to incorporate the territory of the diaspora by force. Thus Serbia's 1991 attack on Croatia was spurred partly by Croatian threats against the Serbian minority.[39] Likewise, Russia's attitude toward the

---

38. On Turkish denial of these murders see Roger W. Smith, "The Armenian Genocide: Memory, Politics, and the Future," in Richard G. Hovannisian, ed. *The Armenian Genocide: History, Politics, Ethics* (New York: St. Martin's, 1992), pp. 1–20; Vahakn N. Dadrian, "Ottoman Archives and Denial of the Armenian Genocide," in Hovannisian, *Armenian Genocide*, pp. 280–310; and Roger W. Smith, "Genocide and Denial: The Armenian Case and Its Implications," *Armenian Review*, Vol. 42 (Spring 1989), pp. 1–38. On the general disappearance of the Armenian people from Turkish historical writings, see Clive Foss, "The Turkish View of Armenian History: A Vanishing Nation," in Hovannisian, *Armenian Genocide*, pp. 250–279.

39. Glenny, "The Massacre of Yugoslavia," pp. 30–31; and Glenny, *The Fall of Yugoslavia*, pp. 12–14, 123.

Russian diaspora will be governed partly by the treatment of the Russian diaspora in their new homelands. Oppressive policies will provoke wider Russian aims.[40]

PERCEPTUAL FACTORS: NATIONALIST SELF-IMAGES AND IMAGES OF OTHERS

The effects of nationalism depend heavily on the beliefs of nationalist movements, especially their self-images and their images of their neighbors. Nations can co-exist most easily when these beliefs converge—when they share a common image of their mutual history, and of one another's current conduct and character. This can be achieved either by common convergence of images on something close to the "truth," or by convergence on the same distortion of the truth. Relations are worst if images diverge in self-justifying directions. This occurs if nations embrace self-justifying historical myths, or adopt distorted pictures of their own and others' current conduct and character that exaggerate the legitimacy of their own cause. Such myths and distortions can expand a nation's sense of its right and its need to oppress its minorities or conquer its diaspora. If carried to extreme such myths can also transform nationalism from symmetrical to asymmetrical—from a purely self-liberating enterprise into a hegemonistic enterprise.[41]

---

40. Even moderate Russian officials have voiced deep concern over the rights of Russian minorities in nearby states. See, for example, Sergei Stankevich, "Russia in Search of Itself," *The National Interest*, No. 28 (Summer 1992), pp. 47–51, at 49–51; and "Four Comments" in ibid. pp. 51–55, at 51–53. They have so far proposed solutions within the framework of international law and institutions: for example, Russian Foreign Minister Andrei Kozyrev suggested in 1992 that the UN establish a mechanism to protect the rights of Russians in non-Slavic former Soviet republics. Thomas Friedman, "Russian Appeals to U.N. to Safeguard Minorities," *New York Times*, September 23, 1992, p. A17. If the rights of these minorities remain otherwise unprotected, however, it seems likely that Russia will act on its own to protect them.

41. In the past I referred to such myth-poisoned nationalism as "hypernationalism." See Stephen Van Evera, "Primed for Peace," *International Security*, Vol. 15, No. 3 (Winter 1990/1991), pp. 7–57, at 47–48n ("Hypernationalism is artificially generated or magnified by chauvinist myths. Conflicts arising from hypernationalism thus derive from the beliefs of nations," not from their circumstances.) However, my usage is narrower than others: see, for example, John Mearsheimer, who defines hypernationalism as the belief that other nationalities are "both inferior and threatening," and as an "attitude of contempt and loathing" toward other nations; Mearsheimer suggests these beliefs can arise from false propaganda or from real experience. John Mearsheimer, "Back to the Future: Instability in Europe After the Cold War," *International Security*, Vol. 15, No. 1 (Summer 1990), pp. 5–56, at 21. Others use the term "hypernationalism" still more broadly to refer to any type of nationalism that spawns aggressive conduct and war. I avoid the term in this paper because it has acquired these several meanings. I regret adding to the confusion, and suggest we settle on a single usage—probably Mearsheimer's, since it has seniority.

Chauvinist mythmaking is a hallmark of nationalism, practiced by nearly all nationalist movements to some degree.[42] These myths are purveyed through the schools, especially in history teaching;[43] through literature; or by political elites. They come in three principal varieties: self-glorifying, self-whitewashing, and other-maligning. Self-glorifying myths incorporate claims of special virtue and competence, and false claims of past beneficence toward others.[44] Self-whitewashing myths incorporate false denial of past wrong-doing against others.[45] Both types of myths can lead a nation to claim a right

---

42. Indeed, the intellectual history of Western nationalisms is largely a record of false claims of special self-virtue and of overwrought blaming of others. See examples in Shafer, *Faces of Nationalism*, pp. 313–342. However, myth is not an essential ingredient of nationalism: nationalism can also rest on a group solidarity based on truth, and the effects of nationalism are largely governed by the degree of truthfulness of the beliefs that a given nationalism adopts; as truthfulness diminishes, the risks posed by the nationalism increase.

43. As Ernst Renan has said, "Getting its history wrong is part of being a nation." Quoted in Hobsbawm, *Nations and Nationalism since 1780*, p. 12.

44. World War I–era European nationalists provide abundant examples of such self-glorification. General Friedrich Bernhardi, the German army's main propagandist, proclaimed in 1912 that the Germans are "the greatest civilized people known to history," and have "always been the standard-bearers of free thought" and "free from prejudice." Friedrich von Bernhardi, *Germany and the Next War*, trans. Allen H. Powles (New York: Longmans, Green, 1914, first published in Germany in 1912), pp. 14, 72. In 1915 German economist Werner Sombart declared that the Germans were "the chosen people of this century," and that this chosenness explained others' hostility: "Now we understand why other people hate us. They do not understand us but they fear our tremendous spiritual superiority." Kohn, *Mind of Germany*, p. 300–301. Richard Dehmel, a German writer, proclaimed in 1914: "We Germans *are* more humane than the other nations; we *do have* better blood and breeding, more soul, more heart, and more imagination." Klaus Schröter, "Chauvinism and its Tradition: German Writers and the Outbreak of the First World War," *Germanic Review*, Vol. 43, No. 2 (March 1968), pp. 120–135, at 126, emphasis in original. In Britain Thomas Macaulay wrote that the British were "the greatest and most highly civilized people that ever the world saw" and were "the acknowledged leaders of the human race in the causes of political improvement." Paul M. Kennedy, "The Decline of Nationalistic History in the West, 1900–1970," *Journal of Contemporary History*, Vol. 8, No. 1 (January, 1973), pp. 77–100, at 81. In the United States Senator Albert Beveridge proclaimed in 1899 that "God . . . has made us the master organizers of the world. . . . He has made us adept in government that we may administer government among savage and senile peoples. . . . He has marked the American people as His chosen nation . . ." Albert K. Weinberg, *Manifest Destiny: A Study of Nationalist Expansionism in American History* (Chicago: Quadrangle, 1963), p. 308. The Soviet government continued this tradition after 1918: the standard Soviet school history text of 1948 claimed that Russian scientists invented the telegraph, steam engine, electric lamp, and the airplane. E.H. Dance, *History the Betrayer: A Study in Bias* (Westport: Greenwood, 1960), pp. 67–68.

45. Innocence can be asserted by denying a barbarous action, or by reinterpreting the action to put a benign "spin" on it. Post-1919 German textbooks illustrate whitewash-by-denial: Weimar German textbooks denied German responsibility for World War I, falsely claiming that "there was no wish for war in Berlin" in 1914, and that "today every informed person . . . knows that Germany is absolutely innocent with regard to the outbreak of the war, and that Russia, France, and England wanted the war and unleashed it." Dance, *History the Betrayer*, p. 62. Nazi-era texts likewise claimed that "England willed the war" in 1914 after having "set Japan on Russia" in 1904. Dance, *History the Betrayer*, p. 57. Whitewash-by-spin is also common. When Nazi forces

to rule others ("we are especially virtuous, so our expansion benefits those we conquer"). They also lead a nation to view others' complaints against them as expressions of ungrateful malice: ("we have never harmed them; they slander us by claiming otherwise"). This can produce conflict-spirals,[46] as the nation responds to others' legitimate complaints with hostility, in expectation that the claimant knows its claims are illegitimate and will back down if challenged. The targets of this hostility, in turn, will take it as further evidence of the nation's inherent cruelty and injustice. Self-glorifying myth, if it contains claims of cultural superiority, can also feed false faith in one's capacity to defeat and subdue others, causing expansionist wars of optimistic miscalculation.

Other-maligning myth can incorporate claims of others' cultural inferiority, false blame of others for past crimes and tragedies, and false claims that others now harbor malign intentions against the nation.[47] Such myths sup-

---

overran Norway and Denmark in 1940 the Nazi party newspaper announced the invasion, but its headline proclaimed "GERMANY SAVES SCANDINAVIA!" William L. Shirer, *The Rise and Fall of the Third Reich: A History of Nazi Germany* (New York: Simon and Schuster, 1960), p. 698n. Similarly, after Soviet forces invaded Afghanistan in 1979 Leonid Brezhnev admitted the action but told the Soviet public: "There has been no Soviet 'intervention' or 'aggression' at all." Rather, Soviet forces were sent to Afghanistan "at its government's request," to defend Afghan "national independence, freedom and honor." L.I. Brezhnev, "Interview for Pravda, January 13, 1980," from *SShA: Ekonomika, Politika, Ideologiya*, No. 2 (February 1980), trans. Joint Publication Research Service, in *U.S.S.R. Report*, No. 75485 (April 14, 1980), p. 3. Japanese imperialists of the 1930s and 1940s claimed Japan was saving China from the "death grip" of the Comintern, and liberating Asia from the Western imperialism. Robert J.C. Butow, *Tojo and the Coming of the War* (Stanford: Stanford University Press, 1969), p. 134; Ienaga, *Pacific War*, pp. 153–154. Earlier a French textbook proclaimed the philanthropy of the French North African empire—"France is kind and generous to the peoples she has conquered." Dance, *History the Betrayer*, p. 44.

46. Thus German whitewashing of German responsibility for World War I helped fuel German hostility toward Europe during the interwar years, and laid the basis for popular German support for Nazi foreign policy. On the post-1918 German "innocence" campaign see Holger H. Herwig, "Clio Deceived: Patriotic Self-Censorship in Germany After the Great War," *International Security*, Vol. 12, No. 2 (Fall 1987), pp. 5–44. A good account of Germany's actual pre-1914 conduct is Imanuel Geiss, *German Foreign Policy, 1871–1914* (Boston: Routledge & Kegan Paul, 1976).

47. For example, Wilhelmine and Nazi German nationalists often asserted others' inherent inferiority. Kaiser Wilhelm II declared in 1913: "the Slavs were not born to rule but to serve, this they must be taught." Fritz Fischer, *War of Illusions: German Policies from 1911 to 1914*, trans. Marian Jackson (New York: W.W. Norton, 1975), p. 222. Historian Heinrich von Treitschke thought the English suffered from "cowardice and sensuality," and the French from "besottedness," while an earlier German textbook declared France was "a fermenting mass of rottenness." Snyder, *From Bismarck to Hitler*, p. 35; Antoine Guilland, *Modern Germany and Her Historians* (Westport: Greenwood Press, n.d., reprint of 1915 ed.), pp. 304, 154, quoting an 1876 text by A. Hummel. Writer Richard Dehmel described an England with "only practical talents but not 'culture'." Schröter, "Chauvinism and its Tradition," p. 125. Later, Hitler thought Russia was "ripe for dissolution" because it was ruled by the Jews, who were "a ferment of decomposition." Jeremy Noakes and Geoffrey Pridham, eds., *Naziism 1919–1945: A History in Documents and*

port arguments for the rightness and necessity of denying equal rights to minorities living in the national territory, and for subjugating peoples further afield. These minorities and distant peoples will appear to pose a danger if they are left unsuppressed; moreover, their suppression is morally justified by their (imagined) misconduct, past and planned.

Self-whitewashing myths are probably the most common of these three varieties.[48] The dangers they pose are proportional to the gravity of the crimes they whitewash. If small crimes are denied, their denial is disrespect that victims can choose to overlook. The denial may even spring from simple ignorance; if so, it conveys little insult. If great crimes are denied, however, their denial conveys contempt for the victims' very humanity. The denial cannot be ascribed to unintended ignorance; if truly great crimes are forgotten, the forgetting is willful, hence it conveys greater insult. And being willful, the denial implies a dismissal of the crime's wrongness, which in turn suggests an ominous willingness to repeat it. As a result, the denial of great crimes provokes greater hostility from the victims than the denial of minor crimes.[49] Thus Croatian historians and politicians who whitewashed the Croatian Ustashi's vast murders of Serbs during World War II were

---

Eyewitness Accounts, Vol. 2 (New York: Schocken, 1988), pp. 615–616. He likewise viewed the United States, in Gerhard Weinberg's paraphrase, as a "mongrel society, in which the scum naturally floated to the top," that "could not possibly construct a sound economy." Gerhard L. Weinberg, "Hitler's Image of the United States," *American Historical Review*, Vol. 69, No. 4 (July 1964), pp. 1006–1021, at 1010.

Wilhelmine German nationalists also falsely accused others of malign intentions. Pan-German nationalists wove what Hermann Kantorowicz later termed a "fairy tale of encirclement" that posited a British-French-Russian plot to destroy Germany. See Geiss, *German Foreign Policy*, pp. 121–127. Imperial Japanese nationalists likewise saw a mythical anti-Japanese "ABCD encirclement" by America, Britain, China, and the Dutch, with the USSR and Germany sometimes thrown in as co-conspirators. See Butow, *Tojo and the Coming of the War*, chapter 8, pp. 188–227. During the Korean War Chinese writers demonized the United States as a "paradise of gangsters, swindlers, rascals, special agents, fascist germs, speculators, debauchers and all the dregs of mankind." President Truman and General Douglas MacArthur became "mad dogs," "blood-stained bandits," "murderers," "rapists," and "savages." At the same time General MacArthur warned that China "has become aggressively imperialistic, with a lust for expansion." John G. Stoessinger, *Nations in Darkness: China, Russia, and America*, 5th ed. (New York: McGraw-Hill, 1990), pp. 50–51.

For an example of falsely blaming others for past tragedies see notes 45 and 46 on the German post-1918 innocence campaign: in making this claim of innocence Germans also blamed others for starting the war.

48. Conversely, other-denigration is less common than both self-whitewashing and self-glorification, but is often implicit in self-glorification (others suffer in comparison to the virtuous self-image: if one's own group is spotlessly virtuous, others look worse by comparison).

49. Moreover, the victims' charges will anger the criminal nation, since it believes itself innocent, hence it views the victims' charges as malicious slander.

playing with especially powerful dynamite:[50] the crimes they denied were enormous, hence their denial had serious ramifications, feeding Serb hostility that led to the Serbo-Croatian war of 1991–92. Likewise, the question of historical responsibility for Stalin's crimes in the former Soviet Union is especially explosive because the crimes in question are so vast.

Why are myths purveyed? They emanate largely from nationalist political elites, for whom they serve important political functions. Some of these functions also serve the nation as a whole, while others serve only the narrow interests of the elite. Self-glorifying myths encourage citizens to contribute to the national community—to pay taxes, join the army, and fight for the nation's defense. These purposes are hard to fault, although the myths purveyed to achieve them may nevertheless have pernicious side-effects. Myths also bolster the authority and political power of incumbent elites: self-glorifying and self-whitewashing myths allow elites to shine in the reflected luster of their predecessors' imagined achievements and the imagined glory of the national institutions they control; other-maligning myths bolster the authority of elites by supporting claims that the nation faces external threats, thus deflecting popular hostility away from national elites and toward outsiders. Myths that serve only these purposes injure intercommunal relations without providing countervailing benefits to the general community.

Although mythmaking is ubiquitous among nationalisms, the scope and character of mythmaking varies widely across nations. Myths flourish most when elites need them most, when opposition to myths is weakest, and when publics are most myth-receptive. Four principal factors govern the level of infection by nationalist myth:

THE LEGITIMACY OF THE REGIME (or, if the national movement remains stateless, the legitimacy of the movement's leaders). As just noted, nationalist myths can help politically frail elites to bolster their grip on power. The temptation for elites to engage in mythmaking is therefore inversely propor-

---

50. After Germany and Italy conquered Yugoslavia in 1941 they established a puppet state, the Independent State of Croatia, under the leadership of the Croatian Ustashi, a nationalist Croat extremist-terrorist organization headed by Ante Pavelic. Without prompting from the Nazis the Ustashi then launched a mass murder campaign against other ethnic groups, killing by one estimate 500,000–700,000 Serbs, 50,000 Jews, and 20,000 Gypsies. Alex N. Dragnich, *Serbs and Croats: The Struggle for Yugoslavia* (New York: Harcourt Brace, 1992), pp. 96, 101–103. Dragnich reports that even the Germans were reportedly horrified by the nature and extent of the killings, and German officials protested to Pavelic (p. 103). On these murders see also Aleksa Djilas, *The Contested Country* (Cambridge: Harvard University Press, 1991), pp. 120–127; he endorses a smaller estimate by Bogoljub Kočović of 234,000 Serbs murdered (p. 126). Noting Croatian denials of the Ustashi's mass murders is Denich, "Unbury the Victims," pp. 5–6.

tional to their political legitimacy: the less legitimate their rule, the greater their incentive to make myths.

A regime's legitimacy is in turn a function of its representativeness, its competence and efficiency, and the scope of the tasks that face it. Unrepresentative regimes will face challenge from under-represented groups, and will sow myths to build the support needed to defeat this challenge.[51] This motive helped fuel the extreme nationalism that swept Europe in the late nineteenth century: oligarchic regimes used chauvinist myths, often spread through the schools, to deflect demands from below for a wider sharing of political and economic power.[52] Corrupt regimes or regimes that lack competence due to underinstitutionalization will likewise deploy chauvinist myths to divert challenges from publics and elites. This is a common motive for mythmaking in the Third World. Finally, regimes that face overwhelming tasks—e.g., economic or social collapse, perhaps caused by exogenous factors—will be tempted to use myths to divert popular impatience with their inability to improve conditions. Thus the Great Depression fueled nationalist mythmaking in some industrial states during the 1930s.[53]

These factors correlate closely with the ebb and flow of nationalist mythmaking through history. Nationalist mythmaking reached high tide in Europe when Europe's regimes had little legitimacy, during 1848–1914. It then fell dramatically as these regimes democratized and their societies became less stratified, which greatly lessened popular challenge to elites.[54]

THE SCOPE OF THE DEMANDS POSED BY THE STATE ON ITS CITIZENRY. The more the regime asks of its citizens, the harder it must work to persuade its

---

51. Such mythmaking has two targets: the public at large, and state instruments of coercion, which may need special motivation to carry out their tasks.

52. Regime illegitimacy provides the largest motive for elite mythmaking when the state cannot rule by pure force: mythmaking is then the elite's only means to preserve its rule. The proximate cause of mythmaking can therefore sometimes be found in the decline of the state monopoly of force, not the decline of elite legitimacy. This was the case in Europe in the nineteenth century: nationalist mythmaking rose with the rise of mass armies and popular literacy, which diminished the capacity of the state to govern by pure coercion. Elites were therefore forced to resort to persuasion, hence to mythmaking. (Mass literacy in this context proved a double-edged sword for newly-literate publics. Literacy enabled mass political mobilization by spreading social knowledge and ideas; this led to popular empowerment, but literacy also made publics easier to control from above, by enabling elites to purvey elite-justifying myths through the written word; this limited or reduced popular power.)

53. Making a similar argument, although casting it in somewhat different terms, is Snyder, "Nationalism and the Crisis of the Post-Soviet State," pp. 14–16.

54. On the decline of nationalistic history in Europe since the world wars see Kennedy, "Decline of Nationalistic History in the West."

citizens to fulfill these demands; this increases its temptation to deploy nationalist myths for purposes of social mobilization. Regimes at war often use myths to motivate sacrifice by their citizens and to justify their cruelties against others.[55] These myths can live on after the war to poison external relations in later years. Mass revolutionary movements often infuse their movements with mythical propaganda for the same reason; these myths survive after the revolution is won.[56] Regimes that are forced by external threats to sustain large peacetime military efforts are likewise driven to use myths to sustain popular support. This is especially true if they rely on mass armies for their defense.[57] Finally, totalitarian regimes place large demands on their citizens, and use correspondingly large doses of myth to induce their acquiescence.

DOMESTIC ECONOMIC CRISIS. In societies suffering economic collapse, mythmaking can take scapegoating form—the collapse is falsely blamed on domestic or international malefactors. Here the mythmaking grows from increased receptivity of the audience: publics are more willing to believe that others are responsible when they are actually suffering pain; when that pain is new and surprising, they search for the hand of malevolent human agents. Germany in the 1930s is the standard example.[58]

THE STRENGTH AND COMPETENCE OF INDEPENDENT EVALUATIVE INSTITUTIONS. Societies that lack free-speech traditions, a strong free press, and free universities are more vulnerable to mythmaking because they lack "truth squads" to counter the nationalist mythmakers. Independent historians can provide an antidote to official historical mythmaking; an independent press is an antidote to official mythmaking about current events. Their absence is a permissive condition for nationalist mythmaking.[59] Wilhelmine Germany

---

55. See, for example, Omer Bartov, *Hitler's Army: Soldiers, Nazis, and the War in the Third Reich* (New York: Oxford University Press, 1991), pp. 106–178, describing the myths purveyed by the Nazi regime to motivate its troops on the Eastern Front.
56. Advancing this argument is Stephen M. Walt, "Revolution and War," *World Politics*, Vol. 44, No. 3 (April 1992), pp. 321–368, at 336–340.
57. For this argument see Posen, "Nationalism, the Mass Army, and Military Power."
58. This hypothesis is widely accepted but has not been systematically tested; more empirical research exploring the relationship between economic downturns and scapegoating would be valuable.
59. The existence of a free press and free universities does not guarantee that myths will be scrutinized; these institutions also require a truth-squad ethos—a sense that mythbusting is among their professional missions. This ethos is often missing among university faculties, who frequently pursue research agendas that have little relevance to the worries of the real world. A discussion that remains valuable is Robert S. Lynd, *Knowledge For What? The Place of Social Science in American Culture* (Princeton: Princeton University Press, 1939). A recent discussion is

illustrates: the German academic community failed to counter the official myths of the era, and often helped purvey them.[60]

Several conclusions follow from this discussion. Democratic regimes are less prone to mythmaking, because such regimes are usually more legitimate and are free-speech tolerant; hence they can develop evaluative institutions to weed out nationalist myth. Absolutist dictatorships that possess a massive military superiority over their citizens are also less prone to mythmaking, because they can survive without it. The most dangerous regimes are those that depend on some measure of popular consent, but are narrowly governed by unrepresentative elites. Things are still worse if these governments are poorly institutionalized, are incompetent or corrupt for other reasons, or face overwhelming problems that exceed their governing capacities. Regimes that emerged from a violent struggle, or enjoy only precarious security, are also more likely to retain a struggle-born chauvinist belief-system.

Conclusion: Predictions and Prescriptions

What predictions follow? These hypotheses can be used to generate forecasts; applied to Europe, they predict that nationalism will pose little risk to peace in Western Europe, but large risks in Eastern Europe.

Most of the nationalisms of the West are satisfied, having already gained states. Western diasporas are few and small, reflecting the relative homogeneity of Western national demography, and Western minorities are relatively well-treated. The historic grievances of Western nationalities against one another are also small—many of the West's inter-ethnic horrors have faded from memory, and the perpetrators of the greatest recent horror—the Germans—have accepted responsibility for it and reconciled with their victims. The regimes of the West are highly legitimate, militarily secure, and economically stable; hence chauvinist mythmaking by their elites is correspondingly

---

Russell Jacoby, *The Last Intellectuals: American Culture in the Age of Academe* (New York: Basic Books, 1987), pp. 112–237. On this problem in political science see Hans J. Morgenthau, "The Purpose of Political Science," in James C. Charlesworth, ed., *A Design for Political Science: Scope, Objectives, and Methods* (Philadelphia: American Academy of Political and Social Science, 1966), pp. 63–79, at 69–74. German academics also cooperated with official German myth-making after World War I; see Herwig, "Clio Deceived."

60. A good survey of German historiography of this era is Snyder, *German Nationalism,* chapter 6 (pp. 123–152). An older survey is Guilland, *Modern Germany and Her Historians.* Also relevant are John A. Moses, *The Politics of Illusion: The Fischer Controversy in German Historiography* (London: George Prior, 1975), chapter 1 (pp. 7–26); and Snyder, *From Bismarck to Hitler,* chapter 3 (pp. 25–35).

rare. The West European nationalisms that caused the greatest recent troubles, those of Germany and Italy, are now clearly benign, and the conditions for a return to aggressive nationalism are absent in both countries. Outsiders sometimes fear that outbreaks of anti-immigrant extremism in Germany signal the return of German fascism, but the forces of tolerance and decency are overwhelmingly dominant in Germany, and the robust health of German democracy and of German academic and press institutions ensures they will remain dominant. As a result nationalism should cause very little trouble in Western Europe.

In the East the number of stateless nationalisms is larger, raising greater risk that future conflicts will arise from wars of liberation. The collapse of Soviet power shifted the balance of power toward these nationalisms, by replacing the Soviet state with weaker successor states. This shift has produced secessionist wars in Georgia and Moldova, and such wars could multiply. The tangled pattern of ethnic intermingling across the East creates large diasporas. Eastern societies have little tradition of respect for minority rights, raising the likelihood that these diasporas will face abuse; this in turn may spur their homelands to try to incorporate them by force. The borders of many emerging Eastern nations lack natural defensive barriers, leaving the state exposed to attack; some borders also lack legitimacy, and correspond poorly with ethnic boundaries. Some new Eastern regimes, especially those in the former Soviet Union, lack legitimacy and are under-institutionalized, raising the risk that they will resort to chauvinist mythmaking to maintain their political viability. This risk is heightened by the regional economic crisis caused by the transition from command to market economies. Evaluative institutions (free universities and a free press) remain weak in the East, raising the risk that myths will go unchallenged. The Soviet regime committed vast crimes against its subject peoples; this legacy will embitter relations among these peoples if they cannot agree on who deserves the blame.[61]

---

61. The emerging nations of the former USSR now stand knee-deep in the blood of Stalin's victims, and in the economic ruin that Bolshevism left behind. If every nation blames only others for these disasters, civil relations among them will be impossible: each will hope to someday settle accounts. Civil relations depend, then, on a convergence toward a common history of the Bolshevik disaster. Things would be best if all converged on a version that blamed the Bolsheviks—who, having vanished, can be blamed painlessly. (Bolshevism would then usefully serve as a hate-soaker—its final, and among its few positive, functions in Soviet history.) Absent that, things would be better if the successor nations agree on how to allocate blame among themselves.

The Eastern picture is not all bleak. The main preconditions for democracy—high levels of literacy, some degree of industrial development, and the absence of a landed oligarchy—exist across most of the East. As a result the long-term prospects for democracy are bright. Moreover, the East's economic crisis is temporary: the conditions for prosperous industrial economies (a trained workforce and adequate natural resources) do exist, so the crisis should ease once the market transition is completed. These relatively favorable long-term prospects for democracy and prosperity dampen the risk that chauvinist mythmaking will get out of hand.[62] The fact that the new Eastern states managed to gain freedom without violent struggles also left them with fewer malignant beliefs, by allowing them to forgo infusing their societies with chauvinist war propaganda. The power and ethnographic structures of the East, while dangerous, are less explosive than those of Yugoslavia: historic grievances and military power coincide less tightly—there is no other Eastern equivalent of Serbia, having both military superiority and large historical grievances; and ethnographic patterns create less imperative for a diaspora-rescue operation by the state most likely to attempt such a rescue, Russia.

---

62. However, in the East's heterogeneous interethnic setting democracy is a mixed blessing: if it takes a strict majoritarian form it can produce majority tyranny and the oppression of minorities, as it has in the past in Northern Ireland and the American Deep South. To produce civil peace in a multi-ethnic setting, democracy must adopt non-majoritarian principles of power-sharing, like those of Swiss democracy. On this question see Arend Lijphart, "Consociational Democracy," *World Politics*, Vol. 21, No. 2 (January 1969), pp. 107–125; Arend Lijphart, *Democracy in Plural Societies: A Comparative Exploration* (New Haven: Yale University Press, 1977); Arend Lijphart, *Democracies: Patterns of Majoritarian and Consensus Government in Twenty-One Countries* (New Haven: Yale University Press, 1984); Arend Lijphart, "The Power-Sharing Approach," in Joseph V. Montville, ed., *Conflict and Peacemaking in Multiethnic Societies* (Lexington, Mass.: Lexington Books, 1990), pp. 491–509; Kenneth D. McRae, "Theories of Power-Sharing and Conflict Management," in Montville, *Conflict and Peacemaking*, pp. 93–106; Jurg Steiner, "Power-Sharing: Another Swiss 'Export Product'?" in Montville, *Conflict and Peacemaking*, pp. 107–114; Hans Daalder, "The Consociational Democracy Theme," *World Politics*, Vol. 26, No. 4 (July 1974), pp. 604–621; Kenneth D. McRae, ed., *Consociational Democracy: Political Accommodation in Segmented Societies* (Toronto: McClelland and Stewart, 1974); and Vernon Van Dyke, "Human Rights and the Rights of Groups," *American Journal of Political Science*, Vol. 18, No. 4 (November, 1974), pp. 725–741, at 730–740. See also James Madison, "The Same Subject Continued . . ." (Federalist No. 10), *The Federalist Papers*, intro. by Clinton Rossiter (New York: New American Library, 1961), pp. 77–84, which addresses the danger of majority tyranny and remedies for it; Madison discusses the risks that arise when "a majority is included in a faction" (p. 80) and the dangers of tyranny by "the superior force of an interested and overbearing majority" (p. 77). Also relevant is Robert M. Axelrod, *Conflict of Interest: A Theory of Divergent Goals with Applications to Politics* (Chicago: Markham, 1970), whose theory of winning coalition membership explains why majoritarian rules distribute power unequally in deeply divided societies.

All in all, however, conditions in Eastern Europe are more bad than good; hence nationalism will probably produce a substantial amount of violence in the East over the next several decades.[63]

What policy prescriptions follow? The Western powers should move to dampen the risks that nationalism poses in the East, by moving to channel manipulable aspects of Eastern nationalism in benign directions. Some aspects of Eastern nationalist movements are immutable (e.g., their degree of intermingling, or the history of crimes between them). Others, however, can be decided by the movements themselves (e.g., their attitude toward minorities, their vision of history, and their willingness to reach final border settlements with others); these can be influenced by the West if the movements are susceptible to Western pressure or persuasion. The Western powers should use their substantial economic leverage to bring such pressure to bear.

Specifically, the Western powers should condition their economic relations with the new Eastern states on these states' conformity with a code of peaceful conduct that proscribes policies that make nationalism dangerous. The code should have six elements: (1) renunciation of the threat or use of force; (2) robust guarantees for the rights of national minorities, to include, under some stringent conditions, a legal right to secession;[64] (3) commitment

---

63. Nationalism is also likely to produce substantial violence in the Third World, largely because a high nation-to-state ratio still prevails there; hence many secessionist movements and wars of secession are likely in the decades ahead. A discussion of the policy issues raised by this circumstance is Halperin, Scheffer, and Small, *Self-Determination in the New World Order;* for a global survey of current self-determination movements see ibid., pp. 123–160.

64. Minority rights should be defined broadly, to include fair minority representation in the legislative, executive, and judicial branches of the central government. The definition of minority rights used in most international human rights agreements is more restrictive: it omits the right to share power in the national government, and includes only the right to political autonomy and the preservation of minority language, culture, and religion. See Edward Lawson, *Encyclopedia of Human Rights* (New York: Taylor & Francis, 1991), p. 1070; on the neglect of minority rights by Western political thinkers, see Vernon Van Dyke, "The Individual, the State, and Ethnic Communities in Political Theory," *World Politics,* Vol. 29, No. 3 (April 1977), pp. 343–369.

When should minority rights be defined to include the right to secession and national independence? Universal recognition of this right would require massive redrawing of boundaries in the East, and would raise the question of Western recognition of scores of now-unrecognized independence movements worldwide. One solution is to recognize the right to secede in instances where the central government is unwilling to fully grant other minority rights, but to decline to recognize the right to secede if all other minority rights are fully recognized and robustly protected. In essence, the West would hold its possible recognition of a right to secede in reserve, to encourage governments to recognize other minority rights. A discussion of the right to secession is Vernon Van Dyke, "Collective Entities and Moral Rights: Problems in Liberal-Democratic Thought," *Journal of Politics,* Vol. 44, No. 1 (February 1982), pp. 21–40, at 36–37. Also relevant is Halperin, Scheffer, and Small, *Self-Determination in the New World Order.*

to the honest teaching of history in the schools,[65] and to refrain from the propagation of chauvinist or other hate propaganda; (4) willingness to adopt a democratic form of government, and to accept related institutions—specifically, free speech and a free press;[66] (5) adoption of market economic policies, and disavowal of protectionist or other beggar-thy-neighbor economic policies toward other Eastern states; and (6) acceptance of current national borders, or agreement to settle contested borders promptly though peaceful means. This list rests on the premise that "peaceful conduct" requires that nationalist movements renounce the use of force against others (element 1), and also agree to refrain from policies that the hypotheses presented here warn against (elements 2–6).

Hypothesis I.4 (see Table 1) warns that the risk of war rises when nationalist movements oppress their minorities; hence the code requires respect for minority rights (element 2). Hypothesis II.6 warns that divergent beliefs about mutual history and current conduct and character raise the risk of war; hence the code asks for historical honesty and curbs on official hate propaganda (element 3). Hypothesis II.6.a warns that illegitimate governments have a greater propensity to mythmake, and hypothesis II.6.d warns that chauvinist myths prevail more often if independent evaluative institutions are weak; hence the code asks that movements adopt democracy (to bolster legitimacy) and respect free speech and free press rights (to bolster evaluation) (element 4). Hypothesis II.6.c warns that economic collapse promotes chauvinist mythmaking; hence the code asks movements to adopt market reforms, on grounds that prosperity requires marketization (element 5). Hypothesis II.3.b warns that the risk of war rises if the borders of emerging nation states lack legitimacy; hence the code asks movements to legitimize their borders through formal non-violent settlement (element 6).[67]

---

65. States should not be asked to accept externally-imposed versions of history in their texts, since no society can arbitrarily claim to know the "truth" better than others. But states could be asked to commit to international dialogue on history, on the theory that free debate will cause views to converge. Specifically, they could be asked to accept the obligation to subject their school curricula to foreign criticism, perhaps in the context of textbook exchanges, and to allow domestic publication of foreign criticisms of their curricula. Schemes of this sort have a long history in Western Europe, where they had a substantial impact after 1945. See Dance, *History the Betrayer*, pp. 127–128, 132, 135–150. This West European experience could serve as a template for an Eastern program.

66. These democratic governments should adopt consociational power-sharing rules, not majoritarian rules; otherwise ethnic minorities will be denied equal political power (see footnote 62.)

67. Such a code could be applied more widely, and serve as the basis for an international regime

The Western powers should enforce this code by pursuing a common economic policy toward the states of the East: observance of the code should be the price for full membership in the Western economy, while non-observance should bring exclusion and economic sanctions.[68] This policy should be married to an economic aid package to assist marketization, also conditioned on code observance.

The Bush and Clinton administrations have adopted elements of this policy, but omitted key aspects. In September 1991, then–Secretary of State James Baker outlined five principles that incorporate most of the six elements in the code of conduct outlined above (only element 3—honest treatment of history—was unmentioned), and he indicated that American policy toward the new Eastern states would be conditioned on their acceptance of these principles.[69] During the spring and summer of 1992 the administration also proposed a substantial economic aid package (the Freedom Support Act) and guided it through Congress.

However, Baker's principles later faded from view. Strangely, the Bush administration failed to clearly condition release of its aid package on Eastern compliance with these principles. It also failed to forge a common agreement among the Western powers to condition their economic relations with the Eastern states on these principles. The principles themselves were not elaborated; most importantly, the minority rights that the Eastern states must protect were not detailed, leaving these states free to adopt a watered-down definition. The Bush administration also recognized several new Eastern governments (e.g., Azerbaijan's) that gave Baker's principles only lip service while violating them in practice.[70] The Clinton administration has largely

on nationalist comportment; a nationalist movement's entitlement to international support would correspond to its acceptance and observance of the code.

68. The Western powers should also offer to help the Eastern powers devise specific policies to implement these principles, and offer active assistance with peacemaking if conflicts nevertheless emerge. Specifically, Western governments and institutions should offer to share Western ideas and experience on the building of democratic institutions; the development of political and legal institutions that protect and empower minorities; the development of market economic institutions; and the best means to control nationalism in education. (On this last point an account is Dance, *History the Betrayer*, pp. 126–150.) Finally, if serious conflicts nevertheless emerge, the West should offer active mediation, as the United States has between Israelis and Arabs.

69. For Baker's principles see "Baker's Remarks: Policy on Soviets," *New York Times*, September 5, 1991, p. A12. Baker reiterated these principles in December 1991; see "Baker Sees Opportunities and Risks as Soviet Republics Grope for Stability," *New York Times*, December 13, 1991, p. A24. Reporting Baker's conditioning of American recognition of the new Eastern governments on their acceptance of these standards is Michael Wines, "Ex-Soviet Leader Is Lauded By Bush," *New York Times*, December 26, 1991, p. 1.

70. See "Winking at Aggression in Baku" (editorial), *New York Times*, February 14, 1992, p. A28.

followed in Bush's footsteps: it continued Bush's aid program, but omitted clear political conditions.[71]

There is still time for such a policy, but the clock is running out. A policy resting on economic sticks and carrots will be too weak to end major violence once it begins; hence the West should move to avert trouble while it still lies on the horizon.

---

71. In April 1993 the Clinton administration forged agreement among the Group of Seven (G7) states (Britain, France, Germany, Italy, Canada, Japan, and the United States) on a $28 billion aid package for the former Soviet Union, and Congress approved a substantial aid package in September 1993. See Serge Schmemann, "Yeltsin Leaves Talks With Firm Support and More Aid," *New York Times,* April 5, 1993, p. 1; David E. Sanger, "7 Nations Pledge $28 Billion Fund To Assist Russia," *New York Times,* April 16, 1993, p. 1; Steven Greenhouse, "I.M.F. Unveils Plan for Soviet Lands," *New York Times,* April 21, 1993, p. A16; and Steven A. Holmes, "House Approves Bill Including 2.5 Billion in Aid for Russians," *New York Times,* September 24, 1993, p. A6. The aid was conditioned on Eastern moves toward marketization, but political conditions were omitted. President Clinton did declared that "we support respect for ethnic minorities," and "we stand with Russian democracy" as he announced the American aid pledge. Schmemann, "Yeltsin Leaves Talks." However, press accounts do not mention explicit political conditions.

Containing Fear

The Origins and Management of Ethnic Conflict

David A. Lake and
Donald Rothchild

Since the end of the Cold War, a wave of ethnic conflict has swept across parts of Eastern Europe, the former Soviet Union, and Africa. Localities, states, and sometimes whole regions have been engulfed in convulsive fits of ethnic insecurity, violence, and genocide. Early optimism that the end of the Cold War might usher in a new world order has been quickly shattered. Before the threat of nuclear armageddon could fully fade, new threats of state meltdown and ethnic cleansing have rippled across the international community.

The most widely discussed explanations of ethnic conflict are, at best, incomplete and, at worst, simply wrong. Ethnic conflict is not caused directly by inter-group differences, "ancient hatreds" and centuries-old feuds, or the stresses of modern life within a global economy. Nor were ethnic passions, long bottled up by repressive communist regimes, simply uncorked by the end of the Cold War.

We argue instead that intense ethnic conflict is most often caused by collective fears of the future. As groups begin to fear for their safety, dangerous and difficult-to-resolve strategic dilemmas arise that contain within them the potential for tremendous violence. As information failures, problems of credible commitment, and the security dilemma take hold, groups become apprehensive, the state weakens, and conflict becomes more likely. Ethnic activists and political entrepreneurs, operating within groups, build upon these fears of insecurity and polarize society. Political memories and emotions also magnify these anxieties, driving groups further apart. Together, these between-group

David A. Lake is Professor of Political Science at the University of California, San Diego, and Research Director for International Relations at the Institute on Global Conflict and Cooperation. Donald Rothchild is Professor of Political Science at the University of California, Davis.

This is an abridged version of two chapters by the authors that will appear in David A. Lake and Donald Rothchild, eds., _Ethnic Fears and Global Engagement: The International Spread and Management of Ethnic Conflict_ (forthcoming). This research was sponsored by the Institute on Global Conflict and Cooperation (IGCC) at the University of California and supported by a generous grant from the Pew Charitable Trusts. An earlier draft of this paper was discussed by IGCC's Working Group on the International Spread and Management of Ethnic Conflict. We are indebted to the members of the working group for many productive discussions over a two-year period. We would especially like to thank Miles Kahler, Arnold Kanter, Charles Kupchan, Charles William Maynes, Barnett Rubin, Timothy D. Sisk, Stephen John Stedman, and John Steinbruner for comments on an earlier draft of this paper.

International Security, Vol. 21, No. 2 (Fall 1996), pp. 41–75
© 1996 by the President and Fellows of Harvard College and the Massachusetts Institute of Technology.

and within-group strategic interactions produce a toxic brew of distrust and suspicion that can explode into murderous violence.

Managing ethnic conflicts, whether by local elites and governments or concerned members of the international community, is a continuing process with no end point or final resolution. It is also an imperfect process that, no matter how well-conducted, leaves some potential for violence in nearly all multi-ethnic polities. Ethnic conflict can be contained, but it cannot be entirely resolved. Effective management seeks to reassure minority groups of both their physical security and, because it is often a harbinger of future threats, their cultural security. Demonstrations of respect, power-sharing, elections engineered to produce the interdependence of groups, and the establishment of regional autonomy and federalism are important confidence-building measures that, by promoting the rights and positions of minority groups, mitigate the strategic dilemmas that produce violence.

International intervention may also be necessary and appropriate to protect minorities against their worst fears, but its effectiveness is limited. Noncoercive interventions can raise the costs of purely ethnic appeals and induce groups to abide by international norms. Coercive interventions can help bring warring parties to the bargaining table and enforce the resulting terms. Mediation can facilitate agreement and implementation. A key issue in all interventions, especially in instances of external coercion, is the credibility of the international commitment. External interventions that the warring parties fear will soon fade may be worse than no intervention at all. There is no practical alternative to active engagement by the international community over the long term.

This essay presents a framework for understanding the origins and management of ethnic conflict. Focusing on the central concept of ethnic fear, we attempt to provide a broad framework for comprehending, first, how the various causes of ethnic conflict fit together and potentially interact and, second, how policies can be crafted to address these causes. Moreover, while our approach is largely "rational choice" oriented, we also seek to examine how non-rational factors such as political myths and emotions interact with the strategic dilemmas we highlight. We recognize that many of the ideas presented here have already appeared in the burgeoning literature on ethnic conflict, and do not claim to be presenting an entirely novel approach, although we note some areas of disagreement with prevailing approaches.

Our analysis proceeds in two steps. The first section examines the inter-group and intra-group strategic dilemmas that produce ethnic violence. Building on this diagnosis, the second section discusses several ways of managing ethnic conflicts both before and after they become violent. We consider, first, confidence-building measures that can be undertaken by local elites and governments—or promoted by members of the international community—to quell real or potential violence and, second, external interventions led by concerned states and organizations. The concluding section highlights several policy initiatives that follow from our analysis.

Strategic Interactions and the Causes of Ethnic Conflict

Most ethnic groups, most of the time, pursue their interests peacefully through established political channels. But when ethnicity is linked with acute social uncertainty, a history of conflict, and fear of what the future might bring, it emerges as one of the major fault lines along which societies fracture.[1] Vesna Pešić, a professor at the University of Belgrade and a peace activist in the former Yugoslavia, says it well: ethnic conflict is caused by the "fear of the future, lived through the past."[2]

Collective fears of the future arise when states lose their ability to arbitrate between groups or provide credible guarantees of protection for groups. Under this condition, which Barry Posen refers to as "emerging anarchy," physical security becomes of paramount concern.[3] When central authority declines, groups become fearful for their survival. They invest in and prepare for violence, and thereby make actual violence possible. State weakness, whether it arises incrementally out of competition between groups or from extremists actively seeking to destroy ethnic peace, is a necessary precondition for violent ethnic conflict to erupt. State weakness helps to explain the explosion of ethnic violence that has followed the collapse of communist regimes in Eastern Europe and the former Soviet Union, and it has also led to violence in Liberia, Somalia, and other African states.

State weakness may not be obvious to the ethnic groups themselves or external observers. States that use force to repress groups, for instance, may appear strong, but their reliance on manifest coercion rather than legitimate

---

1. Kathleen Newland. "Ethnic Conflict and Refugees," in Michael E. Brown, ed., *Ethnic Conflict and International Security* (Princeton, N.J.: Princeton University Press, 1993), p. 161.
2. Vesna Pešić, Remarks to the Institute on Global Conflict and Cooperation (IGCC) Working Group on the International Spread and Management of Ethnic Conflict, October 1, 1994.
3. Barry R. Posen, "The Security Dilemma and Ethnic Conflict," in Brown, *Ethnic Conflict and International Security*, pp. 103–124. See also Jack Snyder, "Nationalism and the Crisis of the Post-Soviet State," in ibid., pp. 79–101.

authority more accurately implies weakness. More important, groups look beyond the present political equipoise to alternative futures when calculating their political strategies. If plausible futures are sufficiently threatening, groups may begin acting today as if the state were in fact weak, setting off processes, discussed below, that bring about the disintegration of the state. Thus, even though the state may appear strong today, concerns that it may not remain so tomorrow may be sufficient to ignite fears of physical insecurity and a cycle of ethnic violence. The forward-looking nature of the strategic dilemmas emphasized here makes the task of forecasting or anticipating ethnic conflicts especially difficult, both for the participants themselves and external actors who would seek to manage them effectively through preventive diplomacy.

Situations of emerging anarchy and violence arise out of the strategic interactions between and within groups. Between groups, three different strategic dilemmas can cause violence to erupt: information failures, problems of credible commitment, and incentives to use force preemptively (also known as the security dilemma). These dilemmas are the fundamental causes of ethnic conflict. Within groups, ethnic activists and political entrepreneurs may make blatant communal appeals and outbid moderate politicians, thereby mobilizing members, polarizing society, and magnifying the inter-group dilemmas. "Non-rational" factors such as emotions, historical memories, and myths can exacerbate the violent implications of these intra-group interactions. Together, these inter-group and intra-group interactions combine, as we explain in this section, to create a vicious cycle that threatens to pull multi-ethnic societies into violence.[4]

STRATEGIC INTERACTIONS BETWEEN GROUPS

Competition for resources typically lies at the heart of ethnic conflict. Property rights, jobs, scholarships, educational admissions, language rights, government contracts, and development allocations all confer benefits on individuals and groups. All such resources are scarce and, thus, objects of competition and occasionally struggle between individuals and, when organized, groups. In

---

4. In this article, we are concerned mostly with internal ethnic conflict. For a discussion of transnational ethnic conflict, and especially its international diffusion and escalation, see David A. Lake and Donald Rothchild, eds., *Ethnic Fears and Global Engagement: The International Spread and Management of Ethnic Conflict* (forthcoming).

societies where ethnicity is an important basis for identity, group competition often forms along ethnic lines.[5]

Politics matter because the state controls access to scarce resources. Individuals and groups that possess political power can often gain privileged access to these goods, and thus increase their welfare.[6] Because the state sets the terms of competition between groups, it becomes an object of group struggle. Accordingly, the pursuit of particularistic objectives often becomes embodied in competing visions of just, legitimate, and appropriate political orders.

In multi-ethnic societies, resource rivalries and the struggle to control state policy produce competing communal interests. In Nigeria, for example, each ethno-regional group looks to the state to favor it when distributing public resources, producing, as Claude Ake observes, an "overpoliticization" of social life which gravely weakens the state itself.[7] In Yugoslavia, Slovenians and Croatians resented the system of federal redistribution to the poorer regions of the country; their publics backed their leaders' expressions of indignation, ultimately fueling the demand for greater political autonomy.[8] When groups conclude that they can improve their welfare only at the expense of others, they become locked into competitions for scarce resources and state power.

Analytically, however, the existence of competing policy preferences is—by itself—not sufficient for violence to arise. Observers too often fail to recognize this important theoretical point and misattribute violence to competition over scarce resources. Violence, after all, is costly for all communal actors: people are killed; factories, farms, and whole cities are destroyed; resources that might have been invested in new economic growth are diverted instead to destructive ends. As violence, and preparing for violence, is always costly, there must exist in principle some potential bargain short of violence that leaves both sides in a dispute better off than settling their disagreements through the use of force; at the very least, the same *ex post* agreement could be reached without the use

---

5. This is, of course, not true as a universal rule. Although ethnic identities are often strong, groups can also form along class, religious, or other lines. The more politically salient ethnicity is, however, the more likely it is that groups will organize on this basis. This is an important way in which the between-group and within-group variables examined here interact.
6. Russell Hardin, *One for All: The Logic of Group Conflict* (Princeton, N.J.: Princeton University Press, 1995), pp. 34–37; and Milton J. Esman, *Ethnic Politics* (Ithaca, N.Y.: Cornell University Press, 1994), p. 216.
7. Claude Ake, "Why Is Africa Not Developing?" *West Africa*, No. 3538 (June 17, 1985), p. 1213.
8. Susan Woodward, *Balkan Tragedy: Chaos and Dissolution After the Cold War* (Washington, D.C.: Brookings, 1995), pp. 69–70.

of force, and the resources that would have been expended in violence divided somehow between the parties *ex ante*.[9] This holds irrespective of the breadth of the group demands or the extent of the antagonisms. The farther apart the policy preferences of the groups are, the greater the violence necessary for one group to assert its will over the other, and the greater the resources that can be saved by averting the resort to force.[10]

Despite appearances, then, competing policy preferences by themselves cannot explain the resort to violence. The divorce between the two halves of Czechoslovakia is a sterling example of two ethnic groups, in conflict over the distribution of resources within their federal state but anxious to avoid the costs of war, developing a mutually agreeable separation to avoid a potentially violent confrontation. For negotiations to fail to bridge the demands of opposing groups, at least one of three strategic dilemmas must exist. Each dilemma alone is sufficient to produce violent conflict. Nonetheless, they typically occur together as a dangerous syndrome of strategic problems.

INFORMATION FAILURES. Because violence is costly, groups can be expected to invest in acquiring knowledge about the preferences and capabilities of the opposing side and bargain hard, but eventually reach an agreement short of open conflict.[11] Groups might even be expected to reveal information about themselves to prevent violence from erupting. When individuals and groups possess private information and incentives to misrepresent that information, competing group interests can produce actual conflict. We refer to this as an information failure. When information failures occur, groups cannot acquire or share the information necessary to bridge the bargaining gap between themselves, making conflict possible despite its devastating effects.

Incentives to misrepresent private information exist in at least three common circumstances. In each, revealing true information undercuts the ability of the group to attain its interests. First, incentives to misrepresent occur when groups are bargaining over a set of issues and believe they can gain by bluffing. By

---

9. James Fearon, "Ethnic War as a Commitment Problem," unpublished manuscript, University of Chicago, 1993; and Fearon, "Rationalist Explanations for War," *International Organization*, Vol. 49, No. 3 (Summer 1995), pp. 379–414.

10. Moreover, a mutually preferred bargain must exist even if the resources available to groups are declining, because violence only further reduces the resource pool relative to possible agreements. For an empirical demonstration of this point, see Valerie Percival and Thomas Homer-Dixon, *Environmental Scarcity and Violent Conflict: The Case of Rwanda* (Washington, D.C.: American Association for the Advancement of Science, 1995).

11. The following two sub-sections draw heavily upon Fearon, "Ethnic War as a Commitment Problem," and "Rationalist Explanations for War," two of the best theoretical works on conflict between organized groups.

exaggerating their strengths, minimizing their weaknesses, and mis-stating their preferences, groups seek to achieve more favorable divisions of resources. Through such bluffs, however, they increase the risk that negotiations will fail and conflicts arise.[12]

Second, groups may be truly aggressive but do not want to be branded as such. They may seek to minimize internal opposition, or to insulate themselves from repercussions in the broader international community. Although typically only minimal sanctions are imposed by other states, most groups seek to avoid the label of an aggressor or violator of international norms and the political isolation that such a classification can carry.

Finally, in conflicts where the groups are simultaneously negotiating and preparing for ethnic war, any attempt to facilitate compromise by having each side explain how it plans to win on the battlefield will seriously compromise the likelihood that it will win should war occur. Thus, groups cannot reveal their strategies or derive accurate predictions of their likely success. Paradoxically, each party is bound by its own self-interest to withhold the information crucial to bringing about an agreement. Concerned that private information they provide on how they intend to protect themselves or attack others will redound to their disadvantage, groups may refrain from revealing the information necessary to forge a mutually satisfactory compromise.[13]

Information failures are possible whenever two or more ethnic groups compete within the political arena. Groups always possess private information and, as these three circumstances suggest, often possess incentives to misrepresent that information. Information failures are thus ubiquitous in ethnic relations. In multi-ethnic societies, states can often communicate and arbitrate successfully between groups and thereby help preclude and resolve information failures. Indeed, communication and arbitration can be understood as two of the primary functions of the state. When effective, states create incentives and a sense of security that allow groups to express their desires and articulate their political aspirations and strategies. Not only do ethnic leaders respond to sidepayments offered by state elites, but—in seeking to curry favor—they are more prepared to provide private information to a "third party" than they are

---

12. In game-theoretic terms, actors will choose to bluff depending upon 1) the beliefs each actor holds about the other's "type" (i.e., the actor is more likely to bluff if it believes the other is "weak" and the second actor believes the first is "strong") and 2) the relative benefits (payoff) and costs (signal) of successful bluffing, unsuccessful bluffing, and not bluffing (i.e., the higher the payoff from success and the smaller the cost of the signal, the more likely the actor is to bluff).
13. Fearon, "Rationalist Explanations for War," p. 400.

to an adversary.[14] As the state weakens, however, information failures become more acute and violence more likely. If one group believes that the other is withholding information, it too may begin to hold back crucial data or antici-pate the failure of negotiations. Groups become suspicious of the intentions of others, and may begin to fear the worst. In this way, information failures and even the anticipation of such failures may drive groups to actions that under-mine the ability of the state to maintain social peace. When this occurs, even previously effective states will begin to unravel. State capabilities, then, are at least partly affected by the magnitude of the information failure and the beliefs and behaviors of the groups themselves.

Information failures cut two ways. On the one hand, all policy differences can be bridged—at least in theory—if the alternative is a costly conflict. Even cultural symbols and practices central to a people's conception of itself as a distinct ethnic group may be negotiable if the known alternative is the outright destruction of the group. On the other hand, strategic incentives to misrepre-sent private information are a primary impediment to peaceful compromise, and these incentives may be present in a wide range of circumstances. Thus, careful mediation by third parties who can probe the true preferences of groups and communicate them to relevant others is important for creating and main-taining cooperative ethnic relations. States able to arbitrate between groups are normally the preferred instrument to this end, but sometimes they too fall victim to the information failures they are designed, in part, to prevent. When this occurs, mediation by outside parties may be required.

PROBLEMS OF CREDIBLE COMMITMENT. Ethnic conflicts also arise because groups cannot credibly commit themselves to uphold mutually beneficial agreements they might reach.[15] In other words, at least one group cannot effectively reassure the other that it will not renege on an agreement and exploit it at some future date. As exploitation can be very costly—up to and including the organized killing of one group by another—groups may prefer to absorb even high costs of war today to avoid being exploited tomorrow.

---

14. We recognize, of course, that the state is not always a neutral third party in domestic disputes, but this simply indicates that the state has already forfeited at least in part the ability to perform this function.

15. Fearon, "Ethnic War as a Commitment Problem"; and Fearon, "Rationalist Explanations for War"; Hardin, *One for All*, p. 143; and Barry R. Weingast, "Constructing Trust: The Political and Economic Roots of Ethnic and Regional Conflict," unpublished manuscript, Stanford University, 1995.

Stable ethnic relations can be understood as based upon a "contract" between groups.[16] Such contracts specify, among other things, the rights and responsibilities, political privileges, and access to resources of each group. These contracts may be formal constitutional agreements or simply informal understandings between elites. Whatever their form, ethnic contracts channel politics in peaceful directions.

Most importantly, ethnic contracts contain "safeguards" designed to render the agreement self-enforcing. They contain provisions or mechanisms to ensure that each side lives up to its commitments and feels secure that the other will do so as well. Typical safeguards include, first, power-sharing arrangements, electoral rules, or group vetoes that prevent one ethnic group from setting government policy unilaterally;[17] second, minority control over critical economic assets, as with the whites in South Africa or Chinese in Malaysia;[18] and third, as was found in Croatia before the breakup of Yugoslavia, maintenance of ethnic balance within the military or police forces to guarantee that one group will not be able to use overwhelming organized violence against the other.[19] These political checks and balances serve to stabilize group relations and ensure that no group can be exploited by the other. In Barry R. Weingast's words, "reciprocal trust can be induced by institutions."[20]

---

16. The term "ethnic contract" was, we believe, coined by Leonard Binder at the first meeting of the IGCC Working Group on the International Spread and Management of Ethnic Conflict, May 13–14, 1994. On relational contracting more generally, see Oliver Williamson, *The Economic Institutions of Capitalism: Firms, Markets, and Relational Contracting* (New York: Free Press, 1985); for an application to inter-state relations, see David A. Lake, "Anarchy, Hierarchy, and the Variety of International Relations," *International Organization*, Vol. 50, No. 1 (Winter 1996), pp. 1–33.
17. Arend Lijphart, *The Politics of Accommodation: Pluralism and Democracy in the Netherlands* (Berkeley: University of California Press, 1967); Donald L. Horowitz, *Ethnic Groups in Conflict* (Berkeley: University of California Press, 1985); Timothy D. Sisk, *Democratization in South Africa: The Elusive Social Contract* (Princeton, N.J.: Princeton University Press, 1995); and Weingast, "Constructing Trust."
18. Heribert Adam and Kogila Moodley, "South Africa: The Opening of the Apartheid Mind," in John McGarry and Brendan O'Leary, eds., *The Politics of Ethnic Conflict Regulation* (New York: Routledge, 1993), pp. 226–250.
19. Misha Glenny, *The Fall of Yugoslavia* (New York: Penguin Books, 1992); and Hardin, *One for All*, pp. 58 and 159.
20. Weingast, "Constructing Trust," p. 15. Aleksa Djilas, "Fear thy Neighbor: The Breakup of Yugoslavia," in Charles A. Kupchan, ed., *Nationalism and Nationalities in the New Europe* (Ithaca, N.Y.: Cornell University Press, 1995), p. 99, argues that the communist party served as the primary safeguard in Yugoslavia, largely through coercion and repression, and that the defeat of the party in the 1990 elections left a political vacuum. He faults the party for not developing "stable institutions" that could have regulated relations among the republics. In "Constructing Trust," on the other hand, Weingast credits Yugoslav President Josip Broz Tito for constructing a set of veto mechanisms institutionalizing trust among the groups.

The terms of the ethnic contract reflect the balance of political power between the groups and their beliefs about the intentions and likely behaviors of one another. Safeguards are crafted to respond to the specific circumstances of each set of groups. However, ethnic contracts can be undermined and problems of credible commitment created by changes in either the ethnic balance of power or the beliefs of groups about others. These changes and their implications are captured in two separate but related models, one by James Fearon that focuses on the balance of political power between groups and one by Weingast that emphasizes beliefs.[21]

The political power of groups is determined by demography, the resources available to each group, and their capacity to organize effectively.[22] More powerful groups have a larger say in setting the terms of the contract. However, for the less powerful group to agree voluntarily to enter and abide by the contract, its interests must also be addressed, including its concern that the more powerful group will try to exploit it and alter the terms of the contract at some future date. Indeed, it is the minority, fearful of future exploitation and violence, that ultimately determines the viability of any existing ethnic contract. When the balance of ethnic power remains stable—and is expected to remain stable—well-crafted contracts enable ethnic groups to avoid conflict despite their differing policy preferences.

However, the ethnic balance of power does evolve over time. As in Lebanon, disparities in population growth rates will eventually alter the balance between groups. Differing access to resources may increase prosperity for some groups and poverty for others, also shifting the ethnic balance. When multi-ethnic polities fragment, as in Yugoslavia and the former Soviet Union, the relevant political space alters rapidly and the various ethnic groups that once counted their numbers on a national scale must now calculate their kin in terms of the new, smaller territorial units, and may find themselves in a stronger or weaker position. It is apprehension over the consequences of any dissolution, for instance, that motivates Protestants in Northern Ireland to hold tenaciously onto union with the largely Protestant United Kingdom rather than merge with the predominantly Catholic state of Ireland. When such changes in the ethnic

21. Fearon, "Ethnic War as a Commitment Problem"; and Fearon, "Rationalist Explanations for War"; see also Fearon, "Commitment Problems and the Spread of Ethnic Conflict," in Lake and Rothchild, *Ethnic Fears and Global Engagement*. See Weingast, "Constructing Trust"; this model is also discussed in Robert H. Bates and Barry R. Weingast, "Rationality and Interpretation: The Politics of Transition," paper presented to the Annual Meeting of the American Political Science Association, Chicago, August 31–September 3, 1995.
22. Hardin, *One for All*, p. 56.

balance of power have not been anticipated, or if the safeguards are overly rigid and cannot be renegotiated easily, the ethnic contract will be at risk of collapse.

Problems of credible commitment arise, as Fearon shows, whenever the balance of ethnic power shifts.[23] As the influence of one side declines, previously enforceable ethnic contracts become unenforceable. The checks and balances that safeguard the agreement today become insufficient tomorrow. Even if the group that is growing stronger promises not to exploit the weaker group in the future, there is nothing to prevent it from breaking its promise when it actually is stronger. Recognizing this, the declining side may choose to fight today rather than accede to an ethnic contract that will become increasingly unenforceable as time progresses.

Independent of changes in the ethnic balance of power, Weingast demonstrates that if information is incomplete and there are costs to becoming a victim in the future, changes in the beliefs of one group about the intentions of another can play a large role in setting the parties on the road to violence.[24] If a group believes that there is even a small chance that it may become a target of a genocidal attack, it may choose conflict over compromise and the risk of future destruction. To provoke conflict, one group need not believe that the other really is aggressive, only fear that it might be. With incomplete information, even small changes in beliefs about the intentions of the other group can generate massive violence.

Information is costly to acquire and, as a result, there is always some uncertainty about the intentions of other groups. Groups compensate for their informational limitations by acting on the basis of prior beliefs about the likely preferences of others (as well as the costs of resorting to violence and other variables). These beliefs are formed through historical experience—the "past," in Pešić's words—and represent each group's best guess about the other's intentions. Groups then update these beliefs as new information becomes available to them. Nonetheless, information is always incomplete and groups are forever uncertain about each other's purposes. Conflict, then, always remains possible in ethnic interactions.

Problems of credible commitment in ethnic relations are universal. Concerned that the balance of power may tip against them or that the other may

---

23. Fearon, "Ethnic War as a Commitment Problem."

24. Weingast, "Constructing Trust"; and Bates and Weingast, "Rationality and Interpretation." The term "beliefs" is used here in its game-theoretic sense to refer to the conditional probability of an actor holding one set of preferences (intentions, in the text; payoffs from a game, more formally) rather than another. Actors form beliefs subjectively, largely on the basis of past interactions.

have hostile intentions, groups worry that agreements made today will not be honored tomorrow. Effective states can help to mitigate these problems of credible commitment by enforcing existing ethnic contracts. When the future risk of exploitation is high, however, current relations and the state itself can quickly unravel. Fearful of the future, weaker groups may resort to preemptive violence today to secure their position in times to come. When this happens, outside peacekeepers or peace enforcers with sufficient military capabilities and political will may be the only way to ensure ethnic peace.

THE SECURITY DILEMMA. Posen has recently extended the concept of the security dilemma, first developed in international relations, to the study of ethnic conflict. In the broadest sense of the concept, the security dilemma is understood to follow axiomatically from anarchy. Under anarchy, states are dependent upon self-help for their security and must therefore maintain and perhaps expand their military capabilities. This can threaten others, who react by maintaining and expanding their capabilities, creating a spiral of arms-racing and hostility. The dilemma follows from the inability of the two sides to observe each other's intentions directly; if each party knew the other was arming strictly for defensive purposes, the potential spiral would be cut short. But because states cannot know the intentions of others with certainty, in Posen's words, "what one does to enhance one's own security causes reactions that, in the end, can make one less secure."[25]

Understood in this broad way, however, the security dilemma more accurately rests on the information failures and problems of credible commitment just discussed. It is the inability both to know with certainty the intentions and abilities of others and to commit credibly not to arm for offensive purposes that drives the spiral. The unique analytic core of the security dilemma lies in situations where one or more disputing parties have incentives to resort to preemptive uses of force. We use the term here to refer to these specific incentives.[26] As Robert Jervis observes, incentives to preempt arise when offensive military technologies and strategies dominate more defensive postures, and thus the side that attacks first reaps a military advantage.[27] The offense is likely to dominate when there are significant military benefits from surprise

---

25. Posen, "The Security Dilemma and Ethnic Conflict," p. 104.

26. We recognize that some readers may prefer the broader use of the term "security dilemma." We believe that the distinctions between information failures, problems of credible commitment, and incentives to use force preemptively are useful and important, and we see no reason to use a less precise catchall term when more precise and analytically refined definitions are available.

27. Robert Jervis, "Cooperation Under the Security Dilemma," *World Politics*, Vol. 30, No. 2 (January 1978), pp. 167–213. See also George H. Quester, *Offense and Defense in the International System* (New York: John Wiley, 1977).

and mobility. Geography will also matter, because some kinds of terrain (such as mountainous areas) and settlement patterns (such as exclusive ethnic zones) are easier to defend than others.[28] When the offense dominates, even *status quo* groups (and states), it follows, may be tempted to launch preemptive strikes to avoid a possibly even worse fate.

When incentives to use force preemptively are strong, the security dilemma takes hold and works its pernicious effects. Fearful that the other might preempt, a group has an incentive to strike first and negotiate later. In ethnic relations, as in international relations, when there are significant advantages to preemption, a cycle of violence can seize previously peaceful groups even as they seek nothing more than their own safety. By the same logic, previously satisfied groups can be driven to become aggressors, destroying ethnic harmony in the search for group security.

STRATEGIC INTERACTIONS WITHIN GROUPS

As we have just shown, strategic interactions between groups create the unstable social foundations from which ethnic conflict arises. Information failures, problems of credible commitment, and the security dilemma demonstrate that even when groups mean well and calculate the costs and benefits of alternatives realistically, conflict can still erupt. Even in "the best of all possible worlds," these strategic dilemmas can produce violent conflict.

Under conditions of actual or potential state weakness, and as the strategic dilemmas described above begin to take hold, two catalysts—ethnic activists and political entrepreneurs—can produce rapid and profound polarization within a multi-ethnic society. Social polarization, in turn, magnifies the strategic dilemmas and potential for conflict described above. As we explain in this section, political memories, myths, and emotions also magnify the polarizing effects of activists and entrepreneurs, further accelerating the vicious cycle of ethnic fear and violence.

All individuals desire to belong to groups, but the strength of this desire differs.[29] In a model of "ethnic dissimilation," Timur Kuran demonstrates that ethnic activists—individuals with especially strong needs to identify with ethnic kin—can manipulate such desires to produce a process of social polarization that is rapid, apparently spontaneous, and essentially unpredictable.[30] By

---

28. Posen, "The Security Dilemma and Ethnic Conflict."
29. Horowitz, *Ethnic Groups in Conflict.*
30. Timur Kuran, "Ethnic Dissimilation and its Global Transmission," in Lake and Rothchild, *Ethnic Fears and Global Engagement.*

persuading others to increase their public ethnic activity in order to maintain standing within the group, Kuran argues, ethnic activists can drive individuals to represent falsely their true preferences. While they might prefer, for instance, not to associate exclusively with members of their own group, individuals are pressed by activists and the social pressures they spawn to alter their behavior in a more "ethnic" direction. In this way, Kuran finds, ethnic activists can cause previously integrated communities to separate along ethnic lines.

Political entrepreneurs—individuals who may not share the beliefs of extremists but who seek political office and power—may reflect the polarization of societies and, through their actions, propel this process further. Ethnicity often provides a key marker for self-aggrandizing politicians seeking to build constituencies for attaining or maintaining political power.[31] Politicians in the middle of the political spectrum or those who court ethnically heterogeneous constituencies are vulnerable, in turn, to political extremists seeking to draw electoral support from only a more ethnically homogeneous and possibly more militant constituency. When faced with the threat of such challenges, even centrist politicians can be driven to embrace a more "ethnic" position and defend communal interests more vigorously, a phenomenon often referred to as ethnic outbidding.[32] Political entrepreneurs can also reinforce processes of social polarization. Like activists, they can highlight and legitimate ethnic associations and affinities and raise the political saliency of ethnicity. In framing issues for the public, moreover, political entrepreneurs can exaggerate the hostility of others and magnify the likelihood of conflict—thereby distorting public debate and images of other groups and driving co-ethnics toward them for power and support. President Slobodan Milošević's control over the media in Serbia, for instance, allowed him to present a one-sided view of Croat violence toward Croatian Serbs.[33] In short, political entrepreneurs both reflect and stimulate ethnic fears for their own aggrandizement.

Many analysts mistakenly focus on social polarization and the role of ethnic activists and political entrepreneurs in fomenting violence as the primary if not sole cause of ethnic conflict. Empirically, it is important to note that social polarization by itself does not necessarily lead to violence; Belgium provides

31. Stephen M. Saideman, "Is Pandora's Box Half-Empty or Half-Full? The Limited Virulence of Secessionism and the Domestic Sources of Disintegration," in Lake and Rothchild, *Ethnic Fears and Global Engagement*.

32. Joseph Rothschild, *Ethnopolitics: A Conceptual Framework* (New York: Columbia University Press, 1981); and Horowitz, *Ethnic Groups in Conflict*.

33. Weingast, "Constructing Trust," p. 20.

a particularly salient example of a polarized society that manages to conduct politics on a peaceful if not necessarily always harmonious basis, partly because the state remains robust enough to prevent significant information failures, problems of credible commitment, and security dilemmas from arising. Ethnic extremists, in turn, are nearly always present, and they can be expected to become prominent whenever at least one of the strategic dilemmas above is initiated. Analytically, ethnic activists and political entrepreneurs are as much a product as a producer of ethnic fears and are dependent for their "success" upon the underlying strategic dilemmas. Nonetheless, they do play an important role in exacerbating ethnic tensions and propelling societies along the road to violence.

The polarization of society is also magnified by such "non-rational" factors as political memories and myths, on the one hand, and emotions, on the other. Political memories and myths can lead groups to form distorted images of others and see others as more hostile and aggressive than they really are. Such myths are often rooted in actual events, and probably could not be long sustained absent a historical basis. Yet, historical events can, over time, evolve into legends that justify the superiority of one group over another, stimulate desires for retribution, or sustain group hatreds. In Africa, following decolonization as well as in the contemporary period, political memories of past conflict have directly contributed to violent encounters, even instances of genocide.[34] In Eastern Europe, political memories and myths have both defined the groups themselves and stimulated acute fears of mutual exploitation. The Croats and Serbs, formerly citizens within the same state and now enemies, have both used history and religion to support a view of the other as a tight ethnic bloc determined on a destructive course and therefore deserving of pitiless retaliation.

Emotions may also cause individuals and groups to act in exaggerated or potentially "irrational" ways that magnify the chances of conflict. Many analysts point to a deep psychological—perhaps even physiological—need for humans to belong to a group.[35] In the process of drawing distinctions, however, individuals often overstate the goodness of their own group while simultaneously vilifying others. Where such emotional biases exist, groups are likely to interpret the demands of others as outrageous, while seeing their own as

---

34. René Lemarchand and David Martin, *Selective Genocide in Burundi*, No. 20 (London: Minority Rights Group, 1974).
35. Horowitz, *Ethnic Groups in Conflict*.

moderate and reasonable; to view the other as inherently untrustworthy, while believing themselves to be reliable; to insist upon adequate safeguards against the possible defection of the other, but interpreting the efforts of others to impose similar restrictions on them as a sign of "bad faith"; to believe that the other is withholding information or deceptive, while they are being open and honest; and so on.

The emotional power of ethnic attachments is typically increased by the unifying effects of what are perceived to be external threats. People who have little in common with others may unite when they feel threatened by external enemies. Thus, the shared identity of the Hutu in Burundi emerged only recently with the Tutsi repressions of 1972.[36] Similarly, in Chechnya, when very disparate interests felt threatened by Russian power, they overcame their differences and made common cause in the face of Russian intervention.

Together, strategic interactions between and within groups can produce environments of fear in which ethnic tensions and conflicts can grow. As Pešić recognizes, it is the future that threatens, but the future is interpreted through the past. While each strategic dilemma alone is sufficient to produce and explain the outbreak of ethnic conflict, they almost always occur simultaneously. Ethnic activists and political entrepreneurs can polarize societies, exacerbating these strategic dilemmas. The tendency toward polarization, in turn, is magnified by political memories and myths and emotions. Combined, these forces create a devastating brew of ethnic rivalry and potential violence.

The Management of Ethnic Conflict

Effective management of ethnic conflicts by local elites and governments and by external states and organizations must reassure minority groups of their physical and cultural safety. To foster stability and constructive ethnic relations, the rights and position of the minority must be secured. Confidence-building measures undertaken by local elites are the most effective instrument to this end, and we discuss these first. In light of group fears and individual ambitions, however, international intervention may be necessary and appropriate either to support local leaders in their confidence-building efforts or to enforce new, externally imposed ethnic contracts. Even so, confidence-building measures and international interventions are imperfect. Unlike other, more optimis-

---

36. Warren Weinstein, "Conflict and Confrontation in Central Africa: The Revolt in Burundi," *Africa Today*, Vol. 19, No. 4 (Fall 1972), p. 27.

tic observers, we see no permanent resolutions, only temporary "fixes." In the end, ethnic groups are left without reliable safety nets. There is no form of insurance sufficient to protect against the dilemmas that produce collective fears and violence. We can only hope to contain ethnic fears, not permanently eliminate them.

CONFIDENCE-BUILDING MEASURES

Confidence-building measures seek to reassure ethnic peoples about their future. To overcome minority fears, confidence-building measures must be appropriate to the needs of those who feel vulnerable to the majority-backed state. The challenge, as I. William Zartman observes, "is to keep the minority/ies from losing."[37] Such safeguards, if handled sensitively over the years, may be able to cope with the central problems of sharing private information and making credible commitments. There are four major trust-building mechanisms for helping ethnic minorities deal with perceived insecurity.

DEMONSTRATIONS OF RESPECT. The security of ethnic peoples is in no small way based on a reciprocity of respect. Unless each side views its opponent as honorable and having legitimate interests, relations are likely to be marred by a history of intended or unintended affronts that widen the social distance between groups and exacerbate fears among ethnic minorities that their children will be relegated indefinitely to second-class status.

Relations in Bosnia, worsened by polarization and increasingly hostile perceptions, have been further aggravated by the contempt Serbs have shown their Muslim adversaries. Describing themselves as the only people in former Yugoslavia "who have the talent, energy, experience, and tradition to form a state," they characterize their adversaries as representing "all that is base, undesirable, and naturally subordinate."[38] In the Sudan, southerners with strong memories of slavery and perceptions of low status bridle at any new evidence of disrespect. Thus, they viewed the Sudanese government's decision to apply Islamic (*Shari'a*) law to them as well as to the Muslims living in the country's north as a confirmation of their second-class status.[39] Their resentment boiled over in 1994, when the minister of state in the president's office, at the mediation talks

---

37. I. William Zartman, "Putting Humpty-Dumpty Together Again," in Lake and Rothchild, *Ethnic Fears and Global Engagement*.

38. Norman Cigar, *Genocide in Bosnia: The Policy of "Ethnic Cleansing"* (College Station: Texas A & M University Press, 1995), pp. 74–75.

39. Amnesty International, *"The Tears of Orphans": No Future Without Human Rights* (New York: Amnesty International, 1995), p. 57.

in Nairobi held by the Inter-Governmental Authority on Drought and Development (IGADD), allegedly treated both the southerners and the IGADD mediators with contempt when rejecting the southerners' call for self-determination and a secular state.[40]

The fears of ethnic minorities may often be overstated. Minorities in Eastern Europe are described as having "an exaggerated fear of the loss of identity," a legacy of distrust of majority authorities that causes them to make broad demands for legal guarantees. The majorities, fearful that this will start them down the slippery slope toward the breakup of their states, refuse to consent to these demands.[41] But to build confidence it is imperative that dominant state elites take minority ethnic resentments and anxieties into account. Those involved in the management of ethnic disputes can learn much from C.E. Osgood's Graduated and Reciprocated Initiatives in Tension Reduction (GRIT) strategy for easing conflict between the superpowers during the Cold War.[42] His suggested approach of repeated overtures without expectations of an immediate tit-for-tat response could stimulate full negotiations between equals. Unless past wrongs are redressed and the sting of disparagement is removed from current ethnic interactions, internal negotiations will remain clouded by an overhang of bitterness and suspicion; minority uncertainty regarding adversary intentions will then contribute to serious conflicts.

POWER-SHARING. Conflict management requires an effort by the state to build representative ruling coalitions. In conceding to ethnic minority leaders and activists a proportionate share of cabinet, civil service, military, and high party positions, the state voluntarily reaches out to include minority representatives in public affairs, thereby offering the group as a whole an important incentive for cooperation. In South Africa, for example, President Nelson Mandela agreed to include power-sharing provisions in the interim constitution in an effort to reconcile the economically dominant local white community as well as to build confidence among mostly white investors abroad. Significantly, this concession was withdrawn in 1996 with the enactment of a new majority rule constitution. National Party leader F.W. de Klerk was quick to describe the ending of multiparty participation in cabinet decision-making as a "mistake" that would cause a loss of confidence in the country.[43]

---

40. *Sudan Democratic Gazette*, No. 53 (October 1994), p. 3.
41. Larry L. Watts, "Ethnic Tensions: How the West Can Help," *World Policy Journal*, Vol. 12, No. 1 (Spring 1995), pp. 92–93.
42. C.E. Osgood, *An Alternative to War or Surrender* (Urbana: University of Illinois Press, 1962).
43. "SA Will Pay Price For New Constitution: FW," *ANC Daily News Briefing*, May 9, 1996, p. 9, as transmitted on gopher://gopher.anc.org.za:70/00/anc/newsbrief/1996/news0509.

Power-sharing can be informal (e.g., Kenya, 1960s) or formal (e.g., Nigeria, 1979), and can take place in authoritarian (e.g., Zambia, 1980s) or democratic (e.g., South Africa, mid-1990s) settings. In both Eastern Europe and Africa, there has been a mixed pattern of "hegemonic exchange" regimes: centrally controlled one- or no-party regimes that allow a limited amount of bargaining to take place between state, ethnic, and other elites. Under the authoritarian administrations of Josip Broz Tito in Yugoslavia or Félix Houphouët-Boigny in Côte d'Ivoire, nationality or ethnic representatives met with the president in cabinet sessions, where strong differences were sometimes aired by group spokespersons behind closed doors. The resulting power-sharing systems are quite diverse, yet they have in common a form of coordination in which a somewhat autonomous state and a number of less autonomous ethnic-based and other interests engage in a process of mutual accommodation in accordance with commonly accepted procedural norms, rules, or understandings.[44] These elite power-sharing arrangements are inevitably fragile and temporary because the communal pillars upon which they rest remain firmly in place and resist the integrative pulls that would lead to countrywide loyalties. Even so, while these arrangements last they provide some security for political and ethnic minorities.

With ethnic balances of power constantly evolving and information limited, these arrangements are necessarily transitional ones. If poorly negotiated and implemented, the incomplete ethnic contracts may eventually be rejected by the groups they are designed to protect. The number of people appointed to the cabinet or civil service, for example, is not in and of itself a guarantee of proportional group influence.[45] When not applied with great care, power-sharing arrangements can backfire. Ethnic elites must be prepared to interact with other elite representatives they find personally repugnant, something difficult to do under normal circumstances but especially so where the norms of collaborative politics are not in place. Where majority-dominated states remain unprepared to respond to legitimate minority demands for full participation in decision-making activities, power-sharing schemes are likely to unravel and become themselves a source of grave insecurity.

ELECTIONS. Although elections represent only a brief episode in a larger political process, they can have enormous influence on inter-group collabora-

---

44. Donald Rothchild, "Hegemonial Exchange: An Alternative Model for Managing Conflict in Middle Africa," in Dennis L. Thompson and Dov Ronen, eds., *Ethnicity, Politics, and Development* (Boulder, Colo.: Lynne Rienner, 1986), p. 72.
45. Robert B. Mattes, "Beyond 'Government and Opposition': An Independent South African Legislature," *Politikon*, Vol. 20, No. 2 (December 1993), p. 76.

tion and conflict. Where favorable circumstances prevail (i.e., an agreement on the rules of the political game, broad participation in the voting process, and a promising economic environment), elections can promote stability. In democratic regimes, where institutionalized uncertainty provides many players with an incentive to participate, the election process can legitimate the outcome.[46] All groups have a reason to organize and, through coalitions with other parties, they are given an opportunity to gain power in the future. This prospect of competing in accordance with the procedural norms of the system can be reassuring to minority interests; not only do they have a chance to advance their individual and collective interests, but they are encouraged by the majority's commitment to the electoral contract. The effect is to preempt conflict.

The implications of elections, however, can also be troubling in multi-ethnic settings. Even where minority groups are represented in the legislature, there is a real possibility that they will remain shut out of the decision-making process. Hence, unless election mechanisms can be linked with other types of political institutions such as multiparty coalitions, regional autonomy, or federalism, they may not be able to provide security against ethnic discrimination. Moreover, when political entrepreneurs seek to outbid their centrist rivals through militant appeals to their ethnic kinsmen, elections can prove very destabilizing, threatening minorities with the possibility of discrimination, exclusion, and even victimization.

Electoral systems have been organized in two main ways to promote inclusive coalitions. First, electoral rules can be set so that candidates are forced to appeal to more than one ethnic group. In an effort to give presidential candidates an incentive to appeal to a broad cross-section of communal groups, for example, both the 1979 and the 1995 (draft) constitutions in Nigeria provided variously that, if there are two candidates for election, a candidate would be deemed to be elected when that person secured a simple majority of the total number of votes cast as well as one-quarter of the votes cast in at least two-thirds of the states. In securing a majority of votes in this multi-ethnic society, moderate appeals, with their overarching themes, were expected to win out over parochial ones.

Second, electoral rules can also be crafted to ensure some minimal representation of all ethnic groups in the society. Those seeking to encourage minority representation in party lists and in ruling coalitions have looked favorably

---

46. Adam Przeworski, *Democracy and the Market* (Cambridge: Cambridge University Press, 1991), p. 26.

on systems of proportional representation (PR). For example, in structuring the elections for the Russian State Duma (the lower chamber of parliament) in 1993, legal drafters provided for a chamber of 450 members, half on the basis of single-member constituencies and half on the basis of PR. Constituencies also vary enormously in size. Such a system ensures the representation of smaller ethnic groups in the State Duma. Similarly, in South Africa, the African National Congress agreed, somewhat reluctantly, to use PR during the transition period to give racial and ethnic minorities a sense of security.[47] Although the PR system seemed cumbersome and failed to generate close links between a member of parliament and his or her constituents, ANC leaders nonetheless agreed to continue use of this mechanism for electing members to the National Assembly under the 1996 Constitution.

The way that state elites structure electoral arrangements is likely to prove critical in building confidence in minority circles. A broad-based electoral formula, like that of Nigeria, and proportional representation are two possible ways of encouraging minority ethnic participation and inclusion; yet they are likely to endure only as long as they retain support among key groups and state elites. If the majority shifts its concern away from the values of representativeness, a change in electoral rules can take place. Unless this change is handled fairly and with extreme sensitivity, it can be perceived by minority groups as inimical to their interests. As a consequence, considerable experience is required before minorities come to see electoral laws as reliable foundations for their security.

REGIONAL AUTONOMY AND FEDERALISM. Political and administrative decentralization can play a role in managing political conflict. By enabling local and regional authorities to wield a degree of autonomous power, elites at the political center can promote confidence among local leaders. Measures on decentralization, regional autonomy, and federalism featured in peace negotiations in Bosnia, Sri Lanka, Cyprus, Sudan, Angola, Mozambique, and South Africa. In each, they provided insurgent militias with an important incentive for responding positively to the government or third-party mediator's proposals for settling the conflict. The U.S.-brokered peace initiative in Bosnia achieved a key breakthrough in the September 1995 negotiations, for example, when the Bosnian government agreed to recognize an autonomous Bosnian Serb entity, called Republika Srpska. In exchange, Serbia and Croatia accepted

---

47. Timothy D. Sisk, "South Africa Seeks New Ground Rules," *Journal of Democracy*, Vol. 4, No. 1 (January 1993), p. 87.

the legal existence of Bosnia and Herzegovina with its present borders and endorsed the division of the country, 51 percent of the territory to the Bosnian government and Bosnian Croats, and 49 percent to the Bosnian Serbs. All three parties perceived control of Bosnia's territory to be critically important for their survival once peace came into effect.

In attempting to create a new balance between state and society, groups turn to decentralization as a means of placing institutional limitations on unbridled central authority. Politically marginalized groups have vivid memories of excessive state penetration and a continuing fear of majority domination. Decentralization and the authority these schemes allow local elites can, therefore, become confidence-building mechanisms that safeguard the place of minorities in the larger society. In Ethiopia, for example, President Meles Zenawi looks to a scheme of ethnic federalism as a means of reversing the repressive, hegemonic practices of previous governments that have led to internal wars.[48] The 1994 Constitution gives the nations making up Ethiopia wide powers, including an unconditional right of self-determination and secession.

Nevertheless, experiments with decentralized systems in India, Pakistan, Cyprus, Sri Lanka, Kenya, Uganda, South Africa, Sudan, and Ethiopia reveal serious practical difficulties in securing majority-backed state acceptance for these attempts to insulate minority interests from central authority. Determined to prevent the division of the state, public officials have taken firm action to avert a weakening of control. In extreme cases, they have revoked previous concessions. Thus, as Yugoslavia began to disintegrate in 1989, Milošević rescinded the autonomous provincial status within Serbia that Tito had given to largely Albanian-populated Kosovo. Sudan's President Gaafar el-Nimeiry, who had been the main advocate of political accommodation with the Southern Sudan Liberation Movement insurgents in 1972, backtracked on his commitments formalized in the Addis Ababa accords and in the late 1970s began to dismantle the federal compromise; to placate hard-line, Muslim elements within his government, Nimeiry intervened in southern regional elections, changed regional boundaries, redivided the southern region, applied *Shari'a* law to non-Muslims, and ultimately abrogated the agreement itself. In both Yugoslavia and Sudan, revocation of concessions on autonomy heightened tensions and led to new violence.

---

48. Cameron McWhirter and Gur Melamede, "Ethiopia: The Ethnicity Factor," *Africa Report*, Vol. 37, No. 5 (September/October, 1992) p. 33.

While regional autonomy and federalism have been used as safeguards, they have had, in some instances, unintended consequences that have actually increased conflict. Despite efforts to decentralize power in South Africa and Ethiopia, the fiscal dominance of the political center has tended to undercut the significance of regional authorities. Moreover, efforts to delineate boundaries have increased conflict between ethno-regional identity groups. In contemporary Russia, the arbitrary way in which internal boundaries divide ethnic peoples has been a major source of tension.[49] In Ethiopia, the regional boundaries set up by the government appear to favor Tigray and the Afars, at the expense of the formerly dominant Amhara and the Somali Isaks in the Awash Valleyland. Unless carefully crafted, decentralization schemes may worsen rather than improve inter-ethnic relations.

CONFIDENCE-BUILDING MEASURES EVALUATED. Confidence-building measures are potentially creative instruments by which states can reassure ethnic minorities. They indicate a sympathetic concern on the part of those in power to the fears and uncertainties of minorities. By acknowledging and showing respect for difference and by agreeing to share resources, state positions, and political power with exposed and vulnerable groups, these measures reduce the perceived risks of association and provide incentives for cooperation with other groups. They can also become the basis over time for a shared sense of common fate among diverse communities. States seeking ethnic accommodations have used confidence-building measures effectively in the past, and they will continue to do so in the future. The international community should encourage states at risk of significant ethnic conflict to make use of confidence-building measures.

However, such confidence-building measures represent conflict management, not conflict resolution. They can reduce some of the factors giving rise to ethnic fears, but they do not alter the basic dilemmas that cause these fears in the first place. The risks in ethnic encounters remain in place, even if papered over by concessions. Because there is always the possibility that groups will adopt more threatening forms of interaction, these confidence-building measures never eliminate the information failures, problems of credible commitment, and security dilemmas that are embedded in ethnic encounters. As Adam Przeworski astutely observes, "if sovereignty resides with the people, the

---

49. Gail W. Lapidus and Renée de Nevers, eds., *Nationalism, Ethnic Identity and Conflict Management in Russia Today* (Stanford, Calif.: Stanford University Center for International Security and Arms Control, 1995), p. 3.

people can decide to undermine all the guarantees reached by politicians around a negotiating table. Even the most institutionalized guarantees give at best a high degree of assurance, never certainty."[50]

EXTERNAL INTERVENTION

If states fail to restrain the incentives for violence rooted in the strategic interactions of groups, it is necessary to turn to the international environment and ask whether external intervention can safeguard minorities against their worst fears. For many observers, sovereignty is linked to responsibility: state elites are expected to guarantee minority rights and provide the means for establishing and maintaining regularized patterns of state-society and inter-ethnic relations. The state, with its monopoly of force, is often in a position, as one South African mediator described it in 1995, to "enforce stability" between local warring parties (in this case, in the East Rand townships in his country). But who will intercede if the state is unable or unwilling to secure the safety of its minority peoples? What forms will this intervention take? Which of the interventions, if any, are likely to have a significant impact on intra-state conflicts?

The principle of sovereignty has never been articulated or respected in the clear-cut manner often assumed by scholars of international relations. As Stephen D. Krasner and Daniel K. Froats demonstrate, states have a long history of intervention in the ethnic (and religious) affairs of others.[51] Many of the treaties settling European affairs in the aftermath of World War I contained provisions obligating states to protect the political and religious rights of minorities within their borders. More recently, the United Nations Charter affirmed an international commitment to basic human rights and fundamental freedoms. UN Secretary General Boutros Boutros-Ghali now believes that "the time of absolute and exclusive sovereignty has passed."[52]

Nonetheless, since 1945 there has been a strong insistence by many countries on the protection of national autonomy afforded by the juridical principle of sovereignty. This emphasis on internal autonomy has often been strongest where states themselves were weakest.[53] Yet today, ethnic conflicts and their

---

50. Przeworski, *Democracy and the Market*, p. 79.

51. Stephen D. Krasner and Daniel K. Froats, "The Westphalian Model and Minority-Rights Guarantees in Europe," in Lake and Rothchild, *Ethnic Fears and Global Engagement*. See also Krasner, "Compromising Westphalia," *International Security*, Vol. 20, No. 3 (Winter 1995/96), pp. 115–151.

52. Boutros Boutros-Ghali, *An Agenda for Peace* (New York: United Nations, 1992), p. 9.

53. Robert H. Jackson and Carl G. Rosberg. "Why Africa's Weak States Persist," *World Politics*, Vol. 35, No. 1 (October 1982), pp. 1–24.

possible spread have thrust issues of "humanitarian" intervention onto the policy agendas of the United States and many other countries. As Edmond Keller indicates, even in Africa, where the norm of juridical sovereignty has been strong, there is a new willingness on the part of state leaders to entertain limitations on the notion of sovereignty, but it remains an open question whether these leaders will be prepared to sanction international interventions directed against their own countries.[54]

External intervention takes three broad forms: noncoercive intervention, coercive intervention, and third-party mediation during both the negotiation and implementation stages. We look briefly at each of these forms, drawing conclusions in each case about their anticipated effects on intra-state conflicts.

NONCOERCIVE INTERVENTION. A sense of alarm over the violation of minority rights taking place in other countries has, at times, prompted outside states and multilateral organizations to protest infractions or exert pressure on the transgressors. Western governments, encouraged by their domestic publics to denounce breaches of human rights in Bosnia, Chechnya, Rwanda, and Sudan, have criticized these abuses through quiet, behind-the-scenes diplomacy and at public fora.

Assertions of international norms are important in raising the costs of unacceptable behavior, especially when their advocates offer an alternative set of interests around which defectors can mobilize and challenge the ensconced ethnic leaders.[55] States are also in a strong position to use inclusion in or exclusion from the international community to reward or punish regimes and ethnic leaders who deviate from internationally accepted norms. The promises of inclusion or the pains of exclusion can at times create strong incentives to behave in a more responsible fashion. Thus Milošević's desire to be accepted by Europeans and North Americans enabled Western diplomats to influence his behavior at the bargaining table, even causing him to make concessions on the emotionally charged issue of Bosnian government control over a unified Sarajevo. Similarly, conditions on membership in international organizations appear to be mitigating ethnic conflicts in Hungary and Romania, while Turkey's desire for acceptance in Europe may be limiting its actions against its Kurdish minority.

---

54. Edmond J. Keller, "Transnational Ethnic Conflict in Africa," in Lake and Rothchild, *Ethnic Fears and Global Engagement*.
55. V.P. Gagnon, Jr., "Ethnic Nationalism and International Conflict: The Case of Serbia," *International Security*, Vol. 19, No. 3 (Winter 1994/95), p. 139.

In South Africa, external protests and sanctions raised the costs of doing business, access to technology and raw materials, and travel. Sanctions physically punished the regime, something that became painfully evident in South Africa's loss of dominance in the air war over Angola, brought on in part by the air force's inability to secure spare parts. The symbolic impact of sanctions was also important because it represented a clear statement of sympathy for black hardship and moral disapproval of apartheid policies by the international community.[56] Above all, international condemnation challenged state and governmental legitimacy. While the costs of sanctions were discomforting and burdensome, they did not hurt the main body of the white constituency sufficiently to alter priorities, until de Klerk's remarkable change of heart on negotiating with the anti-apartheid opposition in the early 1990s.[57]

Given the extreme emotionalism over security issues that brings aggressive ethnic leaders to the fore in the first place, we are skeptical that external appeals, exhortations, and pressures will in and of themselves dissuade determined elites from their abusive courses. Bosnian Serb leader Radovan Karadžić, Bosnian Serb military commander Ratko Mladić, and their ilk remain sufficiently insulated from world pressures that what transpires at diplomatic meetings or in the global press may have little immediate impact on them or their militant followers.

Noncoercive interventions can be helpful in raising the costs of purely ethnic appeals and in structuring the incentives of group leaders prepared to accept international norms for the purposes of recognition, acceptance, and inclusion in the international community. Where conflicts are intense, however, exhortations and international warnings may not deter or end violence. The most that noncoercive intervention can do in such situations is to create a climate in which ethnic appeals and violence are perceived by all as illegitimate and, therefore, marginally less likely to be used.

COERCIVE INTERVENTION. The rise in ethnic conflict today creates new demands and opportunities for coercive intervention by outside states and international organizations.[58] External interventions have two primary effects. First, intervention can alter the internal balance of ethnic power and may lead groups

---

56. Harry R. Strack, *Sanctions: The Case of Rhodesia* (Syracuse, N.Y.: Syracuse University Press, 1978).
57. Sisk, *Democratization in South Africa*.
58. For discussions of the motivations of outside states to intervene in ethnic conflicts, see Michael E. Brown, "Causes and Implications of Ethnic Conflict," in Brown, ed., *Ethnic Conflict and International Security*, pp. 16–20, and Robert Cooper and Mats Berdal, "Outside Intervention in Ethnic Conflicts," in ibid., p. 197.

to moderate their demands. Except perhaps where the sides have reached a "hurting stalemate" and the purpose of the intervention is exclusively to separate the forces and keep the peace, interventions always have political implications.[59] Even in Somalia, where negotiations on establishing a transitional national council led to hopes for a settlement in 1993, the initial humanitarian mission eventually favored one claimant to power (Ali Mahdi Mohamed) over the other (Mohamed Farah Aideed), ultimately causing the politicization of the mission.[60] Typically favoring, by design or default, the weaker side in any internal conflict, external powers reduce the stronger side's chances for success. This, in turn, restrains the stronger party's demands. To the extent that such restraint takes hold, intervention can improve the prospects for agreement. However, the weaker side is likely to increase its demands and ask for more at the bargaining table as its prospects of failure decline and its chances for success improve.[61] For instance, once the NATO countries intervened decisively in September 1995 on behalf of the Bosnian government, and against the Bosnian Serb forces, the latter—pressured by Milošević—quickly moderated their demands and moved towards accepting the territorial partition they had earlier rejected.[62] At the same time, however, the Croats saw new opportunities on the battlefield and at the negotiating table, and the United States and its allies had to exert pressure on the Bosnian government and Croatia not to exploit their increased leverage. With both effects occurring simultaneously in any intervention, the "bargaining gap" between the parties may remain as wide as ever. Unless pressure is exerted on both sides to moderate their demands, intervention by itself will not necessarily enhance the prospects for agreement.

The second primary effect of intervention is to provide guarantees for new ethnic contracts between the warring parties, at least during an interim period. As discussed above, problems of credible commitment hinder the efforts of groups to resolve their differences peacefully. The primary attraction of external

---

59. On "hurting stalemates," see I. William Zartman, *Ripe for Resolution: Conflict and Intervention in Africa* (New York: Oxford University Press, 1985). On the inevitable political implications of intervention, see Caleb Carr, "The Consequences of Somalia," *World Policy Journal*, Vol. 10, No. 3 (Fall 1993), pp. 1–4.
60. John L. Hirsch and Robert B. Oakley, *Somalia and Operation Restore Hope: Reflections on Peacemaking and Peacekeeping* (Washington, D.C.: United States Institute of Peace Press, 1995).
61. Donald Wittman, "How a War Ends: A Rational Model Approach," *Journal of Conflict Resolution*, Vol. 23, No. 4 (December 1979), pp. 743–763.
62. Milošević's role in the October 1995 negotiations carried with it an implied threat: if the Bosnian Serbs refused to be more accommodating at the bargaining table, their Serb kinsmen across the border could further reduce their military support.

intervention is that an outside state can enforce an agreement, thereby providing the necessary credibility that is otherwise lacking. Indeed, when the future risk of exploitation is high, but the declining group is still strong enough to possess some chance of victory, outside enforcers may be the only way to ensure ethnic peace.[63] Thus, in Namibia in 1989, the third-party enforcer was in a position to raise the costs of breaking agreements by monitoring the implementation process, highlighting violations of the peace agreement, and focusing an international spotlight on any breaches that occurred.[64] The lack of any equally effective third-party enforcer in neighboring Angola following the signing of the Bicesse accords, and UNITA President Jonas Savimbi's poor showing in the first round of the 1992 elections, increased incentives to defect from the agreement and resume the civil war.

The promise of the post–Cold War world is that the great powers, freed from the shackles of superpower competition, can now intervene to mitigate ethnic conflicts by providing external guarantees of social order. If the warring parties themselves cannot make credible commitments to uphold their pacts, external powers can lead the groups to peaceful solutions by enforcing any agreement they might reach. The paradox of the post–Cold War world, however, is that absent the bipolar competition that drove them into the far reaches of the globe, the United States and other powers now lack the political will necessary to make a sustained commitment to this role.

The key issue in determining the success of any external guarantee is the commitment of the international community. In a way not sufficiently appreciated by current policy makers in Washington and elsewhere, external guarantees work only when the local parties to the conflict believe that the outside powers are resolved to enforce the ethnic contract in a fair manner into the indefinite future. The behavior of the external powers today is not the crucial factor. Rather, a more fundamental question is whether the warring parties or potential combatants believe the external powers will be there to protect them tomorrow, and in the days and years after that. Absent a belief in the fair-mindedness and stamina of the external powers, intervention in any form will fail to mitigate the conflict.

63. Stephen J. Stedman, *Peacemaking in Civil Wars: International Mediation in Zimbabwe, 1974–1980* (Boulder, Colo.: Lynne Rienner, 1991); and Barbara F. Walter, "The Resolution of Civil Wars: Why Negotiations Fail," unpublished paper, Columbia University, 1995.
64. Virginia P. Fortna, "Success and Failure in Southern Africa: Peacekeeping in Namibia and Angola," in Donald C.F. Daniel and Bradd C. Hayes, eds., *Beyond Traditional Peacekeeping* (New York: St. Martin's, 1995), pp. 282–299.

Unfortunately, even countries with strong interests in intervening often find themselves unable to offer credible external guarantees. Countries vitally affected by the fighting or the outcome either tend to be partisan or are perceived by the combatants as partisan, as was the case with France's intervention in Rwanda in 1994. One or both sides to the conflict, therefore, will doubt the willingness of the outside power to enforce the new ethnic contract in an evenhanded manner, and they will be less likely to reach an effective and enforceable agreement. However, when outside powers have interests in a stable outcome, rather than in the victory or loss of either side, they may be perceived by all as fair-minded facilitators. Britain's role in Zimbabwe in the 1970s is a positive example of an interested party able to work with a coalition of external mediators to push negotiations ahead to a successful outcome.

Countries with weak interests in the conflict, on the other hand, will tend to lack or will be perceived as lacking the political stamina to enforce any new ethnic contract into the future. The United States was unwilling to bear any substantial cost in human lives to guarantee the peace in Somalia, for instance. There are many reasons why states might possess only weak interests in guaranteeing a new ethnic conflict. Most important, political instability abroad is typically broad but shallow in its effects, producing incentives for states to seek to free ride on the efforts of others.[65] This is one plausible interpretation of the hesitancy of the United States in taking a leadership role in Bosnia. In this view, Presidents George Bush and Bill Clinton held back hoping that the Europeans would step forward and carry the financial and military burden; only when the Europeans proved unprepared to assume the costs did the United States take the lead.

Weak commitments produce ambiguous policies that may, in the end, exacerbate rather than resolve conflicts. Public commitments encourage the weaker party to believe that the external power supports it, thereby prompting the group to fight on and hold out for a better deal than its position on the battlefield warrants.[66] Ambiguity and vacillation, however, may simultaneously persuade the stronger party that the external power does not possess sufficient stamina, and that it too may improve its position by continuing to fight. This ambivalent commitment is the true tragedy of the current United States policy in the Balkans. One of the most important lessons from this

---

65. Mancur Olson, *The Logic of Collective Action* (Cambridge, Mass.: Harvard University Press, 1965).
66. Djilas, "Fear thy Neighbor: The Breakup of Yugoslavia," p. 102.

analysis is that if external powers are going to intervene in ethnic conflicts, either alone or in concert with others, they must do so in a way that is credible to the groups involved. An external guarantee that the parties expect will evaporate is no guarantee at all.

THIRD-PARTY MEDIATION. Given the limitations of confidence-building measures and external interventions, there are few alternatives to negotiations if both sides are to be brought into the solution. For a mutually satisfactory peace to take place, a two-step negotiating process is essential: first, among the key elements within each group, and then between the groups themselves. Operating rules must be hammered out in these talks regarding inclusive coalitions, proportionality in recruitment and allocations, autonomy, provisions on electoral competition, and so forth. The ensuing negotiations are likely to be protracted and difficult, largely because the various factions and groups lack a clear chain of command (making commitments difficult to produce) and because they understand fully that the terms they accept will cast a long shadow over their future. But if each of the parties concludes that its alternatives are limited, its present course unduly costly, and its stake in its rival's willingness to cooperate with an agreement significant, they may then begin to negotiate in good faith. External mediators can play an important role in facilitating negotiations by encouraging adversaries to open up channels of communication, to reconsider their alternatives, and to opt for peaceful, negotiated solutions. A mediator's ability to influence the strategies of the adversaries must not be overstated; nevertheless, the ability of a third party to make effective use of pressures and incentives can prove decisive, especially if the parties to the conflict have nowhere else to go.

In intense ethnic disputes, mediators can use a variety of noncoercive and coercive incentives to increase the information available to the adversaries, facilitate a change in their strategies, or find a way to save face. Noncoercive incentives extend benefits or rewards for compliance, while coercive incentives punish or threaten to punish a targeted actor to bring it into line with preferred types of political behavior. Provided that the demands of the two sides are negotiable and neither party can anticipate a military victory, mediators can make use of a package of carrots and sticks in the hopes that the targeted party (or parties) will accept a compromise and thus allow some degree of mutual cooperation to materialize.

Normally, noncoercive incentives will be preferred by third parties, because of their low cost and expected impact. Thus, mediators frequently make use of sidepayments to enlarge the pie and alter the payoff structure, thereby enhancing the benefits of making concessions (as occurred most dramatically in the Egyptian-Israeli negotiations at Camp David in 1978). Third parties can also influence the choices of ethnic minorities by guaranteeing them against possible future abuses at the hands of the majority after an agreement has been reached.

However, when ethnic conflicts grow in intensity and can no longer be resolved by means of rewards, it sometimes becomes necessary for the third party to force movement toward cooperation by means of threats or punishments. These coercive incentives become increasingly punitive as they move from pressure to economic sanctions to military intervention, as occurred at different stages in the Bosnian confrontation. In the contemporary period, only a coalition of mediators seems likely to have the political capacity to create the mix of noncoercive and coercive incentives necessary to overcome a stalemate and move the parties toward a negotiated settlement.

But the scope for third-party initiative at both the negotiation and implementation stages is highly circumscribed. Internal wars are particularly difficult to negotiate, largely because ethnic enmities tend to be so deep and the stakes so high. Data on negotiations indicate that settlements are difficult to achieve and at least as difficult to maintain, even where a third party is prepared to step between the adversaries. Roy Licklider, largely reconfirming earlier studies by Stephen Stedman and Paul Pillar, finds that only 14 out of 57 civil wars between 1945 and 1993 were settled through negotiations.[67] Even with its focus on opening channels of communication and facilitating the flow of information, third-party mediation cannot wholly eliminate potential information failures. The conflicting groups are bound by the same incentives not to reveal all of their private information, even to third parties. Moreover, problems of credible commitment loom large. Barbara Walter suggests that inter-state wars are easier to bring to a negotiated conclusion because the two parties remain on opposite sides of a border; in internal wars, the disputants must re-merge themselves into a single unit and, as a result, face more difficult problems of credible commitment.[68]

The difficulties normally associated with mediation are compounded by the obstacles to implementation. Several laboriously negotiated agreements have

---

67. Roy Licklider, "The Consequences of Negotiated Settlements in Civil Wars, 1945–1993," *American Political Science Review,* Vol. 89, No. 3 (September 1995), p. 684; Stedman, *Peacemaking in Civil Wars,* pp. 5–7; Paul R. Pillar, *Negotiating Peace: War Termination as a Bargaining Process* (Princeton, N.J.: Princeton University Press, 1993), p. 25.
68. Walter, "The Resolution of Civil Wars."

been signed only to fall apart at the implementation stage—for example, in Ethiopia and Eritrea (1962), Sudan (1982), Uganda (1985), Angola (1975, 1992), and Rwanda (1994). A large part of the responsibility for these failures lies with adversary parties and their inability to make credible and reliable commitments. Their distrust of one another's intentions was so deep that the peace agreement crumbled when ambiguity on security-related matters opened the way to renewed confrontation.

However, the failure of these agreements is also partly attributable to the unwillingness of the international community to provide mediators with the economic, logistical, police, and military support needed to oversee the processes of disarmament, integration of the armed forces, repatriation of refugees, and holding of general elections. In addition, the guarantees made to one or more rivals by foreign governments and multilateral organizations have come to lack credibility as local actors now expect the domestic publics of the third-party mediators to lose interest over time in far-off conflicts and retreat from commitments made at the high point of the struggle.

As internal wars reach a hurting stalemate and leaders on both sides perceive an "intolerable situation" with little expectation of military victory, fatigued parties may come to the table and bargain in earnest.[69] Despite the emotionalism and organizational imperatives surrounding civil wars, a number of them— including those in Cambodia, Nicaragua, Zimbabwe, Angola, Namibia, Mozambique, and possibly now Chechnya and Bosnia—have been or are close to being settled by means of negotiations. One must not anticipate too much from mediatory efforts, but a grim outlook is also not appropriate and could be self-fulfilling.

THE LIMITS OF INTERVENTION. External interventions, whether they are non-coercive, coercive, mediatory, or—as is common—a combination of the three, are not likely to solve the underlying strategic dilemmas that produce ethnic fear and violence. Information failures remain possible, despite the efforts of outside actors to facilitate communication and protect the parties from the potentially disastrous consequences of revealing private information. Enforcing ethnic contracts depends upon the credibility of the external parties, who often have far less at stake in the conflict than the warring groups themselves. External actors can seek to raise the costs of using force, in general, and preemptive uses of force, in particular, by punishing groups that strike first; such initiatives or the threat of such initiatives may have a moderating effect

---

69. Zartman, *Ripe for Resolution*, p. 232.

on the security dilemma. Through early action, they may also be able to shape military doctrines and force structures in groups beginning to prepare for self-defense. Nevertheless, once incentives to use force preemptively are in place, outsiders can do little to restrain the security dilemma. In the final analysis, conflict management requires an effort by the local parties to engage in efforts to work out acceptable rules of interaction. External intervention does not by itself create a desire among the parties to restore normal relations. This is not to say that international efforts to contain conflict are not important, only that containment by itself is not a solution.

Toward Practical Initiatives

Most of the time, most ethnic groups live side by side with one another comfortably and amicably. Even in cases where ethnic minorities might otherwise be at risk, states have promoted stable ethnic relations and made concessions on minority group inclusion, participation, autonomy, and access to resources. However, an awareness that regimes can always change their preferences and retract these concessions leaves minorities fearful of the future. Information failures, problems of credible commitment, and the security dilemma lurk in the background of all ethnically divided polities. Conflict always remains a possibility.

Where an element of local anarchy is present and the state is at least potentially weak, a spiral of negative encounters that leads to violence remains a very real possibility. Information failures occur as the state loses its ability to arbitrate between factions, and as groups hold back information and suspect others of doing the same. Problems of credible commitment arise as ethnic contracts collapse and groups come to fear that others will not uphold their promises. Incentives to preempt drive groups to fight first and seek the basis for compromise later. In situations of increasing state weakness, appeals by ethnic activists and political entrepreneurs may awaken long dormant "malignant nationalisms" and lead to escalating violence.[70] In multi-ethnic polities with past histories of conflict and distrust, the social fabric can be very weak and easily torn apart.

In their fear, political minorities, recognizing the state's limited capacity to ensure their physical and cultural safety, look outward to the international

---

70. Stephen Van Evera, "Hypotheses on Nationalism and War," *International Security*, Vol. 18, No. 4 (Winter 1994), p. 8.

community for protection. They hope the international community will restore a balance of power and hence make systematic, state-sanctioned ethnic killing too costly for the hard-line majority leadership to condone. The international response, however, has all too often been feeble and unconvincing.

In the end, and despite the limits on international interventions discussed above, there can be no substitute for greater global commitment and involvement. The international community has already been involved at nearly every stage of some confrontation around the globe. This is a hopeful sign. But so far, many of the international responses have been conducted separately, sporadically, and outside of any comprehensive strategy for achieving ethnic peace, thereby limiting their effectiveness. Recognizing the inherent limits on the ability of international interventions to solve the strategic dilemmas we have identified, as well as the limits of public support in outside states, we recommend three specific avenues of action.

MANAGE INFORMATION

Given the importance of private information and the beliefs that groups hold about the intentions of others, one of the most effective policy instruments in the hands of international actors today is to ensure that objective, unbiased, and balanced information is made widely available in states threatened with intense conflict. This will require a continuing but largely preventive effort. As conflict escalates, outside states and international organizations can consider jamming radios that make inflammatory appeals, as did Radio Télévision Libre des Mille Collines in Rwanda. After the crisis has eased, external actors can use a variety of means, such as radio, fax, and the internet, for sharing information with the warring parties to help verify compliance with new ethnic contracts.

ASSIST "FAILING" STATES

Growing state weakness is a symptom of the strategic dilemmas discussed above. As information failures occur, problems of credible commitment arise, and security dilemmas begin to take hold, groups either turn away from the state or attempt to seize it to further their own quest for security. A decrease in a state's capacity to arbitrate between groups and enforce ethnic contracts is a clear herald of violence. Preventing the breakdown of the state can, in turn, help mitigate the potential for violence. External actors should seek to ensure that confidence-building measures are in place and that elites live up to minimum standards of legal order and political and human rights. The support of the international community for the anti-apartheid struggle in South Africa is a prime example. Trade, financial aid, and other benefits from inclusion in the international community should be linked to the maintenance of minimum international standards of domestic order. In advance of crises, international bodies should also assemble data banks, early warning systems, advance plans for possible mediators, units for peacemaking and enforcement, and personnel to assist in the creation of unified armies. It will be necessary to provide a solid financial basis for such international actions, but the costs will be small compared to the long-run benefits of reduced conflict.

INVEST IN IMPLEMENTATION

Negotiating a peace agreement between warring ethnic groups is only half the job. Implementing the agreement is just as important, and can be more difficult and complex than the negotiations. None of the strategies of external involvement discussed above "solves" the problem of ethnic conflict. Even if external pressure brings the parties to the table and produces an agreement, the underlying strategic dilemmas remain in place. A stable peace can only arise as effective institutions of government are re-established, as the state once again begins to mediate effectively between distrustful ethnic groups, and as the parties slowly gain confidence in the safeguards contained within their new ethnic contracts. This necessarily involves an element of state-building and the possibility of forcible intervention to protect minorities. It is also a slow, incremental process that is likely to require years to bear fruit.

The United States and other countries, individually or collectively, should invest substantially in implementing peace agreements. The very fact that rival parties have consented to an agreement indicates they have jointly come to accept certain outcomes and understandings. At this stage, implementation becomes the decisive factor in the successful creation of internal order. Even when backed by a peacekeeping force, implementing a peace agreement involves a limited commitment on the part of an individual intervener or a coalition of interveners; they are committed to this agreement, not others, and need not fall prey to the inevitable pressures for "mission creep." Successful implementation offers potentially large returns. The alternative is renewed or, in some cases, unending conflict.

Part IV:
International Institutions, War, and Peace

The False Promise of International Institutions

John J. Mearsheimer

Since the Cold War ended, Western policymakers have sought to create security arrangements in Europe, as well as in other regions of the globe, that are based on international institutions. In doing so, they explicitly reject balance-of-power politics as an organizing concept for the post–Cold War world. During the 1992 presidential campaign, for example, President Clinton declared that, "in a world where freedom, not tyranny, is on the march, the cynical calculus of pure power politics simply does not compute. It is ill-suited to a new era." Before taking office, Anthony Lake, the president's national security adviser, criticized the Bush administration for viewing the world through a "classic balance of power prism," whereas he and Mr. Clinton took a "more 'neo-Wilsonian' view."[1]

This approach to international politics rests on the belief that institutions are a key means of promoting world peace.[2] In particular, Western policymakers claim that the institutions that "served the West well" before the Soviet Union collapsed must be reshaped to encompass Eastern Europe as well.[3] "There is

John J. Mearsheimer is a professor in the Political Science Department at the University of Chicago.

This article emerged from a working paper written for "The Changing Security Environment and American National Interests," a project of the John M. Olin Institute for Strategic Studies at Harvard University. I am grateful to Robert Art, Benjamin Frankel, Markus Fischer, Charles Glaser, Hein Goemans, Joseph Grieco, Robert Jervis, Christopher Layne, Eric Lopez, Robert Pape, Ashley Tellis, Bradley Thayer, Ivan Toft, Stephen Van Evera, Stephen Walt, and especially Michael Desch for their most helpful comments.

1. Bill Clinton, "American Foreign Policy and the Democratic Ideal," Campaign speech, Pabst Theater, Milwaukee, Wisconsin, October 1, 1992; Steven A. Holmes, "Choice for National Security Adviser Has a Long-Awaited Chance to Lead," _New York Times_, January 3, 1993.
2. The other prominent theme in Western policymaking circles is the importance of spreading democracy and capitalism across the globe. Prosperous democracies, so the argument goes, do not fight each other. Thus, the aim is to increase the number of stable democracies in the international system. This line of argument is not examined here. For conciseness, international institutions are henceforth referred to simply as institutions.
3. Douglas Hurd, "A New System of Security in Europe," Speech to the Diplomatic and Common-wealth Writers' Association, London, June 2, 1992. Hurd, the British Foreign Secretary, said in this speech: "We have in Western Europe, in the West as a whole, a set of international institutions which have proved their worth for one set of problems—the problems for which they were set up, and now have to be adapted for another. That is the key, the necessary changes in all these institutions are the key to getting the right help, the right reassurance to the countries of central and Eastern Europe." Even Margaret Thatcher, with all her reservations about European institutions, has adopted this theme. She argued days after Iraq invaded Kuwait that, "We must bring

International Security, Winter 1994/95 (Vol. 19, No. 3), pp. 5–49
© 1995 by the President and Fellows of Harvard College and the Massachusetts Institute of Technology.

no reason," according to Secretary of State Warren Christopher, "why our institutions or our aspirations should stop at [the] old frontiers of the Cold War."[4] The institutions he has in mind include the European Community (EC), the North Atlantic Treaty Organization (NATO), the Conference on Security and Cooperation in Europe (CSCE), and the Western European Union (WEU). No single institution is expected to play a dominating role in Europe, however; instead, the aim is to create "a framework of complementary, mutually reinforcing" institutions.[5] "We can promote more durable European security," Christopher claims, "through interlocking structures, each with complementary roles and strengths."[6]

No other region of the world has institutions as extensive and as well-developed as those in Europe. Consequently, Western policymakers trumpet the importance of creating webs of overlapping institutions outside of Europe. Special emphasis is placed on Asia, where there are only a few weak institutions, and where fear of Japan, coupled with the rise of China and the prospect of a further reduction in the American presence, has observers worried about future stability in the region.[7]

There has also been a recent wave of academic interest in institutions. Academic institutionalists, not surprisingly, consider institutions to be a powerful force for stability.[8] Robert Keohane, for example, declares that, "avoiding

the new democracies of Eastern Europe into closer association with the institutions of Western Europe. . . . The European Community has reconciled antagonisms within Western Europe; it should now help to overcome divisions between East and West in Europe." Margaret Thatcher, "Shaping A New Global Community," Speech to the Aspen Institute, Aspen, Colorado, August 5, 1990.
4. Warren Christopher, "Toward a More Integrated World," Statement at the Organization for Economic Cooperation and Development (OECD) Ministerial Meeting, Paris, June 8, 1994. President Clinton and German Chancellor Helmut Kohl share the same view, as Clinton made clear when describing his private talks with Kohl in July 1994: "We know from our experience how half of Europe was integrated through NATO and other institutions that built stability after World War II. At the heart of our discussion today was what we have to do to integrate Europe's other half, the new independent nations." Thomas L. Friedman, "Clinton Sees Germany as Main Partner of the U.S. in Europe," *New York Times*, July 12, 1994.
5. "Interlocking Institutions: The Conference on Security and Cooperation in Europe (CSCE)," NATO Basic Fact Sheet No. 6 (Brussels, June 1994). Also see Jacques Delors, "European Unification and European Security," in *European Security after the Cold War*, Part 1, Adelphi Paper No. 284 (London: International Institute for Strategic Studies [IISS], January 1994), pp. 3–14.
6. Warren Christopher, "The CSCE Vision: European Security Rooted in Shared Values," Statement to the Plenary Session of the Conference on Security and Cooperation in Europe, Rome, November 30, 1993.
7. See Stephen J. Blank, *Helsinki in Asia?* (Carlisle Barracks, Pa.: Strategic Studies Institute, U.S. Army War College, 1993).
8. Stability is simply the absence of wars and major crises.

military conflict in Europe after the Cold War depends greatly on whether the next decade is characterized by a continuous pattern of institutionalized cooperation."[9] Commenting on the aftermath of the Soviet collapse and the end of the Cold War, John Ruggie maintains that "there seems little doubt that multilateral norms and institutions have helped stabilize their international consequences. Indeed, such norms and institutions appear to be playing a significant role in the management of a broad array of regional and global changes in the world system today."[10]

This article examines the claim that institutions push states away from war and promote peace. I concentrate on assessing the major international relations theories that employ institutions as a core concept: liberal institutionalism, collective security, and critical theory.[11] I begin, however, with a brief review of realism, because of the "institutionalist" theories is largely a response to realism, and each directly challenges realism's underlying logic.[12] Realists and institutionalists particularly disagree about whether institutions markedly affect the prospects for international stability. Realists say no; institutionalists say yes. Realists maintain that institutions are basically a reflection of the distribution of power in the world. They are based on the self-interested calculations of the great powers, and they have no independent effect on state behavior. Realists therefore believe that institutions are not an important cause of peace. They matter only on the margins. Institutionalists directly challenge this view of institutions, arguing instead that institutions can alter state preferences and therefore change state behavior. Institutions can discourage states from calculating self-interest on the basis of how every move affects their relative power positions. Institutions are independent variables, and they have the capability to move states away from war.

---

9. Robert O. Keohane, "The Diplomacy of Structural Change: Multilateral Institutions and State Strategies," in Helga Haftendorn and Christian Tuschhoff, eds., *America and Europe in an Era of Change* (Boulder, Colo.: Westview Press, 1993), p. 53.

10. John G. Ruggie, "Multilateralism: The Anatomy of an Institution," *International Organization*, Vol. 46, No. 3 (Summer 1992), p. 561.

11. Prescriptions about how best to maintain peace should rest on general theories about the causes of war and peace. This point is true for both academics and policymakers. Although policymakers are seldom self-conscious in their use of theory, their views about institutions are nevertheless shaped by their implicit preferences for one theory of international relations over another.

12. Keohane, for example, writes, "Institutionalist thinking has focused its critical fire on realism." Robert O. Keohane, "Institutional Theory and the Realist Challenge After the Cold War," in David A. Baldwin, ed., *Neorealism and Neoliberalism: The Contemporary Debate* (New York: Columbia University Press, 1993), p. 271.

Although institutionalists are united in their opposition to realist claims about institutions, each institutionalist theory makes a different argument about how institutions work to alter state behavior. My goal is to evaluate these three theories to determine whether the claim that institutions cause peace is persuasive. That task involves answering four questions: 1) What are institutions? 2) How do they work to cause peace? Specifically, what is the causal logic that underpins each theory? 3) Are these different logics that explain how institutions work compelling? 4) Does the evidence support these theories?

My central conclusion is that institutions have minimal influence on state behavior, and thus hold little promise for promoting stability in the post–Cold War world. The three theories on which the case for institutions is based are all flawed. Each has problems in its causal logic, and all three institutionalist theories find little support in the historical record.

The remainder of this article is organized as follows. I begin with a brief definition of institutions and a   discussion of realism, because each of the institutionalist theories takes its bearings from realism. In the main body of the article, I describe and evaluate liberal institutionalism, collective security, and critical theory. The concluding section considers why institutions are so highly regarded by policymakers and academics, when there is so little evidence that they are an important cause of peace.

What Are Institutions?

There is no widely-agreed upon definition of institutions in the international relations literature.[13] The concept is sometimes defined so broadly as to encompass all of international relations, which gives it little analytical bite.[14] For example, defining institutions as "recognized patterns of behavior or practice around which expectations converge" allows the concept to cover almost every

---

13. Regimes and institutions are treated as synonymous concepts in this article. They are also used interchangeably in the institutionalist literature. See Robert O. Keohane, "International Institutions: Two Approaches," *International Studies Quarterly*, Vol. 32, No. 4 (December 1988), p. 384; Robert O. Keohane, *International Institutions and State Power: Essays in International Relations Theory* (Boulder, Colo.: Westview Press, 1989), pp. 3–4; and Oran R. Young, *International Cooperation: Building Regimes for Natural Resources and the Environment* (Ithaca, N.Y.: Cornell University Press, 1989), chaps. 1 and 8. The term "multilateralism" is also virtually synonymous with institutions. To quote John Ruggie, "the term 'multilateral' is an adjective that modifies the noun 'institution.' Thus, multilateralism depicts a *generic institutional form* in international relations. . . . [Specifically,] multilateralism is an institutional form which coordinates relations among three or more states on the basis of 'generalized' principles of conduct." Ruggie, "Multilateralism," pp. 570–571.

14. For discussion of this point, see Arthur A. Stein, *Why Nations Cooperate: Circumstance and Choice in International Relations* (Ithaca, N.Y.: Cornell University Press, 1990), pp. 25–27. Also see Susan

regularized pattern of activity between states, from war to tariff bindings negotiated under the General Agreement on Tariffs and Trade (GATT), thus rendering it largely meaningless.[15] Still, it is possible to devise a useful definition that is consistent with how most institutionalist scholars employ the concept.

I define institutions as a set of rules that stipulate the ways in which states should cooperate and compete with each other.[16] They prescribe acceptable forms of state behavior, and proscribe unacceptable kinds of behavior. These rules are negotiated by states, and according to many prominent theorists, they entail the mutual acceptance of higher norms, which are "standards of behavior defined in terms of rights and obligations."[17] These rules are typically formalized in international agreements, and are usually embodied in organizations with their own personnel and budgets.[18] Although rules are usually incorporated into a formal international organization, it is not the organization *per se* that compels states to obey the rules. Institutions are not a form of world government. States themselves must choose to obey the rules they created. Institutions, in short, call for the "decentralized cooperation of individual sovereign states, without any effective mechanism of command."[19]

Strange, *"Cave! Hic Dragones:* A Critique of Regime Analysis," in Stephen D. Krasner, ed., *International Regimes,* special issue of *International Organization,* Vol. 36, No. 2 (Spring 1982), pp. 479–496.

15. Oran R. Young, "Regime Dynamics: The Rise and Fall of International Regimes," in Krasner, *International Regimes,* p. 277.

16. See Douglass C. North and Robert P. Thomas, "An Economic Theory of the Growth of the Western World," *The Economic History Review,* 2nd series, Vol. 23, No. 1 (April 1970), p. 5.

17. Krasner, *International Regimes,* p. 186. Non-realist institutions are often based on higher norms, while few, if any, realist institutions are based on norms. The dividing line between norms and rules is not sharply defined in the institutionalist literature. See Robert O. Keohane, *After Hegemony: Cooperation and Discord in the World Political Economy* (Princeton, N.J.: Princeton University Press, 1984), pp. 57–58. For example, one might argue that rules, not just norms, are concerned with rights and obligations. The key point, however, is that for many institutionalists, norms, which are core beliefs about standards of appropriate state behavior, are the foundation on which more specific rules are constructed. This distinction between norms and rules applies in a rather straightforward way in the subsequent discussion. Both collective security and critical theory challenge the realist belief that states behave in a self-interested way, and argue instead for developing norms that require states to act more altruistically. Liberal institutionalism, on the other hand, accepts the realist view that states act on the basis of self-interest, and concentrates on devising rules that facilitate cooperation among states.

18. International organizations are public agencies established through the cooperative efforts of two or more states. These administrative structures have their own budget, personnel, and buildings. John Ruggie defines them as "palpable entities with headquarters and letterheads, voting procedures, and generous pension plans." Ruggie, "Multilateralism," p. 573. Once rules are incorporated into an international organization, "they may seem almost coterminous," even though they are "distinguishable analytically." Keohane, *International Institutions and State Power,* p. 5.

19. Charles Lipson, "Is the Future of Collective Security Like the Past?" in George W. Downs, ed., *Collective Security beyond the Cold War* (Ann Arbor: University of Michigan Press), p. 114.

To answer the three remaining questions about how institutions do or do not work, we must examine the different institutionalist theories separately. However, a brief discussion of realism is in order first.

Realism

Realism paints a rather grim picture of world politics.[20] The international system is portrayed as a brutal arena where states look for opportunities to take advantage of each other, and therefore have little reason to trust each other.[21] Daily life is essentially a struggle for power, where each state strives not only to be the most powerful actor in the system, but also to ensure that no other state achieves that lofty position.

International relations is not a constant state of war, but it is a state of relentless security competition, with the possibility of war always in the background. The intensity of that competition varies from case to case. Although it might seem counterintuitive, states do frequently cooperate in this competitive world. Nevertheless, cooperation among states has its limits, mainly because it is constrained by the dominating logic of security competition, which no amount of cooperation can eliminate. Genuine peace, or a world where states do not compete for power, is not likely, according to realism.

This pessimistic view of how the world works can be derived from realism's five assumptions about the international system. The first is that the international system is anarchic. This does not mean that it is chaotic or riven by disorder.[22] It is easy to draw that conclusion, since realism depicts a world characterized by security competition and war. However, "anarchy" as employed by realists has nothing to do with conflict; rather it is an ordering principle, which says that the system comprises independent political units

---

20. Although realist scholars agree about many aspects of international politics, there are important intellectual disagreements among them. Consider Hans Morgenthau and Kenneth Waltz, probably the two most influential realists over the past fifty years. Morgenthau maintains that states have a will to power, while Waltz begins his theory with the assumption that states merely want to survive and are therefore driven to maximize security. See Hans J. Morgenthau, *Politics Among Nations: The Struggle for Power and Peace*, 5th ed. (New York: Knopf, 1973); and Kenneth N. Waltz, *Theory of International Politics* (Reading, Mass.: Addison-Wesley, 1979). The discussion in this section is based on my own thinking about realism, which is closer to Waltz than to Morgenthau.

21. See Stephen Van Evera, "The Hard Realities of International Politics," *Boston Review*, Vol. 17, No. 6 (November/December 1992), p. 19.

22. See Waltz, *Theory of International Politics*, pp. 88–93. Also see Robert J. Art and Robert Jervis, eds., *International Politics: Anarchy, Force, Imperialism* (Boston: Little, Brown, 1973), part 1; and Helen Milner, "International Theories of Cooperation among Nations: Strengths and Weaknesses," *World Politics*, Vol. 44, No. 3 (April 1992), p. 468.

(states) that have no central authority above them. Sovereignty, in other words, inheres in states, because there is no higher ruling body in the international system. There is no "government over governments."[23]

The second assumption is that states inherently possess some offensive military capability, which gives them the wherewithal to hurt and possibly to destroy each other. States are potentially dangerous to each other. A state's military power is usually identified with the particular weaponry at its disposal, although even if there were no weapons, the individuals of a state could still use their feet and hands to attack the population of another state.

The third assumption is that states can never be certain about the intentions of other states. Specifically, no state can be certain another state will not use its offensive military capability against the first. This is not to say that states necessarily have malign intentions. Another state may be reliably benign, but it is impossible to be certain of that judgment because intentions are impossible to divine with 100 percent certainty. There are many possible causes of aggression, and no state can be sure that another state is not motivated by one of them. Furthermore, intentions can change quickly, so a state's intentions can be benign one day and malign the next. Uncertainty is unavoidable when assessing intentions, which simply means that states can never be sure that other states do not have offensive intentions to go with their offensive military capability.

The fourth assumption is that the most basic motive driving states is survival. States want to maintain their sovereignty. The fifth assumption is that states think strategically about how to survive in the international system. States are instrumentally rational. Nevertheless, they may miscalculate from time to time because they operate in a world of imperfect information, where potential adversaries have incentives to misrepresent their own strength or weakness and to conceal their true aims.

None of these assumptions alone mandates that states will behave competitively. In fact, the fundamental assumption dealing with motives says that states merely aim to survive, which is a defensive goal.[24] When taken together, however, these five assumptions can create incentives for states to think and

---

23. Inis L. Claude, Jr., *Swords Into Plowshares: The Problems and Progress of International Organization*, 4th ed. (New York: Random House, 1971), p. 14.

24. Morgenthau, as emphasized, maintains that states have an innate will to power, and are therefore inherently offensive in their outlook. The argument here is that states begin with a defensive motive, but are forced to think and sometimes act offensively because of the structure of the international system.

sometimes to behave aggressively. Specifically, three main patterns of behavior result.

First, states in the international system fear each other. They regard each other with suspicion, and they worry that war might be in the offing. They anticipate danger. There is little room for trust among states. Although the level of fear varies across time and space, it can never be reduced to a trivial level.[25] The basis of this fear is that in a world where states have the capability to offend against each other, and might have the motive to do so, any state bent on survival must be at least suspicious of other states and reluctant to trust them. Add to this the assumption that there is no central authority that a threatened state can turn to for help, and states have even greater incentive to fear each other. Moreover, there is no mechanism—other than the possible self-interest of third parties—for punishing an aggressor. Because it is often difficult to deter potential aggressors, states have ample reason to take steps to be prepared for war.

The possible consequences of falling victim to aggression further illustrate why fear is a potent force in world politics. States do not compete with each other as if international politics were simply an economic marketplace. Political competition among states is a much more dangerous business than economic intercourse; it can lead to war, and war often means mass killing on the battlefield and even mass murder of civilians. In extreme cases, war can even lead to the total destruction of a state. The horrible consequences of war sometimes cause states to view each other not just as competitors, but as potentially deadly enemies.

Second, each state in the international system aims to guarantee its own survival. Because other states are potential threats, and because there is no higher authority to rescue them when danger arises, states cannot depend on others for their security. Each state tends to see itself as vulnerable and alone, and therefore it aims to provide for its own survival. As Kenneth Waltz puts it, states operate in a "self-help" system. This emphasis on self-help does not preclude states from forming alliances.[26] But alliances are only temporary

---

25. This point is illustrated by the reaction of Britain and France to German reunification at the end of the Cold War. Despite the fact that these three states had been close allies for almost forty-five years, both Britain and France immediately began thinking about the dangers of a united Germany. See David Garnham, "European Defense Cooperation: The 1990s and Beyond," in Dale L. Smith and James Lee Ray, eds., *The 1992 Project and the Future of Integration In Europe* (Armonk, N.Y.: M.E. Sharpe, 1993), pp. 203–205; and Margaret Thatcher, *The Downing Street Years* (New York: HarperCollins, 1993), chaps. 25–26.
26. See Stephen M. Walt, *The Origins of Alliances* (Ithaca, N.Y.: Cornell University Press, 1987).

marriages of convenience, where today's alliance partner might be tomorrow's enemy, and today's enemy might be tomorrow's alliance partner. States operating in a self-help world should always act according to their own self-interest, because it pays to be selfish in a self-help world. This is true in the short term as well as the long term, because if a state loses in the short run, it may not be around for the long haul.

Third, states in the international system aim to maximize their relative power positions over other states.[27] The reason is simple: the greater the military advantage one state has over other states, the more secure it is. Every state would like to be the most formidable military power in the system because this is the best way to guarantee survival in a world that can be very dangerous. This logic creates strong incentives for states to take advantage of one another, including going to war if the circumstances are right and victory seems likely. The aim is to acquire more military power at the expense of potential rivals. The ideal outcome would be to end up as the hegemon in the system. Survival would then be almost guaranteed.

All states are influenced by this logic, which means not only that they look for opportunities to take advantage of one another, but also that they work to insure that other states do not take advantage of them.[28] States are, in other words, both offensively-oriented and defensively-oriented. They think about conquest themselves, and they balance against aggressors; this inexorably leads to a world of constant security competition, with the possibility of war always in the background. Peace, if one defines that concept as a state of tranquility or mutual concord, is not likely to break out in this world.

COOPERATION IN A REALIST WORLD

Although realism envisions a world that is fundamentally competitive, cooperation between states does occur. It is sometimes difficult to achieve, however,

---

27. There is disagreement among realists on this point. Some realists argue that states are principally interested in maintaining the existing balance of power, not maximizing relative power. For examples of this "defensive realism," which contrasts with my "offensive realism," see: Joseph M. Grieco, "Anarchy and the Limits of Cooperation: A Realist Critique of the Newest Liberal Institutionalism," *International Organization*, Vol. 42, No. 3 (Summer 1988), pp. 498–500; Jack L. Snyder, *Myths of Empire: Domestic Politics and International Ambition* (Ithaca, N.Y.: Cornell University Press, 1991), pp. 10–13; and Waltz, *Theory of International Politics*, pp. 126–127. Also see Fareed Zakaria, "Realism and Domestic Politics: A Review Essay," *International Security*, Vol. 17, No. 1 (Summer 1992), pp. 190–196. Morgenthau is also an offensive realist. This disagreement notwithstanding, all realists do believe that states care greatly about the relative balance of power.
28. See Walt, *Origins of Alliances*.

and always difficult to sustain. Two factors inhibit cooperation: relative-gains considerations, and concern about cheating.[29]

States contemplating cooperation must consider how the profits or gains will be distributed among them. They can think about the division in two different ways. They can think in terms of absolute gains, which means each side focuses on maximizing its own profit, and cares little about how much the other side gains or loses in the deal. Each side cares about the other only to the extent that the other side's behavior affects its own prospects for achieving maximum profits. Alternately, states can think in terms of relative gains, which means each side not only considers its individual gain, but also how well it does compared to the other side.

Because states in a realist world are concerned about the balance of power, they must be motivated primarily by relative gains concerns when considering cooperation. While each state wants to maximize its absolute gains, it is more important to make sure that it does better, or at least no worse, than the other state in any agreement. However, cooperation is more difficult to achieve when states are attuned to relative-gains logic, rather than absolute-gains logic. This is because states concerned about absolute gains need only make sure that the pie is expanding and that they are getting at least some portion of the increase, while states that worry about relative gains must care also about how the pie is divided, which complicates cooperative efforts.

Concerns about cheating also hinder cooperation. States are often reluctant to enter into cooperative agreements for fear that the other side will cheat on the agreement and gain a relative advantage. There is a "special peril of defection" in the military realm, because the nature of military weaponry allows for rapid shifts in the balance of power. Such a development could create a window of opportunity for the cheating state to inflict a decisive defeat on the victim state.[30]

These barriers to cooperation notwithstanding, states do cooperate in a realist world. For example, balance-of-power logic often causes states to form alliances and cooperate against common enemies. States sometimes cooperate to gang up on a third state, as the Germans and the Soviets did against Poland in 1939.[31] Rivals as well as allies cooperate. After all, deals can be struck that roughly reflect the distribution of power, and satisfy concerns about cheating.

---

29. See Grieco, "Anarchy and the Limits of Cooperation."
30. Lipson, "International Cooperation," p. 14.
31. Randall L. Schweller, "Bandwagoning for Profit: Bringing the Revisionist State Back In," *International Security*, Vol. 19, No. 1 (Summer 1994), pp. 72–107.

The various arms control agreements signed by the superpowers during the Cold War illustrate this point.

The bottom line, however, is that cooperation takes place in a world that is competitive at its core—one where states have powerful incentives to take advantage of other states. This point is graphically highlighted by European politics in the forty years before World War I. There was much cooperation among the great powers during this period, but that did not stop them from going to war in 1914.[32]

INSTITUTIONS IN A REALIST WORLD

Realists also recognize that states sometimes operate through institutions. However, they believe that those rules reflect state calculations of self-interest based primarily on the international distribution of power. The most powerful states in the system create and shape institutions so that they can maintain their share of world power, or even increase it. In this view, institutions are essentially "arenas for acting out power relationships."[33] For realists, the causes of war and peace are mainly a function of the balance of power, and institutions largely mirror the distribution of power in the system. In short, the balance of power is the independent variable that explains war; institutions are merely an intervening variable in the process.

NATO provides a good example of realist thinking about institutions. NATO is an institution, and it certainly played a role in preventing World War III and helping the West win the Cold War. Nevertheless, NATO was basically a manifestation of the bipolar distribution of power in Europe during the Cold War, and it was that balance of power, not NATO *per se,* that provided the key to maintaining stability on the continent. NATO was essentially an American tool for managing power in the face of the Soviet threat. Now, with the collapse of the Soviet Union, realists argue that NATO must either disappear or reconstitute itself on the basis of the new distribution of power in Europe.[34] NATO cannot remain as it was during the Cold War.

---

32. See John Maynard Keynes, *The Economic Consequences of the Peace* (New York: Penguin Books, 1988), chap. 2; and J.M. Roberts, *Europe, 1880–1945* (London: Longman, 1970), pp. 239–241. There was also significant cooperation between the United States and the Soviet Union during World War II, but that cooperation did not prevent the outbreak of the Cold War shortly after Germany and Japan were defeated.
33. Tony Evans and Peter Wilson, "Regime Theory and the English School of International Relations: A Comparison," *Millennium: Journal of International Studies,* Vol. 21, No. 3 (Winter 1992), p. 330.
34. See Gunther Hellmann and Reinhard Wolf, "Neorealism, Neoliberal Institutionalism, and the Future of NATO," *Security Studies,* Vol. 3, No. 1 (Autumn 1993), pp. 3–43.

Varieties of Institutionalist Theories

There are three institutionalist theories, and each offers a different argument about how institutions push states away from war and help foster stability.[35] Liberal institutionalism is the least ambitious of the three theories. It does not directly address the important question of how to prevent war, but focuses instead on explaining why economic and environmental cooperation among states is more likely than realists recognize. Increased cooperation in those realms is presumed to reduce the likelihood of war, although liberal institutionalists do not explain how. The theory is predicated on the belief that cheating is the main inhibitor of international cooperation, and that institutions provide the key to overcoming that problem. The aim is to create rules that constrain states, but not to challenge the fundamental realist claim that states are self-interested actors.

Collective security directly confronts the issue of how to prevent war. The theory starts with the assumption that force will continue to matter in world politics, and that states will have to guard against potential aggressors. However, the threat of war can be greatly reduced, according to the theory, by challenging realist thinking about state behavior, and substituting in its place three anti-realist norms. First, states should reject the idea of using force to change the status quo. Second, to deal with states that violate that norm and threaten (or start) a war, responsible states must not act on the basis of their own narrow self-interest. Rather, they must suppress the temptation to respond in whatever way would maximize their individual gains, and instead automatically join together to present the aggressor with the threat of overwhelming force. Third, states must trust each other to renounce aggression and to mean that renunciation. They must also be confident that other states will come to their rescue, should they become the target of aggression.

Critical theory is the most ambitious of the theories, as its ultimate aim is to transform the fundamental nature of international politics and to create a world where there is not just increased cooperation among states, but the possibility of genuine peace. Like collective security, but unlike liberal institutionalism,

---

35. Despite these differences among institutionalist theories, proponents of each theory occasionally make favorable reference to the other theories, and thus seem to recognize that all three theories are part of an institutionalist body of literature that takes anti-realism as its main point of reference. See, for example: Charles A. Kupchan and Clifford A. Kupchan, "Concerts, Collective Security, and the Future of Europe," *International Security*, Vol. 16, No. 1 (Summer 1991), pp. 114–161; and Ruggie, "Multilateralism," pp. 561–598.

critical theory directly challenges realist thinking about the self-interested behavior of states. The theory is predicated on the assumption that ideas and
discourse—how we think and talk about international politics—are the driving
forces behind state behavior. It utterly rejects realism's claim that state behavior
is largely a function of the given structure of the external world. For critical
theorists, ideas shape the material world in important ways, and thus the way
to revolutionize international politics is to change drastically the way individuals think and talk about world politics. Intellectuals, especially the critical
theorists themselves, are believed to play a key role in that process.

LIBERAL INSTITUTIONALISM

Liberal institutionalism does not directly address the question of whether
institutions cause peace, but instead focuses on the less ambitious goal of
explaining cooperation in cases where state interests are not fundamentally
opposed.[36] Specifically, the theory looks at cases where states are having
difficulty cooperating because they have "mixed" interests; in other words,
each side has incentives both to cooperate and not to cooperate.[37] Each side
can benefit from cooperation, however, which liberal institutionalists define as
"goal-directed behavior that entails mutual policy adjustments so that all sides
end up better off than they would otherwise be."[38] The theory is of little
relevance in situations where states' interests are fundamentally conflictual and
neither side thinks it has much to gain from cooperation. In these circumstances, states aim to gain advantage over each other. They think in terms of
winning and losing, and this invariably leads to intense security competition,
and sometimes war. But liberal institutionalism does not deal directly with
these situations, and thus says little about how to resolve or even ameliorate
them.

---

36. Among the key liberal institutionalist works are: Robert Axelrod and Robert O. Keohane,
"Achieving Cooperation under Anarchy: Strategies and Institutions," *World Politics,* Vol. 38, No. 1
(October 1985), pp. 226–254; Keohane, *After Hegemony;* Keohane, "International Institutions: Two
Approaches," pp. 379–396; Keohane, *International Institutions and State Power,* chap. 1; Charles
Lipson, "International Cooperation in Economic and Security Affairs," *World Politics,* Vol. 37, No.
1 (October 1984), pp. 1–23; Lisa L. Martin, "Institutions and Cooperation: Sanctions During the
Falkland Islands Conflict," *International Security,* Vol. 16, No. 4 (Spring 1992), pp. 143–178; Lisa L.
Martin, *Coercive Cooperation: Explaining Multilateral Economic Sanctions* (Princeton, N.J.: Princeton
University Press, 1992); Kenneth A. Oye, "Explaining Cooperation Under Anarchy: Hypotheses
and Strategies," *World Politics,* Vol. 38, No. 1 (October 1985), pp. 1–24; and Stein, *Why Nations
Cooperate.*
37. Stein, *Why Nations Cooperate,* chap. 2. Also see Keohane, *After Hegemony,* pp. 6–7, 12–13, 67–69.
38. Milner, "International Theories of Cooperation," p. 468.

Therefore, the theory largely ignores security issues and concentrates instead on economic and, to a lesser extent, environmental issues.[39] In fact, the theory is built on the assumption that international politics can be divided into two realms—security and political economy—and that liberal institutionalism mainly applies to the latter, but not the former. This theme is clearly articulated by Charles Lipson, who writes that "significantly different institutional arrangements are associated with international economic and security issues."[40] Moreover, the likelihood of cooperation is markedly different within these two realms: when economic relations are at stake, "cooperation can be sustained among several self-interested states," whereas the prospects for cooperation are "more impoverished . . . in security affairs."[41] Thus, the theory's proponents pay little attention to the security realm, where questions about war and peace are of central importance.

Nevertheless, there are good reasons to examine liberal institutionalism closely. Liberal institutionalists sometimes assert that institutions are an important cause of international stability. Moreover, one might argue that if the theory shows a strong causal connection between institutions and economic cooperation, it would be relatively easy to take the next step and link cooperation with peace.[42] Some proponents of the theory maintain that institutions contribute to international stability; this suggests that they believe it is easy to connect cooperation and stability.[43] I doubt this claim, mainly because proponents of the theory define cooperation so narrowly as to avoid military issues. Let us assume, however, that liberal institutionalists are attempting to take a

---

39. For examples of the theory at work in the environmental realm, see Peter M. Haas, Robert O. Keohane, and Marc A. Levy, eds., *Institutions for the Earth: Sources of Effective International Environmental Protection* (Cambridge, Mass.: MIT Press, 1993), especially chaps. 1 and 9. Some of the most important work on institutions and the environment has been done by Oran Young. See, for example, Young, *International Cooperation*. The rest of my discussion concentrates on economic, not environmental issues, for conciseness, and also because the key theoretical works in the liberal institutionalist literature focus on economic rather than environmental matters.

40. Lipson, "International Cooperation," pp. 2, 12. Also see Axelrod and Keohane, "Achieving Cooperation Under Anarchy," pp. 232–233; and Keohane, *After Hegemony*, pp. 39–41.

41. Lipson, "International Cooperation," p. 18.

42. I have suggested a possible line of argument in John J. Mearsheimer, "Back to the Future: Instability in Europe After the Cold War," *International Security*, Vol. 15, No. 1 (Summer 1990), pp. 42–44. Also, Charles Glaser makes the connection between cooperation and peace in "Realists as Optimists: Cooperation as Self-Help," *International Security*, Vol. 19, No. 3 (Winter 1994/95), pp. 50–90.

43. Liberal institutionalists assume that cooperation is a positive goal, although they recognize it has a downside as well. See Keohane, *After Hegemony*, pp. 10–11, 247–257; and Keohane, "International Institutions: Two Approaches," p. 393. The virtues and vices of cooperation are not explored in any detail in the liberal institutionalist literature.

giant step toward developing a theory that explains how institutions push states away from war.

CAUSAL LOGIC. Liberal institutionalists claim to accept realism's root assumptions while arguing that cooperation is nevertheless easier to achieve than realists recognize. Robert Keohane, for example, writes in *After Hegemony* that he is "adopting the realist model of rational egoism." He continues: "I propose to show, on the basis of their own assumptions, that the characteristic pessimism of realism does not necessarily follow. I seek to demonstrate that realist assumptions about world politics are consistent with the formation of institutionalized arrangements . . . which promote cooperation."[44] In particular, liberal institutionalists emphasize that states "dwell in perpetual anarchy," and must therefore act as rational egoists in what is a self-help world.[45]

According to liberal institutionalists, the principal obstacle to cooperation among states with mutual interests is the threat of cheating.[46] The famous "prisoners' dilemma," which is the analytical centerpiece of most of the liberal institutionalist literature, captures the essence of the problem that states must solve to achieve cooperation.[47] Each of two states can either cheat or cooperate with the other. Each side wants to maximize its own gain, but does not care about the size of the other side's gain; each side cares about the other side only so far as the other side's chosen strategy affects its own prospects for maximizing gain. The most attractive strategy for each state is to cheat and hope the other state pursues a cooperative strategy. In other words, a state's ideal outcome is to "sucker" the other side into thinking it is going to cooperate, and then cheat. But both sides understand this logic, and therefore both sides will try to cheat the other. Consequently, both sides will end up worse off than if they had cooperated, since mutual cheating leads to the worst possible outcome. Even though mutual cooperation is not as attractive as suckering the other side, it is certainly better than the outcome when both sides cheat.

---

44. Keohane, *After Hegemony*, p. 67; also see p. 29. Similarly, Arthur Stein claims that, "Despite the different conclusions that they draw about the cooperative or conflictual nature of international politics, realism and liberalism share core assumptions." Stein, *Why Nations Cooperate*, p. 8.
45. Oye, "Explaining Cooperation Under Anarchy," p. 1.
46. Cheating is basically a "breach of promise." Oye, "Explaining Cooperation Under Anarchy," p. 1. It usually implies unobserved non-compliance, although there can be observed cheating as well. Defection is a synonym for cheating in the institutionalist literature.
47. The centrality of the prisoners' dilemma and cheating to the liberal institutionalist literature is clearly reflected in virtually all the works cited in footnote 36. As Helen Milner notes in her review essay on this literature: "The focus is primarily on the role of regimes [institutions] in solving the defection [cheating] problem." Milner, "International Theories of Cooperation," p. 475.

The key to solving this dilemma is for each side to convince the other that they have a collective interest in making what appear to be short-term sacrifices (the gain that might result from successful cheating) for the sake of long-term benefits (the substantial payoff from mutual long-term cooperation). This means convincing states to accept the second-best outcome, which is mutual collaboration. The principal obstacle to reaching this cooperative outcome will be fear of getting suckered, should the other side cheat. This, in a nutshell, is the problem that institutions must solve.

To deal with this problem of "political market failure," institutions must deter cheaters and protect victims.[48] Three messages must be sent to potential cheaters: you will be caught, you will be punished immediately, and you will jeopardize future cooperative efforts. Potential victims, on the other hand, need early warning of cheating to avoid serious injury, and need the means to punish cheaters.

Liberal institutionalists do not aim to deal with cheaters and victims by changing fundamental norms of state behavior. Nor do they suggest transforming the anarchical nature of the international system. They accept the assumption that states operate in an anarchic environment and behave in a self-interested manner.[49] In this regard, their approach is less ambitious than collective security and critical theory, which aim to alter important international norms. Liberal institutionalists instead concentrate on showing how rules can work to counter the cheating problem, even while states seek to maximize their own welfare. They argue that institutions can change a state's calculations about how to maximize gains. Specifically, rules can get states to make the short-term sacrifices needed to resolve the prisoners' dilemma and thus to realize long-term gains. Institutions, in short, can produce cooperation.

Rules can ideally be employed to make four major changes in "the contractual environment."[50] First, rules can increase the number of transactions between particular states over time.[51] This *institutionalized iteration* discourages

---

48. The phrase is from Keohane, *After Hegemony*, p. 85.
49. Kenneth Oye, for example, writes in the introduction to an issue of *World Politics* containing a number of liberal institutionalist essays: "Our focus is on non-altruistic cooperation among states dwelling in international anarchy." Oye, "Explaining Cooperation Under Anarchy," p. 2. Also see Keohane, "International Institutions: Two Approaches," pp. 380–381; and Keohane, *International Institutions and State Power*, p. 3.
50. Haas, Keohane, and Levy, *Institutions for the Earth*, p. 11. For general discussions of how rules work, which inform my subsequent discussion of the matter, see Keohane, *After Hegemony*, chaps. 5–6; Martin, "Institutions and Cooperation," pp. 143–178; and Milner, "International Theories of Cooperation," pp. 474–478.
51. See Axelrod and Keohane, "Achieving Cooperation Under Anarchy," pp. 248–250; Lipson, "International Cooperation," pp. 4–18.

cheating in three ways. It raises the costs of cheating by creating the prospect of future gains through cooperation, thereby invoking "the shadow of the future" to deter cheating today. A state caught cheating would jeopardize its prospects of benefiting from future cooperation, since the victim would probably retaliate. In addition, iteration gives the victim the opportunity to pay back the cheater: it allows for reciprocation, the tit-for-tat strategy, which works to punish cheaters and not allow them to get away with their transgression. Finally, it rewards states that develop a reputation for faithful adherence to agreements, and punishes states that acquire a reputation for cheating.[52]

Second, rules can tie together interactions between states in different issue areas. *Issue-linkage* aims to create greater interdependence between states, who will then be reluctant to cheat in one issue area for fear that the victim—and perhaps other states as well—will retaliate in another issue area. It discourages cheating in much the same way as iteration: it raises the costs of cheating and provides a way for the victim to retaliate against the cheater.

Third, a structure of rules can increase the amount of *information* available to participants in cooperative agreements so that close monitoring is possible. Raising the level of information discourages cheating in two ways: it increases the likelihood that cheaters will be caught, and more importantly, it provides victims with early warning of cheating, thereby enabling them to take protective measures before they are badly hurt.

Fourth, rules can reduce the *transaction costs* of individual agreements.[53] When institutions perform the tasks described above, states can devote less effort to negotiating and monitoring cooperative agreements, and to hedging against possible defections. By increasing the efficiency of international cooperation, institutions make it more profitable and thus more attractive for self-interested states.

Liberal institutionalism is generally thought to be of limited utility in the security realm, because fear of cheating is considered a much greater obstacle to cooperation when military issues are at stake.[54] There is the constant threat that betrayal will result in a devastating military defeat. This threat of "swift, decisive defection" is simply not present when dealing with international economics. Given that "the costs of betrayal" are potentially much graver in the military than the economic sphere, states will be very reluctant to accept

---

52. Lipson, "International Cooperation," p. 5.
53. See Keohane, *After Hegemony*, pp. 89–92.
54. This point is clearly articulated in Lipson, "International Cooperation," especially pp. 12–18. The subsequent quotations in this paragraph are from ibid. Also see Axelrod and Keohane, 'Achieving Cooperation Under Anarchy," pp. 232–233.

the "one step backward, two steps forward" logic which underpins the tit-for-tat strategy of conditional cooperation. One step backward in the security realm might mean destruction, in which case there will be no next step—backward or forward.[55]

FLAWS IN THE CAUSAL LOGIC. There is an important theoretical failing in the liberal institutionalist logic, even as it applies to economic issues. The theory is correct as far as it goes: cheating can be a serious barrier to cooperation. It ignores, however, the other major obstacle to cooperation: relative-gains concerns. As Joseph Grieco has shown, liberal institutionalists assume that states are not concerned about relative gains, but focus exclusively on absolute gains.[56] Keohane acknowledged this problem in 1993: "Grieco has made a significant contribution by focusing attention on the issue of relative gains, a subject that has been underemphasized, especially by liberal or neoliberal commentators on the world economy."[57]

This oversight is revealed by the assumed order of preference in the prisoners' dilemma game: each state cares about how its opponent's strategy will affect its own (absolute) gains, but not about how much one side gains relative to the other. In other words, each side simply wants to get the best deal for itself, and does not pay attention to how well the other side fares in the process.[58] Nevertheless, liberal institutionalists cannot ignore relative-gains

---

55. See Roger B. Parks, "What if 'Fools Die'? A Comment on Axelrod," Letter to *American Political Science Review*, Vol. 79, No. 4 (December 1985), pp. 1173–1174.
56. See Grieco, "Anarchy and the Limits of Cooperation." Other works by Grieco bearing on the subject include: Joseph M. Grieco, "Realist Theory and the Problem of International Cooperation: Analysis with an Amended Prisoner's Dilemma Model," *The Journal of Politics*, Vol. 50, No. 3 (August 1988), pp. 600–624; Grieco, *Cooperation among Nations: Europe, America, and Non-Tariff Barriers to Trade* (Ithaca, N.Y.: Cornell University Press, 1990); and Grieco, "Understanding the Problem of International Cooperation: The Limits of Neoliberal Institutionalism and the Future of Realist Theory," in Baldwin, *Neorealism and Neoliberalism*, pp. 301–338. The telling effect of Grieco's criticism is reflected in ibid., which is essentially organized around the relative gains vs. absolute gains debate, an issue given little attention before Grieco raised it in his widely cited 1988 article. The matter was briefly discussed by two other scholars before Grieco. See Joanne Gowa, "Anarchy, Egoism, and Third Images: *The Evolution of Cooperation* and International Relations," *International Organization*, Vol. 40, No. 1 (Winter 1986), pp. 172–179; and Oran R. Young, "International Regimes: Toward a New Theory of Institutions," *World Politics*, Vol. 39, No. 1 (October 1986), pp. 118–119.
57. Robert O. Keohane, "Institutional Theory and the Realist Challenge," in Baldwin, *Neorealism and Neoliberalism*, p. 283. When liberal institutionalists developed their theory in the mid-1980s, they did not explicitly assume that states pursue absolute gains. There is actually little evidence that they thought much about the distinction between relative gains and absolute gains. However, the assumption that states pursue absolute but not relative gains is implicit in their writings.
58. Lipson writes: "The Prisoner's Dilemma, in its simplest form, involves two players. Each is assumed to be a self-interested, self-reliant maximizer of his own utility, an assumption that clearly parallels the Realist conception of sovereign states in international politics." Lipson, "International

considerations, because they assume that states are self-interested actors in an anarchic system, and they recognize that military power matters to states. A theory that explicitly accepts realism's core assumptions—and liberal institutionalism does that—must confront the issue of relative gains if it hopes to develop a sound explanation for why states cooperate.

One might expect liberal institutionalists to offer the counterargument that relative-gains logic applies only to the security realm, while absolute-gains logic applies to the economic realm. Given that they are mainly concerned with explaining economic and environmental cooperation, leaving relative-gains concerns out of the theory does not matter.

There are two problems with this argument. First, if cheating were the only significant obstacle to cooperation, liberal institutionalists could argue that their theory applies to the economic, but not the military realm. In fact, they do make that argument. However, once relative-gains considerations are factored into the equation, it becomes impossible to maintain the neat dividing line between economic and military issues, mainly because military might is significantly dependent on economic might. The relative size of a state's economy has profound consequences for its standing in the international balance of military power. Therefore, relative-gains concerns must be taken into account for security reasons when looking at the economic as well as military domain. The neat dividing line that liberal institutionalists employ to specify when their theory applies has little utility when one accepts that states worry about relative gains.[59]

Second, there are non-realist (i.e., non-security) logics that might explain why states worry about relative gains. Strategic trade theory, for example, provides a straightforward economic logic for why states should care about relative gains.[60] It argues that states should help their own firms gain comparative advantage over the firms of rival states, because that is the best way to insure

---

Cooperation," p. 2. Realists, however, do not accept this conception of international politics and, not surprisingly, have questioned the relevance of the prisoners' dilemma (at least in its common form) for explaining much of international relations. See Gowa, "Anarchy, Egoism, and Third Images"; Grieco, "Realist Theory and the Problem of International Cooperation"; and Stephen D. Krasner, "Global Communications and National Power: Life on the Pareto Frontier," *World Politics*, Vol. 43, No. 3 (April 1991), pp. 336–366.

59. My thinking on this matter has been markedly influenced by Sean Lynn-Jones, in his June 19, 1994, correspondence with me.

60. For a short discussion of strategic trade theory, see Robert Gilpin, *The Political Economy of International Relations* (Princeton, N.J.: Princeton University Press, 1987), pp. 215–221. The most commonly cited reference on the subject is Paul R. Krugman, ed., *Strategic Trade Policy and the New International Economics* (Cambridge, Mass.: MIT Press, 1986).

national economic prosperity. There is also a psychological logic, which portrays individuals as caring about how well they do (or their state does) in a cooperative agreement, not for material reasons, but because it is human nature to compare one's progress with that of others.[61]

Another possible liberal institutionalist counterargument is that solving the cheating problem renders the relative-gains problem irrelevant. If states cannot cheat each other, they need not fear each other, and therefore, states would not have to worry about relative power. The problem with this argument, however, is that even if the cheating problem were solved, states would still have to worry about relative gains because gaps in gains can be translated into military advantage that can be used for coercion or aggression. And in the international system, states sometimes have conflicting interests that lead to aggression.

There is also empirical evidence that relative-gains considerations mattered during the Cold War even in economic relations among the advanced industrialized democracies in the Organization for Economic Cooperation and Development (OECD). One would not expect realist logic about relative gains to be influential in this case: the United States was a superpower with little to fear militarily from the other OECD states, and those states were unlikely to use a relative-gains advantage to threaten the United States.[62] Furthermore, the OECD states were important American allies during the Cold War, and thus the United States benefited strategically when they gained substantially in size and strength.

Nonetheless, relative gains appear to have mattered in economic relations among the advanced industrial states. Consider three prominent studies. Stephen Krasner considered efforts at cooperation in different sectors of the international communications industry. He found that states were remarkably unconcerned about cheating but deeply worried about relative gains, which led him to conclude that liberal institutionalism "is not relevant for global communications." Grieco examined American and EC efforts to implement,

---

61. See Robert Axelrod, *The Evolution of Cooperation* (New York: Basic Books, 1984), pp. 110–113.
62. Grieco maintains in *Cooperation among Nations* that realist logic should apply here. Robert Powell, however, points out that "in the context of negotiations between the European Community and the United States . . . it is difficult to attribute any concern for relative gains to the effects that a relative loss may have on the probability of survival." Robert Powell, "Absolute and Relative Gains in International Relations Theory," *American Political Science Review,* Vol. 85, No. 4 (December 1991), p. 1319, footnote 26. I agree with Powell. It is clear from Grieco's response to Powell that Grieco includes non-military logics like strategic trade theory in the realist tent, whereas Powell and I do not. See Grieco's contribution to "The Relative-Gains Problem for International Relations," *American Political Science Review,* Vol. 87, No. 3 (September 1993), pp. 733–735.

under the auspices of GATT, a number of agreements relating to non-tariff barriers to trade. He found that the level of success was not a function of concerns about cheating but was influenced primarily by concern about the distribution of gains. Similarly, Michael Mastanduno found that concern about relative gains, not about cheating, was an important factor in shaping American policy towards Japan in three cases: the FSX fighter aircraft, satellites, and high-definition television.[63]

I am not suggesting that relative-gains considerations make cooperation impossible; my point is simply that they can pose a serious impediment to cooperation and must therefore be taken into account when developing a theory of cooperation among states. This point is apparently now recognized by liberal institutionalists. Keohane, for example, acknowledges that he "did make a major mistake by underemphasizing distributive issues and the complexities they create for international cooperation."[64]

CAN LIBERAL INSTITUTIONALISM BE REPAIRED? Liberal institutionalists must address two questions if they are to repair their theory. First, can institutions facilitate cooperation when states seriously care about relative gains, or do institutions only matter when states can ignore relative-gains considerations and focus instead on absolute gains? I find no evidence that liberal institutionalists believe that institutions facilitate cooperation when states care deeply about relative gains. They apparently concede that their theory only applies when relative-gains considerations matter little or hardly at all.[65] Thus the second question: when do states not worry about relative gains? The answer to this question would ultimately define the realm in which liberal institutionalism applies.

Liberal institutionalists have not addressed this important question in a systematic fashion, so any assessment of their efforts to repair the theory must be preliminary. What exists are a lengthy response by Keohane to Grieco's original work on relative gains, and two studies responding to Grieco's writ-

---

63. Krasner, "Global Communications and National Power," pp. 336–366; Grieco, *Cooperation among Nations;* and Michael Mastanduno, "Do Relative Gains Matter? America's Response to Japanese Industrial Policy," *International Security*, Vol. 16, No. 1 (Summer 1991), pp. 73–113. Also see Jonathan B. Tucker, "Partners and Rivals: A Model of International Collaboration in Advanced Technology," *International Organization*, Vol. 45, No. 1 (Winter 1991), pp. 83–120.
64. Keohane, "Institutional Theory and the Realist Challenge," p. 292.
65. For example, Keohane wrote after becoming aware of Grieco's argument about relative gains: "Under specified conditions—where mutual interests are low and relative gains are therefore particularly important to states—neoliberal theory expects neorealism to explain elements of state behavior." Keohane, *International Institutions and State Power*, pp. 15–16.

ings by Robert Powell and Duncan Snidal, which Keohane and other liberal institutionalists point to as exemplars of how to think about the relative-gains problem.[66]

Powell and Snidal offer different arguments about when relative-gains considerations are slight. Nevertheless, both are essentially realist arguments.[67] Neither study discusses how institutions might facilitate cooperation, and both explanations are built around familiar realist concepts.

At the root of Powell's argument is the well-known offense-defense balance made famous by Robert Jervis, George Quester, Jack Snyder, and Stephen Van Evera.[68] Powell maintains that relative-gains considerations matter little, and that states act in accordance with liberal institutionalism when the threat of aggressive war is low and "the use of force is no longer at issue."[69] That situation obtains when the cost of aggression is high, which is, in turn, a function of the "constraints imposed by the underlying technology of war."[70] In other words, when the prevailing military weaponry favors the offense, then the cost of war is low, and relative-gains considerations will be intense. Institutions can do little to facilitate cooperation in such circumstances. However, when defensive technology dominates, the cost of initiating aggression is high and the relative-gains problem is subdued, which allows institutions to cause cooperation.

Snidal maintains that relative-gains concerns might not matter much to states even if they face a serious threat of war. The root concept in his argument is

---

66. Keohane, "Institutional Theory and the Realist Challenge," pp. 269–300; Powell, "Absolute and Relative Gains," pp. 1303–1320; and Duncan Snidal, "Relative Gains and the Pattern of International Cooperation," *American Political Science Review*, Vol. 85, No. 3 (September 1991), pp. 701–726. Also see Powell, "Anarchy in International Relations Theory: The Neorealist-Neoliberal Debate," *International Organization*, Vol. 48, No. 2 (Spring 1994), pp. 313–344; Snidal, "International Cooperation among Relative Gains Maximizers," *International Studies Quarterly*, Vol. 35, No. 4 (December 1991), pp. 387–402; and Powell and Snidal's contributions to "The Relative-Gains Problem for International Cooperation," pp. 735–742.

67. On this point, see Sean Lynn-Jones, "Comments on Grieco, 'Realist Theory and the Relative Gains Problem for International Cooperation: Developments in the Debate and the Prospects for Future Research'," unpublished memorandum, December 10, 1992.

68. Robert Jervis, "Cooperation under the Security Dilemma," *World Politics*, Vol. 30, No. 2 (January 1978), pp. 167–214; George H. Quester, *Offense and Defense in the International System* (New York: John Wiley, 1977); Jack Snyder, *The Ideology of the Offensive: Military Decision Making and the Disasters of 1914* (Ithaca, N.Y.: Cornell University Press, 1984); and Stephen Van Evera, "The Cult of the Offensive and the Origins of the First World War," *International Security*, Vol. 9, No. 1 (Summer 1984), pp. 58–107.

69. Powell, "Absolute and Relative Gains," p. 1314; also see p. 1311.

70. Ibid., p. 1312. Powell does not use the term "offense-defense" balance in his article.

the distribution of power in the international system.[71] Specifically, he maintains that in a multipolar system where more than a small number of states have roughly equal power, states will not worry much about relative gains. Increasing the number of states in the system decreases concern for relative gains. "The reason is that more actors enhance the possibilities of protecting oneself through forming coalitions; and, generally, the less well united one's potential enemies, the safer one is."[72] However, he concedes that "the relative gains hypothesis . . . has important consequences for two-actor situations and, where there are small numbers or important asymmetries among larger numbers, it may modify conclusions obtained from the absolute gains model."[73]

I draw three conclusions from this discussion of the liberal institutionalists' efforts to deal with the relative-gains problem. First, even if one accepts Powell and Snidal's arguments about when states largely ignore relative-gains concerns, those conditions are rather uncommon in the real world. Powell would look for a world where defensive military technologies dominate. However, it is very difficult to distinguish between offensive and defensive weapons, and Powell provides no help on this point.[74] Nuclear weapons are an exception; they are defensive weapons in situations of mutual assured destruction.[75] Still, the presence of massive numbers of nuclear weapons in the arsenals of the

---

71. Although Snidal's basic arguments about distribution of power fit squarely in the realist tradition (in fact, Grieco made them in abbreviated form in "Anarchy and the Limits of Cooperation," p. 506), the formal model he develops rests on the non-realist assumption that "gains from cooperation are proportional to the size of the involved states and are shared equally between them." Snidal, "Relative Gains," p. 715. This assumption essentially eliminates the possibility of gaps in gains and thus erases the relative-gains problem. For discussion of this matter, see Grieco's contribution to "The Relative-Gains Problem for International Cooperation," pp. 729–733.
72. Snidal, "Relative Gains," p. 716.
73. Ibid., p. 702.
74. There is general agreement that defensive weapons make conquest difficult and costly, while offensive weapons make conquest cheap and easy. However, there is no recognized set of criteria for assigning specific weapons either offensive or defensive status. See Marion Boggs, *Attempts to Define and Limit "Aggressive" Armament in Diplomacy and Strategy* (Columbia: University of Missouri, 1941); Jack Levy, "The Offensive/Defensive Balance of Military Technology: A Theoretical and Historical Analysis," *International Studies Quarterly*, Vol. 28, No. 2 (June 1984), pp. 219–238; John J. Mearsheimer, *Conventional Deterrence* (Ithaca, N.Y.: Cornell University Press, 1983), pp. 25–27; and Jonathan Shimshoni, "Technology, Military Advantage, and World War I: A Case for Military Entrepreneurship," *International Security*, Vol. 15, No. 3 (Winter 1990/1991), pp. 187–215.
75. See Shai Feldman, *Israeli Nuclear Deterrence: A Strategy for the 1980s* (New York: Columbia University Press, 1982), pp. 45–49; Charles L. Glaser, *Analyzing Strategic Nuclear Policy* (Princeton, N.J.: Princeton University Press, 1990); Jervis, "Cooperation under the Security Dilemma"; and Stephen Van Evera, *Causes of War*, Vol. II: *National Misperception and the Origins of War*, forthcoming), chap. 13.

superpowers during the Cold War did not stop them from engaging in an intense security competition where relative-gains considerations mattered greatly. Very importantly, Powell provides no historical examples to illustrate his central argument. Snidal would look for a multipolar world with large numbers of roughly equal-sized great powers. However, historically we find multipolar systems with small numbers of great powers—usually five or six—and very often significant power asymmetries within them. Snidal offers no historical examples of multipolar systems in which the great powers largely ignored relative-gains considerations.[76]

Second, liberal institutionalism itself has little new to say about when states worry about relative gains. Proponents of the theory have instead chosen to rely on two realist explanations to answer that question: the offense-defense balance and the distribution of power in the system. Thus, liberal institutionalism can hardly be called a theoretical alternative to realism, but instead should be seen as subordinate to it.[77]

Third, even in circumstances where realist logic about relative gains does not apply, non-military logics like strategic trade theory might cause states to think in terms of relative gains. Liberal institutionalist theory should directly confront those logics.

PROBLEMS WITH THE EMPIRICAL RECORD.   Although there is much evidence of cooperation among states, this alone does not constitute support for liberal institutionalism. What is needed is evidence of cooperation that would not have occurred in the absence of institutions because of fear of cheating, or its actual presence. But scholars have provided little evidence of cooperation of that sort, nor of cooperation failing because of cheating. Moreover, as discussed above, there is considerable evidence that states worry much about relative gains not only in security matters, but in the economic realm as well.

---

76. Keohane actually discusses the prospects for stability in post–Cold War Europe in his response to Grieco; see Keohane, "Institutional Theory and the Realist Challenge," pp. 284–291. Surprisingly, his optimistic assessment pays no attention to either Powell or Snidal's arguments, although earlier in that response, he relies on their arguments to "delimit the scope of both realist and institutionalist arguments." See ibid., p. 276.

77. Liberal institutionalists have not always been clear about the relationship between their theory and realism. For example, Keohane makes the modest claim in *After Hegemony* (p. 14) that his theory is a "modification of Realism. Realist theories. . . . need to be supplemented, though not replaced." He made a somewhat bolder claim a few years later, writing that, "despite [certain] affinities with neorealism, neoliberal institutionalism should be regarded as a distinct school of thought." Keohane, *International Institutions and State Power*, p. 8. In that same piece, however, he makes the very bold argument that "we must understand that neoliberal institutionalism is not simply an alternative to neorealism, but, in fact, claims to subsume it." Ibid., p. 15.

This dearth of empirical support for liberal institutionalism is acknowledged by proponents of that theory.[78] The empirical record is not completely blank, however, but the few historical cases that liberal institutionalists have studied provide scant support for the theory. Consider two prominent examples.

Keohane looked at the performance of the International Energy Agency (IEA) in 1974–81, a period that included the 1979 oil crisis.[79] This case does not appear to lend the theory much support. First, Keohane concedes that the IEA failed outright when put to the test in 1979: "regime-oriented efforts at cooperation do not always succeed, as the fiasco of IEA actions in 1979 illustrates."[80] He claims, however, that in 1980 the IEA had a minor success "under relatively favorable conditions" in responding to the outbreak of the Iran-Iraq War. Although he admits it is difficult to specify how much the IEA mattered in the 1980 case, he notes that "it seems clear that 'it [the IEA] leaned in the right direction'," a claim that hardly constitutes strong support for the theory.[81] Second, it does not appear from Keohane's analysis that either fear of cheating or actual cheating hindered cooperation in the 1979 case, as the theory would predict. Third, Keohane chose the IEA case precisely because it involved relations among advanced Western democracies with market economies, where the prospects for cooperation were excellent.[82] The modest impact of institutions in this case is thus all the more damning to the theory.

Lisa Martin examined the role that the European Community (EC) played during the Falklands War in helping Britain coax its reluctant allies to continue economic sanctions against Argentina after military action started.[83] She concludes that the EC helped Britain win its allies' cooperation by lowering

---

78. For example, Lisa Martin writes that "scholars working in the realist tradition maintain a well-founded skepticism about the empirical impact of institutional factors on state behavior. This skepticism is grounded in a lack of studies that show precisely how and when institutions have constrained state decision-making." According to Oran Young, "One of the more surprising features of the emerging literature on regimes [institutions] is the relative absence of sustained discussions of the significance of . . . institutions, as determinants of collective outcomes at the international level." Martin, "Institutions and Cooperation," p. 144; Young, *International Cooperation*, p. 206.

79. Keohane, *After Hegemony*, chap. 10.

80. Ibid., p. 16.

81. Ibid., p. 236. A U.S. Department of Energy review of the IEA's performance in the 1980 crisis concluded that it had "failed to fulfill its promise." Ethan B. Kapstein, *The Insecure Alliance: Energy Crises and Western Politics Since 1944* (New York: Oxford University Press, 1990), p. 198.

82. Keohane, *After Hegemony*, p. 7.

83. Martin, "Institutions and Cooperation." Martin looks closely at three other cases in *Coercive Cooperation* to determine the effect of institutions on cooperation. I have concentrated on the Falklands War case, however, because it is, by her own admission, her strongest case. See ibid., p. 96.

transaction costs and facilitating issue linkage. Specifically, Britain made concessions on the EC budget and the Common Agricultural Policy (CAP); Britain's allies agreed in return to keep sanctions on Argentina.

This case, too, is less than a ringing endorsement for liberal institutionalism. First, British efforts to maintain EC sanctions against Argentina were not impeded by fears of possible cheating, which the theory identifies as the central impediment to cooperation. So this case does not present an important test of liberal institutionalism, and thus the cooperative outcome does not tell us much about the theory's explanatory power. Second, it was relatively easy for Britain and her allies to strike a deal in this case. Neither side's core interests were threatened, and neither side had to make significant sacrifices to reach an agreement. Forging an accord to continue sanctions was not a difficult undertaking. A stronger test for liberal institutionalism would require states to cooperate when doing so entailed significant costs and risks. Third, the EC was not essential to an agreement. Issues could have been linked without the EC, and although the EC may have lowered transaction costs somewhat, there is no reason to think these costs were a serious impediment to striking a deal.[84] It is noteworthy that Britain and America were able to cooperate during the Falklands War, even though the United States did not belong to the EC.

There is also evidence that directly challenges liberal institutionalism in issue areas where one would expect the theory to operate successfully. The studies discussed above by Grieco, Krasner, and Mastanduno test the institutionalist argument in a number of different political economy cases, and each finds the theory has little explanatory power. More empirical work is needed before a final judgment is rendered on the explanatory power of liberal institutionalism. Nevertheless, the evidence gathered so far is unpromising at best.

In summary, liberal institutionalism does not provide a sound basis for understanding international relations and promoting stability in the post–Cold War world. It makes modest claims about the impact of institutions, and steers clear of war and peace issues, focusing instead on the less ambitious task of explaining economic cooperation. Furthermore, the theory's causal logic is flawed, as proponents of the theory now admit. Having overlooked the relative-gains problem, they are now attempting to repair the theory, but their

---

84. Martin does not claim that agreement would not have been possible without the EC. Indeed, she appears to concede that even without the EC, Britain still could have fashioned "separate bilateral agreements with each EEC member in order to gain its cooperation, [although] this would have involved much higher transaction costs." Martin, "Institutions and Cooperation," pp. 174–175. However, transaction costs among the advanced industrial democracies are not very high in an era of rapid communications and permanent diplomatic establishments.

initial efforts are not promising. Finally, the available empirical evidence provides little support for the theory.

COLLECTIVE SECURITY

The theory of collective security deals directly with the issue of how to cause peace.[85] It recognizes that military power is a central fact of life in international politics, and is likely to remain so for the foreseeable future. The key to enhancing stability in this world of armed states is the proper management of military power. As Inis Claude notes, "the problem of power is here to stay; it is, realistically, not a problem to be eliminated but a problem to be managed."[86] For advocates of collective security, institutions are the key to managing power successfully.

Although the theory emphasizes the continuing importance of military force, it is explicitly anti-realist. Its proponents express a distaste for balance-of-power logic and traditional alliances, as well as a desire to create a world where those realist concepts have no role to play.[87]

In the early twentieth century, Woodrow Wilson and others developed the theory of collective security, which formed the basis for the League of Nations. Despite the well-known failings of that particular institution, the theory's popularity remains high. In fact, there has been much interest in collective security in the aftermath of the Cold War.[88] Claude notes, "Whatever their

---

85. The works that best articulate the case for collective security are: Inis L. Claude, Jr., *Power And International Relations* (New York: Random House, 1966), chaps. 4–5; Claude, *Swords Into Plowshares,* chap. 12; and Kupchan and Kupchan, "Concerts and Collective Security." Also see Inis L. Claude, Jr., "Collective Security After the Cold War," in Gary L. Guertner, ed., *Collective Security In Europe and Asia* (Carlisle Barracks, Pa.: Strategic Studies Institute, U.S. Army War College, 1992), pp. 7–27; and Downs, *Collective Security beyond the Cold War.* The best critiques of collective security include: Richard K. Betts, "Systems for Peace or Causes of War? Collective Security, Arms Control, and the New Europe," *International Security,* Vol. 17, No. 1 (Summer 1992), pp. 5–43; Josef Joffe, "Collective Security and the Future of Europe: Failed Dreams and Dead Ends," *Survival,* Vol. 34, No. 1 (Spring 1992), pp. 36–50; Morgenthau, *Politics Among Nations,* pp. 293–306, 407–418; and Arnold Wolfers, *Discord And Collaboration: Essays on International Politics* (Baltimore, Md.: The Johns Hopkins Press, 1962), chap. 12. For a very useful source on collective security, see Maurice Bourquin, ed., *Collective Security,* A Record of the Seventh and Eighth International Studies Conferences (Paris: International Institute of Intellectual Cooperation, 1936).
86. Claude, *Power And International Relations,* p. 6.
87. Consider, for example, how Woodrow Wilson describes pre–World War I Europe: "The day we left behind us was a day of alliances. It was a day of balances of power. It was a day of 'every nation take care of itself or make a partnership with some other nation or group of nations to hold the peace of the world steady or to dominate the weaker portions of the world'." Quoted in Claude, *Power and International Relations,* p. 81.
88. Some examples of recent interest in collective security include: Malcolm Chalmers, "Beyond the Alliance System: The Case for a European Security Organization," *World Policy Journal,* Vol. 7, No. 2 (Spring 1990), pp. 215–250; Downs, *Collective Security beyond the Cold War;* Gregory Flynn and David J. Sheffer, "Limited Collective Security," *Foreign Policy,* No. 80 (Fall 1980), pp. 77–101;

failures, the Wilsonians clearly succeeded in establishing the conviction that collective security represents a brand of international morality vastly superior to that incorporated in the balance of power system."[89]

Curiously, however, it is difficult to find scholarly work that makes the case for collective security without simultaneously expressing major reservations about the theory, and without expressing grave doubts that collective security could ever be realized in practice. Consider the writings of Claude, who is sympathetic to collective security, and has produced some of the most important work on the subject. He wrote in *Power and International Relations*, "I would regard the epithet *unrealistic* as fairly applicable to the theory of collective security." In *Swords into Plowshares*, he maintained that for "men involved in . . . establishing a collective security system . . . their devotion to the ideal has been more a manifestation of their yearning for peace and order as an end than as an expression of conviction that the theory of collective security provides a workable and acceptable means to that end." Finally, Claude wrote in 1992, "I reached the conclusion some thirty years ago that . . . the implementation of collective security theory is not a possibility to be taken seriously."[90]

CAUSAL LOGIC. Collective security starts with the assumption that states behave according to the dictates of realism.[91] The aim, however, is to move beyond the self-help world of realism where states fear each other and are motivated by balance-of-power considerations, even though the theory assumes that military power will remain a fact of life in the international system. For advocates of collective security, institutions are the key to accomplishing this ambitious task. Specifically, the goal is to convince states to base their behavior on three profoundly anti-realist norms.

Kupchan and Kupchan, "Concerts and Collective Security"; Gene M. Lyons, "A New Collective Security: The United Nations and International Peace," *The Washington Quarterly*, Vol. 17, No. 2 (Spring 1994), pp. 173–199; Richard H. Ullman, *Securing Europe* (Princeton, N.J.: Princeton University Press, 1991); and Brian Urquhart, "Beyond the Sheriff's Posse," *Survival*, Vol. 32, No. 3 (May/June 1990), pp. 196–205.

89. Claude, *Power And International Relations*, p. 116. Also see Wolfers, *Discord And Collaboration*, p. 197.

90. Claude, *Power And International Relations*, pp. 203–204; Claude, *Swords Into Plowshares*, p. 283; and Claude, "Collective Security After the Cold War," p. 9. The Kupchans, who are also sympathetic to collective security (see "Concerts and Collective Security"), apparently share Claude's doubts about the theory. After detailing the strengths (pp. 125–137) and flaws (pp. 138–140) of collective security, they abandon the theory and advocate a concert system for Europe (pp. 140–161), which, as discussed below, is fundamentally different from collective security.

91. My thinking about the logic underpinning collective security has been significantly influenced by Bradley A. Thayer, "A Theory of Security Structures," unpublished manuscript, University of Chicago, July 1994.

First, states must renounce the use of military force to alter the status quo. They must not launch wars of aggression, but instead must agree to settle all disputes peaceably. Collective security allows for changes in the status quo, but those changes must come via negotiation, not at the end of a rifle barrel. The theory, as Claude notes, "depends upon a positive commitment to the value of world peace by the great mass of states."[92]

The theory nevertheless recognizes that some states may not accept this norm: if there were universal subscription to the norm, there would be no need for a collective security system to deal with troublemakers, since there would be none.[93] However, the overwhelming majority of states must renounce wars of conquest, or else the system would collapse.

It is difficult to stipulate how many aggressors a collective security system can handle at once before it comes undone. The answer depends on the particular circumstances facing the system, such as: the number of great powers, the distribution of power among them, geography, and whether the aggressors are minor or major powers. The upper limit for aggressive major powers is probably two at any one time, but even then, the system is likely to have difficulty dealing with them. Some collective security systems might even have trouble fighting two minor powers at the same time, since minor powers today are often well-armed. Fighting simultaneous wars against Iraq and North Korea, for example, would be a very demanding task, although the great powers would win them. Ideally, a collective security system would confront only one aggressor at a time, and not too often at that. Claude sums up the matter nicely: "Collective security assumes the *lonely* aggressor; the violator of the world's peace may be allowed an accomplice or two, but in principle the evil-doer is supposed to find himself virtually isolated in confrontation with the massive forces of the international *posse comitatus*."[94]

---

92. Claude, *Swords Into Plowshares*, p. 250.

93. Collective security is often criticized on the grounds that "it is feasible only when it is also unnecessary." In other words, collective security requires that "all members are willing to accept the political status quo," but if that is the case, collective security would be unnecessary since no state, by definition, would cause trouble. Charles L. Glaser, "Why NATO is Still Best: Future Security Arrangements for Europe," *International Security*, Vol. 18, No. 1 (Summer 1993), p. 28. Also see Joffe, "Collective Security and the Future of Europe," pp. 44, 46; and Kupchan and Kupchan, "Concerts and Collective Security," p. 124. This criticism is unfair, however, because the very purpose of a collective security system is to deal with aggressors. If states could be guaranteed that no other state would ever launch an aggressive war, there would be no need for collective security. The theory recognizes that such a guarantee is not possible.

94. Claude, *Power And International Relations*, p. 196.

Second, "responsible" states must not think in terms of narrow self-interest when they act against lonely aggressors, but must instead choose to equate their national interest with the broader interests of the international community. Specifically, states must believe that their national interest is inextricably bound up with the national interest of other states, so that an attack on any state is considered an attack on every state.[95] Thus, when a troublemaker appears in the system, all of the responsible states must automatically and collectively confront the aggressor with overwhelming military power. The aim is "to create automatic obligations of a collective character."[96]

States in a self-help world calculate each move on the basis of how it will affect the balance of power. This narrow sense of self-interest means that states are likely to remain on the sidelines if vital interests are not threatened.[97] This kind of behavior is unacceptable in a collective security world, where there must instead be "a legally binding and codified commitment on the part of all members to respond to aggression whenever and wherever it might occur."[98] A collective security system allows states little freedom of action. The practical effect of this comprehensive system of mutual assistance is that lonely aggressors are quickly confronted with a coalition of overwhelming military strength. For both deterrence and warfighting purposes, this "preponderant power" is far superior to the "minimum winning coalitions" that a troublemaker faces in a balance-of-power world.[99] Once it becomes clear that aggression does not pay, even states reluctant to accept the first norm (the renunciation of aggression) will be more inclined to accept it.

---

95. Woodrow Wilson said in 1916, "We are participants, whether we would or not, in the life of the world. The interests of all nations are our own also. We are partners with the rest. What affects mankind is inevitably our affair as well as the affair of the nations of Europe and of Asia." Quoted in August Heckscher, ed., *The Politics of Woodrow Wilson: Selections from His Speeches and Writings* (New York: Harper, 1956), p. 258.

96. Morgenthau, *Politics Among Nations,* p. 296.

97. A state not at risk might fail to come to the aid of a threatened state because the risks and costs of going to war are too high, or because it has an interest in letting the combatants wear each other down, thus improving its own strategic position. A state not directly at risk might even join forces with the aggressor against the threatened state, so as to gain some of the spoils of victory.

98. Kupchan and Kupchan, "Concerts and Collective Security," p. 119.

99. Traditional alliances have no place in a collective security system. Woodrow Wilson is particularly eloquent on this point: "I am proposing that all nations henceforth avoid entangling alliances which would draw them into a competition of power, catch them in a net of intrigue and selfish rivalry, and disturb their own affairs with influences intruded from without. There is no entangling alliance in a concert of power. When all unite to act in the same sense and with the same purpose, all act in the common interest and are free to live their own lives under a common protection." Quoted in Frederick L. Schuman, *International Politics: An Introduction to the Western State System* (New York: McGraw-Hill, 1933), p. 254.

Third, states must trust each other. States must not only act in accordance with the first two norms, but they must trust that other states will do likewise. If states fear each other, as they do in a realist world, collective security cannot work. States, Claude emphasizes, must "be willing to entrust their destinies to collective security. Confidence is the quintessential condition of the success of the system; states must be prepared to rely upon its effectiveness and impartiality."[100]

Trust is actually the most important of the three norms because it underpins the first two. Specifically, states must be very confident that almost all the other states in the system will sincerely renounce aggression, and will not change their minds at a later date. States also have to be confident that when an aggressor targets them, none of the other responsible states will get cold feet and fail to confront the troublemaker. This element of certainty is of great importance in a collective security system because if it fails to work, at least some of those states that have ignored the balance of power and eschewed alliances are going to be vulnerable to attack.

This discussion of trust raises an additional point about the problems a collective security system faces when it confronts multiple aggressors. The previous discussion focused mainly on the logistical difficulties of dealing with more than one troublemaker. However, the presence of multiple aggressors also raises the question of whether most states in the system are deeply committed to peace, and therefore, whether it makes sense to trust collective security. The more troublemakers there are in the system, the more doubts responsible states are likely to have about their investment in collective security. This same logic applies to suggestions that collective security can get by without requiring that all states join the system. Some argue that one or more states can remain on the sidelines, provided the member states can still confront any troublemakers with overwhelming military force.[101] Although these free-riders are assumed to be non-aggressors, there is no guarantee that they will not later turn to conquest, in which case their free ride might have allowed them to improve significantly their relative power position. This free-rider problem, like the

100. Claude, *Swords Into Plowshares*, p. 255. Also see Claude, *Power And International Relations*, p. 197.
101. See Thomas R. Cusack and Richard J. Stoll, "Collective Security and State Survival in the Interstate System," *International Studies Quarterly*, Vol. 38, No. 1 (March 1994), pp. 33–59; and George W. Downs and Keisuke Iida, "Assessing the Theoretical Case against Collective Security," in Downs, *Collective Security beyond the Cold War*, pp. 17–39.

multiple-aggressor problem, is likely to undermine the responsible states' trust in collective security and thus to cause its failure.

FLAWS IN THE CAUSAL LOGIC. There are two major flaws in collective security theory, and both concern the all-important component of trust. Collective security is an incomplete theory because it does not provide a satisfactory explanation for how states overcome their fears and learn to trust one another. Realists maintain that states fear one another because they operate in an anarchic world, have offensive military capabilities, and can never be certain about other states' intentions. Collective security is largely silent about the first two realist assumptions, as the theory says little about either anarchy or offensive capability.[102] However, it has something to say about intentions, because the theory's first two norms call for states not to aggress, but only to defend. States, in other words, should only have benign intentions when contemplating the use of military force.

However, the theory recognizes that one or more states might reject the norms that underpin collective security and behave aggressively. The very purpose of a collective security system, after all, is to deal with states that have aggressive intentions. In effect, collective security admits that no state can ever be completely certain about another state's intentions, which brings us back to a realist world where states have little choice but to fear each other.

There is a second reason why states are not likely to place their trust in a collective security system: it has a set of demanding requirements—I count nine—that are likely to thwart efforts to confront an aggressor with preponderant power. Collective security, as Claude notes, "assumes the satisfaction of an extraordinarily complex network of requirements."[103]

First, for collective security to work, states must be able to distinguish clearly between aggressor and victim, and then move against the aggressor. However, it is sometimes difficult in a crisis to determine who is the troublemaker and who is the victim.[104] Debates still rage about which European great power, if any, bears responsibility for starting World War I. Similar disputes have followed most other wars.

---

102. Advocates of collective security usually favor widespread arms reductions, but they also recognize that states must maintain a significant offensive capability so that they can challenge an aggressor. For this reason, some scholars suggest that collective security might undermine stability. See Glaser, "Why NATO is Still Best," pp. 30–33.
103. Claude, *Swords Into Plowshares*, p. 250.
104. See Bourquin, *Collective Security*, pp. 295–338.

Second, the theory assumes that all aggression is wrong. But there are occasionally cases where conquest is probably warranted. For example, there are good reasons to applaud the 1979 Vietnamese invasion of Cambodia, since it drove the murderous Pol Pot from power.

Third, some states are especially friendly for historical or ideological reasons. Should a state with close friends be labeled an aggressor in a collective security system, its friends are probably going to be reluctant to join the coalition against it. For example, it is difficult to imagine the United States using military force against Britain or Israel, even if they were branded aggressors by the international community.

Fourth, historical enmity between states can also complicate collective security efforts. Consider that a European collective security system would have to depend heavily on Germany and Russia, the two most powerful states on the continent, to maintain order. However, the idea of Germany, which wrought murder and destruction across Europe in 1939–45, and Russia, which was the core of the Soviet empire, maintaining order in Europe is sure to meet significant resistance from other European states.

Fifth, even if states agree to act automatically and collectively to meet aggression, there would surely be difficulty determining how to distribute the burden. States will have strong incentives to pass the buck and get other states to pay the heavy price of confronting an aggressor.[105] During World War I, for example, Britain, France, and Russia each tried to get its allies to pay the blood price of defeating Germany on the battlefield.[106] Rampant buck-passing might undermine efforts to produce the preponderant military power necessary to make collective security work.

Sixth, it is difficult to guarantee a rapid response to aggression in a collective security system. Planning beforehand is problematic because "it is impossible to know what the alignment of states will be if there is an armed conflict."[107] There are also significant coordination problems associated with assembling a large coalition of states to fight a war. Rapid response becomes even more problematic if the responsible states must deal with more than one aggressor.

105. See Mancur Olson, Jr., and Richard Zeckhauser, "An Economic Theory of Alliances," *Review of Economics and Statistics*, Vol. 48, No. 3 (August 1966), pp. 266–279; and Barry R. Posen, *The Sources of Military Doctrine: France, Britain, and Germany between the World Wars* (Ithaca, N.Y.: Cornell University Press, 1984).
106. David French, *British Strategy and War Aims, 1914–1916* (London: Allen and Unwin, 1986).
107. G.F. Hudson, "Collective Security and Military Alliances," in Herbert Butterfield and Martin Wight, eds., *Diplomatic Investigations: Essays in the Theory of International Politics* (Cambridge, Mass.: Harvard University Press, 1966), p. 177.

It took more than six months for the United States to put together a coalition to liberate Kuwait from Saddam Hussein. As impressive as the American effort was, threatened states are not likely to have much faith in a security system that tells them help is likely to come, but will only arrive months after they have been conquered.

Seventh, states are likely to be reluctant to join a collective security effort because the system effectively transforms every local conflict into an international conflict. States that see conflict around the globe will surely be tempted to cordon off the troubled area and prevent further escalation, as the West has done in the former Yugoslavia.[108] Collective security, however, calls for escalation, even though it is intended for peaceful purposes.

Eighth, the notion that states must automatically respond to aggression impinges in fundamental ways on state sovereignty, and will therefore be difficult to sell. States, especially democracies, are likely to guard jealously their freedom to debate whether or not to fight an aggressor. War is a deadly business, especially if great powers are involved, and few countries want to commit themselves in advance to paying a huge blood price when their own self-interests are not directly involved.

Ninth, there is some contradiction concerning attitudes towards force that raises doubts about whether responsible states would actually come to the rescue of a threatened state. Collective security theory is predicated on the belief that war is a truly horrible enterprise, and therefore states should renounce aggression. At the same time, the theory mandates that states must be ready and willing to use force to thwart troublemakers. However, responsible states find war so repellent that they would renounce it; this raises doubts about their willingness to go to war to stop aggression. Indeed, most advocates of collective security prefer "creative diplomacy and economic sanctions" to military force when dealing with an aggressor state.[109]

In sum, states have abundant reasons to doubt that collective security will work as advertised when the chips are down and aggression seems likely. Should it fail, potential victims are likely to be in deep trouble if they have ignored balance-of-power considerations and placed their faith in collective

---

108. For an example of this line of thinking, see Stephen M. Walt, "Collective Security and Revolutionary Change: Promoting Peace in the Former Soviet Union," in Downs, *Collective Security beyond the Cold War,* pp. 169–195.
109. Robert C. Johansen, "Lessons For Collective Security," *World Policy Journal,* Vol. 8, No. 3 (Summer 1991), p. 562.

security. Recognizing this, states are not likely to place their fate in the hands of other states, but will prefer instead the realist logic of self-help.

PROBLEMS WITH THE EMPIRICAL RECORD. The historical record provides little support for collective security, a point acknowledged by the theory's proponents. The great powers have seriously considered implementing collective security three times in this century: after both World Wars, and after the Cold War. The League of Nations, which was established after World War I, was a serious attempt to make collective security work.[110] It had some minor successes during the 1920s. For example, League mediation resolved the Aaland Islands dispute between Finland and Sweden in 1920, and pressure from the League forced Greek, Italian, and Yugoslav troops out of Albania one year later. The League was much less successful in handling several other conflicts during the 1920s, however: it did not prevent or stop the Greco-Turkish War of 1920–22, or the Russo-Polish War of 1920, and France refused to allow the League to consider its occupation of the Ruhr in January 1923, going so far as to threaten withdrawal from the League if it intervened in the crisis. The League had a mixed record during the 1920s, even though that decade was relatively pacific, and no great power was then bent on aggression.

The international system became increasingly unstable during the 1930s, and the League was seriously tested on six occasions: 1) the Japanese invasion of Manchuria in 1931; 2) the Chaco War of 1932–35; 3) Japan's 1937 invasion of China; 4) Italy's aggression against Ethiopia in 1935; 5) the German occupation of the Rhineland in March 1936; and 6) the Soviet invasion of Finland in 1939. The League failed each test, and was effectively useless by the late 1930s, when the great powers were making the critical decisions that led to World War II.

The United Nations was established in the waning days of World War II to provide collective security around the globe. However, the Soviet-American competition followed on the heels of that war, and the United Nations was therefore never seriously tested as a collective security apparatus during the Cold War.[111]

---

110. The standard history of the League is F.P. Walters, *A History Of The League Of Nations*, 2 vols. (London: Oxford University Press, 1952).

111. See Ernst B. Haas, "Types of Collective Security: An Examination of Operational Concepts," *American Political Science Review*, Vol. 49, No. 1 (March 1955), pp. 40–62; and Kenneth W. Thompson, "Collective Security Reexamined," *American Political Science Review*, Vol. 47, No. 3 (September 1953), pp. 753–772.

Since the Cold War ended, there has been much talk in the West about building a collective security system.[112] The success of the American-led coalition that pushed Iraq out of Kuwait led some experts to conclude that the UN might finally be ready to operate as a collective security institution. In Europe, experts have discussed the possibility of turning NATO, or possibly the CSCE, into a collective security system for the continent. It is too early for conclusive judgments as to whether any of these ideas about collective security will be realized. However, almost all the evidence to date points to failure. Iraq was an unusual case, and no effort is underway to reform the UN so that it can perform true collective security missions.[113] Moreover, the failure of the United States and its European allies either to prevent or to stop the wars in the former Yugoslavia, coupled with NATO's January 1994 decision not to expand its membership eastward, does not bode well for establishing a collective security system in post–Cold War Europe.[114]

FALLBACK POSITIONS. Given the limits of collective security, some of its proponents argue that two less ambitious forms of the theory might be realizable: peacekeeping and concerts. Although they are portrayed as the "budget" version of collective security, some experts think that peacekeeping and concerts might still be a powerful force for international stability.[115]

Peacekeeping, as William Durch notes, "evolved as an alternative to the collective security that the UN was designed to provide but could not."[116]

---

112. See the sources cited in footnote 88.

113. See Adam Roberts, "The United Nations and International Security," *Survival*, Vol. 35, No. 2 (Summer 1993), pp. 3–30; and Claude, "Collective Security After the Cold War," pp. 15–27. For a critical discussion of the performance of the United States and the United Nations in the Gulf War, see Johansen, "Lessons For Collective Security."

114. There is still discussion about extending NATO eastward to include Poland, Hungary, and the two Czechoslovakian remnant states. Russia is deeply opposed to such a move, however, and therefore NATO is not likely to expand eastward in any meaningful way. Regardless, even if those four states joined NATO, the remnant states of the former Soviet Union would still be excluded, and their inclusion would be necessary to transform NATO into an effective collective security system for Europe. For an argument that NATO should not be transformed into a collective security system, see Glaser, "Why NATO is Still Best," pp. 26–33.

115. Regarding peacekeeping, see Mats R. Berdal, *Whither UN Peacekeeping?* Adelphi Paper No. 281 (London: IISS, October 1993), pp. 3–4, 75–77. Concerning concerts, see Kupchan and Kupchan, "Concerts and Collective Security," pp. 151–161; Richard Rosecrance, "A Concert of Powers," *Foreign Affairs*, Vol. 71, No. 2 (Spring 1992), pp. 64–82; and Philip Zelikow, "The New Concert of Europe," *Survival*, Vol. 34, No. 2 (Summer 1992), pp. 12–30.

116. William J. Durch, "Building on Sand: UN Peacekeeping in the Western Sahara," *International Security*, Vol. 17, No. 4 (Spring 1993), p. 151. Also see Berdal, *Whither UN Peacekeeping?*; and William J. Durch, ed., *The Evolution of UN Peacekeeping: Case Studies and Comparative Analysis* (New York: St. Martins, 1993).

However, peacekeeping is not a watered-down version of collective security. It is, instead, a much less ambitious alternative strategy for promoting stability. Peacekeeping entails third party intervention in minor-power civil wars or disputes between minor powers, for the purpose of either preventing war from breaking out or stopping it once it has begun. This intervention can only be accomplished with the consent of the disputants, and third parties cannot use force to affect the behavior of the parties in dispute. Peacekeeping operations must be "expressly non-threatening and impartial."[117] In essence, peacekeeping is mainly useful for helping implement cease-fires in wars involving minor powers. However, the UN's record in performing even that quite limited task is at best mixed.

Peacekeeping has no role to play in disputes between great powers. Moreover, it forbids the use of coercion, which is essential to a collective security system. Its mission is a far cry from the ambitious goals of collective security. Peacekeeping by the UN or by regional organizations like the Organization of African Unity (OAU) can enhance the prospects for world peace only on the margins.[118]

Concerts are sometimes described as an "attenuated form of collective security," or a "reasonable hybrid version of collective security."[119] Charles and Clifford Kupchan maintain that "collective security organizations can take many different institutional forms along a continuum ranging from ideal collective security to concerts."[120] However, the claim that concerts are a less ambitious version of collective security is incorrect.[121] Concerts essentially reflect the balance of power, and are thus largely consistent with realism, whereas collective security, as explained above, is a fundamentally anti-realist theory. Concerts and collective security systems, therefore, reflect different and ultimately incompatible logics. As Quincy Wright reminds us, "The fundamental assumptions of the two systems are different. A government cannot at the

---

117. Berdal, *Whither UN Peacekeeping?* p. 3.
118. For a discussion of the limitations of regional organizations as conflict managers, see S. Neil MacFarlane and Thomas G. Weiss, "Regional Organizations and Regional Security," *Security Studies*, Vol. 2, No. 1 (Autumn 1992), pp. 6–37.
119. Kupchan and Kupchan, "Concerts and Collective Security," p. 120; Betts, "Systems for Peace or Causes of War?" p. 27. Also see Downs, *Collective Security beyond the Cold War*.
120. Kupchan and Kupchan, "Concerts and Collective Security," p. 119.
121. I cannot find evidence that Woodrow Wilson, Inis Claude, or Arnold Wolfers considered concerts to be a limited form of collective security. It appears that the first serious efforts to link collective security with concerts were made in post–Cold War writings on collective security, especially Kupchan and Kupchan, "Concerts and Collective Security."

same time behave according to the Machiavellian assumptions of the balance of power and the Wilsonian assumptions of international organization."[122]

A concert is an arrangement in which great powers that have no incentive to challenge each other militarily agree on a set of rules to coordinate their actions with each other, as well as with the minor powers in the system, often in the establishment of spheres of influence. A concert is a great power condominium that reflects the underlying balance of power among its members. The coordinated balancing that takes place inside a concert does not violate great power self-interest. In fact, when those great powers have a dispute, self-interest determines each side's policy and the concert may collapse as a result.

Concerts are most likely to emerge in the wake of great power wars in which a potential hegemon has been defeated, and power is distributed roughly equally among the victors.[123] Four factors account for this phenomenon. First, the great powers would not have much to gain militarily by attacking each other, given the rough balance of power among them. Second, the victorious powers are likely to have a significant interest in maintaining the status quo, mainly because they are in control and the potential hegemon has been subdued. Third, hegemonic wars are very costly, so the great powers are likely to be war-weary, and deeply interested in avoiding another costly war. Fourth, the victorious great powers worked together to win the war, so the notion of collective action is likely to appeal to them, and carry over into the early postwar years.

Concerts usually last only a few years. The balance of power changes. Defeated powers rise from the ashes. Victorious powers squabble among themselves, especially about how to deal with minor powers. States become less sensitive to the costs of war as time passes.

---

122. Quincy Wright, *A Study Of War*, Vol. 2 (Chicago: University of Chicago Press, 1942), p. 781. Charles Lipson provides an example of how institutionalists try to combine these two incompatible theories. He writes: "Thus, the [post-1815] Concert is a kind of beacon to advocates of collective security . . . not only because it succeeded but because it did so . . . without transforming the self-interested behavior of states." Lipson, "Future of Collective Security," p. 119. However, a system based on the self-interested behavior of states is antithetical to collective security, and therefore, it is difficult to understand how such a system could be considered a "kind of beacon to advocates of collective security." For another example of this problem, see Kupchan and Kupchan, "Concerts and Collective Security," p. 116.

123. See Robert Jervis, "From Balance to Concert: A Study of International Security Cooperation," *World Politics*, Vol. 38, No. 1 (October 1985), pp. 58–79.

The Concert of Europe, which was established after Napoleonic France had finally been subdued, is the only case of a successful concert.[124] Not surprisingly, it is sometimes held up as a model for the post–Cold War world. The Concert worked fairly well from 1815 to 1823, although the great powers did occasionally clash over their dealings with minor powers. After 1823, however, the Concert was unable to function effectively as a coordinating device for the great powers. "The concert existed in an abortive form" until its final collapse as the Crimean War began in 1854.[125] During its heyday, the Concert of Europe reflected the balance of power; states were not compelled to behave in ways that weakened their relative power position. "Maintaining a balance of power," as Richard Betts notes, "remained an important object of the nineteenth-century Concert regime."[126]

In sum, the theory of collective security directly addresses the issue of how to push states away from war and promote peace, and it recognizes that military power plays a central role in international politics. But the theory has several important flaws. It is built on the foundational norm that states should trust each other, but it does not satisfactorily explain how this is possible in an anarchic world where states have military power and uncertain intentions. Furthermore, the historical record provides little support for the theory. The single case of an operative collective security system was the League of Nations, and it was a spectacular failure. Although peacekeeping and concerts are sometimes described as limited but promising versions of collective security, they are of marginal value in promoting peace. Moreover, both peacekeeping and concerts work according to different logics than collective security. In fact, concerts, like alliances, basically reflect the balance of power, and are thus consistent with a realist view of institutions.

---

124. Among the best works on the Concert of Europe are: Richard Elrod, "The Concert of Europe: A Fresh Look at an International System," *World Politics*, Vol. 28, No. 2 (January 1976), pp. 156–174; Edward V. Gulick, *Europe's Classical Balance of Power: A Case History of the Theory and Practice of One of the Great Concepts of European Statecraft* (New York: Norton, 1955); Jervis, "From Balance To Concert"; Harold Nicolson, *The Congress of Vienna: A Study in Allied Unity, 1812–1822* (New York: Harcourt, Brace, 1946); Paul W. Schroeder, *Austria, Great Britain, and the Crimean War: The Destruction of the European Concert* (Ithaca, N.Y.: Cornell University Press, 1972); Harold Temperley, *The Foreign Policy of Canning, 1822–1827: England, the Neo-Holy Alliance, and the New World*, 2nd ed. (London: Thomas Nelson, 1966); and Charles K. Webster, *The Foreign Policy of Castlereagh: Britain and the European Alliance, 1815–1822*, 2nd ed. (London: G. Bell, 1934).
125. The phrase is from Gulick, *Europe's Classical Balance of Power*, p. 22.
126. Betts, "Systems for Peace or Causes of War?" p. 27. The Kupchans readily accept that power politics is part of the warp and woof of daily life in a concert system. See "Concerts and Collective Security," pp. 116, 120, 141–144.

CRITICAL THEORY

Critical theorists[127] directly address the question of how to bring about peace, and they make bold claims about the prospects for changing state behavior.[128] Specifically, they aim to transform the international system into a "world society," where states are guided by "norms of trust and sharing." Their goal is to relegate security competition and war to the scrap heap of history, and create instead a genuine "peace system."[129]

Critical theorists take ideas very seriously. In fact, they believe that discourse, or how we think and talk about the world, largely shapes practice. Roughly put, ideas are the driving force of history. Furthermore, they recognize that

---

127. Critical theory is an approach to studying the human condition that is not tied to a particular discipline. In fact, critical theory was well-developed and employed widely in other disciplines before it began to penetrate the international relations field in the early 1980s. This article does not focus on critical theory *per se*, but examines the scholarly literature where critical theory is applied to international relations. I treat those works as a coherent whole, although there are differences, especially of emphasis, among them. For a general discussion of critical theory, see David Held, *Introduction to Critical Theory: Horkheimer to Habermas* (Berkeley: University of California Press, 1980); and Pauline M. Rosenau, *Post-Modernism And The Social Sciences: Insights, Inroads, and Intrusions* (Princeton, N.J.: Princeton University Press, 1992). Also see Pauline Rosenau, "Once Again Into the Fray: International Relations Confronts the Humanities," *Millennium: Journal of International Studies*, Vol. 19, No. 1 (Spring 1990), pp. 83–110.
128. Among the key works applying critical theory to international relations are: Richard K. Ashley, "The Poverty of Neorealism," *International Organization*, Vol. 38, No. 2 (Spring 1984), pp. 225–286; Ashley, "The Geopolitics of Geopolitical Space: Toward a Critical Social Theory of International Politics," *Alternatives*, Vol. 12, No. 4 (October 1987), pp. 403–434; Robert W. Cox, "Gramsci, Hegemony and International Relations: An Essay in Method," *Millennium: Journal of International Studies*, Vol. 12, No. 2 (Summer 1983), pp. 162–175; Cox, "Social Forces, States and World Orders: Beyond International Relations Theory," *Millennium: Journal of International Studies*, Vol. 10, No. 2 (Summer 1981), pp. 126–155; Cox, "Towards A Post-Hegemonic Conceptualization of World Order: Reflections on the Relevancy of Ibn Khaldun," in James N. Rosenau, and Ernst-Otto Czempiel, eds., *Governance Without Government: Order and Change in World Politics* (New York: Cambridge University Press, 1992), pp. 132–159; Rey Koslowski and Friedrich V. Kratochwil, "Understanding Change in International Politics: The Soviet Empire's Demise and the International System," *International Organization*, Vol. 48, No. 2 (Spring 1994), pp. 215–247; Friedrich Kratochwil and John G. Ruggie, "International Organization: A State of the Art on an Art of the State," *International Organization*, Vol. 40, No. 4 (Autumn 1986), pp. 753–775; Ruggie, "Continuity and Transformation in the World Polity: Toward a Neorealist Synthesis," *World Politics*, Vol. 35, No. 2 (January 1983), pp. 261–285; Ruggie, "Territoriality And Beyond: Problematizing Modernity in International Relations," *International Organization*, Vol. 47, No. 1 (Winter 1993), pp. 139–174; Alexander Wendt, "The Agent-Structure Problem in International Relations Theory," *International Organization*, Vol. 41, No. 3 (Summer 1987), pp. 335–370; Wendt, "Anarchy Is What States Make of It: The Social Construction of Power Politics," *International Organization*, Vol. 46, No. 2 (Spring 1992), pp. 391–425; and Wendt, "Collective Identity Formation and the International State," *American Political Science Review*, Vol. 88, No. 2 (June 1994), pp. 384–396. I use the label "critical theory" to describe this body of literature; other labels are sometimes used, among them constructivism, reflectivism, post-modernism, and post-structuralism.
129. The quotations in this paragraph are from Ashley, "Poverty of Neorealism," p. 285; and Wendt, "Anarchy Is What States Make of It," p. 431.

realism has long been the dominant theory of international politics, and therefore, according to their account of reality, has had substantial influence on state behavior. But critical theorists intend to change that situation by challenging realism and undermining it. Richard Ashley graphically describes their intentions: "Let us then play havoc with neorealist concepts and claims. Let us neither admire nor ignore the orrery of errors, but let us instead fracture the orbs, crack them open, crack them and see what possibilities they have enclosed. And then, when we are done, let us not cast away the residue. Let us instead sweep it into a jar, shine up the glass, and place it high on the bookshelf with other specimens of past mistakes."[130] With realism shattered, the way would presumably be open to a more peaceful world.

Critical theory is well-suited for challenging realism because critical theory is, by its very nature, concerned with criticizing "hegemonic" ideas like realism, not laying out alternative futures. The central aim is "to seek out the contradictions within the existing order, since it is from these contradictions that change could emerge."[131] It is called "critical" theory for good reason. Very significantly, however, critical theory *per se* has little to say about the future shape of international politics. In fact, critical theory emphasizes that, "It is impossible to predict the future."[132] Robert Cox explains this point: "Critical awareness of potentiality for change must be distinguished from utopian planning, i.e., the laying out of the design of a future society that is to be the end goal of change. Critical understanding focuses on the process of change rather than on its ends; it concentrates on the possibilities of launching a social movement rather than on what that movement might achieve."[133]

Nevertheless, international relations scholars who use critical theory to challenge and subvert realism certainly expect to create a more harmonious and peaceful international system. But the theory itself says little about either the desirability or feasibility of achieving that particular end.

---

130. Ashley, "Poverty of Neorealism," p. 286.
131. Robert W. Cox, *Production, Power, and World Order: Social Forces in the Making of World History* (New York: Columbia University Press, 1987), p. 393.
132. Cox, "Post-Hegemonic Conceptualization," p. 139.
133. Cox, *Production, Power, and World Order*, p. 393. The young Karl Marx summed up this approach in 1844: "the advantage of the new trend [is] that we do not attempt dogmatically to prefigure the future, but want to find the new world only through criticism of the old." Karl Marx, "For a Ruthless Criticism of Everything Existing," in Robert C. Tucker, ed., *The Marx-Engels Reader*, 2nd ed. (New York: Norton, 1978), p. 13. Marx's early writings have markedly influenced critical theory. See, for example, Ashley, "Poverty of Neorealism," pp. 226–230; and Cox, "Social Forces," p. 133. Critical theorists, however, disparage Marx's later writings, which lay out a structural theory of politics that has much in common with realism.

CAUSAL LOGIC. Institutions are at the core of critical theory, as its central aim is to alter the constitutive and regulative norms of the international system so that states stop thinking and acting according to realism. Specifically, critical theorists hope to create "pluralistic security communities," where states behave according to the same norms or institutions that underpin collective security.[134] States would renounce the use of military force, and there would instead be "a generally shared expectation of peaceful change."[135] Furthermore, states would "identify positively with one another so that the security of each is perceived as the responsibility of all."[136] States would not think in terms of self-help or self-interest, but would instead define their interests in terms of the international community. In this new world, "national interests are international interests."[137]

Critical theorists have a more ambitious agenda than proponents of collective security. Critical theorists aim to create a world in which all states consider war an unacceptable practice, and are not likely to change their minds about the matter. There do not appear to be any troublemaker states in a pluralistic security community, as there might be in a collective security system. In fact, military power seems to be largely irrelevant in the critical theorists' post-realist world, which has the earmarks of a true "peace system."[138]

For critical theorists, the key to achieving a "postmodern international system" is to alter state identity radically, or more specifically, to transform how states think about themselves and their relationship with other states.[139] In the

134. Emanuel Adler, "Arms Control, Disarmament, and National Security: A Thirty Year Retrospective and a New Set of Anticipations," *Daedalus*, Vol. 120, No. 1 (Winter 1991), pp. 11–18; Ashley, "Geopolitics of Geopolitical Space," pp. 428, 430; and Richard Ned Lebow, "The Long Peace, the End of the Cold War, and the Failure of Realism," *International Organization*, Vol. 48, No. 2 (Spring 1994), pp. 269–277. Wendt uses the term "cooperative security system" in place of "pluralistic security community." See "Anarchy Is What States Make of It," pp. 400–401. Karl Deutsch invented the concept of a pluralistic security community. See Karl W. Deutsch, et al., *Political Community and the North Atlantic Area: International Organization in the Light of Historical Experience* (Princeton, N.J.: Princeton University Press, 1957), pp. 5–9.
135. Ashley, "Geopolitics of Geopolitical Space," p. 430. Also see Adler, "Arms Control, Disarmament, and National Security," p. 11.
136. Wendt, "Anarchy Is What States Make of It," p. 400.
137. Ibid.
138. This outcome is fully consistent with Deutsch's definition of a pluralistic security community: "there is real assurance that the members of that community will not fight each other physically, but will settle their disputes in some other way. If the entire world were integrated as a security community, wars would be automatically eliminated." Deutsch, *Political Community*, p. 5.
139. John G. Ruggie, "International Structure and International Transformation: Space, Time, and Method," in Ernst-Otto Czempiel and James N. Rosenau, eds., *Global Changes and Theoretical Challenges: Approaches to World Politics for the 1990s* (Lexington, Mass.: Lexington Books, 1989), p. 30.

jargon of the theory, "intersubjective understandings and expectations" matter greatly.[140] In practice, this means that states must stop thinking of themselves as solitary egoists, and instead develop a powerful communitarian ethos.[141] Critical theorists aim to create an inter- national system characterized not by anarchy, but by community. States must stop thinking of themselves as separate and exclusive—i.e., sovereign—actors, and instead see themselves as mutually conditioned parts of a larger whole.[142] States, or more precisely, their inhabitants and leaders, should be made to care about concepts like "rectitude," "rights," and "obligations." In short, they should have a powerful sense of responsibility to the broader international community.

A realist might argue that this goal is desirable in principle, but not realizable in practice, because the structure of the international system forces states to behave as egoists. Anarchy, offensive capabilities, and uncertain intentions combine to leave states with little choice but to compete aggressively with each other. For realists, trying to infuse states with communitarian norms is a hopeless cause.

Critical theory, however, directly challenges the realist claim that structural factors are the main determinants of state behavior. In contrast to realism, critical theory assumes that ideas and discourse are the driving forces that shape the world, although it recognizes that structural factors have some, albeit minor, influence.[143] How individuals think about and talk about the world matters greatly for determining how states act in the international system. Ideas matter so much, according to critical theorists, because the world is socially constructed by individual human beings whose behavior is mediated by their thoughts; these thoughts, in turn, are shared by the members of a larger culture. Individuals bear responsibility for shaping the world they inhabit. The

---

140. Wendt, "Anarchy Is What States Make of It," p. 397.

141. "Critical social scientific approaches," as Ashley notes, "are inherently communitarian." See Ashley, "Geopolitics of Geopolitical Space," p. 403; also see pp. 404–407.

142. In a recent article, Alexander Wendt discusses the "emergence of 'international states,' which would constitute a structural transformation of the Westphalian states system." Wendt, "Collective Identity Formation," p. 385.

143. It is important to emphasize that critical theorists do not make a case for pure idealism, where realist structure has little bearing on state behavior. Their argument is much more sophisticated, as they maintain that structure and discourse are inextricably linked together and constantly interact in a dialectical fashion. Structure, they emphasize, both enables and constrains individual behavior. Nevertheless, the key point for critical theorists is that structure is ultimately shaped and reshaped by discourse. In other words, structure may shape our thinking about the world, but structure is ultimately shaped by our discourse. Structure is not an independent material force that shapes how we think and talk about the world. Social reality, in the end, is ultimately a construction of our minds.

world around them is not a given that forces itself upon them. On the contrary, critical theorists argue that ideational forces or "institutions often can change environments."[144] Markus Fischer sums up this crucial point: "In essence, critical theory holds that social reality is constituted by intersubjective consciousness based on language and that human beings are free to change their world by a collective act of will."[145]

Robert Cox's description of the state illustrates how this process of thinking about the world determines how it is structured. "The state," he writes, "has no physical existence, like a building or a lamp-post; but it is nevertheless a real entity. It is a real entity because everyone acts as though it were."[146] Alexander Wendt's discussion of anarchy provides another good example: "Structure," he writes, "has no existence or causal powers apart from process."[147] States, in fact, can think about anarchy in a number of different ways. "Anarchy is what states make of it." Moreover, "self-help and power politics are institutions . . . not essential features of anarchy."

This discussion of how critical theorists think about the state and anarchy points up the fact that realism and critical theory have fundamentally different epistemologies and ontologies, which are the most basic levels at which theories can be compared.[148] Realists maintain that there is an objective and knowable world, which is separate from the observing individual. Critical theorists, on the other hand, "see subject and object in the historical world as a reciprocally interrelated whole," and they deny the possibility of objective knowledge.[149] Where realists see a fixed and knowable world, critical theorists see the possibility of endless interpretations of the world before them. For critical theorists, "there are no constants, no fixed meanings, no secure grounds, no profound secrets, no final structures or limits of history . . . there is only

---

144. Koslowski and Kratochwil, "Understanding Change," p. 226.

145. Markus Fischer, "Feudal Europe, 800–1300: Communal Discourse and Conflictual Practices," *International Organization*, Vol. 46, No. 2 (Spring 1992), p. 430.

146. Cox, "Post-Hegemonic Conceptualization," p. 133.

147. Wendt, "Anarchy Is What States Make of It," p. 395. The subsequent quotations in this paragraph are from ibid. Also see Richard K. Ashley, "Untying the Sovereign State: A Double Reading of the Anarchy Problematique," *Millennium: Journal of International Studies*, Vol. 17, No. 2 (Summer 1988), pp. 227–262.

148. See Cox, "Post-Hegemonic Conceptualization," pp. 132–139; Kratochwil and Ruggie, "International Organization," pp. 763–775; Yosef Lapid, "The Third Debate: On the Prospects of International Theory in a Post-Positivist Era," *International Studies Quarterly*, Vol. 33, No. 3 (September 1989), pp. 235–254; Wendt, "The Agent-Structure Problem," pp. 335–370.

149. Cox, "Post-Hegemonic Conceptualization," p. 135.

interpretation. . . . History itself is grasped as a series of interpretations imposed upon interpretation—none primary, all arbitrary."[150]

Nevertheless, critical theorists readily acknowledge that realism has been the dominant interpretation of international politics for almost seven hundred years. "Realism is a name for a discourse of power and rule in modern global life."[151] Still, critical theory allows for change, and there is no reason, according to the theory anyway, why a communitarian discourse of peace and harmony cannot supplant the realist discourse of security competition and war. In fact, change is always possible with critical theory because it allows for an unlimited number of discourses, and it makes no judgment about the merit or staying power of any particular one. Also, critical theory makes no judgment about whether human beings are "hard-wired" to be good or bad, but instead treats people as infinitely changeable. The key to how they think and behave is the particular "software program" that individuals carry around in their heads, and those can be changed. In essence, critical theorists hope to replace the widely used realist software package with new software that emphasizes communitarian norms. Once that switch has been made, states will cooperate with each other and world politics will be more peaceful.

Most critical theorists do not see ideas and discourses forming at the grass roots and then percolating up to the elites of society. Rather, theirs is a top-down theory, whereby elites play the key role in transforming language and discourse about international relations. Experts, especially scholars, determine the flow of ideas about world politics. It is especially useful, however, if this intellectual vanguard consists of individuals from different states. These transnational elites, which are sometimes referred to as "epistemic communities," are well-suited for formulating and spreading the communitarian ideals that critical theorists hope will replace realism.[152]

Finally, it is worth noting that critical theorists are likely to be quite intolerant of other discourses about international politics, especially realism.[153] Four factors combine to account for this situation. The theory is based on the belief that ideas matter greatly for shaping international politics. Also, it recognizes that particular theories triumph in the marketplace of ideas, and the result is

---

150. Ashley, "Geopolitics of Geopolitical Space," pp. 408–409.
151. Ibid., p. 422.
152. See Adler, "Arms Control"; and Peter M. Haas, ed., *Knowledge, Power, and International Policy Coordination,* special issue of *International Organization,* Vol. 46, No. 1 (Winter 1992).
153. For example, see Ashley, "Poverty of Neorealism," *passim.*

hegemonic discourse. Moreover, although the theory itself does not distinguish between good and bad ideas, critical theorists themselves certainly make that distinction. Furthermore, critical theorists have no historical guarantee that hegemonic discourse will move toward ideas about world politics that they consider sound. Realism, for example, has been the dominant discourse in the international arena for many centuries. Therefore, it makes sense for critical theorists to try to eliminate ideas they do not like, thus maximizing the prospects that their favorite discourse will triumph. Realist thinking, in this view, is not only dangerous, but is the main obstacle critical theorists face in their effort to establish a new and more peaceful hegemonic discourse.[154]

FLAWS IN THE CAUSAL LOGIC.   The main goal of critical theorists is to change state behavior in fundamental ways, to move beyond a world of security competition and war and establish a pluralistic security community. However, their explanation of how change occurs is at best incomplete, and at worst, internally contradictory.[155]

Critical theory maintains that state behavior changes when discourse changes. But that argument leaves open the obvious and crucially important question: what determines why some discourses become dominant and others lose out in the marketplace of ideas? What is the mechanism that governs the rise and fall of discourses? This general question, in turn, leads to three more specific questions: 1) Why has realism been the hegemonic discourse in world politics for so long? 2) Why is the time ripe for its unseating? 3) Why is realism likely to be replaced by a more peaceful communitarian discourse?

Critical theory provides few insights on why discourses rise and fall. Thomas Risse-Kappen writes, "Research on . . . 'epistemic communities' of knowledge-based transnational networks has failed so far to specify the conditions under which specific ideas are selected and influence policies while others fall by the wayside."[156] Not surprisingly, critical theorists say little about why realism has been the dominant discourse, and why its foundations are now so shaky. They certainly do not offer a well-defined argument that deals with this important issue. Therefore, it is difficult to judge the fate of realism through the lens of critical theory.

---

154. Lebow, for example, writes that "Contemporary realists' . . . theories and some of the policy recommendations based on them may now stand in the way of the better world we all seek." Lebow, "The Long Peace," p. 277.
155. My thinking on this matter has been markedly influenced by Hein Goemans.
156. Thomas Risse-Kappen, "Ideas Do Not Float Freely: Transnational Coalitions, Domestic Structures, and the End of the Cold War," *International Organization*, Vol. 48, No. 2 (Spring 1994), p. 187. Also see Koslowski and Kratochwil, "Understanding Change," p. 225.

Nevertheless, critical theorists occasionally point to particular factors that might lead to changes in international relations discourse. In such cases, however, they usually end up arguing that changes in the material world drive changes in discourse. For example, when Ashley makes surmises about the future of realism, he claims that "a crucial issue is whether or not changing historical conditions have disabled longstanding realist rituals of power." Specifically, he asks whether "developments in late capitalist society," like the "fiscal crisis of the state," and the "internationalization of capital," coupled with "the presence of vastly destructive and highly automated nuclear arsenals [has] deprived statesmen of the latitude for competent performance of realist rituals of power?"[157] Similarly, Cox argues that fundamental change occurs when there is a "disjuncture" between "the stock of ideas people have about the nature of the world and the practical problems that challenge them." He then writes, "Some of us think the erstwhile dominant mental construct of neorealism is inadequate to confront the challenges of global politics today."[158]

It would be understandable if realists made such arguments, since they believe there is an objective reality that largely determines which discourse will be dominant. Critical theorists, however, emphasize that the world is socially constructed, and not shaped in fundamental ways by objective factors. Anarchy, after all, is what we make of it. Yet when critical theorists attempt to explain why realism may be losing its hegemonic position, they too point to objective factors as the ultimate cause of change. Discourse, so it appears, turns out not to be determinative, but mainly a reflection of developments in the objective world. In short, it seems that when critical theorists who study international politics offer glimpses of their thinking about the causes of change in the real world, they make arguments that directly contradict their own theory, but which appear to be compatible with the theory they are challenging.[159]

---

157. Ashley, "Geopolitics of Geopolitical Space," pp. 426–427.
158. Cox, "Post-Hegemonic Conceptualization," p. 138. Also see Cox, "Social Forces," pp. 138–149. For other examples, see Ruggie, "Continuity and Transformation," pp. 281–286; and Wendt, "Collective Identity Formation," pp. 389–390.
159. Cox is apparently aware of this problem. After spending eleven pages outlining various objective factors that might shape a new world order, he notes, "It would, of course, be *logically inadmissible*, as well as imprudent, to base predictions of future world order upon the foregoing considerations." Cox, "Social Forces," p. 149, emphasis added. Nevertheless, he then emphasizes in the next few sentences how important those objective considerations are for understanding future world order prospects. He writes: "Their utility is rather in drawing attention to factors which could incline an emerging world order in one direction or another. The social forces generated by changing production processes are the starting point for thinking about possible

There is another problem with the application of critical theory to international relations. Although critical theorists hope to replace realism with a discourse that emphasizes harmony and peace, critical theory *per se* emphasizes that it is impossible to know the future. Critical theory, according to its own logic, can be used to undermine realism and produce change, but it cannot serve as the basis for predicting which discourse will replace realism, because the theory says little about the direction change takes. In fact, Cox argues that although "utopian expectations may be an element in stimulating people to act . . . such expectations are almost never realized in practice."[160] Thus, in a sense, the communitarian discourse championed by critical theorists is wishful thinking, not an outcome linked to the theory itself. Indeed, critical theory cannot guarantee that the new discourse will not be more malignant than the discourse it replaces. Nothing in the theory guarantees, for example, that a fascist discourse far more violent than realism will not emerge as the new hegemonic discourse.

PROBLEMS WITH THE EMPIRICAL RECORD.   Critical theorists have offered little empirical support for their theory.[161] It is still possible to sketch the broad outlines of their account of the past. They appear to concede that realism was the dominant discourse from about the start of the late medieval period in 1300 to at least 1989, and that states and other political entities behaved according to realist dictates during these seven centuries. However, some critical theorists suggest that both the discourse and practice of international politics during the preceding five centuries of the feudal era or central medieval period (800–1300) was not dominated by realism and, therefore, cannot be explained by it.[162] They believe that European political units of the feudal era did not think and therefore did not act in the exclusive and selfish manner assumed by realism, but instead adopted a more communitarian discourse, which guided their

futures. These forces may combine in different configurations, and as an exercise one could consider the hypothetical configurations most likely to lead to three different outcomes as to the future of the state system. The focus on these three outcomes is not, of course, to imply that no other outcomes or configurations of social forces are possible." In other words, Cox does rely heavily on objective factors to explain possible future world orders.

160. Cox, *Production, Power, And World Order*, p. 393.

161. Wendt, for example, acknowledges that, "Relatively little empirical research has been explicitly informed by structuration [critical] theory, which might illustrate its implications for the explanation of state action." Wendt, "The Agent-Structure Problem," p. 362.

162. Ruggie, "Continuity and Transformation," pp. 273–279. Also see Robert W. Cox, "Postscript 1985," in Robert O. Keohane, ed., *Neorealism and Its Critics* (New York: Columbia University Press, 1986), pp. 244–245.

actions. Power politics, so the argument goes, had little relevance in these five hundred years.

Furthermore, most critical theorists see the end of the Cold War as an important watershed in world politics. A few go so far as to argue that "the revolutions of 1989 transformed the international system by changing the rules governing superpower conflict and, thereby, the norms underpinning the international system."[163] Realism, they claim, is no longer the hegemonic discourse. "The end of the Cold War . . . undermined neorealist theory."[164] Other critical theorists are more tentative in their judgment about whether the end of the Cold War has led to a fundamental transformation of international politics.[165] For these more cautious critical theorists, the revolutions of 1989 have created opportunities for change, but that change has not yet been realized.

Three points are in order regarding the critical theorists' interpretation of history. First, one cannot help but be struck by the sheer continuity of realist behavior in the critical theorists' own account of the past. Seven centuries of security competition and war represents an impressive span of time, especially when you consider the tremendous political and economic changes that have taken place across the world during that lengthy period. Realism is obviously a human software package with deep-seated appeal, although critical theorists do not explain its attraction.

Second, a close look at the international politics of the feudal era reveals scant support for the claims of critical theorists. Markus Fischer has done a detailed study of that period, and he finds "that feudal discourse was indeed distinct, prescribing unity, functional cooperation, sharing, and lawfulness."[166] More importantly, however, he also finds "that while feudal actors observed these norms for the most part on the level of form, they in essence behaved like modern states." Specifically, they "strove for exclusive territorial control, protected themselves by military means, subjugated each other, balanced

---

163. Koslowski and Kratochwil, "Understanding Change," p. 215. Also see Lebow, "The Long Peace"; Risse-Kappen, "Ideas Do Not Float Freely"; and Janice Gross Stein, "Political Learning By Doing: Gorbachev As Uncommitted Thinker and Motivated Learner," *International Organization,* Vol. 48, No. 2 (Spring 1994), pp. 155–183. All four of these articles are published together as a symposium on "The End of the Cold War and Theories of International Relations," in the Spring 1994 *International Organization.*
164. Koslowski and Kratochwil, "Understanding Change," p. 217.
165. See, for example, Ruggie, "Territoriality and Beyond," pp. 173–174; Wendt, "Anarchy Is What States Make of It," p. 422; and Wendt, "Collective Identity Formation," p. 393.
166. Fischer, "Feudal Europe," p. 428. Also see the subsequent exchange between Fischer and Rodney Hall and Friedrich Kratochwil in *International Organization,* Vol. 47, No. 3 (Summer 1993), pp. 479–500.

against power, formed alliances and spheres of influence, and resolved their conflicts by the use and threat of force."[167] Realism, not critical theory, appears best to explain international politics in the five centuries of the feudal era.

Third, there are good reasons to doubt that the demise of the Cold War means that the millennium is here. It is true that the great powers have been rather tame in their behavior towards each other over the past five years. But that is usually the case after great-power wars. Moreover, although the Cold War ended in 1989, the Cold War order that it spawned is taking much longer to collapse, which makes it difficult to determine what kind of order or disorder will replace it. For example, Russian troops remained in Germany until mid-1994, seriously impinging on German sovereignty, and the United States still maintains a substantial military presence in Germany. Five years is much too short a period to determine whether international relations has been fundamentally transformed by the end of the Cold War, especially given that the "old" order of realist discourse has been in place for at least twelve centuries.

A close look at the sources of this purported revolutionary change in world politics provides further cause for skepticism. For critical theorists, "the Cold War was fundamentally a discursive, not a material, structure."[168] Thus, if the United States and the Soviet Union had decided earlier in the Cold War that they were no longer enemies, it would have been over sooner.[169] Mikhail Gorbachev, critical theorists argue, played the central role in ending the Cold War. He challenged traditional Soviet thinking about national security, and championed ideas about international security that sounded like they had been scripted by critical theorists.[170] In fact, critical theorists argue that Gorbachev's "new thinking" was shaped by a "transnational liberal internationalist community [epistemic community] comprising the U.S. arms control community, Western European scholars and center-left policy makers, as well as Soviet institutchiks."[171] These new ideas led Gorbachev to end the Soviet Union's "imperial relationship with Eastern Europe," which led to a fundamental change in "the norms of bloc politics and thereby the rules governing super-power relations."[172] In essence, "the changed practices of one of the major

---

167. Fischer, "Feudal Europe," p. 428.
168. Wendt, "Collective Identity Formation," p. 389.
169. This sentence is a paraphrase of Wendt, "Anarchy Is What States Make of It," p. 397.
170. See Koslowski and Kratochwil, "Understanding Change," p. 233.
171. Risse-Kappen, "Ideas Do Not Float Freely," p. 213. Also see ibid., pp. 195–214; and Stein, "Political Learning By Doing," pp. 175–180.
172. Koslowski and Kratochwil, "Understanding Change," pp. 228, 239.

actors . . . [had] system-wide repercussions."[173] Both superpowers "repudiated the notion of international relations as a self-help system and . . . transcended the consequences of anarchy as depicted by realism."[174]

Gorbachev surely played the key role in ending the Cold War, but there are good reasons to doubt that his actions fundamentally transformed international politics. His decision to shut down the Soviet empire in Eastern Europe can very well be explained by realism. By the mid-1980s, the Soviet Union was suffering an economic and political crisis at home that made the costs of empire prohibitive, especially since nuclear weapons provided the Soviets with a cheap and effective means of defense. Many empires collapsed and many states broke apart before 1989, and many of them sought to give to dire necessity the appearance of virtue. But the basic nature of international politics remained unchanged. It is not clear why the collapse of the Soviet Union is a special case.

Furthermore, now that Gorbachev is out of office and has little political influence in Russia, the Russians have abandoned his "new thinking."[175] In fact, they now have an offensively-oriented military doctrine that emphasizes first use of nuclear weapons. More importantly, since the end of 1992, the Russians have been acting like a traditional great power toward their neighbors. The former Soviet Union seems to be an arena for power politics, and Boris Yeltsin's Russia appears to be fully engaged in that enterprise.[176]

Regarding the more modest claim that the end of the Cold War presents an opportunity to move to a world where states are guided by norms of trust and sharing, perhaps this is true. But since critical theorists acknowledge that their theory cannot predict the future, why should we believe their claim, especially

---

173. Ibid., p. 227.
174. Lebow, "The Long Peace," p. 276.
175. See Charles Dick, "The Military Doctrine of the Russian Federation," in *Jane's Intelligence Review*, Special Report No. 1, January 1994, pp. 1–5; Michael C. Desch, "Why the Soviet Military Supported Gorbachev and Why the Russian Military Might Only Support Yeltsin for a Price," *Journal of Strategic Studies*, Vol. 16, No. 4 (December 1993), pp. 467–474; and Stephen Foye, "Updating Russian Civil-Military Relations," *RFE/RL Research Report*, Vol. 2, No. 46 (November 19, 1993), pp. 44–50.
176. See, for example, Thomas Goltz, "Letter from Eurasia: The Hidden Russian Hand," *Foreign Policy*, No. 92, pp. 92–116; Steven E. Miller, "Russian National Interests," in Robert D. Blackwill and Sergei A. Karaganov, eds., *Damage Limitation or Crisis? Russia and the Outside World*, CSIA Studies in International Security No. 5 (Washington, D.C.: Brassey's, 1994), pp. 77–106; Alexei K. Pushkov, "Russia and America: The Honeymoon's Over," *Foreign Policy*, No. 93 (Winter 1993–1994), pp. 77–90; and Bruce D. Porter and Carol R. Saivetz, "The Once and Future Empire: Russia and the 'Near Abroad'," *Washington Quarterly*, Vol. 17, No. 3 (Summer 1994), pp. 75–90.

when it means choosing against realism, a theory that has at least 1200 years of staying power?

Critical theorists have ambitious aims. However, critical theory also has important flaws, and therefore it will likely remain in realism's shadow. Specifically, critical theory is concerned with affecting fundamental change in state behavior, but it says little about how it comes about. Critical theorists do occasionally point to particular causes of change, but when they do, they make arguments that are inconsistent with the theory itself. Finally, there is little empirical evidence to support the claims of critical theorists, and much to contradict them.

Conclusion

Many policymakers as well as academics believe that institutions hold great promise for promoting international peace. This optimistic assessment of institutions is not warranted, however, mainly because the three institutionalist theories which underpin it are flawed. There are serious problems with the causal logic of each theory, and little empirical evidence for any of them. What is most impressive about institutions, in fact, is how little independent effect they seem to have had on state behavior.

We have an important paradox here: although the world does not work the way institutionalist theories say it does or should, those theories remain highly influential in both the academic and policy worlds. Given the limited impact of institutions on state behavior, one would expect considerable skepticism, even cynicism, when institutions are described as a major force for peace. Instead, they are still routinely described in promising terms by scholars and governing elites.

It is beyond the scope of this paper to attempt a detailed explanation of this paradox. Nevertheless, I would like to close with some speculative comments about this puzzle, focusing on the American context.

The attraction of institutionalist theories for both policymakers and scholars is explained, I believe, not by their intrinsic value, but by their relationship to realism, and especially to core elements of American political ideology. Realism has long been and continues to be an influential theory in the United States.[177] Leading realist thinkers such as George Kennan and Henry Kissinger, for

---

177. See Michael J. Smith, *Realist Thought from Weber to Kissinger* (Baton Rouge: Louisiana State University Press, 1986), chap. 1.

example, occupied key policymaking positions during the Cold War. The impact of realism in the academic world is amply demonstrated in the institutionalist literature, where discussions of realism are pervasive.[178] Yet despite its influence, Americans who think seriously about foreign policy issues tend to dislike realism intensely, mainly because it clashes with their basic values. The theory stands opposed to how most Americans prefer to think about themselves and the wider world.[179]

There are four principal reasons why American elites, as well as the American public, tend to regard realism with hostility. First, realism is a pessimistic theory. It depicts a world of stark and harsh competition, and it holds out little promise of making that world more benign. Realists, as Hans Morgenthau wrote, are resigned to the fact that "there is no escape from the evil of power, regardless of what one does."[180] Such pessimism, of course, runs up against the deep-seated American belief that with time and effort, reasonable individuals can solve important social problems. Americans regard progress as both desirable and possible in politics, and they are therefore uncomfortable with realism's claim that security competition and war will persist despite our best efforts to eliminate them.[181]

Second, realism treats war as an inevitable, and indeed sometimes necessary, form of state activity. For realists, war is an extension of politics by other means.

---

178. Summing up the autobiographical essays of 34 international relations scholars, Joseph Kruzel notes that "Hans Morgenthau is more frequently cited than any other name in these memoirs." Joseph Kruzel, "Reflections on the Journeys," in Joseph Kruzel and James N. Rosenau, eds., *Journeys through World Politics: Autobiographical Reflections of Thirty-four Academic Travelers* (Lexington, Mass.: Lexington Books, 1989), p. 505. Although "Morgenthau is often cited, many of the references in these pages are negative in tone. He seems to have inspired his critics even more than his supporters." Ibid.

179. See Keith L. Shimko, "Realism, Neorealism, and American Liberalism," *Review of Politics*, Vol. 54, No. 2 (Spring 1992), pp. 281–301.

180. Hans J. Morgenthau, *Scientific Man vs. Power Politics* (Chicago: University of Chicago Press, 1974), p. 201. Nevertheless, Keith Shimko convincingly argues that the shift within realism, away from Morgenthau's belief that states are motivated by an unalterable will to power, and toward Waltz's view that states are motivated by the desire for security, provides "a residual, though subdued optimism, or at least a possible basis for optimism [about international politics]. The extent to which this optimism is stressed or suppressed varies, but it is there if one wants it to be." Shimko, "Realism, Neorealism, and American Liberalism," p. 297. Realists like Stephen Van Evera, for example, point out that although states operate in a dangerous world, they can take steps to dampen security competition and minimize the danger of war. See Van Evera, *Causes of War*.

181. See Reinhold Niebuhr, *The Children of Light and The Children of Darkness: A Vindication of Democracy and a Critique of Its Traditional Defense* (New York: Charles Scribner's, 1944), especially pp. 153–190. See also Samuel P. Huntington, *The Soldier and the State: The Theory and Politics of Civil-Military Relations* (New York: Vintage Books, 1964).

Realists are very cautious in their prescriptions about the use of force: wars should not be fought for idealistic purposes, but instead for balance-of-power reasons. Most Americans, however, tend to think of war as a hideous enterprise that should ultimately be abolished. For the time being, however, it can only justifiably be used for lofty moral goals, like "making the world safe for democracy"; it is morally incorrect to fight wars to change or preserve the balance of power. This makes the realist conception of warfare anathema to many Americans.

Third, as an analytical matter, realism does not distinguish between "good" states and "bad" states, but essentially treats them like billiard balls of varying size. In realist theory, all states are forced to seek the same goal: maximum relative power.[182] A purely realist interpretation of the Cold War, for example, allows for no meaningful difference in the motives behind American and Soviet behavior during that conflict. According to the theory, both sides must have been driven by concerns about the balance of power, and must have done what was necessary to try to achieve a favorable balance. Most Americans would recoil at such a description of the Cold War, because they believe the United States was motivated by good intentions while the Soviet Union was not.[183]

Fourth, America has a rich history of thumbing its nose at realism. For its first 140 years of existence, geography and the British navy allowed the United States to avoid serious involvement in the power politics of Europe. America had an isolationist foreign policy for most of this period, and its rhetoric explicitly emphasized the evils of entangling alliances and balancing behavior. Even as the United States finally entered its first European war in 1917, Woodrow Wilson railed against realist thinking. America has a long tradition of anti-realist rhetoric, which continues to influence us today.

Given that realism is largely alien to American culture, there is a powerful demand in the United States for alternative ways of looking at the world, and especially for theories that square with basic American values. Institutionalist theories nicely meet these requirements, and that is the main source of their

---

182. It should be emphasized that many realists have strong moral preferences and are driven by deep moral convictions. Realism is not a normative theory, however, and it provides no criteria for moral judgment. Instead, realism merely seeks to explain how the world works. Virtually all realists would prefer a world without security competition and war, but they believe that goal is unrealistic given the structure of the international system. See, for example, Robert G. Gilpin, "The Richness of the Tradition of Political Realism," in Keohane, *Neorealism and Its Critics*, p. 321.
183. Realism's treatment of states as billiard balls of different sizes tends to raise the hackles of comparative politics scholars, who believe that domestic political and economic factors matter greatly for explaining foreign policy behavior.

appeal to policymakers and scholars. Whatever else one might say about these theories, they have one undeniable advantage in the eyes of their supporters: they are not realism. Not only do institutionalist theories offer an alternative to realism, but they explicitly seek to undermine it. Moreover, institutionalists offer arguments that reflect basic American values. For example, they are optimistic about the possibility of greatly reducing, if not eliminating, security competition among states and creating a more peaceful world. They certainly do not accept the realist stricture that war is politics by other means. Institutionalists, in short, purvey a message that Americans long to hear.

There is, however, a downside for policymakers who rely on institutionalist theories: these theories do not accurately describe the world, hence policies based on them are bound to fail. The international system strongly shapes the behavior of states, limiting the amount of damage that false faith in institutional theories can cause. The constraints of the system notwithstanding, however, states still have considerable freedom of action, and their policy choices can succeed or fail in protecting American national interests and the interests of vulnerable people around the globe. The failure of the League of Nations to address German and Japanese aggression in the 1930s is a case in point. The failure of institutions to prevent or stop the war in Bosnia offers a more recent example. These cases illustrate that institutions have mattered rather little in the past; they also suggest that the false belief that institutions matter has mattered more, and has had pernicious effects. Unfortunately, misplaced reliance on institutional solutions is likely to lead to more failures in the future.

The Promise of Institutionalist Theory

Robert O. Keohane and Lisa L. Martin

In his usual direct way, John J. Mearsheimer has sharpened the theoretical issues dividing realist from institutionalist theory, and for this service we are grateful. We are also pleased that he has read the institutionalist literature so thoroughly. He correctly asserts that liberal institutionalists treat states as rational egoists operating in a world in which agreements cannot be hierarchically enforced, and that institutionalists only expect interstate cooperation to occur if states have significant common interests. Hence institutionalist theory does not espouse the Wilsonian concept of collective security—which Charles and Clifford Kupchan refer to as "ideal collective security"—critiqued so well by I.L. Claude thirty years ago.[1] Nor does institutionalism embrace the aspirations to transform international relations put forward by some critical theorists. Like realism, institutionalist theory is utilitarian and rationalistic.[2]

However, Professor Mearsheimer's version of realism has some rather serious flaws. Among them are its penchant for assertions that turn out to be incorrect; its propensity to privilege its own viewpoint, so that in the absence of decisive evidence either way it invariably seems to prevail; its failure to explicate the conditions for the operation of its generalizations; and its logical contradictions, escaped only through verbal sleight-of-hand. We will begin by pointing out such errors from his own recent articles in this journal, then

Robert O. Keohane is Stanfield Professor of International Peace, Harvard University, and author of After Hegemony: Cooperation and Discord in the World Political Economy (Princeton University Press, 1984). Lisa L. Martin is John L. Loeb Associate Professor of Government, Harvard University, and author of Coercive Cooperation: Explaining Multilateral Economic Sanctions (Princeton University Press, 1992).

The authors thank Marc Busch, Chris Gelpi, Andrew Moravcsik, and Celeste Wallander for their valuable comments on an earlier version of this essay.

1. Inis L. Claude, Power and International Relations (New York: Random House, 1962). Mearsheimer relies heavily on Claude's critique in his own discussion of collective security.
2. See Richard K. Ashley, "The Poverty of Neorealism," International Organization, Vol. 38, No. 2 (Spring 1984), pp. 225–286. Ashley included Robert O. Keohane as one of the "neorealists" whose "orrery of errors" he rejected. The fact that Mearsheimer criticized institutionalism and critical theory in the same article should not, therefore, lead readers to believe that there is an intellectual affinity between these two schools of thought. However, the work of "constructivist" theorists such as Alexander Wendt eloquently makes a number of arguments that many institutionalists would accept.

International Security, Vol. 20, No. 1 (Summer 1995), pp. 39–51
© 1995 by the President and Fellows of Harvard College and the Massachusetts Institute of Technology.

examine his major claims about institutionalism. We consider the illusory divide between security and economic issues, the muddled question of "relative gains," and empirical work (admittedly in its early stages) that provides evidence of the significance of international institutions. We conclude that institutions sometimes matter, and that it is a worthy task of social science to discover how, and under what conditions, this is the case.

The Fallacious Logic of Realism

Five years ago Professor Mearsheimer forecast the imminent decline of NATO: "It is the Soviet threat that holds NATO together. Take away that offensive threat and the United States is likely to abandon the Continent, whereupon the defensive alliance it headed for forty years may disintegrate."[3] At the same time, he predicted that "the EC is likely [due to the end of the Cold War] to grow weaker, not stronger with time."[4] Yet now that both NATO and the European Community, now the European Union (EU), are expanding their memberships, and hardly in decline, he abandons specificity for the equally false but more difficult to falsify generalization that "institutions have minimal influence on state behavior and thus hold little prospect for promoting stability in a post–Cold War world."[5]

Professor Mearsheimer demands proof that international institutions matter. Yet he begins his article by reminding us that major governments recently have been emphasizing the value of international institutions; he could have added that they invest significant material and reputational resources in NATO, the EU, and also in organizations such as the General Agreement on Tariffs and Trade (GATT, recently strengthened to create the World Trade Organization) and the North American Free Trade Agreement (NAFTA). Not all international institutions command such resources from governments, but some do. How are we to account for the willingness of major states to invest resources in expanding international institutions, if such institutions are lacking in significance? Mearsheimer suggests that the answer lies in an ideological blindness of American policymakers, whose hostility toward realism drives them to the more congenial institutionalist framework (pp. 47–49). It is difficult to

---

3. John J. Mearsheimer, "Back to the Future: Instability in Europe after the Cold War," *International Security*, Vol. 15, No. 1 (Summer 1990), p. 52.
4. John J. Mearsheimer, "Correspondence: Back to the Future, Part II," *International Security*, Vol. 15, No. 2 (Fall 1990), p. 199.
5. John J. Mearsheimer, "The False Promise of International Institutions," *International Security*, Vol. 19, No. 3 (Winter 1994/95), p. 7. Subsequent references to this article are in parentheses in the text.

square this assertion of a collective delusion with the dominant role of realist theory in policy discussions, or with realism's own precepts about the forces that drive state behavior. In light of states' investments in international institutions, it is fair to turn Mearsheimer's question around: could we not legitimately demand evidence either that leaders of governments are deluded or that NATO and the EU are designed to deceive unsophisticated observers? Mearsheimer assumes that his view is privileged, in the sense that we must accept realism unless overwhelmingly convincing evidence is presented for an alternative view; but the fact that states invest in international institutions make this stance quite problematic.

Institutionalism and realism differ in a number of other respects, one of the most significant of which concerns how they approach social science. A central fault of Mearsheimer's realism as a scientific theory—rather than as rhetoric—is that the conditions for the operation of its "grim picture of world politics" (p. 9) typically are not well-specified. Realism is replete with global generalizations, lacking qualifications about the conditions under which they may be valid. Let us consider two examples from Mearsheimer's own article. First, Mearsheimer writes that "states in a realist world . . . must be motivated *primarily* by relative gains concerns when considering cooperation" (p. 12, emphasis added). But he later admits that this proposition may be false when the threat of aggressive war is low—for instance, when defensive technologies (such as secure second-strike nuclear forces) are prevalent (pp. 23–25). Second, in Mearsheimer's realist world, "every state would like to be the most formidable military power in the system" (p. 12). But since no one thinks that Switzerland, Argentina, or contemporary Britain actually seeks to become "the most formidable military power," what Mearsheimer presumably means to argue is that states with sufficient capabilities always pursue this goal. Even this statement is often false: for example, the United States during the interwar period could reasonably have expected to become the most powerful state in the world, but did not seek such a position. Confronted with such contradictions and anomalies, realism typically retreats from universal rhetoric to *post hoc* and *ad hoc* qualifications, taking into account geography, history, perceptions, and domestic politics.

Institutionalism, in contrast, seeks to state in advance the conditions under which its propositions apply. Our theory may therefore have less appeal to those who require simple "truths," but purportedly scientific theories should specify the conditions under which the theory is expected to hold *a priori*. As Mearsheimer indicates, when state elites do not foresee self-interested benefits from cooperation, we do not expect cooperation to occur, nor the institutions that facilitate cooperation to develop. When states can jointly benefit from cooperation, on the other hand, we expect governments to attempt to construct such institutions. Institutions can provide information, reduce transaction costs, make commitments more credible, establish focal points for coordination, and in general facilitate the operation of reciprocity. By seeking to specify the conditions under which institutions can have an impact and cooperation can occur, institutionalist theory shows under what conditions realist propositions are valid. It is in this sense that institutionalism claims to subsume realism.

Realism's proclivity for bold, unqualified generalizations not only generates anomalies but gets its proponents into logical difficulties. Mearsheimer holds that "institutions have no independent effect on state behavior" (p. 7); that NATO is an institution (p. 13); and that NATO played a role in preventing World War III and helping the West win the Cold War (pp. 13–14). These propositions sound like a classically fallacious syllogism, until one recognizes that there is an escape clause: "NATO was basically a manifestation of the bipolar distribution of power in Europe during the Cold War, and it was that balance of power, not NATO *per se*, that provided the key to maintaining stability on the continent" (p. 14). But liberal institutionalists, who see institutions as rooted in the realities of power and interest, do not argue that NATO could have maintained stability under any imaginable conditions. What we argue is that institutions make a significant difference in conjunction with power realities. Institutions are important "independently" only in the ordinary sense used in social science: controlling for the effects of power and interests, it matters whether they exist. They also have an interactive effect, meaning that their impact on outcomes varies, depending on the nature of power and interests. Mearsheimer is forced to admit the truth of institutional effects with regard to NATO, although for rhetorical purposes he shifts his ground to attack a view that we do not hold: that institutions can prevent war regardless of the structure in which they operate.

Hence Mearsheimer's version of realism is replete with analytical problems. However, it is not our duty here to correct realism's copy-book. In the rest of this brief response, therefore, we focus on the promise of institutionalist theory, and the research directions that we hope will help to realize that promise.

Political Economy vs. Security and the Issue of Relative Gains

Although Mearsheimer has provided an admirable summary of several aspects of institutionalist theory, his version of our argument requires correction on two major points. First, Mearsheimer asserts that institutionalist theory is based on "the assumption that international politics can be divided into two realms—security and political economy—and that liberal institutionalism mainly applies to the latter" (pp. 15–16). Although some institutionalists have made this assertion, it is not the predominant view of the institutionalist literature, and we certainly do not accept it. Secondly, in contrast to Mearsheimer's assertion, our focus is not exclusively on "cheating." Situations of coordination, in which cheating is not a problem but distributional issues are serious, are equally important, although they were underemphasized (but not absent) in the early institutionalist literature.

THE PURPORTED SECURITY VS. POLITICAL ECONOMY DIVIDE

Mearsheimer's assertion that institutionalism employs a "neat dividing line" to separate political economy from security issues is surprising, in view of the attention that he devotes to the volume edited by Kenneth Oye, *Cooperation Under Anarchy*. A major argument of *Cooperation Under Anarchy* is that institutionalist theory can be applied to *both* security and political economy issues. As Robert Axelrod and Robert O. Keohane wrote:

It has often been noted that military-security issues display more of the characteristics associated with anarchy than do political-economic ones. Charles Lipson, for instance, has recently observed that political-economic relationships are typically more institutionalized than military-security ones. This does not mean, however, that analysis of these two sets of issues requires two separate analytical frameworks. Indeed, one of the major purposes of the present collection is to show that *a single framework can throw light on both* [emphasis added].[6]

We share Mearsheimer's view that there is no clean analytical line between economic and security issues, although we do not base our view on the overarching role of relative gains. Institutionalist theory should be highly applicable to security issues because its argument revolves around the role of institutions in providing *information*. This argument is pertinent to realist security arguments, which often rely on worst-case analysis. Realists contend that in an uncertain, anarchic world, states must assume the worst, particularly about others' intentions, when making policy choices. Worst-case analysis

---

6. Robert Axelrod and Robert O. Keohane, "Achieving Cooperation Under Anarchy: Strategies and Institutions," in Kenneth A. Oye, ed., *Cooperation Under Anarchy* (Princeton: Princeton University Press, 1986), p. 227.

implies following policies that do not maximize expected utility for the sake of avoiding terrible outcomes. But if one can secure more information, it may be possible to follow policies that more nearly maximize utility.[7] Realist writers from Kautilya on have stressed the significance of information (intelligence); if institutions can provide useful information, realists should see them as significant. The logic of institutionalist theory is directly applicable to security problems as realists define them.

Hence, if Mearsheimer meant to offer us a "loophole" through which to escape his criticism—that institutionalist theory is only applicable to non-security issues—we emphatically refuse to avail ourselves of his generosity. On the contrary, we hope that, to use Axelrod's phrase, institutionalist theory will gradually "invade" the study of security issues, helping to explain variation in institutional form without denying the validity of many realist insights into power and interests.

RELATIVE GAINS AND INTERNATIONAL COOPERATION

The conclusions we draw from the "relative gains" debate are different from those of Professor Mearsheimer. It is true that when only two states exist and they have perfectly conflicting interests, institutions will not be significant, but this point is obvious. Two issues are more significant: 1) the conditions under which relative gains are important; and 2) the role of institutions when distributional issues are significant—that is, when relative gains are at stake.

It is important to understand the great variation in the extent to which relative gains matter. The major lesson of the recent debate on relative gains is that their importance is *conditional* on factors such as the number of major actors in the system and whether military advantage favors offense or defense.[8] Duncan Snidal has shown that relative gains are unlikely to have much impact on cooperation if the potential absolute gains from cooperation are substantial, or in any context involving more than two states.[9] A valuable aspect of the relative gains debate is that it has made distributional and bargaining issues

---

7. See Celeste A. Wallander, "Balance and Institutions in German-Russian Security Relations after the Cold War," manuscript, Harvard University, 1994; Celeste A. Wallander and Robert O. Keohane, "Toward an Institutional Theory of Alliances," paper prepared for delivery at the Annual Meeting of the International Studies Association, Chicago, Illinois, February 22–25, 1995.
8. See David A. Baldwin, ed., *Neorealism and Neoliberalism: The Contemporary Debate* (New York: Columbia University Press, 1993), p. 323, especially chapters by Joseph Grieco, Duncan Snidal, Robert Powell, and Robert O. Keohane.
9. Duncan Snidal, "Relative Gains and the Pattern of International Cooperation," *American Political Science Review*, Vol. 85, No. 3 (September 1991), pp. 701–726.

more salient than they were in early neoliberal thinking,[10] but if the debate becomes one of "whether" relative gains matter, that value will be dissipated. We need instead to ask under what conditions such distributional conflicts are severe.

What is the role of institutions when distributional issues are important? Contrary to the assertion that institutionalist theory is irrelevant to distributional issues, we argue that distributional conflict may render institutions *more* important. To understand this point, it is essential to distinguish between two problems that states face when they attempt to cooperate. They often worry about the potential for others to cheat, as in a Prisoners' Dilemma. But they also face the problem of coordinating their actions on a particular stable cooperative outcome (solving the problem of multiple equilibria, in game-theoretic terminology). Usually more than one cooperative outcome exists. The states involved may not agree on which of these outcomes is preferred, as each has different distributional implications. Disagreement about the specific form of cooperation is the principal barrier to cooperation in such coordination games. Unless some coordinating mechanism exists, states may fail to capture the potential gains from cooperation. Institutions do not provide the only possible coordinating mechanism.[11] However, in complex situations involving many states, international institutions can step in to provide "constructed focal points" that make particular cooperative outcomes prominent.

Realists interpret the relative-gains logic as showing that states will not cooperate with one another if each suspects that its potential partners are gaining more from cooperation than it is. However, just as institutions can mitigate fears of cheating and so allow cooperation to emerge, so can they alleviate fears of unequal gains from cooperation. Liberal theory argues that institutions provide valuable information, and information about the distribution of gains from cooperation may be especially valuable if the relative-gains logic is correct. Institutions can facilitate cooperation by helping to settle distributional conflicts and by assuring states that gains are evenly divided over

---

10. For development of arguments about the relationship between international regimes and distributional problems, see James D. Morrow, "Modeling the Forms of International Cooperation: Distribution versus Information," *International Organization*, Vol. 48, No. 3 (Summer 1994), pp. 387–423; and James Fearon, "Cooperation and Bargaining Under Anarchy," manuscript, University of Chicago, 1993.

11. For example, Stephen Krasner has argued that coordination problems can be solved by the unilateral exercise of power by the strongest state. Stephen D. Krasner, "Global Communications and National Power: Life on the Pareto Frontier," *World Politics*, Vol. 43, No. 3 (April 1991), pp. 336–366.

time, for example by disclosing information about the military expenditures and capacities of alliance members.

In our view the successful functioning of institutions depends heavily on the operation of reciprocity, both specific and diffuse.[12] States using strategies of reciprocity are engaged in exchange with one another and so require information about the value of their exchanges. Institutionalized reciprocity and distributional concerns are simply two sides of the same coin, reflecting the difficulties of cooperating in a system lacking centralized enforcement and pointing to the need for reliable sources of information if states are to achieve gains from cooperation. Far from leading to the conclusion that institutions are not significant in world politics, the relative-gains debate has led us to understand yet another pathway through which they substantially influence the course of international relations. A crucial step in the institutionalist research program will be to understand the conditions under which institutions can provide the information necessary to serve as reliable solutions to distributional problems.

Empirical Work on the Impact of Institutions

We agree with John Mearsheimer that "more empirical work is needed before a final judgment is rendered on the explanatory power of liberal institutionalism" (p. 26). The point of a new theory is to generate testable hypotheses: liberal institutionalism, like any other theory, only has value insofar as it generates propositions that can be tested against real evidence.

Institutionalist theory conceptualizes institutions both as independent and dependent variables: "institutions change as a result of human action, and the changes in expectations and process that result can exert profound effects on state behavior."[13] Institutional theory has a coherent account of both the creation of institutions and their effects: institutions are created by states *because of* their anticipated effects on patterns of behavior. Early research by institutionalists focused on institutions as dependent variables, examining the conditions under which they are created. Recent research has sought more systematically

---

12. Robert O. Keohane, "Reciprocity in International Relations," *International Organization*, Vol. 40, No. 1 (Winter 1986), pp. 1–27.
13. Robert O. Keohane, *International Institutions and State Power* (Boulder, Colo.: Westview, 1989), p. 10.

to demonstrate that institutions are sometimes significant for political outcomes, and to determine the conditions under which this is the case.[14]

In view of this research program, it should be clear that evidence that
institutions change in response to underlying conditions is hardly a blow
against institutionalist theory. That theory, after all, posits that international
institutions are created in response to state interests, and that their character is
structured by the prevailing distribution of capabilities. The real empirical issue
is how to distinguish the effects of underlying conditions from those of the
institutions themselves. One result of the interdependence between institutions
and underlying forces is that research designed to isolate the impact of institutions is difficult to design and execute. Rarely, if ever, will institutions vary
while the "rest of the world" is held constant. Thus finding the ideal quasi-
experimental situation to test the impact of institutions is not possible.

However, these difficulties do not make it impossible to test the argument
that institutions matter, since changes in underlying conditions and in institutions are not perfectly correlated. Hence it may be worthwhile to search for
instances in which underlying conditions have changed rapidly while institutions have remained relatively constant, or where similar structural changes
confront regions that have different institutional endowments. Another tactic
may be to consider the level of institutional variation itself. The institutionalist
perspective leads us to expect patterned variation in the types of institutions
states construct, since they anticipate that institutions so constructed will constrain them. Analysis of institutional form, such as variations in the institution-
alization of alliances or in the legalization of the international trading system,
should therefore provide valuable evidence for evaluating institutionalist
theory.

Realism's insistence that institutions have only marginal effects renders its
account of institutional creation incomplete and logically unsound, and leaves
it without a plausible account of the investments that states have made in such
international institutions as the EU, NATO, GATT, and regional trading organizations. According to the precepts of realist theory, states act rationally when
they construct institutions, although they know that these institutions will have

---

14. Since institutionalists do not claim that institutions always have a major impact on outcomes,
finding weak institutions hardly constitutes a refutation of institutionalist theory. Hence the
weakness of the International Energy Agency during the 1979 oil crisis, described by Keohane in
After Hegemony: Cooperation and Discord in the World Political Economy (Princeton: Princeton University Press, 1984), is hardly the damning evidence that Mearsheimer claims.

no impact on patterns of cooperation. But what could be the rationale behind devoting resources to structures that will make no difference? Rather than asserting that institutions have no impact, realists must mean that institutions have some effect other than that assumed by liberal institutionalists. Perhaps institutions satisfy the ideological demands of statesmen, or help to pacify inattentive publics. Whatever the rationale, we challenge realists to construct an account of institutional variation and effects that can be tested against the institutionalist alternative. The difference between realism and liberal institutionalism does not lie in whether institutions are independent or dependent variables; it lies in contrasting understandings of *why* institutions are created and *how* they exert their effects.

A number of recent studies establish institutional effects through careful empirical research, guided by institutionalist theory and recognizing potential problems of endogeneity and omitted-variable bias.[15] Ronald B. Mitchell shows that on three different issues involving oil pollution at sea, whether states complied with institutional regulations depended on the nature of the rules. "Clear causal links unambiguously demonstrate that treaty rules independently influenced behavior, with other plausible factors controlled for or absent."[16] New rules on the kinds of tanks that ships are allowed to use, for example, have had a dramatic impact on intentional discharge of oil into the oceans.

The European Court of Justice (ECJ) has also proven a fruitful ground for the study of institutional influence. Anne-Marie Slaughter Burley and Walter Mattli show how the ECJ has had an unexpectedly large impact on the politics of European integration, transforming political into legal issues with the aid of transnational networks of lawyers and judges.[17] The ECJ has gone far to convert the Treaties of Rome into a constitution for the EU, with the result that EU law now reaches deeply into the domestic law of member states. Geoffrey Garrett and Barry Weingast, in another study of the ECJ, show how it resolved problems of multiple equilibria for EU member states by providing constructed

15. On such issues see Gary King, Robert O. Keohane, and Sidney Verba, *Designing Social Inquiry: Scientific Inference in Qualitative Research* (Princeton: Princeton University Press, 1994).

16. Ronald B. Mitchell, *Intentional Oil Pollution at Sea: Environmental Policy and Treaty Compliance* (Cambridge, Mass.: The MIT Press, 1994). See also Ronald B. Mitchell, "Regime Design Matters: Intentional Oil Pollution and Treaty Compliance," *International Organization*, Vol. 48, No. 3 (Summer 1994), pp. 425–458.

17. Anne-Marie Burley and Walter Mattli, "Europe before the Court: A Political Theory of Legal Integration," *International Organization*, Vol. 47, No. 1 (Winter 1993), pp. 41–76. (Anne-Marie Burley now goes by the name Anne-Marie Slaughter.)

focal points in coordination problems.[18] These studies show that institutions have the wide range of effects attributed to them by liberal institutionalists. They change the incentives for states to cheat; they also reduce transaction costs, link issues, and provide focal points for cooperation.

The institutionalist perspective has also been applied with success to the analysis of security regimes. John Duffield has considered NATO as a regional security regime. He finds that NATO made an independent contribution to the "Long Peace" in Europe by drawing boundaries, demonstrating U.S. commitments and making them credible, and facilitating the augmentation of NATO allies' military capabilities.[19] He also finds that the stable norms and rules of NATO led to stability in levels of conventional forces within the regime that cannot be explained by structural theories.[20]

In *Coercive Cooperation*, Lisa Martin showed that the involvement of international organizations in economic sanctions is strongly correlated with high levels of cooperation.[21] Since such a correlation does not establish causality, she also did qualitative work on several cases involving sanctions, including EC sanctions against Argentina during the Falklands War. Mearsheimer considers the Falklands case in isolation from the rest of this research, and dismisses it as "less than a ringing endorsement for liberal institutionalism" on the grounds that concerns about cheating were not involved (p. 25). In fact, Martin does find evidence that states used the EC framework to reduce fears of cheating, in the form of taking advantage of the situation to profit from trade with Argentina.[22] However, the major effect of institutions came through institutionalized linkages that would otherwise have been nonexistent: a linkage between EC budget contributions and the sanctions issue. Prevention of cheating is not the only mechanism by which institutions facilitate cooperation. By creating issue linkages, they allow for more effective retaliation against cheaters and also create scope for mutually-beneficial exchanges. Further evidence for the

---

18. Geoffrey Garrett and Barry R. Weingast, "Ideas, Interests, and Institutions: Constructing the European Community's Internal Market," in Judith Goldstein and Robert O. Keohane, eds., *Ideas and Foreign Policy: Beliefs, Institutions, and Political Change* (Ithaca, N.Y.: Cornell University Press, 1993), pp. 173–206.

19. John S. Duffield, "Explaining the Long Peace in Europe: The Contributions of Regional Security Regimes," *Review of International Studies*, Vol. 20, No. 4 (October 1994), pp. 369–388.

20. John S. Duffield, "International Regimes and Alliance Behavior: Explaining NATO Conventional Force Levels," *International Organization*, Vol. 46, No. 4 (Fall 1992), pp. 819–855.

21. Lisa L. Martin, *Coercive Cooperation: Explaining Multilateral Economic Sanctions* (Princeton: Princeton University Press, 1992).

22. Ibid., p. 143.

EC's role in coordinating sanctions comes from the fact that outside the EC, the only other significant support Britain received came from Commonwealth nations and the United States. In the U.S. case, support was delayed until after the outbreak of war, in distinct contrast to the behavior of EC members.[23] Mearsheimer's dismissal of international institutions implies that linkages are easy to forge when a state desires cooperation, and that cooperation is easy to coordinate even without institutions, yet Britain did not find either to be the case. Even in isolation from the robust statistical results and other case studies reported in *Coercive Cooperation*, the Falklands case illustrates the central role of formal international institutions in enabling states to cooperate to impose multilateral economic sanctions.[24]

Institutions sometimes matter for state policy, but we do not adequately understand in what domains they matter most, under what conditions, and how their effects are exerted. More research on this subject, by students of world politics critical of institutionalist theory as well as by those working from it, is essential, and will be most welcome.

Conclusion

Far from demonstrating the irrelevance of international institutions, Mearsheimer's characterization of conflict in world politics makes institutions appear essential if states are to have any hope of sustained cooperation, and of reaping its benefits. This necessity for institutions does not mean that they are always valuable, much less that they operate without respect to power and interests, constitute a panacea for violent conflict, or always reduce the likelihood of war. Claiming too much for international institutions would indeed be a "false promise." But in a world politics constrained by state power and divergent interests, and unlikely to experience effective hierarchical governance, international institutions operating on the basis of reciprocity will be components of any lasting peace.

---

23. Japan initially refused British pleas to impose sanctions, and took only minor steps following U.S. imposition of sanctions, much later than EC members.

24. The Falklands case cannot be dismissed on grounds that, as Mearsheimer claims, striking a deal was "not difficult." The historical record shows intense conflict, including public protests in some countries and challenges to the sitting government in others. The Thatcher government believed that its survival was at stake in the Falklands War. While perhaps not a "core interest" by realist standards, government survival is surely a fundamental concern of policymakers that could impede cooperation.

The institutionalist research program in international relations is a promising one. The logic of institutionalist theory, with its focus on the informational role of institutions, appears solid. Institutionalists should respond to Mearsheimer's criticisms by better integrating distributional considerations into their models, further specifying the causal mechanisms by which institutions exercise influence, and building on existing empirical work to provide more convincing evidence of institutional effects. Both the questions raised and the provisional answers given by institutionalists, during the relatively short life of this research program, indicate that these tasks may be rewarding. In comparison with the extant alternatives, the promise of institutionalist theory seems bright.

The Promise of Collective Security

Charles A. Kupchan and Clifford A. Kupchan

John J. Mearsheimer's critique of collective security misses its mark for three main reasons. First, Mearsheimer employs so narrow a definition of collective security that he defines away the issues most central to evaluating the peace-causing effects of institutions within the collective security family. Second, he misrepresents how collective security acts to promote stability, by portraying it as based on moralistic principles that violate the logic of power balancing. But collective security is, if nothing else, all about balancing and the aggregation of military force against threats to peace. Indeed, its main advantages over balancing under anarchy are that it provides for more effective balancing against aggressors and that it promotes a more cooperative international environment, thereby making inter-state rivalry and aggression less likely. Third, Mearsheimer's general critique of institutions stems from a theoretical perspective—structural realism—that ignores the extent to which domestic politics, beliefs, and norms shape state behavior. By explaining war and peace solely in terms of power balancing in an anarchic world, Mearsheimer mounts an attack that is at once ahistorical and internally contradictory. We contend that a theoretical perspective that takes power seriously, but not to the exclusion of domestic and ideational variables, offers a richer, more accurate vision of international politics. It is within this vision that collective security has an important role to play in promoting peace and cooperation.

Defining Collective Security

The case for collective security rests on the claim that regulated, institutionalized balancing predicated on the notion of all against one provides more stability than unregulated, self-help balancing predicated on the notion of each for his own. Under collective security, states agree to abide by certain norms and rules to maintain stability and, when necessary, band together to stop

Charles A. Kupchan is Senior Fellow for Europe at the Council on Foreign Relations and a professor at Georgetown University. Clifford A. Kupchan is Senior Foreign Policy Adviser to Congressman Harry Johnston.

The authors would like to thank Richard Betts, George Downs, Peter Katzenstein, Robert Keohane, Lisa Martin, Jack Snyder, and Alexander Wendt for their comments on earlier drafts of this article.

International Security, Vol. 20, No. 1 (Summer 1995), pp. 52–61
© 1995 by the President and Fellows of Harvard College and the Massachusetts Institute of Technology.

aggression. Stability—the absence of major war—is the product of cooperation. In a world of balancing under anarchy, states fend for themselves according to the dictates of a hostile international environment. Stability emerges from competition. The key question is whether regulated balancing predicated upon the notion of all against one, or unregulated balancing predicated upon the notion of each for his own, is more likely to preserve peace. Our task is to show only that collective security is preferable to balancing under anarchy, not that collective security is a panacea or the ultimate answer to preventing war.

In his critique, Mearsheimer focuses only on ideal collective security—a variant in which states make automatic and legally binding commitments to respond to aggression wherever and whenever it occurs. He explicitly excludes from consideration other institutional formulations, such as concerts, that rely on looser and more informal regulation of balancing, arguing that they do not constitute collective security. As a result of this definitional maneuver, Mearsheimer directs his critique at a straw man and fails to engage the core conceptual issue at stake: whether some form of regulated, institutionalized balancing is preferable to unregulated balancing under anarchy.

Of necessity, debate about the value of institutions must focus on generic formulations, not on the performance of a specific institutional variant. Any institution that is predicated upon the principles of regulated balancing and all against one falls into the collective security family. Concerts do retain an undercurrent of competitive, self-help balancing. But they operate in a regulated, norm-governed environment and are predicated on the logic of all against one, not each for his own. Accordingly, our original terminology, which refers to a family of collective security organizations ranging from ideal collective security to concerts, best captures the underlying conceptual issues at stake.[1] Mearsheimer's formulation is, simply put, analytically unsustainable. He insists that concerts are "largely consistent with realism" and logically "incompatible" with collective security, but writes that concerts entail "coordinated balancing" among "great powers that have no incentive to challenge each other militarily [and] agree on a set of rules to coordinate their actions" (p. 35). These features are fundamental attributes of collective security and stand in

---

1. For further discussion, see Richard Betts, "Systems for Peace or Causes of War? Collective Security, Arms Control, and the New Europe," *International Security,* Vol. 17, No. 1 (Summer 1992), pp. 5–43; George Downs and Keisuke Iida, "Assessing the Theoretical Case Against Collective Security," in George Downs, ed., *Collective Security Beyond the Cold War* (Ann Arbor: University of Michigan Press, 1994), pp. 17–21; and Charles Lipson, "Is the Future of Collective Security Like the Past?" in ibid., pp. 105–131.

stark contrast to the inescapable competition and self-help strategies of realist balancing under anarchy.[2]

The Advantages of Collective Security

The advantages of collective security fall into two categories: it provides for more effective balancing against aggressors, and it promotes trust and cooperation.

MORE EFFECTIVE BALANCING AGAINST AGGRESSORS
Perhaps because of confusion over what collective security is, Mearsheimer misunderstands its underlying causal logic. According to Mearsheimer, collective security requires that states "ignore . . . balance-of-power considerations" (p. 33). This characterization is fundamentally mistaken. Collective security addresses head-on the central concern of realists with the competitive nature of the international environment and its propensity to trigger spirals of hostility. Fully aware of the war-causing features of the international system, collective security seeks to provide a more effective mechanism for balancing against aggressors when they emerge, as well as to make aggression less likely by ameliorating the competitive nature of international relations. The challenge for proponents of collective security is not, as Mearsheimer writes, to show that "institutions are the key to managing power successfully" (p. 27). It is to show that there is value added: that institutions are better than no institutions and offer an improvement upon the self-help world of balancing under anarchy.

Collective security provides for more effective balancing against aggressors than balancing under anarchy because, when it works, it confronts aggressors with preponderant as opposed to merely equal force.[3] Under anarchy, only those states directly threatened by the aggressor and states with vital interests in the threatened areas will band together to resist aggression. Under collective

2. See John J. Mearsheimer, "The False Promise of International Institutions," *International Security*, Vol. 19, No. 3 (Winter 1994/95), pp. 5–49. The conceptual muddle caused by Mearsheimer's restrictive definition of collective security is also apparent in his discussion of the empirical record (pp. 33–34). Mearsheimer refers to the League of Nations and the United Nations as collective security organizations. Neither, however, comes close to fulfilling the standards of ideal collective security. The League Covenant and the UN Charter do not entail automatic and binding commitments to respond to aggression with force. Both organizations created inner councils to enhance the influence of the great powers. In these respects, the League and the UN resemble concerts more than they do ideal collective security organizations.
3. See Charles A. Kupchan and Clifford A. Kupchan, "Concerts, Collective Security, and the Future of Europe," *International Security*, Vol. 16, No. 1 (Summer 1991), p. 117, n. 6.

security, other states are likely to join the opposing coalition, both because they have made either explicit or implicit commitments to do so and because they have interests in protecting an international order that they see as beneficial to their individual security.[4] Furthermore, even when it does not work, collective security at its worst (that is, when all member states other than those directly threatened renege on their commitment to resist aggression) is roughly equivalent to balancing under anarchy at its best. Should non-threatened states opt out of collective action, the remaining coalition would consist of the same directly threatened states as the alliance that would form through balancing under anarchy.

The most powerful critique of the argument that collective security at its worst is roughly equivalent to balancing under anarchy at its best is that collective security encourages member states to count on the assistance of others, thereby leaving a directly threatened coalition underprepared for war if the system unravels (p. 30). In a self-help world, the argument runs, the opposing coalition would have known that it was on its own, and prepared accordingly.

Because this critique has been dealt with elsewhere, here we only summarize the main points of rebuttal.[5] First, it is the specter of a collective security organization unraveling on the eve of aggression that causes concern about directly threatened states being left unprepared for war. Yet this scenario is highly improbable; the failure of collective security mechanisms is likely to occur in stages, giving directly threatened states adequate warning that the blocking coalition will not contain its full complement of members. In addition, directly threatened members of a collective security system would be well aware that some of their partners might defect; prudence would dictate the maintenance of force levels greater than those needed should all members

---

4. See ibid., p. 126. Collective security seeks to expand the realm of private interest so that even states whose security is not immediately threatened have a stake in preventing aggression. It does not, as Mearsheimer writes, require that states "not think in terms of narrow self-interest" (p. 29). Rather, it seeks to broaden how states define their self-interest through two different pathways. First, assuming that interests are fixed and confined to realist notions of rational egoism, collective security alters incentives so that states more often find it in their interests to cooperate as opposed to compete. Second, collective security alters the character of state interests themselves, not just the behavior that states adopt to attain those interests. Through processes of learning and socialization, states can come to define their interests in more collective terms. Through its participation in the EU and NATO, for example, Germany has come to define its interests in European rather than in purely national terms. For further discussion, see pp. 57–59 below.
5. See Charles Kupchan, "The Case for Collective Security," in Downs, *Collective Security*, pp. 59–63.

fulfill commitments to collective action. Mearsheimer suggests that, until outright war breaks out, states in a collective security system "must trust each other" and eschew steps to balance against potential aggressors (pp. 29–30). But it is absurd to suggest that collective security—even in its ideal form—requires its members to stand by idly as one among them arms itself to its teeth. As we have argued, concerts are particularly well suited to orchestrating pre-aggression deterrence and the early formation of a preponderant blocking coalition.[6]

Second, states do not set force levels simply by assessing the capabilities of the enemy and determining how much of their own military power is required, given the strength of coalition partners, to achieve preponderance. The level of military capability maintained by a given state is affected by its general threat environment, but also by a complex mix of political and economic considerations. There is no one-to-one ratio between external threat and force level. Rather, as threats increase, governments and publics become generally more willing to devote increased resources to the output of defense goods. Force levels rise with the political will to support the necessary expenditures, not only as military planners calculate what it will take to defeat the enemy. When faced with an increasingly hostile adversary of growing military strength, a directly threatened state in a collective security system would devote more resources to defense, just as it would in an alliance system. Indeed, it may well maintain force levels roughly equivalent to the levels it would maintain as a member of a defensive alliance.

Third, although free riding may contribute to the underproduction of military capability, there is no compelling deductive reason why the free-rider problem should produce a weaker opposing coalition under collective security than under balancing under anarchy.[7] All coalitions, including defensive alliances, can fall prey to free riding. Indeed, the historical example that Mearsheimer uses to illustrate the free-rider problem is that of intra-alliance buck-passing among Britain, France, and Russia during World War I (pp. 31–32). Again, the key question is not whether collective security is flawless, but

---

6. See Kupchan and Kupchan, "Concerts, Collective Security, and the Future of Europe," pp. 138–144. Collective security institutions that do not make responses to aggression automatic and legally binding also take care of Mearsheimer's charge that collective security "transforms every local conflict into an international conflict" by mandating that all members respond to every act of aggression (p. 32). Concerts can play as important a role in orchestrating mutual restraint as in coordinating collective action.

7. For further discussion, see Downs and Iida, "Assessing the Theoretical Case Against Collective Security," pp. 26–29.

whether it deters and blocks aggressors more effectively than balancing under anarchy.[8]

PROMOTING TRUST AND COOPERATION

Assessment of collective security's historical performance poses particular empirical problems because it is when collective security is functioning most effectively that its benefits may be difficult to discern.[9] Collective security is preferable to balancing under anarchy not only because it provides better balancing against aggressors, but also because it fosters an environment in which aggression is less likely to take place. Indeed, its ability to mitigate the rivalry and hostility of a self-help world is one of its key advantages.

Mearsheimer misrepresents collective security's reliance on and promotion of trust among states as one of its chief logical flaws. "Collective security is an incomplete theory," Mearsheimer writes, "because it does not provide a satisfactory explanation for how states overcome their fears and learn to trust one another" (p. 30). We acknowledge that basic compatibility among the great powers in a system is foremost among the conditions necessary for the successful operation of collective security. And this compatibility is a function of the underlying interests and intentions of states, not of their participation in a collective security system. But collective security, through mechanisms we outline in "Concerts, Collective Security, and the Future of Europe" (pp. 130–133) builds on this basic compatibility and reinforces confidence in the inten-

---

8. We acknowledge that it is conceivable that collective security could produce a weaker opposing coalition than balancing under anarchy. At least hypothetically, aggression could take place as a bolt from the blue, or directly threatened states could be dangerously overconfident about the willingness of their coalition partners to join the fray. But for the reasons just enumerated, the risks of such an outcome are low. And these risks are well worth taking in light of collective security's considerable advantages.

9. Mearsheimer incorrectly claims that the empirical record undermines the case for collective security. The Concert of Europe preserved peace in Europe for forty years, not, as Mearsheimer asserts, for eight. The Concert's handling of the Belgian Crisis of 1830–32, the Unkiar-Skelessi question in 1833–34, and the Egyptian Crisis of 1839–41 provides evidence of its successful operation after 1823. It ceased to function only after the revolutions of 1848 destroyed the conditions that enabled it to operate. See Kupchan and Kupchan, "Concerts, Collective Security, and the Future of Europe," pp. 142–143, note 81. The League of Nations enjoyed successes during the 1920s, as Mearsheimer enumerates (p. 33). Admittedly, it failed dramatically to counter Japanese and German aggression during the 1930s. But the existence of the League had virtually nothing to do with the status quo powers' underpreparation for war and their initial inability to deter or stop Germany and Japan. The UN was never seriously tested as a collective security institution because of the Cold War. With the Cold War only recently over, it is too soon to judge whether the UN's effectiveness is on the rise or to determine whether some combination of the Organization for Security and Cooperation in Europe (OSCE, formerly CSCE), NATO, and the Partnership for Peace will emerge as a functioning collective security institution for Europe.

tions of other states, thereby deepening cooperation.[10] It promotes a more benign international environment in which states can devote less attention and fewer resources to ensuring their survival and more to improving their welfare—unless and until an aggressor emerges.[11]

There are profound advantages to institutionalizing a security system that promises to deepen accord among states rather than letting a self-help system take its course and simply hoping that great power conflict does not reemerge. Collective security ameliorates the security dilemma, thereby enhancing stability and reducing the likelihood of unintended spirals of hostility.[12] Collective security would also enable states to focus more on absolute as opposed to relative gains, a condition that Mearsheimer admits would facilitate cooperation (pp. 19–24). A state will focus more on absolute gains when it believes that the relative gains of others will not come back to haunt it. This belief is in turn based on deep-seated assessments of the intentions of those states enjoying relative gains. By building confidence among member states about each others' intentions, collective security thus mitigates the constraints imposed on cooperation by relative-gains considerations.[13] Collective security would not allow its members to focus exclusively on absolute gains, but states would be less concerned about relative gains than in a self-help world.

Finally, collective security institutions would help states define their national interests in ways that contribute to international stability. Especially in post–Cold War Europe, where the strategic landscape is ill-defined and major

---

10. Germany's participation in NATO provides an illustration of this institutional evolution. The Federal Republic became part of NATO because of the strategic objectives it shared with other members. But the current closeness of Germany's relations with its West European neighbors and with the United States is a function not just of shared interests but also of its steady participation in the web of Western institutions. It is hard to imagine that Germany's relations with other established democracies would be as close as they are today had these states been interacting with each other only as like-minded powers in an international environment without institutions.

11. In this sense, it is wrong to argue that collective security works only when it is not needed. On the contrary, it is self-reinforcing; as a collective security organization functions, it promotes the conditions that make it even more effective. The idea is not, as Mearsheimer insists, that states must trust each other and be confident that status quo powers "will not change their minds at a later date" (pp. 29–30). Rather, collective security affords states the opportunity to be more confident about the intentions of others until a given state's behavior proves otherwise.

12. See Kupchan and Kupchan, "Concerts, Collective Security, and the Future of Europe," pp. 133–137.

13. For example, the United States today would be relatively unconcerned should Britain acquire a new offensive weapons system or enjoy a relative gain in a trade deal, not because the United States could best Britain if war broke out or readily find allies to form a blocking coalition, but because it is virtually inconceivable that Britain and the United States would find themselves on opposing sides of a conflict. This confidence in Britain's intentions is a product of decades of close, institutionalized cooperation.

powers are in the midst of reformulating their identities and interests, institutions will shape, and not just be shaped by, the distribution of power. NATO was a response to, not the cause of, the division of Europe into two competing blocs. But the institution has taken on a life of its own despite the collapse of the balance-of-power considerations that led to its formation. NATO continues to enable and encourage Germany to define its interests in European, not national terms. It provides a justification and a vehicle for America's continued military engagement in Europe. Its integrated military structure encourages national military establishments to formulate objectives and strategies that are multinational, not national, in character and outlook.

NATO's future will affect not only how its current members interact with each other, but also how the states of the former Soviet bloc define their security needs. If NATO expands into Central Europe as a defensive military alliance and then stops, it will effectively draw a new dividing line between Europe's east and west. It would be the lines and resultant power blocs created by institutions, not by other political or ideological cleavages, that would help define for Russia what its new sphere of influence is, whether it is a European or a Eurasian power, and whether its relations with NATO will be cooperative or competitive. Instead, Russia should be gradually drawn into a European collective security system, increasing the chances that Russians will come to define themselves as members of a European community of nations, not as outsiders. For reasons of its own, Russia may well veer from the path of democratic reform and pursue foreign policies incompatible with its participation in a collective security system. But taking cautious, prudent steps toward its inclusion unless and until Russia demonstrates malign intentions offers far more promise of preserving peace in Europe than exposing a fragile Russia to the vagaries and insecurities of a self-help world.

The Poverty of Structural Realism

Underlying this debate about the value of international institutions is a fundamental difference of opinion about the causes of war and peace. In the end, our assessment of the promise of collective security stems from a theoretical perspective that is incompatible with Mearsheimer's structural realism. It is therefore appropriate to end this reply by making explicit the precise areas of disagreement.

In Mearsheimer's worldview, all great powers are created equal. When they see the opportunity to do so, great powers will take advantage of one another, fearful of being exploited later if they do not. World War I, World War II, and the Cold War were nothing more and nothing less than great powers acting as they must, given the exigencies of an anarchic, self-help world. From within this worldview, collective security, and international institutions more generally, matter at the margins, if at all. Sooner or later, balance-of-power considerations will override the rules and norms of institutional structures. Collective security organizations may be not only irrelevant, but also dangerous. States that place illusory faith in collective security will find themselves worse off than had they acted as if in a self-help, anarchic setting.

In our worldview, all great powers are not created equal. Although the behavior of major states is heavily influenced by balance-of-power considerations, domestic politics, beliefs, and norms matter too, and not just at the margins. World War I, World War II, and the Cold War came about not from the warp and woof of international competition, but as a result of the emergence of aggressor states—states that for reasons of ideology and domestic politics became predatory and sought power, not security. Wilhelmine Germany, Nazi Germany, and interwar Japan were malign great powers infected with virulent domestic pathologies, not garden-variety great powers dealing with legitimate security concerns. Each commenced an ambitious military buildup and embarked down the path of aggression during peaceful periods in which they faced no imminent security threats. Domestic politics and nationalism, not just the rivalry of a self-help world, were at play. Similarly, the United States and the Soviet Union were not equally to blame for the Cold War. The United States sought its share of wealth and power but, with some notable exceptions, conducted itself as a benign great power. Soviet Russia was the principal aggressor state in the Cold War, driven in part by vulnerability and the search for security, but also by domestic and ideological pathologies.[14]

Our contention that it is not only power politics but also the nature of both domestic and international societies that affects great-power behavior is the basis for our optimism about the promise of collective security. It is conceivable that Russia will emerge as a benign, democratic great power and that all of Europe's major states will share similar values and interests, the underpinnings for the successful functioning of a collective security system. Even Mearsheimer admits that ideational variables can play a role in shaping relationships among

---

14. For discussion of aggressor states and their causes, see Charles Kupchan, *The Vulnerability of Empire* (Ithaca, N.Y.: Cornell University Press, 1994); and Stephen Van Evera, "Primed for Peace: Europe After the Cold War," *International Security*, Vol. 15, No. 3 (Winter 1990/91), pp. 7–57.

states. What, after all, does he mean when he writes that "some states are especially friendly for historical or ideological reasons" (p. 31)? We submit that he is scratching the surface of the poverty of his own theoretical framework, forced to resort to variables other than the balance of power to explain why states sometimes cooperate to the extent they do.

The case for collective security rests not on woolly-headed moralism or naivete about the demands imposed on states by power politics. It rests on a more nuanced understanding of international politics than that offered by structural realism. The post–Cold War era offers an excellent laboratory in which to pit these competing theoretical perspectives against each other. If, one or two decades from now, Russia is a full member of a pan-European collective security body, Mearsheimer will have to recant. If, on the other hand, collective security is given a try but Europe's great powers again fall prey to national rivalries and its multilateral institutions founder, we will have to reconsider not just collective security, but the theoretical suppositions that undergird our confidence in it. Unless collective security is given a chance, however, opportunities to preserve peace in Europe will be missed and unresolved debates between structural realists and institutionalists of various stripes will continue to fill the pages of *International Security.*

The False Premise of Realism

John Gerard Ruggie

John J. Mearsheimer's latest missive in defense of the neorealist homeland targets *tous les azimuts* in the camp of institutionalism.[1] The other contributors to this symposium take up Mearsheimer's treatment of the institutionalist literature. I am concerned here with the policy dimensions of his anti-institutionalist posture.

The brevity of this note permits me only to sketch out three counterpoints to Mearsheimer's analysis. First, U.S. policymakers after World War II went out of their way to ignore the anti-institutionalism that Mearsheimer would have us adopt today. Second, had postwar U.S. policymakers accepted Mearsheimer's views about the irrelevance of international institutions, the international security environment today would not only be different but would pose far greater challenges than it does. Third, the unfavorable view of realism which some U.S. policymakers historically have held is not a product of mushy thinking, as Mearsheimer suggests, but of their grasp of a distinctive feature of America's geopolitical situation which continues to prevail today. These facts register poorly, if at all, on Mearsheimer's neorealist radar screen. As a result, the analytical basis of his *force de frappe* against institutionalism entails serious and potentially dangerous limits as a guide for U.S. foreign policy in the post–Cold War world.

Realism and Institutions after World War II

Postwar America pursued its interests and sought to manage the changing international balance of power; that no one questions. But in doing so, U.S. policymakers also had certain institutional objectives in mind, as evidenced by their stance toward the United Nations, the creation of NATO, and European unification. And at every turn, they faced opposition for this stance from realist anti-institutionalists. I enumerate some of the highlights.

John Gerard Ruggie is Dean of the School of International and Public Affairs at Columbia University.

For helpful comments, I thank Richard Betts, Edward Mansfield, Jack Snyder, Anders Stephanson, Steve Weber, and Mark Zacher.

1. John J. Mearsheimer, "The False Promise of International Institutions," *International Security*, Vol. 19, No. 3 (Winter 1994/95), pp. 5–49.

International Security, Vol. 20, No. 1 (Summer 1995), pp. 62–70
© 1995 by the President and Fellows of Harvard College and the Massachusetts Institute of Technology.

Franklin Roosevelt's initial concept for the organization of the postwar security order was regional: his "four policemen" scheme. But he realized that "the only appeal which would be likely to carry weight with the United States public . . . would be one based upon a world-wide conception."[2] Hence, Roosevelt adopted a hybrid design for the United Nations: a collective security organization based in a concert of power, to be used by, but not against, the permanent members of the Security Council.[3] To be credible, this concert-based system required an enforcement capability. "We are not thinking of a superstate with its own police force and other paraphernalia of coercive power," Roosevelt noted not long before the Dumbarton Oaks conference, at which the major powers agreed upon the enforcement provisions of the UN charter. Instead, he said, they planned to devise a mechanism for "joint action" by national forces.[4] George Kennan, soon to become celebrated as a realist practitioner and then serving in the Moscow embassy, urged "burying" the Dumbarton Oaks proposals. "We are badly enmeshed in our own unsound slogans," he admonished Washington in an unsolicited cable.[5] His advice was ignored. Once Congress approved the charter in December 1945, the major powers proceeded to negotiate hefty UN standby forces.[6] Gradually, these talks fell victim to the emerging cold war.

The Eisenhower administration in 1956 facilitated the invention of the more modest UN collective security mechanism known as peacekeeping. The Suez crisis provided the occasion. When Israel, Britain, and France launched their coordinated attacks against Egypt, Eisenhower was furious. "All right," he instructed his Secretary of State, John Foster Dulles, "Foster, you tell 'em, goddamn it, we're going to apply sanctions, we're going to the United Nations, we're going to do everything that there is so we can stop this thing."[7] Eisenhower did all of that, beginning with U.S.-sponsored UN resolutions calling for an immediate cease-fire and the withdrawal of foreign forces. Under intense U.S. pressure, Britain, France, and Israel claimed that theirs had been a police

2. Cited in Warren F. Kimball, *The Juggler: Franklin Roosevelt as Wartime Statesman* (Princeton: Princeton University Press, 1991), p. 96.
3. Ibid., pp. 103–105.
4. Robert C. Hilderbrand, *Dumbarton Oaks: The Origins of the United Nations and the Search for Postwar Security* (Chapel Hill: University of North Carolina Press, 1990), p. 65.
5. Ibid., p. 250.
6. The final U.S. proposal in mid-1947—by then probably designed to be rejected by the Soviet Union—advocated a total of 20 ground divisions; 1,250 bombers; 2,250 fighters; 3 battleships; 6 carriers; 15 cruisers; 84 destroyers; and 90 submarines. See D.W. Bowett, *United Nations Forces: A Legal Study* (New York: Praeger, 1964), pp. 12–18.
7. Cited in Donald Neff, *Warriors at Suez* (New York: Simon and Schuster, 1983), p. 365.

action, designed to safeguard the Suez Canal, and that they would be willing to turn over their policing functions to a UN force if one were constituted. The UN obliged. With U.S. prodding, Canadian Foreign Minister Lester Pearson proposed a United Nations Emergency Force (UNEF), comprising troops from ten middle-sized and smaller countries.[8] A cease-fire and withdrawal of the invading forces was arranged. Egypt (but not Israel) agreed to accept UNEF on its territory. UNEF, which reached a strength of 6,000, supervised the cease-fire and foreign troop withdrawals, arranged to clear the Suez Canal of war-related blockage, and monitored the Israeli-Egyptian border.

Leading realists of the day objected vigorously to Eisenhower's actions. George Kennan, by then a private citizen, charged that the administration, by opposing its allies at the UN, had allowed "the very foundations of American policy [to be] swept away, the victim of an empty legalism,"[9] by which he meant the concept of collective security Eisenhower invoked on occasion.[10] Hans Morgenthau, the *paterfamilias* of American postwar academic realists, was appalled. "Regardless of the intrinsic merits of [the allies'] military operation," he opined, "once it was started we had a vital interest in its quick and complete success."[11] Arnold Wolfers supported these views.[12] By rejecting realist precepts, however, Eisenhower enabled the UN to devise a limited but nontrivial mode of conflict containment.

International nuclear nonproliferation arrangements, also initiated by the Eisenhower administration, tell a similar story. From the outset, realists have belittled these arrangements, with some going so far as to claim that they induce a false sense of security, thereby making the world worse off.[13] Yet, Secretary Dulles—not known as a liberal internationalist—had it right when

---

8. See Lester B. Pearson, *Mike: The Memoirs of the Right Honourable Lester B. Pearson*, Vol. 2, *1948–1957* (Toronto: University of Toronto Press, 1973), pp. 244–278.
9. George F. Kennan, letter to the editor, *Washington Post*, November 3, 1956, p. A8.
10. Eisenhower exhibited little awareness of the textbook model of collective security that drove the realists to despair, meaning by his occasional use of the term more generically cooperative, institutionalized approaches to dealing with security problems. See Dwight D. Eisenhower, *Waging Peace, 1956–61* (Garden City, N.Y.: Doubleday, 1965).
11. Hans J. Morgenthau, letter to the editor, *New York Times*, November 13, 1956, p. 36.
12. He felt that all had ended well, however, because "the three 'aggressors' did the exceptional thing of restoring the *status quo ante* despite the absence of collective military sanctions." Arnold Wolfers, *Discord and Collaboration* (Baltimore: Johns Hopkins University Press, 1962), p. 187. Wolfers' logic is tortuous, and it also ignores the extensive economic sanctions the United States imposed on Britain. See Diane B. Kunz, *The Economic Diplomacy of the Suez Crisis* (Chapel Hill: University of North Carolina Press, 1991).
13. For a recent rendition of this refrain, see Ted Galen Carpenter, "A New Proliferation Policy," *The National Interest*, No. 28 (Summer 1992), pp. 63–72.

he appealed for Senate approval of the International Atomic Energy Agency statute: "We realize that atomic energy materials and know-how will spread, Agency or no Agency. . . . But a rapid and unsupervised development of nuclear power around the world raises the specter of nuclear weapons ultimately becoming quite general, the byproduct of nuclear power plants."[14] The actual and potential members of the nuclear club today total less than half the number that experts and government officials predicted in the late 1950s and early 1960s.[15] Indeed, in recent years more countries have left the list of problem cases—including Argentina, Brazil, and South Africa—than have joined it. "Virtually every nonproliferation initiative has turned out to be much more effective than expected when it was proposed or designed, and nonproliferation success has been cheaper than expected."[16]

In creating NATO, of all the means available to President Truman for defending Europe from the Soviet threat—unilateral U.S. security guarantees to one, several, or an organization of European states; one or more U.S. bilateral alliances with European states; or a "dumbbell" model linking North American and European alliances—Truman chose the institutional form that most closely approximated collective security commitments. "The signing of the NATO Alliance," Michael Howard has written, "provided a sense that now at last all were for one and one was for all," which is what the concept of collective security has traditionally meant.[17] NATO promised its members equal and unqualified protection under a common security umbrella. At the same time, all members pledged to undertake those measures, including the use of armed force, that they deemed necessary to maintain or restore the security of the collectivity. After the Korean War, an integrated command structure was established within NATO to help execute these pledges.

---

14. Cited in Robert Endicott Osgood, *NATO: The Entangling Alliance* (Chicago: University of Chicago Press, 1962), p. 220.
15. Mitchell Reiss, *Without the Bomb: The Politics of Nonproliferation* (New York: Columbia University Press, 1988), chap. 1.
16. Thomas W. Graham and A.F. Mullins, "Arms Control, Military Strategy, and Nuclear Proliferation," paper presented at the conference on "Nuclear Deterrence and Global Security in Transition," University of California, Institute on Global Conflict and Cooperation, La Jolla, Calif., February 21–23, 1991.
17. Michael Howard, "Introduction," in Olav Riste, ed., *Western Security: The Formative Years* (Oslo: Universitetsforlaget, 1985), p. 16. In an influential essay published a generation ago, Wolfers pointed out the difference between collective self-defense and fully-fledged collective security systems. Arnold Wolfers, "Collective Defense versus Collective Security," in Wolfers, *Discord and Collaboration*, pp. 181–204. NATO, to be sure, is an instance of the former, not the latter. It does not follow, however, as realists typically assume, that there is no principled difference between the NATO form of collective self-defense and an old-fashioned alliance.

Leading realists opposed outright this very feature of NATO, which arguably accounts for its continued efficacy and attraction today. Kennan, as Director of Policy Planning in the State Department, initially felt that no U.S. military commitments to Europe were necessary. But if they had to be made, Kennan preferred what he called a "particularized" rather than a "legalistic-moralistic" form: such commitments should be specific in nature, limited in time, and contingent on discrete exigencies.[18] For Kennan, Article 5 of the North Atlantic Treaty exhibited anything but those attributes. Even though Kennan eventually acquiesced in the creation of NATO, he viewed its "legalistic-moralistic" commitments as barely better than the UN in this regard. In the political arena, Republican Senator Robert A. Taft of Ohio, considered to be "the most powerful single legislator of his day,"[19] lobbied and voted against the North Atlantic Treaty despite being an ardent anticommunist because, as Taft explained: "I do not like the obligation written into the pact which binds us for twenty years to come to the defense of any country, no matter by whom it is attacked and even though the aggressor may be another member of the pact."[20]

Finally, in its posture toward European unification the United States deviated sharply from the core realist maxim that, because today's ally could be tomorrow's adversary, one's ally should not benefit from an alliance relationship so much that it could become a serious competitor another day. In stark contrast, the United States strongly supported European unification. "It was the first time a major power fostered unity rather than discord among nations in a part of the world where it had significant interests."[21] Clearly, as with NATO, this "first" would not have occurred in the absence of the Soviet threat. But equally clear, to all but realists it seems, is that the United States promoted European unification through institutional means that promised to transform the traditional conduct of European international politics, not merely in economic, but also in security affairs.

---

18. See Anders Stephanson, *Kennan and the Art of Foreign Policy* (Cambridge, Mass.: Harvard University Press, 1989), p. 140; David Mayers, *George Kennan and the Dilemmas of U.S. Foreign Policy* (New York: Oxford University Press, 1988), pp. 152–155; and Geir Lundestad, *America, Scandinavia, and the Cold War, 1945–1949* (New York: Columbia University Press, 1980), pp. 172–173, 188–189. Kennan later recalled favoring a "dumbbell" arrangement, with the European countries cooperating on one side, the United States and Canada on the other, but in which they would have been linked, *not* by treaty and a permanent U.S. troop presence in Europe, but merely by a U.S.-Canadian guarantee of assistance in case of Soviet attack. George F. Kennan, *Memoirs: 1925–1950* (Boston: Little, Brown, 1967), pp. 406–407.
19. Lawrence S. Kaplan, *NATO and the United States: The Enduring Alliance* (Boston: Twayne Publishers, 1988), p. 37.
20. Robert A. Taft, *A Foreign Policy for Americans* (Garden City, N.Y.: Doubleday, 1951), pp. 88–89.
21. Armin Rappaport, "The United States and European Integration: The First Phase," *Diplomatic History*, Vol. 5, No. 2 (Spring 1981), p. 121.

General Eisenhower was an early and ardent advocate of a European Defense Community (EDC), and he helped persuade President Truman of its desirability. As president, Eisenhower pushed actively for its establishment: "Only in collective security," he wrote to his friend General Alfred Gruenther during discussions of the EDC, is there "any future for the free world."[22] The Joint Chiefs of Staff came to accept EDC, as did Congress, which proposed to make military aid to EDC countries conditional on the adoption of the treaty.[23] Secretary Dulles told the North Atlantic Council in 1953 that if Europe failed to ratify EDC, "grave doubts" would arise in the United States concerning the future of European security, and America would be obliged to undertake an "agonizing reappraisal" of its role in Europe. The respected realist analyst Robert Osgood was still disturbed by this affair a decade later: "Both sides of the argument displayed almost total indifference to the strategic military considerations," he noted sternly. "Indeed, in the eyes of its principal architects, EDC became as important as an instrument of Franco-German reconciliation as of military security."[24] But that, of course, was the point of U.S. support for EDC, as Franco-German reconciliation was the key to European unification.

After the EDC's failure, the Eisenhower administration turned its attention to nuclear energy as a vehicle for European security integration. It facilitated the creation of EURATOM.[25] It planned ways of sharing nuclear weapons with its NATO allies. And it even explored endowing them with an independent nuclear deterrent.[26] Realists undoubtedly can devise rationalizations of these moves after the fact, but I know of no realist argument that anticipated or recommended them prior to their occurrence.

Roads Not Taken

The preceding discussion suggests that the world today would be significantly different had postwar U.S. policymakers adopted the realists' anti-institutionalist views. NATO almost certainly would not have embodied indivisible

---

22. Cited in Brian R. Duchin, "The 'Agonizing Reappraisal': Eisenhower, Dulles, and the European Defense Community," *Diplomatic History,* Vol. 16, No. 2 (Spring 1992), p. 202.
23. Osgood, *NATO: The Entangling Alliance,* p. 95; and Duchin, "Agonizing Reappraisal," p. 207.
24. Osgood, *NATO: The Entangling Alliance,* pp. 86, 92.
25. Jonathan E. Helmreich, "The United States and the Formation of EURATOM," *Diplomatic History,* Vol. 15, No. 3 (Summer 1991), p. 409.
26. Based on recently opened archives, Steve Weber argues that Eisenhower "intended that [a NATO nuclear] consortium evolve into an integrated and independent nuclear force for the European NATO allies." Steve Weber, "Shaping the Postwar Balance of Power: Multilateralism in NATO," in John Gerard Ruggie, ed., *Multilateralism Matters* (New York: Columbia University Press, 1992), p. 258.

security guarantees, but would instead have taken the form of specific and contingent alliance commitments.[27] As such, it might not have lasted as long as the Cold War did and, if it had, in all likelihood it then would have gone the way of the Warsaw Treaty Organization.[28] Attempts to achieve European unification might well have succumbed to the collective action problems realists and rationalists repeatedly stress, leaving us today with far more competitive European policies in places like ex-Yugoslavia and the former Soviet Union, quite probably considerable instability in the heart of Europe itself, and no 35,000-strong Eurocorps becoming operational in the autumn of 1995. Finally, however weak the UN may be today, even marginal contributions in peacekeeping and nonproliferation usually are better, and in the long run often less costly, than none.

Realism and U.S. Policymakers

Mearsheimer states that "American elites, as well as the American public, tend to regard realism with hostility" (p. 48). The reason, he believes, has to do with values or idealism. This assessment misses the mark. It may accurately characterize Woodrow Wilson, who claimed to find power politics abhorrent, though he exhibited no problem practicing it.[29] But it does not capture the views of Roosevelt, Truman, Eisenhower, or Dulles. Their attitudes toward the institutional dimensions of security policy had less to do with mushy thinking than with geopolitical realities. Curiously, realism's blinders on this issue have caused it to overlook its own explanatory terrain.

America is not now and has never been a relative equal on a continent densely populated by potential adversaries, the European context for which balance-of-power theory and *raison d'état* were first invented. The traditional

---

27. Steve Weber tries carefully to generate "predictions" from today's realist and rationalist theories about NATO's form, based on how these theories calculate states' interests and strategies, and taking into account the facts as they were known to policymakers in 1949. He finds it difficult if not impossible to conjure up NATO's indivisible security guarantees within either theoretical model. See Weber, "Shaping the Postwar Balance of Power," pp. 235–238.

28. For numerous reasons, ranging from differential changes in external threat perception to shifts in domestic politics or simple transaction costs, country-by-country alliance commitments among a large number of states are intrinsically harder to sustain over time than is one single set of generalized commitments; see John Gerard Ruggie, "Multilateralism: The Anatomy of an Institution," in Ruggie, *Multilateralism Matters*, esp. pp. 31–35. In addition to having been imposed by Moscow, the Warsaw Pact was, of course, based on dyadic ties to Moscow.

29. No American president before or since used force more often than Wilson. See Frederick Calhoun, *Power and Principle: Armed Intervention in Wilsonian Foreign Policy* (Kent, Ohio: Kent State University Press, 1986), p. 2.

American aversion to "entangling alliances" is easily understood as a by-product of that geopolitical situation. But it has complicated the task of achieving sustained U.S. involvement for the sake of a stable international security order. Narrowly defined interest calculations would, more often than not, indicate that a crisis in some faraway place was not a vital U.S. concern, until it was too late to avoid the worst of outcomes, including two world wars. And yet the United States could hardly involve itself everywhere all the time.

This foreign policy dilemma has existed for as long as America has been a world power. Teddy Roosevelt employed a mixture of piety, patriotism, and jingoism on behalf of a campaign by "civilized and orderly powers to insist on the proper policing of the world."[30] Wilson hoped to build on America's aversion to entangling alliances a U.S. commitment to what he described as "a universal alliance."[31] Franklin Roosevelt sought to "make Wilsonianism practical" by establishing a universal institutional tripwire but embedding it in a major power concert.[32] Thereafter, the problem was attenuated by the Soviet military threat and communist ideological challenge. But even then, and true to form, Truman and Eisenhower agreed to involve the United States militarily in the defense of Europe *only* within institutional frameworks that promised to transform the organization of European security relations in the direction of a security community, in which the likelihood of future wars (and the necessity for U.S. involvement) would be reduced. *Ideas,* reflecting a fundamental geopolitical fact, not *idealism,* were at play in these endeavors.[33]

Ironically, Henry Kissinger, the canonical figure in the American pantheon of practical realists, has now discovered this dilemma.[34] Without the driving force of the Cold War, Kissinger asks, what will ensure the American involvement that is necessary to create and sustain a stable international security order? *A la carte* interest calculations, he concedes, are unlikely to suffice. "In traveling along the road to world order for the third time in the modern era," Kissinger concludes, U.S. power will need to be coupled with an affirmative vision that rises above mere necessity: "a vision of a future that cannot be

30. In a 1902 speech to Congress, cited by Robert Dallek, *The American Style of Foreign Policy* (New York: Oxford University Press, 1983), p. 35.
31. See, in particular, Wilson's 1917 "Peace Without Victory" speech to the U.S. Senate. Thomas J. Knock, *To End All Wars: Woodrow Wilson and the Quest for a New World Order* (New York: Oxford University Press, 1992), pp. 112–115.
32. Kimball, *The Juggler,* p. 103.
33. For an elaboration, see John Gerard Ruggie, "Third Try at World Order? America and Multilateralism after the Cold War," *Political Science Quarterly,* Vol. 109, No. 4 (Fall 1994), pp. 553–570.
34. Henry A. Kissinger, *Diplomacy* (New York: Simon and Schuster, 1994), esp. chap. 31.

demonstrated when it is put forward and judgments about the relationship between hope and possibility that are, in their essence, conjectural."[35]

Realism and the Future

Realism got a great many things right about the postwar world, but it has failed to grasp the subtle yet integral role of institutionalist objectives in U.S. foreign policy, including security policy. As a result, realism—especially the hyper-realist variant represented by Mearsheimer—is not only wanting but potentially dangerous as a guide to the post–Cold War world. That realism missed the mark on core elements of institutionalism in the structurally far simpler postwar era is *prima facie* grounds for doubting that it will do better—and strong reason to believe that it will do worse—in the more complex and ambiguous international security environment ahead.

Moreover, as the other contributors to this symposium demonstrate, neo-realism also misconstrues key theoretical aspects of institutionalism. And yet, in the policy arena its flawed rationale is invoked routinely to legitimate such serious anti-institutionalist assaults as the national security provisions of the new Republican majority's "Contract With America" (H.R. 7 and the Senate's "Peace Powers Act"), which would virtually foreclose timely and effective U.S. participation in UN peacekeeping operations, and constrain the constitutional prerogatives of the president as commander-in-chief if these were to be exercised through UN means. The echoes of 1919, when unilateralists riding on realist rhetoric joined with a rump of ever-present irreconcilables to defeat Wilson's quest to take the United States into the League of Nations, and thus ushered in an era of costly isolationism, are ominous.

---

35. Ibid., pp. 833–834.

Constructing International Politics

Alexander Wendt

John J. Mearsheimer's "The False Promise of International Institutions"[1] is welcome particularly in two respects. First, it is the most systematic attempt to date by a neorealist to address critical international relations (IR) theory.[2] Second, it reminds neoliberals and critical theorists, normally locked in their own tug-of-war, that they have a common, non-realist interest in the institutional bases of international life.[3] "False Promise" is likely, therefore, to spur productive discussions on all sides.

Unfortunately, it will be hard for most critical theorists to take seriously a discussion of their research program so full of conflations, half-truths, and misunderstandings. However, to some extent misunderstanding is inevitable when anthropologists from one culture first explore another. A dialogue between these two cultures is overdue, and "False Promise" is a good beginning.

Critical IR "theory," however, is not a single theory. It is a family of theories that includes postmodernists (Ashley, Walker), constructivists (Adler, Kratochwil, Ruggie, and now Katzenstein), neo-Marxists (Cox, Gill), feminists (Peterson, Sylvester), and others. What unites them is a concern with how world politics is "socially constructed,"[4] which involves two basic claims: that the fundamental structures of international politics are social rather than strictly material (a claim that opposes materialism), and that these structures

Alexander Wendt is Associate Professor of Political Science at Yale University.

For their exceptionally detailed and helpful comments I am grateful to Mike Barnett, Mlada Bukovansky, Bud Duvall, Peter Katzenstein, Mark Laffey, David Lumsdaine, Sylvia Maxfield, Nina Tannenwald, Jutta Weldes, and the members of the Yale IR Reading Group.

1. John J. Mearsheimer, "The False Promise of International Institutions," *International Security*, Vol. 19, No. 3 (Winter 1994/95). Subsequent references appear in parentheses in the text.
2. Other efforts include Robert Gilpin, "The Richness of the Tradition of Political Realism," *International Organization*, Vol. 38, No. 2 (Spring 1984), pp. 287–304, and Markus Fischer, "Feudal Europe, 800–1300," *International Organization*, Vol. 46, No. 2 (Spring 1992), pp. 427–466.
3. On neoliberalism and critical theory, see Robert Keohane, "International institutions: Two approaches," *International Studies Quarterly*, Vol. 32, No. 4 (December 1988), pp. 379–396, and Wendt, "Collective Identity Formation and the International State," *American Political Science Review*, Vol. 88, No. 2 (June 1994), pp. 384–396. Mearsheimer treats collective security as a third form of institutionalism, but this is unwarranted. Collective security is an approach to international order, arguable on either neoliberal or critical grounds, not a form of institutional analysis.
4. This makes them all "constructivist" in a broad sense, but as the critical literature has evolved, this term has become applied to one particular school.

International Security, Vol. 20, No. 1 (Summer 1995), pp. 71–81
© 1995 by the President and Fellows of Harvard College and the Massachusetts Institute of Technology.

shape actors' identities and interests, rather than just their behavior (a claim that opposes rationalism). However, having these two claims in common no more makes critical theory a single theory than does the fact that neorealism and neoliberalism both use game theory makes them a single theory. Some critical theorists are statists and some are not; some believe in science and some do not; some are optimists and some pessimists; some stress process and some structure.[5] Thus, in my reply I speak only for myself as a "constructivist," hoping that other critical theorists may agree with much of what I say. I address four issues: assumptions, objective knowledge, explaining war and peace, and policymakers' responsibilities.

Assumptions

I share all five of Mearsheimer's "realist" assumptions (p. 10): that international politics is anarchic, and that states have offensive capabilities, cannot be 100 percent certain about others' intentions, wish to survive, and are rational. We even share two more: a commitment to states as units of analysis, and to the importance of systemic or "third image" theorizing.

The last bears emphasis, for in juxtaposing "structure" to "discourse" and in emphasizing the role of individuals in "critical theory" (p. 40), Mearsheimer obscures the fact that constructivists are structuralists. Indeed, one of our main objections to neorealism is that it is not structural enough: that adopting the individualistic metaphors of micro-economics restricts the effects of structures to state behavior, ignoring how they might also constitute state identities and interests.[6] Constructivists think that state interests are in important part con-

---

5. These are far more than differences of "emphasis," as suggested by Mearsheimer's disclaimer, note 127.
6. "Constitute" is an important term in critical theory, with a special meaning that is not captured by related terms like "comprise," "consist of," or "cause." To say that "X [for example, a social structure] constitutes Y [for example, an agent]," is to say that the properties of those agents are made possible by, and would not exist in the absence of, the structure by which they are "constituted." A constitutive relationship establishes a conceptually necessary or logical connection between X and Y, in contrast to the contingent connection between independently existing entities that is established by causal relationships.
The identity-behavior distinction is partly captured by Robert Powell's distinction between preferences over outcomes and preferences over strategies; Robert Powell, "Anarchy in International Relations Theory," *International Organization*, Vol. 48, No. 2 (Spring 1994), pp. 313–344. The main exception to the mainstream neglect of structural effects on state identity is Kenneth Waltz's argument that anarchy produces "like units"; Kenneth Waltz, *Theory of International Politics* (Reading, Mass.: Addison-Wesley, 1979), pp. 74–77. Constructivists think there are more possibilities than this; see Alexander Wendt, "Anarchy is What States Make of It: The Social Construction of Power Politics," *International Organization*, Vol. 46, No. 2 (Spring 1992), pp. 391–425.

structed by systemic structures, not exogenous to them; this leads to a socio-logical rather than micro-economic structuralism.

Where neorealist and constructivist structuralisms really differ, however, is in their assumptions about what structure is made of. Neorealists think it is made only of a distribution of material capabilities, whereas constructivists think it is also made of social relationships. Social structures have three ele-ments: shared knowledge, material resources, and practices.[7]

First, social structures are defined, in part, by shared understandings, expec-tations, or knowledge. These constitute the actors in a situation and the nature of their relationships, whether cooperative or conflictual. A *security dilemma*, for example, is a social structure composed of intersubjective understandings in which states are so distrustful that they make worst-case assumptions about each others' intentions, and as a result define their interests in self-help terms. A *security community* is a different social structure, one composed of shared knowledge in which states trust one another to resolve disputes without war.[8] This dependence of social structure on ideas is the sense in which constructiv-ism has an idealist (or "idea-ist") view of structure. What makes these ideas (and thus structure) "social," however, is their intersubjective quality. In other words, sociality (in contrast to "materiality," in the sense of brute physical capabilities), is about shared knowledge.

Second, social structures include material resources like gold and tanks. In contrast to neorealists' desocialized view of such capabilities, constructivists argue that material resources only acquire meaning for human action through the structure of shared knowledge in which they are embedded.[9] For example, 500 British nuclear weapons are less threatening to the United States than 5 North Korean nuclear weapons, because the British are friends of the United States and the North Koreans are not, and amity or enmity is a function of shared understandings. As students of world politics, neorealists would prob-ably not disagree, but as theorists the example poses a big problem, since it completely eludes their materialist definition of structure. Material capabilities as such explain nothing; their effects presuppose structures of shared knowl-edge, which vary and which are not reducible to capabilities. Constructivism is therefore compatible with changes in material power affecting social relations

---

7. What follows could also serve as a rough definition of "discourse."

8. See Karl Deutsch, et al., *Political Community and the North Atlantic Area* (Princeton: Princeton University Press, 1957).

9. For a good general discussion of this point, see Douglas Porpora, "Cultural Rules and Material Relations," *Sociological Theory*, Vol. 11, No. 2 (July 1993), pp. 212–229.

(cf. Mearsheimer, p. 43), as long as those effects can be shown to presuppose still deeper social relations.

Third, social structures exist, not in actors' heads nor in material capabilities, but in practices. Social structure exists only in process. The Cold War was a structure of shared knowledge that governed great power relations for forty years, but once they stopped acting on this basis, it was "over."

In sum, social structures are real and objective, not "just talk." But this objectivity depends on shared knowledge, and in that sense social life is "ideas all the way down" (until you get to biology and natural resources). Thus, to ask "when do ideas, as opposed to power and interest, matter?" is to ask the wrong question. Ideas always matter, since power and interest do not have effects apart from the shared knowledge that constitutes them as such.[10] The real question, as Mearsheimer notes (p. 42), is why does one social structure exist, like self-help (in which power and self-interest determine behavior), rather than another, like collective security (in which they do not).

The explanatory as opposed to normative character of this question bears emphasis. Constructivists have a normative interest in promoting social change, but they pursue this by trying to explain how seemingly natural social structures, like self-help or the Cold War, are effects of practice (this is the "critical" side of critical theory). This makes me wonder about Mearsheimer's repeated references (I count fourteen) to critical theorists' "goals," "aims," and "hopes" to make peace and love prevail on Earth. Even if we all had such hopes (which I doubt), and even if these were ethically wrong (though Mearsheimer seems to endorse them; p. 40), they are beside the point in evaluating critical theories of world politics. If critical theories fail, this will be because they do not explain how the world works, not because of their values. Emphasizing the latter recalls the old realist tactic of portraying opponents as utopians more concerned with how the world ought to be than how it is. Critical theorists have normative commitments, just as neorealists do, but we are also simply trying to explain the world.

Objectivity

Mearsheimer suggests that critical theorists do not believe that there is an objective world out there about which we can have knowledge (pp. 41ff). This is not the case. There are two issues here, ontological and epistemological.

---

10. On the social content of interests, see Roy D'Andrade and Claudia Strauss, eds., *Human Motives and Cultural Models* (Cambridge: Cambridge University Press, 1992).

The ontological issue is whether social structures have an objective existence, which I addressed above. Social structures are collective phenomena that confront individuals as externally existing social facts. The Cold War was just as real for me as it was for Mearsheimer.

The epistemological issue is whether we can have objective knowledge of these structures. Here Mearsheimer ignores a key distinction between modern and postmodern critical theorists. The latter are indeed skeptical about the possibility of objective knowledge, although in their empirical work even they attend to evidence and inference. Constructivists, however, are modernists who fully endorse the scientific project of falsifying theories against evidence. In an article cited by Mearsheimer, I advocated a scientific-realist approach to social inquiry, which takes a very pro-science line.[11] And despite his claims, there is now a substantial body of constructivist empirical work that embodies a wholly conventional epistemology.[12]

Mearsheimer is right, however, that critical theorists do not think we can make a clean distinction between subject and object. Then again, almost all philosophers of science today reject such a naive epistemology. All observation is theory-*laden* in the sense that what we see is mediated by our existing theories, and to that extent knowledge is inherently problematic. But this does not mean that observation, let alone reality, is theory-*determined*. The world is still out there constraining our beliefs, and may punish us for incorrect ones. Montezuma had a theory that the Spanish were gods, but it was wrong, with disastrous consequences. We do not have unmediated access to the world, but this does not preclude understanding how it works.

Explaining War and Peace

Mearsheimer frames the debate between realists and critical theorists as one between a theory of war and a theory of peace. This is a fundamental mistake.

11. See Alexander Wendt, "The Agent-Structure Problem in International Relations Theory," *International Organization*, Vol. 41, No. 3 (Summer 1987), pp. 335–370; and, for fuller discussion, Ian Shapiro and Alexander Wendt, "The Difference that Realism Makes," *Politics and Society*, Vol. 20, No. 2 (June 1992), pp. 197–223.
12. See, among others, Michael Barnett, "Institutions, Roles, and Disorder," *International Studies Quarterly*, Vol. 37, No. 3 (September 1993), pp. 271–296; David Lumsdaine, *Moral Vision in International Politics* (Princeton: Princeton University Press, 1993); Samuel Barkin and Bruce Cronin, "The State and the Nation," *International Organization*, Vol. 48, No. 1 (Winter 1994), pp. 107–130; Rey Koslowski and Friedrich Kratochwil, "Understanding Change in International Politics," *International Organization*, Vol. 48, No. 2 (Spring 1994), pp. 215–248; Thomas Biersteker and Cynthia Weber, eds., *State Sovereignty as Social Construct* (Cambridge: Cambridge University Press, forthcoming); and Peter Katzenstein, ed., *Constructing National Security* (working title), forthcoming.

Social construction talk is like game theory talk: analytically neutral between conflict and cooperation.[13] Critical theory does not predict peace.[14] War no more disproves critical theory than peace disproves realism. The confusion stems from conflating description and explanation.

The descriptive issue is the extent to which states engage in practices of *realpolitik* (warfare, balancing, relative-gains seeking) versus accepting the rule of law and institutional constraints on their autonomy. States sometimes do engage in power politics, but this hardly describes all of the past 1300 years, and even less today, when most states follow most international law most of the time,[15] and when war and security dilemmas are the exception rather than the rule, Great Powers no longer tend to conquer small ones, and free trade is expanding rather than contracting.[16] The relative frequency of *realpolitik*, however, has nothing to do with "realism." Realism should be seen as an explanation of *realpolitik*, not a description of it. Conflating the two makes it impossible to tell how well the one explains the other, and leads to the tautology that war makes realism true. Realism does not have a monopoly on the ugly and brutal side of international life. Even if we agree on a *realpolitik* description, we can reject a realist explanation.

The explanatory issue is *why* states engage in war or peace. Mearsheimer's portrayal of constructivist "causal logic" on this issue is about 30 percent right. The logic has two elements, structure and agency. On the one hand, constructivist theorizing tries to show how the social structure of a system makes actions possible by constituting actors with certain identities and interests, and material capabilities with certain meanings. Missing from Mearsheimer's account is the constructivist emphasis on how agency and interaction produce and reproduce structures of shared knowledge over time. Since it is not possible here to discuss the various dynamics through which this process takes place,[17] let me illustrate instead. And since Mearsheimer does not offer a

---

13. On the social basis of conflict, see Georg Simmel, *Conflict and the Web of Group Affiliations* (Glencoe, Ill.: Free Press, 1955). This is also why I prefer to avoid the term "institutionalism," since it associates sociality with peace and cooperation.
14. Fischer's suggestion that critical theory predicts cooperation in feudal Europe is based on a failure to understand the full implications of this point; see Fischer, "Feudal Europe, 800–1300."
15. See Louis Henkin, *How Nations Behave* (New York: Council on Foreign Relations, 1979), p. 47.
16. On the inadequacy of "realist" descriptions of international politics, see Paul Schroeder, "Historical Reality vs. Neo-realist Theory," *International Security*, Vol. 19, No. 1 (Summer 1994), pp. 108–148.
17. For a start, see Alexander Wendt, "Collective Identity Formation," and Emanuel Adler, "Cognitive Evolution," in Emanuel Adler and Beverly Crawford, eds., *Progress in Postwar International Relations* (New York: Columbia University Press, 1991), pp. 43–88. The best introduction to processes of social construction remains Peter Berger and Thomas Luckmann, *The Social Construction of Reality* (New York: Anchor Books, 1966).

neorealist explanation for inter-state cooperation, conceding that terrain to institutionalists, let me focus on the "hard case" of why states sometimes get into security dilemmas and war, that is, why they sometimes engage in *realpolitik* behavior.

In "Anarchy is What States Make of It" I argued that such behavior is a self-fulfilling prophecy,[18] and that this is due to both agency and social structure. Thus, on the agency side, what states do to each other affects the social structure in which they are embedded, by a logic of reciprocity. If they militarize, others will be threatened and arm themselves, creating security dilemmas in terms of which they will define egoistic identities and interests. But if they engage in policies of reassurance, as the Soviets did in the late 1980s, this will have a different effect on the structure of shared knowledge, moving it toward a security community. The depth of interdependence is a factor here, as is the role of revisionist states, whose actions are likely to be especially threatening. However, on the structural side, the ability of revisionist states to create a war of all against all depends on the structure of shared knowledge into which they enter. If past interactions have created a structure in which status quo states are divided or naive, revisionists will prosper and the system will tend toward a Hobbesian world in which power and self-interest rule. In contrast, if past interactions have created a structure in which status quo states trust and identify with each other, predators are more likely to face collective security responses like the Gulf War.[19] *History matters*. Security dilemmas are not acts of God: they are effects of practice. This does not mean that once created they can necessarily be escaped (they are, after all, "dilemmas"), but it puts the causal locus in the right place.

Contrast this explanation of power politics with the "poverty of neorealism."[20] Mearsheimer thinks it significant that in anarchy, states cannot be 100 percent certain that others will not attack. Yet even in domestic society, I cannot be certain that I will be safe walking to class. There are no guarantees in life, domestic or international, but the fact that in anarchy war is possible does not mean "it may at any moment occur."[21] Indeed, it may be quite unlikely, as it is in most interactions today. Possibility is not probability. Anarchy as such

---

18. A similar argument is developed in John Vasquez, *The War Puzzle* (Cambridge: Cambridge University Press, 1993).

19. On the role of collective identity in facilitating collective security, see Wendt, "Collective Identity Formation."

20. Richard Ashley, "The Poverty of Neorealism," *International Organization*, Vol. 38, No. 2 (Spring 1984), pp. 225–286.

21. Kenneth Waltz, *Man, the State, and War* (New York: Columbia University Press, 1959), p. 232.

is not a structural cause of anything. What matters is its social structure, which varies across anarchies. An anarchy of friends differs from one of enemies, one of self-help from one of collective security, and these are all constituted by structures of shared knowledge. Mearsheimer does not provide an argument for why this is wrong; he simply asserts that it is.

Other realist explanations for power politics fare somewhat better. Although neorealists want to eschew arguments from human nature, even they would agree that to the extent human-beings-in-groups are prone to fear and competition, it may predispose them to war.[22] However, this factor faces countervailing dynamics of interdependence and collective identity formation, which sometimes overcome it. The distribution of material capabilities also matters, especially if offense is dominant, and military build-ups will of course concern other states. Again, however, the meaning of power depends on the underlying structure of shared knowledge. A British build-up will be less threatening to the United States than a North Korean one, and build-ups are less likely to occur in a security community than in a security dilemma.

In order to get from anarchy and material forces to power politics and war, therefore, neorealists have been forced to make additional, *ad hoc* assumptions about the social structure of the international system. We see this in Mearsheimer's interest in "hyper-nationalism," Stephen Walt's emphasis on ideology in the "balance of threat," Randall Schweller's focus on the status quo–revisionist distinction and, as I argued in my "Anarchy" piece, in Waltz's assumption that anarchies are self-help systems.[23] Incorporating these assumptions generates more explanatory power, but how? In these cases the crucial causal work is done by social, not material, factors. This is the core of a constructivist view of structure, not a neorealist one.

The problem becomes even more acute when neorealists try to explain the relative absence of inter-state war in today's world. If anarchy is so determining, why are there not more Bosnias? Why are weak states not getting killed off left and right? It stretches credulity to think that the peace between Norway and Sweden, or the United States and Canada, or Nigeria and Benin are all due to material balancing. Mearsheimer says cooperation is possible when core interests are not threatened (p. 25), and that "some states are especially friendly

22. For a good argument to this effect, see Jonathan Mercer, "Anarchy and Identity," *International Organization*, Vol. 49, No. 2 (Spring 1995).
23. John J. Mearsheimer, "Back to the Future," *International Security*, Vol. 15, No. 1 (Summer 1990), pp. 5–56; Stephen Walt, *The Origins of Alliances* (Ithaca: Cornell University Press, 1987); Randall Schweller, "Tripolarity and the Second World War," *International Studies Quarterly*, Vol. 37, No. 1 (March 1993), pp. 73–103; and Wendt, "Anarchy is What States Make of It."

for historical or ideological reasons" (p. 31). But this totally begs the question of why in an ostensibly "realist" world states do not find their interests continually threatened by others, and the question of how they might become friends. Perhaps Mearsheimer would say that most states today are status quo and sovereign.[24] But again this begs the question. What is sovereignty if not an institution of mutual recognition and non-intervention? And is not being "status quo" related to the internalization of this institution in state interests? David Strang has argued that those states recognized as sovereign have better survival prospects in anarchy than those that are not.[25] Far from challenging this argument, Mearsheimer presupposes it.

Neorealists' growing reliance on social factors to do their explanatory work suggests that if ever there were a candidate for a degenerating research program in IR theory, this is it.[26] The progressive response (in the Lakatosian sense) would be to return to realism's materialist roots by showing that the background understandings that give capabilities meaning are caused by still deeper material conditions, or that capabilities have intrinsic meaning that cannot be ignored. To show that the material base determines international superstructure, in other words, realists should be purging their theory of social content, not adding it as they are doing.[27] And anti-realists, in turn, should be trying to show how the causal powers of material facts presuppose social content, not trying to show that institutions explain additional variance beyond that explained by the distribution of power and interest, as if the latter were a privileged pre-social baseline.

Responsibility

An important virtue of "False Promise" is that it links neorealism and its rivals to the ethical responsibilities of foreign policymakers. These responsibilities

---

24. Mearsheimer and Waltz both assume sovereignty, without acknowledging its institutional character; see Mearsheimer, "False Promise," p. 11, and Waltz, *Theory of International Politics*, pp. 95–96.
25. David Strang, "Anomaly and Commonplace in European Political Expansion," *International Organization*, Vol. 45, No. 2 (Spring 1991), pp. 143–162.
26. "Degenerating" problem shifts are adjustments to a theory that are *ad hoc*, while "progressive" shifts are those that have a principled basis in its hard core assumptions. See Imre Lakatos, "Falsification and the Methodology of Scientific Research Programmes," in Lakatos and Alan Musgrave, eds., *Criticism and the Growth of Knowledge* (Cambridge: Cambridge University Press, 1970), pp. 91–196.
27. The significance of Dan Deudney's work lies partly in his appreciation of this point; see Dan Deudney, "Dividing Realism: Structural Realism versus Security Materialism on Nuclear Security and Proliferation," *Security Studies*, Vol. 1, Nos. 2 and 3 (1993), pp. 7–37.

depend in part on how much it is possible to change the structure of shared knowledge within anarchy. If such change is impossible, then Mearsheimer is right that it would be irresponsible for those charged with national security to pursue it. On the other hand, if it *is* possible, then it would be irresponsible to pursue policies that perpetuate destructive old orders, especially if we care about the well-being of future generations.

To say that structures are socially constructed is no guarantee that they can be changed.[28] Sometimes social structures so constrain action that transformative strategies are impossible. This goes back to the collective nature of social structures; structural change depends on changing a system of expectations that may be mutually reinforcing. A key issue in determining policymakers' responsibilities, therefore, is how much "slack" a social structure contains. Neorealists think there is little slack in the system, and thus states that deviate from power politics will get punished or killed by the "logic" of anarchy. Institutionalists think such dangers have been greatly reduced by institutions such as sovereignty and the democratic peace, and that there is therefore more possibility for peaceful change.

The example of Gorbachev is instructive in this respect, since the Cold War was a highly conflictual social structure. I agree with Mearsheimer (p. 46) that Soviet nuclear forces gave Gorbachev a margin of safety for his policies. Yet someone else in his place might have found a more aggressive solution to a decline in power. What is so important about the Gorbachev regime is that it had the courage to see how the Soviets' own practices sustained the Cold War, and to undertake a reassessment of Western intentions. This is exactly what a constructivist would do, but not a neorealist, who would eschew attention to such social factors as naive and as mere superstructure. Indeed, what is so striking about neorealism is its total neglect of the explanatory role of state practice.[29] It does not seem to matter what states do: Brezhnev, Gorbachev, Zhirinovsky, what difference does it make? The logic of anarchy will always bring us back to square one. This is a disturbing attitude if *realpolitik* causes the very conditions to which it is a response; to the extent that realism counsels *realpolitik*, therefore, it is part of the problem. Mearsheimer says critical theorists

---

28. Hence, *contra* Mearsheimer, there is nothing problematic about the fact that critical theorists do not make predictions about the future. What happens in the future depends on what actors do with the structures they have made in the past.

29. This is not true of classical realists; for a sympathetic discussion of the latter from a critical standpoint, see Richard Ashley, "Political Realism and Human Interests," *International Studies Quarterly*, Vol. 25, No. 2 (June 1981), pp. 204–237.

are "intolerant" of realists for this reason (p. 42). The ironies of this suggestion aside, what matters is getting policymakers to accept responsibility for solving conflicts rather than simply managing or exploiting them. If neorealism can move us in that direction, then it should, but as I see it, neorealist ethics come down to *"sauve qui peut."*

To analyze the social construction of international politics is to analyze how processes of interaction produce and reproduce the social structures—cooperative or conflictual—that shape actors' identities and interests and the significance of their material contexts. It is opposed to two rivals: the materialist view, of which neorealism is one expression, that material forces *per se* determine international life, and the rational choice–theoretic view that interaction does not change identities and interests. Mearsheimer's essay is an important opening to the comparative evaluation of these hypotheses. But neorealists will contribute nothing further to the debate so long as they think that constructivists are subversive utopians who do not believe in a real world and who expect peace in our time.

A Realist Reply | *John J. Mearsheimer*

$\mathbf{I}$ appreciate the opportunity to respond to the rejoinders to my article on "The False Promise of International Institutions."[1] I begin with a brief restatement of what is at issue between my critics and me. Then I deal in turn with each response.

The Core Issue

The central question raised in "False Promise" is straightforward and widely recognized in the international relations literature: can international institutions prevent war by changing state behavior? Specifically, can institutions push states away from war by getting them to eschew balance-of-power logic, and to refrain from calculating each important move according to how it affects their relative power position?

Realists answer no. They believe that institutions cannot get states to stop behaving as short-term power maximizers. For realists, institutions reflect state calculations of self-interest based primarily on concerns about relative power; as a result, institutional outcomes invariably reflect the balance of power. Institutions, realists maintain, do not have significant independent effects on state behavior. However, realists recognize that great powers sometimes find institutions—especially alliances—useful for maintaining or even increasing their share of world power. For example, it was more efficient for the United States and its allies to balance against the Soviets through NATO than through a less formal and more *ad hoc* alliance. But NATO did not force its member states to behave contrary to balance-of-power logic.

Institutionalists answer yes. They believe that institutions can independently change state behavior. Institutions can cause peace, so the argument goes, by convincing states to reject power-maximizing behavior, and to accept outcomes that might weaken their relative power position. In short, the debate between the institutionalists and me is about whether institutions can have an independent effect on state behavior, or whether instead institutional outcomes

John J. Mearsheimer is a professor in the Political Science Department at the University of Chicago.

1. John J. Mearsheimer, "The False Promise of International Institutions," *International Security*, Vol. 19, No. 3 (Winter 1994/95), pp. 5–49.

International Security, Vol. 20, No. 1 (Summer 1995), pp. 82–93
© 1995 by the President and Fellows of Harvard College and the Massachusetts Institute of Technology.

reflect great power interests, and are essentially tools that great powers employ for their own selfish purposes.

The responses to "False Promise" prompt me to make a brief but important point about the role of alliances in institutional theory. Institutionalists traditionally have focused on what might be called "inner-directed" institutions, i.e., those designed to manage and resolve conflicts among the member states, and to facilitate cooperation among them. Inner-directed institutions seek to cause peace by influencing the behavior of the member states. Thus, the larger the membership, the better the prospects for peace. A collective security system is a good example of an inner-directed institution. At the same time, institutionalists have paid little attention to alliances, which are "outer-directed" institutions. Alliances are not primarily concerned with keeping peace among the member states, much less with coaxing them to violate balance-of-power logic in their behavior. Instead, the target of an alliance's attention is an outside state, or coalition of states, which the alliance aims to deter, coerce, or defeat in war. To the extent that alliances cause peace, they do so by deterrence, which is straightforward realist behavior. Not surprisingly, institutionalists have largely ignored NATO in their writings, and have focused instead on inner-directed institutions such as the European Community (EC) and the International Energy Agency.

I raise this point because the responses by Ruggie and by Keohane and Martin suggest that a crucial change may be occurring in their thinking about institutions. They make frequent reference to NATO in their responses, which implies that alliances are now a central element in institutionalist theory. Thus, the fact that NATO helped deter the Soviet threat is invoked as evidence that institutions cause peace. However, NATO's success in the Cold War cannot be cited as support for institutionalist theory, because deterrence has virtually nothing to do with the long-standing claims of institutionalists. In essence, both Ruggie and Keohane and Martin are shifting the terms of debate, and making realist claims under the guise of institutionalism. This point's significance will become apparent in the following discussion of their responses.

John Ruggie: A Ship Passing in the Night

Ruggie's response does not provide a strong defense of institutionalist theory, because it simply does not address the core issue about institutions raised in "False Promise." Furthermore, his four main arguments about institutions are consistent with realism. He argues that during the early Cold War some realists like George Kennan sometimes gave bad advice about such matters as "the creation of NATO and European unification," and that policymakers wisely ignored that advice. This argument is correct but irrelevant, as it says nothing about whether institutions cause peace by independently affecting state behavior.

Ruggie also makes the realist claim that "postwar America pursued its interests and sought to manage the changing international balance of power," but he adds that "U.S. policymakers also had certain institutional objectives in mind (p. 62)," such as the establishment of NATO. This may be true, but this argument too has little to do with whether institutions cause peace by independently affecting state behavior. Ruggie then argues that the United States fared better waging the Cold War with institutions like NATO than it would have without them. I agree. I believe great powers sometimes use institutions to further their interests. Yet once again, this point does not address the central issue raised in "False Promise": can institutions cause peace by independently affecting state behavior?

Finally, Ruggie occasionally hints that American policymakers proposed ideas that contradict realist logic. But he does not push these arguments very far, and ultimately concedes that those policymakers were motivated by "geopolitical fact, not *idealism*." For example, he argues that, "In creating NATO . . . Truman chose the institutional form that most closely approximated collective security commitments." Ruggie makes it sound like Truman was behaving according to the dictates of Charles and Clifford Kupchan. However, he quickly reverses himself in the subsequent footnote (p. 65), where he writes: "[Arnold] Wolfers pointed out the difference between collective self-defense and fully-fledged collective security systems. . . . NATO, to be sure, is an instance of the former, not the latter."

He also claims that the Eisenhower administration's support of European unification "deviated sharply" from realism. This claim is incorrect. Eisenhower believed that the United States had a security interest in seeing the Soviet Union contained, but he also believed that America's military presence in Europe would be temporary, and that the Europeans would eventually have to fend for themselves against the Soviet threat. He felt that a united Western Europe would achieve this containment better than a divided Western Europe; this policy perspective is consistent with realism. These cases aside, Ruggie gives away the store when he concludes that "the views of Roosevelt, Truman, Eisenhower, or Dulles . . . toward the institutional dimensions of security policy had less to do with mushy thinking than with geopolitical realities."

This conclusion corresponds to a realist view of institutions: U.S. policymakers used NATO and other institutions to improve their relative power position *vis-à-vis* their main adversary, the Soviet Union.

Robert Keohane and Lisa Martin: Realists by Any Other Name . . .

When liberal institutionalism was first articulated in the mid-1980s by Keohane and others, it was a rather straightforward theory that presented a clear alternative to realism. The original theory argued that institutions could independently ease cooperation among states by helping states overcome certain collective action dilemmas. In 1988, however, Joseph Grieco (a realist) published an article in *International Organization* that called into question the original theory's causal logic.[2] Empirical work then began appearing that supported Grieco's claims. Stephen Krasner (another realist) published an article on global communications in *World Politics* (1991) that was an especially damning indictment of liberal institutionalism.[3]

Liberal institutionalists scrambled to repair their theory in the wake of this realist challenge. Keohane and Martin's response is an attempt to describe post-Grieco liberal institutionalism and contrast it with realism. Their bottom line is that realism is a deeply flawed theory, and that modified liberal institutionalism is a superior theory of international politics. However, a careful look at Keohane and Martin's response reveals that liberal institutionalism in its latest form is no longer a clear alternative to realism, but has, in fact, been swallowed up by it. The most recent variant of liberal institutionalism is realism by another name.

There are three principal dimensions to Keohane and Martin's response. First, they build much of their case around the nebulous claim that "institutions matter," a phrase they invoke at least four times. At the same time, they imply that I think institutions are simply irrelevant. This line of argument allows them to ask why states would devote "resources to structures that will make no difference." They claim that my answer must be that it is the result of some "collective delusion." It is fruitless to argue about whether institutions "matter," since the claim is so vague that it has no real meaning. In the end,

---

2. Joseph M. Grieco, "Anarchy and the Limits of Cooperation: A Realist Critique of the Newest Liberal Institutionalism," *International Organization*, Vol. 42, No. 3 (Summer 1988), pp. 485–507.
3. Stephen D. Krasner, "Global Communications and National Power: Life on the Pareto Frontier," *World Politics*, Vol. 43, No. 3 (April 1991), pp. 336–366. Also see Baldev Raj Nayar, "Regimes, Power, and International Aviation," *International Organization*, Vol. 49, No. 1 (Winter 1995), pp. 139–170.

everything matters. The real question, as described in "False Promise," is how, and how much, do institutions affect state behavior? For what it is worth, I believe institutions sometimes matter. After all, great powers use institutions to further their interests. Thus, I find it neither surprising nor inconsistent with realism to discover that states invest modest resources in institutions. But that point hardly addresses the main issue: can institutions get states to eschew short-term gains for long-term benefits?

The second dimension of Keohane and Martin's response is an unsparing criticism of realism, followed by the claim that institutions affect state behavior in ways that contradict realism. They begin their response by going on the offense against realism, suggesting that this "purportedly scientific theory" may not even deserve to be called social science. Nevertheless, their subsequent discussion of institutions is replete with realist arguments. For example, they write, "liberal institutionalists, who see institutions as rooted in the realities of power and interest, do not argue that NATO could have maintained stability under any imaginable conditions. What we argue is that institutions make a significant difference in conjunction with power realities (p. 42)." Later (p. 47) they write, "institutionalist theory . . . after all, posits that international institutions are created in response to state interests, and that their character is structured by the prevailing distribution of capabilities." Both of these quotations could have been taken straight from a Realism 101 lecture. Furthermore, Keohane and Martin hardly mention the argument that institutions can have an independent effect on state behavior. Indeed they write (p. 48) that "the difference between realism and liberal institutionalism does not lie in whether institutions are independent or dependent variables." If that is the case, then it is difficult to see how this latest version of liberal institutionalism presents much of a challenge to realism.

Keohane and Martin make some arguments that might appear to contradict realism, but on close inspection, do not. Regarding the issue of relative gains, for example, they emphasize that "institutions can facilitate cooperation by helping to settle distributional conflicts." There is no question that institutions might help two states divide the gains of cooperation in a way that satisfies both parties. But that task is compatible with realism, because it does not require states to violate balance-of-power logic. In fact, institutions are working in such cases to ensure that agreements reflect the balance of power. Grieco made precisely this point in his 1988 article.[4] Nevertheless, as I emphasized in "False Promise," cooperation and peace are not the same thing. After all, the

---

4. Grieco, "Anarchy and the Limits of Cooperation," pp. 506–507.

Ribbentrop-Molotov pact was a case of international cooperation, but hardly a source of peace.

Finally, virtually all of the tasks that Keohane and Martin assign to institutions can be accomplished without them. For example, there is no reason why two states cannot bargain with each other and use side payments to help alleviate the relative-gains problem. Institutions are not necessary to accomplish this task, although they may sometimes help distribute gains so that the final outcome reflects the balance of power. Keohane and Martin also make much of the fact that institutions facilitate "issue linkage," which sometimes enhances the prospects of cooperation. Martin argues in her study of EC sanctions against Argentina during the Falklands War that Britain was able to secure the cooperation of other European states by linking issues in the context of the EC. This is true, but issue linkage was a commonplace practice in world politics well before institutions came on the scene; moreover, Britain and the other European states could have used other diplomatic tactics to solve the problem. After all, Britain and America managed to cooperate on sanctions even though the United States was not a member of the EC.

The third dimension of Keohane and Martin's response is to offer evidence that institutions can cause peace. However, the evidence they provide to support their claim is especially weak. Studies of oil pollution at sea and the European Court of Justice simply do not tell us much about war and peace. John Duffield's work on NATO is insightful, but it is largely consistent with a realist understanding of that alliance. Duffield certainly does not argue that NATO was formed for non-realist reasons or that it forced member states to violate balance-of-power logic. Keohane and Martin try to excuse the dearth of empirical support for liberal institutionalism by claiming that it is a "new theory." This defense is not persuasive. Liberal institutionalism has been at the center of international relations debates for well over a decade, a lengthy period by academic standards. If there were strong empirical support for liberal institutionalism, some of it should have surfaced by now. In fact, considerable empirical research has been done on the theory. However, most of it undermines liberal institutionalism and supports realism. Thus, it is not surprising that the liberal institutionalists are now converting to realism, but it would clarify matters if they would admit it.

Charles Kupchan and Clifford Kupchan: Mixing Oil and Water

In "False Promise" I examined the standard theory of collective security, which has been in the international relations literature for decades. That theory presents a stark alternative and direct challenge to realism. States behave according to different logics in each theory, and therefore the predictions of each for life in the international system vary greatly as well. I argued in "False Promise" that there are flaws in the logic of collective security, and that there is much historical evidence that it is unworkable in practice. I also argued that concerts, in contrast, are institutions that are compatible with realism, and therefore they work according to a different logic than collective security. Thus, collective security systems and concerts should be regarded as distinct institutional forms.

The Kupchans, for the most part, do not challenge the assessment of the standard version of collective security laid out in "False Promise." They argue instead that I employ a very narrow definition of collective security. The claim is that I set up a straw man by focusing on what they label "ideal collective security." This charge is incorrect. I described and analyzed the standard version of the theory, which has long served as the basis of discussion when scholars debate the merits of collective security. In fact, I considered the same theory that Inis Claude examined in his pathbreaking works on collective security, and not surprisingly, I came to many of the same conclusions that he did.[5]

The Kupchans' response focuses on defending a new version of collective security, which they invented and first articulated in a Summer 1991 *International Security* article, and which incorporates balance-of-power logic.[6] In essence, they attempted to devise a theory of collective security that marries realism with the standard version of collective security. I did not pay much attention to the Kupchans' new theory in "False Promises" because it has a fatal flaw: realism and collective security are incompatible theories which cannot be mixed together to produce a coherent theory of state behavior, because these two theories argue that states behave in fundamentally different and contradictory ways.

The Kupchans have claimed that collective security can take "many different institutional forms along a continuum ranging from ideal collective security to concerts,"[7] and that their goal in their current article is to defend concerts and

5. See Inis L. Claude, Jr., *Swords Into Plowshares: The Problems and Progress of International Organization*, 4th ed. (New York: Random House, 1971); and Claude, *Power And International Relations* (New York: Random House, 1966).
6. Charles A. Kupchan and Clifford A. Kupchan, "Concerts, Collective Security, and the Future of Europe," *International Security*, Vol. 16, No. 1 (Summer 1991), pp. 114–161.
7. Ibid., p. 119.

everything between the two ends of the continuum. It is not clear, however, what institutional forms lie between standard collective security and concerts. The Kupchans provide no description of these other institutional forms, and do not distinguish them from concerts. I will simply refer to them as nameless institutional forms (NIFs). Thus, when the Kupchans defend collective security, they are specifically not defending standard collective security, but are instead defending NIFs and concerts. The distinguishing feature of NIFs and concerts, according to the Kupchans, is that they contain elements of both standard collective security and realism. In essence, the Kupchans mix those polar opposite theories together and claim that the result is a theory that provides the best of both worlds. Not only do "states agree to abide by certain norms and rules to maintain stability and, when necessary, band together to stop aggression," but the world of NIFs and concerts is also one where "the behavior of major states is heavily influenced by balance-of-power considerations."

The Kupchans' efforts notwithstanding, realism and standard collective security cannot be married to each other because the two theories are mutually exclusive. States that are "heavily influenced by balance-of-power considerations" are, by definition, going to be mainly concerned about the balance of power, not about maintaining peace. Some of those states will pursue both offensive and defensive strategies aimed at improving their relative power position. Some states will initiate wars for security reasons. Other times they will be content—for balance-of-power reasons— to remain on the sidelines and let two or more rivals fight a war. There is not going to be a lot of trust in such a world, and states operating in it will often form alliances. Yet the Kupchans also claim that states can act in the spirit of standard collective security, and "abide by certain norms and rules to maintain stability," and that when an aggressor appears on the scene, all of the other states are supposed to "band together to stop aggression." This kind of behavior, however desirable, directly contradicts realism. Contrary to what the Kupchans argue, balancing in a realist world cannot be equated with their notion of balancing under collective security. These two different kinds of balancing behavior are contradictory and incompatible.

There are other problems with the Kupchans' argument. Consider their claim that concerts and NIFs are likely to fail in stages, giving threatened states ample warning time. There is no reason to assume that a collective security system will fail long before a state is attacked, rather than at the moment of attack. And if it fails in stages, the state attacked at the first stage still gets clobbered. The Kupchans, of course, allow states to hedge against this danger, by behaving like realists. But that concession leaves one wondering if maybe they too are realists in disguise.

Alexander Wendt: Missing the Critical Issues

Critical theory, unlike Keohane and Martin's latest version of liberal institutionalism and the Kupchans' version of collective security, offers a distinct and bold challenge to realism. Critical theorists like Wendt make no concessions to realism, and they make no bones about their desire to replace it with a more communitarian and peaceful discourse. That clarity of purpose is all for the good, as it makes it easier to assess the relative merits of the competing theories. Nevertheless, Wendt's response is disappointing, not so much for what it says, as for what it does not say. Specifically, he does not answer the criticisms leveled against critical theory in "False Promise." Instead, he concentrates on describing critical theory, and showing how it differs from realism. This task is necessary, he argues, because I misrepresented critical theory in "False Promise." But, as I discuss below, that charge is false. The key differences between the two theories are not in dispute; rather the debate is over which theory provides the best guide to understanding state behavior.

Wendt begins his response with the charge that my discussion of critical theory in "False Promise" is "full of conflations, half-truths, and misunderstandings." Thus, his response is an opportunity to set the record straight by accurately describing critical theory and showing how it differs from realism. However, there are no important differences between us regarding the essentials of critical theory and realism. Consider two of his examples about how I supposedly distort critical theory.

Wendt maintains that I was wrong to treat critical theory as a "single theory," because "it is a family of theories that includes postmodernists, constructivists, neo-Marxists, feminists, and others." I recognize that there are differences among critical theorists (as there are among realists), and I pointed out this fact in "False Promise" (p. 37). When comparing critical theory with realism, I focused on the common elements within the critical theory literature, because it was neither practical nor necessary to take into account every difference in this large body of scholarship. The question is whether smoothing over the differences resulted in a caricature of critical theory. It does not because, as Wendt acknowledges, critical theorists are united on the key issue at stake between themselves and realists: whether "world politics is socially constructed."

Wendt next argues that I "obscure" the fact that critical theorists, like realists, are structuralists. In fact, he argues that the problem with realism is that "it is not structural enough." Confusion arises, however, out of different uses of the term "structure." There is no question that in "False Promise" I described realism, but not critical theory, as a structural theory. Wendt, however, prefers to call them both structural theories, although it is clear from his discussion of realism and critical theory that "structure" has a completely different meaning for each, and that labeling both theories "structural" does not challenge my description of critical theory in any meaningful way. A brief description of the two theories—using his language about structure—shows that there is no significant disagreement between Wendt and me regarding the essentials of critical theory and realism.

Realists believe that state behavior is largely shaped by the *material structure* of the international system. The distribution of material capabilities among states is the key factor for understanding world politics. For realists, some level of security competition among great powers is inevitable because of the material structure of the international system. Individuals are free to adopt non-realist discourses, but in the final analysis, the system forces states to behave according to the dictates of realism, or risk destruction. Critical theorists, on the other hand, focus on the *social structure* of the international system. They believe that "world politics is socially constructed," which is another way of saying that shared discourse, or how communities of individuals think and talk about the world, largely shapes the world. Wendt recognizes that "material resources like gold and tanks exist," but he argues that "such capabilities . . . only acquire meaning for human action through the structure of shared knowledge in which they are embedded." Significantly for critical theorists, discourse can change, which means that realism is not forever, and that therefore it might be possible to move beyond realism to a world where institutionalized norms cause states to behave in more communitarian and peaceful ways.

The most revealing aspect of Wendt's discussion is that he did not respond to the two main charges leveled against critical theory in "False Promise." The first problem with critical theory is that although the theory is deeply concerned with radically changing state behavior, it says little about how change comes about. The theory does not tell us why particular discourses become dominant, and others fall by the wayside. Specifically, Wendt does not explain why realism has been the dominant discourse in world politics for well over a thousand years, although I explicitly raised this question in "False Promise" (p. 42). Moreover, he sheds no light on why the time is ripe for unseating realism, nor on why realism is likely to be replaced by a more peaceful, communitarian discourse, although I explicitly raised both questions.

Wendt's failure to answer these questions has important ramifications for his own arguments. For example, he maintains that if it is possible to change international political discourse and alter state behavior, "then it is irresponsible to pursue policies that perpetuate destructive old orders [i.e., realism], especially if we care about the well-being of future generations." The clear implication here is that realists like me are irresponsible and do not care much about the welfare of future generations. However, even if we change discourses and move beyond realism, a fundamental problem with Wendt's argument remains: because his theory cannot predict the future, he cannot know whether the discourse that ultimately replaces realism will be more benign than realism. He has no way of knowing whether a fascistic discourse more violent than realism will emerge as the hegemonic discourse. For example, he obviously would like another Gorbachev to come to power in Russia, but he cannot be sure we will not get a Zhirinovsky instead. So even from a critical theory perspective, defending realism might very well be the more responsible policy choice.

The second major problem with critical theory is that its proponents have offered little empirical support for their theory. For example, I noted in "False Promise" that critical theorists concede that realism has been the dominant discourse in international politics from about 1300 to 1989, a remarkably long period of time. Wendt does not challenge this description of the historical record by pointing to alternative discourses that influenced state behavior during this period. In fact, Wendt's discussion of history is obscure. I also noted in "False Promise" that although critical theorists largely concede the past to realism, many believe that the end of the Cold War presents an excellent opportunity to replace realism as the hegemonic discourse, and thus fundamentally change state behavior. I directly challenged this assertion in my article, but Wendt responds with only a few vague words about this issue.

Wendt writes in his response that "if critical theories fail, this will be because they do not explain how the world works, not because of their values." I agree completely, but critical theorists have yet to provide evidence that their theory can explain very much. In fact, the distinguishing feature of the critical theory literature, Wendt's work included, is its lack of empirical content. Possibly that situation will change over time, but until it does, critical theory will not topple realism from its commanding position in the international relations literature.

Conclusion

The discussion of institutions up to now has a distinct academic flavor. However, the debate over whether institutions cause peace is not just a dispute about international relations theory; it also has significant real-world consequences. For example, the Clinton administration and many European policymakers publicly maintain that states should not worry about the balance of power—that is "old thinking," they say—but should instead rely on institutions to protect them. This perspective makes sense only if there is evidence that institutions can get the job done. But so far, the evidence indicates that institutions do not provide a sound basis for building a stable post–Cold War world. Institutions failed to prevent or shut down the recent wars in Bosnia and Transcaucasia, and failed to stop the carnage in Rwanda; there is little reason to think that those same institutions would do better in the next trouble spot. The bottom line on institutions seems clear: despite all the rhetoric about their virtues, there is little evidence that they can alter state behavior and cause peace.

States temporarily led astray by the false promise of institutionalist rhetoric eventually come to their senses and start worrying about the balance of power. Surely Bosnian policymakers now recognize their mistake in trusting institutions like the UN and the EC to pull their chestnuts out of the fire. In the meantime, however, a state that ignores the balance of power can suffer enormous damage. Thus, it would seem to make sense, from both a moral and a strategic perspective, for institutionalists to tone down their claims about the peace-causing effects of institutions until they have solid evidence to support their position.

Part V:
War and Peace in a Changing
International System

Is War Obsolete?

A Review Essay

John Mueller, *Retreat from Doomsday: The Obsolescence of Major War*. New York: Basic Books, 1989.

$\mathbf{T}$he forty-five years that have now passed since the end of World War II without interstate war in Europe is the longest such period in its post-medieval history.[1] Many scholars and commentators have attributed the present "long peace" among the major powers to the deterrent effect of nuclear weapons. When President Ronald Reagan and General Secretary Mikhail Gorbachev agreed that a nuclear war cannot be won and must not be fought, they were only reiterating what has become an almost universally accepted piety in current public and scholarly discussion of international relations.[2]

John Mueller's *Retreat from Doomsday*[3] advances a much stronger thesis: major war was already becoming obsolete by the time of the First World War;

The author thanks Francis Bator, McGeorge Bundy and Marc Trachtenberg for many helpful comments on an earlier draft of this essay. They encouraged him in writing down his speculations without necessarily endorsing them, and read the result with critical eyes.

Carl Kaysen is David W. Skinner Professor of Political Economy in the Program in Science, Technology and Society at the Massachusetts Institute of Technology, and a member of MIT's program in Defense and Arms Control Studies.

1. See J.S. Levy, *War in the Modern Great Power System, 1495–1975* (Lexington: University Press of Kentucky, 1983); and Evan Luard, *War in International Society* (London: I.B. Taurus, 1986). Luard's analysis covers 1400–1984, and includes civil wars, colonial wars and revolts, and some other wars outside the European system. Both Levy and Luard find the nineteenth century—1816–99 in Levy, 1815–1914 in Luard—the most peaceful of the long periods they studied. Luard records the periods of 1815–54 and 1871–1914, forty and forty-three years, as free of major power wars. The longest such period in the eighteenth century was 1720–27, and in earlier centuries war raged even more frequently.
2. See Department of State *Bulletin*, Vol. 86, No. 2106 (January 1988), p. 8, for the joint communiqué at the end of the Reagan-Gorbachev meeting in Geneva, November 19–21, 1985. Agreement is not universal. See for example ch. 4 in Paul Seabury and Angelo Codevilla, *War: Ends and Means* (New York: Basic Books, 1989). See also Richard Pipes, "Why the Soviets Think They Could Fight and Win a Nuclear War," *Commentary*, Vol. 64 (July 1977), pp. 21–34.
3. John Mueller, *Retreat from Doomsday: The Obsolescence of Major War* (New York: Basic Books, 1989); most subsequent references to this book appear parenthetically in the text. See also Mueller, "The Essential Irrelevance of Nuclear Weapons: Stability in the Postwar World," *International Security*, Vol. 13, No. 2 (Fall 1988), pp. 55–79.

International Security, Spring 1990 (Vol. 14, No. 4)
© 1990 by the President and Fellows of Harvard College and of the Massachusetts Institute of Technology.

World War II repeated and reinforced that lesson. The development of nuclear weapons was accordingly irrelevant to the process; it was, so to speak, the flourish under the *finis* at the end of the story.

Mueller's central argument is that war—among "western," modernized nations—has become "subrationally unthinkable."

An idea becomes impossible not when it becomes reprehensible or has been renounced, but when it fails to percolate into one's consciousness as a conceivable option. Thus, two somewhat paradoxical conclusions about the avoidance of war can be drawn. On the one hand, peace is likely to be firm when war's repulsiveness and futility are fully evident—as when its horrors are dramatically and inevitably catastrophic. On the other hand, peace is most secure when it gravitates away from conscious rationality to become a subrational, unexamined mental habit. At first, war becomes rationally unthinkable—rejected because it's calculated to be ineffective and/or undesirable. Then it becomes subrationally unthinkable—rejected not because it's a bad idea but because it remains subconscious and never comes off as a coherent possibility. Peace in other words, can prove to be habit forming, addictive. (p. 240.)

The obsolescence of war, argues Mueller, is thus the result of a change in mental habits through socio-cultural evolution, not a change in the terms of a calculation: "unthinkable," not "unprofitable."

When the whole postwar European security system is rapidly changing, Mueller's claims merit careful consideration. The burden of this essay is that Mueller is right in his result, but that his argument fails to sustain his conclusion. Mueller hardly explains the cultural change that has made wars unthinkable, and fails to explore the interconnections among cultural, political, and economic changes in the evaluation of interstate war. It is because wars of the kind under consideration have become unprofitable, both economically and politically, that they have become unthinkable. Finally, he is too cavalier in his dismissal of the significance of nuclear weapons.

Mueller's Analysis

Mueller sets the stage for his examination of the change in attitudes toward war by probing two other social institutions that have disappeared through a similar cultural change: duelling and slavery. Duelling, for centuries a natural and appropriate response to offense and insult between gentlemen, became ridiculous and therefore unthinkable in the course of the last century (pp. 9–11). Slavery has had a similar fate:

From the dawn of pre-history until about 1788 it had occurred to almost no one that there was anything the least bit peculiar about the institution of slavery. Like war, it could be found just about everywhere, in one form or another, and it flourished in every age . . . . The abolitionist movement that broke out at the end of the century in Britain and the United States was something new, not the culmination of a substantial historical process.

As it happened, it was a new idea whose time had come. . . . Within a century, slavery, and most similar institutions like serfdom, had been all but eradicated from the face of the globe. Slavery had become controversial, then peculiar, then obsolete. (pp. 11–12.)

Mueller refers to the parallels of duelling and slavery several times in later chapters, but more as emblems than explanations.

More directly in point is Mueller's brief account of those nations that have "opted out" of the war system: Holland and Sweden. Both were at one time great powers; both had been militarily strong and active. But, notes Mueller,

After 1713, [Holland] dropped out of the great power system and concentrated on commercial and colonial ventures. . . . For over two-and-one-half centuries, Holland has generally . . . sought to avoid all international war in Europe, a pattern that can be called Hollandization.

Sweden, a Great Power—and a very warlike one—in the seventeenth century lost that status by 1721. . . . Swedish kings tried warfare again a few times between 1741 and 1814 [unsuccessfully]. Thereafter, [they] lost whatever residual enthusiasm for war they could still muster, and . . . have now been at peace for over a century and a half. (p. 20.)

He cites Switzerland, Spain, Denmark and Portugal as other "Hollandized" nations, which at earlier times had been, or, in terms of resources, could have been, Great Powers, but simply opted out.

After a brief discussion of the century-long peace between the United States and Canada, and an even briefer reference to the rise of the liberal state and the absence of war among liberal democracies, Mueller directly addresses his main theme, the changing social evaluation of war.[4] Before World War I, he argues, only a small minority spoke against war. Quakers opposed war as immoral, as they did slavery, religious intolerance, and many other then-

---

4. Mueller fails to cite Michael Doyle's brilliant discussion of why liberal states have never fought with each other. See Doyle, "Kant, Liberal Legacies, and Foreign Affairs", parts 1 and 2 in *Philosophy and Public Affairs*, Vol. 12, No. 3, No. 4 (Summer, Fall 1983), pp. 205–235 and 325–353. I am indebted to Marc Trachtenberg for calling Doyle's work to my attention after reading an earlier draft of this paper. Doyle's argument overlaps my own with respect to changes in the political rewards of war, but is not identical to it.

widespread and socially-approved practices embodying man's inhumanity to man. Non-religious humanists shared these views. So did those who saw war as inimical to commerce and economically ruinous, from Montesquieu, Kant, Buckle, and Adam Smith in the seventeenth and eighteenth centuries to Norman Angell in the twentieth. The majority view, however (or at least the majority of those who recorded their views), approved of war. War was an admirable stage for the display of heroism and virility for the individual and glory for the nation at one end of the spectrum of ideas, and a psychologically inevitable product of aggressiveness rooted in human nature and a necessary element of human progress in social Darwinian terms at the other.

The First World War changed these ideas. The magnitude of the slaughter, the costs to both victors and vanquished, the horribly inhuman and degrading circumstances of combat itself led to a "bone-deep revulsion," a "colossal confirmation [of] the repulsiveness, immorality and futility of war."[5]

According to Mueller, there were three possible lessons to be drawn from the experience of World War I: collective security had somehow to be substituted for individual self-help; military preparations, including newer and more formidable weapons, had to be maintained at a level that would deter war; conflicts had to be negotiated out rather than fought out. Most of the world drew the third lesson.

Unfortunately, Mussolini, Hitler, and the leaders of Japan were socially and culturally outsiders who had not shared the lessons of the First World War. They continued to believe in both the nobility and necessity of war. Mussolini was a foolish romantic pushing an unwilling Italian people into military adventures. The Japanese leadership was an ideological remnant of pre–World War I times, with a romantic view of war and a belief in the positive political and social role of the military in their own great task of modernization. Hitler, with his racist ideology, resentment against Versailles and quest for *Lebensraum*, was an entrepreneurial genius of both politics and war. None of them wanted genuinely to negotiate conflicts: the attempts of the other European states to do so, and the United States to avoid them—in

---

5. Mueller, *Retreat from Doomsday*, p. 55. It is striking that Mueller neither quotes nor cites the novels and memoirs of the twenties that expressed these feelings profoundly and gave them wide circulation: Erich Maria Remarque, *All Quiet on the Western Front;* Robert Graves, *Goodbye to All That;* Henri Barbusse, *Fire;* e.e. cummings, *The Enormous Room;* or Paul Fussell's overview of this literature in *The Great War and Modern Memory* (New York: Oxford University Press, 1975). Nor does Mueller explain why the American Civil War, the first modern war, which was equally costly and bloody relative to its extent, did not have the same effect in changing attitudes.

short, "appeasement"—led to the Second World War. For Mueller, Hitler's leadership in Germany was a necessary condition for the outbreak of war; he is silent on whether it was also sufficient.

The Second World War repeated and reinforced the lessons of the first and this time they were better learned. Among the developed nations there were now no dropouts who had failed to attend class. The atomic bomb played no significant part in these lessons. The war taught that U.S. productive power was itself a great deterrent; Detroit was as important as the atom bomb (pp. 82–84). Further, the actual use of the bomb against Japan was significant only because half of its leadership was already prepared to surrender (pp. 87–88). Finally, the absence of civil war against the occupying Nazis and their puppet governments (beyond the relatively small scale guerrilla resistance in occupied Europe) showed that the population had lost its stomach for war (pp. 91–92).

Roughly half of Mueller's book, chapters 5–9, depicts the major events of the period of the long peace since World War II. Mueller sees the success of containment as reflecting the satisfaction of the victors with and acceptance by the losers of the postwar situation; nuclear weapons are essentially irrelevant. The Korean War was a stabilizing event; it demonstrated the inutility of limited war. Khrushchev's policy of bluster and crisis-creation similarly failed, as did his efforts at seduction of the non-communist world by the examples of Soviet success in competitive economic growth—"we will bury you"—and the space race. The failure of U.S. intervention in Vietnam's civil war was followed by China's abandonment of the Cold War, and in turn by Soviet recognition of its "overreach" in the Third World and the demise of the cold war.

WEAKNESSES AND LIMITATIONS OF MUELLER'S ANALYSIS

Mueller's analysis reveals inadequacies at three different levels. The inadequacies detract least from the author's central argument at the first level, which characterizes the chapters summarized immediately above. These chapters present a curious and inconsistent mixture of Mueller's central thesis with a more conventional, neo-realist analysis of events. The fears of the advocates of containment and the consequent military responses in Korea and Vietnam were, Mueller argues, not all unreasonable at the time (p. 213); thus U.S. intervention in Vietnam may well have prevented a third world war, by stimulating a premature Chinese attempt at a coup in Indonesia. If delayed, the coup attempt might well have succeeded, emboldening Khrushchev and Mao to further use of force and accordingly creating a panic reaction in the United States leading to major war. Mueller recognizes this as speculation, but says it should not be dismissed (pp. 181–187). But Mueller's discussion of the Vietnam War gives almost no attention to the internal situation within South Vietnam. Mueller is unsympathetic to U.S. and West European cold warriors, yet sneers at Congressional constraints on executive action in Vietnam and Africa. He is contemptuous of Soviet performance, yet omits any discussion of why communism might have been attractive in the Third World.

These, however, are superficial flaws that do not detract from the force of Mueller's larger thesis, even if they weaken readers' confidence in the care with which he marshals evidence and advances argument.

At a second and deeper level, Mueller fails to confront the traditional realist and neo-realist argument that war is an inescapable feature of the anarchic international system in which independent states seek power and security. After all, this is one of the dominant models of international relations, if not the dominant one, and Mueller simply does not engage with it.

Kenneth Waltz offers a clear statement of the realist view: conflict is the inevitable result of the structure of the international system.[6] Independent states seeking security in an anarchic system in which war is the *ultima ratio* of statecraft will inevitably be in conflict, and conflict will regularly issue in war, as it has throughout history. However, a bipolar system has better prospects than a multipolar one for stability and the avoidance of war. With formidable nuclear, arsenals on both sides, the prospects for avoiding war become better still; indeed, "the probability of major war among states having nuclear weapons approaches zero."[7] Waltz thus supports Mueller's conclu-

---

6. Kenneth Waltz, "The Origins of War in Neo-Realist Theory," *Journal of Interdisciplinary History*, Vol. 17, No. 3 (Spring 1988), pp. 615–628; Waltz, *Man, the State, and War* (New York: Columbia University Press, 1959); and Waltz, *Theory of International Politics* (Reading, Mass.: Addison Wesley, 1979). The whole of that issue of the *Journal of Interdisciplinary History*, devoted to the "origins and prevention of major wars," has been published as Robert I. Rotberg and Theodore K. Rabb, eds., *The Origin and Prevention of Major Wars* (Cambridge: Cambridge University Press, 1989). A much cruder exposition of a much less subtle realist view is presented by Seabury and Codevilla in *War: Ends and Means*. Combining a primer with a present-oriented polemic, it depicts war as the inevitable consequence of the often ideologically-driven aggressive plans of some states. This situation has persisted through history and will continue in the future, they argue; wars must be expected, prepared for, if possible deterred, and if necessary fought. Neither preparation for war at all levels nor willingness to fight it using all available and imaginable weapons can be avoided, except by submitting to the will of the aggressor.
7. Waltz, "The Origins of War in Neo-Realist Theory," p. 627.

sion, at least for so long as the world of international politics remains bipolar, but for entirely different reasons. And as bipolarity disintegrates, it is not clear where Waltz's argument leads: will the stability effect of "absolute" weapons outweigh the instability of shifting alliances that multipolarity breeds?[8]

Though Mueller essentially dismisses the neo-realist case by ignoring it, he does not hesitate to make use of neo-realist arguments himself. He explains the stability of the post–World War II settlement in essentially neo-realist terms: the war resulted in a stable structure of power (pp. 95–97).

At the third and deepest level, Mueller fails to account for the socio-cultural change that he relies on to explain the "retreat from doomsday." The retreat appears to take place in a vacuum, or at best in a highly rarefied atmosphere in which the forces of technological change, economic change, and change in the internal structures and workings of the polities that fight or avoid wars are barely detectable. In his analysis, social ideas and attitudes seem to change of themselves, or at best to reflect changes in the ideas and attitudes of individuals, aggregated in an unstructured way. But this is not the way the world works. It is to this that the rest of this essay is addressed.

Toward a More Comprehensive Explanation: The Historical Background

Understanding why war has become obsolescent requires an examination of the political and economic calculus of war. A necessary and sufficient, or almost sufficient, condition for the disappearance of war is that all parties concerned calculate a negative cost benefit ratio *ex ante*.[9] No nation will start

8. See also Waltz's essay "Toward Nuclear Peace," pp. 684–712, in Robert Art and Kenneth Waltz, eds., *The Use of Force: Military Power and International Politics*, 3rd ed. (Lanham, Md.: University Press of America, 1988). Focusing on nuclear proliferation rather than directly on multipolarity, Waltz sees it as contributing to an increase in stability rather than the reverse. For the opposite conclusion see Lewis Dunn, "What Difference Will It Make?" in Art and Waltz, *The Use of Force*, pp. 713–725.
9. This condition is almost sufficient in that it appears to omit the possibility of inadvertent war. But inadvertent wars, if they occur at all, occur only in situations of conflict in which at least some of the actors have mobilized military forces and are threatening or contemplating their use. In such a situation, one or more actors must expect that making the threat of war, even allowing for the possibility that it may in fact occur, will produce a positive outcome. See Bruce Bueno de Mesquita, *The War Trap* (New Haven: Yale University Press, 1981), and Bueno de Mesquita, "The Contribution of Expected Utility Theory to the Study of International Conflict," in *Journal of Interdisciplinary History*, Vol. 43, No. 4 (Spring 1988), pp. 629–652 (also in Rotberg and Rabb, *The Origin and Prevention of Major Wars*). Luard, *War in International Society*, devotes chapter 5 to examining the decision processes that led to wars and concludes by asking:

a war unless it expects to gain in some way by doing so. Of course the prospective gain may be a virtual rather than an absolute one: the avoidance of an even greater loss where the alternative course of action requires submission in one way or another to the will of the adversary.

In the starkest and simplest terms, the key proposition of the more comprehensive explanation is that for most of human history, societies were so organized that war could be profitable for the victors, in both economic and political terms. But profound changes in economics and politics in the last century and a half, following the Industrial Revolution, have changed the terms of the calculation.

For millennia, societies were organized around landholding as the chief basis of both economic and political power. Agriculture was the overwhelmingly dominant economic activity; land and relatively unskilled labor were its major inputs, and typically—though not invariably—land was relatively the more scarce. Political power was based on the control of land, the mobilization of agricultural surpluses, and their conversion into military power and symbolic display in the shape of political and religious buildings and ceremonies. For these millennia, most labor was more or less tied to the landholder and land, either institutionally through slavery and serfdom, or less formally through simple immobility.

In such societies, successful war yielded a clear gain: control over territory—additional land and the associated labor force—that added directly to both economic and political power. Compared to the potential returns, costs, at least for the winner, were small. The instruments of war were simple and its scale typically small. The land itself suffered from war at most for one harvest season beyond the war's duration. While there were some losses of labor force in terms of civilian casualties and more in spread of famine and disease, these losses too were usually transient, and in general added little to the ambient levels of famine and disease.

In the political structure characteristic of these societies, the power holders were themselves the warriors, and the connection between those who fought

---

"Can war nonetheless occur accidentally?" His answer: "The evidence of history provides no indication that this is likely. Throughout the whole of the period we have been surveying it is impossible to identify a single case in which it can be said that a war started accidentally: in which it was not, at the time when war broke out, the deliberate intentions of at least one party that war should take place. . . . Whether a decision to make war results from active desire or passive willingness, therefore, it remains the case that the decision, when it occurs, is deliberate and intentional" (p. 232).

wars and those who, in victory, gained from them was direct and immediate. Conversely, the large mass of the population was separated entirely from political power and almost entirely from war. Shifts in political control and rule over the land on which they lived and worked had little effect on ordinary people's lives, except as one of the variations of fortune visited upon them by fate or the gods, like flood, drought, or plague.

In such societies, the romanticization of war and the high value given to the warrior hero were clearly functional. Even without a discussion of causation, it is clear that the social valuation of war corresponded well with its role as an instrument for gaining and enlarging political and economic power for those who both decided on war and waged it.[10] To be sure, this direct connection meant that the warriors and kings who decided on war risked their own lives, and could and did lose them in victory as well as defeat. They confronted this risk sustained not only by ideas of honor and glory, but by familial and dynastic as well as personal bases of reckoning gains and losses.

This is, of course, a highly schematic account, but as a set of stylized facts, it serves well to characterize most of Europe from the ninth to the fifteenth centuries. By the end of the fifteenth century, the scheme needs enlargement. Cities and trade, including overseas trade, became important; the machinery of government became more elaborate, and leaders other than warriors played an important role in it. Professional armies and gunpowder, used in both small arms and artillery, began to play an increasing role in warfare; the mounted knight disappeared; and the scale of war grew.[11] These changes continued, and increased in importance in the next three centuries. Still, the political, economic, and technical parameters remained such that war could still be seen as an enterprise in which possible gains outweighed costs.

Through the eighteenth century, political structures still concentrated power in the hands of a small elite who decided on peace and war; kings

---

10. See Homer's *Iliad,* passim.
11. For changes in the scale of war in the early part of the period, see Luard, *War in International Society,* chap. 2. He divides the time from 1400 into five periods: 1400–1559, the age of dynasties; 1559–1648, the age of religions; 1648–1789, the age of sovereignty; 1789–1917, the age of nationalism; and 1917 to the present, the age of ideology. His first period would correspond to the simple pre-industrial model of society; a more elaborate industrial model covers his next two, and at least part of the fourth. During the first of Luard's periods, wars involved armies ranging from 10–15,000 men on a side at first, rising to 30–40,000 by its end. By the end of the next period they had grown as much as tenfold. In the age of sovereignty wars tended to be smaller, and nothing matched the scale of the Thirty Years War, either in terms of forces mobilized or of relative casualties.

remained centrally important. The great majority of the population was still so distant from the ruling elites as to be almost totally disconnected from them. Land and immobile labor remained important though not as overwhelmingly dominant. The new spheres of economic activity in cities and trade also provided assets capturable by war. The cities themselves contained appropriable wealth in the form of stocks of food, materials, and (handicraft) manufactures. Trade was typically conducted in a mercantilist framework, often by licensed monopolies, so that political rulers retained both a substantial interest in it and control via access to ports and shipping. The scale of war was growing, but the scale of destruction was still small. Cities of course were more vulnerable to destruction than agricultural land, but they often had the option to surrender rather than endure siege and bombardment. Their inhabitants, too, while not tied to the land, were not particularly mobile. This was especially true of the economically most valuable ones, the skilled craftsmen and commercially active traders, who in much of Europe were more closely tied, politically, socially, and culturally, to their cities than to the sovereign king or emperor who nominally ruled them.[12] Thus they sometimes were available as intact or nearly intact spoils of war.

In the late sixteenth and early seventeenth centuries, religion assumed a salience in European wars that it has not had before or since.[13] But religious issues were still intermingled with issues of power, and Catholic sovereigns were often allied with Protestant ones in the wars of the period.

Though the societies of the eighteenth century differed greatly from those of the previous millennia in which the ideas of heroic valor and the romance of war developed, the ideas remained lively among elites, and thus still functional, since these remained the war-deciding, if no longer the chief war-making, classes.

THE GREAT CHANGE

In the nineteenth century, economy, polity, society, and culture were all transformed in ways that fundamentally changed the calculus of war. The

---

12. For the situation in Germany, see Mack Walker, *German Small Towns: Community, State and General Estate, 1648–1871* (Ithaca: Cornell University Press, 1971).
13. Luard found 26 civil wars over religious conflict and the same number of international wars concerned partly with religion in Europe between 1559 and 1648. These were more than half of the civil wars and about half of the international wars in the period. See *War in International Society*, Tables 3 and 4, pp. 36, 37, and also p. 93. Of course the wars of Islamic expansion and the European responses thereto in the Middle East and Spain were also wars of religion.

industrial revolution replaced animal by mechanical and then electric power, natural and traditional materials by steel and manufactured chemicals, and small-scale handicraft by large-scale factory production; transportation and communication sped up by orders of magnitude. By the end of the century, urban outweighed rural populations in half of Europe and, by the middle of the next, in most of the rest of Europe and North America, too. War, too, was industrialized: more powerful weapons, larger and more complexly organized armies, and great improvements in supply, transport, and communication changed its scale and intensity. After the American and French Revolutions, the fundamental basis of political legitimacy changed. The polity became both more inclusive and more integrated. More and more of the population were included in the politically significant classes. The spread of literacy as well as the growth of urban middle classes meant that there was no longer as profound a gulf of thought and feeling separating a small governing elite from a huge mass that belonged almost to a different species. The development of the polity was part of the larger process by which states become nations. The separate, isolated localities and regions of the peasant world were fused into a truly national state. Schooling played a significant role in this process, as did military service, but other less-organized forces, for example, the growth of railroad and road systems, were also important.[14]

The nation-states that were being created at the end of the last century and the first part of the twentieth formed a new kind of polity, culturally as well as politically. They became the chief focus of popular loyalty. The individual citizen identified directly with the nation on the basis of the cultural style he shared with his fellows. This was a literate culture, based on a nationally organized system of education that reached all the nation's inhabitants. The individual's membership in the culture was direct, rather than mediated through membership in smaller sub-groups. Sub-groups existed, of course, but were flexible rather than rigid, and typically did not evoke the same strong identification as the nation. The population was anonymous, fluid, mobile. Homogeneity, literacy, anonymity are the key words for describing the members of the new nation-state.[15]

---

14. See Eugen Weber, *Peasants into Frenchmen, 1870–1914* (Stanford: Stanford University Press, 1976), for detailed examination of this transformation in France.

15. This characterization is drawn from Ernest Gellner, *Nations and Nationalism* (Ithaca: Cornell University Press, 1983). The passage above is adapted from p. 138. Gellner's short book is an incisive, penetrating, and persuasive discussion of how the nation-states of the modern industrial world differ from earlier states, which were typically segmented, often multinational, and

DOES WAR STILL PAY? THE ECONOMIC CALCULUS

All of these nineteenth-century changes affected both the potential gains and the potential costs of war. In the economic sphere, land greatly diminished in importance as a resource. Capital in the tangible forms of machinery, buildings, and the infrastructure of transportation, communication, and urban life, and especially intangible human capital, in the form of the accumulated knowledge and skills of the work force at all levels, became relatively much more important. The integration of all or nearly all of the population into the unified society of the nation-state meant that the mere acquisition of territory did not by itself convey effective control of the resources sited on it, especially the all-important human resources (but of this more below).

The economic balance changed on the cost side as well. Industrialization multiplied both the scale and cost of war; industrial wars involved the whole nation, not the typically small fraction of population and output drawn into earlier wars. World Wars I and II far outweighed anything that had gone before in destructiveness.[16]

Destruction of a significant part of the stock of tangible capital in the battlefield countries was one element, and not even the most important, in the economic costs of the great wars. Loss of life, especially in the cohorts of young men in military service, was significant. Finally, there was the loss of four or five years of economic growth by the diversion to war-making of those resources that would otherwise have created new capital, tangible and human.[17]

---

not at all marked by a common literate culture. Gellner uses this analysis to explain the force of nationalism in the modern world. A more extended summary of Gellner's argument is provided on the last four pages of his book (pp. 139–143). See also his essays collected in Gellner, *Culture, Identity, and Politics* (Cambridge: Cambridge University Press, 1987). Much of the non-economic part of the argument of this essay rests on Gellner's insights.

16. See Levy, *War in the Modern Great Power System*, Table 41, pp. 88–91. The two world wars (102 and 113 in his list) exceeded all others in measures of severity, intensity, and concentration, measured respectively in total battle deaths, battle deaths/population, and battle deaths/nation-year. The nearest competitors in these measures—the Napoleonic Wars, the War of the Spanish Succession, and the Thirty Years War—were far behind.

17. The case of the United States in World War II is exceptional. U.S. involvement came at a time when the economy was operating far below capacity, and started slowly with a buildup to provide equipment and supplies to France and the United Kingdom. Thus the United States was able to increase both war production, including substantial investments in new capacity for making weapons, and civilian consumption. There probably was a gain in total growth in both civilian consumption and investment usable for further growth over what would have been achieved in the absence of war. In contrast, the demographic losses of Britain and France in the First World War have often been seen as a contributing factor to their sluggish economic performance in the 1920s and 1930s.

On the other side of the ledger, the extent to which the conquest of new territory added to the economic strength of the conqueror is questionable. The one-time opportunity for looting—seizure and removal of stocks of materials and finished goods, and movable capital equipment such as vehicles, ships, aircraft, machinery—remained. Compared to pre-industrial times, the available loot was much greater, since industrial societies have a much higher ratio of physical capital stock (other than land) to output than do agricultural-commercial ones. However, assuming that the conqueror aims to retain his conquests for a long period and wring from them a continuing economic surplus, the comparative balance is not so clear. The question is whether the economy of a different society, all or part of another industrial nation, can be effectively incorporated by conquest against the will of its inhabitants. The continuing political hostility of the conquered, and its effects on the level of energy and efficiency with which their economy operates, may lead to poorer results than those the conqueror could have achieved by avoiding the cost of the war and of continuing suppression of the conquered, and instead investing the equivalent in production for home consumption or trade with the rest of the world.

How long does political hostility endure? How high are its economic costs directly in terms of political repression, and indirectly in terms of political strikes, sabotage, low productivity? There has been no systematic study that could provide answers to these questions. Available evidence is fragmentary and non-quantitative.

Perhaps the first example of the conquest of a part of one industrial society by another is the German annexation of Alsace-Lorraine after the Franco-Prussian war. But, despite its forty-year duration, the episode provides no clear lesson. The area certainly functioned as part of the German economy, and was integrated into it to a substantial degree.[18] But on the other side, the primary purpose of the annexation was military. German military investment in garrison troops was high, and German policy did little to promote maximum integration and economic performance. Throughout the pe-

---

18. Alsatian potash was an important input to German agriculture, as were the phosphate by-products of the Thomas steelmaking process, which utilized the minette ores of Lorraine. The use of these ores by the Ruhr steelmakers helped the German steel industry reach first place in world production just before the First World War. Yet the ores came from *French* Lorraine; the boundary had been drawn two decades before the Thomas process came into wide use. Had the process been available in 1871, the Germans might well have sought to draw the boundary differently. I am indebted to Marc Trachtenberg for pointing this out.

riod, conflict continued between German military and civilian authorities, and between the local "particularists" who wished to improve the region's relations to the Reich, and an alliance of Catholic clergy and liberals who were hostile to Protestant, authoritarian Prussia. A clumsy and clumsily managed political structure did nothing to diminish these conflicts. Though three-quarters of the population lived in primarily German-speaking communities, and only one-eighth in primarily French-speaking ones, popular hostility to German rule remained strong. Almost a quarter of the original population migrated to France during this period, but some of this loss was replaced by immigration from Germany. The attempt to apply the German military call-up to the young men of the territories was a failure, with evasion rates running 25 percent or more in the early years after annexation.

The textile industry in Alsace, which earlier had been a European leader, grew much more slowly than it did in other parts of the Reich during the same period. The interests of firms and localities in the other parts of the Reich in restricting competition from the newly-annexed territories were effective in preventing investments in canals and ports, and in slowing the development of railroad connections with France, all of which could have increased productivity in the newly conquered "Reichsland."[19]

It is difficult to strike a balance on the basis of the information available, and even more difficult to speculate definitively what Germany could have achieved with an effective policy directed to promoting the economic and political integration of the territories.

Another example to test the proposition is that of German-occupied Europe between 1940 and 1944. Alan Milward, studying the economics of the Second World War, finds that the conquest and occupation of France was a profitable operation for Germany.[20] On one set of calculations, the levies that the Germans imposed on France rose from some 9–10 percent of French output in 1940 to about a third in 1943, then declined to a quarter in 1944. These flows represented some 3 to 8 or 9 percent of the German GNP in the corresponding years, falling to about 6 percent in 1944. On the basis of a crude estimate of the costs of conquest and occupation, Milward further

---

19. This account is drawn primarily from Dan P. Silverman, *Reluctant Union: Alsace-Lorraine and Imperial Germany, 1871–1918* (University Park: Pennsylvania State University Press, 1972), which appears to be the only recent study. See also Hajo Holborn, *A History of Modern Germany*, Vol. 3, *1840–1945*, (New York: Knopf, 1965).

20. Alan Milward, *War, Economy, and Society, 1939–1945* (Berkeley: University of California Press, 1979), ch. 5, "The Economics of Occupation."

concludes that the returns substantially outweighed the cost.[21] Although showing no similarly comprehensive calculations, Milward concludes that Belgium and the Netherlands also yielded a surplus to the Germans, but Norway did not, because of its smaller economy, dependence on imported raw materials, and the cost of the relatively large number of active German forces stationed there.

The significance of these calculations is unclear. The period is a short one. In France, and to a lesser extent in Belgium, governments and substantial segments of the population were sympathetic to the Nazis, but there was also active resistance in all three countries. The strongest conclusions that these and the other examples sustain is that the question of the economic costs and benefits of conquest is open.

Milward discusses at some length the part played in Germany's calculus of war by German concepts of *Grossraumwirtschaft*, the idea that Germany needed to expand the area it controlled in order to sustain its role as a great military power. More agricultural land was particularly needed, but so was access to raw materials, especially iron ore, bauxite, and oil. There is no easy way to assess how much weight this economic motive had in driving Germany's policy, compared to the mix of desire for revenge for the wrongs of Versailles, racist ideology, Nazi dreams of a New Order, hatred and fear of Bolshevism, and Hitler's simple lust for power. The economic goals were certainly present; that does not say that they were correctly assessed.

Aside from the particular goals of Germany in 1939, access to and control of critical raw materials—oil and metal ores in particular—have often been advanced as economic bases for war. Japanese actions in the thirties provide another example of this type. However, the proposition does not stand up to analysis. Raw material inputs have long been declining in overall economic importance; the ratios of primary production in general, and minerals specifically, to GNP have been steadily declining in industrial countries at least since the First World War. Further, any single material usually has substitutes and, at higher prices, alternative sources of supply. Even crude oil, often cited as indispensable to modern society and modern military power, can be substituted by coal-based synthetics, as Germany did successfully during the Second World War, although at much higher costs. But if the calculation were made of the economic balance between securing these materials by

---

21. Ibid., pp. 137–147, esp. tables 21 and 22, p. 140, and discussion on pp. 144–145.

conquest, and securing them in the ordinary ways by trade or by the search for substitutes and alternate sources of supply, it would be a peculiar situation indeed that gave the advantage to war. The typical discussion of critical materials takes for granted the necessity of wartime access or alternately the threat of hostile denial, thus begging the question of whether they are worth fighting for. But the question should rather be seen as a long-run one: is it cheaper for a nation to secure the supply of raw materials not found within its borders by trade, or by conquest?[22]

DOES WAR STILL PAY? THE POLITICAL CALCULUS

So far, the discussion of how the coming of industrialization has changed the calculus of war has focused on its economic elements. But the political calculus is at least as important, if not more so. It is presidents, prime ministers, and party secretaries who play central roles in making decisions about war and peace, not finance ministers, budget directors, and central bankers. Here, too, the last century-and-a-half has brought a profound trans-formation. Governments have become popular and populist even when not democratic; the welfare of the general population, conceived in a broad sense, is their chief business, and it is to achieving this that they bend their efforts. Of course, this is true *a fortiori* in democratic societies, in which the question, "are you better off now than you were however many years ago?" is always a useful electoral cry for one or another of the political competitors.[23] But even authoritarian and repressive governments in modern societies need the consent, however tacit and grudging, of the mass of the governed. Economic well-being and social peace are the chief elements on which this consent rests.

Making war can rarely contribute positively to these goals. In the short run, the mass of the public bears heavy costs. The public, not a small army of professionals, pays the price in blood, whether as soldiers or as city dwellers subject to attack from the air. They suffer the immediate hardships consequent on wartime economic mobilization. If the arguments above are correct, it is most unlikely that there is compensation in the long run sufficient to outweigh the costs, even to families that have not suffered death or injury.

---

22. These issues are discussed further in E.N. Castle and K.A. Price, eds., *U.S. Interests and Global Natural Resources* (Baltimore: Johns Hopkins University Press, 1983). See especially the essays of McGeorge Bundy and Carl Kaysen.
23. Michael Doyle's two-part article "Kant, Liberal Legacies and Foreign Policy," examines this question at length.

Welfare-oriented societies typically produce leaders who are attuned to and reflect their societies' goals. They compete for their positions by appealing to the public as improvers of public welfare, whether by positive action, or by promising to unleash the natural forces of progress. Peace, not war, is seen as the natural state of affairs by leaders as well as the public. Further, the dominance of the nation-state as a focus of popular sentiment has delegitimated wars of conquest; they are not only unlikely to be profitable, they are viewed as wrong. Gellner quotes Lord Acton: "Thus began a time when the text simply was, that nations would not be governed by foreigners. Power legitimately attained, and exercised with moderation, was declared invalid."[24] Germany's annexation of Alsace-Lorraine exemplified just such an illegitimate change of rule. Current examples are even clearer. The Israeli military occupation of the West Bank and the Soviet-installed regimes in Eastern Europe have all been characterized by an extremely high level of persisting political hostility between their populations and the dominant power.

Economy, Polity, and the Social Evaluation of War

The changes in society, economy, and polity sketched in the preceding pages provide both the context for and a substantial part of the explanation of the cultural change that Mueller invokes as the chief reason for the obsolescence of major war in the industrialized world. New relations of individuals to a new kind of society, new leaders with new conceptions of their task, and new ways of making war explain new ideas about war. An additional question Mueller simply does not address is, what governed the pace of change in the social evaluation of war? Why did the lessons of the First World War require the experience of the Second before they were widely absorbed? Part of the answer is that the two wars themselves were the agents of consummation for the social changes described. The First World War greatly accelerated the disappearance of regimes ruled by hereditary elites that were still imbued with old ideas of war. The experiences of the inter-war years and the Second World War solidified the recognition and acceptance of the guarantee of popular welfare as a major duty of the state.

Viewed another way, the time scale for these changes was surprisingly short. In general, social ideas—cultures—change much more slowly than

---

24. Gellner, *Nations and Nationalism*, p. 159.

social institutions.[25] Although the transformations consequent on industrialization were well underway in the major states of Europe by 1914, the culture of politics was still nearer to that of 1815 than that of 1945. In 1914, when the Germans took the steps that set themselves and the other combatants on the path to war, they hoped for a short war not much different from the other wars they had experienced since 1815. They put their faith in a war plan that called for the rapid defeat of France, and their hope in the neutrality of Britain. The final steps to the Second World War were more compressed in time than those that led to the first: just six years from Hitler's assumption of power to the German invasion of Poland. The responses to his moves by other European nations were reluctant, not eager; there were not two sides pushing for war. If anything, some of the lessons of the first war had been overlearned in France, Britain, and the United States. The cap to all this was the improbable conjuncture of situation and personal talents that brought Hitler to his key role in the process.

To be sure, the cultural transformation is far from complete. Wars still mobilize national sentiments, and create a heightened emotional state with an intensified sense of community and sharing. Even the threat of war or the display of force brings out such feelings. The nationalization and integration of modern societies sketched above reinforces and amplifies these sentiments, and their instant dissemination and multiple reflection in the media does so even more.[26]

A short, small war, ending in victory at little cost in blood or treasure, by mobilizing just these sentiments, can still produce political gains for the leaders who initiate it. The recent Falklands/Malvinas War produced a substantial gain for Prime Minister Thatcher, and the United States' intervention in Grenada—hardly a war—a similar one for President Reagan. But such wars may be hard to choose successfully. As Yehoshafat Harkabi has pointed out, nations that have initiated wars in this century have generally come out the loser.[27]

---

25. See Clifford Geertz, *The Interpretation of Cultures* (New York: Basic Books, 1973), passim.
26. See John Mueller, *War, Presidents, and Public Opinion* (Lanham, Md.: University Press of America, 1985). This is a reprint of the original published in 1973. Mueller traces the public response, as shown in polls, to the actions of Presidents Truman in Korea and Johnson in Vietnam. Initially strongly positive, public opinion declined and turned negative as the wars dragged on and casualties grew.
27. Yehoshafat Harkabi, "Directions of Change in the World Strategic Order," a comment on a paper of the same title given by Karl Kaiser at the 30th Anniversary Conference of the International Institute for Strategic Studies (IISS), in Brighton, and reprinted in *The Changing Strategic*

Broad Arguments and the Evidence, Such As It Is

The foregoing comments on the recentness of change in the social accept-
ability of war are consistent with such quantitative evidence as there is on
the frequency and intensity of war. Melvin Small and David Singer, in their
1982 study *Resort to Arms,* find no trends at all in the frequency or intensity
of wars between 1816 and 1980.[28]

J.S. Levy's longer study of wars in the great power system does identify
some trends. His regression analysis shows that the frequency of wars involving the great powers, measured in terms of 25-year periods, declined
modestly over the 1495–1975 period of his study. So did the duration of wars
and their magnitude, in terms of nation-years of wars. However, their severity in terms of casualties increased.[29]

Organizing his material somewhat differently, Levy compares the five long
periods, "modified centuries," covered by his data: 1500–1599, 1600–1713,
1714–1789, 1816–1899, 1900–1975 (a periodization that excludes the wars of
the French Revolution and Napoleon). The seventeenth century appears as
the most warlike, followed by the sixteenth, the eighteenth, and the twentieth; with the nineteenth most peaceable.[30]

Luard, with a somewhat different periodization and less attempt at refined
measurement, paints a broadly similar picture. His age of nationalism (1789–
1917) is of course more warlike than Levy's nineteenth century, since it
includes the great wars of 1789–1815 and 1914–1917. He too comments on
the peaceable century of 1815–1914 in Europe: Prussia, which led in the
number of its wars, was involved in international war for only five years,
Russia for eight, France for five, Austria for four, and Britain for three.[31] But
relative peaceableness extended only to international wars in Europe. The
same period that saw only twenty-eight international wars in Europe saw
244 wars worldwide, including 107 of colonial conquest or colonial revolt and
47 civil wars in Europe.[32]

Landscape: IISS Conference Papers, 1988, Part II, Adelphi Paper No. 237 (London: IISS, 1989), pp.
21–23. Harkabi makes, in highly compressed form, some of the broader arguments made here.
28. Melvin Small and J. David Singer, *Resort to Arms: International and Civil Wars, 1816–1980*
(Beverly Hills: Sage, 1982).
29. Levy, *War in the Modern Great Power System,* Table 6.3, p. 134.
30. Ibid., Table 6.5, p. 143.
31. See Luard, *War in International Society,* ch. 2 and appendices 1–5.
32. Luard reminds us that the long peace since World War II was a long peace in Europe, not
in the rest of the world, ibid., pp. 72–79.

Does the Nuclear Revolution Matter?

The argument so far has made no mention of the nuclear revolution, and so far is in accord with Mueller's contention that major war between modern nations was on its way to obsolescence before the development of nuclear weapons. However, this is not to accept that the profound revolution in the technology of war brought by nuclear and thermonuclear weapons and long-range ballistic missiles does not matter; quite the contrary. These new technologies of war have amplified the message of this century's war experiences by many decibels, and set it firmly in the minds of the wide public as well as those of political and military leaders. Contemplating what a dozen thermonuclear warheads can do to a modern society, much less a thousand dozen, leads all concerned to a much more subtle, careful, and discriminating calculation of what the national interest is, in any conflict situation, and how it can best be pursued. And all *are* concerned. The downside risks of wrong decisions have become so immense and immediate that it is almost inconceivable that haste and wishfulness will again play the roles in initiating wars that they have in the past. It is equally difficult to think what interest other than sheer survival can be placed on the other pan of the balance, and there is simply no rational way to believe that, in a world of long-range missiles carrying thermonuclear warheads, the initiation of nuclear war is a way to ensure survival.[33] Nor have nuclear weapons made the world safe for non-nuclear war, if it involves the interests of nuclear-armed nations on both sides of a conflict, since the risks of escalation must be counted into a balance already unfavorable to war.

Another way to make clear that the nuclear-missile revolution in military technology has had a profound effect is to imagine, *per impossibile*, that the revolution had taken place in the world of the eighteenth century. Even the most calculating of absolute monarchs, completely focused on their dynastic interests, and totally unconcerned with the welfare of their powerless peasant populations, would nevertheless have had to take a different view of war than they had previously held. The prospect that they themselves, their families, their capitals, and their hunting lodges as well as their palaces would all vaporize in the thermonuclear fire would certainly change their

---

33. See McGeorge Bundy, *Danger and Survival: Choices about the Bomb in the First Fifty Years* (New York: Random House, 1988), for a penetrating and meticulous examination of the cautious behavior of the leaders of the superpowers in periods of tension and moments of crisis.

assessment of the relative virtues of war and peace. The question for this imagined world is whether the elites would have had the time to contemplate the lesson of Hiroshima and Nagasaki, or whether their survivors would have had to learn it by bitter experience.

Concluding Observations

If wars among modern nations truly serve no possible rational purpose, why is there not wide, even universal, recognition of this proposition, especially by the political leadership of these nations? What leads them to persist in supporting large military forces, and building their relations to other nations around military alliances and the threat, if not actual use, of force? These questions can be answered at both a general and a quite specific level.

The general answer is that cultures change much more slowly than technologies and institutions. As Keynes said, most living politicians are slaves of some dead scribbler. Despite Mueller's assertion, war has not yet become "subrationally unthinkable," even though conscious attitudes toward war have indeed changed.

For most governmental and political elites in modern states, the old ideas of military power and "defense" as the core of national sovereignty still carry great weight. Accordingly, providing the capability for war, and being in some sense prepared to use it, still command a large share of the resources and energies of governments. This has been true over a wide range of the political spectrum, wide enough to cover most of the actual and potentially eligible ruling groups. Disarmers and pacifists in opposition have changed their views when they led or joined governments. Those who have maintained these views have remained outsiders and critics, because most of the publics share their governors' views of these questions.

On a more concrete level, the powerful grip of ideology on governments and publics on both sides of the great postwar East-West divide has diverted attention from the changes sketched in the preceding pages. The West has combined abhorrence of communism as a mode of social organization with belief in its inherent expansionism and its goal of conquest. These beliefs, and a reading of the lessons of the 1930s that focused on the failure of will in France, Great Britain, and the United States, have justified the place of military power and the threat of war in the center of our international picture. On the other side of the divide, ideological commitment to the idea that capitalists must and will resist the inevitable triumph of communism, and the fear of capitalist encirclement, together with a reading of history since 1917 that justifies that fear, have produced a complementary world picture.

It is just the revolutionary change in military technology, especially in the last twenty-five years, that has loosened the grip of ideology on both sides of the divide. The self-confessed failure of communist ideology as a blueprint for successful social organization is helping to complete the process, and opening the way to new thinking in the West as well as the East.

Assuming that the foregoing analysis is correct, and assuming further that it can be made widely persuasive (which may be two independent assumptions), does not imply that the world is on the threshold of universal and perpetual peace. Fully modern industrial nations are still in the minority in the world in both number and population. Civil wars, and forms of violent international conflict falling short of war, are widespread and will continue to be so in the foreseeable future.

Nonetheless, this analysis reinforces Mueller's to offer a real basis for hope. The international system that relies on the national use of military force as the ultimate guarantor of security, and the threat of its use as the basis of order, is not the only possible one. To seek a different system with a more secure and a more humane basis for order is no longer the pursuit of an illusion, but a necessary effort toward a necessary goal. The industrialized nations, which are also the most heavily and dangerously armed, must lead the way to this transformation by their own example of changed behavior. That may not be enough to persuade the others, but it is certainly the indispensable first step.

Postscript

The first draft of this essay, ending just above, was finished in the middle of October 1989. At that time, nothing foreshadowed the accelerating pace of revolutionary political change in Eastern Europe shown in each morning's headlines and each evening's broadcasts, not quite two months later. To be sure, the internal politics of the Soviet Union had been undergoing far-reaching changes since Gorbachev's ascension to leadership in 1985, and these changes were having their reflection in Soviet relations with the rest of the world. By last spring, Poland's government had taken the first steps away from the Communists' monopoly of political power by relegitimizing Solidarity and engaging in negotiations about the composition of the government with its leadership. But even in October 1989, no one expected the dizzying changes of November and December.[34]

So far, the focus of change is the internal political order in Poland, Hungary, Czechoslovakia, the German Democratic Republic, Rumania, and Bulgaria. But the first signs of their equally profound international consequences are appearing. The same crowds in the streets of Leipzig and East Berlin that have demanded and achieved the dismissal of their country's Communist leadership are displaying banners reading, "*Ein Volk, Ein Land*" (One People, One Country). The sentiment for German reunification is echoed in more guarded language in Bonn and Washington, and bluntly rejected in Moscow.[35] As seen from Moscow, the simultaneous reunification of Germany and the strengthening of its ties with the West, specifically with NATO, pose a threat to the entire postwar settlement that was finally ratified in Helsinki after twenty-five years of Western denial, and threaten to undo the results of the Second World War. As seen from Washington, a reunification of Germany that required the withdrawal of American and other NATO troops from West Germany as well as Soviet troops from East Germany would mean the destruction of the whole Western security structure that has been arduously built up since the North Atlantic Treaty of 1949.

Both views will have to change. Have not the heads of both governments been saying that the will of the people should prevail? It is clear that a profound transformation of the international structure of power in Europe—and the whole world—is underway. In the past, such changes have regularly been consummated by war. The argument presented in this essay supports the prediction that this time the changes can take place without war (although not necessarily without domestic violence within the states concerned). So far—mid-January—so good. The author and his readers will be eagerly and anxiously testing the prediction each day.

---

34. See, for example, Seweryn Bialer and Michael Mandelbaum, *The Global Rivals* (New York: Vintage Books, 1989). Here two leading students of the Soviet Union and East-West relations write: "Whatever happens in Europe itself, the two military blocs will not dissolve. . . . The Soviet Union will not release its grip on its East European satellites, nor will the West be powerful enough to break that grip by force" (p. 193).

35. See Timothy Garton Ash, "The German Revolution," *New York Review of Books*, December 21, 1989, pp. 14–19. (The article was dated November 21, 1989.)

Economic Interdependence and War

Dale C. Copeland

A Theory of Trade Expectations

$\mathbf{D}$oes economic interdependence increase or decrease the probability of war among states? With the Cold War over, this question is taking on importance as trade levels between established powers such as the United States and Russia and emerging powers such as Japan, China, and Western Europe grow to new heights. In this article, I provide a new dynamic theory to help overcome some of the theoretical and empirical problems with current liberal and realist views on the question.

The prolonged debate between realists and liberals on the causes of war has been largely a debate about the relative salience of different causal variables. Realists stress such factors as relative power, while liberals focus on the absence or presence of collective security regimes and the pervasiveness of democratic communities.[1] Economic interdependence is the only factor that plays an important causal role in the thinking of both camps, and their perspectives are diametrically opposed.

Liberals argue that economic interdependence lowers the likelihood of war by increasing the value of trading over the alternative of aggression: interdependent states would rather trade than invade. As long as high levels of

Dale C. Copeland is Assistant Professor in the Department of Government and Foreign Affairs at the University of Virginia.

For their helpful comments on previous drafts of this article, I would like to thank Robert Art, V. Natasha Copeland, Michael Desch, Angela Doll, John Duffield, Matthew Evangelista, Richard Falkenrath, James Fearon, Joseph Grieco, Atsushi Ishida, Irving Lachow, Alastair Iain Johnston, Andrew Kydd, Jack Levy, Lisa Martin, Michael Mastanduno, John Mearsheimer, Andrew Moravcsik, John Owen, Paul Papayoanou, Stephen Rhoads, Gideon Rose, Richard Rosecrance, Len Schoppa, Herman Schwartz, Randall Schweller, Jitsuo Tsuchiyama, David Waldner, and Stephen Walt. This article also benefited from presentations at the Program on International Politics, Economics, and Security at the University of Chicago; the University of Virginia Department of Government's faculty workshop; the annual meeting of the American Political Science Association, Chicago, September 1995; the Olin security workshop at the Center for International Affairs, Harvard University; and the Center for Science and International Affairs, Harvard University (under whose auspices it was written). All errors remain mine.

1. For a summary of the causal variables in the two schools, see John J. Mearsheimer, "Back to the Future: Instability in Europe After the Cold War," *International Security*, Vol. 15, No. 1 (Summer 1990), pp. 5–56; Robert O. Keohane, "International Liberalism Reconsidered," in John Dunn, ed., *The Economic Limits to Modern Politics* (Cambridge: Cambridge University Press, 1990), pp. 165–194.

International Security, Vol. 20, No. 4 (Spring 1996), pp. 5–41
© 1996 by the President and Fellows of Harvard College and the Massachusetts Institute of Technology.

interdependence can be maintained, liberals assert, we have reason for optimism. Realists dismiss the liberal argument, arguing that high interdependence increases rather than decreases the probability of war. In anarchy, states must constantly worry about their security. Accordingly, interdependence—meaning mutual dependence and thus vulnerability—gives states an incentive to initiate war, if only to ensure continued access to necessary materials and goods.

The unsatisfactory nature of both liberal and realist theories is shown by their difficulties in explaining the run-ups to the two World Wars. The period up to World War I exposes a glaring anomaly for liberal theory: the European powers had reached unprecedented levels of trade, yet that did not prevent them from going to war. Realists certainly have the correlation right—the war was preceded by high interdependence—but trade levels had been high for the previous thirty years; hence, even if interdependence was a necessary condition for the war, it was not sufficient.

At first glance, the period from 1920 to 1940 seems to support liberalism over realism. In the 1920s, interdependence was high, and the world was essentially peaceful; in the 1930s, as entrenched protectionism caused interdependence to fall, international tension rose to the point of world war. Yet the two most aggressive states in the system during the 1930s, Germany and Japan, were also the most highly dependent despite their efforts towards autarchy, relying on other states, including other great powers, for critical raw materials. Realism thus seems correct in arguing that high dependence may lead to conflict, as states use war to ensure access to vital goods. Realism's problem with the interwar era, however, is that Germany and Japan had been even more dependent in the 1920s, yet they sought war only in the late 1930s when their dependence, although still significant, had fallen.

The theory presented in this article—the theory of trade expectations—helps to resolve these problems. The theory starts by clarifying the notion of economic interdependence, fusing the liberal insight that the benefits of trade give states an incentive to avoid war with the realist view that the potential costs of being cut off can push states to war to secure vital goods. The total of the benefits and potential costs of trade versus autarchy reveals the true level of dependence a state faces, for if trade is completely severed, the state not only loses the gains from trade but also suffers the costs of adjusting its economy to the new situation.

Trade expectations theory introduces a new causal variable, the expectations of future trade, examining its impact on the overall expected value of the trading option if a state decides to forgo war. This supplements the static consideration in liberalism and realism of the levels of interdependence at any point in time, with the importance of leaders' dynamic expectations into the future.

Levels of interdependence and expectations of future trade, considered simultaneously, lead to new predictions. Interdependence can foster peace, as liberals argue, but this will only be so when states expect that trade levels will be high into the foreseeable future. If highly interdependent states expect that trade will be severely restricted—that is, if their expectations for future trade are low—realists are likely to be right: the most highly dependent states will be the ones most likely to initiate war, for fear of losing the economic wealth that supports their long-term security. In short, high interdependence can be either peace-inducing or war-inducing, depending on the expectations of future trade.

This dynamic perspective helps bridge the gaps within and between current approaches. Separating levels of interdependence from expectations of future trade indicates that states may be pushed into war even if current trade levels are high, if leaders have good reason to suspect that others will cut them off in the future. In such a situation, the expected value of trade will likely be negative, and hence the value of continued peace is also negative, making war an attractive alternative. This insight helps resolve the liberal problem with World War I: despite high trade levels in 1913–14, declining expectations for future trade pushed German leaders to attack, to ensure long-term access to markets and raw materials.

Even when current trade is low or non-existent, positive expectations for future trade will produce a positive expected value for trade, and therefore an incentive for continued peace. This helps explain the two main periods of détente between the Cold War superpowers, from 1971 to 1973 and in the late 1980s: positive signs from U.S. leaders that trade would soon be significantly increased coaxed the Soviets into a more cooperative relationship, reducing the probability of war. But in situations of low trade where there is no prospect that high trade levels will be restored in the future, highly dependent states may be pushed into conflict. This was the German and Japanese dilemma before World War II.

The article is divided into three sections. The first section reviews liberal and realist theories on the relationship between economic interdependence and the probability of war, and provides a critique of both theories. The second section lays out trade expectations theory. The final section examines the diplomatic historical evidence for the new theory against two significant cases: Germany before World War I and Germany before World War II. The evidence indicates that the new variable, expectations of future trade, helps resolve the anomalies for current theories: in both cases, negative expectations for future trade, combined with high dependence, led leaders into total war out of fear for their long-term economic position and therefore security.

The Liberal and Realist Debate on Economic Interdependence and War

The core liberal position is straightforward.[2] Trade provides valuable benefits, or "gains from trade," to any particular state. A dependent state should therefore seek to avoid war, since peaceful trading gives it all the benefits of close ties without any of the costs and risks of war. Trade pays more than war, so dependent states should prefer to trade not invade. This argument is often supported by the auxiliary proposition that modern technology greatly increases the costs and risks of aggression, making the trading option even more rational.

The argument was first made popular in the 1850s by Richard Cobden, who asserted that free trade "unites" states, "making each equally anxious for the prosperity and happiness of both."[3] This view was restated in *The Great Illusion* by Norman Angell just prior to World War I and again in 1933. Angell saw states having to choose between new ways of thinking, namely peaceful trade, and the "old method" of power politics. Even if war was once profitable, modernization now makes it impossible to "enrich" oneself through force; indeed, by destroying trading bonds, war is "commercially suicidal."[4]

Why do wars nevertheless occur? While the start of World War I just after *The Great Illusion*'s initial publication might seem to refute his thesis, Angell in

---

2. Four other subsidiary liberal arguments, employing intervening variables, are not sufficiently compelling to discuss here. The first suggests that high trade levels promote domestic prosperity, thereby lessening the internal problems that push leaders into war. The second argues that interdependence helps to foster increased understanding between peoples, which reduces the misunderstandings that lead to war. The third asserts that trade alters the domestic structure of states, heightening the influence of groups with a vested interest in peaceful trade. The final argument contends that trade has the "spill-over" effect of increasing political ties between trading partners, thus improving the prospects for long-term cooperation. For an critical analysis of these views, see Dale Copeland, "Economic Interdependence and the Outbreak of War," paper presented to University of Virginia Department of Government's faculty workshop, March 1995.
3. Richard Cobden, *The Political Writings of Richard Cobden* (London: T. Fischer Unwin, 1903), p. 225.
4. Norman Angell, *The Great Illusion*, 2d ed. (New York: G.P. Putnam's Sons, 1933), pp. 33, 59–60, 87–89.

the 1933 edition argued that the debacle simply confirmed the unprofitability of modern wars. He thus upheld the common liberal view that wars, especially major wars, result from the misperceptions of leaders caught up in the outmoded belief that war still pays. Accordingly, his is "not a plea for the impossibility of war . . . but for its futility," since "our ignorance on this matter makes war not only possible, but extremely likely."[5] In short, if leaders fail to see how unprofitable war is compared to the benefits of trade, they may still erroneously choose the former.

Richard Rosecrance provides the most extensive update of the Cobden-Angell thesis to the nuclear era. States must choose between being "trading states," concerned with promoting wealth through commerce, and "territorial states," obsessed with military expansion. Modern conditions push states towards a predominantly trading mode: wars are not only too costly, but with the peaceful trading option, "the benefits that one nation gains from trade can also be realized by others." When the system is highly interdependent, therefore, the "incentive to wage war is absent," since "trading states recognize that they can do *better* through internal economic development sustained by a worldwide market for their goods and services than by trying to conquer and assimilate large tracts of land."[6] Rosecrance thus neatly summarizes the liberal view that high interdependence fosters peace by making trading more profitable than invading.[7]

---

5. Ibid., pp. 59–62, 256.
6. Richard Rosecrance, *The Rise of the Trading State: Commerce and Conquest in the Modern World* (New York: Basic Books, 1986), pp. 13–14; 24–25 (emphasis added); see also Rosecrance, "War, Trade and Interdependence," in James N. Rosenau and Hylke Tromp, eds., *Interdependence and Conflict in World Politics* (Aldershot, U.K.: Avebury, 1989), pp. 48–57; Rosecrance, "A New Concert of Powers," *Foreign Affairs*, Vol. 71, No. 2 (Spring 1992), pp. 64–82.
7. A book often seen as a statement on the peace-inducing effects of interdependence—Robert O. Keohane and Joseph S. Nye, *Power and Interdependence* (Boston: Little, Brown, 1977)—actually contains no such causal argument. For Keohane and Nye, "complex interdependence" is more peaceful by definition: it is "a valuable concept for analyzing the political process" only when military force is "unthinkable" (pp. 29, 24). In the second edition: "since we *define* complex interdependence in terms of [policy] goals and instruments," arguments "about how goals and instruments are affected by the degree to which a situation approximates complex interdependence or realism will be tautological." Thus, "we are left essentially with two dependent variables: changes in agendas and changes in the roles of international organizations." Keohane and Nye, *Power and Interdependence*, 2d ed. (Glenview, Ill.: Scott, Foresman, 1989), p. 255; emphasis in original. The dependent variable of this article—the likelihood of war—is nowhere to be found, which is not surprising, since it is assumed away. Other works on interdependence from the 1970s, which largely examined dependent variables other than war, are discussed in Copeland, "Economic Interdependence and the Outbreak of War."

Realists turn the liberal argument on its head, arguing that economic inter-dependence not only fails to promote peace, but in fact heightens the likelihood of war.[8] States concerned about security will dislike dependence, since it means that crucial imported goods could be cut off during a crisis. This problem is particularly acute for imports like oil and raw materials; while they may be only a small percentage of the total import bill, without them most modern economies would collapse. Consequently, states dependent on others for vital goods have an increased incentive to go to war to assure themselves of contin-ued access of supply.

Neorealist Kenneth Waltz puts the argument as follows: actors within a domestic polity have little reason to fear the dependence that goes with spe-cialization. The anarchic structure of international politics, however, makes states worry about their vulnerability, thus compelling them "to control what they depend on or to lessen the extent of their dependency." For Waltz, it is this "simple thought" that explains, among other things, "their imperial thrusts to widen the scope of their control."[9] For John Mearsheimer, nations that "depend on others for critical economic supplies will fear cutoff or blackmail in time of crisis or war." Consequently, "they may try to extend political control to the source of supply, giving rise to conflict with the source or with its other customers." Interdependence, therefore, "will probably lead to greater security competition."[10]

---

8. One might contend that realists doubt the causal importance of economic interdependence, since relative gains concerns convince great powers to avoid becoming dependent in the first place. Aside from arguments showing why states may cooperate despite concerns for relative gains (see essays by Powell, Snidal, and Keohane in David A. Baldwin, ed., *Neorealism and Neoliberalism: The Contemporary Debate* [New York: Columbia University Press, 1993]; Dale Copeland, "Why Relative Gains Concerns May *Promote* Economic Cooperation: A Realist Explanation for Great Power Interdependence," presented at the annual meeting of the International Studies Association, San Diego, April 1996), the argument is empirically false. Periods of high interdependence have arisen even when the security competition between great powers was particularly intense, such as from 1880 to 1914, as Waltz acknowledges. Kenneth Waltz, "The Myth of Interdependence," in Ray Maghoori and Bennett Ramberg, *Globalism versus Realism* (Boulder, Colo.: Westview Press, 1982), p. 83. Since the reality of high interdependence cannot be argued or assumed away, I focus here on the core realist claim that whenever high levels of interdependence are reached, for whatever reason, war is more likely.
9. Kenneth Waltz, *Theory of International Politics* (New York: Random House, 1979), p. 106.
10. John J. Mearsheimer, "Disorder Restored," in Graham Allison and Gregory F. Treverton, eds., *Rethinking America's Security* (New York: W.W. Norton, 1992), p. 223; Mearsheimer, "Back to the Future," p. 45. See also Robert Gilpin, "Economic Interdependence and National Security in Historical Perspective," in Klaus Knorr and Frank N. Trager, eds., *Economic Issues and National Security* (Lawrence, Kan.: Allen, 1977), p. 29. Adopting the realist argument, but emphasizing how dependence leads states to adopt destabilizing offensive strategies, is Anne Uchitel, "Interdepend-

This modern realist understanding of economic interdependence and war finds its roots in mercantilist writings dating from the seventeenth century. Mercantilists saw states as locked in a competition for relative power and for the wealth that underpins that power.[11] For mercantilists, imperial expansion—the acquisition of colonies—is driven by the state's need to secure greater control over sources of supply and markets for its goods, and to build relative power in the process. By allowing the metropole and the colonies to specialize in production and trade of complementary products (particularly manufactured goods for raw materials), while ensuring political control over the process, colonies "opened up the possibility of providing a system of supply within a self-contained empire."[12]

In this, we see the underpinning for the neorealist view that interdependence leads to war. Mercantilist imperialism represents a reaction to a state's dependence; states reduce their fears of external specialization by increasing *internal* specialization within a now larger political realm. The imperial state as it expands thus acquires more and more of the characteristics of Waltz's domestic polity, with its hierarchy of specialized functions secure from the unpredictable policies of others.

In sum, realists seek to emphasize one main point: political concerns driven by anarchy must be injected into the liberal calculus. Since states must be primarily concerned with security and therefore with control over resources and markets, one must discount the liberal optimism that great trading partners will always continue to be great trading partners simply because both states benefit absolutely. Accordingly, a state vulnerable to another's policies because of dependence will tend to use force to overcome that vulnerability.

---

ence and Instability," in Jack Snyder and Robert Jervis, eds., *Coping with Complexity in the International System* (Boulder, Colo.: Westview Press, 1993), pp. 243–264. For Barry Buzan, since liberal free-trading systems are dependent on a hegemon which invariably declines, such systems are destined to fall into "malevolent" mercantilist practices, as states scramble to control access to goods formerly safeguarded by the hegemon. Avoiding the liberal system altogether, through a "benign" mercantilist system of self-sufficient trading blocs, will be therefore preferred. Buzan, "Economic Structure and International Security: The Limits of the Liberal Case," *International Organization*, Vol. 38, No. 4 (Autumn 1984), esp. pp. 597, 609–623. For a similar argument, see Robert Gilpin, *U.S. Power and the Multinational Corporation* (New York: Basic Books), 1975, p. 259.
11. See Eli F. Heckscher, *Mercantilism*, vol. 2, trans. Mendel Shapiro (London: George Allen, 1931), p. 15; Jacob Viner, "Power Versus Plenty as Objectives of Foreign Policy in the Seventeenth and Eighteenth Centuries," *World Politics*, Vol. 1, No. 1 (October 1948), p. 10; David A. Baldwin, *Economic Statecraft* (Princeton, N.J.: Princeton University Press, 1985), chap. 5.
12. Heckscher, *Mercantilism*, vol. 2, p. 40.

A COMPARISON OF THE LIBERAL AND REALIST PERSPECTIVES
While the liberal and the realist arguments display critical differences, they possess one important similarity: the causal logic of both perspectives is founded on an individual state's decision-making process. That is, while the two camps freely use the term "interdependence," both derive predictions from how particular decision-making units—states—deal with their own specific dependence. This allows both theories to handle situations of "asymmetric interdependence," where one state in a dyad is more dependent than the other. Their predictions are internally consistent, but opposed: liberals argue that the more dependent state is less likely to initiate conflict, since it has more to lose from breaking economic ties;[13] realists maintain that this state is more likely to initiate conflict, to escape its vulnerability.

The main difference between liberals and realists has to do with their emphasis on the benefits versus the costs of interdependence. The realist argument highlights an aspect that is severely downplayed in the liberal argument, namely, consideration of the potential costs from the severing of a trading relationship. Most liberals, if pressed, would probably accept David Baldwin's conceptualization of dependence as the opportunity costs a state would experience should trade end. Yet Baldwin's opportunity costs are only the loss of the benefits from trade received after a state moves from autarchy.[14] It is this understanding of opportunity costs that is followed in the most comprehensive liberal argument for interdependence and peace, that of Rosecrance. There is little sense in Rosecrance's work that a state's decision to specialize and thus to restructure its economy radically can entail huge "costs of adjustment" should trade be later severed, nor that such costs can actually put the state in a far worse position than if it had never moved from autarchy in the first place.[15] This is the concern of realists when they talk about dependence on

---

13. See Keohane and Nye, "World Politics and the International Economic System," in C. Fred Bergsten, ed., *The Future of the International Economic Order* (Lexington: D.C. Heath, 1973), pp. 121–122; Neil R. Richardson and Charles W. Kegley, "Trade Dependence and Foreign Policy Compliance," *International Studies Quarterly*, Vol. 24, No. 2 (June 1980), pp. 191–222.

14. David A. Baldwin, "Interdependence and Power: A Conceptual Analysis," *International Organization*, Vol. 34, No. 4 (Autumn 1980), pp. 478, 482–484, 489; Baldwin, "The Power of Positive Sanctions," *World Politics*, Vol. 24, No. 1 (October 1971), pp. 19–38; Albert O. Hirschman, *National Power and the Structure of Foreign Trade*, exp. ed. (Berkeley: University of California Press, 1980), chap. 2.

15. On the costs of adjustment, see Ruth Arad, Seev Hirsch, and Alfred Tovias, *The Economics of Peacemaking* (New York: St. Martin's Press, 1983), pp. 26–34. Keohane and Nye examine the "costs of adjusting" as an integral part of "vulnerability" interdependence (*Power and Interdependence*, p. 13). Yet they do not establish the original autarchic position as a baseline for examining these costs independently from the benefits of trade forgone; this baseline is incorporated later in

"vital goods" such as oil. A state that chooses not to buy oil from outsiders forgoes certain benefits of trade, but by operating on domestic energy sources, it avoids the heavy penalty experienced by a state that does base its industrial structure on imported oil, only to find itself cut off from supplies.

That Rosecrance minimizes this realist concern is evident. In an explicit effort to refute Waltz's definition of interdependence as "a trading link which 'is costly to break'," Rosecrance contends that "to measure interdependence in this way misses the essence of the concept." His subsequent discussion emphasizes only the benefits that states give up if they choose not to trade (his "opportunity costs"), and makes no mention of any potentially severe costs of adjustment. In fact, he argues that dependence on such things as foreign sources of energy is really no different than relying on outsiders for "fashions" or different makes of cars; if trade is cut off, a state loses only "consumer choice." Recognition that the whole industrial structure of a state might be undermined or destroyed by an adversary's severing of vital trade is absent.[16]

Rosecrance is reluctant to acknowledge realist concerns, perhaps because to do so would imply that dependent states might be more willing to go to war, as realists maintain, while Rosecrance is arguing that they are less willing to do so.[17] This points to a critical distinction between liberalism and realism that illuminates the liberal understanding of why wars ultimately occur. For liberals, interdependence does not have a downside that might push states into war, as realists contend. Rather, interdependence is seen to operate as a restraint on aggressive tendencies arising from the domestic or individual levels. If interdependence becomes low, this restraint is taken away, allowing the aggressive tendencies to dominate. To borrow a metaphor from Plato: for liberals, inter-

---

building the new theory. Liberals also consider "costs" in terms of losses in "autonomy" due to trade ties; see Richard N. Cooper, *The Economics of Interdependence* (New York: McGraw Hill, 1968), pp. 4–12; Rosecrance, *Rise of the Trading State,* pp. 39–41, 235. Note, however, that these are costs that go hand in hand with high trade, not costs that are experienced if trade is cut off. Hence, these losses in autonomy are more accurately considered as a form of sensitivity interdependence— costs incurred when trade is ongoing—rather than as a form of "vulnerability" interdependence so worrying to realists. On this, see Keohane and Nye, "International Interdependence and Integration," in Fred I. Greenstein and Nelson W. Polsby, eds., *Handbook of Political Science,* vol. 8 (Reading, Mass.: Addison-Wesley, 1975), pp. 368–370.

16. Rosecrance, *Rise of the Trading State,* pp. 144–145. In the appendix, an iterated prisoner's dilemma is used to show the "concrete benefits" from trade cooperation. If states decide not to cooperate, they simply "[do] not benefit"; pp. 233–236.

17. Rosecrance occasionally seems to accept that some goods are more vital than others, but even here he reiterates the liberal argument: "Countries dependent on the world economy for markets, assistance, and *critical raw materials* are *doubly hesitant* to embark on military adventures"; ibid., p. 133, emphasis added.

dependence operates like the reins on the dark horse of inner passions; it provides a material incentive to stay at peace, even when there are internal predispositions towards aggression. Remove the reins, however, and these passions are free to roam as they will.[18]

This point becomes clearer as one examines Rosecrance's explanations for the two World Wars. World War II, for Rosecrance, was ultimately domestically driven. The main aggressors saw war as a means to cope with the upheavals flowing from "social discontent and chaos" and the "danger of left-wing revolutions"; given these upheavals, it is "not surprising that the territorial and military-political system [i.e., war] emerged as an acceptable alternative to more than one state." Connecting the Second World War to causes arising from the unit level in the First World War, he continues: "If Germany, Italy, and Japan did not fulfill their territorial ambitions at the end of World War I, they might develop even more nationalistic and solidaristic regimes and try again."[19] With trade and therefore interdependence at low levels in the 1930s, "economics offered no alternative possibility"; it failed to provide what he later refers to as a "mitigat[ing]" or "restraining" influence on unit-level motives for war.[20]

World War I is a problematic case for Rosecrance, as it was for Angell, since the great powers went to war even though trade levels were still high. Like Angell, Rosecrance's main defense of liberalism is that leaders simply did not see how beneficial interdependence was, and how costly war would be. Due to outmoded ideas and unit-level pathologies, they misperceived the situation; hence, interdependence could not operate as it should, as a restraint on aggression. He talks about leaders' obsession with "nationalist ambitions" and "balance of power politics." He suggests that "no pre-1914 statesman or financier was fully aware of the damage that war would do to the European body economic" because of the irrational belief that "[war] would be over very

---

18. See Plato's *Phaedrus* in *Phaedrus and Letters VII and VIII,* trans. Walter Hamilton (Harmondsworth: Penguin, 1973), sections 246–256. The historical roots of this view are explicated in Albert O. Hirschman, *The Passions and the Interests: Political Arguments for Capitalism before its Triumph* (Princeton: Princeton University Press, 1977). He quotes Montesquieu (ibid., p. 73): "It is fortunate for men to be in a situation in which, though their passions may prompt them to be wicked, they have nevertheless an interest in not being so."
19. Rosecrance, *Rise of the Trading State,* pp. 102–103 (see also p. 111). Rosecrance does point out that Germany and Japan apparently went to war also to gain raw materials (ibid., p. 108). He does not argue, however, that these two states were more dependent than other states for such materials; to have done so would suggest the validity of the realist logic.
20. See ibid., pp. 106, 123, 150, 162.

quickly."[21] At one point, he even seems to cast doubt on the efficacy of interdependence as a restraint on aggression:

> One should not place too much emphasis upon the existence of interdependence per se. European nations in 1913 relied upon the trade and investment that flowed between them; that did not prevent the political crisis which led to . . . World War I. Interdependence only constrains national policy if leaders accept and agree to work within its limits.[22]

It thus appears that Rosecrance cannot really envision interdependence as being anything but a "constraint" or "restraint" on unit-level tendencies to aggress. This view is consistent with the general liberal perspective that all wars are ultimately driven by unit-level phenomena such as misperceptions, authoritarianism, ideology, and internal social conflict. Rosecrance's historical understanding of the World War II, for example, would fit nicely with the "democratic peace" literature: had all the states in 1939 been democratic, war would probably not have occurred despite the disrupted global economic situation, but since some states were not democratic, their aggressive domestic forces became unfettered once interdependence had declined. The idea that economic factors by themselves can push states to aggress—an argument consistent with neorealism and the alternative theory I will present below—is outside the realm of liberal thought, since it would imply that purely systemic forces can be responsible for war, largely regardless of unit-level phenomena.[23]

While liberal theory certainly downplays the realist concern for the potential costs of severed trade, it is also clear that realists slight the positive role the benefits of trade can have on a state's choice between peace and war. In the next section, I bring together the liberal emphasis on benefits with the realist emphasis on costs to create a framework for understanding the true level of dependence a state faces. This section also seeks to correct the most significant

---

21. See ibid., pp. 18–19, 88, 96–97, 99, 150.

22. Ibid., p. 141 (see also p. 150). The argument here borders on being non-falsifiable: disconfirming cases where war occurs despite high interdependence can be sidestepped by saying simply that states did not "accept" being peaceful traders. Note as well that if states have already decided to be peaceful, then interdependence is not needed as a restraint.

23. On liberalism's inherently unit-level orientation to conflict, see Andrew Moravcsik, "Liberalism and International Relations Theory," Working Paper, Center for International Affairs, Harvard University, 1992; Michael Howard, *War and the Liberal Conscience* (New Brunswick: Rutgers University Press, 1978). On the democratic peace argument, see Bruce Russett, *Grasping the Democratic Peace* (Princeton: Princeton University Press, 1993).

error in both liberal and realist theories, namely, their lack of theoretical attention to the dynamics of state expectations for the future.

Trade or Invade? A Theory of Trade Expectations

This section introduces the theory of trade expectations. This theory extends liberal and realist views regarding interdependence and war, by synthesizing their strengths while formulating a dynamic perspective on state decision-making that is at best only implicit in current approaches. The strength of liberalism lies in its consideration of how the benefits or gains from trade give states a material incentive to avoid war, even when they have unit-level predispositions to favor it. The strength of realism is its recognition that states may be vulnerable to the potential costs of being cut off from trade on which they depend for wealth and ultimately security. Current theories, however, lack a way to fuse the benefits of trade and the costs of severed trade into one theoretical framework.

More significantly, these theories lack an understanding of how rational decision-makers incorporate the future trading environment into their choice between peace and war. Both liberalism and realism often refer to the future trading environment, particularly in empirical analyses. But in constructing a theoretical logic, the two camps consider the future only within their own ideological presuppositions. Liberals, assuming that states seek to maximize absolute welfare, maintain that situations of high trade should continue into the foreseeable future as long as states are rational; such actors have no reason to forsake the benefits from trade, especially if defection from the trading arrangement will only lead to retaliation.[24] Given this presupposition, liberals can argue that interdependence—as reflected in high trade at any particular moment in time—will foster peace, given the benefits of trade over war. Realists, assuming states seek to maximize security, argue that concerns for relative power and autonomy will eventually push some states to sever trade ties (at least in the absence of a hegemon). Hence, realists can insist that interdependence, again manifest as high trade at any moment in time, drives dependent states to initiate war now to escape potential vulnerability later.

For the purposes of forging strong theories, however, trading patterns cannot be simply assumed *a priori* to match the stipulations of either liberalism or of realism. Trade levels fluctuate significantly over time, both for the system as a

---

24. See Rosecrance, *Rise of the Trading State,* appendix.

whole and particularly between specific trading partners, as the last two centuries demonstrate. Accordingly, we need a theory that incorporates how a state's expectations of its trading environment—either optimistic or pessimistic—affect its decision-calculus for war or peace. This is where the new theory makes its most significant departure. Liberalism and realism are theories of "comparative statics," drawing predictions from a snapshot of the level of interdependence at a single point in time. The new theory, on the other hand, is dynamic in its internal structure: it provides a new variable, the "expectations of future trade," that incorporates in the theoretical logic an actor's sense of the future trends and possibilities.[25] This variable is essential to any leader's determination not just of the immediate value of peace versus war at a particular moment in time, but of the overall expected value of peace and war over the foreseeable future.

From consideration of the expectations-of-future-trade variable along with a state's level of dependence, one can derive a consistent deductive theory of state decision-making showing the conditions under which high interdependence will lead to peace or to war. High interdependence can be peace-inducing, as liberals maintain, as long as states expect future trade levels to be high in the future: positive expectations for future trade will lead dependent states to assign a high expected value to a continuation of peaceful trade, making war the less appealing option. If, however, a highly dependent state expects future trade to be low due to the policy decisions of the other side, then realists are likely to be correct: the state will attach a low or even negative expected value to continued peace without trade, making war an attractive alternative if its expected value is greater than peace. Moreover, since a negative expected value of trade implies a long-term decline in power, even if war is not profitable *per se*, it may be chosen as the lesser of two evils.[26]

---

25. On the differences between comparative statics and dynamic analyses that incorporate the future, see Eugene Silberberg, *The Structure of Economics*, 2d ed. (New York: McGraw-Hill, 1990), chaps. 1, 12, and 18.

26. That is, war is rational if it has either a higher net *positive* value or a lower net *negative* value. The theory thus works regardless of whether states are innately "greedy"—seeking positive gains from war—or simply security-seekers desiring to minimize long-term threats. See Charles L. Glaser, "Political Consequences of Military Strategy: Expanding and Refining the Spiral and Deterrence Models," *World Politics*, Vol. 44, No. 4 (July 1992), pp. 497–538. By connecting the trading environment to fears about relative decline, I draw upon the notion that declining states launch preventive wars to uphold their waning security. Elsewhere, I build a solely power-driven theory showing why states faced with deep and inevitable decline initiate major wars. Dale Copeland, "Neorealism and the Myth of Bipolar Stability: Toward a New Dynamic Realist Theory of Major War," *Security Studies*, Vol. 5, No. 3 (Spring 1996).

The deductive logic of the alternative theory, as with liberalism and realism, centers on an individual state's efforts to manage its own situation of dependence. Consider a two-actor scenario, where one state "A" may trade with another state "B." If state A moves away from the initial position of autarchy to begin trading, and trade is free and open, it will expect to receive the benefits of trade stressed by liberals, namely, the incremental increase in A's total welfare due to trade.[27] Note that a state can still be aware of the "benefits of trade" even if present trade is non-existent, since they represent the potential gains from trade that would accrue to the state should trade levels become high in the future.[28] It is a state's ability to foresee future potential benefits that allows it to attach a high expected value to the peaceful trading option even when current trade levels are low (as long as it expects current restrictions to be relaxed).

When a state trades, it specializes in and exports goods in which it enjoys a comparative advantage, while forgoing the production of other goods, which it then imports. This process of specialization, however, entails potentially large costs of adjustment if trade is subsequently cut off. This is especially so in the modern world if the state becomes dependent on foreign oil and certain raw materials. With the economy's capital infrastructure (machines, factories, transportation systems, etc.) geared to function only with such vital goods, a severing of trade would impose huge costs as the economy struggles to cope with the new no-trade situation.[29] In short, the severing of trade, as realists would argue, would put the state in a situation far worse than if it had never specialized in the first place.

This analysis leads to a clearer understanding of any particular state's total level of "dependence." On a bilateral basis, that level is represented by the sum of the benefits that the state would receive from free and open trade with another state (versus autarchy), and the costs to the state of being cut off from that trade after having specialized (versus autarchy). If state A started with an economy of 100 units of GNP before any trade with B (the autarchic position), and open trade with B would mean economic expansion to a level of 110 units of GNP on an ongoing basis, then the "benefits of trade" could be considered as 10 units. If the specialization that trade entails, however, would mean the

---

27. This is consistent with standard trade theory. See Richard E. Caves and Ronald W. Jones, *World Trade and Payments*, 4th ed. (Boston: Little Brown, 1985), chaps. 3–4.
28. I thank Andrew Moravcsik for discussions on the potential benefits of trade.
29. The capital investments represent "sunk costs" not easily recouped. See Arad, Hirsch, and Tovias, *The Economics of Peacemaking*, pp. 26–28.

economy would fall to 85 units should B sever trade ties, then the "costs of severed trade" would be 15 units versus autarchy. State A's total dependence level would thus be the benefits of trade plus the costs of severed trade after specialization, or 25 units.

The dependence level will itself be a function of such parameters as the overall compatibilities of the two economies for trade, the degree of A's need for vital goods such as oil and raw materials, and the availability of alternative suppliers and markets. Thus if A's need for trade with B is great because the economies are highly compatible (say, in terms of mutual comparative advantages), B has valuable natural resources that A lacks, and A has few other countries to turn to, then A's dependence can be considered high.[30]

In deciding between peace and war, however, a state can not refer simply to its dependence level. Rather, it must determine the overall expected value of trade and therefore the value of continued peace into the foreseeable future. The benefits of trade and the costs of severed trade on their own say nothing about this expected value. Dynamic expectations of future trade must be brought in. If the state has positive expectations that the other will maintain free and open trade over the long term, then the expected value of trade will be close to the value of the benefits of trade. On the other hand, if the state, after having specialized, comes to expect that trade will be severed by the trading partner, then the expected value of trade may be highly negative, that is, close to the value of the costs of severed trade. In essence, the expected value of trade may be anywhere between the two extremes, depending on a state's estimate of the expected probability of securing open trade, or of being cut off.[31]

This leads to a crucial hypothesis. For any given expected value of war, we can predict that the lower the expectations of future trade, the lower the

---

30. On the importance of alternatives, see Baldwin, "Interdependence and Power," p. 482; Keohane and Nye, *Power and Interdependence*, p. 13. It is worth remembering that alternative suppliers and markets are only valuable in reducing A's dependence if A can get access to them. If B is able not only to sever bilateral trade, but also to blockade A to prevent third-party trading, then A effectively has no alternatives and is therefore dependent. This was the situation for Japan *vis-à-vis* the United States before 1941 regarding oil imports.

31. This line of reasoning is developed formally in Dale Copeland, "Modelling Economic Interdependence and War: A Theory of Trade Expectations," paper presented at the annual meeting of the American Political Science Association, Chicago, September 1995. It is consistent with consideration of the "probability of transaction" as a determinant of expected national income in Arad, Hirsch, and Tovias, *The Economic of Peacemaking*, pp. 37–43, although they do not employ expectations of future trade as a theoretical variable affecting the likelihood of war.

expected value of trade, and therefore the more likely it is that war will be chosen.

It is important to note that the expected value of trade will not be based on the level of trade at a particular moment in time, but upon the stream of expected trade levels into the future. It really does not matter that trade is high today: if state A knows that B will cut all trade tomorrow and shows no signs of being willing to restore it later, the expected value of trade would be negative. Similarly, it does not matter if there is little or no trade at present: if state A is confident that B is committed to freer trade in the future, the expected value of trade would be positive.

The fact that the expected value of trade can be negative even if present trade is high, due to low expectations for future trade, goes a long way towards resolving such manifest anomalies for liberal theory as German aggression in World War I. Despite high levels of trade up to 1914, German leaders had good reason to believe that the other great powers would undermine this trade into the future; hence, a war to secure control over raw materials and markets was required for the long-term security of the German nation. Since the expected value of trade can be positive even though present trade is low, due to high expectations for future trade, we can also understand such phenomena as the periods of détente in U.S.-Soviet relations during the Cold War (1971–73 and after 1985). While East-West trade was still relatively low during these times, the Soviet need for Western technology, combined with a growing belief that large increases in trade with the West would be forthcoming, gave the Soviets a high enough expected value of trade to convince them to be more accommodating in superpower relations.[32]

In making the final decision between peace and war, however, a rational state will have to compare the expected value of trade to the expected value of going to war with the other state.

The expected value of war, as a realist would emphasize, cannot be ascertained without considering the relative power balance. As one state moves from a position of relative inferiority in economic and military power to relative superiority, the expected value of war will move from negative to positive or even highly positive. This proposition follows directly from the insights of deterrence theory: the larger the state in relative size, the higher the probability of winning a victory, while the lower the costs of fighting the war.[33]

---

32. The U.S.-Soviet Cold War case is covered in Copeland, "Modelling Economic Interdependence and War."
33. See Alexander L. George and Richard Smoke, *Deterrence in American Foreign Policy: Theory and Practice* (New York: Columbia University Press, 1974), chaps. 2–3.

Hence, if victory entails occupying the other state and absorbing its economy, war can take on a very positive expected value when a large power attacks a small state.[34] For example, if Iraq had been allowed to hold on to Kuwait after its August 1990 invasion, war for Iraq would certainly have "paid." Similarly, Czechoslovakia was an easy and attractive target for Germany by 1938–39, as were the other smaller states of Europe, and evidence suggests that war against these nations was indeed profitable for the Nazis.[35] On the other hand, war between more equal great powers is likely to have a much lower or even negative expected value. The Spartan leadership took Sparta into war against Athens in 431 BC, for example, under no illusions that war would be a profitable venture.[36] While the Athenian economy presented a large prize should victory be attained, war with a near-equal adversary could be expected to be very costly, with a low likelihood of victory.

Where we would anticipate a low or negative expected value to the option of war, the expectations-of-future-trade variable should have a determinant effect on the likelihood of war. If state A has positive expectations for future trade with B, and A and B are roughly equal in relative power, then state A will assign a high expected value to continued peaceful trade, will compare this to the low or negative expected value for invasion, and will choose peace as the rational strategy. The higher A's dependence and the higher the expectations for future trade, the higher the expected value for peaceful trade, and therefore the more likely A is to avoid war. But if state A is dependent and has negative expectations for future trade with B, then the expected value of trade will be very low or negative. If the expected value for trade is lower than the expected value for invasion, war becomes the rational choice, and this is so even when the expected value of invasion is itself negative: war becomes the lesser of two evils.[37]

---

34. This is developed formally in Copeland, "Modelling Economic Interdependence and War."
35. See Peter Liberman, "Does Conquest Pay? The Exploitation of Occupied Industrial Economies" (Ph.D. diss., Massachusetts Institute of Technology, 1991).
36. Thucydides, *The Peloponnesian War*, trans. Rex Warner (Harmondsworth: Penguin, 1954), Book 1, lines 80–88.
37. When one state is very large and the other very small, it is harder to sort out the effects of interdependence from the effects of relative power, at least in actual cases of war. The expected value of war for the superior state is likely to be quite positive anyway, and thus will tend to overshadow the expected value of trade even when the state has positive expectations of future trade. Here, the superior state simply chooses war as the "greater of two goods." This choice would not be altered by any diminution of trade expectations; indeed, war would simply be even more rational as the expected value of trade (and therefore peace) falls. War in such a situation of marked power imbalance and low expectations of future trade is thus overdetermined; it would be difficult to tell whether war occurred because of the positive expected value of war, the negative expected value of trade, or both. Thus, in my empirical analysis, I examine cases where great powers

Until now, I have talked about state A's "expectations of future trade" as though they were an essentially exogenous, that is, as though state B, in its willingness to trade with A, were not affected by A's behavior. If, however, state A, by making political, military, or economic concessions, can induce B to relax trading restrictions, then A's low expectations for future trade may be raised.

This suggests that the effects of diplomacy and bargaining need to be integrated into any extended historical analysis.[38] The probability of B trading with A is never completely independent of A's actions, since there is always some concession that A could make to get B to commit to higher trade levels over the long term. But the problem for A is that B's price for high trade may be unacceptable in that it undermines A's internal stability or its external power position. To take an extreme example, if B were to demand, as the price for higher trade, that A unilaterally disarm and allow B to occupy A with its army, it is hard to imagine A accepting such a deal. If B remains unwilling to budge from such an exorbitant demand, then it is fair to say that A's pessimistic expectation for future trade is exogenous; there is little A can do, short of national suicide, to improve the likelihood of trade.

Thus state A, in estimating B's probability of trading with A, will refer to many indicators suggesting how "reasonable" B will be into the future, that is, how willing B will be to trade, and at what price. One may think of these indicators simply as causal factors affecting the variable "expectations of future trade." Such systemic factors as B's economic competitiveness, B's rate of depletion of raw materials and energy reserves (affecting its future export ability), and military pressures constraining B's trade with A will be important. German leaders before World War I, for example, had good reason to believe that Britain would be forced to move to imperial preference to protect its empire from the German economic challenge and to lend support to its entente partners. Japanese leaders in the late 1930s recognized that the United States would have to cut back on oil and iron exports to Japan as U.S. reserves were

---

attacked great powers in long and costly total wars. While these cases do not cover the universe of wars, they do isolate the role of economic interdependence and changing expectations of future trade in the outbreak of war.

38. Given space constraints, my case studies in this article do not provide a full analysis of the bargaining dynamic. For an analysis of interstate economic bargaining, see Baldwin, *Economic Statecraft*, chap. 6; R. Harrison Wagner, "Economic Interdependence, Bargaining Power, and Political Influence," *International Organization*, Vol. 42, No. 3 (Summer 1988), pp. 461–483. Note also that there may be a causal feedback loop, whereby increasing fears of war lead others to reduce trade, which in turn heightens the incentive of dependent states to initiate war. These and other issues involving the endogeneity of trade expectations are addressed more fully in my book manuscript, "Economic Interdependence and War."

depleted or needed to supply a military buildup (even one directed only at Germany). Such systemic pressures on B to reduce trade with A will foster negative expectations of future trade among A's leaders.

But domestic and personal factors can also play a significant role in the exogenous rise or decline in B's likelihood of trading with A, indicating that the assumption that B is a "unitary actor" must be relaxed to some degree when examining history.[39] In 1972, for example, the Soviets saw Nixon and Kissinger as firmly in control of American policy, and therefore able to carry through on commitments to increase East-West trade. Two years later, however, such a positive expectation for future trade could not be sustained in the wake of Watergate and the reassertion of Congressional power, at least at a price which was reasonable to the Soviets. This had much to do with the failure of détente, as I argue elsewhere.[40]

A comparison of the arguments of trade expectations theory with those of liberal and realist theory is presented in Table 1. To summarize: liberals contend that high economic dependence, as manifest in high trade levels, reduces a state's likelihood of initiating war by providing a material "constraint" on unit-level forces for aggression. Low dependence will increase this likelihood, since this constraint on unit-level motives for war is removed. Realists argue that high dependence heightens the probability of war as dependent states struggle to reduce their vulnerability. In the realist world, however, low dependence should have no impact on the likelihood of war or peace; that is, other factors should become causally determinant of war. Still, since economic interdependence is at least eliminated as a possible source of conflict, realists

---

39. Note that state A, the decision-making unit in the theory, can still be treated as a rational unitary actor *responding* to the observed domestic forces on the other side.

40. See Copeland, "Modeling Economic Interdependence and War," pp. 62–66. International trade institutions such as the General Agreement on Tariffs and Trade (GATT), by lowering transaction costs and facilitating the punishment of cheaters, may be an additional means to build positive expectations for future trade. Indeed, for some liberals, peace may only be likely when both interdependence and effective global institutions co-exist and reinforce one another; Keohane, "International Liberalism Reconsidered," p. 183. While such institutions may indeed affect trade expectations, they are unlikely to be as significant in history as the systemic and domestic factors just discussed, for the simple reason that these institutions are a creation of the post–World War II era. Moreover, since concerns for war and peace revolve mostly around the great powers, and powers like Soviet Union and China have been historically excluded from trade institutions like GATT, such institutions cannot account for fluctuations in the levels of tension between the United States and these powers since 1945. Finally, the institutional approach overlooks *bilateral* diplomacy as the principal mechanism through which expectations of trade change; consider the United States and Japan up to December 1941, or the United States and Japan today. Accordingly, while my argument recognizes the contribution institutions can make to the improvement of future trade expectations, the focus both theoretically and empirically remains fundamentally non-institutional.

Table 1. The Competing Theories.

	Core Liberal Theory (e.g., Rosecrance)	Core Realist Theory (e.g., Waltz, Mearsheimer)	Trade Expectations Theory (Copeland)
Nature of the system	Anarchy	Anarchy	Anarchy
Nature of the state	Generally a rational, unitary calculator of costs/benefits, but may also have aggressive, unit-level drives	Rational, unitary actor seeking to reduce vulnerability to improve security	Rational, unitary actor calculating the *expected* stream of benefits and costs *over the foreseeable future*, to maximize wealth and therefore security
Analytical focus	The individual state's concern for its own dependence	The individual state's concern for its own dependence	The individual state's concern for its own dependence
State's decision for war or peace driven by	Benefits of trade (the "gains from trade" from specialization)	Costs of severed trade (the costs of adjustment after being cut off, due to specialization)	Benefits of trade *and* costs of severed trade, *plus* expectations of future trade
Ultimate reason that state goes to war	If level of dependence low (i.e., trade is low), "restraint" on unit-level aggressive tendencies removed	High dependence creates a systemic incentive to use force to overcome vulnerability	High dependence and pessimistic expectations for future trade, creating a low or *negative* expected value for trade
Reason for state choosing to stay at peace	If level of dependence high (i.e., trade is high), then high dependence "restrains" by making benefits of trade greater than value of war	Low dependence removes another systemic incentive for war	High dependence and optimistic expectations for future trade, creating a high expected value for trade

NOTE: All three theories recognize that relative power affects the value of the "invade" option; hence, Table 1 focuses on aspects of the "trade" option that affect the decision for war or peace.

would predict that the overall likelihood of war should fall when mutual dependence is low.

In other words, both liberals and realists believe that a situation of low dependence eliminates "dependence" as a causal variable. But since liberals argue that unit-level forces are always ready to be let loose (in the absence of a community of democratic nations), the termination of high dependence takes away the previous restraint on such forces, and therefore the probability of war rises dramatically. For realists, the causes of war come from systemic factors, including a state's dependence (as well as relative power, etc.); therefore, since high dependence will tend to push a state into war, the absence of dependence gives the state one less systemic reason to aggress.

The new theory departs from the two other approaches by incorporating both the level of dependence and the dynamic expectations of future trade. It is somewhat consistent with realism in that low dependence implies little impact on the prospects for peace or war: if there are few benefits from trade and few costs if trade is cut off, then trade does not matter much in the state's decision to go to war. As with realism, however, the elimination of a factor that might otherwise push a state into war suggests that the probability of war should be less when dependence is low.[41]

When dependence is high, peace will be promoted only when the state has positive expectations of future trade. Here, the liberal logic applies, whereby the positive benefits of trade give the dependent state the incentive not to disrupt a profitable peace. If, however, expectations of future trade fall, then realist concerns about the downside of interdependence—the costs of being cut off—enter in, dramatically increasing the likelihood that the dependent state will initiate war. Importantly, the decision for war does not hinge on what the present trade levels are; rather, it is leaders' expectations for the future that drive whether the expected value of trade is positive and peace-inducing or negative and war-inducing.

---

41. Trade expectations theory, like realism, is a systemic theory; it assumes no unit-level drives towards aggression. While expectations may seem like a unit-level factor, remember that these are expectations of an external phenomenon, namely, the other's propensity to trade into the future; the causal source of behavior comes from outside, not from within, the actor. See Waltz, *Theory of International Politics*, p. 60. One might also argue that domestic and individual level factors within a state can distort expectations, but I simply assume that such misperceptions are minimal for purposes of building a deductive theory; this assumption can be later relaxed if so desired.

Historical Evidence

This section explores how expectations of future trade affected the decisions for war in two cases: Germany and World War I, and Germany and World War II.[42] These cases were chosen for two reasons. First, total wars between great powers minimize the problem of overdetermination that occurs when cases of great powers attacking small powers are included.[43] Second, since Germany lost these wars, internal documents are available to reveal the decision-making processes of aggressing states. If we want to go beyond correlation to causation, we must test the causal mechanism linking variables; that is, we have to see if leaders took their nations into war for the reasons hypothesized.[44]

---

42. Given space limitations, my "best case" among the major wars of this century, Japan and World War II, is covered elsewhere; Copeland, "Modelling Economic Interdependence and War." I show that Japanese leaders—military, civilian, and the emperor himself—reluctantly moved towards a consensus for war with the United States and Britain due to progressively more devastating U.S.-British trade sanctions. Japan, due to its small size, was almost completely dependent on outside sources for the raw materials and oil that supported its industrial structure. As American and British trade restrictions began to increase after 1930, and especially after a series of embargoes starting in 1939, Japan shifted from a primary concern with the Soviet threat to the need for control of raw materials in South East Asia. After the U.S., British, and Dutch severed all oil trade to Japan in July–August 1941, Japanese leaders agreed that unless oil imports were restored, economic decline would imperil long-term security. Hence, following the failure of desperate diplomatic initiatives in November 1941 to secure renewed trade, the plan for all-out war was accepted by the emperor. In short, Japan's extreme dependence, coupled with very negative expectations for future trade, pushed the country into a war that almost all recognized would have great costs and a low probability of success. See Nobutaka Ike, trans. and ed., *Japan's Decision for War: Records of the 1941 Policy Conferences* (Stanford: Stanford University Press, 1967).
43. See note 37, above. To minimize the selection bias of focusing just on the wars themselves, I also look at the periods before the wars began, to see how incentives for aggression changed as independent variables did.
44. Empirical analyses so far have been primarily correlational studies, finding that high trade tends to be associated with lower conflict. Mark J. Gasiorowski, "Economic Interdependence and International Conflict: Some Cross-national Evidence," *International Studies Quarterly*, Vol. 30, No. 1 (March 1986), pp. 22–38; Mark J. Gasiorowski and Solomon W. Polachek, "Conflict and Interdependence: East-West Trade and Linkages in the Era of Detente," *Journal of Conflict Resolution*, Vol. 26, No. 4 (December 1982), pp. 709–729; Polachek, "Conflict and Trade," *Journal of Conflict Research*, Vol. 24, No. 1 (March 1980), pp. 55–78; William J. Domke, *War and the Changing Global System* (New Haven: Yale University Press, 1988), chap. 5; Edward D. Mansfield, *Power, Trade, and War* (Princeton: Princeton University Press, 1994), chap 4. These studies, however, provide no documentary evidence that leaders considered trade levels in deciding between war and peace. It is thus hard to know whether the correlation is spurious or illuminating. While the result seems to support liberalism over realism, it is also consistent with trade expectations theory: high trade should be associated with lower conflict in those instances where expectations for future trade are also positive. Given their suspect methodologies, one should also be cautious about quickly dismissing realism. The correlation of trade with less conflict in the first three studies is not surprising, since dyads of small states are included to build the sample. Such states tend to have very high trade/GNP ratios. See Stephen D. Krasner, "State Power and the Structure of International Trade," *World Politics*, Vol. 28, No. 3 (April 1976), p. 328. However, they are deterred from war by their

Exploring internal decision-making in some detail, I show how trade expectations theory helps solve the empirical puzzles for liberalism and realism.

GERMANY AND THE OUTBREAK OF WORLD WAR I

Germany had been one of the few great powers trying to buck the trend towards protectionism in the early and mid-1890s. Recognizing that German industrial products could now match the goods of any state, Chancellor Caprivi set in place policies to expand German trade in Europe and overseas. Other great powers, however, indicated their opposition to any German *penetration pacifique*. Severe tariffs from the United States (McKinley tariff, 1890) and France (Meline tariff, 1892) were certainly worrisome. Even that bastion of free trade—Britain—indicated after 1895 that its fear of rising German commercial strength would soon lead to a reversal of policy. In 1896, the British had raided the Transvaal region of South Africa, jeopardizing German commercial interests. In mid-1897, Canada slapped a discriminatory tariff on non-British goods, contrary to the 1865 Most Favored Nation treaty between Germany and the British empire. Despite Germany's protest, the British, far from making amends, upheld the Canadian decision and then renounced the 1865 treaty in July 1897. Soon after this Joseph Chamberlain opened talks with British colonies on the possible formation a general imperial preference system.[45]

German expectations for future trade reflected these developments. On July 31, 1897, the Prussian minister in Munich informed Chancellor von Hohenlohe that public opinion saw the British "denunciation" of the 1865 treaty as "the prelude to a close trade relationship of England with her colonies." The kaiser's marginal comments indicated his agreement that "the denunciation is the beginning of a revolution in the whole system of British commercial policy." For the kaiser, any suggestion that the target of British action was the United States was "nonsense"; clearly "it is against Germany." He continued, "now that the superiority of German industry is recognized, [the British] will soon make efforts to destroy it."[46]

---

very size. Note as well that all of these tests simply assume that the trade/GNP ratio alone is an adequate measure of the core concept, dependence. Given the concern of realism and trade expectations theory for the costs of severed trade, a proper test must also include such factors as dependence on others for vital goods and availability of alternative sources of supply.

45. See Paul M. Kennedy, *The Rise of Anglo-German Antagonism, 1860–1914* (London: Ashfield, 1980), chaps. 12–14.

46. Quoted from *German Diplomatic Documents, 1871–1914*, vol. II, trans. E.T.S. Dugsdale (New York: Harper and Brothers, 1930), pp. 486–487.

The "main worry" of German leaders during the late 1890s, as Fritz Fischer recounts, "remained . . . the extreme protectionist tariffs of the United States and the plans for a British customs association."[47] The German naval buildup after 1898 was partly designed to protect German trade, particularly imports of raw materials and food. Cecil notes that there was widespread recognition in Germany that with its fast growing population, Germany "could no longer subsist on native-grown foodstuffs" and that a strong navy was needed as "a necessary bulwark against starvation."[48]

German leaders had good reason to worry about the dependability of outside suppliers. In the decade and a half before the war, dependence on trade for vital goods increased dramatically, driven by phenomenal growth in both population and industrial size. Domestic oil production, for example, had gone up 140 percent from 1900 to 1913, but still accounted for only ten percent of total German oil needs. The state went from being a net exporter of iron ore as late as 1897 to relying on outsiders for close to 30 percent of its needs by 1913, despite domestic production increases of 120 percent. By 1913, over 57 percent of Germany's imports were in the form of raw materials, versus 44 percent in 1903 and 41 percent in 1893. All this was occurring at a time when Germany's ratio of trade to GNP was rising to new heights: from 32 percent in 1900, to 36 percent in 1910, to almost 40 percent in 1913.[49]

Of great concern as well were the growing French, Russian, and British efforts to obstruct German commerce. After 1897, Britain and the United States worked in tandem to preclude German colonial gains: despite Germany's efforts, for example, it received nothing from the dissolution of the Spanish empire. In both Moroccan crises, 1905 and 1911, Britain helped France thwart greater German economic penetration of Africa. In fact, from 1898 to 1913, the colonial territory Germany had been permitted to acquire was only one-

---

47. Fritz Fischer, *War of Illusions: German Policies from 1911 to 1914*, trans. Marian Jackson (New York: W. W. Norton, 1975), p. 7.

48. Lamar Cecil, *Albert Ballin: Business and Politics in Imperial Germany* (Princeton: Princeton University Press, 1967), p. 149. It was at this time that German leaders implemented the concepts of *Weltpolitik* and *Mitteleuropa* as responses to growing foreign protectionism. *Weltpolitik* sought "the attainment of secure external supplies of raw materials at regulated prices," while *Mitteleuropa*, its continental counterpart, envisioned the development of "an organized and protected system of economic exchanges between an industrial Germany and an agricultural periphery in central and eastern Europe." See Woodruff D. Smith, *The Ideological Origins of Nazi Imperialism* (New York: Oxford University Press, 1986), pp. 65, 78.

49. See B.R. Mitchell, *European Historical Statistics, 1750–1975*, 2d rev. ed. (New York: Facts on File, 1981), pp. 514, 821 on trade/GNP; pp. 393, 439 on oil; pp. 409, 445–446 on iron ore. See W.F. Bruck, *Social and Economic History of Germany from William II to Hitler, 1888–1938* (Cardiff: Oxford University Press, 1938), p. 110, on raw materials.

seventh that acquired by the United States, a state less often thought of as "imperialist."[50]

In the Middle East, the British worked actively to minimize German economic penetration. In 1907, they agreed with Russia to divide Persia into spheres of influence as part of a campaign to restrict any extension of German power via the proposed Berlin–Baghdad Railway. The Russian ambassador reported to Moscow in August 1910, "England is less interested in what happens in Persia than in preventing any other Power, except England and Russia, from playing any role there. This applies particularly to Germany and Turkey."[51] Just before the war, England worked out a tacit deal with the Americans, giving them a sphere of influence over Latin American oil, in return for British domination of the Middle Eastern oil reserves.[52] By these means, the Germans were effectively denied control over oil imports at a time when only 10 percent of Germany's growing oil requirements was supplied by internal production.

Two other areas concerned the Germans: raw materials and food. With Germany becoming a net importer of iron ore after 1897, French ore became increasingly important: German ore imports from France had increased almost sixty-fold from 1900 to 1913 as Sweden, Germany's main supplier, moved to establish export quotas. German industry invested heavily in the mines of Northern France, and by 1913, directly controlled about 10 to 15 percent of French ore reserves.[53]

The French government took steps to stop this economic penetration, delaying further concessions to German companies in early 1912 and then halting them altogether in December 1913. This came at a time when German capital in general was being shut out of both the French and Russian markets. It is not surprising, therefore, that German industrialists in 1913 would openly speak to the Italian Minister of Commerce "of the need to lay their hands on the iron ore basin of French Lorraine; war seemed to them a matter for industry."[54]

---

50. Holger H. Herwig, *Politics of Frustration: The United States in German Naval Planning, 1889–1941* (Boston: Little, Brown, 1976), p. 9.
51. Quoted in G. Lowes Dickinson, *The International Anarchy, 1904–1914* (New York: Century, 1926), p. 261; see also chap. 10.
52. See Fiona Venn, *Oil Diplomacy in the Twentieth Century* (New York: St. Martin's, 1986), chap. 2; Daniel Yergin, *The Prize: The Epic Quest for Oil, Money, and Power* (New York: Simon and Schuster, 1991), pp. 153–163.
53. Fischer, *War of Illusions*, pp. 321–322; see also Hans W. Gatzke, *Germany's Drive to the West* (Baltimore: Johns Hopkins Press, 1950), pp. 30–38.
54. Quoted in Fischer, *War of Illusion*, p. 326; see also pp. 322–326.

Expectations for the critical food trade were also deteriorating in the last years before the war. Imports of foodstuffs from 1890 to 1913 grew at an average of 4.8 percent a year, well above the overall economic growth rate of 3.9 percent. The Anglo-German naval arms race reflected fears on each side that the other might blockade imports to starve the adversary into submission. British plans for such a blockade were well-advanced in the last decade before the war, and "[the] threat to Germany was a real one."[55]

Thus German leaders after 1897 were increasingly worried about great power economic as well as military encirclement. Their declining expectations of future trade on the eve of World War I are revealed by the extensive documentary work of Fischer.[56] His evidence shows a clear relation between initial German war aims and the increasing economic anxieties of a diverse group of individuals before July 1914. The shared fear was that German industry, increasingly dependent on outsiders for vital goods, would be strangled by the growing economic restrictions imposed by adversaries. Since these powers had extensive imperial possessions, they could afford to adopt closed economic policies; Germany lacked such an alternative. As neomercantilist Gustav Schmoller in 1900 put it, the Russian, British, and American world empires, "with their greed for land, their power at sea and on land, their trade," want to put all others "into an economic straitjacket and to smother them."[57]

By 1911, after the failures of the second Moroccan crisis and "in response to the protectionist trends in the United States, Britain, and Russia," Germany "turned again to the idea of a central European economic area as a defensive measure."[58] Concern for economic security was tangible, transcending ideological and party lines. Future chancellor and National Liberal Stresemann stated in early 1913 that Germany must seek to "create a self-sufficient economic area, so as to make sure of our raw material requirements and to protect our exports." Basserman of the Centre Party in mid-1912 stated that "our trade declines more and more in certain places where we are pushed out or where it keeps its end up only with difficulties." Even the Social Democrat Hildebrand would write in 1911, "from a socialist standpoint the acquisition of colonial domains has become an acute economic necessity for Germany." Indeed,

---

55. Avner Offer, *The First World War: An Agrarian Interpretation* (Oxford: Oxford University Press, 1989), p. 322; chaps. 15–21; pp. 325–326, 335. By 1906, Germany was importing about 20 per cent of its annual grain consumption (p. 230).
56. While Fischer's goal is to show that domestic causes for the war were predominant, much of his evidence actually indicates that German leaders were driven by systemic concerns, namely the safeguarding of German economic security. Fischer, *War of Illusions*, pp. viii–ix.
57. Quoted in ibid., p. 35.
58. Fischer's words, ibid., p. 10.

Fischer shows that after 1906 the Social Democratic party moved from opposition to acceptance of German colonial expansion.[59]

These views paralleled those within the government. Walter Rathenau, who was the influential head of the department of military raw materials in the War Ministry in August 1914, was arguing by December 1913 that Germany's raw material base was too "narrow," and that it depended on "the mercy of the world market as long as [Germany] did not itself possess sufficient raw material sources." In April 1914, Albert Ballin noted that the "expansion of our foreign markets is increasingly threatened," and in the oil-rich Near East in particular, "we have been thrown out of the most important regions there."[60]

The declining expectations of future trade contributed to the pervasive sense of general decline felt by the German leadership in July 1914. Extensive evidence shows that German leaders brought on world war for "preventive" motives, namely to forestall the rise of powers such as Russia.[61] Economic factors reinforced these motives. If France and Russia could be defeated, valuable areas in Europe would be incorporated under German tutelage, guaranteeing the raw materials and markets needed for future German economic power and therefore security; without major war, the economic policies of German adversaries would push Germany further into decline over the long term.

These aims were revealed in the so-called "September Program," which was finalized by Chancellor Bethmann Hollweg on September 9. The plan stated that the "general aim of the war" was "security for the German Reich in west and east for all imaginable time." Russia "must be thrust back as far as possible," while France would become "economically dependent on Germany, secur[ing] the French market for our exports." France's "ore-field of Briey, which is necessary for the supply of ore for our industry, [would] be ceded," and a "central European economic association," including central Europe, France, Poland, and "perhaps Italy, Sweden, and Norway," would be formed. And while members would be "formally equal," "in practice [the association] will be under German leadership and must stabilize Germany's economic dominance over *Mitteleuropa*."[62]

---

59. Quotations in ibid., pp. 234, 250–253.
60. Quoted in ibid., pp. 238, 450.
61. For a summary, see Dale Copeland, "Realism and the Origins of Major War" (Ph.D. diss., University of Chicago, 1993), chaps. 3 and 4.
62. Quoted in Fritz Fischer, *Germany's Aims in the First World War* (New York: W. W. Norton, 1967), pp. 103–104.

This blunt programme for German economic hegemony in Europe was clearly consistent with the pre-war call for a *Mitteleuropa*, and it reflected the work of Bethmann and his associates through the months of July and August 1914. Rathenau, now in charge of raw materials for the Reich, was particularly influential. On August 1, 1914, he submitted to Bethmann a long memorandum arguing that "only a Germany reinforced by 'Mitteleuropa' would be in a position to maintain herself as an equal world power between the world powers of Britain and the United States on the one side and Russia on the other," and war, if necessary, would help to achieve this "essential objective."[63] The date shows that the report must have been prepared during the height of the July crisis, demonstrating that the September program reflected pre-war objectives, rather than a post-hoc scramble to justify the reality of war.

Of particular concern were German iron ore interests in France. On August 26, Bethmann sought information on the size of the ore deposits in French Lorraine, and soon after agreed to consider annexation of French mines "in a final peace treaty." Aware of pre-war French discrimination against German companies, in the September Program he wrote that any commercial treaty with a defeated France "must secure for us financial and industrial freedom of movement in France in such a fashion that German enterprises can no longer receive different treatment from [the] French."[64] Russian pre-war trade restrictions were also to be torn down. Bethmann noted in an October 22, 1914, memo to Delbrück, secretary of state in the Reich Interior Office, that after the war Russia "would have imposed on it a long-term commercial treaty which would mean a lowering of Russian industrial tariffs."[65]

It is important to note the widespread agreement during the September–October period that despite likely opposition from industrial and agricultural interests, Germany needed to create a free-trade zone within Europe after victory in order to compete against the remaining world powers. In a September 13 memo to Bethmann, Delbrück argued that "only a Europe without customs barriers [controlled by Germany] can effectively face the vast producing potential of the transatlantic world."[66] In October, von Falkenhausen, counsellor at the Prussian Ministry of Agriculture, wrote that economic hegemony

---

63. Ibid., pp. 101 and 11. The first part of the quote is Fischer's paraphrase from the document; the words "essential objective" Fischer takes from the document itself. Bethmann was clearly impressed by the memo; he circulated it throughout the department. Ibid., p. 101.
64. Quoted in Fischer, *War of Illusions*, p. 533; Fischer, *Germany's Aims*, p. 104.
65. Fischer's words summarizing the document, *War of Illusions*, p. 538.
66. Quoted in ibid., p. 540.

in Europe was needed to "match the great, closed bodies of the United States, the British, and the Russian Empires," in order to compete "over the conditions of the admission of each to the markets of the others."[67] Also in October, an adviser to Delbrück, Schoenebeck, argued that the "final great aim" in the war was "to create a great central European economic area which allows us to maintain our place in the economic struggle of the nations and prevents us from declining into economic impotence in the face of the increasingly closed and assertive economic world empires—Great Britain with its colonies, the United States, Russia, Japan and China."[68]

Thus increasingly pessimistic German trade expectations had much to do with the German willingness to bring on a major war in July 1914. With Britain shutting Germany out of the oil-rich Middle East and resource-rich Africa, with France threatening Germany's access to iron ore, and with high French and Russian tariff levels limiting German economic growth versus "economic empires" like Britain and the United States, German leaders felt that only a major war would provide the economic dominance of Europe needed for long-term German survival.

GERMANY AND THE START OF WORLD WAR II

There is great continuity between German decision-making up to World War I and up to World War II in terms of the causal role of economic factors.[69] This derives from one overriding fact: Germany in the 1930s, as before World War I, was a state capable of great military power, but its small territory possessed few natural resources compared with the great powers surrounding it. In consequence, Germany would always remain highly dependent on outsiders for the food and raw materials vital to its economic health, unless it expanded. Moreover, since the surrounding great powers were better able to fashion self-sustaining imperial realms, should they ever move in this direction by closing their borders to trade—as they began to do in the early 1930s—long-term German economic viability and therefore security would be threatened. These two realities implied that Germany's potential military superiority might

---

67. Quoted in ibid., p. 539.
68. Quoted in Fischer, *War of Illusions*, p. 539 and *Germany's Aims*, p. 251.
69. In showing this continuity, I do not mean to minimize the atrocities committed by the Nazi regime. Rather, while Hitler's *means* were far more evil than Wilhelmine Germany's, many of his *ends* in terms of economic and territorial security were essentially the same. The most important contribution to the "continuity" argument in modern historiography is Fritz Fischer's work and the work of his followers in the "Hamburg School." See also Smith, *Ideological Origins*.

have to be used, as in World War I, to generate the territorial mass needed for survival against what in 1914 were referred to as the "economic world empires."

The strategic obsessions of Adolf Hitler and the Nazi regime revolved around this dilemma which the first World War had failed to solve. In *Mein Kampf*, Hitler foresaw that, because Germany's small size constrained its "living space" (*Lebensraum*), its dependence on foreign states for food would only increase as the population grew faster than the yields on arable land.[70] By the mid-1930s, his anxiety shifted somewhat: Germany's problem was not simply the supply of food, but even more seriously, the supply of raw materials needed for industrial strength. This dual problem could be overcome by one strategy: war against the system, with the acquisition of Russian land west of the Urals as the prime territorial objective. By destroying Russia, in one stroke Germany could acquire the land needed for vital food and raw materials, while preventing the rise of the state most likely to overwhelm Germany in the future.[71]

Even if we question critical aspects of Hitler's worldview, it is important to note not only that his strategic objectives mirrored much of pre-1914 thinking, but that without his mass appeal and the loyalty of subordinates, Hitler could not have initiated world war. Would Hitler's arguments have made as much sense to his followers, if Germany had possessed the land mass of Russia or the British empire, or if world trade had not been disrupted by the Great Depression? Implicit in what follows is the argument that had Germany been less dependent on vital goods, and had expectations for future trade not been so pessimistic following U.S., British, and French efforts to create closed trading blocs, it would have been much more difficult for Hitler to pull Germany into war: the expected value of the trading option would have been much higher— or at least not as negative—thus dampening the necessity for war.

Immediately after Hitler's accession to power, Nazi economic policy was guided by the so-called "Reformers," a group of economists calling for the creation of a self-sufficient "large economic area" (*Grosswirtschaftsraum*) protected by tariff barriers.

This campaign was prompted by the collapse of the international trading system in the wake of the slump, the revival of world-wide protectionism, and

---

70. Hitler, *Mein Kampf*, trans. Ralph Manheim (Boston: Houghton Mifflin, 1925), pp. 131–140. For the pre-1914 origins of the idea of *Lebensraum*, see Smith, *Ideological Origins*, chap. 5.
71. On Hitler's fears of the rise of Russia, see Hitler, *Mein Kampf*, chap. 24.

specifically, the creation of imperial or regional preference areas. . . . If Germany's economy was to compete with those of the United States, the British Empire, and Japan, it would need to create a rival economic bloc.[72]

This was akin to the pre–World War I concept of *Mitteleuropa*, an idea actively resuscitated by the Brüning and Papen governments after 1930 in response to the collapse of world trade.[73]

Nevertheless, from 1933 to 1936, when the economy was overseen by Hjalmar Schacht, the president of the Reichsbank, Germany did not proceed immediately towards greater self-sufficiency. Keynesian deficit spending, including mass rearmament, produced an immediate economic revival that required marked increases in the input of raw materials, which generally came from abroad. The massive wave of protectionism that followed the U.S. Smoot-Hawley tariffs of 1930, however, created a major constraint: since Germany could not sell its exports abroad, foreign currency could not be raised to pay for the imports of raw materials.

By June 1934, Hitler was being told that the "raw materials situation [was] becoming daily more acute," and that there was a "drain of foreign exchange."[74] The problem was particularly acute since much of Germany's raw material was coming from British colonies or dominions that had entered into the British imperial preference system. Part of the "New Plan" of September 1934 was to reorient German trade away from the British Empire and towards smaller European countries and South America, where supplies would be more secure.[75]

The New Plan solved the balance-of-payments problem for 1935, but by late 1935, world economic upheavals had shifted the terms of trade against Germany; import prices had risen 9 percent while export prices dropped by 9 percent. In other words, Germany had to sell 18 percent more just to import the same amount.[76] By 1936, Hitler decided to move towards greater autarchy in preparation for the war he saw as necessary for Germany's long-term economic viability. This decision was embodied in the "Four-Year Plan" of August 1936. Imports were to be restricted to goods that could not be acquired within Germany, while a program to synthesize oil and later rubber was initiated.

---

72. From J. Noakes and G. Pridham's summary notes, *Nazism 1919–1945: A Documentary Reader*, vols. 2 and 3 (Exeter, U.K.: University of Exeter, 1988), pp. 259–260.
73. Ibid., p. 260.
74. Ibid., Doc. No. 181, p. 270.
75. Ibid., p. 274. See also Hirschman, *National Power*, part II.
76. Noakes and Pridham, *Nazism, 1919–1945*, p. 277.

Since the plan was opposed by Schacht and others, Hitler composed a lengthy memorandum to his key subordinates in August, explicating his rationale. Germany, he wrote, was engaged in a struggle for its very survival. Germany's situation was dire: "We are overpopulated and cannot feed ourselves from our own resources. . . . It is equally impossible for us at present to manufacture artificially certain raw materials which we lack in Germany or to find substitutes for them." Germany needed to act to relieve its dependence on "foodstuffs and raw materials," and the solution "lies in extending our living space, that is to say, extending the sources of raw materials and foodstuff of our people."[77]

Hitler recognized that Germany could try to satisfy its dependence by importing the necessary goods, yet this required selling exports to get imports. The world economic environment was not amenable to this strategy.

(a) Since the German people will be increasingly dependent on imports for their food and must similarly, whatever happens, import a proportion at least of certain raw materials from abroad, every effort must be made to facilitate these imports. (b) An increase in our own exports is possible in theory but in practice hardly likely. *Germany does not export to a political or economic vacuum, but to areas where competition is very intense.* . . . Since imports of food on the whole cannot be substantially reduced and are more likely to increase, an adjustment must be found in some other way.

Hitler's solution was therefore to seek "100 percent self-sufficiency . . . in every sphere where it is feasible," to save precious foreign currency for the importation of food and any raw materials that could not be found or synthesized within Germany.[78]

The problem of raw material dependence turned out to be more intractable than Hitler imagined. Through vast investments, Germany was able to increase production of synthetic fuel by 130 percent from 1936 to 1939. In 1938, however, still only about 10 percent of German petroleum need was met by domestic production; the other 90 percent was coming from outside, primarily the West Indies, the United States, and Rumania. In the same year, two-thirds of iron ore requirements came from outside. By the outbreak of war itself, Germany still relied on outsiders for fully one-third of all raw material needs.[79]

---

77. Ibid., Doc. No. 185, pp. 283–284.
78. Ibid., Doc. No. 185, pp. 284–286 (emphasis added).
79. Oil figures from Robert Goralski and Russell W. Freeburg, *Oil and War: How the Deadly Struggle for Fuel in WWII Meant Victory or Defeat* (New York: William Morrow, 1987), p. 26; iron ore from Mitchell, *European Historical Statistics*, pp. 446, 410; raw materials from Noakes and Pridham,

Expectations for future trade were not getting any better after 1935. British and French moves towards imperial preference solidified. The League of Nations' attempt to impose oil sanctions on Italy after its attack on Ethiopia, while ultimately unsuccessful, also suggested how the "have" great powers would react should the "have-nots" seek changes in the status quo. And sometimes vital imports were suddenly cut off for no apparent reason, or due to uncontrollable domestic factors in the supplying nation. In February 1936, for example, the Soviet Union stopped all oil deliveries to Germany, citing only "difficulties with foreign payments."[80] Such actions could only have further reduced Hitler's estimate of the value of the trading option.

By 1937, the critical decision for war had been made. On November 5, 1937, Hitler brought together his top four military leaders and the Foreign Minister for what is generally considered to be the most important "war council" meeting prior to the war.[81] The issue at hand was whether Germany's "space" problem could be solved by "means of autarchy" or by "increased participation in the world economy." The first was infeasible, since complete autarchy "could not be maintained." Hitler then launched into a discussion of the trading option as a means to German long-term security. To "participation in the world economy," he said, "there were limitations which we were unable to remove. The establishment of Germany's position on a secure and sound foundation was obstructed by market fluctuations, and commercial treaties afforded no guarantee for their actual observance." Countries that Germany formerly relied on for food were now industrializing, implying that they could no longer meet German food needs. Germany was also living in "an age of economic empires," and Hitler compared Germany to others with small territories, such as Japan and Italy, where "economic motives underlay the urge for expansion." Unfortunately, "for countries outside the great economic empires, opportunities for economic expansion were severely obstructed."

Nazism 1919–1945, p. 291. On German efforts to reduce dependence through increased trade ties with China and Eastern Europe, and through intervention in the Spanish Civil War, see Gerhard L. Weinberg, *The Foreign Policy of Hitler's Germany: Starting World War II* (Chicago: University of Chicago Press, 1980), chaps. 1, 5 and 7; David E. Kaiser, *Economic Diplomacy and the Origins of the Second World War* (Princeton: Princeton University Press, 1980); Robert H. Whealey, *Hitler and Spain: The Nazi Role in the Spanish Civil War, 1936–1939* (Lexington: University Press of Kentucky, 1989); Berenice A. Carroll, *Design for Total War: Arms and Economics in the Third Reich* (The Hague: Mouton, 1968).
80. Yergin, *The Prize*, p. 332.
81. See Noakes and Pridham, *Nazism 1919–1945*, p. 680.

Admitting that the economic stimulus provided by rearmament "could never form the basis of a sound economy over a long period," Hitler elaborated the supply dilemma:

There was a pronounced military weakness in those states which depend for their existence on foreign trade. As our foreign trade was carried on over the sea routes dominated by Britain, it was a question rather of security of transport than of foreign exchange, which revealed in time of war the full weakness of our food situation. The only remedy, and one which might seem to us visionary, lay in the acquisition of greater living space.[82]

This living space "can be sought only in Europe"; this was "not a matter of acquiring population but of gaining space for agricultural use. Moreover, areas producing raw materials can be more usefully sought in Europe, in immediate proximity to the Reich, than overseas."[83] Germany, he said, would have to acquire territory from others through force. He then laid out three possible contingency plans, all of which envisioned war by 1943–45 at the latest, before German military power would be past its peak.[84]

From this meeting, it is clear that the two conditions outlined by trade expectations theory as determinant of war—high dependence and low expectations for future trade—were present in the German case by the late 1930s.[85] In such a situation, even if the expected value of invasion is low or negative,[86] the value of the status quo trading option tends to be even lower; major war then becomes the lesser of two evils, especially when the negative expected value of trade only exacerbates anticipated decline. While no one would want

---

82. Ibid., Doc. No. 503, pp. 681–683.
83. Ibid., Doc. No. 503, pp. 682–683.
84. Ibid., Doc. No. 503, pp. 684–685.
85. One might discount Hitler's language as mere talk necessary to justify his true driving force, which was his lust to dominate others; see Hans J. Morgenthau, *Scientific Man Versus Power Politics* (Chicago: University of Chicago Press, 1946). Even if this were true, however, it begs the question of why he felt his four key military leaders would need to hear an elaborate economic rationale for war. We thus return to the point that without the support of his subordinates, Hitler could not have initiated war; calculated aggression, therefore, had to have a logical end. It is also clear that the majority of Hitler's military leaders were not simply brain-washed dupes of Nazi ideology, but accepted the necessity of major war on strategic grounds. See the essays in Correlli Barnett, ed., *Hitler's Generals* (New York: Quill, 1989); John J. Mearsheimer, *Conventional Deterrence* (Ithaca: Cornell University Press, 1983), chap. 4; Dale Copeland, "Deterrence, Reassurance, And Machiavellian Appeasement: Was the Second World War Inevitable?" paper presented at *Security Studies* conference on "Deterrence after the Cold War: Theoretical Perspectives and Policy Implications of Enduring Rivalries," Naval Postgraduate School, Monterey, Calif., September 1995.
86. On May 23, 1939, Hitler told his top military officials that while Germany must "aim at a short war," it "must also be prepared for a war of 10–15 years' duration." Noakes and Pridham, *Nazism 1919–1945*, Doc. No. 539, p. 738.

to understate important unit-level reasons for the war (Hitler's personality, the nature of the Nazi regime, its racist ideology, etc.), Germany's systemic economic situation was a fundamental cause. Like Japan in 1930s, Germany's small territorial size, highly industrialized economy, and growing population meant that it would always be dependent on other great powers for goods vital to its long-term well-being. This would be so despite German efforts to achieve relative autarchy. With the world economy going through significant fluctuations, and with large economic empires like the United States and Britain shutting off trade with have-not nations like Germany, it was not surprising that "participation in the world economy" was not seen as the means to achieve Germany's long-term security.

Thus, Hitler's calculations contained a certain tragic rationality eerily similar to those of German decision-makers in 1914. Moreover, German military leaders, most of whom were in positions of authority before Hitler assumed power, also accepted his logic. Disagreements with the military were mostly over tactics, not grand-strategic objectives: there was almost universal acceptance of the notion that Germany, to survive as a nation, had to overcome its severe dependence on others by grabbing the raw materials and fertile territory of other states.

Conclusion

This article offers a new theory to build upon liberal and realist approaches to economic interdependence and war. The other two approaches highlight important causal elements of interdependence—liberalism, the benefits of trade, and realism, the potential costs of severed trade—but neither specifies the conditions under which these elements will operate. By introducing a dynamic factor, expectations of future trade, the new theory shows when high levels of dependence lead to peace or to war. When expectations for trade are positive, leaders expect to realize the benefits of trade into the future and therefore have less reason for war now; trade will indeed "constrain." If, however, leaders are pessimistic about future trade, fearing to be cut off from vital goods or believing that current restrictions will not be relaxed, then the negative expected value of peace may make war the rational strategic choice.

A few practical implications of this new theoretical framework for the post–Cold War world can be briefly noted. In anticipating likely areas of conflict, one should look for situations in which powers have both high levels of dependence on outsiders and low expectations for trade. Both China and Japan, as emerging great powers, may soon satisfy these conditions. China's economy is growing at a yearly rate many times that of most other powers, and its domestic sources of raw materials are struggling to keep pace; within the next couple of years, for example, China will have to begin importing oil.[87] As it continues to modernize its armed forces, it will gradually gain the strength necessary to press its territorial claims.[88]

Japan has never truly overcome the problem it faced before World War II, namely, its overwhelming dependence on others for the vital minerals and oil needed to sustain its modern industrial economy. While U.S. hegemony in the region has allowed Japan to flourish since 1945, one can imagine the fears that would arise in Tokyo should the United States ever reduce its naval and military presence in the Far East (for budgetary or other reasons). Japan would be compelled to try to defend its raw material supply routes, setting off a spiral of hostility with regional great powers like China, India, Russia, and perhaps the United States itself.[89]

Russia still has significant economic ties with the states of the former Soviet Union, and is, in particular, dependent on pipelines through Ukraine and Belarus to sell its natural gas to Western European customers. These states in turn depend on Russia for their energy supplies.[90] Should Ukraine use threats to turn off the pipelines as political leverage, low expectations for future trade might push Russia to reoccupy its former possession in order to mitigate its economic vulnerability.

American and European dependence on Middle East's oil exports, combined with plummeting expectations for future trade, were probably the key factors leading the United States and Europe to unite against Iraq in 1990–91. It is not hard to envision future scenarios in the Persian Gulf involving fundamentalist Iran or a resurgent Iraq that could dictate a repeat of the Gulf War, this time with perhaps far more devastating consequences.

The key to moderating these potential conflicts is to alter leaders' perceptions of the future trading environment in which they operate. As the Far Eastern

---

87. See Nicholas D. Kristof, "The Rise of China," *Foreign Affairs*, Vol. 72, No. 5 (November/ December 1993), p. 64.

88. China has already staked a claim to the potentially oil rich and much disputed Spratly Islands in the South China Sea. See Gerald Segal, "East Asia and The 'Constrainment' of China," *International Security*, Vol. 20, No. 4 (Spring 1996), pp. 107–135. William H. Overholt, *The Rise of China: How Economic Reform is Creating a New Superpower* (New York: Norton, 1993).

89. For an exaggerated but still insightful analysis of this, see George Friedman and Meredith Lebard, *The Coming War with Japan* (New York: St. Martin's Press, 1991).

90. See Erik Whitlock, "Ukrainian-Russian Trade: The Economics of Dependency," *Radio Free Europe/Radio Liberty Research Report*, Vol. 2, No. 43 (October 29, 1993), pp. 38–42.

situation of the late 1930s showed, the instrument of trade sanctions must be used with great care when dealing with states possessing manifest or latent military power. Economic sanctions by the United States against China for human rights violations, for example, if implemented, could push China toward expansion or naval power-projection in order to safeguard supplies and to ensure the penetration of Asian markets. Sanctions against Japan could produce the same effect, if they were made too strong, or if they appeared to reflect domestic hostility to Japan itself, not just a bargaining ploy to free up trade.

The value of maintaining an open trading system through the new World Trade Organization (WTO) is also clear: any significant trend to regionalization may force dependent great powers to use military force to protect their trading realms. In this regard, my analysis tends to support the liberal view that international institutions may help reinforce the chances for peace: insofar as these institutions solidify positive expectations about the future, they reduce the incentive for aggression. Yet trade expectations between great powers are usually improved without formal institutions being involved, simply as the result of smart bilateral diplomacy. Nixon and Kissinger achieved just that when they negotiated the 1972 trade treaty with the Soviets. Conversely, trade expectations can be shattered by poor bilateral diplomacy even within the context of an overarching international regime. American trade sanctions against China or Japan tomorrow, for example, might produce profound political-military tension, even under the new WTO framework. The existence of formal institutions, therefore, does not do away with the need for intelligent great power foreign policy between individual great powers.

This article began with the question of whether high economic interdependence between states after the Cold War might help preserve the peace. For liberals confident that a new day is dawning for the international system, this analysis sounds a strong note of caution. It is the very states that are the *most* dependent on others that are likely to lead the system into war, should their leaders become pessimistic about the continuation of trading relations that so determine their wealth and security. But my argument also rejects the stark view of realists who automatically equate continued high interdependence with conflict: if leaders can sustain positive expectations for the future, then trading will indeed seem more rational than invading. To a large degree, whether interdependence leads to war or to peace thus becomes a question of political foresight. Those leaders who understand that an adversary's decisions rest not on the static situation of the present, but on the dynamic expectations for the future, will be better able to avoid the tragedy of war.

Environmental Scarcities and Violent Conflict

Evidence from Cases

Thomas F. Homer-Dixon

Within the next fifty years, the planet's human population will probably pass nine billion, and global economic output may quintuple. Largely as a result, scarcities of renewable resources will increase sharply. The total area of high-quality agricultural land will drop, as will the extent of forests and the number of species they sustain. Coming generations will also see the widespread depletion and degradation of aquifers, rivers, and other water resources; the decline of many fisheries; and perhaps significant climate change.

If such "environmental scarcities" become severe, could they precipitate violent civil or international conflict? I have previously surveyed the issues and evidence surrounding this question and proposed an agenda for further research.[1] Here I report the results of an international research project guided by this agenda.[2] Following a brief review of my original hypotheses and the project's research design, I present several general findings of this research that led me to revise the original hypotheses. The article continues with an account of empirical evidence for and against the revised hypotheses, and it concludes with an assessment of the implications of environmentally induced conflict for international security.

Thomas F. Homer-Dixon is Assistant Professor of Political Science and Director of the Peace and Conflict Studies Program at the University of Toronto. From 1990 to 1993, he was co-director and lead researcher of the Project on Environmental Change and Acute Conflict.

Portions of this article have been drawn from Thomas Homer-Dixon, Jeffrey Boutwell, and George Rathjens, "Environmental Scarcity and Violent Conflict," *Scientific American,* February 1993; and from Homer-Dixon, "Environmental Scarcity and Global Security" *Headline Series* (New York: Foreign Policy Association, 1993). The author thanks the participants in the Project on Environmental Change and Acute Conflict, especially project co-directors Jeffrey Boutwell and George Rathjens. The Donner Canadian Foundation funded the article's preparation.

1. Thomas Homer-Dixon, "On the Threshold: Environmental Changes As Causes of Acute Conflict," *International Security,* Vol. 16, No. 2 (Fall 1991), pp. 76–116.
2. The three-year Project on Environmental Change and Acute Conflict brought together a team of thirty researchers from ten countries. It was sponsored by the American Academy of Arts and Sciences and the Peace and Conflict Studies Program at the University of Toronto.

International Security, Vol. 19, No. 1 (Summer 1994), pp. 5–40
© 1994 by the President and Fellows of Harvard College and the Massachusetts Institute of Technology.

In brief, our research showed that environmental scarcities are already contributing to violent conflicts in many parts of the developing world. These conflicts are probably the early signs of an upsurge of violence in the coming decades that will be induced or aggravated by scarcity. The violence will usually be sub-national, persistent, and diffuse. Poor societies will be particularly affected since they are less able to buffer themselves from environmental scarcities and the social crises they cause. These societies are, in fact, already suffering acute hardship from shortages of water, forests, and especially fertile land.

Social conflict is not always a bad thing: mass mobilization and civil strife can produce opportunities for beneficial change in the distribution of land and wealth and in processes of governance. But fast-moving, unpredictable, and complex environmental problems can overwhelm efforts at constructive social reform. Moreover, scarcity can sharply increase demands on key institutions, such as the state, while it simultaneously reduces their capacity to meet those demands. These pressures increase the chance that the state will either fragment or become more authoritarian. The negative effects of severe environmental scarcity are therefore likely to outweigh the positive.

General Findings

Our research was intended to provide a foundation for further work. We therefore focused on two key preliminary questions: does environmental scarcity cause violent conflict? And, if it does, how does it operate?

The research was structured as I proposed in my previous article. Six types of environmental change were identified as plausible causes of violent intergroup conflict:

- greenhouse-induced climate change;
- stratospheric ozone depletion;
- degradation and loss of good agricultural land;
- degradation and removal of forests;
- depletion and pollution of fresh water supplies; and
- depletion of fisheries.

We used three hypotheses to link these changes with violent conflict. First, we suggested that decreasing supplies of physically controllable environmental resources, such as clean water and good agricultural land, would provoke interstate "simple-scarcity" conflicts or resource wars. Second, we hypothesized that large population movements caused by environmental stress would induce "group-identity" conflicts, especially ethnic clashes. And third, we suggested that severe environmental scarcity would simultaneously increase economic deprivation and disrupt key social institutions, which in turn would cause "deprivation" conflicts such as civil strife and insurgency.

Two detailed case studies were completed for each of the three research hypotheses.[3] By selecting cases that appeared, *prima facie*, to show a link between environmental change and conflict, we sought to falsify the null hypothesis that environmental scarcity does not cause violent conflict. By carefully tracing the causal processes in each case, we also sought to identify how environmental scarcity operates, if and when it is a cause of conflict. The completed case studies were reviewed at a series of workshops of leading experts; in light of these findings, I revised the original hypotheses, identified common variables and processes across the cases, and examined the revised hypotheses in light of the case-study evidence. The project's conclusions were reviewed by a core team of experts. The following are four general findings of this research effort.

RESOURCE DEPLETION AND DEGRADATION
Of the major environmental changes facing humankind, degradation and depletion of agricultural land, forests, water, and fish will contribute more to social turmoil in coming decades than will climate change or ozone depletion.

When analysts and policymakers in developed countries consider the social impacts of large-scale environmental change, they focus undue attention on climate change and stratospheric ozone depletion.[4] But vast populations in the developing world are already suffering from shortages of good land, water, forests, and fish; in contrast, the social effects of climate change and ozone depletion will probably not be seen till well into the next century. If

---

3. On simple-scarcity conflicts, we examined water in the Jordan and Nile River basins and the Southern African region; on environmentally induced group-identity conflicts, we focused on Bangladesh-Assam and the Miskito Indians in Nicaragua; and on economic decline and civil strife, we studied the Philippines and China. Researchers in the project also investigated the 1989 conflict in the Senegal River basin, the 1969 Soccer War between El Salvador and Honduras, the rise of the Sendero Luminoso in Peru, migration and civil strife in Haiti, and migration from black homelands in South Africa.
4. For example, see David Wirth, "Climate Chaos," *Foreign Policy*, No. 74 (Spring 1989), pp. 3–22; and Neville Brown, "Climate, Ecology and International Security," *Survival*, Vol. 31, No. 6 (November/December 1989), pp. 519–532.

these atmospheric problems do eventually have an impact, they will most likely operate not as individual environmental stresses, but in interaction with other, long-present resource, demographic, and economic pressures that have gradually eroded the buffering capacity of some societies.

Mexico, for example, is vulnerable to such interactions. People are already leaving the state of Oaxaca because of drought and soil erosion. Researchers estimate that future global warming could decrease Mexican rainfed maize production up to forty percent. This change could in turn interact with ongoing land degradation, free trade (because Mexico's comparative advantage is in water-intensive fruits and vegetables), and the privatization of communal peasant lands to cause grave internal conflict.[5]

ENVIRONMENTAL SCARCITY

Environmental change is only one of three main sources of scarcity of renewable resources; the others are population growth and unequal social distribution of resources. The concept "environmental scarcity" encompasses all three sources.

Analysts often usefully characterize environmental problems as resource scarcities. Resources can be roughly divided into two groups: non-renewables, like oil and iron ore, and renewables, like fresh water, forests, fertile soils, and the earth's ozone layer. The latter category includes renewable "goods" such as fisheries and timber, and renewable "services" such as regional hydrological cycles and a benign climate.

The commonly used term "environmental change" refers to a human-induced decline in the quantity or quality of a renewable resource that occurs faster than it is renewed by natural processes. But this concept limits the scope of environment-conflict research. Environmental change is only one of three main sources of renewable-resource scarcity. The second, population growth, reduces a resource's per-capita availability by dividing it among more and more people.[6] The third, unequal resource distribution, concentrates a

---

5. Diana Liverman, "The Impacts of Global Warming in Mexico: Uncertainty, Vulnerability and Response," in Jurgen Schmandt and Judith Clarkson, eds., *The Regions and Global Warming: Impacts and Response Strategies* (New York: Oxford University Press, 1992), pp. 44–68; and Diana Liverman and Karen O'Brien, "Global Warming and Climate Change in Mexico," *Global Environmental Change*, Vol. 1, No. 4 (December 1991), pp. 351–364.
6. Peter Gleick provides a potent illustration of the effect of population growth on water scarcity in Table 3 of "Water and Conflict: Fresh Water Resources and International Security," *International Security*, Vol. 18, No. 1 (Summer 1993), p. 101.

resource in the hands of a few people and subjects the rest to greater scarcity.[7] The property rights that govern resource distribution often change as a result of large-scale development projects or new technologies that alter the relative values of resources.

In other words, reduction in the quantity or quality of a resource shrinks the resource pie, while population growth divides the pie into smaller slices for each individual, and unequal resource distribution means that some groups get disproportionately large slices.[8] Unfortunately, analysts often study resource depletion and population growth in isolation from the political economy of resource distribution.[9] The term "environmental scarcity," however, allows these three distinct sources of scarcity to be incorporated into one analysis. Empirical evidence suggests, in fact, that the first two sources are most pernicious when they interact with unequal resource distribution.

We must also recognize that resource scarcity is, in part, subjective; it is determined not just by absolute physical limits, but also by preferences, beliefs, and norms. This is illustrated by a debate about the role of population growth and resource scarcity as causes of the conflict between the Sandinista government and the Miskito Indians in Nicaragua.[10] Bernard Nietschmann argues that the Nicaraguan state's need for resources to sustain the country's economic and agricultural development caused environmental degradation to spread from the Pacific to the Atlantic coast of the country. As this happened, indigenous Miskitos in the east came into conflict with the central government. Sergio Diaz-Briquets responds that the Sandinistas expropriated Miskito lands because of ideology, not scarcity. The Atlantic coastal region was largely ignored by the Nicaraguan state under Somoza. Following the revolution, the Sandinistas had ample newly expropriated land to distribute to their followers; but the new government—guided by Marxism—saw the Miskitos as a backward people with a competing worldview and a precapitalist mode of production, whose land rightfully belonged to a state that was removing impediments to the historical progress of the working class.

---

7. The second and third types of scarcity arise only with resources that can be physically controlled and possessed, like fish, fertile land, trees, and water, rather than resources like the climate or the ozone layer.
8. Since population growth is often a main cause of a decline in the quality and quantity of renewable resources, it actually has a dual impact on resource scarcity, a fact rarely noted by analysts.
9. James Boyce, "The Bomb Is a Dud," *The Progressive*, September 1990, pp. 24–25.
10. Bernard Nietschmann, "Environmental Conflicts and Indigenous Nations in Central America," paper prepared for the Project on Environmental Change and Acute Conflict (May 1991); and Sergio Diaz-Briquets, "Comments on Nietschmann's Paper," ibid.

Figure 1. Resource Capture and Ecological Marginalization.

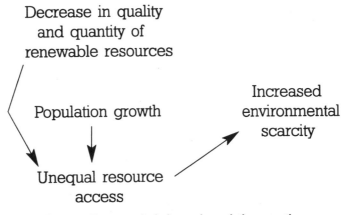

Resource Capture: Resource depletion and population growth cause unequal resource access.

The gap between the two views can be bridged by noting that scarcity is partly subjective. Marxist ideology encouraged the Sandinistas to adopt a strategy of state-directed industrialization and resource-use; this led them to perceive resources as more scarce than had the Somoza regime.

INTERACTION OF SOURCES OF ENVIRONMENTAL SCARCITY
The three sources of environmental scarcity often interact, and two patterns of interaction are particularly common: "resource capture" and "ecological marginalization" (see Figure 1).

A fall in the quality and quantity of renewable resources can combine with population growth to encourage powerful groups within a society to shift resource distribution in their favor. This can produce dire environmental scarcity for poorer and weaker groups whose claims to resources are opposed by these powerful elites. I call this type of interaction "resource capture." Unequal resource access can combine with population growth to cause migrations to regions that are ecologically fragile, such as steep upland slopes, areas at risk of desertification, and tropical rain forests. High population densities in these areas, combined with a lack of knowledge and capital to

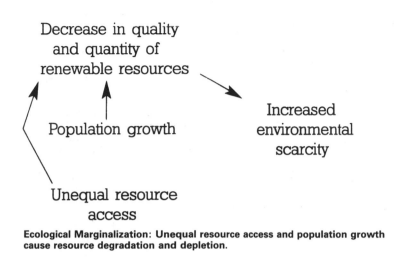

Ecological Marginalization: Unequal resource access and population growth cause resource degradation and depletion.

protect local resources, causes severe environmental damage and chronic poverty. This process is often called "ecological marginalization."[11]

RESOURCE CAPTURE. Events in the Senegal River valley in 1989 illustrate resource capture. The valley demarcates the border between Senegal and Mauritania in West Africa. Senegal has fairly abundant agricultural land, but much of it suffers from high to severe wind and water erosion, loss of nutrients, salinization because of overirrigation, and soil compaction caused by intensification of agriculture.[12] The country has an overall population density of 38 people per square kilometer and a population growth rate of 2.8 percent; in 25 years the population will double.[13] In contrast, except for the Senegal Valley along its southern border and a few oases, Mauritania is

11. Jeffrey Leonard, "Overview," *Environment and the Poor: Development Strategies for a Common Agenda* (New Brunswick, N.J.: Transaction, 1989), p. 7. For a careful analysis of the interaction of population and land distribution in El Salvador, see chap. 2 in William Durham, *Scarcity and Survival in Central America: The Ecological Origins of the Soccer War* (Stanford, Calif.: Stanford University Press, 1979), pp. 21–62.

12. Global Assessment of Soil Degradation, *World Map on Status of Human-Induced Soil Degradation*, Sheet 2, Europe, Africa, and Western Asia (Wageningen, the Netherlands: United Nations Environment Programme [UNEP], International Soil Reference Centre, 1990).

13. Nafis Sadik, *The State of the World Population 1991* (New York: United Nations Population Fund, 1991), p. 24; World Resources Institute [WRI], *World Resources 1992–93* (New York: Oxford University Press, 1992), pp. 246 and 262.

largely arid desert and semiarid grassland.[14] Its population density is very low at about 2 people per square kilometer, but the growth rate is 2.9 percent. This combination of factors led the Food and Agriculture Organization (FAO) and two other organizations in a 1982 study to include both Mauritania and Senegal in their list of "critical" countries whose croplands cannot support their current and projected populations without a large increase in agricultural inputs, such as fertilizer and irrigation.[15]

Normally, the broad floodplains fringing the Senegal River support productive farming, herding, and fishing based on the river's annual floods. During the 1970s, however, the prospect of chronic food shortages and a serious drought encouraged the region's governments to seek international financing for the Manantali Dam on the Bafing River tributary in Mali, and the Diama salt-intrusion barrage near the mouth of the Senegal River between Senegal and Mauritania. These dams were designed to regulate the river's flow to produce hydropower, expand irrigated agriculture, and provide river transport from the Atlantic Ocean to landlocked Mali, which lies to the east of Senegal and Mauritania.

But the plan had unfortunate and unforeseen consequences. Anticipation of the new dams sharply increased land values along the river in areas where high-intensity agriculture would become feasible. The elite in Mauritania, which consists mainly of white Moors, then rewrote legislation governing land ownership, effectively abrogating the rights of black Africans to continue farming, herding, and fishing along the Mauritanian riverbank.[16]

---

14. Despite popular perception and the past claims of the United Nations Environment Programme, many experts now believe that the African Sahel (which includes southern Mauritania) is a robust ecosystem that does not exhibit extensive human-induced desertification. There is no clear southward march of the Sahara desert, and ecosystem recovery can be rapid if there is adequate rainfall and a reduction in grazing pressures. See "The Ebb and Flow of the Sahara," *New York Times*, July 23, 1991, p. B9. Overgrazing across the western Sahel, and the consequent migration of people from the region, appear to arise from the expansion of sedentary farming and population growth that together concentrate pastoralists on smaller areas of land (an example of ecological marginalization). In general, pastoralists are weak in the face of modern African states; state development since decolonization has often changed property rights at their expense. See Olivia Bennett, ed., *Greenwar: Environment and Conflict* (London: Panos, 1991), chap. 3, pp. 33–53.
15. G.M. Higgins, et al., *Potential Population Supporting Capacities of Lands in the Developing World*, Technical Report of Project INT/75/P13, "Land Resources of the Future," undertaken by the UN Food and Agriculture Organization (FAO) in collaboration with the International Institute for Applied Systems Analysis (IIASA) and the UN Fund for Population Activities (Rome, 1982), Table 3.5, p. 137.
16. Michael Horowitz, "Victims of Development," *Development Anthropology Network*, Bulletin of the Institute for Development Anthropology, Vol. 7, No. 2 (Fall 1989), pp. 1–8; and Horowitz, "Victims Upstream and Down," *Journal of Refugee Studies*, Vol. 4, No. 2 (1991), pp. 164–181.

There has been a long history of racism by white Moors in Mauritania towards their non-Arab, black compatriots. In the spring of 1989, the killing of Senegalese farmers by Mauritanians in the river basin triggered explosions of ethnic violence in the two countries. In Senegal, almost all of the 17,000 shops owned by Moors were destroyed, and their owners were deported to Mauritania. In both countries several hundred people were killed and the two nations nearly came to war.[17] The Mauritanian regime used this occasion to activate the new land legislation, declaring the Mauritanians who lived alongside the river to be "Senegalese," thereby stripping them of their citizenship; their property was seized. Some 70,000 of the black Mauritanians were forcibly expelled to Senegal, from where some launched raids to retrieve expropriated cattle. Diplomatic relations between the two countries have now been restored, but neither has agreed to allow the expelled population to return or to compensate them for their losses.

We see here the interaction of two sources of human-induced environmental scarcity: degradation of the land resource and population pressures helped precipitate agricultural shortfalls, which in turn encouraged a large development scheme. These factors together raised land values in one of the few areas in either country that offered the potential for a rapid move to high-intensity agriculture. A powerful elite then changed property rights and resource distribution in its own favor, which produced a sudden increase in resource scarcity for an ethnic minority, expulsion of the minority, and ethnic violence.

The water shortage on the occupied West Bank of the Jordan River offers a similar example of how population growth and excessive resource consumption can promote resource capture. While figures vary, Israel's average annual supply of renewable fresh water is about 1,950 million cubic meters (mcm).[18] Current Israeli demand, including that of settlements in the occupied territories and Golan Heights, exceeds this supply by about ten percent. The deficit is covered by overpumping aquifers. As a result, water tables in some parts of Israel and the West Bank have dropped. This can cause the

---

17. Jacques Belotteau, "Senegal-Mauritanie: les graves evenements du printemps 1989," *Afrique Contemporaine*, No. 152 (April 1989), pp. 41–42.
18. Miriam Lowi, "West Bank Water Resources and the Resolution of Conflict in the Middle East," Occasional Paper No. 1, Project on Environmental Change and Acute Conflict (September 1992); see also Lowi, "Bridging the Divide: Transboundary Resource Disputes and the Case of West Bank Water," *International Security*, Vol. 18, No. 1 (Summer 1993), pp. 113–138; and Natasha Beschorner, "Water and Instability in the Middle East," Adelphi Paper No. 273 (London: International Institute for Strategic Studies [IISS], Winter 1992/93).

exhaustion of wells and the infiltration of sea water from the Mediterranean.[19] Israel's population growth in the next thirty years, even without major immigration from the former Soviet Union, will probably cause the country's water demand to outstrip supply by at least forty percent.[20]

Over half of Israel's water comes from aquifers, and the rest from river flow, floodwater, and waste-water recycling. Two of the three main aquifers on which Israel depends lie principally underneath the West Bank, although their waters drain into Israel. About forty percent of the groundwater Israel uses (and therefore about a quarter of its sustainable supply) originates in occupied territory. To protect this important source, the Israeli government strictly limits water use by Jewish settlers and Arabs on the West Bank. But there is a stark differential in water access between the groups: on a per capita basis, settlers consume about four times as much as Arabs. Israel restricts the number of wells Arabs can drill in the territory, the amount of water Arabs are allowed to pump, and the times at which they can draw irrigation water. Since 1967, Arabs have not been permitted to drill new wells for agricultural purposes, although the Mekorot (the Israeli water company) has drilled more than thirty wells for settlers' irrigation.

Arab agriculture in the region has also suffered because some Arab wells have become dry or saline as a result of deeper Israeli wells drilled nearby. These Israeli water policies, combined with the confiscation of agricultural land for settlers as well as other Israeli restrictions on Palestinian agriculture, have encouraged many West Bank Arabs to abandon farming and move to towns.[21] Those who have done so have mostly become either unemployed or day laborers within Israel. The links between these processes and the recent unrest in the occupied territories are unclear; many political, economic, and ideological factors operate. But it seems reasonable to conclude that water scarcity and its consequent economic effects contributed to the grievances behind the *intifada* both on the West Bank and in Gaza.

---

19. There appears to be an impending crisis, for example, from salinization of aquifers beneath the Gaza Strip, where the pressure on water resources is "rapidly becoming intolerable"; Beschorner, "Water and Instability," pp. 14–15. The Gaza aquifers are connected to the coastal aquifer that is vital to Israel. Salinization can cause irreversible physical changes in aquifers; even if replenished with fresh water, their capacity is reduced. See Fred Pearce, "Wells of Conflict on the West Bank," *New Scientist*, June 1, 1991, pp. 37–38.

20. Lowi, "West Bank Water Resources," p. 34.

21. Since 1967, the irrigated area on the West Bank has dropped from 27 percent of the total cultivated area to 3.5–6 percent. Beschorner, "Water and Instability," pp. 14 and 78.

ECOLOGICAL MARGINALIZATION. The Philippines offers a good illustration of ecological marginalization. There, inequalities in access to rich agricultural lowlands combine with population growth to cause migration to easily degraded upland areas; erosion and deforestation contribute to economic hardship that spurs insurgency and rebellion.

Spanish and American colonial policies in the Philippines left behind a grossly unfair distribution of good cropland in lowland regions, an imbalance perpetuated since independence by a powerful landowning elite.[22] Since World War II, green-revolution technologies have greatly increased lowland production of grain for domestic consumption, and of cash crops such as sugar, coconut, pineapple, and bananas that help pay the country's massive external debt. This has raised demand for agricultural labor on large farms, but not enough to compensate for a population growth rate of 2.5 to 3.0 percent per annum. Together, therefore, inequalities in land access and growth in population have produced a surge in agricultural unemployment.

With insufficient rural or urban industrialization to employ this excess labor, there has been unrelenting downward pressure on wages.[23] Economically desperate, millions of poor agricultural laborers and landless peasants have migrated to shantytowns in already overburdened cities, such as Manila. Millions of others have moved to the least productive—and often most ecologically vulnerable—territories, such as steep hillsides.[24] In these uplands, settlers use fire to clear forested or previously logged land. They bring with them little knowledge or money to protect their fragile ecosystems, and their small-scale logging, production of charcoal for the cities, and slash-and-burn farming often cause horrendous environmental damage, particularly water erosion, landslides, and changes in the hydrological cycle.[25] This has set in motion a cycle of falling food production, the clearing of new plots,

---

22. The best cropland lies, for the most part, in the coastal plains of the archipelago's islands. Landowning and manufacturing elites are closely linked, and their relative economic power has actually grown since independence: the top 10 percent of the country's families controlled 37 percent of the nation's total income in 1985, up from 27 percent in 1956. See Richard Kessler, *Rebellion and Repression in the Philippines* (New Haven: Yale University Press, 1989), p. 18.

23. Using a standardized figure of 100 for 1972, average real wages dropped from 150 in the early 1950s to about 100 in 1980. Kessler, *Rebellion and Repression*, p. 26.

24. A full account can be found in Maria Concepción Cruz, et al., *Population Growth, Poverty, and Environmental Stress: Frontier Migration in the Philippines and Costa Rica* (Washington, D.C.: WRI, 1992).

25. World Bank, *Philippines: Environment and Natural Resource Management Study* (Washington, D.C.: World Bank, 1989). Erosion rates can exceed 300 tons per hectare per year, ten to twenty times the sustainable rate.

and further land degradation. There are few new areas in the country that can be opened up for agricultural production, so even marginally fertile land is becoming hard to find in many places, and economic conditions are often desperate for the peasants.[26]

The situation in the Philippines is not unique. Ecological marginalization occurs with striking regularity around the planet, affecting hundreds of millions of people in places as diverse as the Himalayas, Indonesia, Costa Rica, Brazil, and the Sahel.

SOCIAL AND TECHNICAL INGENUITY

Societies are more able to avoid turmoil if they can adapt to environmental scarcity so that it does not cause great suffering. Strategies for adaptation fall into two categories, and both depend on adequate social and technical ingenuity. First, societies can continue to rely on their indigenous resources but use them more sensibly and provide alternative employment to people who have limited resource access. For example, economic incentives like increases in resource prices and taxes can reduce degradation and depletion by encouraging conservation, technological innovation, and resource substitution. Family planning and literacy campaigns can ease population-growth induced scarcity. Land redistribution and labor-intensive rural industries can relieve the effects of unequal access to good cropland.

Second, the country might "decouple" itself from dependence on its own depleted environmental resources by producing goods and services that do not rely heavily on those resources; the country could then trade the products on the international market for the resources it no longer has at home. Such decoupling might, in fact, be achieved by rapidly exploiting the country's environmental resources and reinvesting the profits in capital, industrial equipment, and skills to permit a shift to other forms of wealth creation. For instance, Malaysia could use the income from over-logging its forests to fund a modern university system that trains electrical engineers and computer specialists for a high-technology industrial sector.

If either strategy is to succeed, a society must be able to supply enough ingenuity at the right places and times. Two kinds are key. Technical ingenuity is needed to develop, for example, new agricultural and forestry technologies that compensate for environmental loss. Social ingenuity is needed

---

26. Gareth Porter and Delfin Ganapin, Jr., *Resources, Population, and the Philippines' Future: A Case Study,* WRI Paper No. 4 (Washington, D.C.: World Resources Institute, 1988).

to create institutions and organizations that buffer people from the effects of scarcity and provide the right incentives for technological entrepreneurs. Social ingenuity is therefore often a precursor to technical ingenuity. The development and distribution of new grains adapted for dry climates and eroded soils, of alternative cooking technologies to compensate for the loss of firewood, and of water conservation technologies depend on an intricate and stable system of markets, legal regimes, financial agencies, and educational and research institutions.

In the next decades, the need for both technical and social ingenuity to deal with environmental scarcities will rise sharply. Population growth, rising average resource consumption, and persistent inequalities in access to resources ensure that scarcities will affect many environmentally sensitive regions with a severity, speed, and scale unprecedented in history. Resource-substitution and conservation tasks will be more urgent, complex, and unpredictable, driving up the need for technical ingenuity. Moreover, solving these problems through market and other institutional innovations (such as changes in property rights and resource distribution) will require great social ingenuity.

At the same time that environmental scarcity is boosting the demand for ingenuity, however, it may interfere with supply. Poor countries start at a disadvantage: they are underendowed with the social institutions—including the productive research centers, efficient markets, and capable states—that are necessary for an ample supply of both social and technical solutions to scarcity. Moreover, their ability to create and maintain these institutions may be diminished by the very environmental stress they need to address, because scarcity can weaken states, as we shall see, and it can engender intense rivalries between interest groups and elite factions.[27]

Evidence Bearing on the Hypotheses

The findings described above led me to revise the original three hypotheses by redefining the independent variable, "environmental scarcity." I narrowed the range of environmental problems that were hypothesized to cause conflict, so as to deemphasize atmospheric problems and focus instead on for-

---

27. For a full elaboration of the argument in this section, see Homer-Dixon, "The Ingenuity Gap: Can Developing Countries Adapt to Environmental Scarcity?" paper prepared for the Project on Environmental Change and Acute Conflict (March 1994).

ests, water, fisheries, and especially cropland. I expanded the scope of the independent variable to include scarcity caused by population growth and resource maldistribution as well as that caused by degradation and depletion. And I also incorporated into the variable the role of interactions among these three sources of scarcity.

Our research project produced the following empirical evidence bearing on the three hypotheses thus revised.

HYPOTHESIS 1: SIMPLE-SCARCITY CONFLICTS BETWEEN STATES

There is little empirical support for the first hypothesis that environmental scarcity causes simple-scarcity conflicts between states. Scarcities of renewable resources such as forests and croplands do not often cause resource wars between states. This finding is intriguing because resource wars have been common since the beginning of the state system. For instance, during World War II, Japan sought to secure oil, minerals, and other resources in China and Southeast Asia, and the 1991 Gulf War was at least partly motivated by the desire for oil.

However, we must distinguish between non-renewable resources such as oil, and renewable resources. Arthur Westing has compiled a list of twelve conflicts in the twentieth century involving resources, beginning with World War I and concluding with the Falklands/Malvinas War.[28] Access to oil or minerals was at issue in ten of these conflicts. Just five conflicts involved renewable resources, and only two of these—the 1969 Soccer War between El Salvador and Honduras, and the Anglo-Icelandic Cod War of 1972–73— concerned neither oil nor minerals (cropland was a factor in the former case, and fish in the latter). However, the Soccer War was not a simple-scarcity conflict between states; rather it arose from the ecological marginalization of Salvadorean peasants and their consequent migration into Honduras.[29] It is evidence in support, therefore, of our second and third hypotheses (below), but not for the first. And, since the Cod War, despite its name, involved very little violence, it hardly qualifies as a resource war.

States have fought more over non-renewable than renewable resources for two reasons, I believe. First, petroleum and mineral resources can be more

---

28. Arthur Westing, "Appendix 2. Wars and Skirmishes Involving Natural Resources: A Selection from the Twentieth Century," in Arthur Westing, ed., *Global Resources and International Conflict: Environmental Factors in Strategic Policy and Action* (Oxford: New York, 1986), pp. 204–210.
29. See Durham, *Scarcity and Survival.*

directly converted into state power than can agricultural land, fish, and forests. Oil and coal fuel factories and armies, and ores are vital for tanks and naval ships. In contrast, although captured forests and cropland may eventually generate wealth that can be harnessed by the state for its own ends, this outcome is more remote in time and less certain. Second, the very countries that are most dependent on renewable resources, and which are therefore most motivated to seize resources from their neighbors, also tend to be poor, which lessens their capability for aggression.

Our research suggests that the renewable resource most likely to stimulate interstate resource war is river water.[30] Water is a critical resource for personal and national survival; furthermore, since river water flows from one area to another, one country's access can be affected by another's actions. Conflict is most probable when a downstream riparian is highly dependent on river water and is strong in comparison to upstream riparians. Downstream riparians often fear that their upstream neighbors will use water as a means of coercion. This situation is particularly dangerous if the downstream country also believes it has the military power to rectify the situation. The relationships between South Africa and Lesotho and between Egypt and Ethiopia have this character.[31]

The Lesotho case is interesting. Facing critical water shortages, South Africa negotiated in vain with Lesotho for thirty years to divert water from Lesotho's mountains to the arid South African province of Transvaal. In 1986 South Africa gave decisive support to a successful military coup against Lesotho's tribal government. South Africa declared that it helped the coup because Lesotho had been providing sanctuary to guerrillas of the African National Congress. This was undoubtedly a key motivation, but within months the two governments reached agreement to construct the huge Highlands Water Project to meet South Africa's needs. It seems likely, therefore, that the desire for water was an ulterior motive behind South African support for the coup.[32]

---

30. Peter Gleick, "Water and Conflict," Occasional Paper No. 1, Project on Environmental Change and Acute Conflict (September 1992); and Gleick, "Water and Conflict: Fresh Water Resources and International Security," *International Security*, Vol. 18, No. 1 (Summer 1993), pp. 79–112.

31. In 1980, Egyptian President Anwar el-Sadat said, "If Ethiopia takes any action to block our right to the Nile waters, there will be no alternative for us but to use force"; quoted in Norman Myers, "Environment and Security," *Foreign Policy*, No. 74 (Spring 1989), p. 32. See also chap. 6, "The Nile River," in Thomas Naff and Ruth Matson, eds., *Water in the Middle East: Conflict or Cooperation?* (Boulder, Colo.: Westview, 1984), pp. 125–155.

32. "Pretoria Has Its Way in Lesotho," *Africa Report* (March–April, 1986), pp. 50–51; Patrick

However, our review of the historical and contemporary evidence shows that conflict and turmoil related to river water are more often internal than international. The huge dams that are often built to deal with general water scarcity are especially disruptive. Relocating large numbers of upstream people generates turmoil among the relocatees and clashes with local groups in areas where the relocatees are resettled. The people affected are often members of ethnic or minority groups outside the power hierarchy of their society, and the result is frequently rebellion by these groups and repression by the state. Water developments can also induce conflict over water and irrigable land among a country's downstream users, as we saw in the Senegal River basin.[33]

HYPOTHESIS 2: POPULATION MOVEMENT AND GROUP-IDENTITY CONFLICTS
There is substantial evidence to support the hypothesis that environmental scarcity causes large population movement, which in turn causes group-identity conflicts. But we must be sensitive to contextual factors unique to each socio-ecological system. These are the system's particular physical, political, economic, and cultural features that affect the strength of the linkages between scarcity, population movement, and conflict.

For example, experts emphasize the importance of both "push" and "pull" factors in decisions of potential migrants.[34] These factors help distinguish migrants from refugees: while migrants are motivated by a combination of push and pull, refugees are motivated mainly by push. Environmental scarcity is more likely to produce migrants than refugees, because it usually develops gradually, which means that the push effect is not sharp and sudden and that pull factors can therefore clearly enter into potential migrants' calculations.

Migrants are often people who have been weak and marginal in their home society and, depending on context, they may remain weak in the receiving society. This limits their ability to organize and to make demands. States play

Laurence, "A 'New Lesotho'?" *Africa Report* (January–February 1987), pp. 61–64; "Lesotho Water Project Gets Under Way," *Africa Report* (May–June 1988), p. 10. See also Charles Okidi, "Environmental Stress and Conflicts in Africa: Case Studies of African International Drainage Basins," paper prepared for the Project on Environmental Change and Acute Conflict (May 1992).
33. See Thayer Scudder, "River Basin Projects in Africa," *Environment*, Vol. 31, No. 2 (March 1989), pp. 4–32; and Scudder, "Victims of Development Revisited: The Political Costs of River Basin Development," *Development Anthropology Network*, Vol. 8, No. 1 (Spring 1990), pp. 1–5.
34. Astri Suhrke, "Pressure Points: Environmental Degradation, Migration, and Conflict," Occasional Paper No. 3, Project on Environmental Change and Acute Conflict (March 1993).

a critical role here: migrants often need the backing of a state (either of the receiving society or an external one) before they have sufficient power to cause conflict, and this backing depends on the region's politics. Without it, migration is less likely to produce violence than silent misery and death, which rarely destabilizes states.[35] We must remember too that migration does not always produce bad results. It can act as a safety valve by reducing conflict in the sending area. Depending on the economic context, it can ease labor shortages in the receiving society, as it sometimes has, for instance, in Malaysia. Countries as different as Canada, Thailand, and Malawi show the astonishing capacity of some societies to absorb migrants without conflict.

Even accounting for such contextual factors, events in Bangladesh and Northeast India provide strong evidence in support of the second hypothesis. In recent decades, huge numbers of people have moved from Bangladesh to India, producing group-identity conflicts in the adjacent Indian states. Only one of the three sources of environmental scarcity—population growth—seems to be a main force behind this migration. Even though Bangladesh's cropland is heavily used, in general it is not badly degraded, because the annual flooding of the Ganges and Brahmaputra rivers deposits nutrients that help maintain the fertility of the country's floodplains.[36] And while land distribution remains highly unequal, this distribution has changed little since an initial attempt at land reform immediately following East Pakistan's independence from the British.[37]

But the United Nations predicts that Bangladesh's current population of 120 million will nearly double, to 235 million, by the year 2025.[38] Cropland, at about 0.08 hectares per capita, is already desperately scarce. Population density is over 900 people per square kilometer (in comparison, population density in neigboring Assam is under 300 per square kilometer). Since virtually all of the country's good agricultural land has been exploited, population growth will cut in half the amount of cropland available per capita by 2025. Land scarcity and the brutal poverty and social turmoil it engenders have been made worse by flooding (perhaps aggravated by deforestation in

---

35. Ibid.
36. The relationship between flooding and soil fertility is ill-understood. See James Boyce, "Birth of a Megaproject: Political Economy of Flood Control in Bangladesh," *Environmental Management*, Vol. 14, No. 4 (July/August 1990), pp. 419–428, especially p. 424.
37. James Boyce, *Agrarian Impasse in Bengal: Institutional Constraints to Technological Change* (Oxford: Oxford University Press, 1987), p. 9.
38. Sadik, *The State of the World Population 1991*, p. 43.

the Himalayan watersheds of the region's major rivers); by the susceptibility of the country to cyclones; and by the construction by India of the Farakka Barrage, a dam upstream on the Ganges River.[39]

People have been moving around this part of South Asia in large numbers for centuries. But the movements are increasing in size. Over the last forty years, millions have migrated from East Pakistan or Bangladesh to the Indian states of Assam, Tripura, and West Bengal. Detailed data are scarce, since both India and Bangladesh manipulate their census data for political reasons, and the Bangladeshi government avoids admitting there is large out-migration, because the question causes friction with India. But by piecing together demographic information and experts' estimates, we concluded that migrants from Bangladesh have expanded the population of neighboring areas of India by 12 to 17 million, of which only 1 or 2 million can be attributed to migration induced by the 1971 war between India and Pakistan that created Bangladesh. We further estimate that the population of the state of Assam has been boosted by at least 7 million people, to its current total of 22 million.[40]

This enormous flux has produced pervasive social changes in the receiving regions. It has altered land distribution, economic relations, and the balance of political power between religious and ethnic groups, and it has triggered serious intergroup conflict. Members of the Lalung tribe in Assam, for instance, have long resented Bengali Muslim migrants: they accuse them of stealing the area's richest farmland. In early 1983, during a bitterly contested election for federal offices in the state, violence erupted. In the village of Nellie, Lalung people massacred nearly 1,700 Bengalis in one five-hour rampage.[41]

---

39. Controversy surrounds the question of whether Himalayan deforestation contributes to flooding; see Centre for Science and Environment (CSE), *Floods, Flood Plains, and Environmental Myths* (New Delhi: CSE, 1991), especially pp. 68–69. On the Farakka Barrage, Ashok Swain writes: "It has disrupted fishing and navigation [in Bangladesh], brought unwanted salt deposits into rich farming soil, affected agricultural and industrial production, changed the hydraulic character of the rivers and caused changes in the ecology of the Delta." See Swain, "Environmental Destruction and Acute Social Conflict: A Case Study of the Ganges Water Dispute," Department of Peace and Conflict Research, Uppsala University (November 1992), p. 24.
40. Sanjoy Hazarika, "Bangladesh and Assam: Land Pressures, Migration, and Ethnic Conflict," Occasional Paper No. 3, Project on Environmental Change and Acute Conflict (March 1993), p. 52–54.
41. "A State Ravaged," *India Today*, March 15, 1983, pp. 16–21; "Spillover Tension," *India Today*, March 15, 1983, pp. 22–23. The 1991 Indian Census showed that Assam's population growth rate has declined; the conflicts in Assam in the early 1980s appear to have encouraged many migrants from Bangladesh to go to West Bengal instead.

In Tripura, the original Buddhist and Christian inhabitants now make up less than 30 percent of the state's population. The rest are Hindu migrants from either East Pakistan or Bangladesh. This shift in the ethnic balance precipitated a violent insurgency between 1980 and 1988 that diminished only after the government agreed to return land to dispossessed Tripuris and to stop the influx of Bangladeshis. But, as the migration has continued, this agreement is in jeopardy.[42]

There are important features unique to this case. Within Bangladesh, key "push" factors include inheritance practices that divide cropland into smaller plots with each generation, and national and community water-control institutions that sharply limit agricultural output and keep peasants from gaining full benefit from some of the most fertile land in the world.[43] On the "pull" side, the standard of living in India is markedly better, and Indian politicians have often encouraged Bangladeshi migration to garner their votes. Furthermore, in the Ganges-Brahmaputra region, the concept of nation-state is often not part of the local culture. Many people think of the region as "greater Bengal," and state borders do not figure heavily in the calculations of some migrants, especially when there are receptive family, linguistic, and religious groups across the frontier. Finally, during the colonial period, the British used Hindus from Calcutta to administer Assam, and Bengali became the official language. As a result, the Assamese are particularly sensitive to their loss of political and cultural control in the state.

While such contextual factors are important, they cannot obscure the fact that land scarcity in Bangladesh, arising largely from population growth, has been a powerful force behind migration to neighboring regions and communal conflict there.[44]

HYPOTHESIS 3: ECONOMIC DEPRIVATION, INSTITUTIONAL DISRUPTION,
AND CIVIL STRIFE
Empirical evidence partially supports the third hypothesis that environmental scarcity simultaneously increases economic deprivation and disrupts key

---

42. Hazarika, "Bangladesh and Assam," pp. 60–61.
43. Boyce, *Agrarian Impasse.*
44. See Shaukat Hassan, "Environmental Issues and Security in South Asia," Adelphi Paper No. 262 (London: IISS, Autumn 1991), pp. 42–43; P.C. Goswami, "Foreign Immigration into Assam," in B.L. Abbi, ed., *Northeast Region: Problems and Prospects of Development* (Chandigarh, India: Centre for Research in Rural and Industrial Development), pp. 35–59; and Susanta Dass, *Spotlight on Assam* (Chanderpur, India: Premier Book Service, 1989).

social institutions, which in turn causes "deprivation" conflicts such as civil strife and insurgency. Environmental scarcity does produce economic deprivation, and this deprivation does cause civil strife. But more research is needed on the effects of scarcity on social institutions.

Resource degradation and depletion often affect economic productivity in poor countries and thereby contribute to deprivation. For example, erosion in upland Indonesia annually costs the country's agricultural economy nearly half a billion dollars in discounted future income.[45] The Magat watershed on the northern Filipino island of Luzon—a watershed representative of many in the Philippines—suffers gross erosion rates averaging 219 tons per hectare per year; if the lost nutrients were replaced by fertilizer, the annual cost would be over $100 per hectare.[46] Dryland degradation in Burkina Faso reduces the country's annual gross domestic product by nearly nine percent annually because of fuelwood loss and lower yields of millet, sorghum, and livestock.[47]

Vaclav Smil has estimated the combined effect of environmental problems on China's economic productivity.[48] The main burdens he identifies are reductions in crop yields caused by pollution of water, soil, and air; higher human morbidity from air pollution; farmland loss because of construction and erosion; nutrient loss and flooding due to erosion and deforestation; and timber loss arising from poor harvesting practices. Smil calculates the current cost to be at least 15 percent of China's gross national product, and he is convinced that the toll will rise steeply in the next decades.[49] Although China's economy is booming, much of the new wealth is concentrated in the

---

45. Robert Repetto, "Balance-Sheet Erosion—How to Account for the Loss of Natural Resources," *International Environmental Affairs*, Vol. 1, No. 2 (Spring 1989), pp. 103–137.
46. This estimate does not include the economic costs of lost rooting depth and increased vulnerability to drought, which may be even larger. See Wilfrido Cruz, Herminia Francisco, and Zenaida Conway, "The On-Site and Downstream Costs of Soil Erosion in the Magat and Pantabangan Watersheds," *Journal of Philippine Development*, Vol. 15, No. 1 (1988), p. 88.
47. Ed Barbier, "Environmental Degradation in the Third World," in David Pearce, ed., *Blueprint 2: Greening the World Economy* (London: Earthscan, 1991), Box 6.8, p. 90.
48. Vaclav Smil, "Environmental Change as a Source of Conflict and Economic Losses in China," Occasional Paper No. 2, Project on Environmental Change and Acute Conflict (December 1992).
49. It is hard to judge gross economic activity in China and convert these figures into dollars. Perhaps because of this, the World Bank has not increased its estimates of per capita annual GNP in line with the rapid expansion of the Chinese economy. Smil suggests that the Bank's current annual figure of $370/capita may be too low by a factor of four. This judgment is supported by recent re-evaluations of China's GNP by the International Monetary Fund. See World Bank, *World Development Report, 1992* (New York: Oxford University Press, 1992), p. 218; and Steven Greenhouse, "New Tally of World's Economies Catapults China into Third Place," *New York Times*, May 20, 1993, p. A1.

coastal provinces, especially around Hong Kong; many other parts of the country remain terribly poor.

I originally hypothesized that scarcity would undermine a variety of social institutions. Our research suggests, however, that one institution in particular—the state—is most important. Although more study is needed, the multiple effects of environmental scarcity, including large population movements and economic decline, appear likely to weaken sharply the capacity and legitimacy of the state in some poor countries.

First, environmental scarcity increases financial and political demands on governments. For example, to mitigate the social effects of loss of water, soil, and forest, governments must spend huge sums on industry and infrastructure such as new dams, irrigation systems, fertilizer plants, and reforestation programs. Furthermore, this resource loss can reduce the incomes of elites directly dependent on resource extraction; these elites usually turn to the state for compensation. Scarcity also expands marginal groups that need help from government by producing rural poverty and by displacing people into cities where they demand food, shelter, transport, energy, and employment. In response to swelling urban populations, governments introduce subsidies that drain revenues, distort prices, and cause misallocations of capital, which in turn hinders economic productivity. Such large-scale state intervention in the marketplace can concentrate political and economic power in the hands of a small number of cronies and monopolistic interests, at the expense of other elite segments and rural agricultural populations.

Simultaneously, if resource scarcity affects the economy's general productivity, revenues to local and national governments will decline. This hurts elites that benefit from state largesse and reduces the state's capacity to meet the increased demands arising from environmental scarcity. A widening gap between state capacity and demands on the state, along with the misguided economic interventions such a gap often provokes, aggravates popular and elite grievances, increases rivalry between elite factions, and erodes the state's legitimacy.

Key contextual factors affect whether lower economic productivity and state weakening lead to deprivation conflicts. Civil strife is a function of both the level of grievance motivating challenger groups and the opportunities available to these groups to act on their grievances. The likelihood of civil strife is greatest when multiple pressures at different levels in society interact to increase grievance and opportunity simultaneously. Our third hypothesis says that environmental scarcity will change both variables, by contributing to economic crisis and by weakening institutions such as the state. But numerous other factors also influence grievance and opportunity.

Contrary to common belief, there is no clear correlation between poverty (or economic inequality) and social conflict.[50] Whether or not people become aggrieved and violent when they find themselves increasingly poor depends, in part, upon their notion of economic justice. For example, people belonging to a culture that inculcates fatalism about deprivation—as with lower castes in India—will not be as prone to violence as people believing they have a right to economic wellbeing. Theorists have addressed this problem by introducing the variable "relative deprivation."[51] But there is little correlation between measures of relative deprivation and civil conflict.[52]

Part of the problem is that analysts have commonly used aggregate data (such as GNP/capita and average educational levels) to measure individual deprivation.[53] In addition, more recent research has shown that, to cause civil strife, economic crisis must be severe, persistent, and pervasive enough to erode the legitimacy or moral authority of the dominant social order and system of governance. System legitimacy is therefore a critical intervening variable between rising poverty and civil conflict. It is influenced by the aggrieved actors' subjective "blame system," which consists of their beliefs about who or what is responsible for their plight.[54]

Serious civil strife is not likely to occur unless the structure of political opportunities facing challenger groups keeps them from effectively expressing their grievances peacefully, but offers them openings for violence against authority.[55] The balance of coercive power among social actors affects the

---

50. Some of the best studies of this question have focused on the relationship between poverty and urban violence in the United States. See William Ford and John Moore, "Additional Evidence on the Social Characteristics of Riot Cities," *Social Science Quarterly*, Vol. 51, No. 2 (September 1970), pp. 339–348; and Robert Jiobu, "City Characteristics and Racial Violence," *Social Science Quarterly*, Vol. 55, No. 1 (June 1974), pp. 52–64.

51. People are said to be relatively deprived when they perceive a widening gap between the level of satisfaction they have achieved (usually defined in economic terms) and the level they believe they deserve. Deprivation is said to be relative to some subjective standard of equity or fairness; the size of the perceived gap depends upon the beliefs about economic justice held by the individual. See Ted Gurr, *Why Men Rebel* (Princeton: Princeton University Press, 1970).

52. Steven Finkel and James Rule, "Relative Deprivation and Related Theories of Civil Violence: A Critical Review," in Kurt and Gladys Lang, eds. *Research in Social Movements, Conflicts, and Change* (Greenwich, Conn.: JAI, 1986), pp. 47–69.

53. Ibid.

54. These beliefs are grounded in historical and economic experience. See, for example, James Scott, *The Moral Economy of the Peasant: Rebellion and Subsistence in Southeast Asia* (New Haven: Yale University Press, 1976), pp. 1–11.

55. Homer-Dixon, "On the Threshold," pp. 105–106 and 109–111.

probability of success and, therefore, the expected costs and benefits of different actions by the state, its supporters, and challenger groups. A state debilitated by corruption, by falling revenues and rising demand for services, or by factional conflicts within elites will be more vulnerable to violent challenges by political and military opponents; also vital to state strength is the cohesiveness of the armed forces and its loyalty to civil leadership.[56]

Challengers will have greater relative power if their grievances are articulated and actions coordinated through well-organized, well-financed and autonomous opposition groups. Since grievances felt at the individual level are not automatically expressed at the group level, the probability of civil violence is higher if groups are already organized around clear social cleavages, such as ethnicity, religion, or class. These groups can provide a clear sense of identity and act as nuclei around which highly mobilized and angry elements of the population, such as unemployed and urbanized young men, will coalesce. Conversely, if economic crisis weakens challenger groups more than the state, or affects mainly disorganized people, it will not lead to violence.

Factors that can influence both grievance and opportunity include the leadership and ideology of challenger groups, and international shocks and pressures such as changes in trade and debt relations and in costs of imported factors of production such as energy.[57] The rapid growth of urban areas in poor countries may have a similar dual effect: people concentrated in slums can communicate more easily than those in scattered rural villages; this may reinforce grievances and, by reducing problems of coordination, also increase the power of challenger groups. Research shows, however, surprisingly little historical correlation between rapid urbanization and civil strife;[58] and the exploding cities of the developing world have been remarkably quiescent in recent decades. This may be changing: India has lately witnessed ferocious urban violence, often in the poorest slums, and sometimes directed at new

---

56. See Farrokh Moshiri, "Revolutionary Conflict Theory in an Evolutionary Perspective," in Jack Goldstone, Ted Gurr, and Farrokh Moshiri, eds., *Revolutions of the Late Twentieth Century* (Boulder, Colo.: Westview, 1991), pp. 4–36; and Goldstone, "An Analytical Framework," ibid., pp. 37–51.
57. For a review of some of these factors, see Jack Goldstone, "Theories of Revolution: The Third Generation," *World Politics*, Vol. 32, No. 3 (April 1980), pp. 425–453.
58. Wayne Cornelius, Jr., "Urbanization As an Agent in Latin American Political Instability: The Case of Mexico," *American Political Science Review*, Vol. 63, No. 3 (September 1969), pp. 833–357; and Abdul Lodhi and Charles Tilly, "Urbanization, Crime, and Collective Violence in 19th-Century France," *American Journal of Sociology*, Vol. 79, No. 2 (September 1973), pp. 296–318.

migrants from the countryside.[59] In Egypt, fundamentalist opposition to the government is located in some of the most desperate sectors of Cairo and other cities such as Asyut.

The Philippines provides evidence of the links between environmental scarcity, economic deprivation, and civil strife. The country has suffered from serious strife for many decades, usually motivated by economic stress.[60] Today, cropland and forest degradation in the uplands sharply exacerbates this economic crisis. The current upland insurgency—including guerrilla attacks and assaults on military stations—is motivated by the poverty of landless agricultural laborers and farmers displaced into the remote hills, where the central government is weak.[61] During the 1970s and 1980s, the communist New People's Army and the National Democratic Front found upland peasants receptive to revolutionary ideology, especially where coercive landlords and local governments left them little choice between rebellion and starvation. The insurgency has waned somewhat since President Marcos left, not because economic conditions have improved much in the countryside, but because the democratically elected central government is more legitimate and the insurgent leadership is ideologically rigid.

Contextual factors are key to a full understanding of this case. Property rights governing upland areas are, for the most part, either nonexistent or very unclear. Legally these areas are a public resource, and their "open access" character encourages in-migration. Yet many upland peasants find themselves under the authority of concessionaires and absentee landlords who have claimed the land. Neither peasants, nor concessionaires, nor landlords, however, have secure enough title to have incentive to protect the land from environmental degradation. Increasing external debt encouraged the Marcos government, under pressure from international financial agencies, to adopt draconian stabilization and structural adjustment policies. These caused an economic crisis in the first half of the 1980s, which boosted

---

59. Sanjoy Hazarika, "Week of Rioting Leaves Streets of Bombay Empty," *New York Times*, January 12, 1993, p. A3.
60. The Huk rebellion in the late 1940s and early 1950s provides some of the best evidence for the link between economic conditions (especially unequal land distribution) and civil strife in the Philippines. See Benedict Kerkvliet, *The Huk Rebellion: A Study of Peasant Revolt in the Philippines* (Quezon City, Philippines: New Day Publishers, 1979); and E.J. Mitchell, "Some Econometrics of the Huk Rebellion," *American Political Science Review*, Vol. 63, No. 4 (December 1969), pp. 1159–1171.
61. Celso Roque and Maria Garcia, "Economic Inequality, Environmental Degradation and Civil Strife in the Philippines," paper prepared for the Project on Environmental Change and Acute Conflict (1993).

agricultural unemployment, reduced opportunities for alternative employment in urban and rural industries, and gave a further push to migration into the uplands.[62]

Finally, the insurgents gained adherents because they built on indigenous beliefs and social structures to help the peasants define their situation and focus their discontent. The most successful rebellions in Filipino history have drawn on peasants' millenarian vision—rooted in their Catholicism—of "an idealized pre-Spanish condition of wholeness."[63] The current insurgency has been particularly potent because it mingles "the spiritual search for liberation and the political search for independence, into the overarching quest for Filipino identity."[64] This has provided peasants with an alternative moral system to the traditional patron-client relationship between peasants and landowners. The feudal norms imposed obligations on landowners, which gave peasants rudimentary economic security, but disintegrated with the commercialization of agriculture and the urbanization of elites in the early and mid-twentieth century.[65]

Causal processes like those in the Philippines can be seen around the planet: population growth and unequal access to good land force huge numbers of rural people into cities or onto marginal lands. In the latter case, they cause environmental damage and become chronically poor. Eventually these people may be the source of persistent upheaval, or they may migrate yet again, stimulating ethnic conflicts or urban unrest elsewhere.

The rise of the Sendero Luminoso rebellion in Peru can be attributed to a subsistence crisis caused, in part, by such a process of ecological marginalization.[66] The country's mountainous southern highlands are not suitable for farming. The hills are steep, and the soil is thin and dry. Nonetheless, during

---

62. Maria Concepción Cruz and Robert Repetto, *The Environmental Effects of Stabilization and Structural Adjustment Programs: The Philippines Case* (Washington, D.C.: World Resources Institute, 1992). See also Francisco Lara, Jr., "Structural Adjustments and Trade Liberalization: Eating Away Our Food Security," *PPI Research Papers* (Quezon City: Philippine Peasant Institute [PPI], 1991); and Robin Broad, *Unequal Alliance, 1979–1986: The World Bank, the International Monetary Fund, and the Philippines* (Quezon City: Ateneo de Manila University Press, 1988).

63. Kessler, *Rebellion and Repression,* pp. 24–25.

64. Ibid.

65. Ibid, pp. 16–19. See also Reynaldo Clemena Ileto, *Pasyon and Revolution: Popular Movements in the Philippines, 1840–1910* (Manila: Ateneo de Manila University Press, 1979).

66. Cynthia McClintock, "Why Peasants Rebel: The Case of Peru's Sendero Luminoso," *World Politics,* Vol. 37, No. 1 (October 1984), pp. 48–84; and McClintock, "Peru's Sendero Luminoso Rebellion: Origins and Trajectory," in Susan Eckstein, ed., *Power and Popular Protest: Latin American Social Movements* (Berkeley: University of California Press, 1989), pp. 61–101.

the colonial period, Indian peoples in the region were displaced onto hillsides when Spanish settlers seized richer valley lands. In the 1970s, the Velasco government undertook a sweeping land-redistribution program. But people in the highlands benefited little, because the government was reluctant to break up large agricultural enterprises that generated much of the country's export earnings.

Natural population growth and a lack of good land or jobs elsewhere boosted population densities in the southern highlands. The department of Ayacucho saw density increase from 8.1 people per square kilometer in 1940 to 12.1 in 1980. Cropland availability dropped below .2 hectare per capita.[67] These densities exceed sustainable limits, given the inherent fragility of the region's land and prevailing agricultural practices. Cropland has therefore been badly degraded by erosion and nutrient depletion.

Cynthia McClintock notes that, "if population increases while the soil deteriorates, food production per-capita can be expected to decline."[68] Wealth in the region is almost entirely derived from subsistence agriculture. Family incomes—already among the lowest in Peru—dropped sharply in real terms in the 1970s and 1980s; in 1980, per-capita income in the Peruvian highlands was 82 percent of the 1972 level. This poverty resulted in declining caloric intake; in 1980 people in the southern highlands had less than 70 percent of the daily requirement set by the FAO. In 1983, a drought made the subsistence crisis even worse, and production of the staple crop of potatoes fell by 40–50 percent.

While government policies were partly responsible for the long-term income decline in the Peruvian highlands, the particularly harsh drop in the southern region was a result of population pressures, poor land, and the lack of alternative sources of income. The peasants' sense of deprivation was increased by the land reform in the 1970s, which raised their expectations in vain. There is thus a strong correlation between areas suffering severe poverty and areas of Sendero Luminoso strongholds: "the sine-qua-non element" of these strongholds is "the subsistence crisis in the country's southern highlands during the early 1980s."[69]

In terms of contextual factors, Ayacucho offered special opportunities to insurgents. It is physically remote, which reduced the government's control,

---

67. McClintock, "Why Peasants Rebel," pp. 61 and 63.
68. Ibid., p. 63.
69. Ibid., p. 82.

and it has a major university that served as an organizational base for radicals that became the core of Sendero. The university's remoteness also meant that students were disproportionately from the peasantry, and could therefore return to their communities with ease; moreover, they were less likely to find professional jobs on graduation. The relative power of the government was also weakened, ironically, by the land reform, which caused large landowners to leave the region. The Velasco regime did not fill the vacuum with new political and security institutions, in part because an economic downturn later in the decade reduced the government's resources for the task.

McClintock believes that the poverty of these regions condemns the country to chronic, long-term turmoil. The government may be civilian, but is unlikely to be very democratic, and will confront "virtually constant revolutionary and criminal violence."

A COMBINED MODEL
There are important links between the processes identified in the second and third hypotheses. For example, although population movement is sometimes caused directly by scarcity, more often it arises from the greater poverty caused by this scarcity. Similarly, the weakening of the state increases the likelihood not only of deprivation conflicts, but of group-identity conflicts.

It is useful, therefore, to bring the hypotheses together into one model of environment-conflict linkages (Figure 2). Decreases in the quality and quan-

Figure 2. Some Sources and Consequences of Environmental Scarcity.

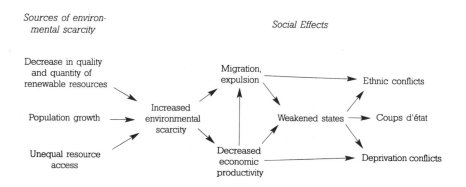

Figure 3. Environmental Scarcity in the Philippines.

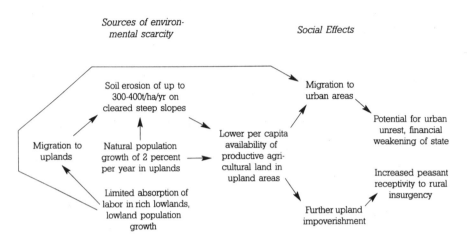

NOTE: The variables and linkages in Figure 3 map onto Figure 2, with the source of scarcity on the left and the forms of conflict on the right.

tity of renewable resources, population growth, and unequal resource access act singly or in various combinations to increase the scarcity, for certain population groups, of cropland, water, forests, and fish. This can reduce economic productivity, both for the local groups experiencing the scarcity and for the larger regional and national economies. The affected people may migrate or be expelled to new lands. Migrating groups often trigger ethnic conflicts when they move to new areas, while decreases in wealth can cause deprivation conflicts such as insurgency and rural rebellion. In developing countries, the migrations and productivity losses may eventually weaken the state which in turn decreases central control over ethnic rivalries and in-creases opportunities for insurgents and elites challenging state authority. Figure 3 shows how these linkages work in the Filipino case.

South Africa and Haiti illustrate this combined model. In South Africa, apartheid concentrated millions of blacks in some of the country's least productive and most ecologically sensitive territories, where population dens-ities were worsened by high natural birth rates. In 1980, rural areas of the Ciskei homeland had 82 people per square kilometer, whereas the surrounding Cape Province had a rural density of 2. Homeland residents had little capital and few resource-management skills and were subject to corrupt and abusive local governments. Sustainable development in such a situation was impossible, and wide areas were completely stripped of trees for fuelwood, grazed down to bare dirt, and eroded of top soil. A 1980 report concluded that nearly 50 percent of Ciskei's land was moderately or severely eroded, and nearly 40 percent of its pasturage was overgrazed.[70]

This loss of resources, combined with a lack of alternative employment and the social trauma caused by apartheid, created a subsistence crisis in the homelands. Thousands of people have migrated to South African cities, which are as yet incapable of adequately integrating and employing these migrants. The result is the rapid growth of squatter settlements and illegal townships that are rife with discord and that threaten the country's move to democratic stability.[71]

In Haiti, the irreversible loss of forests and soil in rural areas deepens an economic crisis that spawns social strife, internal migration, and an exodus of "boat people." When first colonized by the Spanish in the late fifteenth century and the French in the seventeenth century, Haiti was treasured for its abundant forests. Since then, Haiti has become one of the world's most dramatic examples of environmental despoliation. Less than two percent of the country remains forested, and the last timber is being felled at four percent per year.[72] As trees disappear, erosion follows, worsened by the steepness of the land and by harsh storms. The United Nations estimates that at least 50 percent of the country is affected by topsoil loss that leaves the land "unreclaimable at the farm level."[73] So much soil washes off the slopes that the streets of Port-au-Prince have to be cleared with bulldozers in the rainy season.

Unequal land distribution was not a main cause of this catastrophe. Haiti gained independence in 1804 following a revolt of slaves and ex-slaves against

70. Francis Wilson and Mamphela Ramphele, *Uprooting Poverty: The South African Challenge* (New York: Norton, 1989); George Quail, et al., *Report of the Ciskei Commission* (Pretoria: Conference Associates, 1980), p. 73.

71. See Mamphela Ramphele and Chris McDowell, eds., *Restoring the Land: Environment and Change in Post-Apartheid South Africa* (London: Panos, 1991); and Chris Eaton, "Rural Environmental Degradation and Urban Conflict in South Africa," Occasional Paper of the Peace and Conflict Studies Program, University of Toronto, June 1992.

72. WRI, *World Resources, 1992–93*, p. 286.

73. Global Assessment of Soil Degradation, *World Map on Status of Human-Induced Soil Degradation*, Sheet 1, North and South America.

the French colonial regime. Over a period of decades, the old plantation system associated with slavery was dismantled, and land was widely distributed in small parcels.[74] As a result, Haiti's agricultural structure, unique to Latin America, has 73 percent of cropland in private farms of less than 4 hectares.[75]

But inheritance customs and population growth have combined to produce scarcity, as in Bangladesh. Land has been subdivided into smaller portions with each generation. Eventually the plots cannot properly support their cultivators, fallow periods are neglected, and greater poverty prevents investment in soil conservation. The poorest people leave for steeper hillsides, where they clear the forest and begin farming anew, only to exhaust the land in a few years.[76] Many peasants try to supplement their falling incomes by scavenging wood for charcoal production, which contributes to further deforestation.

These processes might have been prevented had a stable central government invested in agriculture, industrial development, and reforestation. Instead, since independence Haiti has endured a ceaseless struggle for power between black and mulatto classes, and the ruling regimes been solely interested in expropriating any surplus wealth the economy generated. Today, over 60 percent of the population is still engaged in agriculture, yet capital is unavailable for agricultural improvement, and the terms of exchange for crop production favor urban regions.[77] The population growth rate has actually increased, from 1.7 percent in the mid-1970s to over 2 percent today: the UN estimates that the current population of 6.75 million will grow to over 13 million by 2025.[78] As the land erodes and the population grows, incomes shrink: agricultural output per capita has decreased ten percent in the last decade.[79]

Analysts agree that rising rural poverty has caused ever-increasing rural-rural and rural-urban migration. In search of work, agricultural workers move

---

74. Thomas Weil, et al., *Haiti: A Country Study* (Washington, D.C.: Department of the Army, 1982), pp. 28–33.
75. Anthony Catanese, "Haiti's Refugees: Political, Economic, Environmental," *Field Staff Reports*, No. 17 (Sausalito, Calif.: Universities Field Staff International, Natural Heritage Institute, 1990–91), p. 5.
76. Elizabeth Abbott, "Where Waters Run Brown," *Equinox*, Vol. 10, No. 59 (September/October 1991), p. 43.
77. Marko Ehrlich, et al., *Haiti: Country Environmental Profile, A Field Study* (Washington, D.C.: U.S. Agency for International Development, 1986), pp. 89–92.
78. WRI, *World Resources, 1992–93*, p. 246.
79. Ibid., p. 272.

from subsistence hillside farms to rice farms in the valleys. From there, they go to cities, especially to Port-au-Prince, which now has a population of over a million. Wealthier farmers and traders, and even those with slimmer resources, try to flee by boat.

These economic and migration stresses are undoubtedly contributing to civil strife. In the aftermath of the collapse of "Baby Doc" Duvalier's regime in 1986, the poor unleashed their vengeance on those associated with the regime, in particular on Duvalier's gangs of enforcers, the *tontons macoutes*. During his election campaign and his short tenure as president, Jean-Bertrand Aristide reportedly encouraged poor slum-dwellers to attack Haiti's elite. Fearful of uprisings, the current military regime has ferociously oppressed the country's poor and peasantry. Even if the present political stalemate is resolved, Aristide is returned to power, and international sanctions are lifted, Haiti will be forever bear the burden of its irreversibly ravaged environment, which may make it impossible to build a prosperous, just, and peaceful society.

THE CAUSAL ROLE OF ENVIRONMENTAL SCARCITY
Environmental scarcity often acts as a powerful long-term social stressor, but does it have any independent role as a cause of conflict? Many analysts assume that it is no more than a fully endogenous intervening variable linking political, economic, and social factors to conflict. By this view, environmental scarcity may be an important indicator that political and economic development has gone awry, but it does not merit, in and of itself, intensive research and policy attention at the expense of more fundamental political and economic factors.

But the cases reviewed here highlight three reasons why this view is wrong. First, as we saw in the Senegal and Jordan basins, environmental scarcity can itself be an important force behind changes in the politics and economics governing resource use. In both cases, scarcity caused powerful actors to increase in their own favor the inequities in the distribution of resources. Second, ecosystem vulnerability is often an important variable contributing to environmental scarcity, and this vulnerability is, at least in part, an independent physical factor: the depth of soils in the Filipino uplands and the vulnerability of Israel's aquifers to salt intrusion are not functions of human social institutions or behavior. Third, in many parts of the world— including regions of the Philippines, Haiti, Peru, and South Africa—environmental degradation has crossed a threshold of irreversibility. Even if enlightened social change removes the original political, economic, and cultural causes of the degradation, it will be a continuing burden on society. Once irreversible, in other words, environmental degradation becomes an exogenous variable.

Implications for International Security

Environmental scarcity has insidious and cumulative social impacts, such as population movement, economic decline, and the weakening of states. These can contribute to diffuse and persistent sub-national violence. The rate and extent of such conflicts will increase as scarcities worsen.

This sub-national violence will not be as conspicuous or dramatic as inter-state resource wars, but it will have serious repercussions for the security interests of both the developed and the developing worlds. Countries under such stress may fragment as their states become enfeebled and peripheral regions are seized by renegade authorities and warlords. Governments of countries as different as the Philippines and Peru have lost control over outer territories; although both these cases are complicated, it is nonetheless clear that environmental stress has contributed to their fragmentation. Fragmentation of any sizeable country will produce large outflows of refugees; it will also hinder the country from effectively negotiating and implementing international agreements on collective security, global environmental protection, and other matters.

Alternatively, a state might keep scarcity-induced civil strife from causing its progressive enfeeblement and fragmentation by becoming a "hard" regime that is authoritarian, intolerant of opposition, and militarized. Such regimes are more prone to launch military attacks against neighboring countries to divert attention from internal grievances. If a number of developing countries evolve in this direction, they could eventually threaten the military and economic interests of rich countries.

A state's ability to become a hard regime in response to environmentally induced turmoil depends, I believe, on two factors. First, the state must have sufficient remaining capacity—despite the debilitating effects of scarcity—to mobilize or seize resources for its own ends; this is a function of the internal organizational coherence of the state and its autonomy from outside pressures. Second, there must remain enough surplus wealth in the country's ecological-economic system to allow the state, once it seizes this wealth, to pursue its authoritarian course. Consequently, the countries with the highest probability of becoming "hard" regimes, and potential threats to their neighbors, are large, relatively wealthy developing countries that are dependent on a declining environmental base and that have a history of state strength. Candidates include Indonesia and, perhaps, Nigeria.

Our research suggests that environmental pressures in China may cause the country's fragmentation.[80] This is not the received wisdom: most experts have been distracted by the phenomenal economic expansion in China's coastal areas; they have tended to project these trends onto the rest of the country and to neglect the dangers posed by resource scarcities.[81] The costs of misreading of the Chinese situation could be very high. China has over one-fifth of the world's population, a huge military with growing power-projection capability, and unsettled relations with some of its neighbors. The effects of Chinese civil unrest, mass violence, and state disintegration could spread far beyond its borders.

Chinese fertility rates peaked at the height of the cultural revolution between 1969 and 1972. Population growth will peak at about 17 million per year in the mid-1990s, as the babies born during the cultural revolution reach their reproductive years. In the late 1980s and early 1990s, specialists tempered their optimism about Chinese ability to bring population growth down to replacement rate.[82] Market liberalization in the countryside undermined the one-child policy. In rural areas state coercion seemed less effective, and peasants enriched by market reforms could more easily pay fines. In some provinces, therefore, it became common for families to have two or three children. The most recent evidence, however, suggests that Chinese authorities have renewed their commitment to controlling population growth. In response to often extremely coercive measures by low-level officials, fertility rates have fallen below two children per woman for the first time.[83] But

---

80. Smil, "Environmental Change as a Source of Conflict and Economic Losses in China"; Jack Goldstone, "Imminent Political Conflict Arising from China's Environmental Crises," Occasional Paper No. 2, Project on Environmental Change and Acute Conflict (December 1992).
81. See, for example, Barber Conable and David Lampton, "China: The Coming Power," *Foreign Affairs*, Vol. 72, No. 5 (Winter 1992/93), pp. 133–149. In their assessment of the pressures on contemporary China, the authors devote only half a sentence to demographic and environmental stresses.
82. Griffith Feeney, et al., "Recent Fertility Dynamics in China: Results from the 1987 One Percent Population Survey," *Population and Development Review*, Vol. 15, No. 2 (June 1989), pp. 297–321; Shanti Conly and Sharon Camp, "China's Family Planning Program: Challenging the Myths," *Country Study Series*, No. 1 (Washington, D.C.: Population Crisis Committee, 1992).
83. Nicholas Kristof, "China's Crackdown on Births: A Stunning, and Harsh, Success," *New York Times*, April 25, 1993, p. A1.

experts are not sure that this accomplishment can be sustained for long, and even if it is, China's population will continue to grow well into the next century.

Only two poor populous countries in the world have less arable land per capita than China: Egypt and Bangladesh. In fact, 300 million people in China's interior have even less arable land than the Bangladeshis. China has little scope to expand irrigated and arable land, although it might be able to increase the intensity of irrigation in some places. Consequently, continued population growth and loss of cropland mean that China will have 25 percent less arable land per capita by 2010. Moreover, the remaining land will often be of declining quality: every year the country loses as much nitrogen and phosphorous from soil erosion as it applies in inorganic fertilizer. Vaclav Smil notes that many experts and senior authorities in China are frightened by the environmental situation, believing the country has already crossed key thresholds of unsustainability. Grain is a constant preoccupation of the leadership, and imports even into rich areas may soon be necessary. Already, tens of millions of Chinese are trying to migrate from the country's interior and northern regions, where water and fuelwood are desperately scarce and the land is often badly damaged, to the booming coastal cities. Smil expects bitter disputes among these regions over migration and water sharing.

Jack Goldstone has estimated the consequences of these stresses for social stability. He notes that population and resource pressures led to widespread civil violence in China during the Ming and Qing dynasties.[84] The current regime recognizes that such pressures will cause mounting grievances in the worst-affected regions. "The rapidly growing population of the north and west cannot be fed and employed within those regions," Goldstone writes. "There is not sufficient land, nor sufficient water, to provide for the additional hundreds of millions that will be born in the next decades."[85] If large-scale migration out of the region is blocked, deprivation conflicts in the northwest are likely. Coupled with merchant and worker resistance in the major cities, they would probably lead to the fall of the central government. If the migration is diverted into China's southern countryside, deprivation and group-identity conflicts are likely to result there.

The only realistic policy is to permit movement to the wealthy coastal cities. Coastal areas must therefore be allowed to continue their rapid eco-

84. For a full analysis, see Jack Goldstone, *Revolution and Rebellion in the Early Modern World* (Berkeley: University of California Press, 1991).
85. Goldstone, "Imminent Political Conflicts Arising from China's Environmental Crises," p. 52.

nomic growth to absorb surplus labor. But, Goldstone argues, the Beijing government will have great difficulty maintaining economic and political control over this process. Economic liberalization helps to mobilize the population by dissolving long-standing social relations, and this weakens the Communist Party's ability to micro-manage Chinese society. Moreover, the Party is divided from the very non-Party elites that are rapidly expanding because of economic growth, including student, business, and professional groups. Further growth will depend on private domestic investment, which will encourage these elites, and also workers in private industry, to demand democratization and responsiveness of the regime. The Party has also been weakened by deep internal disagreements over the rate and degree of economic and political liberalization; suspicions about the reliability of the Army; and worker discontent that remains high throughout the country.

Divisions within the regime and among elites, combined with an increasingly mobilized population, create greater opportunities for challenges to central authority. But resource and population pressures force the regime to pursue policies, such as further economic liberalization, that only weaken it more. Goldstone believes that long-term stability would be more likely if China were to begin serious democratization soon, but he is not sanguine. Central authorities will probably refuse to recognize their loosening grip on the society, and this will eventually prompt secessionist movements in Moslem lands to the west and Tibet in the South. Sichuan may also seek independence. "Once the glue of unified communist rule dissolves, China may once again, as it has so often in its history following the fall of unifying dynasties, experience a decade or even century-long interregnum of warring among regional states."[86]

Conclusions

Our research shows that environmental scarcity causes violent conflict. This conflict tends to be persistent, diffuse, and sub-national. Its frequency will probably jump sharply in the next decades as scarcities rapidly worsen in many parts of the world. Of immediate concern are scarcities of cropland, water, forests, and fish, whereas atmospheric changes such as global warm-

---

86. Ibid., p. 54.

ing will probably not have a major effect for several decades, and then mainly by interacting with already existing scarcities.

The degradation and depletion of environmental resources is only one source of environmental scarcity; two other important sources are population growth and unequal resource distribution. Scarcity often has its harshest social impact when these factors interact. As environmental scarcity becomes more severe, some societies will have a progressively lower capacity to adapt. Of particular concern is the decreasing capacity of the state to create markets and other institutions that promote adaptation. The impact of environmental scarcity on state capacity deserves further research.

Countries experiencing chronic internal conflict because of environmental stress will probably either fragment or become more authoritarian. Fragmenting countries will be the source of large out-migrations, and they will be unable to effectively negotiate or implement international agreements on security, trade and environmental protection. Authoritarian regimes may be inclined to launch attacks against other countries to divert popular attention from internal stresses. Any of these outcomes could seriously disrupt international security. The social impacts of environmental scarcity therefore deserve concerted attention from security scholars.

The Utility of Force in a World of Scarcity

$\mathbf{F}$rom the dawn of modern history to the mid-twentieth century, relations between states were conducted in an atmosphere darkened by the ever present possibility of violence. Although moral conceptions imposed some restraints on the actions of statesmen, in the absence of a world government and firm moral consensus, issues could rarely be settled solely by appeals to reason and justice. Coercion, not persuasion, was thus an all-too-frequent means of resolving disputes, and because the resort to force could never be completely precluded, organized violence became the most effective form of coercion and the ultimate arbiter in world politics. Even when disputes were ended through negotiation, the threat of force still lay in the background and shaped the results profoundly. As Nicholas Spykman concluded in the grim world of the early 1940s, world politics is power politics and the ultimate form of power in that domain is military force.[1]

In the past five decades, however, the great powers have shown increasing reluctance to employ force overtly against one another or even against weaker states. Their apparent hesitation has led several sophisticated observers of international affairs to conclude that the once-central role of armed force is rapidly diminishing, perhaps soon to the point of irrelevance. The central assertion of these authors is that the costs, risks, and difficulties in applying force are rising while the benefits derived therefrom are declining.[2] This optimistic school has presented an impressive case with important implications for

John Orme is Professor of Politics at Oglethorpe University in Atlanta, Georgia, and author of Deterrence, Reputation, and Cold War Cycles (London: Macmillan, 1992). He is at work on a book exploring why international rivals make peace.

The author would like to thank Dan Kaufman, Michael Mazarr, Brad Stone, the Emory Seminar on International Security, and several anonymous readers for their comments. None bears any responsibility for the errors of fact or interpretation that remain.

1. Nicholas J. Spykman, *America's Strategy in World Politics* (New York: Archon, 1970), p. 18.
2. Leading representatives of this school include Klaus Knorr, *The Power of Nations* (New York: Basic Books, 1975); John Mueller, *Retreat from Doomsday: The Obsolescence of Major War* (New York: Basic Books, 1989); Richard Ullman, *Securing Europe* (Princeton, N.J.: Princeton University Press, 1991); Richard Rosecrance, *The Rise of the Trading State: Commerce and Conquest in the Modern World* (New York: Basic Books, 1986); Evan Luard, *The Blunted Sword: The Erosion of Military Power in Modern World Politics* (New York: New Amsterdam, 1988); Francis Fukuyama, *The End of History and the Last Man* (New York: Avon, 1992); and Max Singer and Aaron Wildavsky, *The Real World Order* (Chatham, N.J.: Chatham House, 1993).

International Security, Vol. 22, No. 3 (Winter 1997/98), pp. 138–167
© 1997 by the President and Fellows of Harvard College and the Massachusetts Institute of Technology.

the future of international politics, the academic study of international relations, and the conduct of U.S. foreign and defense policy. It deserves a serious and systematic response. The aim of this article is to provide it. It commences with a critical review and synthesis of the arguments that have been offered to sustain the conclusion that force is declining in utility. The following three sections, which comprise the bulk of the article, then describe, explain, and analyze the consequences of three ongoing developments that may confound optimistic expectations by increasing the ease and value of territorial acquisition and thereby heighten the importance of military force in world politics. These trends are the revolution in military affairs (RMA), the coming surge in world population, and the spread of industrialization to the developing nations. The concluding section considers the prospect that, at some point in the next century, the international arena could return to a Hobbesian state of war.

Grounds for Optimism

Many observers have attributed the diminished visibility of military force above all else to the presence of nuclear weapons. Not only do these fearsome devices act as mutual deterrents, they maintain, but the prospect that even the most limited use of force could set in motion a process of unintended and uncontrollable escalation discourages the resort to violence at any level. The unprecedented destructiveness of the atomic bomb has compelled states to resolve conflicts through tests of will rather than overt violence. These contests are won by the side that conveys an image of superior credibility and determination. Because states are usually more committed to preserving their territory and independence than their opponents are to aggrandizement, the defender enjoys an enormous advantage. Furthermore, the victor in a nuclear war would find the radioactive "inheritance" in his possession afterward small recompense for the devastation the enemy could visit on his own land. Hence nuclear force is so "useful" for the defense of territory that it reduces conventional offensive forces to impotence, thereby eliminating the risk of attack and freezing the territorial status quo.[3]

Yet it is difficult to reject a priori the possibility that if nuclear weapons were generally perceived to be so destructive as to be unusable states would no

---

3. Robert Jervis, *The Meaning of the Nuclear Revolution* (Ithaca, N.Y.: Cornell University Press, 1989), pp. 19–22, 29–35, 227–228; and Shai Feldman, *Israeli Nuclear Deterrence: A Strategy for the 1980s* (New York: Columbia University Press, 1982), pp. 31–32.

longer be intimidated from initiating conventional wars by the prospect of escalation.[4] Although the "balance of interests" may indeed favor the defender in most instances, it is certainly conceivable that a leader with a high tolerance for risk, strong domestic support, or extraordinary thespian talent could create an all-too-credible impression among his opponents that he is more committed to altering the status quo than they are to preserving it, particularly if the defenders were attempting to extend deterrence beyond their borders. Had Britain and France possessed nuclear weapons in 1936, for example, would they have been able to deter a nuclear-armed Hitler from occupying the Rhineland, achieving *Anschluss* with Austria, or seizing the Sudetenland? In any case, nuclear powers have been challenged by *conventional* force frequently enough since 1945 to raise serious doubts about the reliability of nuclear deterrence. Consider the following anomalies: China's attack on the United States, 1950; China's on the Soviet Union, 1969; Vietnam's on China, 1979; Argentina's on Britain, 1981; and Pakistan's on India or vice versa. For A.F.K. Organski and Jacek Kugler, to maintain that nuclear weapons deter conflict at all levels in light of such evidence is "to believe in magic."[5]

The absence of war between the Soviet Union and the United States, the "long peace" of the Cold War, has often been attributed to the presence of nuclear weapons. But the U.S. arsenal was too small in the late 1940s and too conspicuously unsuccessful in deterring Soviet encroachment on Eastern Europe to provide an entirely convincing explanation. It is often forgotten that the division of Europe stemming from the diplomatic deadlock at Yalta satisfied the basic security objectives of both the Soviet Union (protection against a renascent Germany) and the United States (preservation of a balance of power in Europe) simultaneously. Although both hoped for something better—the Soviets, for revolution in the West, and the Americans, for self-determination in the East—neither would have been strongly inclined to risk another conflict on the scale of World War II to improve the Yalta system, even if nuclear weapons had never been invented. The stability of Cold War Europe thus rested to an important degree on the weakness of any incentive to alter the status quo. Were nuclear weapons to be introduced into a situation where two rivals find it more difficult to achieve their fundamental objectives simultaneously, nuclear deterrence would be put to a much sterner test.

---

4. Mueller, *Retreat from Doomsday*, pp. 236–240.
5. A.F.K. Organski and Jacek Kugler, *The War Ledger* (Chicago: University of Chicago Press, 1980), pp. 147–179, quotation on p. 179.

John Mueller believes that force soon will be obsolescent, but his conclusion does not stand or fall solely on the effects of the nuclear revolution. Atomic weapons, he contends, have served mainly to underscore what was already abundantly clear by 1945: conventional war as fought twice on the European continent had already become so destructive as to be virtually useless as an instrument of foreign policy. Fission bombs destroyed Hiroshima faster but no more thoroughly than conventional ordnance had leveled Dresden and Tokyo. Eliminating the bomb in order to fight total conventional war, Mueller reasons, would simply mean jumping from the fiftieth rather than the fifty-first story of a building.[6]

Even when the risks of escalation are deemed controllable or acceptable, the economic and political costs of battle appear to have increased. War not only requires costly expenditures on increasingly expensive weapons systems, but can also rupture mutually beneficial commercial relations. The strong, it is often said, can no longer effortlessly impose their will on the weak as in the nineteenth century. Advanced military powers now face more effectively organized peoples inspired by intense nationalism, such as those in Vietnam and Afghanistan, who are difficult to subdue by any morally acceptable means. Public opinion among the most advanced states has grown much more critical of the use of force, although there is not complete consensus as to why. Mueller asserts that human lives—and not only those of one's own soldiers but those of the enemy—are simply valued more highly than in the past.[7] Some scholars contend that a "postmodern culture" of individualism, cosmopolitanism, and distrust of government has prevented potential great powers from developing and projecting military might as they once did. Others suggest that television has magnified the psychological impact of any loss of life, rendering democracies increasingly squeamish about casualties.[8] In any case, the revulsion of the American public to the deaths of several U.S. soldiers on October 3, 1993, in Mogadishu and the long hesitation of the European powers to intervene in Bosnia demonstrate the low tolerance of democratic publics for casualties on distant (or even proximate) battlefields. In this climate of opinion, it is difficult for leaders to present a compelling rationale for the employment of force and to carry out the action without facing heavy political damage.

---

6. Mueller, *Retreat from Doomsday*, p. 116.
7. Ibid., p. 9; and Rosecrance, *Rise of the Trading State*, p. 131.
8. Barry Buzan and Gerald Segal, "The Rise of 'Lite Powers': A Strategy for the Postmodern States," *World Policy Review*, Vol. 13, No. 3 (Fall 1996), pp. 3–4; and David Shukman, *Tomorrow's War: The Threat of High-Technology Weapons* (New York: Harcourt, Brace, 1996), pp. 177–180, 211.

The potential gains from the use of force also appear much less attractive than in the past. Many of the most important issues of the present and future do not depend on who occupies a given territory, but rather on what is done on that territory. In these cases, which would include such crucial matters as trade, monetary policy, environmental protection, and human rights, the threat of force would usually be implausible and in any case ineffective. The predominant form of conflict since 1945, according to Evan Luard, has been "low-intensity conflict" within (and not between) states. The aim in most of these situations is not to destroy the enemy, but rather to persuade the population of the merits of one's system of government. "Even the most powerful states on earth, armed with all the vast array of modern weaponry, cannot easily convince by acts of force." Rather, it is "political factors," such as the effectiveness of governments and the strength of nationalist sentiment, that are decisive.[9]

The overriding objective of the most advanced states, in the eyes of Mueller and many other observers, is economic prosperity. Yet it is not immediately clear why the populations of advanced industrial societies, blessed with more material goods than at any time in human history, should focus so intently on wealth as their object. On closer examination, it appears that the importance of wealth as a motivation in foreign policy and in life more generally has increased not in absolute but only in relative terms. That is, other goals now matter less than before.[10] This point has been developed much more explicitly by Francis Fukuyama, who maintains that the political strength of "atavistic" social classes injected an aristocratic urge for glory into the counsels of state in the otherwise bourgeois societies of nineteenth-century Europe. With the destruction of those classes and the rise of democracy, demands for "megalothymia" (recognition of oneself or one's state as greater than others) have been largely eliminated from politics. Further, democracies satisfy the common man's yearning for recognition more satisfactorily than any previous regime and are thus likely to proliferate. Perhaps because of this, democracies are not driven as other political regimes have been by a desire for collective honor. Only wealth remains as a goal.[11]

---

9. Luard, *Blunted Sword*, pp. 2, 7–20, 181–182.
10. Mueller's analogy between the decline of dueling and the obsolescence of war suggests as much. See Mueller, *Retreat from Doomsday*, pp. 13, 219–222, 227, 233–234.
11. Fukuyama, *End of History*, pp. 173, 185–190, 255–275, 283, 314–315, 328–336.

The use of violence might still be conceivable under these conditions for economic motives, but in the view of Richard Rosecrance, force is unattractive even for this object. Violence on the scale of the world wars would ravage the property coveted by a rational aggressor so completely that it would scarcely be worth acquiring, and if anything other than extraction of basic resources were expected, the cooperation of the subject population would be nearly impossible to elicit. (Slaves can be compelled to dig for ore, but not to program computers.) War does not pay, not only because the costs of acquisition are so high, but also because the value of the conquest is so low.[12]

Finally, the advantages of acquisition are much less apparent than in preceding epochs. Additional "living space" is no longer necessary, as settlement is now urbanized; nor required for farm land, now that such a small proportion of the population is employed in agriculture; nor for raw materials, because they constitute such a small percentage of the value added through manufacturing; nor for defense, as modern weaponry affords adequate protection.[13] Most important, the alternatives to territorial expansion are now much more attractive. In the preindustrial past, rising population eventually produced diminishing returns to investment and stagnant standards of living. The only route to riches under these conditions was the acquisition of additional territory. The application of scientific and technical knowledge for the enhancement of productivity now provides societies an escape from the dilemma of diminishing returns.[14] The expansion of production at home appears to be a much faster and safer path to prosperity than conquest abroad, and if all the requisites of an industrial economy are not present within one's borders, trade is also a cheaper and easier method of acquiring them than imperialism. Military force has been, first and foremost, a means of taking and holding territory. The smaller the benefits that can be derived from the occupation of land, the smaller will be the reward to those who have invested in military might.[15]

These arguments echo an observation offered long ago, at the beginning of the modern age, by Francis Bacon:

---

12. Rosecrance, *Rise of the Trading State*, pp. 32–37, 128; and Knorr, *Power of Nations*, pp. 123–126.
13. Ullman, *Securing Europe*, pp. 23–27. Ullman recognizes that this holds true for the industrialized states only.
14. Robert Gilpin, *War and Change in International Politics* (Cambridge, U.K.: Cambridge University Press, 1981), p. 71
15. Rosecrance, *Rise of the Trading State*, pp. 13–14, 24–25, 129, 139, 159–160; and Ullman, *Securing Europe*, p. 23.

It will, perhaps, be as well to distinguish three species and degrees of ambition. First, that of men who are anxious to enlarge their own power in their country, which is a vulgar and degenerate kind; next, that of men who strive to enlarge the power and empire of their country over mankind, which is more dignified but not less covetous; but if one were to endeavor to renew and enlarge the power and empire of mankind in general over the universe, such ambition (if it may be termed) is both more sound and more noble than the other two. Now the empire of man over things is founded on the arts and sciences alone, for nature is only to be commanded by obeying her.[16]

For Bacon, the striving for wealth through the application of scientific knowledge to production alleviates scarcity and provides a peaceful alternative to the pursuit of wealth by means of force. Thus, in the words of Hans Morgenthau, "The empire of man over nature replaces the empire of man over man."[17]

Thomas Hobbes's depiction of the state of nature in Part 1, Chapter 13 of *Leviathan*[18] is widely viewed as the foundation of modern realism. According to Hobbes, the fundamental interests of actors in a state of nature—"gain, safety, and reputation"—cannot be attained simultaneously by two different individuals, or, by extension, two different governments; hence a state of nature will always become a state of war. But if the yearning for glory has ceased to animate us, if wealth can be achieved without the exercise of military power, and if defense dominates offense on the battlefield, the range of issues over which conflict could arise has narrowed decisively. The anxieties that have fostered insecurity should then ease and the preoccupation with security diminish. The state of nature should no longer tend toward a state of war. In the past, military strength has afforded great powers influence not only over those they can coerce but also over those who needed their protection. The farther international affairs moves from Hobbesian anarchy, the less states will need this sort of protection and the weaker will be the influence enjoyed by states that can provide it.

Many will find this an attractive vision of the future. But is it a realistic one? The optimists have advanced a linear view of history. Secular forces are at work, they believe, that are bringing a permanent and irreversible decline in the efficacy of military force. But are there other forces in play that could hinder this transformation of the state of nature, halt the demilitarization of national

---

16. Francis Bacon, *Novum Organum*, First Book, Section 129.
17. Hans Morgenthau, *Scientific Man and Power Politics* (Chicago: University of Chicago Press, 1946), p. 43.
18. Thomas Hobbes, *Leviathan* (Harmondsworth, U.K.: Penguin, 1968).

and international politics, and perhaps restore to military force its once central role in world affairs? In which direction, then, are the tides of history running? These are the questions to which I now turn.

The Revolution in Military Affairs

Many military analysts believe that the application of information technology is bringing about a change in the practice of warfare as profound as those resulting from gunpowder and nuclear weapons.[19] The term "military revolution" was coined by historian Michael Roberts in 1955 to convey the importance of the changes in military organization and strategy conceived and implemented by Maurice of Nassau and Gustavus Adolphus between 1560 and 1660. Usage has since broadened to mean any epochal shift in military technique, organization, and strategy. The military revolutions of the past have had a profound impact on the evolution of domestic society, the balance of power, the conduct of war, and the prospects for peace.[20] The revolutions initiated by Napoleon and the German high command of the 1930s, for example, shifted the balance decisively to the offense and made possible their grasp for dominion on a continental scale. The revolution in military affairs now in progress may be no less far-reaching in its consequences. The technological bases of the ongoing revolution are dramatic improvements in the accuracy and range of weaponry, the acuity of reconnaissance and surveillance, the ease of deception and suppression of the enemy's defenses, and the effectiveness of command and control. If exploited effectively by changes in organization and doctrine, these innovations promise both to ease the restraints against the use of force and to increase substantially its efficacy, particularly when applied against adversaries who have not mastered this way of war.[21]

19. James FitzSimonds and Jan van Tol, "Revolutions in Military Affairs," *Joint Forces Quarterly*, No. 4 (Spring 1994), pp. 25–27; Dan Gouré, "Is There a Military-Technological Revolution in America's Future?" *Washington Quarterly*, Vol. 16, No. 4 (Autumn 1993), pp. 177–181; William Perry, "Desert Storm and Deterrence," *Foreign Affairs*, Vol. 70, No. 4 (Fall 1991), p. 66–69; International Institute for Strategic Studies, *Strategic Survey 1995–1996* (London: International Institute for Strategic Studies, 1996), pp. 31–32; and Andrew Krepinevich, "Cavalry to Computer: The Pattern of Military Revolutions," *National Interest*, No. 37 (Fall 1994), pp. 30, 40.
20. Michael Roberts, "The Military Revolution, 1560–1660," in Clifford J. Rogers, ed., *The Military Revolution Debate* (Boulder, Colo.: Westview, 1995); and Krepinevich, "Cavalry to Computer," pp. 30–31.
21. Michael Mazarr, *The Military Technical Revolution: A Structural Framework* (Washington, D.C.: Center for Strategic and International Studies, 1993), pp. 15–21, 59–60; William Owens, "Introduction," in Stuart E. Johnson and Martin Libicki, eds., *Dominant Battlespace Knowledge: The Winning*

Although the information revolution in warfare was only in its initial stages in 1991, the Gulf War provided ample evidence of the opportunities and dangers it may bring. The most impressive weapon in action during the Gulf conflict was the F-117A fighter-bomber. F-117As flew only 2 percent of U.S. sorties in the Gulf War but accounted for 40 percent of the damage done to strategic targets. Overall, more than 80 percent of the bombs dropped by F-117As are thought to have hit their target, and none of the aircraft was shot down. In a comparative case study of twenty-four sorties, the Gulf War Air Power Survey (GWAPS) found that F-111Es using unguided Mk-82 bombs destroyed two targets in twelve sorties with 168 bombs, while F-117As struck twenty-six targets successfully in their twelve sorties with only twenty-eight precision-guided bombs.[22] These remarkable results were attained through a combination of stealth and precision. During the raids on Germany and Japan, the average error probable was measured at best in thousands of feet and sometimes in miles. F-16s have far better navigation systems than B-29s, but achieved an accuracy of only 200 feet dropping unguided bombs from 17,000 feet. Laser-guided munitions, on the other hand, attained an accuracy of one to two feet during the Gulf War, and 85 percent of the smart bombs dropped landed within ten feet of their target. As one U.S. Air Force officer remarked, the question was no longer which building to target but which room—or in some instances, which part of the room.[23]

Edge (Washington, D.C.: National Defense University Press, 1995), pp. 4–5; Joseph Nye Jr. and William Owens, "America's Information Edge," *Foreign Affairs*, Vol. 75, No. 2 (March/April 1996), p. 23; Eliot A. Cohen, "A Revolution in Warfare," *Foreign Affairs*, Vol. 75, No. 2 (March/ April 1996), p. 44; Steven Metz and James Kievet, *Strategy and the Revolution in Military Affairs* (Carlisle, Penn.: Strategic Studies Institute, 1995); Jeffrey Cooper, *Another View of the Revolution in Military Affairs* (Carlisle, Penn.: Strategic Studies Institute, 1994); Michael Mazarr, *The Revolution in Military Affairs* (Carlisle, Penn.: Strategic Studies Institute, 1994); Michael Vickers, "The Revolution in Military Affairs and Military Capabilities," in Robert Pfaltzgraff and Richard Schultz, eds., *War in the Information Age* (McLean, Va.: Brassey's, forthcoming 1997); and Perry, "Desert Storm and Deterrence," pp. 66–69.
22. James Winnifield, Preston Niblack, and Dana J. Johnson, *A League of Airmen* (Santa Monica, Calif.: RAND, 1994), p. 247; Perry, "Desert Storm and Deterrence," p. 76; R.A. Mason, "The Air War in the Gulf," *Survival*, Vol. 33, No. 3 (May/June 1991), p. 215; and Thomas Keaney and Eliot A. Cohen, *Gulf War Air Power Survey: Summary Report* (Washington, D.C.: U.S. Government Printing Office, 1993), p. 243.
23. Edward Luttwak, "Air Power in U.S. Military Strategy," in Richard Schultz and Robert Pfaltzgraff, eds., *The Future of Air Power in the Aftermath of the Gulf War* (Maxwell Air Force Base, Ala.: Air University Press, 1992), pp. 19–20; and Richard Hallion, *Storm over Iraq: Air Power and the Gulf War* (Washington, D.C.: Smithsonian Institution Press, 1992), pp. 188–189, 212, 264. The initial claims for munitions may have been exaggerated. "One target, one kill" lethality was not achieved during the Gulf War because of the inaccuracy of bomb damage assessment. See U.S. General Accounting Office, *Operation Desert Storm: Evaluation of the Air War*, U.S. GAO/PEMD-96-10

Accuracy makes weapons more lethal to targets but less destructive to their surrounding communities. Iraq suffered remarkably few civilian casualties (1,500–2,000 dead according to U.S. estimates) in view of the intensity of the coalition raids.[24] In the words of a Dutch human rights observer, "What struck me most was how little damage allied air raids had actually caused to civilian areas, relative to the amount of bombs said to have been dropped. Especially in Baghdad, the bombing was eerily precise." One peace activist found the Iraqi capital to be "a city whose homes and offices were almost entirely intact," but noted that some of her colleagues were lamenting that smart bombs do not "produce the kinds of images that mobilize peace movements."[25] The fateful correlation between military efficacy and random devastation that had increasingly characterized war over the past centuries has been decisively broken. War will not become antiseptic—it will still involve smashing things and hurting people—but it should be possible to wage it in the future without the massive damage to civilian life and property that has occurred in all major conflicts of the twentieth century, from the Great War to Vietnam.

The impressive improvements in the accuracy of weapons mean that more of what is seen can be destroyed, and with the expected enhancements in sensors, more of the enemy's forces will be seen. During the Gulf War, systems such as JSTARS (joint surveillance target attack radar system) and AWACS (airborne warning and control system) provided the Coalition with an unprecedented understanding of developments on the battlefield. Because their target acquisition technology is radar based, they can provide real-time coverage over an extensive area in nearly all weather conditions. A state possessing RMA technology will begin a future war with superior sensors that permit its commander to see the enemy's forces much better than his are seen. This "information dominance" should allow the commander to bring the enemy under threat while his own forces remain much less vulnerable. Once the RMA power has demonstrated the ability to kill nearly all of what it sees, simply communicating to the enemy that "we know where you are" may be enough

---

(Washington, D.C.: U.S. GAO, July 1996). Improvements here are likely. The Lacrosse radar-imaging satellite can already penetrate clouds, although only over a limited area, and the Department of Defense's research efforts are intended to provide wide area, all-weather, day and night, foliage-penetrating coverage for both target acquisition and prompt bomb damage assessment by early in the next century. See *Defense Science and Technology Strategy* (Washington, D.C.: Department of Defense, Director of Defense Research and Engineering, July 1992), pp. II-8, II-16.

24. Mason, "Air War," p. 225; and Hallion, *Storm over Iraq*, pp. 190–193.

25. Quotations from Jeffrey Record, *Hollow Victory* (McLean, Va.: Brassey's, 1993), p. 112; and Hallion, *Storm over Iraq*, pp. 199–200.

to persuade them to surrender or withdraw. Even if the more visionary plans for nonlethal force cannot be brought to fruition, the advantages of information dominance, in combination with the enhanced protection afforded to civilians by smart weapons, may do much to diminish humanitarian and moral objections to the use of force.

Even the most humane of peoples are more concerned about the lives of their own soldiers than those of opposing civilians and combatants. Here, too, the results of the Gulf War suggest that restraints on the use of force are likely to ease. Early computer estimates projected 40,000 U.S. casualties, with 10,000 of them fatalities; in the event, U.S. forces suffered only 148 killed out of 540,000 participants. During the Vietnam War the United States lost one plane in every twenty-five sorties. Twenty-seven aircraft were lost in the Gulf War, one for every 750 sorties, against an opponent who had invested very heavily in air defense.[26] Some observers contend that this astonishing outcome was an anomaly arising from unusual circumstances and thus provides no clear indication of future trends. The battlefield was a flat and featureless desert that was easily scanned and ideal for mobile warfare, and Saddam Hussein was an incompetent strategist and uninspiring leader who first exposed his forces to six weeks of bombardment, then failed to anticipate the main direction of the Coalition's attack. The troops themselves, it is alleged, were poorly motivated, poorly led, and poorly trained. Stephen Biddle, for example, contends that if the Republican Guards had dug in their tanks more skillfully at the Battle of 73 Easting, they would have inflicted very heavy casualties on the Coalition. Smart weapons, it seems, are particularly lethal only to dumb opponents. In short, Iraq was the perfect battlefield and Saddam Hussein and his troops, "the perfect enemy."[27]

Although peculiarities of circumstance no doubt contributed to the disproportionate ratio of casualties, they alone cannot explain it. In point of fact, the weather during the Gulf conflict was the worst in the region in fifteen years, and identification of the enemy would have been very difficult under such conditions without the aid of JSTARS.[28] Furthermore, the better Iraqi divisions,

---

26. Freedman and Karsh, *Gulf Conflict*, pp. 302–303, 391; and Record, *Hollow Victory*, p. 84.

27. Michael Mazarr, Don Snider, and James Blackwell Jr., *Desert Storm: The Gulf War and What We Learned* (Boulder, Colo.: Westview, 1993), pp. 113–114; John Mueller, "The Perfect Enemy: Assessing the Gulf War," *Security Studies*, Vol. 5, No. 1 (Autumn 1995), pp. 77–117; and Stephen Biddle, "Victory Misunderstood: What the Gulf War Tells Us about the Future of Conflict," *International Security*, Vol. 21, No. 2 (Fall 1996), pp. 149–151, 158–161, 166–168.

28. Robert Scales Jr., *Certain Victory* (Washington, D.C.: U.S. Army, 1993), pp. 169, 371–372.

unlike the Kurdish and Shi'ite conscripts entrenched on the border, displayed determination and courage on several occasions, though to no avail. The only Iraqi offensive of the war, the attack on al-Khafji on January 29–30, turned into a debacle for the 5th Mechanized Division. Although considered to be one of Iraq's finest, it proved incapable of coordinating complex maneuvers (some units ended up lost in the desert) and was pounded relentlessly from the air. In the pivotal tank confrontations at the end of the ground campaign on February 25–27, the Republican Guards were repeatedly surprised, in some instances caught eating lunch, or with their tanks facing the wrong direction, or even with their tanks' batteries removed to power heaters and lights. Incompetence alone cannot account for this. The Coalition's air campaign had disrupted the Iraqis' communications, blinded them, and stripped them of air cover. In a war of movement, they were desperately vulnerable.[29] During these battles the unusually inclement weather sometimes grounded Coalition aircraft, but the crews of the United States' M1 tanks, possessing not only superior armor and longer-range guns but also thermal sights, were still able to peer through the rain and mist to locate and destroy enemy tanks. Even in encounters where Pentagon analysts judged their defensive positions to be well prepared, the hapless Iraqis were still routed.[30]

Future opponents may be luckier or more competent than Iraq, but RMA powers will continue to enjoy decisive advantages over their adversaries. Three advantages merit emphasis here. First, accuracy means that pilots can accomplish much more with fewer missions and thus greatly reduced risk. Second, most of the "searching" during the Vietnam War was done by highly vulnerable ground forces and most of the "destroying" by less vulnerable air power. Improvements in sensors should make it much easier to locate the enemy without putting ground forces at risk in this way.[31] Third, long-range precision strikes launched from stealthy platforms should make possible "disengaged combat" in which RMA forces will be able to inflict heavy damage

29. William Taylor and James Blackwell Jr., "The Ground War in the Gulf," *Survival*, Vol. 33, No. 3 (May/June 1991), pp. 234–235, 243; Lawrence Freedman and Efraim Karsh, *The Gulf Conflict 1990–1991* (Princeton, N.J.: Princeton University Press, 1993), p. 324; Keaney and Cohen, *GWAPS*, "Operations and Effectiveness," Vol. 2, p. 224; Rick Atkinson, *Crusade* (Boston: Houghton Mifflin, 1993), p. 465; Thomas A. Keaney, "The Linkage of Air and Ground Power in the Future of Conflict," *International Security*, Vol. 22, No. 2 (Fall 1997), pp. 148–149; and Scales, *Certain Victory*, p. 373.
30. Atkinson, *Crusade*, pp. 252, 466–467; Norman Friedman, *Desert Victory* (Annapolis, Md.: Naval Institute Press), p. 234; and *Conduct of the Persian Gulf War: Final Report to Congress*, April 1992, pp. 277–281.
31. Libicki, "DBK and Its Consequences," in Johnson and Libicki, *Dominant Battlespace Knowledge*, pp. 39–41.

on the enemy at minimal risk. By targeting the enemy's longest-range systems first, RMA forces should be able to close on the enemy gradually while remaining nearly invulnerable to counterattack. The military effectiveness and limited costs in life of these tactics should do much to overcome the reluctance of democratic publics to commit their forces to battle.

U.S. professional soldiers, as measured not only by their performance on the battlefield but also through reliable quantitative indices such as desertions, demonstrated vastly superior morale to the Iraqi conscripts facing them.[32] Complex weapons systems require high levels of training that cannot easily be provided to draftees: "Smart weapons require smart soldiers."[33] The more expensive the technology of war and the more difficult it is to master, the greater is the advantage of quality over quantity on the battlefield. Hence the day of the conscript soldier has passed. This, too, has important implications for the utility of force. Democracies will probably never cease to agonize over the resort to war, but in the event, it will be much easier to dispatch career soldiers who have voluntarily agreed to risk their lives than conscripts who are compelled to serve. Moreover, it may soon be possible to substitute military machines for soldiers in many tasks. Dozens of pilotless aircraft, or unmanned aerial vehicles, were deployed in the Gulf War for the purpose of surveillance, and they will probably dominate airborne reconnaissance in the future. Cruise missiles also played a vital role in the initial assault on Iraq's air defenses. Deep strikes of this sort, which achieve high levels of accuracy without putting at risk the lives of pilots, are expected to figure prominently in future war plans. The U.S. Army's *STAR: 21* study predicts that its core military platform of the twenty-first century, analogous to the tank in this one, "may well be an unmanned system."[34]

If the RMA does indeed fulfill the hopes of its proponents, not only will the moral and political restraints against the use of force ease, but the prospects for successful offensive action at reasonable cost will also improve, for several reasons. One of the most important sources of friction in the past has been the fog of battle, the literal or figurative obscurity of the events on the battlefield

---

32. Taylor and Blackwell, "The Ground War in the Gulf," p. 240; and Record, *Hollow Victory*, p. 80.
33. William Odom, *America's Military Revolution: Strategy and Structure after the Cold War* (Washington, D.C.: American University Press, 1993), p. 54; and Mazarr, *Revolution in Military Affairs*, p. 29.
34. Vickers, "The Revolution in Military Affairs and Military Capabilities"; Shukman, *Tomorrow's War*, pp. 177–185; and Gouré, "Is There a Military-Technological Revolution in America's Future?" p. 180.

to the military leadership, which has made it impossible for them to employ their forces with complete effectiveness. At times, soldiers have roamed the field of battle for all intents and purposes beyond the control of the commander, and the issue was settled more by chance than strategy. One of the most important of all aspects of the RMA is the promise that new sensors and communication nodes will disperse the fog of war through quantum improvement in the quality of intelligence and the effectiveness of communications. Technologies such as the global positioning system, digital radios, defense communications satellites, AWACS, and JSTARS afforded Coalition commanders unparalleled situational awareness during the Gulf War. Although friction can never be reduced to zero, the results attained from a given force should be greatly enhanced and the uncertainties that have made war "the province of chance" much diminished. It may thus be possible to achieve decisive military superiority over less sophisticated opponents without a quantitative advantage or even with lesser numbers. Under such conditions, arms control treaties that attempt to discourage aggression by equalizing force levels will afford states much less protection.

It has always been necessary in the past for the offense to concentrate its forces at one point in order to break through the defense. Such forces then became vulnerable to counterattack, which is why defense has always in some measure had the advantage over offense. Already, widely dispersed systems can rain down fire at a specific point when effectively directed. With continued improvements in the range and accuracy of weaponry and the effectiveness of command and coordination, it will become increasingly possible for the offense to concentrate fire but not forces before the enemy, which may shift the eternal contest between offense and defense decisively in favor of the attacker.

If and when the time comes to concentrate force, this will happen at unprecedented speed. Heavy armor will be increasingly vulnerable on future battlefields. With further advances in materials technology and electronics, however, it should be possible to decrease the weight of tanks and other instruments of land warfare by eliminating some of the crew and reducing the armor, relying instead on stealth and improved range for protection against the enemy. This improvement in punch for pound will not only enhance the survivability of major land platforms, but will also make possible much more rapid engagement on the battlefield. As mobility increases, so too does the attractiveness of offensive action.

Finally, stealth strengthens the attacker by restoring the prospects for surprise, perhaps close to the levels prevailing before the invention of radar, while accuracy radically diminishes the number of aircraft and tonnage of bombs needed to destroy a given set of targets. These capabilities may enable an RMA power to paralyze and demoralize the enemy without destroying his forces in detail by incapacitating key logistical, communications, and defense systems. The Gulf War provides impressive although perhaps not conclusive evidence of the effectiveness of strategic bombing when implemented with advanced technology. Skeptics correctly point out that strategic bombing alone did not compel Saddam Hussein to withdraw from Kuwait—only the imminent destruction of the Republican Guards accomplished that—but its indirect contribution was nonetheless substantial.[35] F-117s, Tomahawk cruise missiles, and fighters equipped with radiation-seeking missiles neutralized Iraq's formidable air defenses in the first days of the war, guaranteeing the Coalition command of the air through the duration of the campaign. The attrition of Iraq's forces, by means such as the innovative and deadly "tank plinking" by F-111s, was thereby greatly facilitated.[36] Coalition aircraft also destroyed fifty of Iraq's bridges, reduced its electricity generation to 15 percent of prewar capacity, and shut down its oil refineries altogether in a matter of weeks with only a small fraction of the sorties that were necessary for the same purposes against Nazi Germany or Vietnam. The loss of electrical power presented insurmountable difficulties for nearly every Iraqi military activity, and the resulting interdiction of the Kuwaiti Theater of Operations (KTO) gave rise to severe shortages that contributed heavily to the demoralization of the unfortunate conscripts whom Saddam Hussein positioned on the border.[37] Iraq was by no means uniquely vulnerable in this respect. The number of key production targets is limited even in larger, more advanced societies, and most will remain highly vulnerable to strategic attack.

The strikes against Iraq's leadership, and command, control, and communications, and intelligence (C^3I) did not eliminate Saddam Hussein and apparently did not completely sever communications between Baghdad and the

---

35. Robert Pape, *Bombing to Win: Air Power and Coercion in War* (Ithaca, N.Y.: Cornell University Press, 1996), chapters 7, 9; and Scales, *Certain Victory*, pp. 366–368.
36. Perry, "Desert Storm and Deterrence," pp. 73–75; and Mazarr, Snider, and Blackwell, *Desert Storm*, pp. 93, 97, 107, 121–122.
37. Keaney and Watts, *GWAPS*, Vol. 2, "Operations and Effectiveness," pp. 224–225, 303; Colonel John Warden, "Employing Air Power in the Twenty-first Century," in Schultz and Pfaltzgraff, *The Future of Air Power in the Aftermath of the Gulf War*, pp. 71–79; Hallion, *Storm over Iraq*, pp. 191–193; and Freedman and Karsh, *Gulf Conflict*, pp. 321–322, 389.

KTO. They did, however, eliminate Iraq's capacity to coordinate complex ground-force operations in the Kuwaiti theater, as was evident from the confusion at al-Khafji. Although the damage to Iraq's C^3I did not induce Saddam to yield, it left his forces nearly powerless to react effectively to the Coalition's massive flanking maneuver.[38] Destruction of the enemy's means of gathering intelligence and controlling his forces generally produces a tremendous shock effect and it did so in the Gulf War, demoralizing and befuddling the Iraqi troops. Future opponents may judge continued resistance to be fruitless once they have been deprived of the ability to command their forces and to see the enemy. Quick and relatively bloodless victories would then be possible through the early elimination of the enemy's C^3I and other strategic targets. The mere threat of destroying the enemy's armed forces piece by piece and inflicting pain on civilians may not be sufficient to compel surrender—it was not with Saddam—but, at the very least, successful strategic bombing substantially increases the prospects and lowers the costs of victory for an RMA power. One caveat is in order, however. Some analysts contend that the decentralization of telecommunications, proliferation of unmanned reconnaissance vehicles, and widening access to global positioning satellites will render other societies less vulnerable to attacks on C^3I, making information dominance harder to achieve in the future than it was in the Gulf.[39]

For Colonel John Warden, a leading advocate of strategic bombing, the upshot of these developments is that "offense again has clearly assumed the dominant position in warfare."[40] For Jeffrey Cooper, they will make possible "the return of Clausewitzian decisive victories in place of attrition warfare." Would these assertions still hold true if an advanced RMA power were to confront a less advanced state armed with unconventional weapons, or a

---

38. Freedman and Karsh, *Gulf Conflict*, p. 324; Taylor and Blackwell, "The Ground War in the Gulf," pp. 234–235, 243; *GWAPS*, Vol. 2, pp. 224, 288–289, quotation on p. 343; Atkinson, *Crusade*, p. 465; and Scales, *Certain Victory*, p. 373. Coalition attacks on C^3I were less than totally successful for three reasons. First, Iraq's communications system was hardened to withstand nuclear war (Warden, "Employing Air Power," p. 57). Second, the Iraqis took effective countermeasures, including the threat of death sentences for users of two-way radios in Kuwait. Reliance on underground cables, however, led to the "collapse" of their system when they were forced to move by Coalition forces (*GWAPS*, Vol. 2, pp. 223–234). Third, the Coalition may have opted to leave some lines of communication open in order to monitor the enemy or find its leadership (Pape, *Bombing to Win*, pp. 239–240).
39. Eliot A. Cohen, "The Meaning and Future of Air Power," *Orbis*, Vol. 39, No. 2 (Spring 1995), pp. 193–196.
40. Warden, "Employing Air Power," in Schultz and Pfaltzgraff, *The Future of Air Power*, p. 79, also 60–61, 80; Jeffrey Cooper, "Dominant Battlespace Awareness and Future Warfare," in Johnson and Libicki, *Dominant Battlespace Knowledge*, p. 115; see also Vickers, "The Revolution in Military Affairs and Military Capabilities," p. 6.

technological peer? It is possible, although admittedly this is a strong claim— that the current RMA will at least partially reverse the consequences of the nuclear revolution. U.S. Army Lieutenant General William Odom (ret.), for example, has suggested that "the Gulf War, if it has implications for nuclear war, would seem to reinforce the view that nuclear weapons are being transcended in their importance to modern warfare by new weapons technologies."[41] Modern conventional munitions should be capable of assuming many of the missions heretofore assigned to nuclear weapons, including the demanding task of countering an enemy's atomic arsenal. One aim of the "Defense Counterproliferation Initiative," announced by the Clinton administration on December 7, 1993, is to enable the United States to disarm an enemy possessing weapons of mass destruction by means of a preemptive strike with conventional ordnance. Technology such as precision-guided weapons, earth-penetrating warheads and sensors, and special munitions designed to destroy unconventional weapons could make this possible.[42] As a last resort, nuclear deterrence may suffice. The United States faced an opponent in the Gulf War, after all, who possessed chemical weapons, and not only were these weapons not used, they were not even distributed to field commanders, apparently because Saddam had been warned explicitly by then-Secretary of State James Baker.[43] Eventually, the combination of a conventional first strike, theater ballistic missile defense, and nuclear deterrence may effectively negate the importance of a small or medium-sized nuclear force.

The RMA should weaken resistance to the use of force by limiting the damage done to the enemy's society, eliminating reliance on conscripts, and improving the prospects for early victory at reasonable cost. The possession of these capabilities by a power strongly committed to the international status quo should discourage conventional aggression and exert a profoundly stabilizing influence on world politics. Aggressors may seek to challenge the United States with asymmetrical strategies, but the most obvious of these—guerrilla war and terrorism—are not well adapted for the seizure of territory.[44] Conven-

---

41. Odom, *America's Military Revolution*, pp. 61–62; also Mazarr, *Revolution in Military Affairs*, p. 32. Vickers, in "The Revolution in Military Affairs and Military Capabilities," pp. 13–14, is more guarded.
42. Joseph Pilat and Walter Kirchner, "The Technological Promise of Counterproliferation," *Washington Quarterly*, Vol. 18, No. 1 (Winter 1995), pp. 155–156, 160–161; Mazarr, *Revolution in Military Affairs*, pp. 31–32; and Hallion, *Storm over Iraq*, p. 266.
43. Freedman and Karsh, *Gulf Conflict*, pp. 397–398.
44. Caveat from Brian Nichiporuk and Carl Builder, *Information Technologies and the Future of Land Warfare* (Santa Monica, Calif.: RAND, 1995), pp. 49–52, and Cohen, "A Revolution in Warfare," p. 51; rebuttal from Bevin Alexander, *The Future of Warfare* (New York: Norton, 1995), pp. 46,

tional force will remain useful as long as these conditions obtain precisely because it will not have to be used very frequently. The United States' monopoly of the RMA cannot last indefinitely, however, given that the civilian technologies on which it is based are already spreading rapidly. (Twenty nations can already produce precision-guided munitions).[45] The uneven progress of military technology and organization invariably gives rise to large inequalities of power between states. When such improvements have also strengthened offensive force against defense, the ability of leading states to seize territory has been decisively enhanced.[46] The same technologies that permitted the United States to regain Kuwait at low cost would also allow a future revisionist power to inflict a rapid and decisive defeat on an adversary without destroying its economy. Hence, the diffusion of the information-based RMA should increase the utility of force for offensive purposes and widen opportunities for territorial expansion, provided of course that other RMA powers are willing to stand aside.

If, on the other hand, the United States or some other defender of the status quo were to intervene against a technological peer, what would be the result? The possible course and outcome of a war between two RMA powers is obviously difficult to predict, but it is an issue that must eventually be faced. Presumably the accuracy of weapons would mean that losses to civilians would remain modest as long as mutual restraint were to hold. Improvements in intelligence and in the lethality of weaponry, however, could make such an engagement as sanguinary for soldiers as the trenches of the Western front. The potentially high rates of attrition could lead to a gruesome stalemate on the battlefield or, alternatively, induce a degree of caution on both sides that would preclude a decisive result.[47] Furthermore, in a battlespace where nearly everything that is seen is destroyed, remaining invisible to the enemy would become the key to survival. Because forces on the move generate much more data for the opponent's sensors and offense is impossible without movement, taking territory could be much more difficult than holding it. Hence, Martin

---

219–220. According to the Director of Defense Research's report, sensors may soon be capable of penetrating foliage, which may alter the view that the U.S. military "does not do jungles." *Defense Science and Technology Strategy*, p. II-16.

45. Earl Tilford, *The Revolution in Military Affairs: Prospects and Cautions* (Carlisle, Penn.: Strategic Studies Institute, 1995), p. 16; Alexander, *Future of Warfare*, pp. 79–82; and Krepinevich, "Cavalry to Computer," pp. 37–42.

46. Gilpin, *War and Change in International Politics*, pp. 61–63.

47. Mazarr, *Revolution in Military Affairs*, pp. 19–20, quotation at p. 16; and Metz and Kievit, *Strategy and the Revolution in Military Affairs*, p. 24.

Libicki maintains, defense would dominate offense if two RMA powers faced each other.[48] Libicki assumes that sensors will improve faster than will stealth, however, and this may not prove to be the case. Further development of stealth or countersensor technology, including improvements by adversaries of the United States, is certainly conceivable. Even a temporary advantage in concealment over detection could shift the advantage swiftly to the attacker. Thus far, according to Richard Hallion, there appears to be no truly effective countermeasure to the stealth fighter and there may never be. Eighty years after the invention of the submarine, he notes, it still remains difficult to detect.[49] Other factors will also favor the aggressor. The enhanced mobility of land forces and the capacity to concentrate fire without concentrating force, as aforementioned, should strengthen the offense; but most important of all, the initiator may hope that a preemptive attack on the opponent's C3I systems and air defenses will yield early information dominance and a quick and relatively easy victory. Indeed, the fear that the opponent might launch such an attack first could be a persuasive argument for preemption.

Population Growth and Its Consequences

The RMA can be expected to ease the restraints, reduce the costs, and increase the effectiveness of the use of force for some purposes, and may shift the strategic advantage from the defender to the attacker. If so, large-scale conventional warfare will become more feasible than it has been at any time since the advent of blitzkrieg. The attractiveness of war, however, depends not only on the productivity of military capabilities but also on the ends for which they are employed. Mueller and Fukuyama maintain that the yearning for honor through conquest has vanished; while the descendants of Francis Bacon and Adam Smith believe that war is "irrational" because trade and industrialization are more effective means of achieving prosperity. Will there, then, be anything to fight about in the future? A second trend in contemporary history, the enormous expansion of world population now in process, suggests that we have no grounds for complacency.

---

48. Libicki, "DBK and Its Consequences," pp. 40–41, 45.
49. Ibid.," pp. 34–36. For rebuttals, see Alexander, *Future of Warfare*, p. 50; Warden, "Employing Air Power," p. 81; Vickers, "The Revolution in Military Affairs and Military Capabilities," pp. 11–12; Gouré, "Is There a Military-Technological Revolution in America's Future?" p. 180; and Hallion, *Storm over Iraq*, p. 249.

The world's inhabitants now number approximately 5.6 billion. Because of the comparative youth of much of the current population, even if replacement fertility were achieved immediately, the expansion would not cease until 2050, when it would reach 8.5 billion. Estimates of the ultimate peak population vary widely, of course, but the United Nations' medium projection is 10 billion by 2050, nearly double the current total.[50] The earth's population is increasingly concentrated in cities. By 2025, Latin America is expected to be 85 percent urban and Africa will have an urban majority. Unless nearly miraculous rates of economic development are achieved, much of this urban population will remain impoverished. Half of the residents of cities such as Delhi, Nairobi, and Manila are already living in slums.[51] These developments may hold profound significance for international security.

Mueller has concluded that the reluctance to employ force has its origins in a higher valuation of human life, but provides no clear explanation for this occurrence. It is possible, of course, that this shift in moral thinking has no material cause at all and has evolved through a gradual process of moral enlightenment over the centuries. If so, one wonders why it took an entire millennium after the introduction of the humanitarian ideals of the New Testament into Western societies for this increased valuation of human life to take root. Edward Luttwak has provided a simple but compelling answer. As long as women bore six or seven children and usually lost several to disease or malnutrition, he says, adults were inured to death and could bear with some equanimity the loss of one or two of their sons in battle. Once societies achieved replacement levels of fertility, the death of a child became a shocking abnormality and an irreplaceable loss.[52] More than any other factor, this may explain why advanced industrial societies have been reluctant to suffer casualties recently on the battlefield. In the developing world outside China, however, the average number of children per family is still 4.4, and replacement levels of fertility are not expected to occur in India until 2030 and in Africa until 2050.[53] If Luttwak's hypothesis is correct, these societies should remain more prone to violence until that stage is reached.

---

50. George Moffett, *Critical Masses: The Global Population Challenge* (New York: Viking, 1994), pp. 7–9.
51. Ibid., pp. 29–32.
52. Edward Luttwak, "Where Are the Great Powers?" *Foreign Affairs*, Vol. 73, No. 4 (July/August, 1994), p. 115.
53. Moffett, *Critical Masses*, pp. 8–9.

Rapid population growth and urbanization have been associated throughout the modern era with violent upheavals in domestic politics that have brought to power belligerent autocracies hostile to the prevailing international order. William McNeill contends that the 44 percent rise in population between 1715 and 1789 first destabilized France's old regime by filling the cities and countryside with desperate men, then provided its successor with both the means and the motive for expansion. Because the *grande armée* was raised by conscription and fed by foraging off the land, Napoleon quite literally exported France's population problem and in so doing created a force that was not only larger but much more mobile than that of his enemies.[54] In the years after the French Revolution, peasant rebellion demolished the old order and prepared the way for totalitarian regimes in Russia, China, and elsewhere. Eric Wolf's research has shown that one common thread in all of these revolutionary situations was the explosive growth of population leading to immiseration of the rural poor. In European Russia, for example, the population rose from 36 million in 1796 to 129 million in 1900. In China the numbers swelled from the already enormous figure of 265 million in 1775 to 430 million in 1850 and then to 600 million during the 1940s.[55] According to Jack Goldstone, all of the major upheavals in modern Chinese history (the collapse of the Ming dynasty, the Taiping rebellion, and the revolutions of 1911 and 1949) were preceded by a sharp deterioration in the land to labor ratio.[56]

The threat of peasant rebellion may remain with us for some time, as the recent uprising in Chiapas, Mexico, suggests, but the most dangerous class of the next century will probably be the urban poor of the less developed countries. It is they who formed the shock troops of the Iranian Revolution and who now provide the mass base of support for Islamist movements in the Arab world.[57] Their existence calls into question the optimistic predictions of Fukuyama and others that the end of history and the universal spread of democracy are at hand. The prospects for democracy must remain highly

---

54. William C. McNeill, *The Pursuit of Power* (Chicago: University of Chicago Press, 1982), pp. 145–146, 185–187, 192–200.
55. Eric Wolf, *Peasant Wars of the Twentieth Century* (New York: Harper and Row, 1968), pp. 281–282.
56. Jack Goldstone, "The Coming Chinese Collapse," *Foreign Policy*, No. 99 (Summer 1995), pp. 36–38.
57. Olivier Roy, *The Failure of Political Islam* (Cambridge, Mass.: Harvard University Press, 1994), pp. 53–55; Robert Kaplan, "The Coming Anarchy," *Atlantic Monthly* (February 1994), p. 66; and Robert Kaplan, *The Ends of the Earth* (New York: Random House, 1996), pp. 8–9, 32–33, 107–108, 350–351.

uncertain in countries whose capitals are ringed by wretched, importunate mobs. The more pertinent question may not be whether democracy can be sustained in such unfavorable circumstances, but rather whether these states will collapse into chaos or successfully mobilize and channel the discontent of the urban poor through extremist ideologies for a program of foreign aggression.[58]

Since the defeat of Hitler and Imperial Japan, the conquest of nature has provided a surer and safer path to enrichment than the conquest of territory. How much farther can the conquest of nature proceed? The harvest from the oceans is already at its limit; if more fish were removed than at present, stocks would diminish to the point where future catches would fall. On land, the outlook is more ambiguous, but recent statistics are not encouraging: the production of cereals dropped from 342 kilograms in 1984 to 326 kilograms per capita in 1990. The causes of this decline are manifold and will not be easily remedied. The amount of land under cultivation peaked in 1981 and has since fallen 8.5 percent. The speed of urbanization makes it likely that this trend will continue. Yields also appear to be reaching their limits. From 1950 to 1984, they doubled; but in the 1990s the global rate of improvement has slowed to 0.5 percent, which is less than one-third the rate of increase of population. Heavier fertilizer application has functioned as a substitute for land in the past, but its use also declined between 1989 and 1993, in part because of changes in government policy but also because after a point yields simply do not seem to respond much to additional fertilization. Irrigation, another crucial input, peaked in 1978 and has since declined 6 percent. The inflation-adjusted cost of the large-scale engineering projects needed to expand irrigation (i.e., dams, canals, and reservoirs) doubled in India from 1950 to 1980, which suggests that investment in irrigation is also strongly subject to diminishing returns. A repetition of the "green revolution" does not appear to be in prospect.[59]

The situation in China is particularly worrisome. China has one-fifth of the world's population but only 7 percent of its farmland (only Egypt and Bang-

58. Kaplan, "The Coming Anarchy," pp. 60, 74–75; Kaplan, *Ends of the Earth*, pp. 117, 125–126, 267, 272, 349–350; and Thomas Homer-Dixon, "Environmental Scarcity and Violent Conflict," *International Security*, Vol. 19, No. 1 (Summer 1994), p. 36. Homer-Dixon and Jack Goldstone foresee civil strife rather than interstate war as the likeliest result of growing scarcity. Both are quoted in Kaplan, *Ends of the Earth*, pp. 349–350.
59. Lester R. Brown and Hal Kane, *Full House* (New York: Norton, 1994), pp. 75–88, 96–97, 122–123, 136; Nikos Alexandratos, *World Agriculture: Towards 2010* (Chichester, U.K.: Wiley, 1995), p. 7; Gary Gardner, "Preserving Agricultural Resources," in Lester R. Brown et al., *State of the World 1996* (New York: Norton, 1996), pp. 79–84; and Sandra Postel, *Last Oasis: Facing Water Scarcity* (New York: Norton, 1992), pp. 40, 50–52; quotation in Moffett, *Critical Masses*, p. 74.

ladesh have less arable land per inhabitant), and much of this is of poor quality. Its share of the world's fresh water is also 7 percent, most of it in the south. These resources are already under heavy stress. By 1993, 100 of China's cities were experiencing severe water shortages, and in 1995 the Yellow River dried up 385 miles from the Pacific Ocean. The water table is falling at a rate of one meter per year in parts of northern China, including Beijing, where one-third of the wells are said to be dry.[60] Two Chinese scholars, having reviewed the studies of their country's carrying capacity conducted since the 1950s, concluded in 1988 that "the long-term strategic goal of China's population policy should be to limit the population below one billion, or ideally, below 700 million."[61] But China's population is expected to increase another 490 million by 2030 to reach 1.6–1.7 billion, while prosperity is enabling its inhabitants to "move up the food chain" and consume more meat, eggs, and beer. Lester Brown reckons that the combination of these trends will nearly double China's demand for grain by the year 2030. The prospects for meeting this demand from domestic sources he judges to be extremely unfavorable. He estimates that China's grain deficit will total some 207 million tons if there is no further increase in consumption of eggs, meat, and beer, and will rise to 369 million tons if grain consumption per capita increases to 400 kilograms yearly. This figure is nearly double the 200 million tons of grain that was available on world markets in 1994.[62]

Other observers are more sanguine. The International Food Policy Research Institute expects China's production of wheat, corn, and rice to rise 90 percent, 80 percent, and 54 percent by 2020, while the U.S. Department of Agriculture (USDA) projects 1 percent growth per year to 2020 in Chinese grain production. But even if China is able to meet the USDA's projection, it will still fall well short of the 33 percent rise in demand projected by Mei Fungquan of the Chinese Academy of Agricultural Science by 2010. Chinese government experts remain optimistic publicly about the long run but concede that grain

---

60. Homer-Dixon, "Environmental Scarcity and Violent Conflict," p. 38; Goldstone, "The Coming Chinese Collapse," p. 36; Megan Ryan and Christopher Flavin, "Facing China's Limits," in Lester R. Brown et al., *State of the World 1995* (New York: Norton, 1995), pp. 117–118; Martin Walker, "China and the New Era of Resource Scarcity," *World Policy Journal*, Vol. 13, No. 1 (Spring 1996), p. 10; and Postel, *Last Oasis*, pp. 34–35, 54.

61. Joel E. Cohen, *How Many People Can the Earth Support?* (New York: Norton, 1995), p. 224.

62. Lester Brown, *Who Will Feed China?* (New York: Norton, 1995), pp. 36, 45–46, 54–56, 71, 77–78, 94–97. A new rice strain developed in the Philippines promises to increase production 25 percent, but this would cover world population growth for only three years. Brown, "The Acceleration of History," in Brown et al., *State of the World 1996*, p. 11.

imports, perhaps 70 million tons by the year 2000, will be needed to bridge the gap in the near future.[63] Even if exporters prove capable of meeting the rising demand from China and other developing world importers, this will not necessarily produce a calming effect on world politics. Interdependence has in some instances intensified rather than moderated the conflicts between states. Japan's desire to escape dependence on the United States, for example, led to the attack on Pearl Harbor in 1941. Were the Chinese to become heavily dependent on the United States for grain, they would, at the very least, bid up the price of food and exacerbate poverty and food insecurity elsewhere. China would be compelled to pay the bill for the imports of grain by releasing a torrent of labor-intensive exports on world markets. Taiwan's exports average about $3,800 per capita. For China to gain only $500 per capita, its exports would have to rise from $85 billion (in 1994) to $750 billion, which is twice Japan's current total. It is not obvious that China's trading partners could absorb exports on such a scale without being besieged by demands for protection.[64] One may doubt, however, whether the current Chinese leadership or any future one would choose to place their country in a position where one dry month in Kansas could create shortages in Chinese cities or where they would be vulnerable to political pressure enforced with the threat of embargoes by grain exporters. The Chinese will not soon forget that 30 million died of starvation as a consequence of Mao Zedong's reckless social engineering in the late 1950s. China's minister of agriculture, Liu Jiang, stated emphatically in 1995 that "grain is an important product, which . . . is of great significance to social stability and national security. . . . China must not be dependent on the world market for grain."[65]

The more fundamental problem is that even if the Chinese are willing to accept dependence on the global market, the grain may simply not be available. The United Nations' Food and Agricultural Organization (FAO), whose analysts are much less Malthusian than Brown, expects a slowdown in the

---

63. Mei estimates that demand for grain in China will increase from 450 million tons in 1993 to 600 million in 2010, a 33 percent increase. One percent compounds to about 18.4 percent in seventeen years. Mei Fungquan, "Sustainable Food Production and Food Security in China," in *Food for All* (Bangkok: Food and Agriculture Organization Regional Office for Asia and the Pacific, 1995), p. 34; Margit Adam, "Can China Feed Its People? The Answer May Be No, then Yes," *FAO Review*, Vol. 27, No. 5 (September/October 1995), pp. 26–29.

64. Walker, "China and the New Era of Resource Scarcity," p. 11; Paul Kennedy, *Preparing for the Twenty-first Century* (New York: Random House, 1993), pp. 176–177. Export estimates from Goldstone, "The Coming Chinese Collapse," pp. 49–50.

65. Brown, *Who Will Feed China?* pp. 38, 102–104, 117, 122–123, 133; quoted in Adam, "Can China Feed Its People?" p. 28.

expansion of grain output among developing countries from the 3.0 percent annual growth of the 1960s to 1.8 percent up to 2010 and 1.3 percent thereafter. Output per capita may not increase at all. Land is being lost not only to urbanization but also to soil degradation (principally through erosion), which has already damaged 15 percent of the world's agricultural land severely and is continuing at an alarming pace. Improvements in productivity will probably also slow. Biotechnology may increase the resistance of plants to pests or permit wheat to be grown in salty soils, but it is not expected to generate quantum increases in yields. Undesirable side effects of the green revolution such as waterlogged soils, salinization, and resistance to pesticides continue to threaten the progress of the past generation. For these reasons, both the FAO and the International Food Policy Research Institute expect the developing countries' demand for food to outstrip their supply, necessitating an increase in food imports from 90 million metric tons today to between 160 and 180 tons by 2010. The FAO remains confident, however, that there is sufficient slack capacity in the developed economies to meet this demand, particularly if former communist countries succeed in reforming agriculture and become net exporters.[66]

This confidence may be misplaced. Global water utilization has tripled since 1950 to reach 4,340 cubic kilometers, two-thirds of which goes for irrigation. Assuming constant consumption per capita (which is optimistic), an additional 780 cubic kilometers will have to be tapped to meet projected demand by 2025. It is not altogether clear where this water will be found. China, India, Iran, Libya, Pakistan, and Saudi Arabia are all withdrawing groundwater faster than it is replenished by rainfall, and U.S. farmers have also been drawing water from the aquifers under the Great Plains and the Central Valley of California at rates that are unsustainable. The expected doubling of the world's urban population will sharpen the competition among agriculture, industry, and

---

66. Alexandratos, *World Agriculture: Towards 2010*, pp. 45, 79–80, 88, 119–120, 169–170, 178–179; Pierre Crosson, "Future Supplies of Land and Water for World Agriculture," in Nural Islam, ed., *Population and Food in the Early Twentieth Century* (Washington, D.C.: International Food Policy Research Institute, 1995), pp. 155–157; Peter Oram and Benhat Hojjati, "The Growth of Existing Agricultural Technology," in Islam, *Population and Food*, pp. 167, 174–175; Mercedita Agcaoili and Mark Rosegrant, "Global and Regional Food Supply, Demand, and Trade Prospects to 2010," in Islam, *Population and Food*, p. 70; Nural Islam, "Overview," in Islam, *Population and Food*, pp. 2–4; Donald Mitchell and Merlinda Ingco, "Global and Regional Food Demand and Supply Prospects," in Islam, *Population and Food*, pp. 52–56; Vaclav Smil, "How Many People Can the Earth Feed?" *Population and Development Review*, Vol. 20, No. 2 (June 1994), pp. 266, 277–278, 279–280; Paarlberg, "Rice Bowls and Dust Bowls," pp. 128–129; Adam, "Can China Feed Its People?" p. 28; Gardner, "Preserving Agricultural Resources," pp. 81–83, 87; and Postel, *Last Oasis*, pp. 53, 58.

residential use, most likely to the detriment of agriculture. Water tables are already falling rapidly under developing world metropolises such as Mexico City and Bangkok. Because 60 percent of the water drawn for irrigation is thought to be wasted, there is ample scope for conservation, but at some point, water will pose an inescapable constraint on the expansion of population and the enhancement of human welfare.[67]

Plants release large amounts of water in the process of photosynthesis, and little can be done to reduce the rate of transpiration. A minimum of approximately 200 tons of water is thus required each year to produce a daily diet of 2,000 calories of wheat. Plausible estimates of the total amount of fresh water available for human use vary from 9,000 to 14,000 cubic kilometers. If the higher figure proves to be correct, then, according to the calculations of Joel Cohen, 2,000 calories daily can be supplied to about 12 billion people. If the world holds 9,000 cubic kilometers, as the FAO estimates, then, according to Cohen's model, the world's fresh water will support at most 2 billion people at the current United States level of consumption (10,000 calories per day directly and indirectly) and will provide little more than an average of 1,500 daily calories per capita to a population of 10 billion, a level of subsistence close to starvation.[68] Recall that the United Nations' medium estimate for global population is 10 billion by 2050 and a maximum of 11.5 billion at some point in the twenty-second century.[69]

The Spread of Industrialization

The pressure of population on global food supplies coincides with a third secular trend, the spread of industrialization to the late-developing south, especially East Asia. Together, the two are placing ever greater demands on the earth and its resources. In view of this, one may well ask, as does Martin Walker, whether "the vast majority of the planet will ever be able to realize the levels of food and energy consumption that have become routine in North

---

67. Sandra Postel, "Forging a Sustainable Water Strategy," in Brown et al., *State of the World 1996*, pp. 41–44; Brown, *Who Will Feed China?* pp. 104–115; Brown, "Acceleration of History," pp. 5, 9, 15, 17; Postel, *Last Oasis*, pp. 33–34, 39, 53–54, 99, 112, 166; Gardner, "Preserving Agricultural Resources," pp. 81, 86–87. Under experimental conditions plants transpire much less water at elevated levels of carbon dioxide, however. Postel, *Last Oasis*, p. 92.
68. Cohen, *How Many People Can the Earth Support?* pp. 307–318, 362; Postel, *Last Oasis*, p. 28; the FAO estimate is from the Technical Background Paper, "The Critical Role of Water," paragraph 2.4, prepared for the World Food Summit in Rome, November 1996.
69. Moffett, *Critical Masses*, pp. 7–9.

America, Western Europe, and Japan over the past 50 years?"[70] Petroleum may soon present a serious bottleneck. In 1994 China consumed five barrels of oil per capita each day; the United States, fifty-three. China's need for oil is certain to increase as its industrialization proceeds and the Chinese begin to acquire the trappings of Western consumerism, especially the automobile. If China's demand for oil doubles in ten years—a conservative assumption—its total consumption will equal that of the United States. China has extensive domestic reserves in the Tarim Basin, but these are remote and will be difficult to develop. To meet this rising demand, China will probably have to import 16 million barrels per day, which is twice the current production of Saudi Arabia. India's demand is also rising rapidly and will probably match that of Western Europe by the same year. At a minimum, the Asian giants' thirst for petroleum is likely to drive up the price of energy and set in motion the inflationary forces that have been contained so successfully in Europe and America in the last decade. It may pose strategic dangers as well. The great majority of China's oil will be derived from the Persian Gulf. To safeguard this supply, Kent Calder speculates, China will deploy a blue water navy to patrol the sea-lanes and will seek strategic partnership with two of the countries with the greatest reserves—Iran and Iraq—policies with "unsettling implications" for Japan, the United States, and the rest of Asia.[71]

Even more significant, potentially, are the recent findings of the Intergovernmental Panel on Climate Change (IPCC). The body, which was founded under United Nations auspices and includes 2,500 scientists from around the world, released a report in 1995 stating that global temperatures have been rising over the past 100 years, that human activity is probably responsible for some of this increase, and (certainly by implication) that global temperature may continue to rise to the point where it will present serious risks to human life if no action is taken to forestall it. The panel predicted that temperatures will rise 1.44–6.3 degrees Fahrenheit if no further measures are implemented to slow greenhouse emissions, and added that human-induced warming might represent only 50–70 percent of the actual increase in temperature.[72] Plenty of evidence to the contrary can be adduced;[73] but even if the likelihood of catastrophic warming

70. Walker, "China and the New Era of Resource Scarcity," p. 11.
71. Kent Calder, "Asia's Empty Gas Tank," *Foreign Affairs*, Vol. 75, No. 2 (March/April 1996), pp. 58–60; and Walker, "China and the New Era of Resource Scarcity," p. 9.
72. William K. Stevens, "Experts Confirm Human Role in Global Warming," *New York Times*, September 10, 1995; William K. Stevens, "Scientists Say Earth's Warming Could Set Off Wide Disruptions," *New York Times*, September 18, 1995.
73. See Gregg Easterbrook, *A Moment on the Earth* (New York: Penguin, 1995), pp. 278–281.

is not large, it would be imprudent to dismiss these warnings and abandon efforts to stem the accumulation of greenhouse gases in the atmosphere. Here, too, China's role will be crucial. The IPCC estimates that if China continues to burn coal at current rates, by 2025 it will be emitting more greenhouse gases than Canada, Japan, and the United States combined.[74] Persuading the Chinese and other long-impoverished peoples to curtail their industrial development while North Americans, Europeans, and Japanese continue to enjoy their accustomed standard of living will be no easy task.

The State of War

Predictions of the imminent obsolescence of force appear to be premature. Whether the twenty-first century will witness a revival in the desire for military glory is not clear, but it is conceivable that the world will enter a post-Baconian age in which economic growth no longer provides a solvent to conflicts within and between states. Even if the consequences of the accumulation of greenhouse gases prove to be relatively mild, cheap energy, fertile land, and fresh water will not be obtainable in endless abundance in the coming decades. The combination of environmental threats and resource constraints may eventually bring a fundamental alteration in the basic conditions of international politics. When the empire of man over nature can no longer be easily extended, then the only way for one people to increase its standard of living is by redistributing the sources or fruits of industry from others to themselves. The surest way to do so is by extending man's empire over man. If the population surge continues to outpace improvements in agricultural productivity and if industrialization drives up the cost of resources or presses the world's capacity to absorb pollution beyond its limits, additional land will become desirable and perhaps, for some states, indispensable. As the value of land increases, so too does the value of the primary means of taking and holding it: diminishing returns in the economy implies increasing returns to the military.

The information revolution in warfare will simultaneously evolve and disperse across the planet at a pace and in a manner that are unforeseeable, in all likelihood widening the disparities in power between states and perhaps in some instances strengthening the initiator of war decisively against the defender. The next two generations may thus be fated to live in an era where the technology of destruction is progressing much faster than the technology of

---

74. Ibid., p. 313.

production. Under circumstances such as these, it is likely that the premises of the "trading state" policy of nations such as Japan and Germany will come under serious reexamination. Trade offers a viable substitute for political control over markets and sources of raw materials only as long as the international economy remains open and physical threats do not impede the flow of goods. Even if disruption were initially confined to a "zone of turmoil,"[75] it is difficult to believe, for example, that Japan, South Korea, Italy, and France would remain unconcerned if China or North Africa lapsed into chaos or militarism. If developed countries in the "zone of peace" do not attempt to achieve security by unilateral measures but continue to rely on protection by others, the value of that protection will increase proportionately to the degree of danger to their economic interests, as will the diplomatic and economic "return" to military power.

The hunger for resources, by one count, has set states on the path of expansion at least twelve times in this century.[76] Will statesmen of the future seek to enlarge their territories in order to alleviate the economic distress of their peoples? The most ominous scenario would clearly be a conjunction of the capability and need to seize territory in one state, most likely one of the larger and more successful developing countries. Much, of course, is contingent. If the overall impact of the RMA has been overstated or if improvements in sensor capabilities outpace stealth, the dominance of defense may persist indefinitely; if Chinese statistics are completely fallacious, if water and soil conservation efforts succeed, or if biotechnology produces some pleasant surprises, many more mouths may be fed than at present; and if oil reserves are more plentiful and the effects of greenhouse emissions less severe than is now feared, the empire of man over nature may be extended further. One condition is unalterable, however. There is only so much fresh water on the planet, and hence there must eventually be a limit to the amount food available to nourish the human species.[77]

The state of nature does not tend to a state of war if the fundamental motives of those in it do not drive them into conflict. But "if any two men desire the same thing, which nevertheless they cannot both enjoy," Hobbes observed coldly, "they become enemies." Whether this irreducible struggle obtains de-

---

75. The terms are from Singer and Wildavsky, *The Real World Order*, chapters 1–3.
76. Arthur Westing, "Appendix 2," in Arthur Westing, ed., *Global Resources and International Conflict* (Oxford, U.K.: Oxford University Press, 1986), pp. 204–209.
77. If energy were to become cheap enough to permit massive desalinization of sea water, even this constraint could be escaped, but this is not likely soon. Postel, *Last Oasis*, p. 45.

pends not only on the wisdom and virtue of the actors but also on factors beyond their immediate control. If we or our descendants live in a world where offense holds the advantage over defense, where a swelling population is exceeding its means of comfortable subsistence, and where industry is pressing against natural constraints, such "enemies" will abound. Life for many will be poor, nasty, brutish, and short, though, alas, not solitary. Realism will remain our best guide and, as Hobbes warned, clubs will be trumps. The affairs of nations and the collisions of interests, passions, and ideals between peoples will be decided, as they have been so often in the past, by the implements of war and those who wield them.

International Security

The Robert and Renée Belfer Center for
Science and International Affairs
John F. Kennedy School of Government
Harvard University

Articles in this reader were previously published in
International Security, a quarterly journal sponsored and
edited by The Robert and Renée Belfer Center for Science and
International Affairs at the John F. Kennedy School of
Government at Harvard University, and published by MIT
Press Journals. To receive subscription information about the
journal or find out more about other readers in our series,
please contact The MIT Press Journals Department at Five
Cambridge Center, Fourth Floor, Cambridge, MA,
02142-1493.